Comparative Morphology of Vascular Plants

A Series of Biology Books

EDITORS: *Douglas M. Whitaker, Ralph Emerson, George W. Beadle* (1946–1961)

CURT STERN
Principles of Human Genetics. (Second Edition)

JAMES BONNER AND ARTHUR W. GALSTON
Principles of Plant Physiology

ADRIAN M. SRB AND RAY D. OWEN
General Genetics

EVELYN L. OGINSKY AND WAYNE W. UMBREIT
An Introduction to Bacterial Physiology. (Second Edition)

CHESTER A. LAWSON, RALPH W. LEWIS, MARY ALICE BERMESTER, GARRETT HARDIN
Laboratory Studies in Biology: Observations and Their Implications

LEONARD MACHLIS AND JOHN G. TORREY
Plants in Action: A Laboratory Manual of Plant Physiology

C. L. PORTER
Taxonomy of Flowering Plants

N. J. BERRILL
Growth, Development, and Pattern

GARRETT HARDIN
Biology: Its Principles and Implications

GRETCHEN L. HUMASON
Animal Tissue Techniques

HARRY W. SEELEY, JR. AND PAUL J. VANDEMARK
Microbes in Action: A Laboratory Manual of Microbiology

WILLIAM A. JENSEN
Botanical Histochemistry: Principles and Practice

PETER ABRAMOFF AND ROBERT G. THOMSON
Laboratory Outlines in Biology

WAYNE W. UMBREIT
Modern Microbiology

GUNTHER S. STENT
Molecular Biology of Bacterial Viruses

THEODORE HOLMES BULLOCK AND G. ADRIAN HORRIDGE
Structure and Function in the Nervous Systems of Invertebrates

ADRIANCE S. FOSTER AND ERNEST M. GIFFORD, JR.
Comparative Morphology of Vascular Plants

COMPARATIVE MORPHOLOGY OF VASCULAR PLANTS

BY ADRIANCE S. FOSTER

University of California, Berkeley

AND ERNEST M. GIFFORD, Jr.

University of California, Davis

Drawings by EVAN L. GILLESPIE

W. H. FREEMAN AND COMPANY

 San Francisco and London

Preface

Preparing a modern textbook that will adequately and interestingly display to both student and teacher the present state of knowledge of the comparative morphology of vascular plants is indeed a formidable and challenging task. The divergence in opinion as to how the vast body of morphological knowledge accumulated during the past century should be presented in university or college courses is clearly reflected in certain recent texts. Some authors restrict themselves to a very detailed treatment of the structure, reproduction, and evolution of lower vascular plants. Others present a more elementary treatment of vascular plants as a whole, together with a survey of the entire plant kingdom. Because there are such wide variations in teaching methods and in the content of botanical curricula in colleges and universities, each type of book undoubtedly serves a purpose and has value. But we believe that today there is a great need for a textbook, which, in addition to providing a purely factual description of all the main groups of vascular plants, will also display clearly the procedures, general principles, and objectives of comparative morphology. This volume has been written and organized from this point of view. We hope that our text will in some measure orient and vitalize the teaching of plant morphology and that it will also emphasize the important relationships between morphology, taxonomy, and experimental morphogenesis.

The present volume has grown from teaching experience, and it is primarily intended to function as the text for an advanced one-semester course in plant morphology—a course such as that taught by the authors for many years at the University of California consisting of two lectures and six hours of laboratory work per week for a period of 15 weeks. However, this book is, in our judgment, also sufficiently comprehensive for use in a year course at either the senior or graduate level.

Because of the excessive fragmentation which all the classical fields of botany are now experiencing, it seems essential at the outset to discuss in broad terms the nature and objectives of the science of plant morphology. This we have attempted to do in the opening chapter, which also includes pertinent discussions of the concept of homology in plants and of the major lines of evidence upon which morphological interpretations are based. We believe the student requires this type of introduction—frequently omitted from modern texts—before he can be expected to pursue with any motivation the inevitable details of comparative morphology.

The student of plant morphology may, as can easily happen in any science, miss the forest because of the trees. To avoid this common difficulty insofar as possible, a series of orientation chapters (Chapters 2 through 6) are introduced before presentation of the comparative morphology of the several groups of vascular plants. In these chapters we have attempted to summarize and to appraise (1) the salient morphological features and common plan of the reproductive cycle in vascular plants, (2) the general organography and anatomy of the vegetative sporophyte, and (3) the structure and development of sporangia, gametangia, and embryos. The essential subject matter of these chapters could serve as the basis for the early lectures in a course in plant morphology. But we hope also that the frequent cross-referencing between these introductory chapters and later portions of the book may more closely relate *morphological principles* to the discussions of the structure and reproduction in specific types of vascular plants.

For reasons that are briefly explained in Chapter 2, we have adopted the designation "Tracheophyta" as representing the vascular plant "division" of the plant kingdom, and under this division we recognize four major subdivisions: *Psilopsida, Lycopsida, Sphenopsida,* and *Pteropsida.* In the light of continuous changes in viewpoint and nomenclature regarding the major taxa of vascular plants, the classification followed in this book may be criticized as too conservative or as outmoded. We believe, however, that there is considerable pedagogic value in this taxonomic scheme and that teachers who maintain a different viewpoint can readily adapt our presentation of comparative morphology to their own philosophy regarding the number of divisions or phyla within the vascular plants.

In each of the chapters dealing with the subdivisions or orders of vascular plants we have striven for a full and balanced treatment of the subject. Particularly with reference to those chapters on the Psilopsida, Lycopsida, and Sphenopsida, considerable paleobotanical information has been included in order to provide a historical background for the more extended discussions of the surviving types in these groups. In all chapters in this book citations to standard works and to published articles pertinent to a given topic are made directly in the text, and the complete references are listed alphabetically at the end of each chapter. Of course there is no pretense that these collectively represent a definitive bibliography. But it is believed that the references given will indicate the source of most of the interpretations adopted and will at the same time provide the student and teacher with the necessary clues to the voluminous literature relating to the morphology of vascular plants.

Illustrations are an essential component of a textbook in plant morphology, and the numerous drawings, diagrams, and photographs in this book have been carefully selected to aid the student to grasp the salient points developed in each chapter. Some of the figures are based upon original drawings and photomicrographs prepared by the authors. The great majority of the line drawings, however, have been redrawn from published articles and books by the skillful pen of Mr. Evan L. Gillespie, to whom we express our deep appreciation for enthusiastic, imaginative, and intelligent cooperation. The sources of all borrowed illustrations are indicated in the figure legends, and we are indebted to the various authors and publishers for permission to reproduce them. Special acknowledgment is made to Dr. Katherine Esau for permission to use a number of the illustrations in her book, *Plant Anatomy* (John Wiley and Sons, Inc., N. Y.). We also thank Mr. Victor Duran, who made several of the original photomicrographs, and Dr. T. E. Weier, who kindly provided a number of the photographs used in the chapter on the Coniferales.

Although the authors assume full responsibility for the viewpoints and statements in this book, special acknowledgments are due to those individuals who have offered advice and suggestions in the preparation of the manuscript. In particular we are greatly obliged to Professor Ralph H. Wetmore of Harvard University, who critically reviewed the entire manuscript and offered many valuable suggestions for its improvement. Mr. Howard J. Arnott, who served as the senior author's teaching assistant in plant morphology, and Dr. Marion S. Cave read portions of the original manuscript and were extremely helpful in discussing certain aspects of our presentation. Two of the editors of the Biology Series, Dr. George W. Beadle and Dr. Ralph Emerson, reviewed the manuscript, and we are grateful for their help and valuable suggestions. Lastly, we are happy to pay deserved tribute to our wives, Helen V. Foster and Jean D. Gifford, for their unfailing patience and for their assistance with the proofreading.

December 1958   ADRIANCE S. FOSTER
Berkeley   ERNEST M. GIFFORD, JR.

Contents

Chapter

Contents

Chapter

Chapter

1 THE SCIENCE OF PLANT MORPHOLOGY

The extraordinary diversity in the form, stature, and habit of plants is a familiar fact of experience which is recognized by even the scientifically untrained observer. The "sea-weeds" of the ocean, the lowly "mosses" and graceful "ferns" of the woodlands, the towering cone-bearing trees of the northern forests, and the infinitely varied flowering plants of orchard and garden all are recognized as different kinds of plants by the layman, on the basis of more or less superficial criteria or earmarks.

Casual inspection of the *surface aspects* of plants, however, is a highly unreliable method for either separating plants into natural groups or gaining a proper understanding of the nature and relationships of their parts. Thus, for example, the small green plants floating on the surface of ponds or garden pools are often commonly lumped together as "pond scum," "algae" or even "moss," because of their small size and the absence of conspicuous flowers. However, rigorous scientific study of such a population of aquatic plants from the standpoint of morphology would show that it contains not only algae (in the scientific sense) but also aquatic ferns and minute flowering plants! With respect to the recognition of external similarities and differences among land plants, superficial observation often leads to equally incorrect conclusions. Frequently a wide variety of totally unrelated plants are called ferns by the layman, because they have divided or pinnatifid leaves. From a broad, comparative-morphological standpoint it is clear that the true ferns are remarkably diversified as to leaf form and that their distinguishing characteristics are based on subtle but reliable similarities of structure and method of reproduction. And last there is confusion in the mind of the untrained observer in regard to flowering plants. With an understandable mental picture of a conspicuous and brightly-colored garden or hothouse type of flower, the layman often fails to realize that the reproductive structures of grasses and of many trees and shrubs are flowers. This commonly leads to a wholly erroneous notion of the nature of reproduction in even the most common plants and to an astonishing underestimation of the diversity in form and habit of the flowering plants as a whole.

In marked contrast with such undisciplined regard of form and structure, the science of plant morphology attempts, by rigorous techniques and meticulous observations, to probe beneath these surface aspects of plants—in short, to explore and to compare those *hidden aspects* of form, structure, and reproduction which constitute the basis for the interpretation of similarities and differences among plants. One of the most fruitful results of early morphological studies was the recognition that a relatively few fundamental types of organs underly the construction of the plant body. Thus, the leaf, stem, and root were regarded as the principal types of vegetative organs, the size, form, proportions, and arrangement of which are subject to the most varied development or modification. As knowledge of the reproductive cycles of plants increased, sporangia and gametangia were added to this short list of major organ categories, and the importance of a broad comparative study of the resemblances, or homologies, of plant organs thus became established. Let us examine more closely the notion of homology as it is used in the interpretation of plant form and structure.

The Concept of Homology

The essence of the idea of homology was expressed in the writings of the great poet and philosopher Goethe, to whom we also owe the word "morphology" (literally the science of form). Goethe sought for the nature of the morphological relationships among the various kinds of leafy appendages in higher plants. In his celebrated essay, *Metamorphosis in Plants*, published in 1790, he concluded that no real boundary exists between such organs as cotyledons, foliage leaves, bracts, and the organs of the flower—all are expressions of the same type of organ; i.e., the leaf (Arber, 1946). Although Goethe's theory has been criticized as an example of idealistic morphology, it has proved an extremely astute viewpoint and indeed constitutes the theoretical basis for the current view that the flower is a determinate axis with foliar appendages (see, Chapter 18).

The rapid expansion of botanical knowledge which occurred in the nineteenth century emphasized the importance of the concept of homology and the need for interpreting homologies in the broadest possible light. Goethe's ideas, and the earlier observations of K. F. Wolff (1759) on the origin of leaves at the growing point of the shoot, paved the way to a better understanding of serial homology in plants. With reference to a shoot, this term designates the equivalence in *method of origin* and *positional relationships* of the successive foliar appendages of a shoot. Thus, a bud scale is considered serially homologous with a foliage leaf because, like the latter, it arises as a lateral outgrowth from the shoot apex. Classical as well as modern ontogenetic studies have shown the very close resemblances in detail of origin and early histogenesis among the varied types of foliar organs of both vegetative and flowering shoots. Moreover, the different types of foliar appendages in the same plant are often interconnected by intermediate forms or transitional organs. On the other hand, the concept of general homology in plants is much more difficult to demonstrate ontogenetically (see Mason, 1957, for a critical discussion). This is so because, unlike higher animals, plants are characterized by an open type of growth—a plant embryo is not a miniature of the adult, and hence homologies based on the resemblance in position, development, and form of two organs in different kinds of plants may be open to serious question. The cotyledons of seed plants occur at the first node of the embryo and in that respect may be held to be homologous with one another. But whether, for example, *all* foliage leaves in vascular plants at large are homologous is a question which is by no means easily resolved, either from an ontogenetic or phylogenetic point of view (see Chapter 3).

The question of homologies in plants was placed in an entirely new position as the result of the publication in 1859 of Charles Darwin's classic, *The Origin of Species*. His theory of the rôle of natural selection in producing the gradual adaptive changes in the form and organography of both plants and animals exerted a profound effect on all questions of homologies. The goal of morphology now became very clear: the interpretation of form and structure from a historical (i.e., phylogenetic) point of view. Resemblances or homologies between organs were to be viewed as the result of descent from a common ancestral "type." Thus, the strong trend toward the phylogenetic interpretation of form and structure which arose during the latter part of the past century has continued to this day. In addition to its effect on all concepts of homology, the phylogenetic approach to morphology has provided the basis for a more realistic and natural classification of the plant kingdom.

It is evident that reliable interpretations require consideration of evidence that is derived from a wide variety of sources. Morphological theories increase in probability in relation to the extent to which collateral lines of evidence can be harmonized with one another. This chapter may therefore be most appropriately concluded by a brief, critical review of the sources of evidence which should be considered and evaluated in interpreting any problems of form and structure in plants.

Sources of Evidence in Morphological Interpretation

Adult Form and Structure

By far, the most voluminous data of comparative morphology have resulted from the study of the form of the adult plant.* Information derived from such study has contributed significantly to our knowledge of the wide variations in: (1) the form, venation, and phyllotaxy (arrangement on the axis) of foliar organs, (2) the patterns of branching of root and shoot systems, and (3) the morphological construction of such spore-producing structures as sporophylls, strobili, and flowers. During the second half of the nineteenth century, increasing emphasis was placed upon the study of the primary vascular system of the plant as the key to the interpretation of the morphological nature or homology of plant organs. The wide and continued use today of vascular patterns in morphology is based upon the fundamental assumption that the

---

* Strictly speaking, the term "adult" cannot have the same meaning for individual higher plants as it does for individual animals, e.g., vertebrates. In vertebrates the process of embryogeny yields a truly adult organism in which normally no additional organs are produced during the lifetime of the individual. But in vascular plants the continued activity of embryonic regions or meristems at the tips of shoots and roots results in an open system of growth that is characterized by the formation of new organs throughout the life span of the individual (Fig. 1-1). Moreover, in many vascular plants the vascular cambium makes more or less extensive periodic additions to the secondary vascular system of the older portions of stems and roots. For convenience in exposition therefore, adult will designate fully developed organs or plant tissues rather than the plant as a whole.

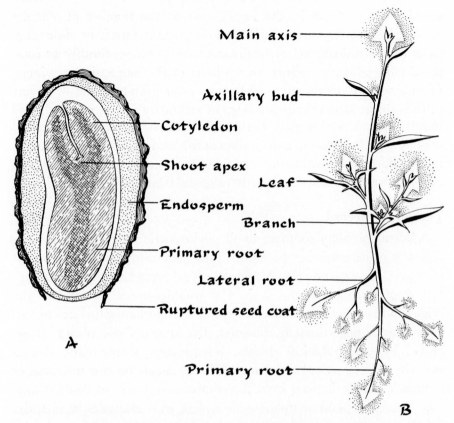

Main axis

Axillary bud

Cotyledon

Shoot apex

Leaf

Endosperm

Branch

Primary root

Lateral root

Ruptured seed coat

A

Primary root

B

Figure 1-1 Open system of growth in vascular plants. **A,** longisection of seed of a dicotyledon showing simple organography of embryo; **B,** diagram showing the open pattern of terminal growth and the progressive formation of organs in the shoot and root systems of a young sporophyte. [A, redrawn from Avery, *Amer. Jour. Bot.* 20:309, 1933.]

primary vascular system is more stable, or conservative, in a phylogenetic sense, than other tissue systems and hence is reliable as a criterion in morphological interpretation. Considerable support for this assumption is provided not only from comparative study of living plants but also by the beautifully preserved patterns of vasculation in the vegetative and reproductive structures of extinct plants. Among the many examples which might be given of the use of vascular anatomy in the determination of homologies, the following are outstanding: the morphological interpretation of floral organs (see Chapter 18 for details); the interpretation of the phylogenetic development of the leaf traces in vascular plants (that is, the significance of the number of vascular stands which diverge into a leaf at a node); and the patterns of development of the primary xylem in the stem and root in primitive as compared with advanced plants. In addition to the emphasis on primary vascular systems, much attention has also been given to extensive surveys of the minute structure or histology of secondary xylem, or wood. The results of such surveys have been applied in the appraisal of the taxonomic aspects of genera and families in the seed plants, and particularly in the effort to determine the origin and trends of evolutionary specialization of tracheids and vessels (Metcalfe and Chalk, 1950; Bailey, 1954).

The Fossil Record

A salient problem common to all phylogenetic interpretations is the difficulty of determining the sequence in the evolutionary development of organs, tissues, and cells. A complete fossil record of the evolutionary history of the sporangium or the leaf would provide evidence of the origin and trends of specialization of these important structures in vascular plants; unfortunately, however, the known fossil record, as revealed by paleobotanical studies, is extremely fragmentary. Consequently, phylogenetic theories are still based largely on circumstantial or indirect evidence derived from the comparative study of living plants. The history of plant morphology is replete with examples of how the same series of morphological types has been interpreted by some investigators as a sequence of *advancing complexity,* and by others as a series in *progressive reduction.* In other words, the decision whether a given structure is primitive or advanced depends upon the interpretation of the apparently "simple" forms in the series; that is, these forms may be regarded as either the beginnings or as terminal specializations. Many simple forms which were regarded in the past as primitive now seem to be specialized because of profound evolutionary reduction. Therefore it is clear that inferences regarding the phylogenetic nature of an organ must be based upon the wise evaluation of the evidence from extinct as well as living types of plants. New paleobotanical discoveries will continue to force morphologists to reconsider and revise many of the so-called classical viewpoints that are based solely on living plants.

Aside from impressions or casts of leaves, stems, and other structures, the most important type of fossil material consists of the partially or fully preserved remains of the organs and tissues of vascular plants. The epidermis (including its distinctive stomata) is often beautifully preserved and has been utilized by Florin (1931) in his highly significant studies on the evolutionary history of gymnosperms. Much has also been learned about the structure of the conducting systems in the earliest land plants, and this information furnishes a realistic background for theoretical interpretations of patterns of vasculation in living plants (Bower, 1935). Reproductive structures such as sporangia, spores, cones, fruits, and seeds are also found in a remarkably good state of preservation, and their careful study by paleobotanists and morphologists has contributed significantly to our reconstruction of plant life in the ancient world and to continued revisions of the relationship and classification of plants (Arnold, 1947).

In concluding this brief discussion, it must be emphasized that the facts revealed by the fossil record have demonstrated the probability of parallel evolution or homoplasy in plants. These terms indicate independent origin and evolutionary development, in widely separated groups, of apparently similar structures. An excellent example of parallel evolution is the independent development of seeds in a number of clearly distinct groups of plants. Some of these groups, such as the Bennettitales, represent extinct gymnosperms and there is little evidence that this order constituted the ancestral stock from which other groups of modern seed-bearing plants arose. If one accepts the idea of parallel evolution—and many facts could be cited in its support—it is clear that great caution must be observed in postulating a monophyletic origin (i.e., from the same ancestral stock) of such fundamental morphological structures as leaves, seeds, or sporangia. All of these structures may have originated in more than one way in the evolution of various groups of living and extinct plants.

Ontogeny

A highly important source of evidence for morphological interpretation is derived from the study of ontogeny—the actual development of a plant or of one of its component organs, tissues, or cells from the primordial stage to maturity. Histogenesis is a phase of ontogenetic study concerned with the origin of cells and tissues, and embryogenesis and organogenesis are concerned with the history of development of embryos and organs, respectively. It should be emphasized, however, that the boundaries between these lines of ontogenetic study are drawn largely as a matter of convenience in dealing with the varied aspects of development characteristic of the plant as a whole.

Ontogeny, like phylogeny, is thus concerned with origins and with stages in development. The attractiveness of ontogenetic study lies in the ability of the investigator to reconstruct, with considerable accuracy and completeness, the sequence of changes in form and structure which actually occur between the primordial phase of an organ and its mature functional stage. Phylogeny—which is concerned with the sequence of changes in form and structure that have occurred in the past—is, as we have seen, limited in its reconstructions by the exceedingly fragmentary nature of the fossil record.

The importance of detailed ontogenetic information is clearly shown in the interpretation of the life cycles of vascular plants. Since the classical studies of Hofmeister (1862) on Alternation of Generations, it has been repeatedly verified that each of the two generations (sporophyte and gametophyte) begins ontogenetically as a single cell. The spore, which results from meiosis, is the primordial cell which develops into the gametophyte, while the zygote, resulting from gametic union or fertilization, is the starting point of the sporophyte. Thus Alternation of Generations, which is one of the most profound generalizations in plant morphology, rests upon the results of ontogenetic study. (See Fig. 2-1.)

Ontogenetic studies have also proved essential to the solution of many special morphological problems. For example, the distinction between the two main types of sporangia in vascular plants is based primarily upon differences in their method of origin and early development (Chapter 4). Likewise, the numerous studies of the past century and of today on the ontogeny of foliar organs have shed important light on the morphological interpretation of such structures as stipules, bud scales, and particularly, floral organs (Foster 1928, 1935). Within the past two decades there has been a notable renaissance of interest in the classical problems of structure and growth of the apical meristems of vascular plants. These studies have not only greatly extended our knowledge of organogenesis and histogenesis but have also emphasized the need for an experimental approach to problems of development in plants (Gifford, 1954; Wardlaw, 1952; Torrey, 1955).

Despite the demonstrated value of ontogenetic evidence, there are certain limitations to the ontogenetic interpretation of morphological problems which must be clearly understood. One of the most important of these limitations concerns the assumed occurrence of recapitulation in plants. According to the theory of recapitulation, the ontogeny of an organism tends—in abbreviated fashion—to repeat or recapitulate its evolutionary history. A frequently cited example of so-called recapitulation in plants is the development in seedlings of juvenile leaves which differ conspicuously in size, form, and venation from the foliage characteristic of the adult phase of the same plant. However, whether these juvenile leaves provide a reliable clue to the morphology of the ancestral leaf type in any given case is open to serious question. In general, ontogenetic sequences, whether in the succession of foliar types in the young plant or the stages in the ontogeny of an organ or tissue, do not fully or accurately depict the complex path of evolutionary history, and recapitulatory hypotheses should always be made with great caution (Sahni, 1925). This is true, because ontogenetic sequences vary so widely in their extent and character. In some instances the ontogeny of a structure may be relatively protracted, thus permitting the phylogenetic evaluation of a well-defined series of stages. Vessel elements, for example, acquire their characteristic perforations late in ontogeny and their early development may closely resemble that of tracheids from which they undoubtedly have phylogenetically evolved. Very commonly, however, the ontogenetic history of a structure may be conspicuously abbreviated or telescoped and therefore may be of little or no value in phylogenetic questions.

In conclusion, it is well to realize the important interrelationship between the processes of ontogeny and phylogeny (Mason, 1957). Evolution or phylogeny involves historical change, but from our present point of view "change" is effected by factors which cause the gradual or abrupt modification of ontogenetic processes. A mature tracheid does not give rise to a vessel element, nor does a simple leaf give rise to a complex leaf. On the contrary, evolutionary changes in either tracheary cells or in foliar organs are the result of progressive modifications in the ontogeny of such structures. As Bailey (1944) has so clearly said: "Both comparative and developmental morphology will be more productive of valid generalizations when problems of mutual interest are attacked from a broadened viewpoint of the phylogeny of modified ontogenies in the vascular plants as a whole."

Physiology and Morphogenesis

If plant morphology is regarded as a phase of botanical science exclusively concerned with the description and phylogenetic interpretation of form and structure, it might seem to have little or nothing to do with those dynamic activities of plants that fall within the designation of plant physiology. But is not the wide separation which has developed between morphology and physiology not only artificial but highly undesirable? Goebel (1900) in his monumental *Organography of Plants* adopted the position that "the form and function of an organ stand in the most intimate relation to each other." A similar point of view was followed by Haberlandt (1914) in his attempt to classify and to characterize the tissue systems of plants on a functional basis. Abundant evidence exists that the interpretation of form and structure cannot logically be divorced from function. Sporangia and gametangia in vascular plants are complex multicellular organs, the structure, ontogeny and phylogeny of which constitute important morphological problems. But these organs are more than merely structural features of plants—they are also functionally essential, the sporangia producing spores which give rise to gametophytes and the gametangia forming sperms and eggs that are indispensable to the normal sexual reproduction of a plant. A further illustration of the interrelationships between structure and function is provided by the tracheids and vessel elements in the xylem of vascular plants. These two types of cells vary widely in their form and structure, and they furnish valuable criteria for the broad morphological interpretation of the xylem in vascular plants as a whole. But tracheids and vessels physiologically serve as the major water-conducting elements in plants, and their evolutionary specialization is clearly related to this important function (Bailey, 1953). As a final example of the correlation between structure and function, we may mention the foliage leaves of vascular plants. These organs—although highly diversified in shape, size, and details of anatomy—serve as the major photosynthetic structures of the majority of vascular plants.

It should be clear from these few illustrations that the morphological and functional aspects of plant organs and tissues are indeed interrelated. Although the adaptive or functional significance of many anatomical characters in plants has by no means been experimentally demonstrated, the rigid separation of form from function is, as Goebel remarked, a position which leads to "altogether unfruitful speculations."

We have attempted to show in this chapter that morphology has been largely concerned with determining *what* a given structure represents (i.e., its homology), and *how* it arises—ontogenetically or phylogenetically. But this leaves unanswered many fundamental biological questions: Why is the process of organ and tissue formation characterized by such an orderly series of integrated developmental stages? Why do fertilized eggs in the various groups of vascular plants develop into entirely different types of organized embryos which, in turn, develop into quite dissimilar adult sporophytic plants? Why do the structurally similar primordia which arise at the shoot apex develop into such diversified appendages as bud scales, foliage leaves, and floral organs? And why, during histogenesis, do certain cells originating from the same meristem, pursue such radically different paths of differentiation? Finding answers to these and similar questions in causal morphology is the goal of experimental morphogenesis, which is one of the most rapidly developing fields in modern botanical science.

The experimental morphogenetic approach to problems of form and structure is based essentially on a variety of techniques which are used in determining the factors (genetical, biophysical, and biochemical) which condition or "determine" a given type of developmental pattern. With modern methods it has been possible to perform delicate surgical operations on the living shoot apex—operations involving incisions or the removal of portions of the apex or of young leaf primordia. The response of the mutilated apex, if it survives, can then be followed and sections can be made to determine the pattern of differentiation of the remaining cells and organ primordia. Experiments of this nature have been made on ferns (Wetmore and Wardlaw, 1951) as well, as on angiosperms (Ball, 1950, 1952a, 1952b) and the results have been applied to the causal interpretation of histogenesis and organogenesis in vascular plants (Chapter 13). Investigators have also had success in growing detached shoot or root apices in suitable culture media and in testing the effects of various biochemical and biophysical factors on their development. (Wetmore 1953, 1956; Torrey, 1955). In the case of certain lower and higher vascular plants, it has been possible to raise entire plants in culture from a detached shoot apex.

Morphogenetic experiments on the apical meristems of shoots and roots, as well as the numerous recent investigations on *in vitro* cultures of cells, tissues, and organs, all are concerned with the potentialities of isolated parts of a plant for independent growth and differentiation. Such studies hold considerable promise for a better understanding of the genesis of form and structure in plants, but a detailed evaluation of the results thus far obtained cannot be attempted in this book. For extensive discussions on plant morphogenesis and some reference to the voluminous literature, see White (1943); Maheshwari (1950); Wardlaw (1952, 1955); Wetmore (1953, 1956); Ball (1956a, 1956b); Torrey and Shigemura (1957); Steeves, Gabriel, and Steeves (1957); Steeves and Sussex (1957).

In conclusion it is worthwhile emphasizing that experimental morphogenesis is a synthetic science, one which must involve the coordination of the evidence of comparative morphology, genetics, biochemistry, biophysics, and ontogeny. But we must remember that the experimental approach should be made within the frame of reference provided by the actual range in form and structure of the diversified types of living plants. This morphological framework is, as we have seen, the end product of an incredibly long period of plant evolution. There is therefore great need, as Wardlaw (1952) has pointed out, for a continuous effort to integrate the data and concepts of comparative morphology with our knowledge of the specific factors, which at present seem to condition or control the unfolding of form and structure in plants.

References

Arber, A. 1946. Goethe's Botany. *Chronica Botanica.* 10:67-124.

Arnold, C. A. 1947. *An Introduction to Paleobotany.* McGraw-Hill, New York.

Bailey, I. W. 1944. The development of vessels in angiosperms and its significance in morphological research. *Amer. Jour. Bot.* 31:421-428.

——. 1953. Evolution of the tracheary tissue of land plants. *Amer. Jour. Bot.* 40:4-8.

——. 1954. *Contributions to Plant Anatomy.* Chronica Botanica Co., Waltham, Mass.

Ball, E. 1950. Isolation, removal, and attempted transplants of the central portion of the shoot apex of *Lupinus albus* L. *Amer. Jour. Bot.* 37:117-136.

——. 1952a. Morphogenesis of shoots after isolation of the shoot apex of *Lupinus albus*. *Amer. Jour. Bot.* 39:167-191.

——. 1952b. Experimental division of the shoot apex of *Lupinus albus* L. *Growth* 16:151-174.

——. 1956a. Growth of the embryo of *Ginkgo biloba* under experimental conditions. I. Origin of the first root of the seedling *in vitro*. *Amer. Jour. Bot.* 43:488-495.

——. 1956b. Growth of the embryo of *Ginkgo biloba* under experimental conditions. II. Effects of a longitudinal split in the tip of the hypocotyl. *Amer. Jour. Bot.* 43:802-810.

Bower, F. O. 1935. *Primitive Land Plants.* Macmillan, London.

Darwin, C. 1859. *The Origin of Species.* (Ed. 6. J. Murray, 1875) London.

Florin, R. 1931. Untersuchungen zur Stammesgeschichte der Coniferales und Cordaitales. *Svenska. Vetensk. Akad. Handl.* Ser. 5. 10:1-588.

Foster, A. S. 1928. Salient features of the problem of bud-scale morphology. *Biol. Rev.* 3:123-164.

——. 1935. A histogenetic study of foliar determination in *Carya Buckleyi var. arkansana*. *Amer. Jour. Bot.* 22:88-147.

Gifford, E. M., Jr. 1954. The shoot apex in angiosperms. *Bot. Rev.* 20:477-529.

Goebel, K. 1900. *Organography of Plants.* Eng. Ed. Part I. Clarendon Press, Oxford.

Goethe, J. W., von. 1790. *Versuch die Metamorphose der Pflanzen zu erklären.* Gotha.

Haberlandt, G. 1914. *Physiological Plant Anatomy*, Macmillan, London.

Hofmeister, W. 1862. *On the Germination, Development and Fructification of the Higher Cryptogamia and on the Fructification of the Coniferae.* Published for the Ray Society by Robert Hardwicke, London.

Maheshwari, P. 1950. *An introduction to the Embryology of Angiosperms.* McGraw-Hill, New York.

Mason, H. L. 1957. The concept of the flower and the theory of homology. *Madroño* 14:81-95.

Metcalfe, C. R., and L. Chalk. 1950. *Anatomy of the Dicotyledons.* 2 v. Clarendon Press, Oxford.

Sahni, B. 1925. The ontogeny of vascular plants and the theory of recapitulation. *Jour. Ind. Bot. Soc.* 4:202-216.

Steeves, T. A., H. P. Gabriel, and M. W. Steeves. 1957. Growth in sterile culture of excised leaves of flowering plants. *Science,* 126:350-351.

Steeves, T. A., and I. M. Sussex. 1957. Studies on the development of excised leaves in sterile culture. *Amer. Jour. Bot.* 44:665-673.

Torrey, J. G. 1955. On the determination of vascular patterns during tissue differentiation in excised pea roots. *Amer. Jour. Bot.* 42:183-198.

Torrey, J. G., and Y. Shigemura. 1957. Growth and controlled morphogenesis in pea root callus tissue grown in liquid media. *Amer. Jour. Bot.* 44:334-344.

Wardlaw, C. W. 1952. *Phylogeny and Morphogenesis.* St. Martin's Press, New York.

————. 1955. *Embryogenesis in Plants.* Wiley, New York.

Wetmore, R. H. 1953. The use of "in vitro" cultures in the investigation of growth and differentiation in vascular plants. *Brookhaven Symposia in Biol.* No. 6:22-40.

————. 1956. Growth and development in the shoot system of plants. Paper No. VIII, from "Cellular mechanisms in differentiation and growth." Princeton University Press, Princeton, N. J.

Wetmore, R. H., and C. W. Wardlaw. 1951. Experimental morphogenesis in vascular plants. *Ann. Rev. Plant Phy.* 2:269-292.

White, P. R. 1943. A *Handbook of Plant Tissue Culture.* The Jaques Cattell Press, Lancaster, Pa.

Wolff, C. F. 1774. *Theoria Generationis.* Editio nova. Halle a.d. Saale.

Chapter

2 THE SALIENT FEATURES OF VASCULAR PLANTS

One of the most significant events in the long evolutionary development of the plant kingdom was the origin of the first land plants. These organisms, which in all probability arose from some ancient group of green algae, are believed by many students of evolution to have been extremely simple in organography. Perhaps they closely resembled such apparently primitive plants as the Devonian *Rhynia* and *Horneophyton* (see Fig. 7-1). The conquest of the land must have been a long, hazardous, and costly process of slow adjustment to a new and inhospitable environment, and many of the steps in that early trial and error period may always remain unknown to science. But when one compares the organography, anatomy, and spore development of such ancient forms as *Rhynia* with the morphology of a modern angiosperm, the magnitude of the changes which accompanied evolution on the land becomes evident. *Rhynia* was a rootless, leafless plant that was low in stature, and it had a simple and primitive vascular system. The reproductive structures of the sporophyte were crude sporangia located at the tips of the aerial branches, and they produced spores which were alike in form and size. In contrast, a present-day angiosperm, e.g., a modern dicotyledonous tree, is an extremely complex organism. In addition to its chief vegetative organs (root, stems and leaves), such a plant develops flowers, fruits, and seeds and exhibits a highly evolved vascular system which is periodically renewed and augmented by the activity of a vascular cambium. Obviously *Rhynia* and the woody angiosperm share certain general morphological features (photosynthetic, spore-producing and vasculated sporophytes) but differ profoundly in the degree and type of development of other morphological characters.

15

In this chapter an effort will be made to select and to describe briefly the salient morphological features that are common to most living vascular plants. Such preliminary analysis and orientation seems indispensable as an approach to the more detailed treatment of comparative morphology as presented in subsequent chapters. For convenience in exposition, the definitive features of sporophyte and gametophyte generations will be described separately.

Sporophyte Generation

The normal origin of this generation is from the zygote, a diploid cell which results from the fertilization of the egg by a sperm (Fig. 2-1). There is considerable variation in vascular plants with respect to the length of the period of attachment and physiological dependency of the young multicellular sporophyte upon the gametophyte generation. In certain lower vascular plants, for example *Lycopodium*, sporophytes may remain connected to the gametophyte for several years. By contrast, the period of dependency of the sporophyte in heterosporous plants, for example *Selaginella*, and seed plants is very brief and is usually limited to the phase of embryogeny. Ultimately, in *all types* of vascular plants the sporophyte gains physiological independence and develops into the dominant, typically photosynthetic, phase of the life cycle. *This physiological independence and dominance of the sporophyte constitutes one of the most definitive characters of all vascular plants.*

From an organographic viewpoint, the sporophyte typically consists of a shoot system (usually aerial) made up of stems and various types of foliar organs and of roots. The latter vary widely in their origin during embryogeny and later phases of growth—they are absent only from the Psilotaceae and certain highly specialized aquatic and parasitic plants. Shoots and roots are theoretically capable of unlimited apical growth, branching, and organ formation because of the maintenance at their tips of apical meristems. This capacity for continued indefinite apical growth is not found in the small dependent sporophytes of mosses and liverworts and hence represents a fundamentally important distinction between these organisms and all vascular plants (see Fig. 1-1).

From an anatomical viewpoint, one of the most definitive features of

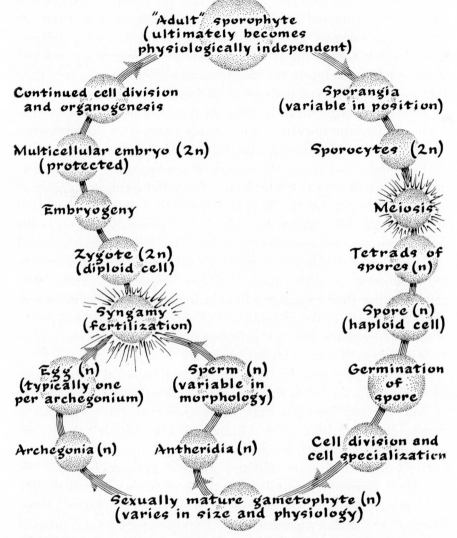

Figure 2-1 Alternation of sporophyte and gametophyte generations in the complete life cycle of vascular plants. (The processes and structures represented are discussed in detail in the text.)

the sporophyte is the presence of a vascular system. Indeed, the occurrence in the xylem, or water-conducting part of this system, of cells known as tracheids is responsible for the designation of all vascular plants as "Tracheophyta." (See Bailey, 1953, for a discussion of the evolution of tracheary tissue.) As will become evident in subsequent chapters, the form and arrangement of the vascular system varies not only among different groups of tracheophytes, but among different organs of the same plant as well. Because of its remarkably well-preserved condition in fossils, the vascular system often provides important clues to relationships and to trends of phylogenetic development. Except for the vein endings, which in leaves or floral organs consist largely of tracheary cells, the vascular system consists typically of two distinctive tissues: phloem, the definitive conducting elements of which are the sieve elements; and xylem, the important conducting or tracheary elements of which are the tracheids and the vessel elements. The basic difference between the two types of xylem cells is that the tracheid is an imperforate cell, whereas the ends of vessel elements ontogenetically develop one or more openings or perforations. A series of superposed vessel elements constitutes a vessel. Vascular tissues are essential to the conduction of water, mineral solutes, and soluble organic compounds—upon their coordinated functioning depends the normal physiology and growth of the sporophyte. Evidently, in the early occupation of the land by plants, the rapid evolution of an effective vascular system must have been of primary importance.

Although typical vascular tissue, in the morphological sense just defined, is usually limited to the sporophyte generation, the gametophyte of *Psilotum* may develop a weak, discontinuous central strand of tracheids (Holloway 1938, 1939; Bierhorst, 1953). This is indeed a remarkable fact, one which warrants serious consideration in any effort to interpret the evolutionary relationships between sporophyte and gametophyte generations. In this respect it is of further interest to note that tracheary tissue has also been observed in certain fern gametophytes. Examples of vasculated gametophytes clearly deserve careful cytological and experimental study (see Manton, 1950). According to Steil (1939, pp. 439-440), "one of the first and best evidences of apogamy in ferns is the appearance of tracheids just back of the apical notch of the prothallium."

The characteristic reproductive organ of the sporophyte is the sporangium. As will be shown in detail in Chapter 4, sporangia differ significantly in their position, methods of origin and development, and mature structure including sporangial wall and spore type. These differences provide reliable criteria, in many instances, for classifying vascular plants. From the standpoint of reproduction (i.e., spore formation) such diverse structures as the sporophylls of lower heterosporous plants and the stamens and carpels of the angiosperm flower are fundamentally similar. However, whether these structures are homologous in a morphological sense is a question which must be reserved for later discussion.

Gametophyte Generation

The normal origin of this generation is from a spore, which, in turn, is a product of the meiotic (reductional) divisions of spore mother cells in the sporangium (see Fig. 2-1). In certain lower vascular plants, such as some species of *Lycopodium, Equisetum,* and most of the ferns, the gametophyte is a free-living photosynthetic plant; in others, such as *Psilotum, Tmesipteris,* and many species of *Lycopodium,* the gametophyte is subterranean, devoid of chlorophyll, and apparently dependent upon the presence of an endophytic fungus for its existence. In marked contrast, the gametophytes of gymnosperms and angiosperms are much smaller and are physiologically dependent upon the sporophyte generation. Aside from these morphological and physiological variations, the chief importance of the gametophyte is the production of male gametes (or sperms) and female gametes (or eggs). These gametes are developed in distinctive multicellular gametangia in all lower vascular plants, the sperms arising in antheridia and the solitary egg developing within the archegonium. In angiosperms, the male and female gametes are produced directly by the greatly reduced and modified gametophytes, and morphologically definable sex organs are not developed. The position, ontogeny, and structure of gametangia and gametes furnish important characters used in the comparison and classification of the groups of lower vascular plants. A full discussion of the comparative morphology of gametangia is presented in Chapter 5.

Alternation of Generations

Alternation is a consistent feature of all groups of tracheophytes and hence represents the basic pattern of reproduction in these dominant plants of the modern world. Figure 2-1 represents schematically the structures and processes common to the complete life cycle of lower vascular plants. The student must understand this generalized life cycle clearly before he becomes involved in the infinite variations of detail which occur in the cycle of reproduction of specific genera or groups of plants.

Because the sporophyte generation is the obvious and dominant phase of the life cycle, we may properly begin our analysis of Fig. 2-1 with the zygote. This diploid cell results from the union of a male gamete with the egg, a process occurring in the archegonia of lower vascular plants, including the majority of gymnosperms, and in the female gametophyte of angiosperms. The next event is the process of embryogeny, which involves the production from the zygote of a multicellular embryo, the early development, form, and organography of which are often specific in a given group. By means of further growth and differentiation from the shoot and root apices of the embryo, the adult and independent sporophyte is developed. The general organography and vasculation of the sporophyte have already been outlined in this chapter. Ultimately, as shown in Fig. 2-1, the sporophyte plant forms sporangia in which spore-mother cells, or sporocytes, are produced. These cells, like all normal cells of the vegetative sporophyte, are diploid. However, each sporocyte can by meiotic division give rise to a tetrad or group of four haploid spores. When circumstances are favorable a spore germinates and by cell division and cell specialization produces the gametophyte generation. As we have already seen, this phase in the life cycle varies considerably in size and physiology—its salient function is the production of sperms and eggs. The union—called fertilization or syngamy —between a male gamete and an egg, restores the diploid chromosome number and produces the zygote from which a new sporophyte plant may develop.

It should be clear from this description that the alternation of sporophytic and gametophytic generations in the life cycle is normally coordinated with a periodic doubling followed by a halving in chromosome number. The diploid zygote $(2n)$ from which the sporophyte arises contains twice the number of chromosomes typical of the spore (n) which produces the gametophyte. Is this difference in chromosome number of spore and zygote a clue to the remarkable morphological and functional differences between the generations which arise from these cells? Or, to ask the question another way: Are syngamy and meiosis always essential processes in the production of the sporophyte and gametophyte, respectively? Either apparently deserves a negative answer, because many cases are now known (especially among ferns and also angiosperms) of diploid gametophytes and haploid sporophytes. Diploid gametophytes may arise, *without the intervention of spores*, directly from the leaf of a sporophyte. This phenomenon is termed apospory. Aposporous gametophytes may arise spontaneously in nature but they can also be artificially induced by culturing detached leaves or pinnae under conditions favorable to regeneration. Very commonly, aposporous gametophytes bear functional antheridia and archegonia, and chromosome studies have shown the remarkable fact that their gametes are diploid and the sporophyte resulting from their union is tetraploid ($4n$). On the other hand, sporophytes may arise, *without the act of fertilization*, directly from one or from several cells of the gametophyte: This phenomenon is termed apogamy. The cell from which an apogamous sporophyte originates may be a vegetative cell of the gametophyte or one of the component cells (exclusive of the egg cell) of the archegonium. Depending upon the chromosome number of the gametophyte (i.e., whether normal n or aposporous $2n$) the apogamous sporophyte may be haploid or diploid.

The occurrence of apogamy and apospory definitely reduces the value of the use of chromosome number in the precise morphological definition of the sporophyte and gametophyte generations in plants. But there still remains the greater problem of the phylogenetic origin of alternating generations in the vascular plants. A very widespread view, developed and championed in great detail by Bower (1935) holds that in an evolutionary sense the sporophyte generation is a new phase which became interpolated in the life cycle "between the successive events of syngamy and meiosis." In short, the sporophyte arose from the postponement of meiosis which resulted in the interpolation, by vegetative growth, of a post-sexual diploid phase. This interpretation is commonly designated the Antithetic Theory of Alternation, although Bower himself prefers the term Interpolation Theory. In contrast to this, the Homologous Theory of Alternation postulates that sporophyte and gametophyte are fundamentally alike in nature—that they represent, to quote Eames (1936, p. 393), "correlative phases in the life cycle of the plants which have arisen by modification of an original single phase which was sexual." The Homologous Theory thus assumes that vascular plants arose from an ancestral algal stock in which morphologically similar sporophytic and gametophytic phases were already differentiated. According to Eames, the simple alga-like sporophytes of certain members of the Psilophytales and the marked resemblances between the sporophyte and gametophyte of certain living primitive types (*Psilotum* and *Tmesipteris*) furnish strong evidence supporting the Homologous Theory. In this regard, future paleobotanical discoveries may reveal the nature of the gametophyte generation in the earliest land plants, and hence contribute to a better understanding of the origin of those trends of evolutionary specialization which underly alternation of generations in the tracheophytes.

Classification of Vascular Plants

This chapter may be appropriately concluded by a brief discussion of the scheme of classification adopted in this book. In our opinion, the vascular plants as a whole constitute that major group or division of the plant kingdom which has been designated Tracheophyta (Eames, 1936). This term literally means tracheid plants, and thus emphasizes the universal occurrence of tracheary tissue as a component of the vascular system of the sporophyte. Within the Tracheophyta we recognize the following four principal subdivisions:

1. Psilopsida. This subdivision includes the living genera *Psilotum* and *Tmesipteris* as well as the extinct Paleozoic psilophytes (see Chapter 7).

2. Lycopsida. This subdivision comprises the living genera *Lycopodium, Phylloglossum, Selaginella,* and *Isoetes* and the extinct lycopods of the Paleozoic (see Chapter 8).

3. Sphenopsida. This subdivision largely comprises extinct Paleozoic plants and the single, living genus *Equisetum* (see Chapter 9).

4. Pteropsida. This is the largest and most comprehensive of the subdivisions of the Tracheophyta and comprises the living and extinct ferns (Filicinae) and seed plants (Gymnospermae and Angiospermae). Pteropsid plants are discussed in detail in Chapters 10-19.

Since this book is primarily a text in comparative morphology, the arguments pro and con as to the taxonomic merits of such a classification can receive only brief consideration (Just, 1945). Admittedly, the broad designation of Tracheophyta may carry the implication that plants with a definable vascular system constitute a natural and monophyletic line of evolution. On this subject much has been written, but the evidence at present is far from conclusive. Indeed, if one assumes that the major groups of vascular plants—many of which extend with considerable sharpness back to the Paleozoic—originated from separate psilophyte or even algal stocks, Tracheophyta does not represent a phylogenetic division of the plant kingdom. This point of view is clearly reflected in the classification of vascular plants into a series of phyla and sub-phyla (Tippo, 1942), and the segregation of the lower, non-seed-bearing vascular plants into four major divisions (Smith, 1955). All schemes for classifying and designating the higher taxonomic categories or taxa of plants are, of course, subject to revision in the light of new paleobotanical discoveries, and hence no claim is made that the classification employed here represents more than a convenient scheme which has certain facts in its favor. From a purely legalistic viewpoint, the Eighth International Botanical Congress (held in Paris, 1954) states that "the principles of priority and typification do not apply to names of taxa above the rank of order." However, this Congress did recommend that divisional names for all plants except Fungi should end in *Phyta*, a recommendation which is followed in the divisional name Tracheophyta.

In regard to the classification adopted here, a brief discussion of the basis for the recognition of the subdivision Pteropsida is essential. Many current texts—both elementary and advanced—segregate vascular plants into two principal groups: Pteridophyta, comprising the lower non-seed-bearing vascular plants, and Spermatophyta, or seed plants. This familar and convenient classification has been widely criticized because first, it groups psilophytes, lycopods, and horsetails as allies of the ferns, a procedure that is not justifiable on morphological grounds, and second, it separates the ferns from all seed-bearing plants, a disposition which is regarded by many morphologists, from a phylogenetic standpoint, as wholly unnatural. The fact that certain Paleozoic fern-like plants (e.g., the Pteridosperms), previously classified as pteridophytes, reproduced by means of seeds constitutes a good argument in favor of grouping ferns (in the broad sense of primitive as well as modern types) in the same major group with seed plants. This is the taxonomic basis for the establishment of the Pteropsida, and the student is referred to Eames (1936, pp. 400-407) and Arnold (1947, pp. 11-12) for a more detailed discussion of the subject.

References

Arnold, C. A. 1947. *An Introduction to Paleobotany.* McGraw-Hill, New York.

Bailey, I. W. 1953. Evolution of the tracheary tissue of land plants. *Amer. Jour. Bot.* 40:4-8.

Bierhorst, D. W. 1953. Structure and development of the gametophyte of *Psilotum nudum. Amer. Jour. Bot.* 40:649-658.

Bower, F. O. 1935. *Primitive Land Plants.* Macmillan, London.

Eames, A. J. 1936. *Morphology of Vascular Plants. Lower Groups.* McGraw-Hill, New York.

Holloway, J. E. 1938. The embryo and gametophyte of *Psilotum triquetrum.* A preliminary note, *Ann. Bot. N. S.* 2:807-809.

————. 1939. The gametophyte, embryo, and young rhizome of *Psilotum triquetrum* Swartz. *Ann. Bot. N. S.* 3:313-336.

International Code of Botanical Nomenclature (Adopted by 8th Int. Bot. Congress, Paris, July, 1954). International Bureau for Plant Taxonomy and Nomenclature. Utrecht. 1956.

Just, T. 1945. The proper designation of the vascular plants. *Bot. Rev.* 11: 299-309.

Manton, I. 1950. *Problems of Cytology and Evolution in the Pteridophyta.* Cambridge University Press, London.

Smith, G. M. 1955. *Cryptogamic Botany. Vol. II. Bryophytes and Pteridophytes.* Ed. 2. McGraw-Hill, New York.

Steil, W. N. 1939. Apogamy, apospory, and parthenogenesis in the pteridophytes. *Bot. Rev.* 5:433-453.

Tippo, O. 1942. A modern classification of the plant kingdom. *Chronica Botanica* 7:203-206.

Chapter

3 THE VEGETATIVE SPOROPHYTE

This chapter briefly reviews those features of the vegetative sporophyte of vascular plants which enter most commonly into morphological comparisions and interpretations. For the convenience of the student, the material is presented in five categories: (1) the contrasts between shoot and root, (2) the methods of branching or ramification of shoots, (3) the concept of microphylls and megaphylls, (4) the comparative anatomy of the sporophyte, and (5) the Stelar Theory. Each of these topics is extremely comprehensive in factual content and also is complex because of the conflicting theories which seek to unify and to explain their varied aspects. Hence the necessarily brief treatments are intended to orient the beginner in plant morphology rather than to provide a definitive résumé of the various topics.

Shoots and Roots

In the great majority of living vascular plants the developing embryo gives rise to a leafy stem, or shoot, and a primary root. Further development of the young sporophyte results, through the activity of apical meristems, in the formation of additions to the original shoot and root components, for example, the production of lateral branches in the primary shoot, the development of new roots adventitiously from the stem, and the ramification of the primary root. (See Fig. 1-1.)

From the standpoints of organography, function, and anatomy, shoots and roots are conspicuously divergent systems. Roots develop no superficial appendages other than the absorbing root hairs and are to be regarded as naked axes; their chief functions are the absorption of water and solutes, and anchorage. In contrast, shoots have a jointed or segmental organography because the axis or stem bears conspicuous lateral appendages, or leaves; these structures are extraordinarily variable in size, form, and anatomy, and very probably have originated phylogenetically in at least two distinct ways, as will be discussed later in the chapter. The chief functions of shoots are photosynthesis, storage, and reproduction; the last is associated with the development from the shoot system of such structures as sporangia, strobili, and flowers.

In regard to apical growth and branching, roots and shoots differ in several important respects. The root apex consists of a root cap which functions as a protective buffer to the delicate meristem which lies beneath it. This subterminal meristem of roots is the point of origin of two different patterns of cell formation. One adds new cells outwardly to the root cap, the other contributes the cells which become a part of the root body (Fig. 3-1, A). As we have already mentioned, roots are devoid of foliar appendages. Except for hairs, the only lateral appendages which may occur are lateral roots, and these structures, unlike the usually superficially developed branches of the shoot, originate deep within the tissue of the parent root. In marked contrast to the root apex, the apex of the shoot consists of the terminal meristem itself, and no cap of tissue comparable to a root cap is developed. Aside from giving rise to the primary stem tissues, a very important function of the shoot apex is the formation of new leaves (Fig. 3-1, B). Leaves originate as primordia (singular, primordium) by means of localized cell division and cell extension at discrete loci or nodes on the flanks of the shoot apex. Leaf primordia typically arise in acropetal sequence; that is, the succession is toward the apex, which means the youngest stages in leaf development are found nearest the summit of the meristem. In addition to their acropetal order of development, the primordia of leaves are laid down usually in an orderly and often distinctive arrangement or phyllotaxis with reference to the stem. In some plants the leaf primordia are formed in pairs, successive pairs being at right angles to one another (decussate phyllotaxis) or in groups of three or more (whorled phyllotaxis); perhaps most commonly, a single leaf occurs at each node— an arrangement designated alternate-spiral. Although consideration of such varied phyllotactic patterns is important, the causal factors responsible for them are still poorly understood. (See Wardlaw, 1952, pp. 390-419, for a résumé of experimental studies on phyllotaxis.)

The differentiation between distinct root and shoot systems in most

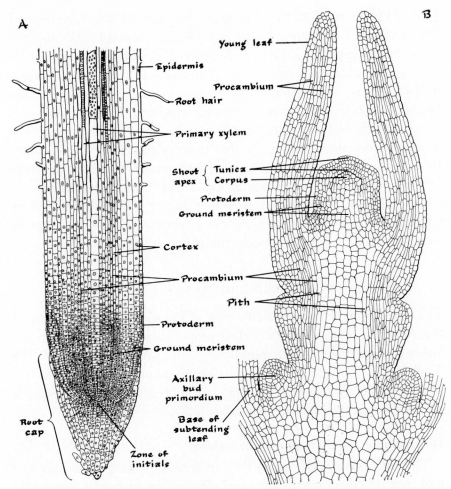

Figure 3-1 Longisections showing the apical meristems and the origin of the primary meristematic tissues in the root and shoot of angiosperms. **A,** root tip of *Hordeum sativum*; **B,** shoot tip of *Hypericum uralum*. [A, redrawn from *A Textbook of General Botany*, Ed. 4, by R. M. Holman and W. W. Robbins. N. Y.: John Wiley and Sons, Inc., 1951; B, redrawn from Zimmermann, *Jahrb. f. wiss. Bot.* 68:289, 1928.]

living tracheophytes is of considerable interest from an evolutionary viewpoint. It is now rather generally agreed that such an organographic and anatomical differentiation did not exist in the Devonian Psilophytales; on the contrary, these early land plants were devoid of roots, and some of them (*Horneophyton* and *Rhynia*) also lacked foliar organs

(Fig. 7-1). In such archaic organisms portions of the underground system of stems apparently served physiologically as roots. The modern survivors of the psilopsid line—*Psilotum* and *Tmesipteris*—are likewise rootless and, moreover, exhibit very primitive leaf-like structures. Both of these genera show absolutely no trace in their embryogeny of a suppressed or abortive root, a fact that adds weight to the belief that they are primitively rootless plants (see Chapter 7). From such considerations it seems reasonable to postulate that roots originated phylogenetically from the leafless axes of early types of land plants. However, the steps in the further evolutionary divergence of roots from primitive shoots, which led to the acquisition of a root cap, a prevalent internal or endogenous origin of branches, and the retention of a primitive type of vascular system, are unfortunately completely obscure today.

Types of Branching in Shoots

The types of branching or ramification of the sporophyte, especially of the shoot, are quite varied, and their proper classification and interpretation are important to both morphology and taxonomy. (Domin, 1923; Troll, 1937). From the broadest possible morphological viewpoint, two principal types (under each of which are subtypes) of ramification are recognized: dichotomous or dichopodial, and monopodial.

Dichotomous or Dichopodial Branching

True dichotomy results from the subdivision of the growing shoot or root apex into two more or less equal sister apices; each apex pursues its own individual growth for a time, and then may fork or dichotomize as before (Fig. 3-2, A, C). Troll calls this kind of dichotomy isotomous branching (Fig. 3-3, A, B). Successive dichotomies may be in planes more or less at right angles to each other, resulting in a cruciate system, which is illustrated very clearly in *Psilotum* (Chapter 7, Fig. 7-3, A). More commonly, however, the successive dichotomies occur in the same plane, and a flat system of forked branches results. This condition, known as flabellate dichotomy, occurs in certain species of *Lycopodium* and *Selaginella* with dorsiventral shoots (Chapter 8, Fig. 8-10, A). Dichotomous branching is usually regarded as the most primitive method of ramification of the sporophyte in vascular plants. It was apparently the prevailing mode of branching in the extremely archaic Psilophytales and today it is restricted largely to the shoots and roots of those plants which are regarded as primitive (*Psilotum, Tmesipteris, Isoetes,* and many species of *Lycopodium* and *Selaginella*). The occurrence of dichotomy in the shoot systems of certain ferns appears rather well established (Bower, 1935) but in other pteropsid plants (i.e., the gymnosperms and angiosperms) dichotomous branching is rare or, more usually, entirely absent.

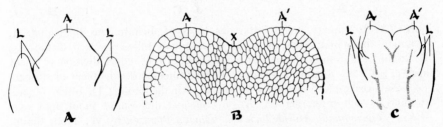

Figure 3-2 Dichotomous branching in *Lycopodium alpinum.* **A,** vegetative shoot apex (A) with leaf primordia (L); **B,** dichotomous division of a reproductive shoot apex (x) into two new apices, (A and A′); **C,** later stage in dichotomy of vegetative shoot apex. [From *Vergleichende Morphologie der höheren Pflanzen* by W. Troll. Berlin: Gebrüder Borntraeger, 1937.]

Monopodial Branching

In this type of ramification the main shoot axis or stem is conspicuous and lateral branches develop from axillary buds situated some distance behind the main shoot apex (Fig. 3-1, B). Thus, instead of repeated forking of the shoot apex, which is typical of dichotomous branching, monopodial branching is characterized by the dominance of the main axis over its laterals. Monopodial branching is the prevalent type of ramification throughout the seed plants, but it occurs also in certain of the lower groups of vascular plants. A striking example is the genus *Equisetum,* many species of which develop conspicuous whorls of branches. However, these branches originate from buds which alternate in position and number with the whorled leaves at each node (see Chapter 9).

Both the dichotomous and monopodial branch systems may be modified or disguised to some degree by unequal development of successive branches. For example, dichotomy of the shoot apex may be followed

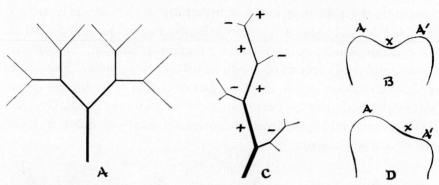

Figure 3-3 Isotomous and anisotomous types of dichotomous branching. **A**, isotomous branching, showing equal development following each dichotomy; **B**, origin of isotomous branch primordia (A, A′) by equal division of shoot apex (x); **C**, anisotomous branching, showing unequal development of stronger (+) and weaker (−) branches following each dichotomy; **D**, origin of anistomous branch primordia (A, A′) by unequal division of shoot apex (x). [From *Vergleichende Morphologie der höheren Pflanzen* by W. Troll: Berlin, Gebrüder Borntraeger, 1937.]   ,

by a very unequal growth of the two shanks—one may develop very strongly and surpass or overtop the other which is thus left behind as a short and apparently lateral shoot (Fig. 3-3, D). If this pattern of unequal or anisotomous branching is consistently followed throughout shoot growth, a pseudomonopodium, or sympodium, results, as shown in Fig. 3-3, C. This condition, with intergradations between it and regular flabellate dichotomy, is characteristic of many species of *Lycopodium* and *Selaginella* (see Rzehak, 1956, for an experimental study of pseudomonopodial branching in *Selaginella*). Sympodial growth is also characteristic of many fundamentally monopodial branch systems in the angiosperms. Here, one of the axillary buds near the main shoot apex gives rise to a precocious, vigorous side shoot which soon overtops the main shoot in its growth; the pattern of development is then repeated for each successively developed lateral shoot. The result is an apparent monopodium that actually consists of a series of superposed lateral branches which collectively may resemble a single axis.

Microphylls and Megaphylls

Interpretation of the morphology and evolutionary history of the leaves of vascular plants constitutes a fundamental problem that has attracted much attention during the present century. Leaves, regardless of their size, form, or structure, arise as lateral protuberances from the shoot apex and at maturity represent the typical lateral appendages of the axis or stem (see Fig. 1-1). From an ontogenetic viewpoint, a leaf is a determinate organ. In contrast to the theoretically unlimited or open type of apical growth characteristic of the stem, the apical growth of the leaf primordium in most plants ceases early in ontogeny and is followed by a phase of tissue specialization and enlargement which culminates in the production of the final shape and structure of the adult foliar organ (Foster, 1936). The question is: How did the distinction between an indeterminate axis and its lateral foliar appendages arise during the evolutionary history of vascular plants? The answer to this question is particularly important in the light of paleobotanical studies on the Psilophytales, a group of Devonian and Silurian plants which includes the simplest vascular plants known to science. The sporophytes of certain members of the Psilophytales (*Rhynia* and *Horneophyton*) comprised a system of dichotomously branched axes which were entirely devoid of leaves. If, as is widely believed, the aerial branches of such archaic plants are truly the prototypes of the modern leafy shoot, it logically follows that the stem preceded the leaf in evolution. Although current interpretations vary as to *how* determinate foliar appendages phylogenetically developed from a system of naked axes, it is generally agreed that evolutionary processes produced two morphologically different types of leaves: microphylls and megaphylls. Let us now examine the salient features of these two major classes of foliar organs and the manner in which they may have evolved in the lower vascular plants.

Morphological Contrasts

MICROPHYLLS. The microphyll, as its name suggests, is often a very small leaf (as, for example, are the leaves of certain species of *Lycopodium* and *Selaginella*) but it may attain considerable length, as it does in certain species of *Isoetes* (Chapter 8). The definitive character of the microphyll which distinguishes it from the megaphyll is its extremely simple vascular system. As shown in Fig. 3-4, C, at the node of a microphyllous shoot a single strand of vascular tissue—the leaf trace—diverges from the edge of the stele or vascular cylinder of the stem and extends as an unbranched mid-vein from the base to the apex of the leaf. It must be emphasized that the divergence of the single leaf trace at the node of a microphyll is *not* associated with a corresponding break or *leaf gap* in the stele of the axis. In short, as discussed more fully in Chapter 10, the development of microphylls is closely correlated with stems that possess a protostelic type of vascular cylinder.

On the basis of this character, microphylls occur typically in all members of the Lycopsida and in certain genera of the Psilophytales and are possibly represented (at least anatomically) by the univeined leaves of *Equisetum* in the Sphenopsida. The morphology of the appendages in the living order Psilotales is more difficult to interpret. In *Psilotum* the appendages are very small scale-like structures devoid of veins, but in *Tmesipteris* all of the larger appendages are traversed by a single unbranched mid-vein. Such variations in the Psilotales may be indicative

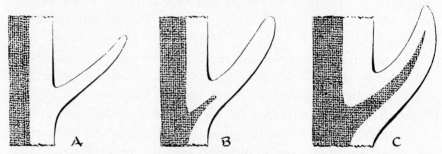

Figure 3-4 Evolutionary development of microphylls in the Psilophytales. **A,** *Psilophyton princeps* with primitive enation devoid of vascular tissue; **B,** *Asteroxylom* with rudimentary leaf trace (shaded) extending to base of enation; **C,** *Arthrostigma*, microphyll with single vascular strand. [From *Primitive Land Plants* by F. O. Bower. London: Macmillan and Co. Ltd., 1935.]

of various levels in the phylogenetic development of microphylls from emergences. For further details of microphyllous development in the Psilotales refer to Chapter 7.

In certain genera of the Lycopsida a small scale-like outgrowth, termed the ligule, develops near the adaxial base of each of the vegetative microphylls and sporophylls (Fig. 8-15). On the basis of the presence or absence of ligules, lycopsid plants can be arranged in two series: the "Ligulatae," which includes the living genera *Selaginella* and *Isoetes* as well as the members of the extinct order Lepidodendrales, all of which are characterized by ligulate leaves and ligulate sporophylls; and the "Eligulatae" in which ligules are absent, as in the living genera *Lyco-*

podium and *Phylloglossum* and possibly the extinct genus *Lycopodites*.

The ligule appears very early in the ontogeny of a microphyll and is initiated from a single surface cell in *Isoetes* whereas in *Selaginella* it originates from several short rows of superficial cells (Harvey-Gibson, 1896; Hsü, 1937). At maturity the ligule in each genus is a surprisingly complex organ, considering its small size and short life. The base or foot region is to some extent sunken in the tissue of the microphyll and consists of the sheath, a layer of cells continuous with the epidermis of the leaf or sporophyll, and the glossopodium, which is particularly well-developed in *Selaginella* and consists of a wedge-shaped group of large, highly vacuolated prismatic cells (see Fig. 8-13). According to Dunlop (1949) the sheath cells of the ligule of *Isoetes macrospora* possess well-defined Casparian strips and thus resemble typical endodermal cells; a less conspicuous Casparian strip also occurs on the walls of the sheath cells of the ligule of *Selaginella rupestris*. In *Isoetes engelmanni*, investigated in great detail by Smith (1900), the foot region of the ligule becomes very massive and its lateral portions grow upwardly and downwardly as pairs of horn-like processes. We have observed a comparable situation in other species, but a fuller investigation of the ontogeny of the ligule in *Isoetes* is highly desirable. In both *Selaginella* and *Isoetes* the free exserted portion of the ligule, prior to its death, is composed largely of relatively small, densely staining, polygonal-shaped cells. From a functional standpoint, it is believed that ligules are secretory organs which, by exuding water and possibly mucilage, serve to keep young leaves and sporangia in a moist condition. The frequent development of tracheid-like cells (transfusion tissue) between the ligule sheath and the adjacent vein of the microphyll indicates the possibility of direct conduction of water to the base of the ligule. Phylogenetically, the origin and homology of the ligule are very obscure problems. But the considerable antiquity of ligules is shown by their presence in certain of the extinct lycopods of the Paleozoic Era.

MEGAPHYLLS.   The megaphyll (also called macrophyll by some authors), illustrated by the large and usually pinnatifid leaf of the ferns, is fundamentally distinguished from the microphyll by its complex venation and by the relation of its leaf trace or traces to a well-defined leaf gap in the stele of the stem (Fig. 3-5). In a few living genera of

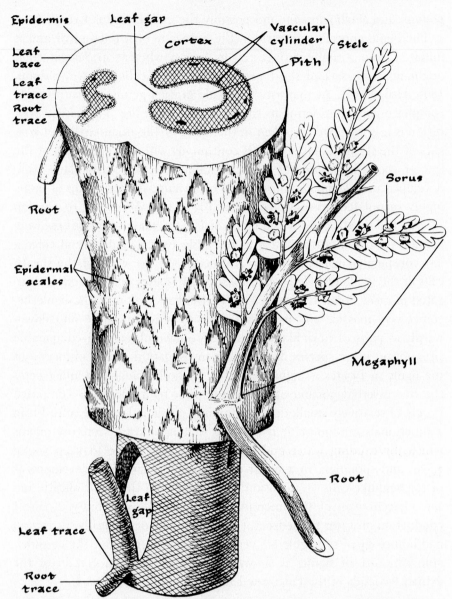

Figure 3-5 Organography and general vascular anatomy of a small portion of a fern shoot. A pinnatified megaphyll with its abaxial sori is seen in surface view at right. Note that the divergence of a leaf trace into a megaphyll (shown at the top and bottom of the figure) is associated with a leaf-gap in the stele of the stem. [From *The Anatomy of Woody Plants* by E. C. Jeffrey. Chicago: The University of Chicago Press, 1917.]

ferns the vascular system of the stem is a protostele. In the majority of ferns, however, the presence of megaphyllous leaves is correlated with some type of siphonostele; that is, a central pith is enclosed by a continuous or dissected cylinder of vascular tissue. (For a detailed discussion of stelar morphology in the ferns see Chapter 13.) In contrast with the univeined microphyll, the venation of the lamina of a megaphyll consists of a somewhat complex system of branching vascular strands. It is generally agreed that in ferns the most primitive pattern of venation consists of a series of dichotomously branched veinlets which terminate freely without anastomoses (i.e., interconnections) at the margins of the lamina (Bower 1935). This open dichotomous venation is connected by transitional patterns with the more highly evolved, complex types of closed or reticulate venation found in the leaves of both eusporangiate and leptosporangiate ferns (Fig. 13-4).

Phylogenetic Origin

As Bower (1935, p. 548) has clearly pointed out, the evolutionary meaning of the morphological differences between microphylls and megaphylls "can only be solved by comparison between various types living and fossil, aided where possible by reference to individual development." On this basis Bower concluded that the microphylls and megaphylls of lower vascular plants represent the result of separate paths in foliar evolution.

According to Bower, microphylls originated as enations or superficial lateral outgrowths from the naked stems or axes of primitive members of the Psilophytales. At the earliest stage in evolution, as exemplified by *Psilophyton*, the enation was a small scale or spine-like outgrowth devoid of a leaf trace or vein, as shown by Fig. 3-4, A. At a more advanced stage, as in *Asteroxylon*, the enation was provided with a rudimentary leaf trace which terminated at the base of the appendage (Fig. 3-4, B). Further extension of the leaf trace into the appendage resulted in a primitive univeined microphyll, as shown in *Drepanophycus* [*Arthrostigma* (Fig. 3-4, C)]. Additional support for the enation theory of the microphyll is found in the shoots of the living psilopsids. In both *Psilotum* and *Tmesipteris* the young sporophytic axis is naked; in *Psilotum* all of the appendages formed later in shoot development remain devoid of veins; in *Tmesipteris* the adult foliar organ develops a

single well-defined mid-vein. To summarize, Bower's theory holds that
enation leaves or microphylls represent an upgrade progression from
leaflessness rather than downgrade steps of reduction (Fig. 3-4). The
contrary (and, at present, less widely accepted) view of Zimmermann
(1954) maintains that microphylls, including the scale-like emergences
of *Asteroxylon* or *Psilotum*, represent the culmination of a process of
reduction from lateral dichotomously branched systems of axes or
telomes.

Today there appears to be rather widespread acceptance of the theory
that the megaphylls of ferns originated phylogenetically as a result of the
specialized development of dichotomous branch systems. The first sug-
gestion of the cladode (i.e., stem) nature of the megaphyll was made by
Lignier (1903), and this idea was subsequently developed in considerable
detail by Bower (1935) and ultimately became a basic feature of Zimmermann's Telome Theory. (Zimmermann, 1930; Wilson, 1953.) According to Bower, the first step toward the differentiation between axis
and cladode leaves (megaphylls) was a gradual change from the original
pattern of *equal dichotomous branching* in psilophytalean plants to a
sympodial type of growth. This consisted in the *unequal development*
of the sister branches of a dichotomy, one continuing growth as the main
axis, the other becoming laterally displaced and representing the pre-
cursor of a megaphyll. Subsequent flattening, and the fusion or webbing
of the divisions of the repressed or overtopped lateral branch systems, is
then assumed to have brought about a clear distinction between cladode
leaves borne laterally upon a well-defined central axis or stem. As stated
by Bower (1935, p. 625) the "history of the origin of the Cladode Leaf
is thus quite distinct in its initial steps from that of the microphyllous or
enation leaf."

The Telome Theory

The phylogenetic concept that megaphylls evolved from subordinated
branch systems has been utilized also by Zimmermann (1930, 1953, 1954)
in connection with his widely exploited Telome Theory. According to
this theory, the most primitive vascular plant was composed entirely of a
system of telomes. A telome is the ultimate terminal portion of a
dichotomizing axis and may bear a sporangium (fertile telome) or be
sterile (sterile telome, termed by Zimmermann a "phylloid"). Fertile and

sterile telomes may develop in separate or combined groups called telome trusses. In Zimmermann's opinion the vegetative shoot of megaphyllous plants evolved by the operation of a relatively few elementary processes, among the most important of which are *overtopping, planation,* and *webbing.* The relation of these processes to the evolution of the mega- phyll is shown diagrammatically in Fig. 3-6. Beginning with a leafless and dichotomously branched plant such as *Rhynia,* unequal dichotomous branching resulted in the overtopping of the weaker branch by its more aggressive sister branch; this process was repeated at each point of a major dichotomy and resulted in the initial distinction between axis and leaves (Fig. 3-6, A, B). The subordinated lateral branches at first dichotomized in more than one plane; later, as the result of planation, branching became restricted to a single plane (Fig. 3-6, C). The final step in megaphyll evolution, according to the Telome Theory, consisted in the fusion or webbing of the separate telomes of an overtopped lateral branch into a flat, primitive lamina characterized by a simple type of open dichotomous venation (Fig. 3-6, D). Subsequent fusions be- tween the veinlets produced varied types of reticulate venation.

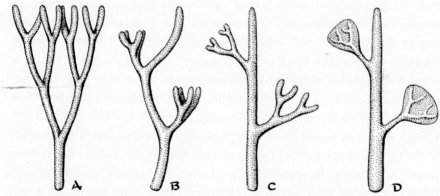

Figure 3-6 The phylogenetic origin and development of the megaphyll accord- ing to the telome theory. **A,** isotomous branch system, without distinction be- tween axis and megaphylls; **B,** unequal dichotomy or "overtopping," the weaker branches representing initial stages in megaphyll evolution; **C,** dichot- omous branching of primitive megaphylls in a single plant ("planation"); **D,** union between forked divisions of megaphylls ("webbing") has produced a flat, dichotomously veined lamina. [Adapted from *Cryptogamic Botany, Vol. II. Bryophytes and Pteridophytes* by G. M. Smith. N. Y.: McGraw-Hill Book Company, Inc., 1955.]

Zimmermann and certain other morphologists (e.g., Florin, 1938-1945; Wilson, 1942) have extended the telome concept beyond the level of the ferns to the interpretation of the foliar and reproductive organs of both gymnosperms and angiosperms (see Wilson, 1953, for a detailed review). Although from the standpoint of vasculation the leaves of gymnosperms and angiosperms qualify as megaphylls (Chapter 18), other contemporary morphologists are more skeptical of the value of the telome concept, particularly with reference to the efforts which have been made to extend it to the interpretation of the morphology of angiosperms (Bailey, 1949, 1956).

Comparative Anatomy of the Sporophyte

It should be evident by now that the organographic evolution of the sporophyte has reached various levels in the different groups of living vascular plants. In the Psilotaceae and Lycopodiaceae, many ancient features such as dichotomous branching and microphylls are still in evidence. By contrast, the living Pteropsida exhibit a much higher level of organ specialization, including the development of large complex leaves and the presence of monopodial branching. Paleobotanical evidence reveals that a similar complex and variable evolution of cell types and tissues also has occurred. Indeed, one of the most important achievements in paleobotany has been the discovery and description of the well-preserved anatomy of several ancient groups of vascular plants. This has made possible at least the beginning of a true phylogenetic interpretation and classification of cell types and tissues (Hofmann, 1934; Foster, 1949, 1956a). It seems reasonable to conclude this chapter with a brief review of the outstanding aspects of sporophyte anatomy. Of course this résumé should in no sense, be regarded as a satisfactory condensation of the vast subject matter of plant anatomy (Esau, 1953), but we hope that it will provide the indispensable orientation needed by the student in his introductory approach to the comparative anatomy of stem, leaf, and root.

Sachs' Classification of Tissue Systems

One of the most useful schemes for understanding the general topographical anatomy of the adult sporophyte was devised by the celebrated German botanist, Julius von Sachs (1875). The great merit of his classification is its simplicity and its wide applicability to the primary structure of the stem, leaf, and root. According to Sachs, the early phylogenetic development of vascular plants resulted in the differentiation of three principal systems of tissues: the external epidermal and cork layers collectively termed the Dermal System; the strands of conducting phloem and xylem tissue which compose the Fascicular System; and the remaining internal tissue or tissues designated the Fundamental or Ground Tissue System. Sachs emphasized that each of these tissue systems may comprise the most varied cell types and that his scheme of classification was concerned with the broadest possible contrast between systems of tissues (see Foster, 1949, for a critical discussion of Sachs' scheme of classifying tissue systems).

Figure 3-7 shows diagrammatically the application of Sachs' classification and terminology to the gross anatomy of the stem, leaf, and root of flowering plants. This figure indicates plainly that the fascicular tissue system is the most variable of the three, from the standpoint of its pattern of development within plant organs. In stems the fascicular system appears either as a central cylinder of phloem and xylem or in the form of vascular bundles arranged in a cylinder or scattered throughout the ground tissue system (see Fig. 3-7, A; also Fig. 18-6). The form of the fascicular system of the leaf ranges from one to many bundles or a

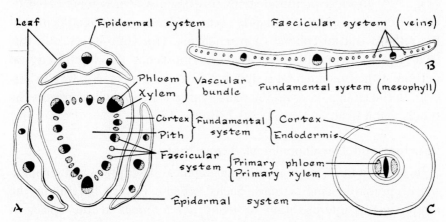

Figure 3-7 Diagrams (based on *Linum usitatissimum*) illustrating the positions and patterns of the epidermal, fascicular, and fundamental tissue systems in the vegetative organs of a dicotyledon. **A,** transection of stem and three leaf bases; **B,** transection of lamina of leaf; **C,** transection of root. [Redrawn from *Plant Anatomy* by K. Esau. N. Y.: John Wiley and Sons, Inc., 1953.]

cylinder in the petiole, to a complex series of veins, usually arranged in a single plane, in the lamina (Fig. 3-7, B; also Fig. 18-5). In the root the pattern of the fascicular system is very distinctive, consisting of a radial and alternate series of phloem and xylem strands; commonly the latter are joined at their inner edge to form a solid core of xylem as shown in Fig. 3-7, C.

In contrast with these diverse patterns exhibited by the fascicular system, the form and arrangement of Sachs' other tissue systems are comparatively simple. The dermal system, in all foliar organs and in young stems and roots, is represented by the epidermis (Fig. 3-7; also Figs. 18-5, 18-6). Typically this is a single layer of superficial cells which are tightly joined except for the stomatal openings; in some groups of dicotyledons the leaf may develop on one or both surfaces a multiple epidermis consisting of two or many layers of cells, all of which have originated from the subdivision of the original surface layer of cells (Fig. 3-9, C). In the stems and roots of many vascular plants the epidermis is eventually sloughed away by the development beneath it of cork. Like the cells of the epidermis, cork cells are compactly arranged and it is only at certain areas known as lenticels that well-developed intercellular air-space systems are found. Situated below the dermal system and external to or surrounding the fascicular system is the fundamental tissue system (Fig. 3-7). In most pteropsid stems this tissue system is represented by the cortex—a cylinder of tissues between epidermis and the phloem, and the pith—a central column of parenchyma. (see Fig. 3-7, A; also Fig. 18-6, A.) The stems of the *Lycopsida* and most roots develop the cortical portion of the fundamental system but lack a pith (Fig. 3-7, C; also Fig. 8-4). In the lamina of leaves the photosynthetic mesophyll represents the fundamental tissue system (Fig. 3-7, B; Fig. 18-5).

Structure and Development of Tissue Systems

In addition to its value in the topographical description and comparison of primary tissue systems, Sachs' scheme is very helpful in the morphological interpretation of *tissue development* at the apices of shoots and roots. Apical meristems, as shown by the numerous researches of the past decade, are extraordinarily variable in their histology (see Foster, 1949, pp. 42-48; Esau, 1953; Gifford, 1954, for literature on the subject). In some plants, for example, *Equisetum* and the leptosporangiate ferns, a single well-defined apical cell occupies the tip of the axis and represents the ultimate point of origin of all the meristematic tissue of the apex of root and shoot (see Fig. 9-4). However, the shoot apices of *Lycopodium,* of certain eusporangiate ferns, and of a great many gymnosperms possess several superficial apical initials. And finally, the shoot apices of the angiosperms have a typical stratified arrangement of cells, the outer layer or layers representing the tunica, which surrounds a central mass of meristem designated the corpus; in this type of apex, the number and position of individualized apical initials is very uncertain in most cases (Fig. 3-1, B). Despite the histological differences among the types of apices in vascular plants, an essentially similar pattern of early histogenesis or tissue formation, is common to all of them. This consists in the ultimate segregation, behind the apex of shoot and root, of three primary meristematic tissues: the protoderm, the procambium, and the ground meristem (Fig. 3-1). These tissues are the precursors of the epidermal, fascicular, and ground tissue systems, respectively, and their salient features may now be briefly examined.

THE EPIDERMIS. The protoderm, derived from the cells of the shoot or root apex, is a uniseriate layer of dividing cells that ultimately forms the epidermis of mature organs (Figs. 3-1, 3-8, 3-9). Certain protoderm cells enlarge, acquire cutinized outer walls, and differentiate as the typical epidermal cells of leaves and stems. In many plants large numbers of protoderm cells develop into the various types of epidermal appendages or trichomes; common examples of trichomes are root hairs and the various kinds of hairs so commonly seen on leaves and stems. The stomata are characteristic of the epidermal system of foliage leaves, and many types of stems, floral organs, and fruits (Fig. 18-5, B). Paleobotanical evidence shows clearly that stomata were present in such ancient and simple vascular plants as the Psilophytales. Stomata develop by the division and differentiation of certain protoderm cells into pairs of guard cells between which a stomatal opening or pore is formed (Fig. 3-8). In many plants two or more of the cells bordering upon the stoma are distinctive in form and are termed subsidiary cells (Fig. 3-8, C; Fig. 16-7). The student should understand that the epidermis of fossil plants, and particularly the arrangement and structure of its stomata, provides very important clues as to the phylogeny and relationships of extinct

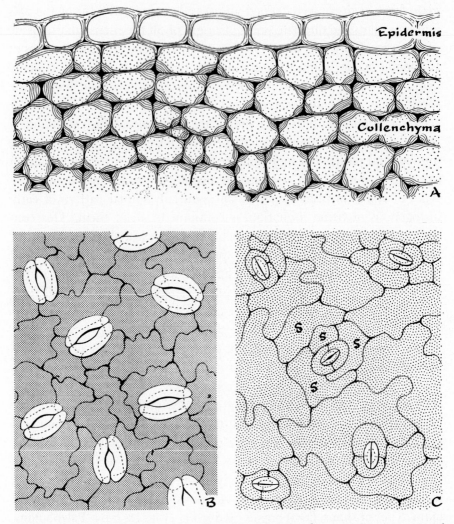

Figure 3-8 **A,** transection of epidermis and collenchyma tissue in stem of *Cucurbita*; **B,** surface view of stomata in lower epidermis of leaf of *Capsicum*; **C,** surface view of stomata with subsidiary cells (*s*) in lower epidermis of leaf of *Sedum*. [A-C, redrawn from *Plant Anatomy* by K. Esau. N. Y.: John Wiley and Sons, Inc., 1953; B, courtesy Artschwager.]

tracheophytes. An excellent illustration of the phylogenetic importance of epidermal structure is found in the detailed comparisons between the stomata of living and extinct gymnosperms made by Rudolf Florin (1931).

THE FUNDAMENTAL TISSUE SYSTEM. This system of tissues originates from the ground meristem and, as mentioned before, is represented by the tissues found in the cortex of stems and roots, the pith of pteropsid stems, and the mesophyll of foliar organs (Fig. 3-1). In contrast with the elongated and often spindle-shaped procambial cells, ground meristem cells, prior to differentiation, are polyhedral cells which closely approximate tetrakaidecahedra (14-sided bodies) in form. Cells of this type very commonly enlarge, become separated by intercellular spaces, and mature into the parenchyma tissue, which often is the principal component of the fundamental tissue system. But additional cell types and tissues may originate from unspecialized ground meristem and become part of the fundamental tissue system of plant organs. A common example of this is collenchyma tissue, which is very frequently developed in the outer region of the cortex of stems and in the subepidermal region of petioles (Fig. 3-8, A). In the ontogeny of collenchyma the ground meristem cells divide and elongate, ultimately producing compact strands or a cylinder of living cells with unevenly thickened primary walls; very commonly the thickest portions of the wall are laid down at the angles or corners where several collenchyma cells meet. Regarded functionally, collenchyma tissue provides support and flexibility for growing organs and at maturity is characterized by considerable tensile strength.

Another extremely common type of tissue in the fundamental tissue system is sclerenchyma, which is composed of cells with thick, lignified secondary walls. Two fairly well-demarcated cell types are included under sclerenchyma: fibers, which typically are conspicuously elongated cells with pointed ends, and sclereids, which are polygonal (the so-called stone cells), columnar, or profusely branched in form. At maturity fibers very commonly are dead cells, devoid of protoplasts, and occur as strands or cylinders of tightly joined cells which evidently are of considerable importance in providing mechanical strength to plant organs (Fig. 3-9, A). Sclereids may occur in compact masses in various parts of the fundamental tissue system, but they also occur as isolated cells or idioblasts. In the leaves of many dicotyledons, branched idioblastic sclereids are frequently diffuse in their distribution in the mesophyll (Fig. 3-9, B), but in certain genera the sclereids are terminal, or restricted in occurrence to the vein endings (Fig. 3-9, C). (See Foster, 1949, 1956b, for further details and references to the literature on foliar sclereids.)

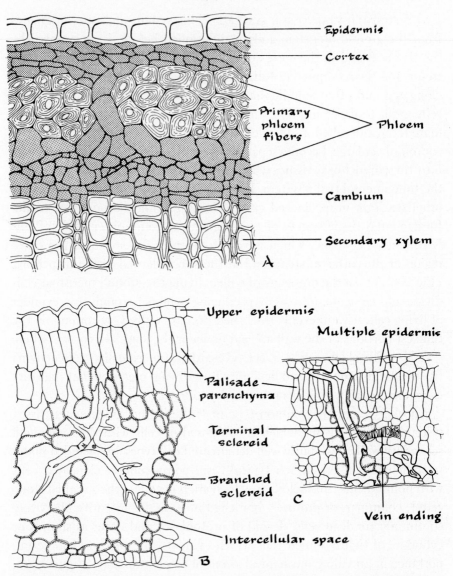

Figure 3-9 A, transection of stem of *Linum usitatissimum* illustrating position of strands of primary phloem fibers; **B,** transection of portion of lamina of *Trochodendron aralioides* showing a branched sclereid; **C,** transection of a portion of lamina of *Mouriria Huberi,* showing a columnar, ramified terminal sclereid. [A, redrawn from *Plant Anatomy* by K. Esau. N. Y.: John Wiley and Sons, Inc., 1953; B, redrawn from Foster, *Amer. Jour. Bot.* 32:456, 1945; C, redrawn from Foster, *Amer. Jour. Bot.* 34:501, 1947.]

THE FASCICULAR TISSUE SYSTEM. From what we have said regarding the variable patterns of the fascicular system, a corresponding variability is to be anticipated in the patterns of procambium formation in young organs. In the young, terminal regions of many stems (particularly the stems of gymnosperms and angiosperms) and in differentiating leaves the procambium consists of discrete cellular strands composed of elongated cells (Fig. 3-1, B); each strand matures as a vascular bundle composed of primary phloem and primary xylem tissue, as shown in Figs. 3-10, and 3-11. In the stems of certain lower vascular plants (*Lycopodium*, and certain ferns) and in many roots, the procambium is a central core or column of tissue from which the vascular cylinder, devoid of pith, originates (Fig. 3-1, A). A discussion of the complex problem of the origin and development of primary vascular tissues from the procambium is entirely beyond the scope of this book (see Esau, 1954, for a review of the subject and literature references), but certain aspects of vasculation in plants are essential to our presentation of comparative morphology and merit brief discussion here.

The first of these general problems concerns the general structure of primary xylem and the meaning of the terms protoxylem and metaxylem. According to the best of modern usage, protoxylem designates the pole of earliest developed primary xylem and includes all tracheary tissue which differentiates (i.e., completes its growth and secondary wall development) during the period of organ elongation. Tracheary elements of the protoxylem, as shown in Fig. 3-10, often develop their secondary walls as a series of rings (annular elements) or as one or more spiral bands (spiral elements). The metaxylem is the remaining portion of the primary xylem which completes its differentiation, after the organ in which it occurs has ceased to elongate. Metaxylem cells, also shown in Fig. 3-10, usually have more extensively developed secondary walls which commonly appear as a series of connected bars (scalariform elements) or a network (reticulate elements), or else the wall is pitted.

It must be emphatically stated that the primary xylem may consist wholly of tracheids or of both tracheids and vessel elements. The type of secondary wall pattern is therefore not necessarily correlated with the presence or absence of vessel elements. The primary xylem of certain species of *Selaginella* and of the fern *Pteridium* contains well-defined

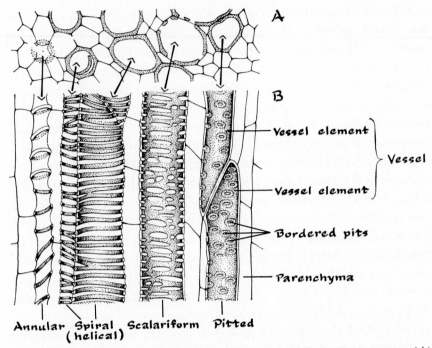

Figure 3-10 A portion of the primary xylem of *Aristolochia* in transverse (A) and longisectional (B) view. Note diversity in types of secondary wall patterns of tracheary elements in progressing from protoxylem at left to metaxylem at right. [From *Plant Anatomy* by K. Esau. N. Y.: John Wiley and Sons, Inc., 1953.]

vessels; these conducting structures also occur in the primary xylem of many monocotyledons and dicotyledons. (See Bailey, 1944, 1957; and Cheadle, 1953, for a discussion of the evolution of vessels.)

A second problem involves the direction of radial maturation of successive procambial cells during the differentiation of the primary xylem. In the roots of all vascular plants, and in the stems of *Psilotum* and the *Lycopsida*, the first protoxylem cells to acquire secondary walls occur at the outermost edge of the procambial cylinder; these cells establish the future pattern of xylem differentiation which occurs *centripetally* or toward the center of the axis. Primary xylem of this type is termed exarch and is regarded as the most primitive condition in vascular plants (Fig. 3-11, A). In the stems of modern seed plants, however, the protoxylem begins its development from the innermost procambial cells—those situated next to the pith—and the remainder of the process of primary xylem differentiation occurs *centrifugally* or toward the periphery of the stem (Fig. 3-11, B). This type of primary xylem is termed endarch xylem and is believed to be the most highly advanced condition. Lastly, in the leaf and stem bundles of many ferns the primary xylem is mesarch. This means that the protoxylem begins development within the procambial strand and that further xylem formation occurs centripetally as well as centrifugally; consequently, at maturity the protoxylem cells are surrounded by the metaxylem, as can be seen in Fig. 3-11, C. The distinction between exarch, endarch, and mesarch xylem thus appears to be of considerable importance, not only among different groups of vascular plants but even between the root and stem of the same plant. Since the xylem of extinct plants is often well-preserved in fossils, the recognition of the position of the protoxylem in relation to the metaxylem is a matter of considerable significance in paleobotanical interpretation.

A third problem in regard to the structure of vascular tissues concerns the phloem. The primary phloem of vascular plants is characterized by the presence of specialized conducting cells known as sieve elements. The definitive feature of these elements, at least in angiosperms, is the

Figure 3-11 Directions of radial maturation of tracheary elements in the primary xylem of vascular plants. **A,** exarch primary xylem; **B,** endarch primary xylem; **C,** mesarch primary xylem. [Redrawn from *The Anatomy of Woody Plants* by E. C. Jeffrey. Chicago: The University of Chicago Press, 1917.]

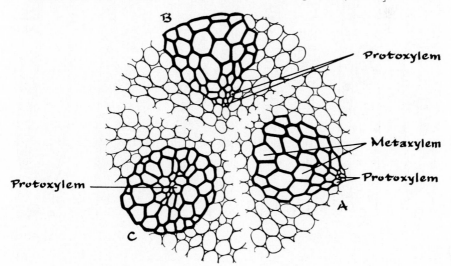

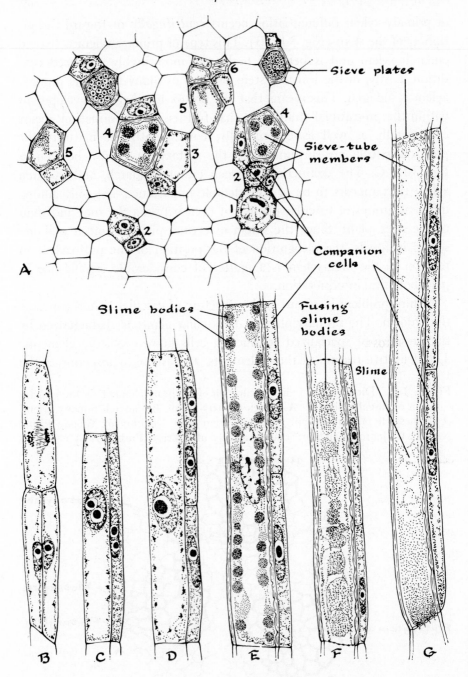

absence at maturity of a nucleus and the presence of more or less specialized sieve areas or sieve plates in the walls (Fig. 3-12, A, G). A sieve area is a modified portion of the primary wall traversed by connecting strands of protoplasm, each of which at an early stage in development is surrounded by a cylinder of substance termed callose. Prior to the death and obliteration of sieve elements, the sieve fields (and the coarser sieve plates) are usually entirely covered with callose. In the angiosperms the sieve elements occur in superposed series collectively designated sieve tubes. Each sieve-tube member is associated with one or more nucleated companion cells (Fig. 3-12, A, C-G). In addition to the definitive sieve elements, primary as well as secondary phloem may contain parenchyma cells, sclereids, and fibers. For detailed treatments of the ontogeny and structure of both primary and secondary phloem, consult Esau, Cheadle, and Gifford, 1953; and Esau, 1950, 1953.

Lastly, the concept of secondary vascular tissues and their demarcation from the primary vascular system needs to be considered. Secondary vascular tissues are produced from the vascular cambium, and since the cells of both phloem and xylem are often arranged in radial rows this system of tissues often is clearly demarcated from the more irregular pattern of cells of the primary vascular system. (See Fig. 3-9 A; also Fig. 16-8, A.) But the criterion of orderly versus irregular cell arrangement is not always valid; in some angiosperms and gymnosperms the tracheary cells of the primary as well as the secondary xylem are in regular radial alignment (Fig. 18-6, A). As a consequence, the boundary between the primary and secondary vascular systems can be only approximately determined even when the entire ontogenetic development has been studied. Secondary growth by means of a vascular cambium has repeatedly arisen during the evolution of vascular plants. Many extinct groups of the tracheophytes (for example, *Lepidodendron* and *Cala-*

Figure 3-12 Differentiation of sieve-tube members and their associated companion cells in *Cucurbita*. **A**, transection of phloem, the successive numbers (*1-6*) designating stages in development of sieve-tube members and companion cells; **B-G**, corresponding stages in development as seen in longisectional view. Note the disappearance of the nucleus (**E-F**) and the development of sieve plates at the ends of the sieve-tube members. [Redrawn from *Plant Anatomy* by K. Esau. N. Y.: John Wiley and Sons, Inc., 1953.]

mites; see Fig. 9-11, C) showed conspicuous secondary growth, and secondary growth is a prominent feature of all living gymnosperms and of a large number of the angiosperms. However, most of the lower vascular plants of today such as the Psilotaceae, the majority of the Lycopsida, *Equisetum,* and the majority of ferns, are devoid of cambial activity. In these organisms, as in most of the monocotyledons, the fascicular system is entirely primary and derived ontogenetically from the procambium.

The Stelar Theory

During the latter half of the nineteenth century the increasing emphasis placed on the importance of the vascular system in morphological interpretation led to the formulation of the Stelar Theory. This theory, which was developed by Van Tieghem and his students (Van Tieghem and Douliot, 1886) has had far-reaching effects on modern concepts of the morphology and evolution of the primary vascular system and hence deserves our attention. According to Van Tieghem, the primary structure of the stem and root are fundamentally similar in that each organ consists of a central stele enveloped by the cortex, the outer layer of which is represented by the epidermis. The term "stele" was used in a collective sense by Van Tieghem to designate not only the primary vascular tissues but also the so-called conjunctive tissues associated with them: pericycle, vascular rays, and, when it occurs, the pith tissue (Fig. 3-13).

One of the critical—and in the light of modern studies, controversial —aspects of the Stelar Theory is the nature of the anatomical boundaries which separate the cortex from the stele. Van Tieghem considered that the inner boundary of the cortex is represented by the endodermis, a cylinder of living cells which, from a strict histological viewpoint, are characterized by the presence of Casparian strips. These strips or bands represent chemically modified portions of the radial- and end-walls of the endodermal cells and are thought to contain both lignin and suberin.

In roots and in the stems of many of the lower vascular plants an endodermis is present and represents a tangible boundary between cortex and stele (Fig. 7-5, A). But an endodermis, in the sense just defined, is not present in the stems of a large proportion of the seed plants,

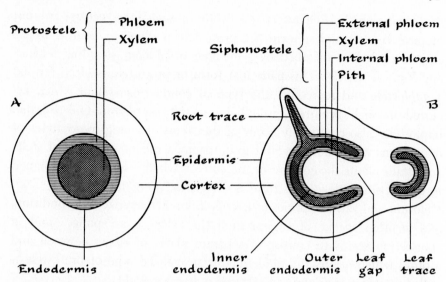

Figure 3-13 Types of steles in the stems of vascular plants. **A,** the protostele; **B,** the siphonostele. [Redrawn from *The Anatomy of Woody Plants* by E. C. Jeffrey. Chicago: The University of Chicago Press, 1917.]

especially woody types, and in these cases the limits between cortex and stele are more difficult to establish. The pericycle likewise fluctuates in its occurrence in vascular plants and the entire concept of pericycle and pericyclic fibers has been critically re-examined in recent years from an ontogenetic viewpoint (see especially Esau, 1950). Although the pericycle is a recognizable cylinder of cells at the outer edge of the stele of roots and the stems of lower vascular plants, ontogenetic studies have shown that the so-called pericycle in the stems of many angiosperms represents actually the outermost portion of the primary phloem. In such instances the pericyclic fibers are morphologically a part of the protophloem and consequently there is no independent tissue zone separating the cortex from the stele (Fig. 3-9, A).

Despite the absence of consistent histological boundaries between the cortex and stele, the value of the Stelar Theory as a unified concept has been widely recognized and has led to efforts to classify and interpret phylogenetically the varied types of vascular cylinders that occur in stems and roots.

It is now rather generally agreed that from a phylogenetic as well as an ontogenetic standpoint the most primitive type of stele is the *protostele*, which is characterized by the absence of a central column of pith. In its simplest form the protostele is merely a central strand of primary xylem sheathed by a cylinder of phloem (see Fig. 3-13, A and Fig. 7-2, A, C). This particular form of protostele is often termed a *haplostele* and represents the type of conducting system which occurred in such primitive psilophytes as *Horneophyton* and *Rhynia*; haplosteles also commonly occur in the stems of young sporophytes of many ferns which develop later in ontogeny a medullated type of stele. In certain plants the contour of the core of xylem is lobed or starshaped in transectional view—this form is designated an *actinostele* (Fig. 7-4). *Psilotum* and various species of *Lycopodium* characterize this condition, and in other species of *Lycopodium* the xylem is a "sponge" and in transection seems to consist of separate plates of tissue between and around which occurs the phloem; this specialized type of protostele is called the *plectostele* and is illustrated in Fig. 8-4, C, D.

A stele with a central column of pith is regarded phylogenetically as an advance in anatomical development and is termed a *siphonostele* (Fig. 3-13, B). Siphonosteles are characteristic of the stems of most members of the Pteropsida (see Chapter 10). Considerable difference of opinion has prevailed among morphologists as to the method of phylogenetic origin and development of a pith. One theory, championed by the American anatomist E. C. Jeffrey (1917, pp. 283-291) holds that the pith is always *extrastelar* in origin—that it represents the inclusion of the fundamental tissue into the core of xylem. The opposed extreme view is that the pith is *stelar* in origin and represents degraded tracheary elements. Evidence for this view is furnished by the existence of protosteles in which the central region consists of both tracheids and parenchyma cells; this type of vitalized protostele is presumed to typify a stage in the phylogenetic reduction of the centermost tracheary elements to parenchyma (Fig. 13-14, A). Today there is good reason to believe that medullated steles have originated in both of these ways. In other words, similar-appearing siphonosteles may have resulted either by the gradual inclusion of areas of cortical parenchyma or by the phylogenetic reduction of the original tracheids to parenchyma (see especially Bower, 1911).

The histological structure of the siphonostele varies widely. In certain fern genera (*Adiantum*, *Marsilea*, and *Dennstaedtia*) the cylinder of primary xylem is bordered internally as well as externally by phloem tissue. Furthermore, two endodermal cylinders are developed, one separating the cortex from the external phloem, the other situated between the internal phloem and the pith (see Fig. 13-15). This condition is termed amphiphloic, and a stele with this construction is specifically designated as a *solenostele* (Gwynne-Vaughan, 1901). The solenostele is often used to support the theory that the siphonostele has arisen by the invasion of the xylem by extra-fascicular tissues; i.e., endodermis, pericycle, and phloem. In certain highly specialized angiosperm families such as Asclepiadaceae and Solanaceae, internal phloem is developed at the periphery of the pith. However, it is very probable that the amphiphloic condition in this case is a mark of extreme anatomical specialization rather than an example of the persistence of a primitive fernlike stelar structure. Most commonly, at least in seed plants, the stele of the stem consists of only an external cylinder of phloem enclosing the xylem; this condition is designated ectophloic (see Fig. 16-8, A).

The most highly evolved siphonosteles are those in which the primary vascular tissues (in transectional view) appear as a ring or a scattered series of vascular bundles. If a solenostele in a lower vascular plant is dissected in this manner, the stele is termed a *dictyostele* (Brebner, 1902). In this case the strands are interconnected, forming a tubular network, and each strand is concentric in structure, consisting of a central strip of xylem completely surrounded by phloem (Fig. 13-16, A). The term meristele is often used to designate such a concentric strand of vascular tissue. If evolutionary modification has culminated in the dissection of an ectophloic siphonostele, a *eustele* results. This type of vascular system is widespread in the seed plants, and the interconnected strands composing it are called collateral bundles; these consist of a strand of xylem flanked externally by phloem tissue, as shown in Fig. 3-7, B, and in Fig. 18-6, A. If the stele of an angiosperm stem with internal phloem is conspicuously dissected, the individual vascular strands are frequently bicollateral in structure and consist of a median strip of xylem flanked on each side by phloem.

In all siphonosteles fairly conspicuous strips of parenchyma known as gaps develop at various points in the vascular cylinder. The Pteropsida, except for protostelic ferns and a few angiosperms, are distinguished specifically from the other phyla of vascular plants by the presence of leaf gaps (Chapter 10). These parenchymatous areas occur above the point of divergence of the vascular strands or leaf traces to the bases of the leaves (Figs. 3-5 and 3-13, B). In dissected steles such as the highly dissected dictyosteles typical of some ferns, and in eusteles, parenchymatous areas between the vascular strands vary in number and vertical extent, and sometimes tend to overlap within each internode; doubtless some of these areas are merely interfascicular strips of parenchyma without consistent relationship to the leaf-trace system. In contrast with the development of leaf gaps in the Pteropsida, the shoots of microphyllous plants (Psilopsida, Lycopsida, and Sphenopsida) are devoid of such structures. This is apparent in Fig. 3-4, C. In microphyllous plants with siphonosteles the only gaps present are branch gaps, which are related to the divergence of the vascular strands to the lateral branches. Siphonosteles devoid of true leaf gaps have been termed cladosiphonic in contrast with the phyllosiphonic condition in the Pteropsida (Jeffrey, 1910).

References

Bailey, I. W. 1944. The development of vessels in angiosperms and its significance in morphological research. *Amer. Jour. Bot.* 31:421-428.

————. 1949. Origin of the angiosperms: need for a broadened outlook. *Jour. Arnold Arboretum* 30:64-70.

————. 1956. Nodal anatomy in retrospect. *Jour. Arnold Arboretum* 37:269-287.

————. 1957. The potentialities and limitations of wood anatomy in the study of the phylogeny and classification of the angiosperms. *Jour. Arnold Arboretum* 38:243-254.

Bower, F. O. 1911. On medullation in the pteridophyta. *Ann. Bot.* 25:555-574.

————. 1935. *Primitive Land Plants.* Macmillan, London.

Brebner, G. 1902. On the anatomy of *Danaea* and other Marattiaceae. *Ann. Bot.* 16:517-552.

Cheadle, V. I. 1953. Independent origin of vessels in the monocotyledons and dicotyledons. *Phytomorphology* 3:23-44.

Domin, K. 1923. Dichotomy and chorisis. A morphological study. *Bull. Int. Acad. Sci. Boheme.* 3:1-10.

Dunlop, D. W. 1949. Casparian strips in *Isoetes macrospora*. *Bull. Torrey Bot. Club* 76:134-135.

Esau, K. 1950. Development and structure of the phloem tissue. II. *Bot. Rev.* 16:67-114.

———. 1953. *Plant Anatomy.* Wiley, New York.

———. 1954. Primary vascular differentiation in plants. *Biol. Rev.* 29: 46-86.

Esau, K., V. I. Cheadle, and E. M. Gifford, Jr. 1953. Comparative structure and possible trends of specialization of the phloem. *Amer. Jour. Bot.* 40:9-19.

Florin, R. 1931. Untersuchungen zur Stammesgeschichte der Coniferales und Cordaitales. *Svenska. Vetensk. Akad. Handl.* Ser. 5. 10:1-588.

———. 1938-1945. Die Koniferen des Oberkarbons und des unteren Perms. *Paleontographia* 85B: Heft 1-8.

Foster, A. S. 1936. Leaf differentiation in angiosperms. *Bot. Rev.* 2:349-372.

———. 1949. *Practical Plant Anatomy.* Ed. 2. Van Nostrand, New York.

———. 1956a. Characteristics of main cell types: Seed Plants. Table 123, pp. 148-149. *Handbook of Biological Data.* Carpenter Lithographic and Printing Co., Springfield, Ohio.

———. 1956b. Plant idioblasts: remarkable examples of cell specialization. *Protoplasma* 46:184-193.

Gifford, E. M., Jr. 1954. The shoot apex in angiosperms. *Bot. Rev.* 20: 477-529.

Gwynne-Vaughan, D. T. 1901. Observations on the anatomy of solenostelic ferns. I. *Loxsoma. Ann. Bot.* 15:71-98.

Harvey-Gibson, R. J. 1896. Contributions towards a knowledge of the anatomy of the genus *Selaginella,* Spr. Part II. The ligule. *Ann. Bot.* 10:77-88.

Hofmann, E. 1934. *Paläohistologie der Pflanze.* J. Springer, Wien.

Hsü, J. 1937. Anatomy, development and life history of *Selaginella sinensis.* I. Anatomy and development of the shoot. *Bull. Chinese Bot. Soc.* 3:75-95.

Jeffrey, E. C. 1910. The Pteropsida. *Bot. Gaz.* 50:401-414.

———. 1917. *The Anatomy of Woody Plants.* University of Chicago Press, Chicago.

Lignier, O. 1903. Equisétales et Sphenophyllales. Leur origine filicinéenne commune. *Bull. Soc. Linn. Normandie.* Ser. 5. 7:93-137.

Rzehak, H. 1956. Zum Übergipfelungsprozess. Entwicklungsphysiologische Experimente an *Selaginella Martensii. Zeitsch. f. Botanik* 44:265-288.

Sachs, J., von. 1875. *Textbook of Botany.* Clarendon Press, Oxford.

Smith, R. W. 1900. The structure and development of the sporophylls and sporangia of *Isoetes. Bot. Gaz.* 29: 225-258, 323-346.

Troll, W. 1937. *Vergleichende Morphologie der höheren Pflanzen.* Bd 1. Erster Teil, Lieferung 2. Gebrüder Borntraeger, Berlin.

Van Tieghem, P. and H. Douliot. 1886. Sur la polystelie. *Ann. Sci. Nat. Bot.* Ser. 7. 3:275-322.

Wardlaw, C. W. 1952. Phylogeny and Morphogenesis. St. Martin's Press, New York.

Wilson, C. L. 1942. The telome theory and the origin of the stamen. *Amer. Jour. Bot.* 29:759-764.

———. 1953. The telome theory. *Bot. Rev.* 19:417-437.

Zimmermann, W. 1930. *Die Phylo-* *genie der Pflanzen.* Erster Teil. G. Fischer, Jena.

———. 1953. Die Urlandpflanzen (Psilophyten) und ihre Bedeutung für die Stammesgeschichte. *Natur-* *wiss. Monatsschrift* 61:175-187.

———. 1954. Uber die mikrophyllen "Psilophyten," ihre Entstehung und Bedeutung für die Stammesge-schichte. *Paläont. Zeitschrift* 28:-56-66.

Chapter

4 SPORANGIA

One of the salient and definitive features of the sporophyte generation in vascular plants is the production of more or less numerous spore sacs or sporangia. In marked contrast with a moss or a liverwort, wherein the entire sporophyte normally forms only a single, non-septate sporangium, vascular plants are poly-sporangiate, and the number of sporangia and spores developed by a single individual may be enormous. For example, Bower (1908) has estimated that a single, well-developed male shield fern (*Nephrodium filix-mas*) may produce approximately 50,000,000 spores in a single season. Obviously, for a larger plant, such as a full-grown pine or fir tree, the total number of pollen grains would reach astronomical figures. The so-called sulphur showers which are familiar phenomena each year in regions of coniferous forests are really countless yellow pollen grains that have been released from the sporangia of cones and are buoyed by wind currents. From a broad biological point of view, the apparently wasteful overproduction of spores, especially by lower vascular plants and wind-pollinated seed plants, actually tends to compensate for the high proportion of spores that do not survive after dispersal from the parent plant. Thus, as is true also of the prodigious development of gametes in animals and in many kinds of plants, it seems that over-production of spores is a device for insuring the perpetuation of the race.

All normal sporangia of vascular plants share one important feature: they are *the* specific regions of the sporophyte where reductional division or meiosis occurs. This process can be localized further to the sporocytes, or spore mother cells, which are the essential components of any im-mature sporangium. Each sporocyte is normally a diploid cell which, as a result of meiotic divisions, yields a group of four spores known as a spore tetrad (Fig. 4-1). Aside from this functional identity, however, the sporangia in the various vascular plant groups differ widely in position, form, size, structure, and method of development. In a given group, or even in certain genera, the position, structure, and ontogeny of the sporangium provide consistent and useful criteria for morphological comparison and taxonomic utilization. Indeed, such major groups of the tracheophytes as the Psilopsida, Lycopsida, Sphenopsida, and Filicineae are sharply distinguished from one another on the basis of sporangium morphology alone. Among the living Filicineae, the leptosporangiate ferns are a very vivid example of a large, biologically successful group of plants that differ from all other vascular plants in the details of the development and structure of their sporangia (Chapter 13, p. 270).

It should now be clear that sporangia are structures which, although conservative in their functional aspects, vary considerably in other ways. This points to a long, complex evolutionary history, the details of which may never become entirely clear. However, as paleobotanical research continues, fossilized sporangia in a fair state of preservation continually become available for study and comparison. Such sporangia throw considerable light on the morphology and evolution of the sporangia of modern vascular plants, as will be explained in Chapter 7.

In this chapter the important topographical, ontogenetic, and structural features of the sporangia of the lower groups of vascular plants are emphasized. The purpose is to provide the student with a general conspectus of the subject and an orientation, both of which will be indispensable in his survey of the comparative morphology of the Psilopsida, Lycopsida, Sphenopsida, and Filicineae. Later chapters will discuss sporangium morphology in the gymnosperms and angiosperms.

Position of Sporangia

The evidence provided by such extinct Psilophytalean genera as *Horneophyton* and *Rhynia* indicates that sporangia antedated leaves in evolution (Chapter 7). In other words, the most primitive and elemental type of sporangium appears to have been a cauline (i.e., belonging to the stem) structure and, at least in the Psilophytales, was merely a sporogenous tip of the axis. Among living vascular plants, cauline sporangia occur, according to recent interpretation, in *Psilotum* and *Tmesipteris,* the living representatives of the Psilopsida, and in *Equi-*

setum. In *Equisetum* the sporangia occur in circular groups attached to the under surface of peltate sporangiophores. These sporangium-bearing structures may represent condensed, highly modified fertile branches, but a completely satisfactory interpretation of their evolutionary history has not yet been offered (Chapter 9).

In other groups of vascular plants the sporangia are evidently related to leaves. A foliar structure which subtends or bears one or more sporangia is termed a sporophyll. Throughout the ferns, particularly the leptosporangiate types, the sporophylls are, to varying degrees, photosynthetic organs and are often large and pinnatifid like the sterile foliage leaves or fronds. In some genera, however, special areas of the frond, or even complete leaves, are devoted exclusively to spore production and are usually non-photosynthetic. In the sporophylls of leptosporangiate ferns the sporangia typically are segregated into discrete groups, known as sori, at the margins or on the abaxial surface of the lamina (Chapter 13). There exists wide fluctuation in respect to the number of sori produced by a fern sporophyll and the number of sporangia in each sorus. Sporangial number and spore output are of course tremendous in the huge sporophylls of tree ferns.

Certain groups of vascular plants are distinguished by the fact that the sporophylls, instead of being intermingled with ordinary foliage leaves, are aggregated into a compact conelike structure termed a strobilus. The Lycopsida is a particularly instructive group in which various degrees of development and distinctness of the strobilus are strikingly displayed. In all lycopsid plants a solitary sporangium is associated with each sporophyll and is either situated in its axil, as in *Selaginella,* or attached adaxially to the basal region of the sporophyll, as in certain species of *Lycopodium* and all members of the genus *Isoetes.* Most species of *Lycopodium,* like members of the genus *Selaginella,* develop well-defined strobili which are borne at the tips of main or lateral shoots. But in *L. lucidulum* and *L. selago,* for example, the sporangia occur in poorly defined patches or zones which alternate with purely vegetative regions of the shoot system (see Chapter 8). The viewpoint is now generally held that the strobiloid forms of *Lycopodium* represent an evolutionary development from the morphological condition represented in such a species as *L. selago.* In the genus *Isoetes* a definable strobilus distinct from the vegetative part of the plant likewise is absent. A high proportion of the quill-like leaves are fertile and bear large solitary microsporangia or megasporangia on their adaxial bases; however, many of the functionally sterile leaves actually develop rudimentary or abortive sporangia. Such an authority as Bower (1908, p. 165) states that "after the first sporangia appear, the whole plant may be regarded as a strobilus, imperfectly differentiated, as in the selago type, into fertile parts and parts sterile by abortion or by complete suppression."

The gymnosperms predominantly are a strobiloid group within the Pteropsida, and in the cycads and certain of the conifers the strobili (cones) are exceptionally large. The flowers of many angiosperms, particularly certain members of the Magnoliaceae and Ranunculaceae, are also remarkably similar to strobili in their general organography and function. However, a discussion of the strobili and sporangia of seed plants, must be deferred until later chapters.

Structure of Sporangia

From the broadest possible structural standpoint, the mature sporangium in lower vascular plants consists fundamentally of one or of many spores enclosed by a protective wall (Fig. 4-1). In discussing the morphology and ontogeny of sporangia, "wall" is used to designate the layer or layers of cells, distinct in origin from the sporocytes, that constitute the sterile protective jacket of the sporangium. When a sporangium is sunken within the stem or the sporophyll the wall is merely an external multilayered cover which is not sharply demarcated from the adjacent sterile tissue. But in emergent sporangia the wall is much more clearly defined; furthermore, in this type the spore-producing portion of the sporangium is very often borne on a definite stalk (Fig. 4-1, f'). In addition to its protective rôle, the wall of most sporangia is definitely related to the method of dehiscence or splitting open of the spore case. Certain of the surface cells of the sporangia of many lower vascular plants are unevenly thickened and collectively form a distal plate, a ridge, or an incomplete ring; these varied cell patterns constitute dehiscence mechanisms, the biophysical and biochemical operation of which deserves much more investigation than has been accorded it in the past (Goebel, 1905). Undoubtedly, the most specialized and

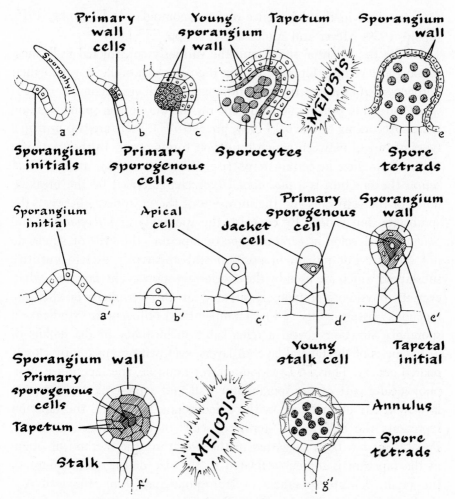

Figure 4-1 Ontogeny and structure of the two principal types of sporangia in vascular plants. *a-e*, the eusporangium; *a'-g'*, the leptosporangium. (See text for detailed discussion of this diagram.)

familiar dehiscence mechanisms are the annulus and stomium of the sporangium in advanced leptosporangiate ferns (see Fig. 13-9, I). In these plants the transverse rupture of the thin sporangium wall, and the slow recurving of the annulus and the upper half of the capsule, is followed by the return of the latter approximately to its former position with a sudden jerk that hurls the dry spores a distance of 1-2 centimeters from the parent plant. (For detailed descriptions of the physical mechanism involved in the dehiscence of fern sporangia see Ursprung, 1915; Ingold, 1939; Meyer and Anderson, 1940, pp. 237-238.)

Besides the essential spores and the variously constructed wall, most sporangia develop a tapetum during the early or middle stages in their ontogeny. From a functional standpoint, the tapetum consists of cells which probably provide nourishment for the developing sporocytes and spores. According to Goebel (1905, pp. 596-597), there are two principal types of tapeta between which transition forms occur. In the sporangia of the Psilotales, in certain ferns (e.g., Ophioglossales), and in *Equisetum* the tapetum is a *plasmodial type* characterized by the breaking down of the cell walls and the intrusion of the protoplasts between the sporocytes and spores. By contrast, the sporangia of *Lycopodium* and *Selaginella* develop a *secretion type* of tapetum, the cells of which do not separate but remain in position and apparently excrete nutritive substances which are used by the developing spores. The tapetum, whatever its physiological type, is situated at the periphery of the sporogenous tissue (Fig. 4-1). Comparative ontogenetic studies on sporangia, however, reveal a remarkable inconstancy in the details of histogenesis of the tapetal layer or layers, even within apparently closely related genera. Thus, in *Lycopodium*, for example, the tapetum is morphologically part of the sporangium wall and represents its innermost layer. On the other hand, in the allied genus *Selaginella* the tapetum represents the outermost "sterilized" cells of the sporogenous tissue. Possibly, as has been suggested in the literature, the method of origin of the tapetum is somehow related to the size of the sporangium. In the small, delicate sporangia of leptosporangiate ferns the wall is a single cell layer, and the tapetal cells develop in a most precise manner from the large tetrahedral primary sporogenous cell (Fig. 4-1, e'-f'). But in *Isoetes*, notable for the enormous size of the sporangium, the tapetum originates in part from the innermost layer of the wall and in part from the surface cells of the remarkable trabeculae which almost completely partition the sporangial cavity.

Ontogeny and Classification of Sporangia

Our present terminologies and classification of sporangia in vascular plants are based upon the important researches of the great German morphologist Karl Goebel. In a paper published in 1881 he suggested that there are two principal types of sporangia: the eusporangium and the leptosporangium. The former type arises ontogenetically from several initial cells, and, at least before final maturation, develops a wall of several layers of cells. The eusporangium, as Goebel discovered, is the prevailing type throughout vascular plants. In contrast, the leptosporangium arises from a single parent cell or initial, and its wall is composed of but a single layer of cells. This more delicate type of sporangium, as Goebel correctly supposed, is restricted to the most highly advanced families of ferns which are now commonly called the leptosporangiate ferns.

Goebel's (1880, 1881) emphasis on ontogeny as a basis for the interpretation and classification of sporangia has had far-reaching effects, and the numerous researches since his original work have tended generally to support the distinction which he made between eusporangia and leptosporangia. In this regard the extensive and very detailed ontogenetic studies of F. O. Bower, the distinguished British morphologist and student of the ferns, deserve particular mention. Although recognizing the distinctions which can usually be made between the eusporangiate and leptosporangiate methods of sporangial development, Bower (1889, 1891, 1935) has drawn attention repeatedly to the existence of intermediate patterns of sporangial ontogeny, as illustrated in the ferns by the family Osmundaceae. Such transitional conditions, which will be described later in this chapter, justify, in Bower's opinion, the belief that the eusporangiate and leptosporangiate modes of development represent the end points of a continuous morphological series and that a rigid morphological distinction should not be made between them. This series, he believes, also represents the probable phylogenetic development of sporangia which, at least in the ferns, began with the eusporangiate condition and terminated in the highly evolved leptosporangium. For convenience in presentation, the salient features of the ontogeny and structure of selected examples of eusporangia and leptosporangia will be treated separately.

The Eusporangium

In all lower vascular plants and in the microsporangia of certain conifers (Allen, 1946) the parent cells or initials of the eusporangium are superficial in position. Sometimes these initials are referred to as epidermal cells, but this seems an inappropriate term for the highly meristematic cells from which the sporangium arises. The first step in the development of the sporangium consists in the division of the initials by walls parallel to the surface (Fig. 4-1, b). Divisions in this plane are termed periclinal, and they result in the formation of an outer and an inner series of cells. In a very general sense, these two series of cells represent the starting points for the sporangium wall and the sporogenous tissue, respectively. Because of this, the outer series is commonly called jacket cells, or primary wall cells, or parietal cells, and the inner series primary sporogenous cells (Fig. 4-1, b). But the intensive studies of Bower and other investigators show that the first periclinal divisions in the sporangium initials do not always sharply define the future sporogenous tissue. On the contrary, further additions to the potential spore-forming cells may be made by periclinal divisions in the original outer cell series; moreover, the number of surface cells which function as parent cells for the sporogenous tissue may be somewhat variable even within a single genus. A few selected genera in the lower vascular plants will serve to illustrate the general eusporangiate pattern and some of its variants; see Fig. 4-1 for the general scheme of ontogeny. We may appropriately begin our discussion with the Lycopsida (Fig. 8-5).

In the genus *Lycopodium*, which has been thoroughly investigated by Bower, the number of rows of surface cells which collectively function as sporangium initials varies from one in *L. selago* to as many as three in *L. alpinum*. Periclinal divisions in the initials result in a rather clear-cut distinction between (1) an outer cell layer which by further periclinal and anticlinal divisions (i.e., divisions resulting in new walls oriented perpendicular to the surface) builds up the several-layered wall, and (2) an inner fertile layer of potentially sporogenous cells from which by irregularly oriented planes of division the sporocytes ultimately arise (Fig. 4-1, b, c). Occasionally, according to Bower, periclinal divisions in the superficial cells resulting from the first periclinal divisions may contribute additional cells to the sporogenous tissue. The ontogeny of the sporangium in *Selaginella* likewise conforms closely to the typical eusporangiate pattern and in all fundamental details resembles the early phases of sporangium development in *Lycopodium*. This is of particular interest since it shows that the mode of initiation and early development of a sporangium, is not correlated with the condition of either homospory or heterospory. On the contrary, both young microsporangia and megasporangia in *Selaginella* are eusporangiate in type and become distinguishable only as the result of the breakdown of all but one or a very few megasporocytes in the future megasporangium (see Fig. 8-13). The difference in method of origin of the tapetum in the sporangia of *Lycopodium* and *Selaginella* has already been mentioned, and it is illustrated in Chapter 8.

As might be anticipated on the basis of its enormous size at maturity, the sporangium of *Isoetes* arises from a relatively large number of superficial initials; in certain species investigated by Bower four to five rows of surface cells of the sporophyll function as parent cells. Although all the internal cells produced by the earliest periclinal divisions are potentially sporogenous, extensive areas of sporogenous tissue eventually fail to reach their developmental possibilities and give rise to the remarkable trabeculae, so distinctive of both the microsporangia and megasporangia of *Isoetes* (Chapter 8). As in certain species of *Lycopodium*, additions to the primary sporogenous cells may be made in *Isoetes* by subsequent periclinal divisions in the overlying surface cells.

In *Equisetum*, the only living member of the extremely ancient sphenopsid line, the sporangia develop by the eusporangiate method. However, according to Bower (1935, p. 183), a generous portion of the primary sporogenous tissue is referable in origin to the inner derivatives of a single surface cell. But the first periclinal division of the sporangial initial does not delimit all the future sporogenous cells; additions are made to the fertile area by further periclinal divisions in the original and adjacent surface cells (Fig. 9-6). Likewise, in the Ophioglossaceae and Marattiaceae, which are designated as the eusporangiate ferns, a considerable portion or all of the primary sporogenous tissue of the sporangium originates from a single inner derivative of a superficial initial (Bower, 1935; Campbell, 1911, 1918). But, as in *Equisetum*, surface cells adjacent to this initial contribute to the formation of the multiseriate wall of the sporangium.

Finally, mention should be made of the massive sporangia in the living genera of the Psilopsida. In *Psilotum* and *Tmesipteris* the sporangia develop by the eusporangiate method, but the number of surface initials concerned in the formation of the primary sporogenous tissue is difficult to determine. The sporangial development in both of these genera agrees with that of *Equisetum* and *Ophioglossales* in one interesting respect—in all of them a considerable portion of the potentially sporogenous cells disintegrates, producing a plasmodium-like liquid in which the surviving sporocytes divide meiotically and produce spores (see Fig. 7-6).

In concluding this discussion of the eusporangium, a few remarks about the mature wall and the ripe spores are in order. Although all typical eusporangia have a wall two or more layers thick at a middle stage in ontogeny, the *inner wall layers* (including of course the tapetum when this is of parietal origin) commonly become stretched, compressed, and ultimately destroyed. Thus, at maturity the walls of many eusporangia—for example, in *Equisetum, Lycopodium*, and *Selaginella* —may appear to consist of only a single layer of cells. But in *Psilotum*, in *Tmesipteris*, and very strikingly in *Botrychium* (a member of the eusporangiate ferns) the mature sporangium wall is multi-layered.

The output of spores from eusporangia in both homosporous and heterosporous plants is variable but is frequently much greater than that in the leptosporangium. Estimates of spore number are made by counting (in serial sections) the number of spore-mother cells and multiplying by 4. Such counts reveal that in certain homosporous types the numbers are in the hundreds, or in the thousands in various eusporangiate ferns. Apparently, the greatest spore output occurs in the microsporangia of *Isoetes*, where it is estimated that from 150,000 to 1,000,000 spores may develop in a single microsporangium.

The form of spores is quite variable and often is of considerable diagnostic value. Tetrahedral spores, with conspicuous triradiate ridges, are characteristic of most species in the Lycopsida, whereas bilateral spores are characteristic of *Psilotum* and *Tmesipteris*. In *Equisetum* the spores are unique because of four band-like appendages, or elaters, that are developed on the surface of each spore (see Fig. 9-5, B, C). These elaters are hygroscopic, coiling around the spore when the air is moist but uncoiling when it is dry. If the spores encounter alternating moist and dry air the elaters coil and uncoil repeatedly; this is believed to facilitate the dispersal of the spores from the open sporangium.

The Leptosporangium

The salient ontogenetic feature of the typical leptosporangium is its origin from a single superficial initial cell (Fig. 4-1, a', and Fig. 13-9). Although this parent cell divides into two cells by means of a transverse or somewhat oblique division wall, the lower cell plays no role in the development of the sporangium. On the contrary, it is from the outer cell that the entire sporangium (stalk, wall, tapetum, and spores) takes origin (Fig. 4-1, a'-g' shows a general scheme of ontogeny). This outer cell functions at first like a tetrahedral apical cell: by means of a series of vertical-oblique divisions parallel to three of its sides it builds up a variable number of segments. The lower segments develop into the slender three-rowed stalk, and the three uppermost segments give rise to a part of the wall of the sporangium. The growth of the apical cell ultimately is terminated when it divides periclinally by a curved wall into an outer cap or jacket cell and an inner primary sporogenous cell (Fig. 4-1, d'). The jacket cell, together with the uppermost derivatives of the original apical cell, gives rise by anticlinal divisions to the one-layered wall of the leptosporangium. Concomitantly, the primary sporogenous cell divides by walls parallel to its sides, forming four tapetal initials which by means of periclinal and anticlinal divisions ultimately produce a two-layered tapetum (Fig. 4-1, e'-f'). The large, remaining inner cell forms the sporocytes. Maturation of the leptosporangium includes the eventual disintegration of the tapetum, meiosis, and the development of the spore tetrads, the elongation of the stalk cells, and the ultimate rupture of the sporangium wall (Fig. 13-9). In all of the advanced families of the leptosporangiate ferns the annulus is vertical and the dehiscence of the capsule transverse or brevicidal. But in the phylogenetically less evolved groups, such as the Gleicheniaceae, the annulus is transverse to transverse-oblique, and the dehiscence is longitudinal or longicidal (Chapter 13).

Although there is considerable variation in the average spore output of the leptosporangia in the various families, the number is, in general, less than for eusporangia. In none of the genera for which Bower made spore countings does the number of spores per sporangium equal the huge numbers produced by the sporangia in the Lycopsida or in eusporangiate ferns. In typical leptosporangia the number of spores is a direct power of two: 16, 32, 64, 128, 256, and 512. According to Bower (1935, p. 427) "in the vast majority of the leptosporangiate ferns each capsule contains 64 spores or less." Such numbers as 24 or 48, though not direct powers of two, do occur and are the result of reductions in the number of cell divisions which lead to the formation of sporocytes. Mature fern spores often exhibit various types of wall sculpturing which may be of value in taxonomic differentiation. In certain highly evolved fern groups a special deposit known as the perispore occurs on the spore wall. This has been shown to have considerable systematic value (Wagner, 1952).

As stated earlier in this chapter, development and structure of the stalk of the sporangium in the Osmundaceae do not easily fit the scheme of either a typical leptosporangium or a typical eusporangium (Williams, 1928). In the first place, as shown in Fig. 4-2, A, B, the form of the initial cell from which the sporogenous cell, tapetum, and wall originate is variable. Sometimes the cell is truncated at the base, thus resembling the form of comparable cells in a eusporangium; at other times, in the same sorus, the cell is pointed at the base as in a typical leptosporangiate fern. Secondly, Fig. 4-2 reveals the fact that the entire sporangium cannot be traced in origin to a single cell, as can a typical leptosporangium.

Figure 4-2 Development of sporangia in the Osmundaceae. **A-B,** *Todea barbara,* illustrating variations in early stages of differentiation; **C,** *Osmunda regalis,* longisection of sporangium showing wall, tapetum, sporogenous tissue and, massive stalk. [From *Primitive Land Plants* by F. O. Bower. London: Macmillan and Co., Ltd., 1935.]

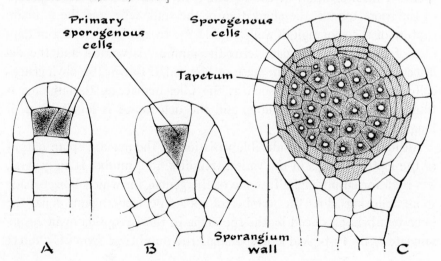

On the contrary, neighboring cells contribute, as they do in a eusporangium, to the development of the massive stalk which contrasts strikingly with its more slender counterpart in a typical leptosporangium (compare Fig. 4-1, f′ with Fig. 4-2, C, and Fig. 13-9, I). Lastly, the spore output in the transitional sporangia of the Osmundaceae is, in general, higher than in ordinary leptosporangiate ferns; in *Osmunda regalis*, for example, it ranges from 256 to 512.

Summary and Conclusions

There are two principal types of vascular plant sporangia—eusporangia, and leptosporangia—and they are distinguished by their method of origin and development, their wall structure, and their spore output (Fig. 4-1).

Typical eusporangia originate in lower vascular plants from a series of superficial parent cells or initials which, by periclinal division, give rise to primary wall cells (external series) and primary sporogenous cells (internal series). To varying degrees, further additions from superficial cells may be made to the underlying sporogenous tissue. In most eusporangia a nutritive layer or tapetum is developed either from the sporogenous tissue or from the innermost layer of the sporangium wall. The eusporangium, prior to complete maturity, develops a wall two or more layers thick, although at the time of dehiscence the inner wall layers may be crushed or obliterated. The spore output of eusporangia is high and variable.

By contrast, a typical leptosporangium originates from a single parent cell which first produces the stalk and then, by a curved periclinal division, is subdivided into a jacket or wall-producing cell and an internal primary sporogenous cell. The latter produces four tapetal initials, then gives rise to a relatively small number of sporocytes. The dehiscence of leptosporangia is either transverse or longitudinal and the spore output small and usually some power of two. The Osmundaceae are an example of ferns in which the ontogeny and structure of the sporangium is somewhat intermediate between that of typical leptosporangia and eusporangia (Fig. 4-2).

What general conclusions can be drawn from the existence of these two, well-defined morphological types of sporangia? Do they represent independent and parallel types, or can they be related in a phylogenetic sense? The widespread occurrence of the eusporangiate condition throughout vascular plants, including two of the living orders of ferns, would indicate the eusporangium as the fundamental condition. That it indeed may represent the elemental and truly primitive type of spore case is suggested by its appearance in the living members of the Psilopsida and in Paleozoic ferns. As arranged by Bower (1935), a very persuasive series of ontogenetic patterns seems to exist which serves to bridge the gap between eusporangiate and leptosporangiate ferns and to demonstrate the derived nature of the latter group.

One of the most important conclusions regarding the morphology of sporangia was expressed by Bower (1896, p. 8), who stated that the study of the sporangia of a given plant should be carried out in the light of a full knowledge of the segmentation of its apical meristems. This means that the mode of origin and pattern of development of sporangia should be viewed not as isolated phenomena but as a part of the general ontogeny of the plant—and an effort should be made to test the assumption that correlations between sporangial ontogeny and apical segmentation in the shoot do exist. It is now clear that Bower's hypothesis is very commendable.

Throughout lower vascular plants the surface cells of the shoot apex divide to varying degrees in the periclinal plane and thus do not collectively form a discrete surface layer. For this reason, internal cells of the apex and of the foliar primordia can be traced in origin to superficial cells or initials. As we have seen, this is precisely the pattern of origin of the sporangia, which differ ontogenetically only in the number of parent cells which produce them.

Much remains to be done in the way of testing Bower's idea with reference to the seed plants. In certain gymnosperms the microsporangium initials, like those of eusporangia in lower groups, are superficial cells (Chapter 16). This is correlated with the relative frequency of periclinal divisions in the surface cells of the shoot apex of many different kinds of gymnosperms (Allen, 1946). In the angiosperms the initials of the microsporangia represent hypodermal cells in the anther, overlaid by a well-defined epidermis (Chapter 19). This condition, in turn, seems to be well correlated with the existence of a sharply defined external cell layer in the shoot apices of most angiosperms.

References

Allen, G. S. 1946. The origin of the microsporangium of *Pseudotsuga*. *Bull. Torrey Bot. Club* 73:547-556.

Bower, F. O. 1889. The comparative examination of the meristems of ferns as a phylogenetic study. *Ann. Bot.* 3:305-392.

————. 1891. Is the Eusporangiate or the Leptosporangiate the more primitive type in the ferns? *Ann. Bot.* 5: 109-134.

————. 1896. *Studies in the morphology of spore-producing members. II. Ophioglossaceae.* Privately printed, London.

————. 1908. *The origin of a Land Flora.* Macmillan, London.

————. 1935. *Primitive Land Plants.* Macmillan, London.

Campbell, D. H. 1911. The Eusporangiatae. The comparative morphology of the Ophioglossaceae and Marattiaceae. Carnegie Institution of Washington, Publication No. 140. Washington, D. C.

————. 1918. *The Structure and Development of Mosses and Ferns.* Ed. 3. Macmillan, New York.

Goebel, K. 1880. Beiträge zur vergleichenden Entwickelungsgeschichte der Sporangien. *Bot. Zeit.* 38:545-552, 561-571.

————. 1881. Beiträge zur vergleichenden Entwickelungsgeschichte der Sporangien. *Bot. Zeit.* 39:681-694, 697-702, 713-719.

————. 1905. *Organography of Plants.* Eng. Ed. by I. B. Balfour. Part II. Clarendon Press, Oxford.

Ingold, C. T. 1939. *Spore Discharge in Land Plants.* Clarendon Press, Oxford.

Meyer, B. S. and D. B. Anderson. 1940. *Plant Physiology.* Van Nostrand, New York.

Ursprung, A. 1915. Uber die Kohäsion des Wassers in Farnannulus. *Ber. Deutsch. Bot. Ges.* 33:153-162.

Wagner, W. H., Jr. 1952. The fern genus *Diellia*. *Univ. California Publ. Bot.* 26:1-212.

Williams, S. 1928. Sporangial variation in the Osmundaceae. *Trans. Roy. Soc. Edinburgh.* 55:795-805.

Chapter

5 GAMETANGIA

Throughout the vascular plants sexual reproduction is achieved by the pairing of morphologically unlike gametes.

In all lower vascular plants the male gamete, usually termed the sperm or spermatozoid, is a motile, flagellated cell that requires liquid water to reach the passive, non-motile egg. From an evolutionary point of view such motile sperms, like their counterparts in liverworts and mosses, exemplify the persistence of the kind of gamete typical of many aquatic thallophytes. In contrast with the somewhat casual dispersal of flagellated sperms in lower groups of the tracheophytes, modern seed plants, because of the development of a pollen tube by the male gametophyte, do not depend on water for transportation of sperms—the pollen tube conveys the male gametes directly to the immediate vicinity of the egg. This is true of *Ginkgo* and the cycads, which have retained flagellated sperms, but it is particularly significant in all the remaining living groups of gymnosperms and angiosperms where the male gametes are devoid of flagella.

In all the lower groups of vascular plants the sex cells are normally produced in separate organs or gametangia. Many instances have been recorded, in the literature, of bisexual gametangia that contain both eggs and sperms, and these remarkable structures will be discussed in more detail later in the chapter. But normal gamete development involves the production of distinctive, unisexual gametangia. The male gametangium, or antheridium, produces the sperms, which vary in number from four in *Isoetes* to several thousand in certain eusporangiate ferns. The female gametangium, or archegonium, is quite different in that typically it produces only a single, non-motile egg which at the time of fertilization is situated at the base of the archegonial canal; the canal provides the channel through which the sperm must pass to reach the female gamete.

Antheridia and archegonia, as is true of the functionally equivalent sex organs of the Bryophyta, are complex organs consisting of a jacket

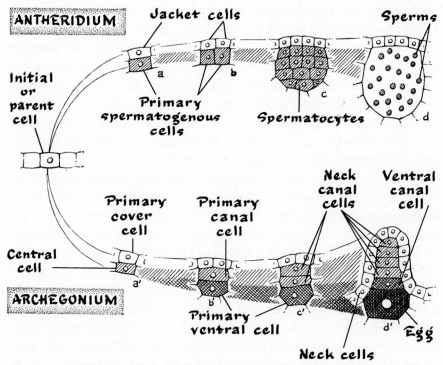

Figure 5-1 Ontogeny and structure of gametangia in lower vascular plants (exclusive of the leptosporangiate ferns): *a-d*, the antheridium; *a'-d'*, the archegonium. Note the similarity in the mode of origin and the first stage in development of the two types of sex organs.

(usually 1 cell thick) of sterile cells which encloses and shelters the gametes. This is illustrated in Fig. 5-1. Such construction is quite unlike the simple unicellular sex organs that are typical of the thallophytes, and it has led to speculation regarding the evolutionary history of gametangia and the possible homology between antheridia and archegonia. (These two problems will be discussed in some detail at the close of the chapter.)

As is true of sporangia, an exceptional amount of attention has been devoted to the ontogeny and comparative structure of gametangia in all of the main vascular plant groups. One of the most interesting results of comparative research is the discovery that with respect to gamete production the archegonium is a remarkably uniform sex organ. Isolated cases have been reported of archegonia with several eggs, but generally only a single functional gamete is formed, as can be seen in Fig. 5-1, d'. On the basis of this standardized structure, plants with archegonia are very commonly designated collectively as Archegoniatae. Included in this group are the Bryophyta, all lower vascular plants, including the ferns, and the majority of the gymnosperms. In the gymnosperms archegonia are modified in structure, but ontogenetically and structurally they are strictly comparable with the archegonia of the lower groups. In angiosperms the egg is produced in a highly specialized embryo sac, and archegonia as definable organs are absent.

With reference to the evolutionary origin and modification of sex organs in vascular plants, it is interesting to note that antheridia, as definable multicellular organs, are restricted to the lower groups and, unlike archegonia, do not occur in living gymnosperms. This contrast between antheridium and archegonium seems to be correlated with the marked reduction in size of the male gametophyte generation in all heterosporous, lower vascular plants and in the seed plants. In the microgametophytes of *Selaginella* and *Isoetes*, for example, only a single antheridium is produced, whereas in gymnosperms the equivalent structure is further reduced to a few vegetative cells and usually two male gametes. This trend toward the elimination of sterile cells culminates in the male gametophyte of angiosperms, which normally consists of a single vegetative nucleus and two male gametes. Doubtless, the evolution of the pollen tube was a very significant factor in the drastic reduction of the antheridium to a few cells. On the other hand, the persistence of the archegonium as a distinct organ even among the relatively advanced gymnosperms is related to the larger size of the megagametophyte and to the prime biological importance of the archegonium as an organ which produces the egg and shelters the young embryo (Chapter 6).

This chapter is devoted largely to a general account of the position, structure, ontogeny, and homologies of the antheridium and the archegonium. As was the intent of the previous chapter on sporangia, this treatment is intended to provide orientation for the student by emphasizing those fundamental aspects (of gametangia) which are of biological and morphological importance. Further details of the morphology of gametophytes and sex organs will be given in later chapters that deal with specific groups of plants.

Position of Gametangia

It will be desirable first to contrast the gametophytes and sex organs of homosporous and heterosporous lower vascular plants. In the former the gametophyte is exosporic—i.e., free-living and not enclosed by the spore wall—whereas in all heterosporous groups the micro- and megagametophytes are endosporic—i.e., entirely or for the most part enclosed by the wall of the microspore or megaspore, respectively. These differences are important from a biological as well as a morphological standpoint, and there is little doubt that the relatively large exosporic type of gametophyte represents the original and primitive condition. We may therefore begin with this type.

Exosporic gametophytes are typically monoecious, which means they produce or have the capacity to produce both types of gametangia. In some instances the environmental conditions surrounding the developing gametophyte are decisive with respect to the type or types of sex organs which are produced. Unfavorable growing conditions, such as commonly result from crowded masses of gametophytes, may cause inhibition of archegonia. This is true of the prothallia of *Equisetum* and some if not all of the leptosporangiate ferns where weak or impoverished gametophytes form only antheridia.

The gametangia of exosporic gametophytes are usually embedded in the vegetative tissue of the prothallus. This is always the case with the venter or egg-containing portion of the archegonium, but the antheridium is less consistent. In the homosporous members of the Lycopsida, in *Equisetum*, and in the eusporangiate ferns the sterile jacket of the antheridium protrudes slightly above the surface, and the spermatogenous tissue is deeply sunken. But in the Psilotales and the leptosporangiate ferns the antheridia are conspicuously emergent organs. From the standpoint of ontogeny, however, the emergent antheridia of *Psilotum* and *Tmesipteris* are quite like the embedded type, whereas in the higher groups of leptosporangiate ferns the antheridium is a more highly evolved and reduced organ, as will be shown later in this chapter.

The distribution pattern of antheridia and archegonia varies considerably and is correlated to some degree with the form and level of evolu-

tionary development of the gametophyte. In the fleshy, radial, nonphotosynthetic gametophytes of *Psilotum* and *Tmesipteris* the two kinds of
gametangia are intermingled and tend to occur over the entire surface
of the gametophyte (Fig. 7-9, A). An intermingling of sex organs also
occurs in certain presumably primitive species of *Lycopodium*—for example, *L. lucidulum* (Spessard, 1922)—but in other members of this
genus the antheridia and archegonia are formed in distinct patches or
clusters on the upper surface of the gametophyte (Chapter 8). With
reference to the thalloid, dorsiventral, photosynthetic type of gametophyte characteristic of the Marattiaceae and leptosporangiate ferns,
several somewhat intergrading patterns of sex-organ distribution occur.
In *Marattia* and *Angiopteris*, according to Campbell (1918), the
archegonia are confined to the lower surface of the prominent midrib of
the prothallus, whereas the antheridia, although more abundant below,
develop on both surfaces. A more standardized plan of distribution of
gametangia seems to prevail in the higher groups of leptosporangiate
ferns. Here, both kinds of sex organs are commonly restricted to the
lower surface with the archegonia limited to the cushion of tissue situated behind the notch of the heart-shaped prothallus; the more numerous antheridia occur near the basal end of the prothallus as well as on the
wings (Fig. 13-19, A).

Endosporic gametophytes, since they are restricted to heterosporous
plants, are usually strictly dioecious. As mentioned before, the male
gametophyte is extremely reduced in structure, consisting in *Selaginella*
and *Isoetes* of a single vegetative prothallial cell and one antheridium.
The megagametophyte, by contrast, is more robust, consisting of a mass
of food-storing tissue which usually fills the cavity of the megaspore and
which, at least in *Selaginella*, is exposed by the cracking of the spore
wall along the triradiate ridge (Fig. 8-19, A). The small archegonia are
restricted in occurrence to the surface of the protuberant cushion of
gametophyte tissue below the cracked region of the spore wall.

Structure of Gametangia

The initiation and ontogenetic development of gametangia will be outlined comparatively later in this chapter. But now, by way of orientation,
we will describe the cellular structure of antheridia and archegonia as

they approach the stage of functional maturity. Throughout this discussion we will refer frequently to Fig. 5-1.

Antheridium

In the embedded type of antheridium a well-defined sterile jacket or cover is always present. Because this layer is instrumental in the mechanism of sperm discharge, Goebel has proposed that it be designated the "opercular layer." This term is appropriate because, generally, one or more centrally located cells of this layer separate or become broken, thus creating an opening through which the sperms can escape. In the antheridia of many species of *Lycopodium* and in the eusporangiate ferns there is normally only a single cell in the antheridial jacket which is ruptured at maturity. This opercular cell (also termed the cap cell) is commonly triangular when seen in surface view, although it may be four-sided or irregular in contour. The situation in *Equisetum* requires much further study. Some authors (for instance, Campbell, 1918) describe a single opercular cell, and others (Goebel, 1905) maintain that considerable variation occurs within the genus. In *E. limosum*, for example, a relatively large opening is produced by the pulling apart of a group of centrally placed cells. By contrast, in *E. pratense* there are, it is said, only two opercular cells "which then separate from one another in the middle somewhat after the manner of the guard-cells in a stoma." The mechanism of separation or rupturing of opercular cells is poorly understood—Goebel has suggested that the dehiscence may be attributable to the swelling of mucilaginous substances deposited in them. Most commonly, the jacket or opercular layer of embedded antheridia is only a single cell in thickness. But in *Botrychium* and *Helminthostachys*—members of the Ophioglossaceae—the jacket consists of two layers of cells except at the center where several cells, including the opercular cell, remain undivided. According to Campbell (1918), only the single opercular cell is destroyed when the sperms are released.

In the emergent type of antheridium the jacket is always a single layer of cells in thickness. Some variation occurs in the total number of cells which constitute this layer in the various families of the leptosporangiate ferns, although there is usually developed but a single cap or opercular cell. At one end of the series are the apparently highly specialized antheridia of the Polypodiaceae, the jacket here consisting of two ring-like cells and a terminal opercular cell. At the other extreme are the massive complex antheridia of the Gleicheniaceae, wherein the jacket may consist of as many as ten or twelve cells, one of which functions as an opercular cell (Stokey, 1950, 1951).

This discussion of antheridial morphology may be closed appropriately by a brief résumé of the structure and number of sperms produced in the various groups of lower vascular plants. It is a well-established fact that there are two principal types of sperms, based upon the number of flagella developed. In *Lycopodium* and *Selaginella* the sperms are bi-flagellate and in this respect are quite unlike the prevailingly multi-flagellate sperms developed in all other groups including *Ginkgo* and the cycads. Since the spermatozoids of many algae are biflagellate, consider-able interest, from the standpoint of evolution, is attached to the similar condition in *Lycopodium* and *Selaginella.* The taxonomic (and possibly phyletic) importance of the number of flagella developed by sperms is illustrated by the genus *Isoetes.* On the basis of its solitary foliar euspo-rangia, its ligulate sporophylls, and its heterospory, *Isoetes* is commonly regarded as a member of the *Lycopsida,* allied in many respects to *Selaginella.* But the sperms of *Isoetes* are multiflagellate, and in this respect they are quite unlike the male gametes of either *Lycopodium* or *Selaginella.* As mentioned earlier in the chapter, the number of sperms formed by a single antheridium varies widely according to the genus or group of plants. *Isoetes* produces only four sperms from each micro-gametophyte. In contrast, the sperm output is in the hundreds in some leptosporangiate ferns (e.g., *Gleichenia*) and may reach several thou-sand, according to Campbell, in the antheridium of *Ophioglossum pendulum.*

In Bower's (1935) opinion, there is a close parallel between the out-put of sporocytes and the number of spermatocytes, when one compares the sporangia and antheridia of eusporangiate and leptosporangiate ferns. In the first group there tends to be a relatively high number of spore-mother cells and spermatocytes, but in the advanced leptosporangiates there is a marked reduction in number of both spores and male gametes. These differences, Bower believes, show that the progressive refinement in structure of spore-bearing structures has been extended in a compara-ble manner to the sex organs.

Archegonium

Just prior to its complete maturation a typical archegonium consists of the neck, which projects conspicuously above the surface of the gametophyte, and the so-called axial row of cells. The upper members of this row are enclosed by the neck, and the lowermost cells, including the egg, are sunken in the tissue of the gametophyte, as shown by Fig. 5-1, d'. The venter, or basal embedded portion of the archegonium, contains the ventral canal cell and the egg. In members of both the eusporangiate and leptosporangiate ferns the venter is demarcated from adjacent prothallial cells by a rather discrete cellular jacket, but in many vascular plants the cells bounding the lower portion of the axial row of the archegonium are not morphologically distinguishable from other cells of the gameto-phyte. The archegonial neck, which is the morphological and functional equivalent of the jacket of the antheridium, is structurally uniform, usually comprising four vertically arranged rows of cells. The number of cell rows or tiers is remarkably consistent, despite the wide variation in the total number of cells which compose the neck. Without doubt, the longest necks are found in the archegonia of certain species of *Lycopodium*. These contrast markedly with the very short and scarcely projecting archegonial necks in eusporangiate ferns, in prothallia of *Lycopodium* grown *in vitro*, and in *Isoetes* and *Selaginella*.

From a morphological viewpoint, the most important and significantly variable part of the immature archegonium is the axial row (Fig. 5-1). In certain species of *Lycopodium* the so-called axial row may actually consist of a partially or completely double series of cells. This seems to be the usual condition in *L. obscurum* var. *dendroideum*, according to Spessard (1922), and it has been recorded for other species by Lyon (1904). More commonly, however, the axial row is composed of a single series of cells, the function and morphological significance of which deserve full discussion at this point. As mentioned, the lowest cell in the axial row is the egg itself, and this normally is the only component of the row which survives, all the others disintegrating as the archegonium reaches full maturity. The cell located directly above the egg is known as the ventral canal cell; this cell ontogenetically is a sister cell of the egg and in exceptional cases apparently functions as a gamete. All the remaining cells of the axial row, situated above the ventral canal cell, are termed neck canal cells and on theoretical grounds may be regarded as potential gametes also.

From a comparative viewpoint it is possible to arrange the archegonia of lower vascular plants in a *reductional series,* beginning with those in which there are many neck canal cells (e.g., *Lycopodium*) and culminating in the condition where only a single binucleate neck canal cell is formed (this occurs in many leptosporangiate ferns). Whether this series actually corresponds to the general phylogenetic development of the archegonium is difficult to determine, since in admittedly primitive types like *Psilotum* and *Tmesipteris* there may be only two or possibly only a single binucleate neck canal cell. The behavior of the ventral canal cell also is variable and hence of considerable comparative interest. In many lower vascular plants it is a well-defined cell, differing from the egg cell in its smaller size and more flattened form. But in the Ophioglossaceae, which also apparently represent an ancient stock of vascular plants, a distinct ventral canal cell (Campbell, 1911) proves difficult to demonstrate, even by careful ontogenetic study. This is true too in many gymnosperms where the ventral canal cell may be represented by only a short-lived nucleus. Furthermore, in these plants neck canal cells have been entirely eliminated and the mature archegonium consists of a small neck of one or several cell tiers and a huge egg (Chapters 15 and 16).

Very little systematic investigation has been devoted to the mechanism of the opening of the archegonial neck. According to Campbell (1918), when the archegonium opens in leptosporangiate ferns "the terminal cells diverge widely and the upper ones are often thrown off." Goebel (1905) found that the four large terminal cells of the archegonial neck of *Equisetum* become strongly reflexed as they separate from one another, although still remaining attached to the adjacent tier of neck cells. As noted previously, all members of the axial row except the egg cell disintegrate, thus producing a canal through which the motile sperm can pass. In ferns it has been shown that malic acid exerts a chemotactic stimulus upon the spermatozoids; it appears that this organic acid or some other substance is present in the exudate from the open neck of the archegonium and this orients the sperm towards the neck and thence to the egg. Further experimental studies on the nature of the substances which may react in this way on male gametes are highly desirable. (See

Ward, 1954, for an interesting account of the opening of antheridia and
archegonia in the leptosporangiate fern *Phlebodium.*)

Ontogeny of Gametangia

Despite the striking divergence between fully developed antheridia and
archegonia, both kinds of sex organs are remarkably alike in their method
of initiation and in the earliest stages of their ontogeny. In all investigated cases each type of gametangium originates from a single surface
cell of the gametophyte, as can be seen in Fig. 5-1. Whether there are
definable cytological differences between the parent cells of antheridia
and those of archegonia is a question that has never been intensively
studied. Spessard (1922) in his description of the gametophyte of
Lycopodium lucidulum, where the sex organs are intermingled, states
that "it is impossible to distinguish an antheridium from an archegonium
in the very earliest stages of their development. There are some indications that the archegonial initial is slightly larger and longer than the
antheridial initial, but this is so uncertain that it is useless as a criterion."
A similar close resemblance between antheridial and archegonial initials
is found also in other groups, such as *Psilotum* (Bierhorst, 1954) and the
Marattiaceae; the latter are used by Goebel (1928) and Bower (1935) to
illustrate the morphological equivalence of sex organs in vascular plants.

In addition to their identical mode of origin, antheridia and archegonia begin their development by the periclinal division of the parent
cells (Fig. 5-1, a, a'). With reference to the embedded type of antheridium, this results in an outer *jacket cell,* the anticlinal subdivision of
which produces the opercular layer, and an inner *primary spermatogenous cell* (sometimes referred to as the primary androgonial cell)
from which the usually numerous spermatocytes and ultimately the
sperms originate (Fig. 5-1, a-d). There is a comparable distinction between outer sterile cells and inner potentially fertile cells, due to the
first periclinal division of an archegonial initial (Fig. 5-1, a'). In this
case, the outer cell or *primary cover cell,* by means of two successive
anticlinal divisions at right angles to one another, produces a quartet of
cells from which, by transverse divisions, the four vertical rows of the
archegonial neck are developed. The inner of the two derivatives of the
archegonial initial may first produce a *basal cell,* as in many ferns, and

then serve as the parent cell of the axial row, or, as is more commonly the case, it may function directly without first forming a basal cell. In either instance, the parent cell of the axial row is usually designated as the *central cell* (Fig. 5-1, a').

The presence or absence of a basal cell is not a consistent feature of archegonium development within a family or even a genus. The Marattiaceae furnish a good example of the degree of fluctuation that may exist. In *Danaea*, for example, and in *Angiopteris evecta* a basal cell is consistently absent (Haupt, 1940). On the other hand, the presence or absence of a basal cell varies from species to species in the genus *Marattia* (Stokey, 1942). Apparently a basal cell is commonly developed in the young archegonia of leptosporangiate ferns; here, by means of a few anticlinal divisions, it contributes cells to the lower portion of the jacket of the archegonial venter (Fig. 13-19).

This description analyzes the early similarities and differences in the ontogenetic history of the gametangia. A brief discussion is in order of the method of origin of the component cells of the axial row in the archegonium and the comparative ontogeny of the emergent types of antheridia in the leptosporangiate ferns. Let us first examine the development of the cells in the axial row of the archegonia of various plants.

The central cell, in the archegonia of lower vascular plants, divides periclinally into an outer *primary canal cell* and an inner *primary ventral cell* (Fig. 5-1, b'). From the former, one or as many as sixteen neck canal cells originate. As already explained, the most extensive development of neck canal cells occurs in certain species of *Lycopodium* where anticlinal divisions may result in a double series, or, if wall formation is inhibited, a single row of binucleate elements may occur. When only a few neck canal cells are formed these usually are in a superposed row. But the archegonium of certain species of *Equisetum* quite regularly develops two laterally placed neck canal cells. The primary ventral cell is believed to function in some cases as an egg. Perhaps more typically, however, it divides periclinally forming the evanescent *ventral canal cell* and the basally situated *egg* (Fig. 5-1, d'). In the gymnosperms, as mentioned, neck canal cells are not developed. On the contrary, the central cell functions as the initial from which the large egg and the transitory ventral canal cell (or its nucleus) originate.

There remains for final consideration the ontogeny of the antheridium in leptosporangiate ferns, which differs in several interesting respects from that characteristic of embedded antheridia. Some of the differences parallel to a remarkable degree the ontogenetic differences between leptosporangia and eusporangia that have been described in Chapter 4. Perhaps one of the most definitive ontogenetic features of the emergent type of antheridium in leptosporangiate ferns is the fact that the first division wall of the initial does not set apart an outer sterile and an inner fertile cell. On the contrary, the formation of the primary spermatogenous cell is delayed until two or more sterile cells have been cut off by the antheridial initial. In such primitive fern groups as the Gleicheniaceae and Osmundaceae the antheridial initial, by means of alternating oblique divisions, first produces a series of basal cells which constitute the short stalk and the lower portion of the antheridial jacket. Ultimately the initial becomes divided by a curved periclinal wall into an outer *jacket cell* and an inner *primary spermatogenous cell*. From the former, by anticlinal divisions, the upper part of the antheridial jacket including an opercular cell is formed, and the spermatocytes develop from the subdivision of the primary spermatogenous cell. The periclinal wall, which sets apart the spermatogenous cell from the sterile jacket initial, is a remarkable parallel with the similarly oriented wall delimiting the primary wall and primary sporogenous cells of a young leptosporangium.

The early ontogeny of the more delicate emergent antheridium of the highly specialized Polypodiaceae likewise results first in the production of sterile cells. These, however, are fewer in number and of unusual shape. According to the classical interpretation, the antheridial initial divides by means of a funnel-shaped wall into an outer "ring cell" and a central cell. The latter divides by a curved periclinal wall into an outer jacket cell and the internal primary spermatogenous cell. A curved anticlinal division in the jacket cell subdivides the latter into a second ring-shaped cell and a centrally located opercular cell. Certain details in this interpretation have been challenged by Davie (1951), who contends that the first division wall in the antheridial initial is straight or only slightly concave and not funnel-shaped (Fig. 5-2, B). By increasing turgor within the upper of the two cells this wall becomes bent downward until it comes nearly in contact with the original basal wall of the antheridial initial (Fig. 5-2, E, F). Meanwhile, the upper cell divides

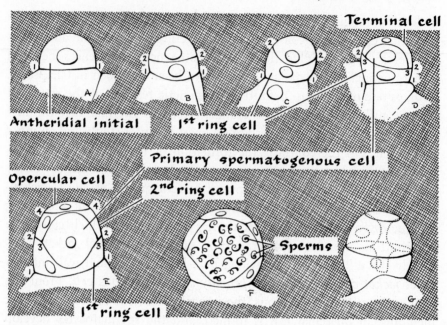

Figure 5-2 Ontogeny of the antheridium in *Pityrogramma calomelanos.* **A,**
formation of the antheridial initial; **B,** two-celled stage; **C,** two-celled stage in
which the first wall (2-2) is becoming depressed; **D,** three-celled stage, consisting of a terminal cell, a primary spermatogenous cell and the first ring cell;
E, transverse division of terminal cell by wall *4-4* has produced the opercular
cell and the second ring cell; **F,** mature antheridium with sperms; **G,** three
dimensional view of antheridium (which has discharged its sperms) to show
form of the ring cells. [Redrawn from Davie, *Amer. Jour. Bot.* 38:621, 1951.]

into the terminal cell and the primary spermatogenous cell (Fig. 5-2,
D). Transverse division of the terminal cell produces a cap or opercular
cell and the second ring cell (Fig. 5-2, E). As the primary spermatogenous cell enlarges, its upper convex wall is forced into contact with the
inner wall of the opercular cell (Fig. 5-2, E, F). At this stage the jacket
of the antheridium consists of three cells: two rings cells and an opercular
cell. But as a result of the contacts established between certain walls, the
antheridium may appear in median longisectional view to have a five-
celled jacket (see Fig. 5-2, F, G; also Fig. 13-19, I).

Homology and Phylogenetic Origin of Gametangia

In the two preceding sections the structure and ontogeny of the sex
organs in lower vascular plants have been described in considerable de-

tail. Can any general conclusion be reached as to the evolutionary significance of the points of resemblance between antheridia and archegonia? Many morphologists believe that the close similarity in mode of initiation and early development of the two kinds of gametangia is evidence of their homology. Each arises from a single parent cell, and each, at a very early stage, exhibits a sharp distinction between external sterile cells and internal fertile ones. What then is the reason for the marked reduction in the number of functional gametes to a single basal cell in the archegonium?

Very possibly, as many writers have pointed out, this reduction indicates that the archegonium is the more specialized of the two gametangia and that it originated in evolution from a more generalized polygametic organ. The antheridium seems in many ways to correspond to such a hypothetical primitive gametangium. On this line of reasoning, the archegonium would be regarded as a highly modified and reduced organ in which a series of potential gametes—the entire axial row—are the morphological equivalents of the spermatocytes of the antheridium. But in modern archegonia all except one of these potential gametes are destroyed in the production of the archegonial canal. Some evidence that the archegonium formerly may have been more antheridial-like in structure is furnished by unusual or abnormal archegonia in the Bryophyta (Holferty, 1904; Meyer, 1911) as well as in lower vascular plants (Lyon, 1904; Spessard, 1922). The archegonia of *Lycopodium complanatum*, for example, very often show from fourteen to sixteen neck canal cells, each of which is binucleate. This might be interpreted as an atavistic trend towards the multiplication of potentially fertile cells.

But the most remarkable structures are the bisexual gametangia that have been observed in various liverworts and mosses and also in certain species of *Lycopodium*. These organs resemble archegonia in their form but contain spermatogenous tissue as well as typical axial-row cells. In *Lycopodium lucidulum*, according to Spessard's investigations, the spermatogenous tissue may occupy either the neck or the venter of an abnormal archegonium. Great care must always be observed in the interpretation, especially from an evolutionary standpoint, of transitional forms between two kinds of organs. But taken in conjunction with the evidence from ontogeny the aberrant archegonia lend further strength to the idea that both antheridia and archegonia have evolved from a rather general, undifferentiated, and probably polygametic sex organ. The details of the evolutionary process may always remain obscure, especially because it is difficult to derive the gametangia of living Archegoniates from the sexual "organs" of any of the green algae (Davis, 1903; Lyon, 1904). With reference to the possible relationship between the gametangia of Bryophytes and lower vascular plants, Goebel (1905, p. 187) makes the following interesting conclusion: "The structure of the sexual organs is alike in its outlines in Bryophyta and Pteridophyta, but shows in the development and in the ultimate details so many differences that we have evidently here to deal with two phyletic series of which the higher has not been derived from the lower, but arising at an early period from simple similar primitive forms they have followed separate paths."

References

Bierhorst, D. W. 1954. The gametangia and embryo of *Psilotum*. *Amer. Jour. Bot.* 41:274-281.

Bower, F. O. 1935. *Primitive Land Plants*. Macmillan, London.

Campbell, D. H. 1911. The Eusporangiatae. The comparative morphology of the Ophioglossaceae and Marattiaceae. Carnegie Institution of Washington, Publication No. 140. Washington, D. C.

————. 1918. *The Structure and Development of Mosses and Ferns*. Ed. 3. Macmillan, New York.

Davie, J. H. 1951. The development of the antheridium in the Polypodiaceae. *Amer. Jour. Bot.* 38:621-628.

Davis, B. M. 1903. The origin of the archegonium. *Ann. Bot.* 17:477-492.

Goebel, K. 1905. *Organography of Plants*. Eng. Ed. by I. B. Balfour. Part II. Clarendon Press, Oxford.

————. 1928. *Organographie der Pflanzen*. Ed. 3. Erster Teil. G. Fischer, Jena.

Haupt, A. W. 1940. Sex organs of *Angiopteris evecta*. *Bull. Torrey Bot. Club.* 67:125-129.

Holferty, G. M. 1904. The archegonium of *Mnium cuspidatum*. *Bot. Gaz.* 37: 106-126.

Lyon, F. 1904. The evolution of the sex organs of plants. *Bot. Gaz.* 37: 280-293.

Meyer, K. 1911. Zur Frage von der Homologie der Geschlechtsorgane und der Phylogenie des Archegoniums. *Biol. Zeitschr.* 2:178-185.

Spessard, E. A. 1922. Prothallia of Lycopodium in America. II. *L. lucidulum* and *L. obscurum* var. *dendroideum. Bot. Gaz.* 74:392-413.

Stokey, A. G. 1942. Gametophytes of *Marattia sambucina* and *Macroglossum Smithii. Bot. Gaz.* 103:559-569.

———. 1950. The gametophyte of the Gleicheniaceae. *Bull. Torrey Bot. Club.* 77:323-339.

———. 1951. The contribution by the gametophyte to classification of the homosporous ferns. *Phytomorphology* 1:39-58.

Ward, M. 1954. Fertilization in *Phlebodium aureum* J. Sm. *Phytomorphology* 4:1-17.

Chapter

6 EMBRYOGENY

The term embryogeny designates the successive steps in the growth and differentiation of a fertilized egg or zygote into a young sporophyte. Although no sharp limits can be set, it will be convenient to distinguish between the early definitive stages in embryogeny and the later phases of growth during which the organs of the embryo arise and become functionally significant.

In all the Archegoniatae (including the majority of gymnosperms) fertilization and the first critical phases of embryogeny occur within the shelter provided by the venter of the archegonium and the adjacent gametophytic tissue. At this first period the polarity (i.e., the distinction between the apex and the base) of the embryo is determined by highly specified planes of division in the zygote, as will be described in detail later in the chapter. The period of enlargement and organ development which follows results, in lower vascular plants, usually in the formation of a shoot apex together with one or more leaves, a root, a well-defined foot, and, in many genera, a suspensor. The foot serves as a haustorial organ which attaches the embryo to the nutritive tissue of the gameto-phyte. In the majority of archegoniate plants the apex of the young embryo faces inwardly toward the gametophytic tissue and away from the neck of the archegonium, as can be seen in Fig. 6-1, B, C. An embryo of this type illustrates strikingly the intimate nutritive relationship be-tween it and the gametophyte since, during enlargement and organo-genesis, it must digest its way through a considerable volume of gametophytic tissue before emerging at the surface of the thallus. Ulti-mately, in contrast with the permanently dependent embryos of all the Bryophyta, the embryo of lower vascular plants becomes free from the nursing gametophyte and grows into an independent sporophyte. In the majority of the gymnosperms and in angiosperms the embryo is shed from the parent plant in a somewhat dormant condition, is enveloped

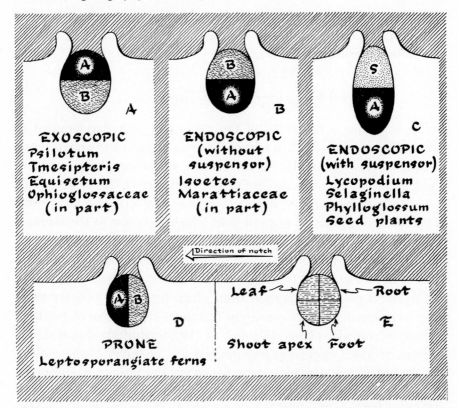

Figure 6-1 Main types of polarity in the development of the embryo in lower vascular plants. In all figures, the apical pole (cell A) is shown in black and the basal pole (cell B) is shaded. **A,** exoscopic polarity; **B,** endoscopic polarity without a suspensor; **C,** endoscopic polarity with a suspensor; **D,** orientation of two-celled embryo in leptosporangiate ferns; **E,** quadrant stage in embryogeny in leptosporangiate ferns illustrating points of future origin of leaf, shoot apex, root, and foot.

by a protective cover, and is often provided with a special nutritive tissue or endosperm; here the embryo constitutes the essential part of that remarkable structure which we term a seed (see Chapters 14 and 19).

In this chapter the discussion will be restricted mainly to the principles of comparative embryogeny as illustrated by the lower vascular plants. As in the discussions of gametangia and sporangia, our intent is to provide orientation for the student and to illuminate those significant details of embryogeny which will be given later when we consider the morphology of special tracheophyta groups. For an account of the embryogeny of seed plants, the student should consult Chapters 14-17 and Chapter 19, which include descriptions of the embryos of selected gymnosperms and angiosperms.

General Organography of Embryos

Before beginning a discussion of the origin and early development of embryos we must have a clear idea of the main categories of organs found in the embryos of vascular plants. From a broad morphological viewpoint, as has been repeatedly emphasized by Bower (1922, 1935), a very young embryo is somewhat filamentous or spindle shaped, and consists of two definable poles: the apical pole, which gives rise to the terminal meristem or shoot apex and one or more leaves, and the basal pole, which in many groups of the lower vascular plants is represented by the suspensor. Let us now examine these components of the embryo.

The apical pole is the portion from which the first or primary shoot takes its origin; it is a very consistent feature of the embryo of the large majority of vascular plants. In much of the literature dealing with the embryos of lower vascular plants the first leaf or leaves of the embryo are designated as cotyledons, a term which we, the authors, would prefer to restrict to the first foliar organs of the embryos of seed plants (Wagner, 1952, p. 45). The size of the first leaf or leaves of the embryo in lower vascular plants fluctuates widely; in some genera—for example, *Lycopodium*—they are very small and rudimentary, whereas in others— *Isoetes, Botrychium virginianum,* and many leptosporangiate ferns— the first leaf is large, precociously developed, and may even be significantly photosynthetic (see Fig. 6-2). In seed plants, as will be described later, the number of cotyledons ranges from one to many.

As stated above, the base of the embryo in certain genera is represented by the suspensor; this structure, highly developed in most gymnosperms and found also in the embryos of angiosperms, is extremely variable in its occurrence in lower vascular plants (Fig. 6-2). The family Ophioglossaceae furnishes an excellent illustration, because in *Ophioglossum* and several species of *Botrychium* a suspensor is absent, whereas in other species of the latter and in *Helminthostachys* it is evident. Variation is found also in the *Lycopsida,* where two of the genera— *Lycopodium* and *Selaginella*—have embryos with suspensors, and *Isoetes* has none (Chapter 8). The morphological interpretation of the suspensor and its correlation with the type of polarity in the embryo will be discussed later, but here it should be noted that the suspensor is a temporary organ, the growth and enlargement of which serve to force the embryo into intimate contact with the nutritive tissue of the gametophyte.

In addition to the shoot apex, leaf primordia, and suspensor, the embryo of most vascular plants acquires a root. The most interesting

Figure 6-2 Variations in form and position of the organs of the embryos in lower vascular plants. **A,** *Selaginella spinulosa;* **B,** *Selaginella Martensii;* **C,** *Lycopodium selago;* **D,** *Lycopodium clavatum;* **E,** *Lycopodium cernuum;* **F,** *Isoetes;* **G,** *Equisetum. F,* foot; *L,* leaf; *R,* root; *S,* suspensor; *Sa,* shoot apex. [Redrawn from *Primitive Land Plants* by F. O. Bower. London: Macmillan and Co. Ltd., 1935.]

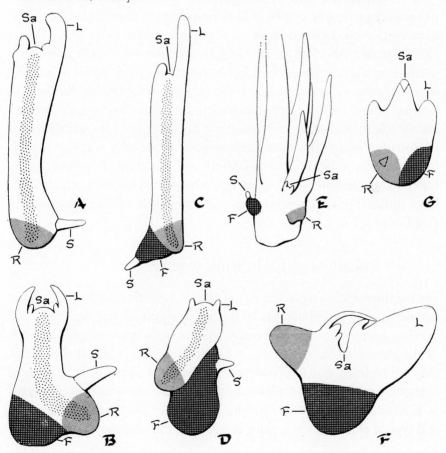

exceptions to this general rule occur in *Psilotum* and *Tmesipteris*. The embryos of these archaic and presumably very primitive plants are crude and entirely devoid of any evidence of a root. As stated in Chapter 7, the absence of any sign of a root in the embryo of *Psilotum* and *Tmesipteris* is regarded as excellent evidence that the rootless adult sporophyte of the Psilotales is a primitive and not a derived condition. In the embryos of all other lower vascular plants the root is a strictly lateral organ, with respect to the main vertical axis of the embryo, as shown in Fig. 6-2. This contrasts markedly with the condition typical of most seed plants where the root tip lies in the same vertical axis as the shoot apex, being situated between the shoot apex and the suspensor (see Chapter 14-17 and Chapter 19). Bower (1922) designates the position of the root in the embryos of gymnosperms and angiosperms as median.

There remains for brief consideration the so-called foot of the embryo, whose occurrence and degree of development vary more than that of the suspensor, even within species of the same genus (Fig. 6-2). Bower (1935) regards the foot as an "opportunist growth" which arises in a position convenient for performing its function as a suctorial or nursing organ. In some embryos, such as those of *Selaginella, Isoetes, Equisetum, Ophioglossum,* and the leptosporangiate ferns, the foot is conspicuous, and its role in anchoring and conveying nutrients from the gametophyte is evident. Perhaps the most impressive example of a suctorial foot is found in the embryos of *Tmesipteris* and *Psilotum*. Here the entire lower half of the embryo develops into a haustorial structure which sends lobes and irregular processes deep into the tissue of the gametophyte (see Chapter 7).

Polarity and Early Embryogeny

During the middle and latter part of the nineteenth century much labor was devoted by morphologists to tracing in minute detail the origin and development of the organs of many types of embryos. One of the results of the close attention given the sequence and planes of cell division in growing embryos was the concept that there is a single or basic plan of segmentation throughout plant embryogeny. In particular, the embryos of *Equisetum* and leptosporangiate ferns were considered fundamental and typical of all embryos, since it was held that the major organs, leaf, stem, root, and foot could be traced back to specific quadrants (i.e., quarter sections) formed at the very beginning of embryonic develop- ment. In the light of our extended knowledge of embryos of all the major groups of vascular plants it is now evident that great variation exists with respect to the definition of these so-called quadrants and their rôle in organogenesis, and that the study of embryogeny should be pursued in as flexible a manner as possible, with due regard to the effect of such external factors as gravity, light, and nutrition on the embryonic pattern (Ward, 1954; Wardlaw, 1955). In short, there is need for a broadened organographic attack on the problems of comparative embryology and a proper recognition of the dangers of rigid histogenetic and organo- genetic interpretations.

According to Bower (1908, 1922, 1935), who has paved the way toward a more dynamic biological understanding of embryogeny the first step in the development of the embryo is the definition of its axial polarity. Except for the leptosporangiate ferns, to be discussed later, the first division wall in the zygote is approximately transverse to the long axis of the archegonium and results in a definite distinction between the future apex and base of the embryo. However, two types of polarity arise from this first division of the zygote. In the more common polarity type, termed *endoscopic,* the apical pole—cell A in Fig. 6-1, B, C—is directed toward the base of the archegonium; in the opposed or *exoscopic* type the apex faces outward toward the neck of the arche- gonium—cell A in Fig. 6-1, A.

The occurrence of these two main types of embryo polarity in vascular plants at large poses some interesting morphological and phylogenetic questions. The endoscopic type occurs in *Lycopodium, Selaginella, Isoetes,* certain of the eusporangiate ferns, and *all* seed plants. The less- frequent exoscopic polarity characterizes the embryogeny of *Psilotum, Tmesipteris, Equisetum,* and some members of the Ophioglossaceae. Thus, the distribution of endoscopic and exoscopic polarity follows to some extent the major groups within the lower vascular plants, although both patterns may be encountered within the confines of a single genus, as is the case in *Botrychium.* In a strict sense, the embryos of most of the investigated members of the leptosporangiate ferns do not fall into either the endoscopic or exoscopic categories because the first division wall in the zygote tends to be parallel to the long axis of the archegonium, as can be seen in Fig. 6-1, D. Consequently, the apical and basal poles of the embryo tend to be oriented laterally with respect to the archegonial axis, and the embryo is prone rather than vertical or curved with respect to the prothallus, as shown by Fig. 6-1, E. A further discussion of the distinctively oriented embryo of leptosporangiate ferns will be given after we describe the origin of the suspensor in various types of embryos.

The presence of a suspensor is invariably correlated with an endoscopic type of polarity. Figure 6-3 illustrates schematically the method of origin of the suspensor in the endoscopic type of embryogeny characteristic of *Lycopodium, Selaginella,* and certain of the eusporangiate ferns. The zygote divides by a transverse wall I-I into two cells as shown in Fig. 6-3, A. The upper cell (labeled S) is directed toward the neck of the archegonium and represents the parent cell of the future suspensor, which may enlarge without further division or give rise to a short multicellular filamentous suspensor. The lower cell (labeled EM), termed the embryonic cell, subsequently gives rise to the main body of the embryo. The plane of the first division of the embryonic cell may be transverse, yielding a hypobasal cell (in contact with the suspensor) and

Figure 6-3 Successive stages in early development of an endoscopic type of embryo with a suspensor. **A,** the first division of the zygote is transverse (wall I-I) and yields a suspensor cell (S) directed toward the archegonial neck and an embryonic cell (EM) directed inwardly; **B,** transverse division of embryonic cell (wall II-II) has produced an epibasal (E) and a hypobasal (H) cell; **C,** the octant stage, resulting from two successive vertical divisions of the epibasal and hypobasal cells.

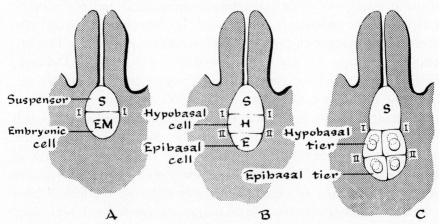

an epibasal cell (Fig. 6-3, B). Two successive vertical divisions in each of these cells results in an eight-celled embryo, consisting of an epibasal tier and a hypobasal tier (Fig. 6-3, C). Although this tiered arrangement of cells apparently is characteristic of the young embryos of many vascular plants, the sequence of wall formation in the embryonic cell appears to fluctuate. In various species of *Lycopodium*, for example, the plane of the first division wall in the embryonic cell is vertical rather than transverse; each of the two cells then divides in a similar plane yielding a group of four cells—a quadrant stage. Transverse divisions of each of these quadrant cells then results in the formation of an eight-celled embryo comprising an epibasal and a hypobasal tier. The variable rôle of the epibasal and hypobasal cell tiers in the subsequent development of the organs of the embryo will be reserved for later discussion.

In embryos devoid of a suspensor the zygote itself functions directly as the embryonic cell, and its first division results, as before, in an epibasal and a hypobasal cell (Wardlaw 1955, p. 22). But in contrast with the invariably endoscopic polarity of embryos with a suspensor, the suspensorless types vary widely as to the orientation of the epibasal cell or apical pole. *Isoetes* and certain genera in the Marattiaceae (*Christensenia, Marattia, Angiopteris*) lack suspensors, yet are characterized by endoscopic polarity. On the other hand, as we have mentioned, all exoscopic embryos (for example, those of *Tmesipteris, Psilotum, Equisetum,* and *Ophioglossum*) are devoid of a suspensor, and in them the epibasal region faces outward toward the neck of the archegonium. To repeat, the orientation of the suspensorless embryo in the leptosporangiate ferns is neither strictly endoscopic nor exoscopic because the first or the basal wall is longitudinal rather than transverse, as can be seen in Fig. 6-1, D. In this case, the apical pole of the young embryo is directed toward the apex of the prothallus but is transverse with reference to the long axis of the archegonium. There appears to be no entirely satisfactory explanation for the anomalous orientation of the embryo in leptosporangiate ferns. Bower (1935) has pointed out that gravity may play a role in determining the plane of the first division of the zygote. In any event, an interesting result of the position of the embryo is that the first leaf and the first root emerge from beneath the lower surface of the gametophyte rather than penetrating the thallus as is the case with endoscopic embryos (Chapter 13).

Origin and Development of Organs

Following the early definition of polarity and the establishment of an
eight-celled embryo, the young sporophyte enters upon a phase of enlargement and organ formation. We may properly ask at this point
whether the organs common to most embryos, such as root, first leaf,
shoot apex, and foot, always arise in a uniform manner from specific
sectors or regions of the embryo. If we restrict ourselves to the evidence
furnished by classical accounts of the embryogeny of leptosporangiate
ferns, this question would be answered in the affirmative. It is said that
in these plants the shoot apex, first leaf, first root, and foot originate
from specific quadrants of the embryo (Fig. 6-1, E). However, this
interpretation, as will be discussed in more detail in Chapter 13,
has been challenged in recent years on the grounds that it postulates a rigid correspondence between the position of organs of the
embryo and the pattern of cellular differentiation arising from each
of the original embryo quadrants. The foot, for example, as described by Ward (1954), originates in *Phlebodium* from cells derived
from both of the anterior or epibasal sectors of the embryo. (See Wardlaw 1955, pp. 142-146 for further critical comments on the classical interpretation of embryogeny in leptosporangiate ferns.)

A precise type of organogenesis referrable to definable quadrants is
believed to exist also in the suspensorless embryo of *Equisetum*. According to the classical investigations of Sadebeck (1878) on *E. arvense* and
E. palustre, the outer epibasal tier of the embryo forms the shoot apex
and the first whorl of leaves, and the foot and root originate from derivatives of the hypobasal tier (Fig. 9-8, A, B). While there now appears
some doubt whether the root in *Equisetum* is always of hypobasal origin,
there is little question as to the discrete method of origin of shoot and
foot, respectively, from the epibasal and hypobasal tiers.

In contrast with *Equisetum* and the leptosporangiate ferns, organogenesis in the embryos of other lower vascular plants follows no clear-cut
uniform or standardized pattern (Fig. 6-2). The shoot apex and the first
foliar appendages show the greatest constancy of all the parts of the
embryo because they invariably arise from the epibasal tier. According
to the analysis of various embryonic patterns made by Bower, the shoot

apex originates as nearly as possible at the geometrical center of the epibasal half of the embryo. In terms of cells, this center corresponds very closely to the point of intersection of the octant walls and is plainly defined in those cases where a single definitive apical cell is produced by obliquely oriented divisions (see Fig. 9-8). Foliar organs, whatever their size, number, or arrangement, likewise originate from the epibasal half of the embryo. In many cases, these primary leaves are arranged in a pair or a whorl around the embryo apex, thus resembling the relation of later leaf primordia of the sporophyte to the shoot apex. But in some embryos, particularly in *Isoetes* and in members of the Ophioglossaceae, the first leaf is unusually large and, because of its precocious growth, tends to displace the shoot apex to the side or even to cause a delay in its initiation.

With reference to its place and time of origin, the root is, without question, the most variable organ of the embryo. Sometimes it arises

Figure 6-4 Embryos of three species of *Selaginella* showing variability in the position of the root with reference to other organs. **A,** *S. denticulata;* **B,** *S. Poulteri;* **C,** *S. Galeottii.* [Redrawn from *Primitive Land Plants* by F. O. Bower. London: Macmillan and Co. Ltd., 1935.]

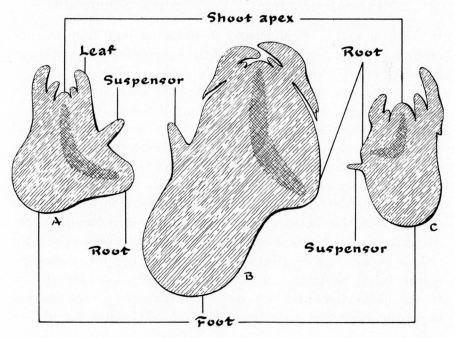

jointly with the first leaf and shoot apex from the epibasal half of the embryo. This is true of the embryos of *Isoetes* and many members of the Ophioglossaceae and Marattiaceae. In other instances, such as in certain species of *Selaginella*, the primary root develops from the hypobasal portion of the embryo. In addition to its variable point of origin, the position of the first root with reference to other organs of the embryo is inconstant, as is shown very clearly in the genus *Selaginella*. In *S. denticulata* the root lies on the same side of the embryo as the suspensor, and in *S. poulteri* it lies on the side opposite the suspensor; finally, in *S. galeotii* the root, while on the same side as the suspensor, lies between the suspensor and the shoot apex. These relationships are shown in Fig. 6-4.

With reference to the foot, it is evident that while this portion of the embryo arises from all or a part of the cells of the hypobasal tier, its form and degree of development fluctuate even within members of the same genus. This is illustrated in both *Lycopodium* and *Selaginella*, the individual species of which differ considerably in regard to the prominence of the foot (see Fig. 6-2).

Embryogeny from a Phylogenetic Standpoint

In this final section of the chapter it will be appropriate to examine briefly the phylogenetic implications of those various aspects of embryogeny which have been presented.

First, we may raise the question of the historical aspects and evolutionary significance of the two principal types of embryo polarity. Which is the prior condition, the exoscopic or the endoscopic? One might assume, in agreement with the viewpoint of Bower, that an endoscopic embryo with a suspensor represents the "primitive spindle" form, from which the suspensorless types have taken origin. According to Bower, the abolition of the suspensor has taken place repeatedly and independently, as evidenced by its variable occurrence in such families as the Marattiaceae and Ophioglossaceae and in the Lycopsida. Once the embryo became free of a suspensor its former obligatory endoscopic polarity might be retained, if this were selectively advantageous from the standpoint of nutrition, or a complete inversion to the exoscopic type of polarity might take place. Bower (1935, p. 533) states that such an inversion of polarity has occurred phylogenetically in *Ophioglossum* and *Botrychium lunaria*. Goebel (1928, p. 225) also holds that a rotation in polarity from endoscopic to exoscopic is admissable in some cases. On the other hand, the occurrence of exoscopic polarity in such primitive vascular plants as *Tmesipteris* and *Psilotum*, as well as throughout the Bryophyta, might equally well suggest that endoscopic polarity, which is typical of the majority of higher vascular plants, is the derived condition (MacMillan, 1898). At present there is absolutely no evidence that the embryos of *Tmesipteris* and *Psilotum* originally possessed suspensors and hence were endoscopic. Very likely, these phyletic questions are not answerable with our present knowledge of embryogeny and plant phylogeny.

There is great need for an intensive experimental attack on the problem of the polarity of embryos. In certain of the Hepaticae it seems clear that the orientation of the archegonium is not a determining factor since, regardless of whether it is upright, horizontal, or pendent, the embryo is strictly exoscopic. Probably, as Bower has suggested, the basal nutrition of the young embryo in these cases is an important factor in maintaining the exoscopic polarity. Almost no experimental work seems to have been done on the factors which might influence or control the polarity of the embryo in vascular plants. Genera such as *Botrychium*, in which the polarity varies with the species, would be particularly interesting to study from a morphogenetic viewpoint.

With reference to the complex problems posed by organogenesis in embryos, several significant points deserve emphasis. During recent decades there has been a conspicuous awakening of interest in the cellular organization and patterns of growth and differentiation of apical meristems. The shoot apex in particular has been explored in a great variety of vascular plants, and the general conclusion reached is that there is no real basis for a rigid and highly deterministic interpretation of either histogenesis or organogenesis (see Foster, 1949; Esau, 1953; Gifford, 1954). A similar flexible viewpoint seems entirely justified in the comparative and phyletic study of embryos. In other words, although correspondence may exist between the origin of organs and the pattern of cell divisions this is not necessarily an obligatory relationship. Furthermore, it should be recalled that a plant embryo, unlike its counterpart in higher animals, is very far from being a miniature of the adult organism.

On the contrary, vascular plant sporophytes are characterized by an open type of growth and organogenesis because of the maintenance of embryonic areas or meristems at the tips of all shoots and roots. This open type of growth—or "continued embryogeny" as Bower terms it—has its beginning in the embryo itself, which thus foreshadows the morphology of the adult plant in only the most general fashion. For these reasons, phylogenetic interpretations of plant embryos should be made with due regard to the possible effects of gravity, light, and the source and type of nutrition on the polarity and pattern of development of the young encapsulated sporophyte (Wardlaw, 1955).

References

Bower, F. O. 1908. *The Origin of a Land Flora*. Macmillan, London.

———. 1922. The primitive spindle as a fundamental feature in the embryology of plants. *Proc. Roy. Soc. Edinburgh*. 43:1-36.

———. 1935. *Primitive Land Plants*. Macmillan, London.

Esau, K. 1953. *Plant Anatomy*. Wiley, New York.

Foster, A. S. 1949. *Practical Plant Anatomy*. Ed. 2. Van Nostrand, New York.

Gifford, E. M., Jr. 1954. The shoot apex in angiosperms. *Bot. Rev.* 20: 477-529.

Goebel, K. 1928. *Organographie der Pflanzen*. Ed. 3. Erster Teil. G. Fischer, Jena.

MacMillan, C. 1898. The orientation of the plant egg, and its ecological significance. *Bot. Gaz.* 25:301-323.

Sadebeck, R. 1878. Die Entwicklung des Keimes der Schachtelhalme. *Jahrb. wiss. Bot.* 11:575-602.

Wagner, W. H., Jr. 1952. The fern genus *Diellia. Univ. California Publ. Bot.* 26:1-212.

Ward, M. 1954. The development of the embryo of *Phlebodium aureum* J. Sm. *Phytomorphology* 4:18-26.

Wardlaw, C. W. 1955. *Embryogenesis in Plants*. Wiley, New York.

Chapter

7 THE PSILOPSIDA

The importance of a well-developed vascular system (xylem and phloem) to a land plant cannot be overemphasized. Establishment of such a system in a land plant, as we have mentioned in Chapter 3, makes possible its continued existence because pathways are present for the transport of raw materials and manufactured food. Since the evolutionary modification of a vascular system has extended over countless ages it is important to examine that group of plants which is considered primitive among vascular plants.

The earliest known record of a representative number of vascular plants goes back approximately 350 million years to the Devonian period of the long Paleozoic era, although certain vascular plants from Australia have been described and assigned to even the Silurian period (approximately 380 million years ago). During much of the Paleozoic a climate prevailed, which might be described as temperate and somewhat seasonal, comparable to that of the coastal regions of California and Oregon. In the animal world higher invertebrates were becoming specialized; fishes, amphibians, and reptiles made their appearance, and by the end of the Paleozoic amphibians were well-established.

Factual information concerning a member of a very ancient group of plants dates back to 1858 when Sir William Dawson described a plant (*Psilophyton princeps*) of Devonian age discovered in Gaspé, Quebec. Because Dawson's description was based upon rather fragmentary evidence, some doubt existed as to the morphological interpretation of the remains. It was not until almost 60 years later that the real significance of this plant was understood. From 1917 to 1921 a series of articles was published by Kidston and Lang (1917) describing well-preserved plants from deposits of Devonian age in the Rhynie chert beds, Aberdeenshire, Scotland. These paleobotanists realized that there were similarities between *Psilophyton* and their discoveries, and the order Psilophytales was established to include all of these presumably primitive extinct plants.

Since these earlier studies, the sporophytes of additional extinct genera have been discovered in such widely separated places as Norway, China, and Australia. No information is available regarding the nature of the gametophyte generation, although the possibility of its discovery is hopefully anticipated.

Classification

Most authorities are in agreement on the general taxonomic treatment of the Psilopsida in that two orders are recognized: Psilophytales, extinct plants, and Psilotales, living plants. The abbreviated outline of classification presented here is intended to serve as a guide for further elaboration upon the morphology of selected members of each order.

Several genera are assigned to the Psilophytales, but we, the authors, will adopt the type method and describe only three of them in some detail. The remains of these plants have been found in a remarkably good state of preservation (for example, *Rhynia* and *Asteroxylon*). Whether they represent the most primitive type of organization can be argued, and this is indeed questioned by some botanists. Nevertheless, they display by their morphology the type of organization typical of psilophytalean plants. Descriptions of additional genera can be found in standard texts on paleobotany (to mention but three: Arnold, 1947; Gothan and Weyland, 1954; Mägdefrau, 1953), and in the research paper of Kräusel (1936).

PSILOPSIDA: Sporophyte with vascular tissue; plant body consisting of a dichotomously branched stem, often with foliar appendages; roots absent; sporangia eusporangiate and homosporous.

PSILOPHYTALES: Extinct plants; plant body was simple, very typically dichotomously branched, and consisted of a rhizome and aerial stems; stems were naked or had small appendages; vascular system was generally protostelic; sporangia were homosporous and terminal.

RHYNIACEAE: Prostrate cylindrical rhizome with upright dichotomously branched stems; vascular system a haplostele; foliar appendages absent. *Rhynia, Horneophyton.*

ASTEROXYLACEAE: Dichotomously branched subterranean rhizome devoid of appendages; aerial stem portion clothed with small leaf-like appendages; vascular system of aerial stem actinostelic.

Asteroxylon.

PSILOTALES: Living plants, dichotomously branched with underground rhizome and aerial stems; aerial portion may have small scale-like appendages or larger leaf-like structures; vascular cylinder protostelic to siphonostelic; sporangia two- or three-chambered, terminal on side branches; eusporangiate and homosporous.

PSILOTACEAE: Characteristics as for Psilotales.

Psilotum, Tmesipteris.

Psilophytales

Rhyniaceae: Rhynia

ORGANOGRAPHY. The two species of this genus, R. *Gwynne-Vaughani* and R. *major*, are well-known because numerous specimens of them have been found in the Scotland deposits. As mentioned previously, the preservation of these specimens is so excellent that they have yielded valuable information concerning the form and internal structure of the plants. *Rhynia major* was a vascular plant that grew in marshy swamps to a maximum height of about 50 cm (see Fig. 7-1). Each stem was approximately 5 mm in diameter. The plant body consisted of an underground rhizome upon which tufts of absorbing rhizoids occurred. Roots were absent. The aerial portion (stem), which was merely a continuation of a part of the underground system, branched dichotomously and was devoid of appendages. Growth of the plant was apparently initiated by apical meristems located at the tips of the branches. Elongate cylindrical sporangia terminated many of the ultimate dichotomies.

ANATOMY. The stem of *Rhynia* possessed epidermal, fundamental, and vascular tissue systems (Chapter 3)—an organization that is characteristic of not only the other members of the Psilopsida but also the more-advanced modern vascular plants.

The entire branch system was covered by an epidermis with a thick cuticle on its outer surface. Stomata were present on the aerial portion. Internal to the epidermis was a broad cortex comprising parenchyma cells which probably functioned as the photosynthetic tissue. A slender vascular cylinder occupied the center of the axes (Fig. 7-2, A) and was composed of a cylinder of primary xylem surrounded by a cylinder of primary phloem. This disposition of vascular tissue is designated specifi-

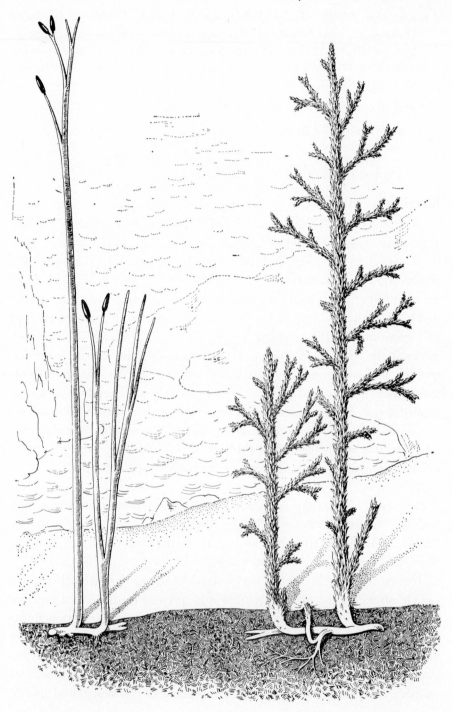

cally as a haplostele, as mentioned in Chapter 3. The xylem contained tracheids with annular thickenings, as interpreted by Lang, whereas the phloem consisted of thin-walled elongate cells.

The presumably indehiscent sporangia (Fig. 7-2, B) that terminated certain branches were, in some specimens, approximately 4 mm in diameter and 12 mm long. A rather massive sporangial wall, with a heavy cuticle on the outer surface, enclosed spores which were formed in tetrads. From all appearances, *Rhynia* was homosporous and the sporangium was of the eusporangiate type.

Rhyniaceae: Horneophyton

Considerable information has been obtained regarding *Horneophyton*, the other genus in the family, which often is found with *Rhynia* in the Rhynie chert. The underground portion of *Horneophyton* consisted of a lobed rhizome from which arose the aerial dichotomously branched stems. The underground tuberous body lacked a vascular system. Groups of rhizoids located on the surface undoubtedly functioned in absorption. The aerial stem had a vascular system similar to that of *Rhynia*. Sporangial position and organization were very similar to those of *Rhynia*, differing only in the occurrence of a sterile columella in the sporangial locule.

Asteroxylaceae: Asteroxylon

ORGANOGRAPHY. The structure and appearance of this genus were quite different from that of the other two genera and merit specific attention. *Asteroxylon mackiei* was larger than *Rhynia* (Fig. 7-1), and its reconstruction has been more difficult because preservation was more fragmentary. The plant had a naked dichotomously branched subterranean rhizome. Small branch systems were present which probably functioned in anchorage and absorption. At intervals the tips of some dichotomies became upright, bearing numerous, closely appressed, small, leaf-like appendages. The main upright axes exhibited irregular or obscure dichotomous branching, whereas smaller local branch systems dis-

---

Figure 7-1 Diagrammatic restoration of two members of the Psilophytales. Left, *Rhynia major*; right, *Asteroxylon mackiei*. [Redrawn from Kidston and Lang, *Trans. Roy. Soc. Edin.*, Vol. 52, Part IV, 1921.]

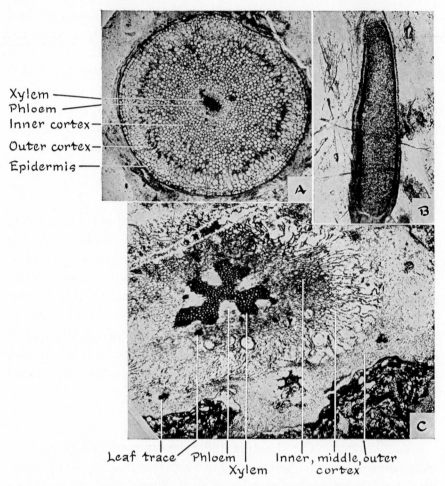

Xylem ——
Phloem ——
Inner cortex —
Outer cortex —
Epidermis ——

Leaf trace Phloem   Inner, middle, outer
               Xylem   cortex

Figure 7-2   Anatomy of the Psilophytales. **A**, transection of the stem of *Rhynia Gwynne-Vaughani;* **B**, longisection, sporangium of *Rhynia Gwynne-Vaughani* (note numerous spores in the sporangial cavity); **C**, transection, central portion of the stem of *Asteroxylon mackiei.* [From Kidston and Lang, *Trans. Roy. Soc. Edin.* Vols. 51-52, 1917-1921.]

played more regular dichotomous growth. The fertile region, devoid of appendages, is thought to have been the continuation of an upright axis, branching dichotomously with sporangia at the terminus of each ultimate dichotomy.

ANATOMY.   The internal anatomy of the rhizome portion was similar to that of *Rhynia,* although the fundamental and vascular tissue systems of the upright portions (Fig. 7-2, C) were more complex in structure and arrangement. The shoot was covered by an epidermis with thick outer walls, which was interrupted in places by the presence of stomata. The cortex was differentiated into three general regions: the outer, middle, and inner portions. The outer cortex was composed of homogeneous and compact parenchyma; the middle layer was highly lacunate; and the inner portion was compact and homogeneous. Occupying the central region of the stem was the vascular cylinder, which may be designated as an actinostele (Chapter 3). Primary xylem in the form of a fluted cylinder occupied the center of the stem. Protoxylem occurred near the extremities of the lobes but was surrounded on all sides by metaxylem, making the xylem mesarch in development. There were some annular tracheids in the protoxylem, but most of the xylem cylinder was composed of helically thickened tracheids; no xylem parenchyma was present. Primary phloem occurred between the lobes of xylem and in a thin layer opposite the xylem lobes. "Leaf" traces, departing from the vicinity of the lobes, passed obliquely through the cortex and ended abruptly near the base of each leaf-like appendage. These traces were concentric; that is, each trace consisted of primary xylem surrounded on all sides by primary phloem. In one species, A. *elberfeldense*, the vascular cylinder was siphonostelic in lower portions of the aerial stem.

Sporangia, occupying the tips of ultimate dichotomies, were pear-shaped, possessed a thick epidermal layer, and opened by a specific dehiscence mechanism. These plants were homosporous and presumably displayed the eusporangiate type of development.

Psilotales

Psilotaceae—Sporophyte Generation of Psilotum

ORGANOGRAPHY. *Psilotum*, consisting of two species, *P. nudum* (Fig. 7-3, A) and *P. flaccidum*, is pantropical and subtropical in distribution, reaching north to Florida, Bermuda, and Hawaii. The plant occurs as an epiphyte on tree ferns, on coconut trunks, or at the base of trees, or it may be terrestrial, growing in soil or among exposed rocks. *Psilotum nudum* (*P. triquetrum*) grows remarkably well under greenhouse conditions and is cultivated in most botanical gardens in the temperate regions. Depending upon its location and environment, the sporophyte of *P. nudum* may be pendent or erect, dwarfed (8 cm high), or reach a height of 75-100 cm. The plant body consists of a basal branched rhizome system which is generally hidden beneath the soil or humus, and a slender, upright, green aerial portion which is freely and dichotomously

Figure 7-3 Organography of *Psilotum nudum.* **A,** habit of plant grown under greenhouse conditions; **B,** portion of ultimate dichotomy of shoot showing three-lobed sporangia and their associated appendages.

branched and which bears small appendages and sporangia (Fig. 7-3, B).
The branched rhizome system, which bears numerous small scales, grows
by means of apical meristems located at the tips of ultimate branches.
According to the recent studies of Bierhorst (1954b), the degree of
branching of the rhizome is directly related to the effects of obstacles
which the apical meristem encounters in its growth through the soil. No
structure is present which could be interpreted anatomically as a root,
although the underground rhizome system anchors the plant and serves
as an absorptive surface. A mycorrhizal intracellular fungus, gaining
entrance through rhizoids, is present in cells of the outer cortex (Verdoorn, 1938; Bierhorst, 1954b). This fungus may be related intimately
to the physiology of the plant. Any one of the rhizome tips may turn
upward and by apical growth produce an aerial branch system. The
basal part of the shoot may be cylindrical with longitudinal ribs, whereas
the more distal aerial stems are provided with three longitudinal ridges.

STEM ANATOMY. The apical meristem of rhizomes and aerial
branches is reported to have a single, large, wedge-shaped apical cell
(Ford, 1904; Bierhorst, 1954b; Marsden and Wetmore, 1954) which
divides repeatedly, giving rise to additional meristematic cells which
differentiate eventually into tissues comprising the three primary tissue
systems.

The lower portions of the aerial system as well as the more distal
regions are covered by an epidermis, as shown in Fig. 7-4, in which the
outer tangential cell walls are heavily cutinized and covered by a definite
cuticle. Stomata are present mainly in areas between the longitudinal
ribs (Zimmermann, 1927). Internal to the epidermis there is a rather
broad cortex which can be resolved into three regions (Fig. 7-4). The
outer portion, directly beneath the epidermis, consists of elongated,
lobed parenchyma cells with intercellular spaces between the vertical
rows. Starch grains are present in great numbers. Internal to this zone
there is a band of vertically elongated and thick-walled cells, with small
intercellular air spaces and few or no starch grains. In the lower portions
of the aerial stems the walls of these cells apparently become lignified.
In progressing from this zone to the vascular cylinder, the cell walls
become thinner and thinner and less lignified with an increase in the
number of starch grains per cell.

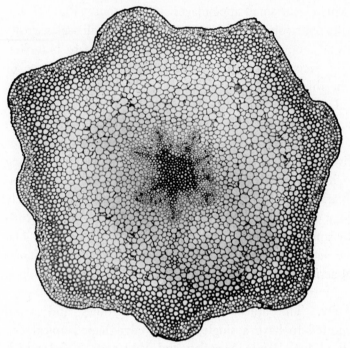

Figure 7-4 Transection (near base of aerial shoot) of stem of *Psilotum nudum*. Note stomata in epidermis, differences in thickness of cell walls in outer and inner cortex, and the lobed central core of xylem.

The boundary between the fundamental tissue (cortex) system and the vascular cylinder is marked by the endodermis (see Fig. 7-4; also Fig. 7-5, A), a very distinctive layer in that a conspicuous Casparian strip is present in the radial and end walls of the vertically elongated cells. Occupying the center of the rhizome in *P. nudum* is a slender cylinder of primary xylem which may be greatly reduced in small axes (Bierhorst, 1954b) and is a ridged or fluted cylinder in the aerial branches. Near the transition region from rhizome to aerial stem this cylinder may have as many as 10 lobes (Bower, 1935; Pitot, 1950), whereas a smaller number are present in the more distal parts of the aerial branch system (Figs. 7-4; 7-5, A). At levels where several xylem lobes are present the center of the stem in *P. nudum* is generally occupied by elongate sclerenchymatous cells. Partially disorganized protoxylem tracheids, with helical or scalariform thickenings, occupy the extreme tips of the xylem lobes in aerial branches while the remainder is composed of metaxylem with scalari-

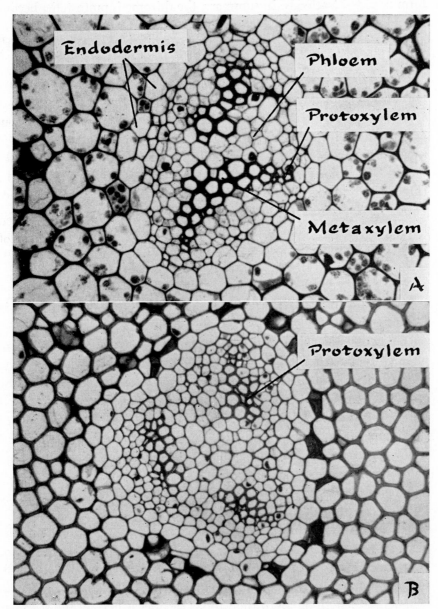

Figure 7-5 Stem anatomy of the Psilotales. **A,** transection of the vascular cylinder and adjacent cortex of a small aerial stem of *Psilotum nudum;* **B,** transection near the base of an aerial branch of *Tmesipteris tannensis.*

form or pitted tracheids. In summary, the rhizome is protostelic, becoming an exarch siphonostele throughout a considerable portion of the aerial branch system; the upper branches may, however, be strictly actinostelic.

Unlike the xylem, the component parts of the primary phloem have not been thoroughly investigated. Internal to the endodermis is a cylinder of parenchyma-like cells, generally one layer thick, which is designated as the pericycle. Internal to the pericycle is a cylinder of irregularly spaced, smaller, somewhat more angular cells—the sieve elements (Fig. 7-5, A). These cells are elongate, often lignified at the corners, and possess many spherical bodies as part of their cell contents (Ford, 1904; Stiles, 1910; Esau, *et al*, 1953). The structure and distribution of sieve areas in the cells are imperfectly known. Most of the tissue in the bays between the xylem arms is composed of elongate parenchyma cells.

"LEAF" ANATOMY. As mentioned earlier, the "foliar" appendages in *Psilotum* are small scale-like structures which are irregularly distributed on the aerial stem (Fig. 7-3, B). Internally the appendage consists of photosynthetic parenchyma cells which are continuous, lower down, with similar tissue of the stem. There is no vascular bundle in the appendage of *P. nudum*, although in *P. flaccidum* a "leaf" trace ends at the base of the foliar structure. The morphological interpretation of these appendages is presented in Chapter 3. No stomata are present in the epidermis. Grouped generally on the upper part of the stems are bilobed appendages, each of which is associated with a three-lobed sporangium.

SPORANGIUM. The morphological interpretations of the spore-producing structure in the Psilotales are varied and controversial; see, for example, Solms-Laubach, 1884; Bower, 1894, 1935; Eames, 1936; Smith, 1955; Campbell, 1940; Zimmermann, 1930; Bierhorst, 1956. To comment at length on all of the various theories is beyond the scope of this book. Thus, only a descriptive account, based upon the most reliable sources, will be presented together with selected interpretive theories.

The sporangium of *Psilotum* in the mature condition is generally a

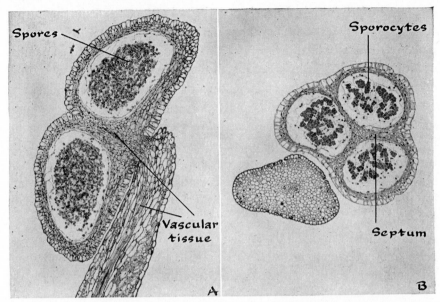

Figure 7-6 Sporangia of the Psilotales. **A**, longisection, bilocular sporangium of *Tmesipteris tannensis*; **B**, transection, triocular sporangium of *Psilotum nudum*; note that the sporocytes are surrounded by an irregular fluid-like tapetum.

three-lobed structure (Fig. 7-3, B; and Fig. 7-6, B), 2-3 mm wide, and closely surrounded by a forked, foliar appendage. Each lobe of the sporangium, corresponding to an internal spore chamber, exhibits loculicidal dehiscence at maturity.

In early stages of development it is difficult to determine whether a lateral primordium will become simply a single vegetative appendage or whether it will become eventually a "fertile" branch (Bower, 1894, 1935). For *Psilotum* it was reported by Bower that a lateral appendage is differentiated earlier than the associated sporangial structure; the latter arises on the adaxial side of the original appendage. In a recent study Bierhorst (1956) concludes that the original appendage is, in fact, the sporangial or spore-producing apparatus and that the subjacent leaf-like lobe is a lateral outgrowth on the "fertile axis." (At this juncture the term sporangium is avoided; the reason for this treatment will be made clear in the discussion to follow.) According to Bierhorst, the primordium of the fertile axis exhibits apical growth. The sites of future sporangial locules become apparent early through periclinal divisions in separate surface initials. In each case these divisions result in the setting apart of primary wall initials and primary sporogenous cells. By repeated periclinal and anticlinal divisions of the primary wall initials a sporangial wall of four or five layers is produced. Derivatives of the primary sporogenous cells divide in many planes to form the sporogenous tissue (Fig. 7-7). The entire sporogenous mass does not become converted into sporocytes; only irregular groups of sporocytes function, and the remaining disintegrate and undoubtedly serve as a nourishing fluid in which the functional sporocytes and spores develop (Fig. 7-6, B). As is true of other plants with eusporangiate development, numerous spores are formed. Individual spores are bilaterally symmetrical with a reticulate wall pattern.

Unlike the foliar appendages, the sporangial axis is vasculated. A vascular bundle extends into the partition between locules and may continue nearly to the apex of this so-called fertile axis.

INTERPRETATIONS OF THE SPORANGIUM. The spore-producing structure in the Psilotales has been interpreted by some investigators as being a synangium—that is, the fusion product of two or more sporangia. Others consider the foliar appendage of *Psilotum* to be a sporophyll bearing a trilocular sporangium. A third school of thought interprets the sporangium as occupying the terminus of a short or lateral branch. According to the last interpretation, the sporangium is therefore fundamentally trilocular, cauline in nature, and terminal in position. Prototypes for such an interpretation may eventually be found among the Psilophytales. Developmentally, the spore-producing organ does not resemble the type of ontogeny displayed by plants possessing synangia— that is, the early independent development of sporangia and their subsequent fusion; the presence of vascular tissue in the sporangium of *Psilotum* would tend to support the axial concept of the sporangium. The sporangial axis has often been compared with the sporangiophore in the Equisetales (Chapter 9) and, such a comparison has more meaning than the concept of the fundamentally foliar position of the sporangium. Lastly, serious consideration should be given to the thought provoking concept that perhaps each unit of the fertile axis (foliar and sporangial) represents phylogenetically a condensation of a more elaborate branch system (see Chapter 3; also Bierhorst, 1956).

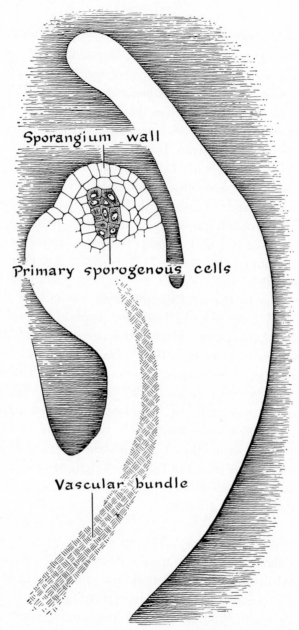

Figure 7-7 A developing sporangium and its associated appendage in *Psilotum nudum*. The details of only one locule are shown. The vegetative stem is to the left.

Psilotaceae—Sporophyte Generation of Tmesipteris

ORGANOGRAPHY.   We have devoted considerable space to a detailed description of the sporophyte of *Psilotum* because we believe that there is more material of this genus generally available for teaching purposes in most institutions than there is of *Tmesipteris*. However, a descriptive treatment of the order would be incomplete without consideration of the interesting genus *Tmesipteris*.

In contrast with *Psilotum*, which is widespread in its distribution, *Tmesipteris* is confined to Australia, New Caledonia, New Zealand, and other islands of the South Pacific Ocean. *Tmesipteris tannensis* (Fig. 7-8) generally grows as a pendulous epiphyte, 5-20 cm long, on the trunks of tree ferns or other trees, but often it may be found on mounds of humus. One form, *T. Vieillardia*, has been described as an erect terrestrial plant (Sahni, 1925). Organization of the sporophyte is very similar to that of *Psilotum*, with a branching rhizome system and an aerial shoot portion. However, significant morphological differences do exist between the genera. Each aerial shoot of *Tmesipteris* may exhibit only one dichotomy. The "foliar" appendages are scale-like at the base, gradually increasing in size toward the tip. The majority of appendages are larger than those of *Psilotum*, and are flat and broadly lanceolate with a mucronate tip. The larger leaves are supplied with a single, unbranched vascular bundle. The bases of the leaves are strongly decurrent, and the distinction between stem and leaf is difficult to determine, particularly near the tip, since often a foliar appendage terminates the axis. Roots are absent—a feature, it will be recalled, characteristic of the Psilopsida as a whole.

STEM ANATOMY.   The rhizome is protostelic, gradually becoming siphonostelic in the aerial system (Fig. 7-5, B) with five or more protoxylem poles surrounded almost entirely by metaxylem (Sykes, 1908). The primary xylem of aerial branches is mesarch in development, in contrast with *Psilotum* in which the primary xylem is exarch. More distally from the base of the stem of *Tmesipteris* there may be a smaller number of xylem strands which display an irregular arrangement due to the departure of leaf traces from the vascular cylinder. Protoxylem and metaxylem are composed of scalariform tracheids. The center of the stem

Figure 7-8 The pendent aerial branches of *Tmesipteris tannensis*. Sporangia can be seen near the tip of the branch to the right. In many of the appendages, the single unbranched midvein is evident.

consists of parenchyma-like cells which may have relatively thick walls. External to the strands of xylem is a cylinder of phloem in which the sieve elements are made evident by the presence of spherical inclusions and heavily lignified cell walls. These cells are reported as having tapering ends with numerous sieve areas on their lateral walls (Sykes, 1908). A characteristic endodermis is present in the rhizome, but in the aerial portions no such definable layer is evident. Between the phloem cylinder and an inner layer of cortex, the cells of which contain brown tanniferous or phlobaphene materials, is a zone two or three cells wide which physiologically may represent endodermis and pericycle (Fig. 7-5, B).

The cortex is composed of a compact tissue of parenchyma cells with evenly thickened, often lignified, cell walls. There may be small groups of photosynthetic parenchyma directly beneath the epidermis; the other tangential walls of the latter are cutinized and covered by a definite cuticle.

LEAF ANATOMY. As mentioned earlier, the foliar appendages of *Tmesipteris* are larger than those of *Psilotum* and, moreover, exhibit a more diversified anatomy. The flattened appendage is covered by a uniseriate epidermis with cutinized outer tangential cell walls in which some of the thickening is laid down in the form of striations; stomata are conspicuously developed in both epidermal layers. The internal ground tissue is uniformly arranged, consisting of lobed parenchyma cells. The single concentric vascular bundle, located centrally, is composed of several protoxylem elements surrounded incompletely by metaxylem which, in turn, is enclosed by phloem. As in the aerial stem, no definable endodermis is present, although a compact zone of parenchyma cells occupies the expected position of such a layer.

SPORANGIUM. As in *Psilotum*, the study of the sporangium in *Tmesipteris* is beset with difficulties of interpreting the mature structure as well as the ontogenetic progressions which are the bases for establishing phylogenetic sequences.

The mature two-lobed sporangium of *Tmesipteris* is interpreted as occupying the terminus of a short lateral branch, although the axis tip is upturned and the sporangium appears to be adaxial (Fig. 7-6, A). The two foliar appendages that are attached to the fertile axis just below the sporangium extend some distance beyond the sporangium. The single vascular bundle of the axis divides into three strands at the level of the foliar appendages. The lateral bundles traverse the appendages, whereas the median strand continues up the axis, ending ultimately in a trichotomy. The two lateral traces in the sporangium traverse the margins of the sporangium, and the central strand ends medianly in the septum (Fig. 7-6, A) between the two sporangial locules (Sykes, 1908).

According to Bierhorst (1956), the development of the fertile axis is similar to that in *Psilotum:* appearance of a primordium near the vegetative shoot tip, apical growth of the primordium, appearance of separate sporangial initials, and the formation of the two foliar appendages from a common outgrowth on the original fertile axis. Subsequent development also is similar to that in *Psilotum*, with the ultimate development of a sporangium with two thick-walled locules devoid of a well-defined tapetum and containing a large number of spores. Dehiscence of each locule is effected through the formation of a longitudinal cleft down the top of each lobe.

Before closing this section on the sporophyte generation, the studies on culturing tips of the aerial branches of *Psilotum* should be mentioned. If the tips of mature aerial branches are grown on agar substrate to which is added suitable nutrients, the axes become more like the rhizome both in external morphology and anatomy (Marsden and Wetmore, 1954). This is interesting because it poses the question of causal relationships. It would seem that the absence of the endophytic fungus is not sufficient evidence for the differential behavior of normal aerial and underground apices. The observed change may be due to the nutritional substrate on which the apex was grown.

Gametophyte Generation

The nature of the gametophyte generation long remained a serious gap in our knowledge of vascular plants; only in the twentieth century has it been discovered and described [Lawson, 1917a (*Tmesipteris*); Darnell-Smith, 1917; Bierhorst, 1953 (*Psilotum*)]. The gametophyte plant or prothallus of both genera is a small structure, ranging from .5 mm to 2.00 mm in diameter, and is several millimeters in length, growing on the trunks of tree ferns or in the crevices of rocks; sometimes it is subterranean in its habitat. Original descriptions were based upon collections made at the natural habitat, and attempts to culture the prothallia were never successful. However, only recently (Moseley and Zimmerly, 1949; Zimmerly and Banks, 1950; Bierhorst, 1953) were sexually

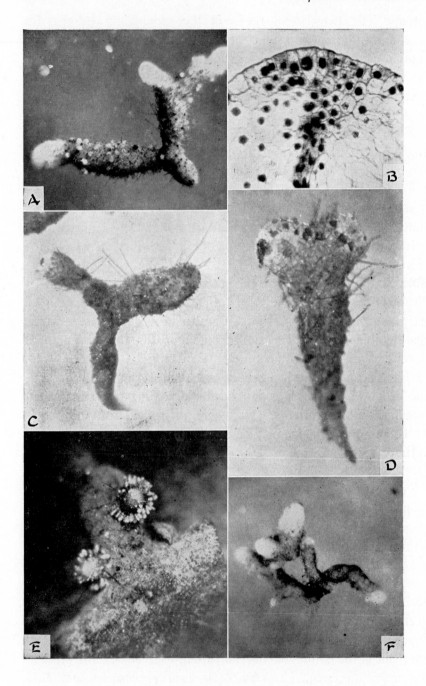

mature gametophyte plants of *Psilotum nudum* discovered growing in pots at the base of ferns which had for many years been in a conservatory. Mature individual plants resemble pieces of the sporophyte rhizome in that they are brown, radially symmetrical, often dichotomously branched but frequently irregularly branched, and invested with rhizoids (Fig. 7-9, A). As is true of underground sporophytic axes, the branching of gametophytic plants is correlated to a considerable degree with apical injury, which results in the establishment of lateral axes (Bierhorst, 1953).

ANATOMY AND CYTOLOGY.   Growth of a prothallium is initiated by apical cells located at the tips of the ultimate dichotomies (Fig. 7-9, B). Branching is restricted, and configuration and growth of the prothallus seemingly are determined in a large measure by surrounding objects. The gametophyte is devoid of chlorophyll, living a saprophytic existence, and is presumably aided by the presence of an endophytic fungus (one of which, in *Psilotum*, is probably *Chladochytrium tmesipteridis*) which gains entrance through the rhizoids and invades nearly all cells of the plant (this can be seen in Fig. 7-11, A, B, D).

All cells of the prothallus are parenchymatous; however, there are instances in *Psilotum* where annular and scalariform or scalariform-reticulate tracheids, surrounded by phloem and an endodermis, have been shown to occupy the center of the prothallus (Holloway, 1938, 1939; Bierhorst, 1953). Such gametophytes are clearly the gamete-producing generation, because antheridia and archegonia are present on their surfaces. Originally the presence of vascular tissue in the gameto-phytes was thought to be only of physiological importance, but cyto-logical investigations revealed a deeper significance to the problem. In *Psilotum* it has been reported that the prothallia are perhaps diploid in chromosome number instead of haploid. Most of the sporophytes of this

---

Figure 7-9 Gametophytes and rhizomes of *Psilotum nudum*. **A,** gametophyte showing meristematic apices (white) and prominent globular antheridia; **B,** longisection, apex of gametophyte (note large apical cell); **C,** young sporo-phyte of gemmae origin (gemmae are vegetative propagules formed both on rhizomes and gametophytes); **D,** young gametophyte of gemma origin (dark areas are presumably archegonia); **E,** clusters of gemmae on a sporophytic rhizome; **F,** gametophyte with attached sporophyte (two large apices). [Courtesy Dr. D. W. Bierhorst.]

genus, then, are tetraploid (having four sets of chromosomes). So far, a wild diploid sporophyte has been reported only from Ceylon (Manton, 1950). The results of recent investigations indicate that the haploid number of chromosomes in *Psilotum* is from 52 to 54, while $n = 200$ or over in *Tmesipteris*. However, a count of $n = 100$, ± 10, has just recently been reported for a race of *Psilotum* (Bierhorst, 1953), which possibly supports the concept that polyploidy is operative. However, it should be emphasized that the presence of vascular tissue in the gameto-phytic plant, regardless of its chromosome number, is unusual among vascular plants. The external similarity between gametophyte and sporo-phyte rhizome, coupled with the presence of vascular tissue in the gametophyte, provides additional evidence for the Homologous Theory as it relates to origin of the alternation of generations. This we have discussed in Chapter 2.

GAMETANGIA. Sex organs (antheridia and archegonia) are scattered over the surface of the gametophyte and are intermingled (Fig. 7-9, A). Young sex organs begin development very close to the apices of the gametophyte; however, young organs may be found also among the more mature ones. The first indication of antheridial development is the presence of a periclinal division in a single surface cell, which sets aside an outer jacket initial and an inner primary spermatogenous cell (Hollo-way, 1918; Lawson, 1917b; Holloway, 1939). By anticlinal divisions a single-layered jacket of several cells is produced enclosing a developing spermatogenous mass in which cell divisions occur in many planes. Ulti-mately the antheridium projects above the surface (see Fig. 7-11, A) much as in leptosporangiate ferns, although antheridial ontogeny is similar to that of *Lycopodium, Equisetum,* and eusporangiate ferns. Each spermatocyte or sperm-mother cell eventually becomes a spirally coiled, multiflagellate sperm and escapes through an opercular cell on the side of the antheridium (Bierhorst, 1954a).

The archegonium likewise is initiated from a single superficial cell, as can be seen in Fig. 7-10, A. An initial periclinal division sets aside an outer cover cell and an inner central cell (Fig. 7-10, B). The cover cell undergoes two successive anticlinal divisions, and by further divisions of these cells and their derivatives, four rows of neck cells, consisting of

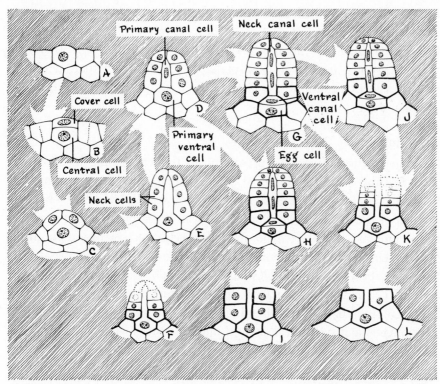

Figure 7-10 Archegonium development in *Psilotum nudum*. Early development follows a uniform scheme (*A-E*), whereas there is considerable variation in subsequent steps (*F-L*). A mature archegonium has only one or two tiers of neck cells, the others slough off during development. (Consult text for details.) [Redrawn from Bierhorst, *Amer. Jour. Bot.* 41:274, 1954.]

from four to six tiers, are produced. The central cell divides periclinally to form the primary canal cell and the primary ventral cell (Fig. 7-10, D). The primary canal cell may divide to form two neck canal cells, although in most instances walls separating the two nuclei have not been observed (Fig. 7-10, G, J). There are also some indications that the central cell functions directly as the egg (Bierhorst, 1954a). The archegonial necks are straight, and the venter is embedded in the gametophyte. As the archegonia approach maturity the cell walls between certain tiers of neck cells become cutinized and the upper part of the neck is sloughed off (Fig. 7-10, F, K). In *Tmesipteris* the neck may break off flush with the surface of the gametophyte, whereas in *Psilotum* a smaller number of tiers may be lost. With the sloughing off of the upper portion of the neck and the disintegration of the axial row a passageway is created for the entrance of the motile sperms (Fig. 7-10, I, L). Bierhorst (1954a) reports that fertilization perhaps precedes the actual "decapitation" of the archegonium. Fertilization is accomplished by the union of sperm and egg.

The Embryo

In the method of early segmentation of the zygote, and in the structure and subsequent development of the embryo, there is close similarity between *Psilotum* and *Tmesipteris* (Holloway, 1921, 1939). The first division of the fertilized egg results in a wall being placed at right angles to the long axis of the archegonium. The cell directed toward the neck of the archegonium is the epibasal cell, the lower is the hypobasal cell. Since members of the Psilotales are illustrative of exoscopic polarity, the epibasal cell may be designated the apex, and the hypobasal cell the base (Chapter 6). The epibasal cell will ultimately give rise to the sporophyte shoot system (aerial and underground), while the hypobasal cell (base) will produce the foot—a structure that anchors the young sporophyte securely to the gametophyte.

By repeated cell divisions the shoot portion increases in size, and an apical cell is established at the distal end. Further vertical growth of the shoot is due in a large measure to the activity of this apical cell; frequently in *Tmesipteris* two apical cells are present on the flanks of the shoot, resulting in two precociously formed horizontal branches. Concomitant with embryo development the gametophyte forms a calyptra-like outgrowth through which the young sporophyte eventually emerges (Fig. 7-11, D). While the shoot portion is assuming form the foot enlarges by repeated cell divisions, sending haustorial outgrowths into the gametophyte tissue. The foot, by virtue of its position and organization, is well suited for the functions of anchorage and absorption until the shoot becomes physiologically independent.

To recapitulate, the young sporophyte consists of an axis (rhizome), with vascular tissue, which may be uniaxial or precociously branched, and an enlarged bulb-like foot embedded in the gametophyte. Ultimately the shoot becomes detached from the foot and the gametophyte through a separation layer in the vicinity of the original boundary between shoot

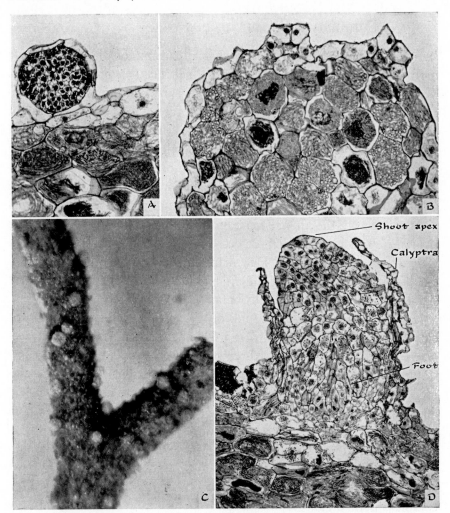

Figure 7-11 Gametangia and embryo of *Psilotum nudum*. **A**, section of nearly mature antheridium, showing jacket layer and spermatocytes; **B**, transection of gametophyte showing two mature archegonia (consult text and Fig. 7-10 for details of development; note that most cells of the gametophyte contain hyphae of an endophytic fungus); **C**, portion of a gametophyte with emergent antheridia; **D**, developing embryo attached to gametophyte by enlarged foot. [From slides prepared by Dr. D. W. Bierhorst.]

and foot. Throughout all of the differentiation process this original boundary is clearly discernible. The rhizome continues to elongate and branch, and eventually ultimate dichotomies emerge above the soil or humus and develop into aerial branches.

Summary and Conclusions

In this chapter we have presented a discussion of the comparative morphology of the living and certain extinct members of the Psilopsida. This subdivision of the Tracheophyta is of particular interest and significance from an evolutionary standpoint because: (1) it includes some of the simplest, least specialized, and probably most primitive of known vascular plants; (2) some of the extinct members may well represent the type of early land plants from which the more highly developed sporophytes of ferns and other lower vascular plant groups have originated; and (3) the extremely simple vascular system of ancient psilopsid plants gives a clue as to the arrangement and histology of primitive conducting tissues in land plants. Well-preserved fossil remains of the Psilopsida were discovered in rocks of Devonian and Silurian age, and the reconstruction and description of these dawn land plants is one of the most significant achievements of paleobotany.

In the relatively brief account of the extinct order Psilophytales, emphasis has been placed on three well-known genera: *Rhynia, Horneophyton,* and *Asteroxylon.* All three genera were plants of relatively low stature and are believed to have been devoid of roots. In *Rhynia* and *Horneophyton* the aerial portions of the sporophyte consisted of slender, leafless, dichotomously branched axes or stems, some of which terminated in solitary, thick-walled, homosporous sporangia. The vascular system in the axes of *Rhynia* and *Horneophyton* was a simple haplostele, consisting of a central strand of tracheids surrounded by a cylinder of phloem-like tissue. The sporophyte of *Asteroxylon* was more complex, both organographically and anatomically. In this genus the lower portions of the aerial axes bore small, numerous, crowded leaf-like appendages. Leaf traces extended from the edge of the lobed vascular cylinder (actinostele) through the broad cortex and terminated at the bases of the appendages but did not enter them. The veinless appendages of *Asteroxylon* have been regarded as typifying a step in the evolution of microphylls. As in *Rhynia* and *Horneophyton,* the sporangia of *Asteroxylon* were homosporous and occurred at the tips of leafless fertile branches.

The greater part of the chapter has been devoted to the description and comparison of *Psilotum* and *Tmesipteris,* the two living genera classified in the order Psilotales. The sporophytes of these genera agree in certain respects—for example, in the absence of roots and in the dichotomous pattern of branching. But marked differences occur between them, with respect to other organographic and anatomical characteristics. The aerial vegetative stems of *Psilotum* bear small and inconspicuous scale-like appendages devoid of veins, whereas in *Tmesipteris* relatively large leaf-like appendages, with well-defined midveins, occur in the upper portions of the aerial shoots. The stele near the base of aerial stems of *Psilotum* consists of a lobed cylinder of exarch xylem (enclosing a central mass of sclerenchyma) and an external cylinder of phloem tissue. In contrast, the aerial stem of *Tmesipteris* develops a siphonostele consisting of a central pith surrounded by a dissected cylinder of mesarch xylem which, in turn, is enclosed by a cylinder of phloem.

The mature homosporous eusporangia of the Psilotales are subtended by paired appendages and consist of three (*Psilotum*) or two (*Tmesipteris*) lobes or spore chambers separated by partitions of sterile tissue known as septa. In contrast with the sporangia of the great majority of vascular plants, vascular tissue extends from the axis into the septa of the sporangia in both *Psilotum* and *Tmesipteris*. Whether the sporangium in either genus is a compound structure or synangium composed of fused sporangia is a debatable question. Also, the morphological significance of the paired or forked appendage at the base of the sporangium has been the subject of various interpretations. According to one current idea, the sporangium is terminal on a short lateral axis, a view supported by the extension of vascular tissue into the septum. Other interpretations of the sporangia of *Psilotum* and *Tmesipteris* have been briefly discussed in this chapter.

The mature gametophytes of *Psilotum* and *Tmesipteris* are very small, dichotomously branched cylindrical structures which superficially resemble fragments of the rhizome of the sporophyte. Gametophytes are either wholly subterranean or they are buried in the crevices of rocks or in the mat of roots on the stems of tree ferns. In very recent years, intensive developmental and cytological studies made on the gametophytes of *Psilotum* have revealed and clarified many points of unusual interest. Chlorophyll is not found in the cells of the gametophyte, and this structure lives as a saprophyte apparently assisted by the presence of an endophytic fungus which gains entrance through the rhizoids and which is found within most of the interior cells. Unlike the non-vasculated gametophytes of most other vascular plants, certain gametophytes in *Psilotum* develop a central strand of xylem and phloem enclosed by an endodermis. The significance of vascular tissue in the gametophyte generation of *Psilotum* with reference to the Homologous Theory of Alternation of Generations has been briefly discussed.

Sexual reproduction in the Psilotales is achieved by the union between the egg and a multiflagellate sperm. The gametophyte is monoecious, and the antheridia and archegonia are scattered and intermingled over its surface. After fertilization the zygote divides by a transverse wall and gives rise to an embryo with exoscopic polarity. The cells directed toward the neck of the archegonium initiate the shoot system, and the basal cells of the embryo produce a conspicuous foot which sends out haustoria into the adjacent tissues of the gametophyte. Ultimately the rootless young sporophyte becomes detached from the gametophyte and develops independently into a new plant.

References

Arnold, C. A. 1947. *An Introduction to Paleobotany*. McGraw-Hill, New York.

Bierhorst, D. W. 1953. Structure and development of the gametophyte of *Psilotum nudum*. Amer. Jour. Bot. 40:649-658.

———. 1954a. The gametangia and embryo of *Psilotum nudum*. Amer. Jour. Bot. 41:274-281.

———. 1954b. The subterranean sporophytic axes of *Psilotum nudum*. Amer. Jour. Bot. 41:732-739.

———. 1956. Observations on the aerial appendages in the Psilotaceae. *Phytomorphology* 6:176-184.

Bower, F. O. 1894. Studies in the morphology of spore-producing members: Equisetinae and Lycopodineae. *Phil. Trans. Roy. Soc. London.* 185B:473-572.

———. 1935. *Primitive Land Plants*. Macmillan, London.

Campbell, D. H. 1940. *The Evolution of the Land Plants (Embryophyta)*. Stanford University Press, Stanford, California.

Darnell-Smith, G. P. 1917. The gametophyte of *Psilotum*. *Trans. Roy. Soc. Edin.* 52:79-91.

Eames, A. J. 1936. *Morphology of Vascular Plants. Lower Groups*. McGraw-Hill, New York.

Esau, K., V. I. Cheadle, and E. M. Gifford, Jr. 1953. Comparative structure and possible trends of specialization of the phloem. *Amer. Jour. Bot.* 40:9-19.

Ford, S. O. 1904. The anatomy of *Psilotum triquetrum*. *Ann. Bot.* 18:589-605.

Gothan, W. and H. Weyland. 1954. *Lehrbuch der Paläobotanik.* Akademie-Verlag, Berlin.

Holloway, J. E. 1918. The prothallus and young plant of *Tmesipteris. Trans. Proc. N. Z. Inst.* 50:1-44.

———. 1921. Further notes on the prothallus, embryo, and young sporophyte of *Tmesipteris. Trans. Proc. N. Z. Inst.* 53:386-422.

———. 1938. The embryo and gametophyte of *Psilotum triquetrum.* A preliminary note. *Ann. Bot. N. S.* 2:807-809.

———. 1939. The gametophyte, embryo, and young rhizome of *Psilotum triquetrum* Swartz. *Ann. Bot. N. S.* 3:313-336.

Kidston, R. and W. H. Lang. 1917. On Old Red Sandstone plants showing structure, from the Rhynie Chert Bed, Aberdeenshire. Parts I-V. *Trans. Roy. Soc. Edin.* 51-52. 1917-1921.

Kräusel, R. 1936. Neue Untersuchungen zur paläozoischen Flora: Rheinische Devonfloren. *Ber. Deut. Bot. Gesell.* 54:307-328.

Lawson, A. A. 1917a. The prothallus of *Tmesipteris tannensis. Trans. Roy. Soc. Edin.* 51:785-794.

———. 1917b. The gametophyte generation of the Psilotaceae. *Trans. Roy. Soc. Edin.* 52:93-113.

Mägdefrau, K. 1953. *Päleobiologie der Pflanzen. Zweite Auflage.* G. Fischer, Jena.

Manton, I. 1950. *Problems of Cytology and Evolution in the Pteridophyta.* Cambridge University Press, London.

Marsden, M. P. F. and R. H. Wetmore. 1954. *In vitro* culture of the shoot tips of *Psilotum nudum. Amer. Jour. Bot.* 41:640-645.

Moseley, M. F., Jr., and B. C. Zimmerly. 1949. *Psilotum* gametophytes matured under greenhouse conditions from self-sown spores. *Science* 110:482.

Pitot, A. 1950. Sur l'anatomie de *Psilotum triquetrum* Sw. *Inst. franc. d'Afrique Noire, Paris.* 12:315-334.

Sahni, B. 1925. On *Tmesipteris Vieillardi* Dangeard, an erect terrestrial species from New Caledonia. *Phil. Trans. Roy. Soc. London.* 213B:143-170.

Smith, G. M. 1955. *Cryptogamic Botany. Vol. II. Bryophytes and Pteridophytes.* Ed. 2. McGraw-Hill, New York.

Solms-Laubach, H. Grafen zu. 1884. Der Aufbau des Stockes von *Psilotum triquetrum* und dessen Entwicklung aus der Brutknospe. *Ann. Jard. Bot. Buitenzorg.* 4:139-194.

Stiles, W. 1910. The structure of the aerial shoots of *Psilotum flaccidum* Wall. *Ann. Bot.* 24:373-387.

Sykes, M. G. 1908. The anatomy and morphology of *Tmesipteris. Ann. Bot.* 22:63-89.

Verdoorn, F. 1938. *Manual of Pteridology.* Martinus Nijhoff, The Hague.

Zimmerly, B. C. and H. P. Banks. 1950. On gametophytes of *Psilotum.* (Abstract) *Amer. Jour. Bot.* 37:668.

Zimmermann, W. 1927. Die Spaltoffnungen der Psilophyta und Psilotales. *Ztschr. für Bot.* 19:129-170.

———. 1930. *Die Phylogenie der Pflanzen.* G. Fischer, Jena.

Chapter

8 THE LYCOPSIDA

The Lycopsida is a well-defined group of vascular plants consisting of fossil and living representatives. The known history of this group extends from the Paleozoic era to the present. There are four living genera with more than 900 species which occur in various parts of the world under varied climatic conditions. The living genera consist of the "ground pine" or club moss *Lycopodium* (Figs. 8-1, 8-2); the club moss *Selaginella* (shown in Fig. 8-10); the small, tuberous plant *Phylloglossum* (Fig. 8-3), which is greatly restricted in its distribution; and the quillwort *Isoetes* (shown in Fig. 8-21, A).

All of these genera can be classified as small plants, some being erect, others living as epiphytes or growing as creepers along the ground or producing underground rhizomes. In contrast with these plants of modest stature, many of the ancient lycopods (*Lepidodendron*) were good-sized trees, and their vegetative structures and spores constituted an important part of coal (see Fig. 8-20). The importance of this assemblage of vascular plants certainly cannot be measured in terms of the present economic value of living members, but rather by the striking morphological unity of the entire group and its value in the interpretation of phylogenetic trends in vascular plants.

The vegetative sporophyte is differentiated into a shoot, consisting of stems and leaves, and a root system. Reminiscent of the group Psilopsida, the shoot system of many forms is dichotomously branched or modified into a pseudomonopodium (Chapter 3). Occasionally the axis may be unbranched (as in *Phylloglossum*). The arrangement of leaves is fundamentally spiral with modifications (decussate, whorled) characteristic of certain species. Leaves of living genera are generally small, whereas those of certain extinct forms were considerably larger. Whatever the arrangement or form of the leaves, each one is generally traversed by a single unbranched vascular bundle. Such a leaf is designated a microphyll (Chapter 3). Each leaf of certain genera, such as *Selagi-*

Figure 8-1 *Lycopodium lucidulum.* Note the sporangia (white structures) in the axils of certain leaves along the upper half of each branch and the clusters of bulbils (structures for vegetative propagation) on the uppermost portion of each shoot.

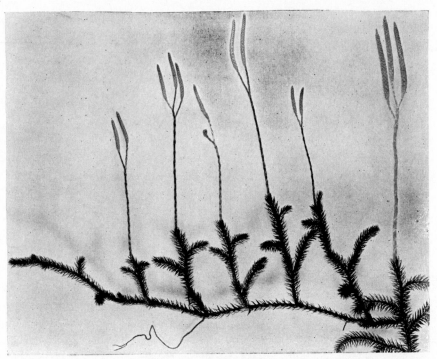

Figure 8-2 *Lycopodium clavatum.* Portion of a plant to show type of branching and the presence of strobili on determinate side branches. A root is evident along the lower edge of the main axis.

nella, Lepidodendron, and *Isoetes,* has a curious tongue-like appendage on its adaxial side termed the ligule (Figs. 8-14 and 8-21).

The vascular cylinder of the stem in most living species is protostelic. The primary xylem is exarch in development and consists primarily of tracheids with scalariform pitting. Whether the vascular cylinder is a protostele or a siphonostele, there are no breaks in the vascular tissue at the point of departure of leaf traces. No leaf gaps exist (Chapter 3). In a stem with a siphonostele a branch gap is present in the vascular cylinder of the main axis only at the point of divergence of the branch trace. The Lycopsida are therefore only cladosiphonic. In most genera the roots, arising adventitiously from rhizomes (e.g., in *Lycopodium*) or other specialized structures (e.g., *Selaginella*), branch dichotomously. In *Isoetes* there is a definite, perennial, root-producing meristem. Although the formation of secondary tissues was very common in ancient lycopods, this feature is characteristic of only one living genus—*Isoetes.*

A feature that unifies the entire group is the position of the eusporangium. Sporangia, occurring singly with each sporophyll, are attached to the adaxial side or are located in the axil of each sporophyll. The conditions of homospory and heterospory are coexistent in the group; heterosporous forms always produce endosporic gametophytes, homosporous forms produce only exosporic gametophytes.

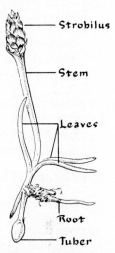

Classification

LYCOPSIDA: Sporophyte differentiated into leaf, stem, root and eusporangium; microphylls ligulate or eligulate; one sporangium attached to or associated with each sporophyll; no leaf gaps; exarch xylem predominates; protostelic or siphonostelic; some have secondary growth.

Figure 8-3 Habit sketch, *Phylloglossum drummondii.* The tuber is a vegetative reproductive body and is capable of developing into a typical plant under favorable environmental conditions.

LYCOPODIALES: Living and extinct plants; sporophytes with primary growth only, no vascular cambium; leaves eligulate; majority have definite strobili; homosporous.

LYCOPODIACEAE: Living and extinct plants; herbaceous; microphylls not forked at tips; many with definite strobili; exosporic gametophytes; biflagellate sperms in the living genus *Lycopodium.*

Lycopodium, Phylloglossum, Lycopodites (extinct).

PROTOLEPIDODENDRACEAE: Extinct, of Devonian age; with primary growth only; forked leaves and sporophylls; no definite strobili formed; no gametophytes known.

Protolepidodendron.

SELAGINELLALES: Living and extinct plants; with primary growth only; no vascular cambium; microphyllous with ligule; definite strobili formed; heterosporous; gametophytes endosporic; sperms biflagellate in living members.

SELAGINELLACEAE: characteristics as in Selaginellales.

Selaginella, Selaginellites (extinct).

LEPIDODENDRALES: Extinct plants; tree-like and most, if not all, with secondary growth; microphyllous with ligule; large root stocks (rhizophores) formed; heterosporous; sporophylls grouped into strobili; some forming seed-like structures.

Selected genera: *Lepidodendron, Stigmaria* (form genus for rhizophores), *Sigillaria, Lepidostrobus* (form genus for strobili), *Lepidocarpon* (form genus for strobili).

ISOETALES: Living and extinct plants; sporophytes have short, corm-like stem; secondary growth; perennial root-producing meristem; ligulate microphylls; heterosporous; endosporic gametophytes; sperms multiflagellate in living members.

ISOETECEAE: Characteristics as in Isoetales.

Isoetes, Isoetites (extinct).

PLEUROMEIALES: Extinct plant; upright unbranched stem with ligulate microphylls grouped at its upper end; upper end of axis terminates in a strobilus; subaerial rhizophore; heterosporous.

PLEUROMEIACEAE: Characteristics as in Pleuromeiales

Pleuromeia.

Lycopodiales

Lycopodiaceae

This family includes two living genera, *Lycopodium* and *Phylloglossum.* The former, the club moss, is worldwide in distribution, with species occurring in such varied climatic zones as arctic and tropic. Most of the species (about 200) of *Lycopodium* are tropical, but certain ones occur in the temperate regions of the world. *Phylloglossum,* a highly reduced and specialized monotypic plant, is restricted to Australasia (Fig. 8-3). *Lycopodites,* a fossil lycopod of the Carboniferous period, resembled the modern club moss in many respects.

Lycopodium

Some of the species are erect shrubby plants (Fig. 8-1), or they may have a trailing or creeping habit (Fig. 8-2), or they may grow as epiphytes. Most of the tropical species have the last growth habit.

ORGANOGRAPHY. Whether a given species is erect in form or consists of a prostrate rhizome portion, branching is fundamentally dichotomous. The branches of a dichotomy may be equal, continuing to grow and to dichotomize, or the branches of a dichotomy may be unequal, one branch overtopping the other. The weaker branch system may grow for a few years, generally becoming determinate, and these determine branches may develop strobili (Fig. 8-2). This mode of branching is termed a pseudomonopodium, and it reaches its highest development in forms with a prostrate, rhizome-like main axis. The leaves of *Lyco-podium* are eligulate microphylls which may be small (2-10 mm long) or in other cases may become 2 or 3 cm long. Phyllotaxy is usually spiral but may be decussate or whorled. In many forms the leaf bases are decurrent. In many of the creeping species dorsiventrality accompanied by anisophylly is characteristic of the lateral determinate branches.

Adventitious roots, which arise endogenously, occur along the lower side of the stem in prostrate forms (Fig. 8-2). In the upright forms these roots may be initiated near the shoot tip and subsequently grow downward through the cortex, emerging at the base of the plant (Fig. 8-4, A). After the root emerges from the stem it may branch freely in a dichotomous fashion. No lateral endogenous roots are formed.

Sporangia always occur singly on the adaxial surface of the sporophylls or in their axils. The sporophylls may be aggregated into definite strobili and may be quite different from vegetative leaves (Fig. 8-2). In many species, however, "fertile" areas alternate with "sterile" regions along the stems, the sporophylls resembling ordinary foliage leaves (Fig. 8-1).

STEM ANATOMY. The mature stem is covered by a uniseriate epidermis. The cortex is highly variable in thickness and structure (Fig. 8-4, A, C). In some species it remains parenchymatous, and in others the cells of specific regions undergo sclerification. Large air space systems may be present. Between the cortex and vascular cylinder there is an endodermis, the cells of which in the mature state are not easily recognized. During early development, however, these cells form Casparian strips and can be identified. Since the cell walls of the endodermis generally become thickened, the transition to the parenchyma cells of the pericycle is abrupt. The pericyclic cylinder may be two or three cells wide or comprise a rather broad tissue zone.

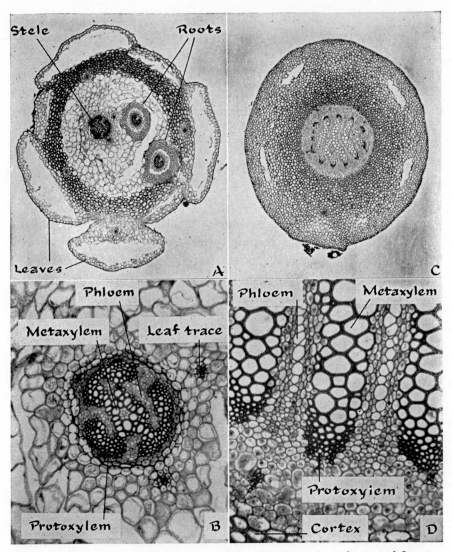

Figure 8-4   Stem anatomy in *Lycopodium*. **A,** transection of stem of *Lycopodium selago*; **B,** details of actinostele in *L. selago*; **C,** transection of stem of *Lycopodium sp.* showing plectostele; **D,** details of portion of stele in **C.**

With the possible exception of the ferns, nowhere in lower vascular plants is there such variation in the pattern of primary xylem and phloem in stems as is found in *Lycopodium*. The same species and even the same individual may show great variation during ontogeny (Hill, 1914, 1919; Wardlaw, 1924). In the mature plant body the vascular cylinder may be actinostelic with the primary phloem occupying the regions between the radiating arms of primary xylem (Fig. 8-4, B). In other species the primary xylem and phloem form strands of tissue which in transverse section appear as alternating bands of xylem and phloem; this type of vascular cylinder is designated a plectostele (Fig. 8-4, D). In still other forms the central mass of xylem may be modified such as to form numerous strands of xylem and phloem, or a complete ring of xylem may surround the phloem tissue (Ogura, 1938). It should be remembered that the seemingly isolated strands of xylem or phloem actually are interconnected. This can be demonstrated if their course is followed throughout the stem.

Ontogenetically it has been demonstrated that the young sporophyte in most species is actinostelic. As growth of the sporophyte continues and the stem increases in size there is generally a change in the pattern of xylem and phloem. The actinostelic condition may persist with the formation of more protoxylem poles; or any of the configurations described above may result. In the smaller branches there may be a return to an actinostelic arrangement with only a few protoxylem points (Holloway, 1909; Jones, 1905; Chamberlain, 1917).

The tracheids in the protoxylem are generally smaller and have either annular or helical secondary wall patterns, whereas those of the metaxylem are larger with predominately scalariform pitting. The phloem consists of sieve cells and parenchyma cells. The sieve cells are elongate with sieve areas distributed over the lateral walls as well as on the end walls.

Before leaving this discussion of stem anatomy it is important to describe the early formation and differentiation of primary vascular tissues in order to gain a fuller understanding of shoot development. The apical meristem of the shoot tip is reported to consist of a group of initials (Turner, 1924; Härtel, 1938) which by periclinal and anticlinal divisions gives rise to the three primary meristematic tissues: protoderm, ground meristem, and procambium, the derivatives of which differentiate into epidermis, cortex, and vascular tissue, respectively. The centrally located procambium extends very close to the shoot apex, a feature characteristic of many lower vascular plants (Wetmore, 1943). The cells of the procambium are elongate, and divide longitudinally and frequently in the transverse plane.

To understand subsequent development, particularly vascular differentiation, an examination of transverse stem sections taken at successive levels from the apex is essential. A transverse section of a shoot very near the tip reveals the vascular cylinder to be a compact core of procambial cells. Very early, however, the future xylem and phloem regions are blocked out through the differential maturation of cells. Cells located at the periphery of the stele differentiate into tracheids of the protoxylem; that is, a secondary wall is laid down by each cell, and eventually the protoplast degenerates and disappears. At the same level, differentiated cells of the protophloem can be identified. Even at this relatively early stage the identification of regions which will become metaxylem and metaphloem is readily possible. Centripetal to the protoxylem and protophloem poles, bands of cells (if characteristic of the species) identified by their shape, increased size and vacuolation as compared with surrounding cells will be the future metaxylem and metaphloem regions. Irreversible differentiation of these cells generally occurs after elongation of the stem ceases.

LEAF ANATOMY.   Initiation of the leaf is reported to take place in a single surface cell on the flank of the apical meristem (Turner, 1924). Growth in length, lateral extension of the midrib region, and maturation of tissues produce the mature leaf. The formation of a leaf is associated with the extension of procambium into its base from the existing central core of differentiating vascular tissue (Härtel, 1938). Differentiation of cells within this original procambial tract produces a mesarch bundle, termed a leaf trace in its course through the cortex, and an unbranched midvein within the leaf itself. Leaf traces are generally attached to lateral flanges on the protostele of the stem axis. The mature leaf is generally small, ovate to lanceolate in outline, and without a definable petiole. A transverse section of the mature foliage leaf reveals a well-developed epidermal layer, with stomata occurring generally on both surfaces, although certain anisophyllous species have stomata restricted to one surface. The mesophyll in many species is composed of more or less isodiametric cells with a conspicuous intercellular air space system.

ROOT.   Except for the ephemeral primary root of the young sporophyte, the roots of actively growing plants arise adventitiously from the stem very near the growing tip. These roots, which arise endogenously from the pericycle (Roberts and Herty, 1934), do not break through the cortex and epidermis immediately but often traverse the cortex for some distance before emerging. Since roots arise acropetally along the stem, many roots may be found in the stem cortex of the aerial portion of erect and epiphytic species (Fig. 8-4, A). In certain species (e.g., *L. pithyoides*) as many as 52 roots may be counted at one level (Stokey, 1907). Only near the base of the stem do these roots emerge. In prostrate forms the roots take a more direct course from the stem axis to the exterior. After emerging from the stem, a root branches dichotomously, often with great regularity; no lateral endogenous roots are formed.

In propagating species of *Lycopodium* it is important to (1) obtain a portion of the plant with intact roots, or (2) use the upper portion of a shoot tip (since roots are initiated near the tip), or (3) secure a portion of the stem with arrested roots which emerge from the stem cortex on contact with a moist surface. Arrested roots may be identified as mounds on the under side of the stem of a prostrate form (Roberts and Herty, 1934). Stokey (1907) has reported that four distinct groups of initials are present in the root apical meristem: a calyptrogen giving rise to the root cap; a tier of initials contributing to the developing protoderm; a group of initials giving rise to the cortex; and a set of initials for the vascular cylinder. Procambial differentiation results in a root that is often diarch. However, in some species (for example, *L. clavatum*) the root resembles the stem in the arrangement of xylem and phloem, and, except for size, it is difficult to distinguish between the two organs. The primary xylem is exarch in development.

SPORANGIUM. One of the definitive characteristics of the Lycopsida is the association of one sporangium with each sporophyll; each sporangium is located on the adaxial side of a sporophyll or in its axil. In certain species of *Lycopodium* (for example, *L. lucidulum, selago*) the sporophylls are similar to vegetative leaves (Fig. 8-1). No definite strobili are formed, but rather there are "fertile" areas on the stem alternating with vegetative or "sterile" regions (Case, 1943). In species considered to be advanced the sporophylls are aggregated into definite cone-like structures or strobili; the sporophylls of such cones may be quite unlike vegetative leaves in size, shape, and color, and they may exhibit other specializations which are related to sporangial protection and spore dispersal. These strobili may occur on leafy stems or they may be elevated on lateral branches which have very small, scale-like leaves unlike those of the vegetative shoot (Figs. 8-2, 8-6, A).

Developmentally the sporangium is of the eusporangiate type; that is, its origin is from a group of surface cells which divide periclinally (Fig. 8-5). The outer cells of such divisions form the multilayered wall, and the inner derivatives the sporogenous cells. The innermost layer of

Figure 8-5   A-D, ontogeny of the sporangium in *Lycopodium clavatum.* Note that initiation of the sporangium takes place in surface cells by periclinal divisions, setting aside primary wall and primary sporogenous cells (**A, B**). The tapetum ultimately arises from inner cells of the sporangium wall.

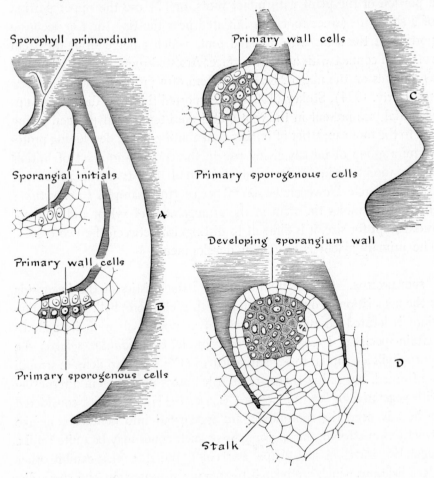

Sporophyll primordium

Primary wall cells

Sporangial initials

Primary sporogenous cells

Primary wall cells

Developing sporangium wall

Primary sporogenous cells

Stalk

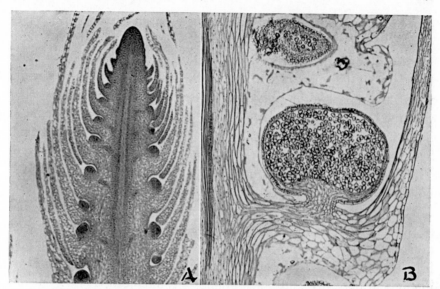

Figure 8-6 **A,** longisection of entire young strobilus of *Lycopodium clavatum*. Developing sporangia can be seen near the bases of sporophylls; **B,** a mature sporangium of *Lycopodium sp.* attached to sporophyll; note numerous spores and the overarching abaxial extension of the sporophyll above; the cone axis is to the left.

the sporangial wall functions as the tapetal layer. For a complete account of eusporangial development refer to Chapter 4.

Mature sporangia of most species are kidney shaped, are yellow to orange, and have a short stalk. As mentioned earlier, there are some very interesting relationships among position of mature sporangia, line of dehiscence, and specialization of the sporophyll. In certain species (e.g., *L. lucidulum*) the mature sporangium is axillary in association with a relatively unmodified sporophyll. Dehiscence is longitudinal and in the same plane as the expanded sporophyll. In other species—those with definite strobili—the mature sporangia are foliar in position, and the sporophylls are imbricated and have abaxial extensions (Fig. 8-6, B). Dehiscence in this instance is transverse, the opening being between the sporophyll and the abaxial extension of the sporophyll directly above. In still other forms the sporangia are axillary, protected as in the latter example by sporophyll modifications, and open by transverse dehiscence. Whether the sporangium is protected or not, it is evident that the line of dehiscence occurs in such a position as to insure efficient dispersal of spores (Sykes, 1908).

Meiosis occurs in the sporocytes, resulting in the formation of spore tetrads. The spores are exceedingly small, light in color, and have thin walls. The spore wall in many species is sculptured, exhibiting various patterns. A triradiate ridge, present on the inner face of each spore, is indicative of the mutual contact between members of a spore tetrad. Spore morphology is useful in delimiting subgroups within the genus. (See Tryon, 1949, for several interesting plates of photographs illustrating differences in spore wall ornamentation.)

The spores of certain species of *Lycopodium* are collected and sold as "lycopodium powder." This powder has been used in the manufacture of fireworks, but its use as a dusting powder on surgical gloves and pills has been discouraged; apparently the spores of *L. clavatum* cause inflammations in operative and other wounds (Whitebread, 1941).

CHROMOSOME NUMBERS. In recent years some information has accumulated on the chromosome numbers of the lower vascular plants. In *Lycopodium* the chromosome number ranges from $n = 14$ to $n = 78$. In one species—*L. selago* (from Europe)—the diploid number is 260, and at meiosis there are many unpaired chromosomes which may indicate hybridity (Dunlop, 1949; Manton, 1950). It has been suggested that chromosome differences are so great in *Lycopodium* that species in the genus are equivalent to genera in other groups of plants. *Phylloglossum drummondii*, the monotypic genus referred to previously, has a $2n$ chromosome number of 502 to 510 with many univalents being present at metaphase I (Blackwood, 1953).

THE GAMETOPHYTE. Depending on the species of *Lycopodium*, the spores may germinate immediately or after a delay of several years. A gametophyte plant of the first type (*L. alopecuroides, cernuum, inundatum*), generally found on the surface of the substrate, is ovoid to cylindrical, with green aerial branches; the entire plant may not be over 3 mm long (Fig. 8-7, B). Rhizoids occur on the colorless basal end. An endophytic fungus, entering the gametophyte plant early in development, is present in most species, occupying a definite region within the prothallus. The sex organs generally occur near the bases of the aerial lobes. The time interval between spore germination and appearance of sex organs may vary from eight months to one year (Treub, 1884; Chamberlain, 1917; Koster, 1941; Eames, 1942).

After spore germination and when 6-8 cells have been formed, gametophytes of the second type enter into a rest period of a year or more. Apparently, further development is dependent on the entrance of a fungus, presumed to be a phycomycete. If this infection does not occur, all further growth ceases (Bruchmann, 1910). Physiologically, the fungus must supply certain substances vital for proper growth of the gametophyte plant. Subsequent development to a stage in which mature sex organs are present may require ten years or more (Eames, 1942). The development of these later stages takes place beneath the surface of the ground or within a layer of humus. The prothallus (e.g., in *L. complanatum, clavatum*) is an oblong structure, ultimately becoming carrot-shaped or disc-shaped, with a convolute margin (Fig. 8-7, A, C). But in epiphytic species the prothallus may be cylindrical, branched, and more attenuated. All of the subterranean prothallia are colorless or yellowish to brown, developing chlorophyll only in those portions of the gametophyte that become exposed near the surface (Spessard, 1922).

The subterranean forms are long-lived (from 10 to 25 years), being continuously increased in size by a marginal ring of meristematic tissue. Old gametophytes may be up to 2 cm in length or width.

In species with the green, annual type of prothallus, antheridia and archegonia are generally intermingled (Chamberlain, 1917), whereas in the subterranean forms the sex organs are segregated into definite groups (Fig. 8-9, A) except in certain species (Spessard, 1922). In the course of development, antheridia generally appear first near the middle of the crown of the prothallus. Initiation of archegonia and more antheridia then occurs in the immediate derivatives of the meristematic ring (Fig. 8-9, A).

The dependence of *Lycopodium* species on the infection of the gametophyte by a fungus presents an interesting physiological problem. It has been possible to culture gametophytes, particularly the annual type, to maturity by sowing the spores on soil taken from the original habitat (see Koster, 1941). Wetmore and Morel (1951a) were able to culture to maturity, in the laboratory under sterile conditions, the gametophyte of *L. cernuum* (a green, annual type with associated fungus).

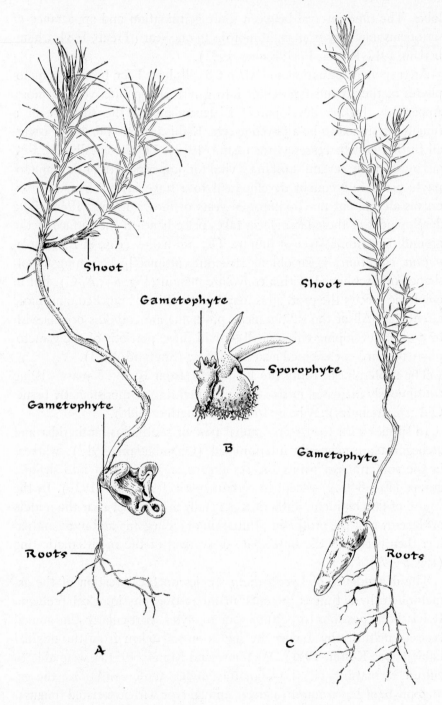

Shoot

Gametophyte

Sporophyte

Gametophyte

Shoot

Gametophyte

Roots

Roots

B

A

C

After sterilizing the spore coat with calcium hypochlorite, the spores were sown on a culture solution containing minerals and glucose. In some cultures the upright branches became club-shaped, while in others a filamentous "pin-cushion" type resulted (Fig. 8-8, A, B). After six months of continued growth, under regulated conditions, antheridia and archegonia were formed. Sporophytes developed in many instances (Fig. 8-8, C, D). It may be assumed that the balanced nutrient solution contained substances that are supplied by the fungus under natural conditions. Through further experimentation it was found that under the action of the growth regulating substance, napthaleneacetic acid, a developing gametophyte is transformed into masses of undifferentiated parenchyma similar to that obtained in culturing the tissues of higher plants.

The ontogeny of gametangia in *Lycopodium* has been described in detail in Chapter 5. We will only re-emphasize here that a remarkable similarity in development exists in the early stages of ontogeny of the sex organs—namely initiation in a single surface cell by a periclinal division, which sets aside the sterile jacket cell and the primary spermatogenous cell of the antheridium, and a division which forms the primary cover cell and the central cell of the young archegonium. The latter cell is the progenitor of the axial row (Fig. 8-9, B, C-E). At maturity an antheridium consists of a sterile jacket or "opercular layer," one cell thick, enclosing many small sperm-mother cells. Each spermatocyte matures into a biflagellate sperm which closely resembles the sperms of bryophytes and certain algae. The archegonia of surface living, green, short-lived prothallia have only three or four tiers of neck cells (Treub, 1884) and usually one neck canal cell, whereas, according to Spessard (1922), archegonia of the subterranean forms have long necks with six or more neck canal cells (Fig. 8-9, B). In either case the venter is embedded in the gametophyte tissue. In certain forms a doubling of the axial row may occur (Spessard, 1922), or archegonia may be formed with exceedingly long necks (see Chapter 5 for further details).

Figure 8-7 Gametophytes of *Lycopodium*. **A,** subterranean gametophyte of *Lycopodium clavatum*, with attached sporophyte; **B,** the sub-aerial or terrestrial type, *L. laterale*; **C,** subterranean type, *L. complanatum*. [A and C redrawn from specimens supplied by Dr. A. J. Eames; B, redrawn from Chamberlain, *Bot. Gaz.* 63:51, 1917.]

Figure 8-8 *In vitro* cultures of *Lycopodium cernuum.* **A,** gametophyte with club-shaped branches (note rhizoids on upright branches); **B,** an older pincushion-like gametophyte; **C,** gametophytes with young sporophytes attached in two culture tubes at the left; **D,** sporophytes with young cones (tips of uppermost branches at left) and roots; a portion of the gametophyte can be seen at the base of each plant. [Courtesy Dr. Ralph H. Wetmore.]

With the degeneration of the neck canal cells and the ventral canal cell a passageway is created for the entrance of the motile biflagellate sperms, which reach the archegonium by swimming through a film of water on the surface of the gametophyte. The results of one study indi-

Figure 8-9 **A,** longisection of the gametophyte of *Lycopodium clavatum* showing the position of antheridia and archegonia, and one embryo; **B,** stages in development of an archegonium, *L. selago;* **C-E,** stages in ontogeny of an antheridium, *L. clavatum;* **F-I,** development of the embryo, *L. selago* (mouth of the archegonium is directed toward the top of the page). (Consult text for details.) [A, redrawn from *Syllabus der Pflanzenfamilien* by Engler and Gilg, Berlin: Gebrüder Borntraeger, 1924; B, G, H, I, redrawn from Bruchmann, *Flora* 101:220, 1910; C-E adapted from *Morphology of Vascular Plants. Lower Groups* by A. J. Eames. N. Y.: McGraw-Hill, 1936.]

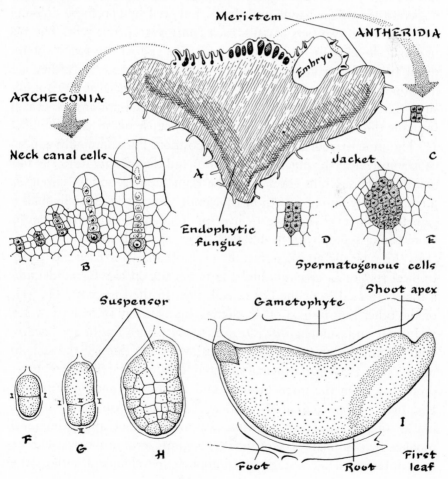

cate that free citric acid or salts of citric acid may play a role in the attraction of sperms to the archegonia (Bruchmann, 1909b).

THE EMBRYO. Embryogeny is correlated, to some degree, with the type of gametophyte, but closer examination reveals a common basic plan. To gain an understanding of embryogeny we will begin with a species possessing an underground prothallus (Fig. 8-9, F-I). The embryo in *Lycopodium* is endoscopic, that is, the shoot apex is directed away from the mouth of the archegonium. The first division of the zygote is transverse to the long axis of the archegonium, setting aside an apex, cell A, and a base, cell B (see Fig. 6-3). Cell B undergoes no further divisions, and becomes a suspensor. Cell A then divides at right angles to the original wall, and this is followed by two more divisions which result in two tiers of cells, each consisting of four cells. The tier of four cells next to the suspensor will give rise to the foot, and the distal tier will produce the first leaf and shoot apex. By further cell division and cell enlargement the foot becomes changed in orientation, since the first leaf and shoot apex grow laterally and upward, eventually breaking through the gametophyte near the meristematic zone (Fig. 8-9, I). The primary root is variable in its position, but commonly appears exogenously near the juncture of the foot and the primary leaf. The foot maintains close connection with the gametophyte and is important physiologically during growth of the young sporophyte. Sexually mature gametophytes may continue to live for some time, supporting one or more young sporophytes in different stages of development.

In the typically green, surface living prothallia (for example, in the tropical species *L. cernuum* and the temperate species *L. inundatum*) a foot is formed from the tier of cells next to the suspensor. The cells of the other tier, instead of developing immediately into the first leaf and shoot apex, undergo divisions in many planes forming a "neutral body," termed a protocorm, which pushes its way through the gametophyte. This green parenchymatous body develops leaf-like structures— protophylls—on the upper surface, and rhizoids on the lower surface. Eventually certain cells at the surface of the protocorm begin functioning as an apical meristem, giving rise to the shoot apex which will produce the "normal" type of shoot. The protocorm in these species has been interpreted as a stage of sporophyte development interpolated between the gametophyte and the "typical" adult sporophyte. (A detailed treatment can be found in Bower, 1935; Goebel, 1930.) For a more complete discussion of embryogeny, refer to Chapter 6.

Protolepidodendraceae

In conformity with the policy outlined earlier, an attempt will be made to present, for each major group, descriptions of a selected number of fossil plants which seem to be related to the group under consideration.

In the Upper Devonian period of the Paleozoic era there grew a small herbaceous plant, *Protolepidodendron*, which exhibited lycopodiaceous characteristics (Kräusel and Weyland, 1932). The shoot system consisted of a prostrate rhizome-like portion and an erect branch system. Many of the upright branches underwent limited dichotomous branching. The growth habit was much like certain species of *Lycopodium*. The shoot systems were clothed with small, eligulate leaves which were forked at the tips; the foliar appendages of some erect branches had a single sporangium located on the adaxial side away from the axil of the sporophyll. The stem was protostelic, with evidence that primary xylem was mesarch in development. Apparently no secondary vascular tissue was formed.

Another genus of even an earlier age is *Baragwanathia longifolia*, discovered in Australia and assigned to the Silurian period. In growth form, *Baragwanathia* probably resembled *Protolepidodendron* and species of *Lycopodium*, although the habit of the plant has not been definitely established because the remains are too fragmentary. The plant had a dichotomously branched shoot system which was composed of axes with spirally arranged leaves from ½ to 1 mm wide, and 4 cm long. Sporangia were seemingly axillary in position, but whether they were actually located on the adaxial side of the sporophylls or attached directly to the stem above the axil has not been determined. Sporophylls were grouped near the tips of the plant but did not form morphologically distinct strobili. In contrast with the scalariform tracheid, which is the prevailing type in the Lycopsida, the tracheids in *Baragwanathia* are reported to have had annular thickenings (Arnold, 1947).

Both *Protolepidodendron* and *Baragwanathia* possess structural features which definitely relate them to the lycopsid line rather than to the

Psilopsida. The coexistence of these simple lycopodiaceous genera with the Psilophytales points to the primitiveness of the Lycopsida and the desirability of seeking vascular plant remains of a period even earlier than the Silurian. In the final analysis the Psilopsida and Lycopsida may prove to be parallel groups, rather than having a linear line of descent. Their true vascular ancestors may well have been present in the Cambrian.

Selaginellales–Selaginellaceae: *Selaginella*

General Characteristics

The genus *Selaginella*, often referred to as the small club moss or spikemoss, is widely distributed over the earth. But even though the genus includes more than 700 species, it does not form a conspicuous part of the world's vegetation. Whereas many species of *Lycopodium* may be relatively large and coarse, most species of *Selaginella* are small and often delicate. It is in the tropics that *Selaginella* is most abundantly represented, being found generally on the ground in damp, shaded localities. Some species occur in cold climates, and many others inhabit temperate zones, growing in damp areas or even occupying exposed rocky ledges. One species, *S. lepidophylla*, cespitose in habit, has become adapted to existence on a Mexican desert and to the arid regions of southwestern United States. In these cases, the entire plant forms a tight ball during periods of drought; in the presence of moisture the branches expand and lie flat on the ground. This species is commonly known as the resurrection plant. *Selaginella* is a greenhouse favorite, and is often used as a border plant. Species of this genus growing together in a greenhouse present an array of color shades—dark to light green, bluish—and some are iridescent.

Growth Form

In growth habit there is considerable variation, although most species can be referred to two or perhaps three growth types. Some species are

Figure 8-10 Two species of *Selaginella* displaying contrasting growth forms. **A,** *S. kraussiana*, a creeping or scrambling type (note rhizophores along main shoot near points of branching); **B,** *S. emelliana*, a form with strong rhizomes and large compound upright branch systems.

erect and even shrubby; others form tufts or mounds and quite often possess leaves that are uniform in size and shape. The leaves are fundamentally spirally arranged, although they generally lie in four vertical rows. In other species the plant may be flat, creeping along the surface of the ground or scrambling over shrubs (Fig. 8-10, A). Still others have a strongly developed rhizomatous stem with large, frond-like side branches which stand erect (Fig. 8-10, B). In the last two types anisophylly (the production of small and large leaves) is often a very prominent feature. In all species branching is fundamentally of the flabellate dichotomous type; the overall growth pattern is pseudomonopodial.

Peculiar prop-like structures, originating from the stem at points of branching, are evident to even an untrained observer. These structures, termed rhizophores, bearing roots at their distal ends, are of great morphological interest (see Fig. 8-10, A; also Fig. 8-11, B); more will be said of their morphological interpretation in a later section of this chapter.

Stem Anatomy

The epidermis consists of cells in which the outer cell walls are cutinized. Stomata are said to be lacking. In many species there are several layers of thick-walled cells beneath the epidermis, which merge gradually with thin-walled chlorophyllous cells of the inner cortex. In most species showing a radial type of growth pattern, as well as in the dorsiventral species, the trailing stem or the prostrate rhizome possesses a protostele (Fig. 8-11, A). A haplostelic condition is a characteristic feature in plants with the radial type of growth, whereas the stele in the dorsiventral species is often a ribbon-shaped vascular strand, as seen in transverse section. In species having a radial type of growth habit the haplostelic condition is characteristic of the lower portion, and the upper portion of the stem may have an actinostelic organization or even become siphonostelic if the center of the stele becomes parenchymatous (Bruchmann, 1909a). The ribbon-shaped protostele in the rhizome of dorsiventral species may be replaced in the upright branches by a number of concentric bundles (meristeles); according to some interpretations each of these bundles is regarded as a distinct stele and stems with this condition are termed "polystelic."

In still other species the rhizome may be solenostelic, and the upright

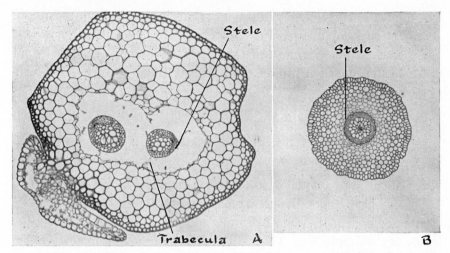

Figure 8-11 Stem (**A**) and rhizophore (**B**) anatomy of *Selaginella*. In a transection of a stem only a few trabeculae appear in the plane of section.

branches may have as many as 10-15 separate meristeles. Experimentally it has been shown that by placing an upright branch of the latter type in a horizontal position, a return to the solenostelic condition is brought about in the newly developed portion of the shoot (Wardlaw, 1924). Whatever the stelar configuration, the composite vascular cylinder or each meristele, as the case may be, is supported in a large air-space system by radially elongated endodermal cells designated *trabeculae* (Fig. 8-11, A). These cells have the characteristic Casparian strips. If the air-space system is large, each support or trabecula may consist of several cortical cells as well as the endodermal cell.

The student should recognize the fact that, in descriptions of changing vascular patterns in the stem, stelar configurations at any given level are merely a reflection of the growth patterns of the apical meristem in relation to development of the entire shoot. The vascular system of a shoot is an interconnected network and should be visualized as such.

Irrespective of stelar organization, the primary xylem is exarch in development, and the metaxylem consists primarily of tracheids with scalariform pitting. Several years ago (Duerden, 1934) certain species were shown to possess vessels, a feature considered formerly to be one of the distinctive characteristics of angiosperms. Not only do certain species of *Selaginella* have vessels, but this type of tracheary structure is found in at least one genus in the ferns and in certain gymnospermous genera (for example, *Ephedra, Gnetum*). The phloem of *Selaginella* has been described as comprising sieve cells and parenchyma cells, but this tissue has not been subjected to detailed studies using modern techniques.

Leaf Anatomy

Leaves of all species are small, attaining a length of a few millimeters. In form the leaves may be ovate, lanceolate, or orbicular. Although spiral arrangement is a common feature in *Lycopodium*, most species of *Selaginella* have leaves that are arranged in four rows along the stem. As mentioned earlier, the shoots of most species are dorsiventral, and the leaves are anisophyllous (Fig. 8-10, A). Two rows of small leaves occur on the dorsal side of the stem, and two rows of larger leaves occur on the ventral side. On close examination, a small tongue-like structure, the ligule, can be observed on the adaxial side of each leaf near the base; more will be said later concerning the development of this structure. Anatomically the mature leaf may vary considerably. The cells of the two epidermal layers may be similar, or in some species they may be somewhat different (Hsü, 1937). Some species have bristles or short hairs extending out from the epidermis. The mesophyll may consist of a distinct palisade layer and spongy parenchyma, or the entire mesophyll may be a reticulum of lacunate parenchyma. Generally stomata occur on the abaxial surface, although in certain species they are present on both surfaces (Harvey-Gibson, 1897). The small median vascular bundle of the leaf is collateral; the xylem consists primarily of tracheids with helical thickenings.

To gain an understanding of the growth of the entire shoot system (stem and leaves) it is necessary to examine the shoot apical meristem. In certain investigated species the shoot is terminated by an apical cell (Barclay, 1931; Hsü, 1937). This apical cell is tetrahedral and appears as an inverted pyramid in longitudinal sectional views of the shoot apex (Fig. 8-12). Through divisions of this apical cell, derivative cells are produced on the three "cutting" surfaces. Each of these cells (segments) undergoes a periclinal division, forming an outer and an inner cell. The outer cell, by further divisions, will produce the epidermis and cortex. Endodermis, pericycle, and vascular tissues are derived ultimately from

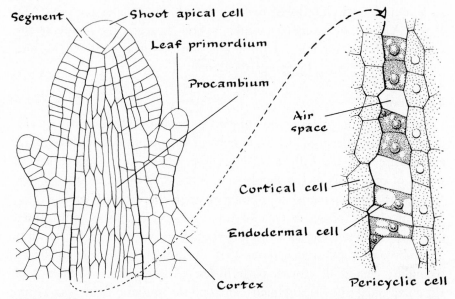

Figure 8-12 Stem development in *Selaginella sinensis*. Longisection of the shoot tip (left), and early development of trabeculae (endodermal cells) and of the air space system surrounding the vascular cylinder (right); endodermal cells become separated from one another and undergo radial extension. [Redrawn from Hsü, *Bull. Chinese Bot. Soc.* 3:75, 1937.]

derivatives of the inner cell (Fig. 8-12). Certain other species are reported to have two adjoining apical initial cells at the shoot tip (Williams, 1931).

Leaves have their origin in surface cells located along the flanks of the apical meristem. After leaf initiation a period of apical growth ensues, which is followed by generalized growth and cellular differentiation. Throughout early development the leaf is traversed by a procambial strand which is in continuity with the vascular cylinder of the stem (Hsü, 1937). Procambial cells eventually differentiate into primary xylem and primary phloem of the leaf bundle.

The ligule (Fig. 8-14), located on the adaxial side of each leaf, makes its appearance through periclinal divisions in the embryonic cells of the protoderm. A detailed account of ligule development is presented in Chapter 3.

Of considerable interest is the large size attained by chloroplasts in this genus. Depending on the species, each mesophyll cell may have one large, cup-shaped chloroplast or from four to six smaller plastids (Ma, 1930). A single unbranched vascular bundle traverses the length of the mature leaf (microphyll). The bundle consists of a few tracheids and sieve cells surrounded by compact parenchyma cells.

The Root

Except for the primary root of the young sporophyte, most species have roots that occur at the distal ends of rhizophores. The rhizophore, a structure that normally is without appendages and which arises at points of branching of the shoot, is an interesting organ (Fig. 8-10, A). It originates from a meristem, termed an angle-meristem (Cusick, 1954). The rhizophore possesses no root cap, and occasionally is transformed into a leafy shoot. Cusick considers the angle-meristem to be basically an embryonic shoot and believes that rhizophore formation involves a secondary change of growth pattern when the regulatory influence of the main axial apex is modified. Rhizophore formation can also be induced experimentally by applying indole-acetic acid to the cut end of a stem (Williams, 1937). The rhizophore is generally unbranched, but on contact with the substrate roots are formed endogenously at the distal end. These roots branch dichotomously and have the recognized anatomical characteristics of true roots. The root is fundamentally monarch.

The Strobilus

Unlike *Lycopodium*, all species of *Selaginella* form strobili or cones. Strobili occur terminally on side branches, although in some forms the cone apical meristem may continue meristematic activity, producing vegetative leaves (Sykes and Stiles, 1910). All sporophylls of a strobilus are generally alike (although not differing from vegetative leaves as much as in certain species of *Lycopodium*) and are arranged in four distinct rows. The sporophylls may fit tightly together, or the vertical distance between sporophylls may be greater, the entire strobilus being a lax or open type of cone.

Because *Selaginella* is heterosporous, sporangia are of two types: microsporangia and megasporangia (Fig. 8-13). The sporophylls associated with these two types of sporangia are then either microsporophylls or megasporophylls. The one mature sporangium associated with each

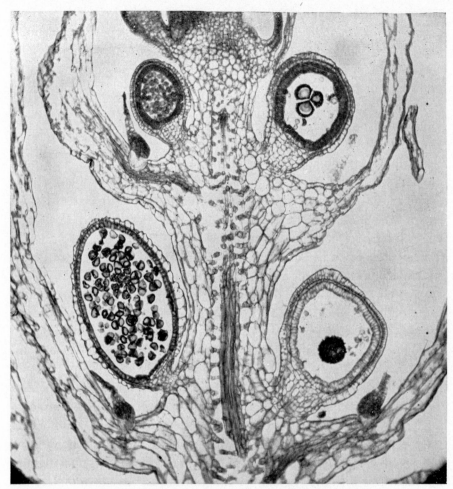

Figure 8-13 Portion of longisection of strobilus of *Selaginella sp.* showing late stages in development of sporangia. At upper left, a microsporangium with microsporocytes; note median sectional view of ligule. At lower left, a mature microsporangium with numerous microspores. Three megaspores, surrounded by degenerating sporocytes, are evident in megasporangium at upper right. The megasporangium at lower right is nearly mature, and at this level of section a single megaspore is seen. (Consult Fig. 8-14 for details of early ontogeny of sporangium in *Selaginella.*)

sporophyll is generally axillary in position, although its origin may be from cells of the axis or the base of the sporophyll (Lyon, 1901; Bower, 1935; Campbell, 1940). There is considerable variation in distribution of sporangia within the strobili of different species. Strobili may consist

entirely of microsporangia or of megasporangia (Mitchell, 1910). However, the mixed condition (either without order or arranged in definite
patterns) is more common. The lower portion of a strobilus may consist of megasporangia and the upper portion of microsporangia, or the
two types of sporangia may be mixed indiscriminately. A common arrangement is two vertical rows of each type. In certain species (e.g., *S.
kraussiana*) only one megasporangium is present at the base of each
strobilus.

Mature microsporangia are generally obovoid or reniform, and often
are reddish to bright orange. Megasporangia are larger than microsporangia and frequently are lobed, conforming in outline to the large
spores within them. The megasporangia are characterized by lighter
colors: whitish-yellow, or light orange.

The site of sporangial initiation, whether microsporangia or megasporangia are considered, is in surface cells of the axis, directly above the
sporophyll, or in cells near the base of the sporophyll on the adaxial side.
Whether two, three, or more than three surface initials are involved
(Bower, 1935; Campbell, 1940; Goebel, 1930), periclinal divisions in
these initials separate an outer tier of cells—the primary wall cells—and
an inner tier—the primary sporogenous cells (Fig. 8-14, A, B). By
repeated anticlinal and periclinal divisions of the primary wall cells, a
two-layered sporangial wall is formed. The primary sporogenous cells
divide periclinally, the outer cells eventually becoming the tapetum; the
inner cells, by dividing in various planes, produce the sporogenous tissue
(Fig. 8-14, C). Undoubtedly cells located at the base of the sporangium,
not identified with the original periclinal divisions, serve to complete the
continuity of the tapetum (Fig. 8-14, D).

In summary, a sporangium at this stage consists of an immature
sporangial wall of two layers, a short stalk, and a conspicuous tapetal
layer enclosing sporocytes which normally round off and separate from
each other prior to the meiotic divisions (Fig. 8-14, D). Up to this developmental stage, microsporangia and megasporangia are indistinguishable, but as development continues the two types become clearly defined.
If a sporangium is to become a microsporangium, a large percentage of
the sporocytes undergo meiosis to form tetrads of microspores (Fig.
8-13). In a potential megasporangium all megasporocytes disintegrate
except one; this sporocyte immediately divides meiotically, forming four

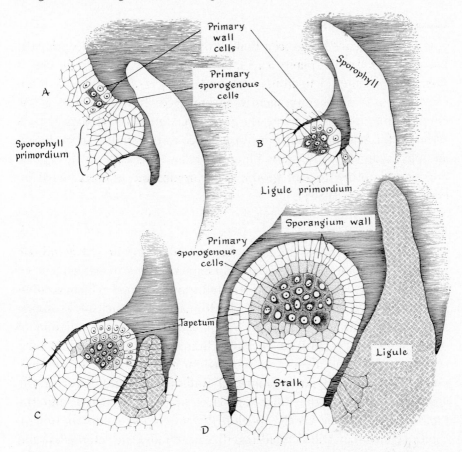

Figure 8-14 **A-D,** early ontogeny of a sporangium in *Selaginella sp.* Periclinal divisions in surface cells set aside primary wall and primary sporogenous cells (**A, B**). The tapetum is formed from outer sporogenous cells (**C, D**). Note precocious development of ligule. Whether the sporangium in **D** would have become a microsporangium or a megasporangium is not evident morphologically at this stage of development. However, physiological specialization may have occurred.

megaspores. Frequently one or more megaspores do not mature. In certain species more than one megasporocyte is functional; eight, twelve, and even more megaspores have been recorded (Duerden, 1929). An analysis of the stored food in megaspores of *Selaginella* indicates that 48 percent of the contents is fatty material, 0.43 percent is nitrogenous, and 1.26 percent is mineral matter (Sosa and Sosa-Bourdouil, 1940).

Chromosome Numbers

It is in the genus *Selaginella* that chromosome numbers exceptionally low for lower vascular plants are found. Furthermore, the minute size of their chromosomes (1 micron, or less, in length) is of considerable interest; $n = 9$ is a number frequently encountered. If we visualize a low chromosome number as being the primitive state, the cytological facts recorded for *Selaginella* take on importance in our studies of evolution and phylogeny. Low chromosome numbers have persisted in this genus, but in some other ancient groups the chromosome numbers have increased (Manton, 1950).

Gametophytes

In the genus *Lycopodium,* it will be recalled, spores do not germinate until their liberation from the sporangium. Also, most species of *Lycopodium* have a long and protracted growth period which is interpolated between germination and the formation of a mature exosporic gametophyte with sex organs. In *Selaginella,* however, germination of microspores and megaspores begins while they are still within their respective sporangia. In a microsporangium at a late stage of development the radial and inner tangential walls of the outer layer of the sporangium thicken; the inner wall layer becomes stretched, and the tapetum may still be visible. Within the microsporangium the microspores (which may still be held together in tetrads) are tetrahedral and have developed a thick outer wall which may be laid down in the form of varied spines or projections. The first division of the microspore re-

Figure 8-15 Development (from left to right) of the microgametophyte in *Selaginella kraussiana.* Early stages of development may occur within the microsporangium prior to sporangium dehiscence. [Redrawn from Slagg, *Amer. Jour. Bot.* 19:106, 1932.]

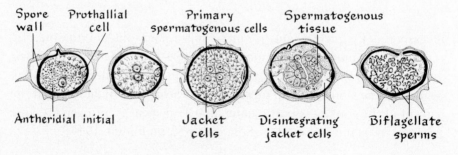

Spore wall | Prothallial cell | Primary spermatogenous cells | Spermatogenous tissue

Antheridial initial | Jacket cells | Disintegrating jacket cells | Biflagellate sperms

sults in the formation of a small prothallial cell and a large antheridial initial (Fig. 8-15). The antheridial initial becomes subdivided by several divisions in various planes. This results in the establishment of a sterile jacket enclosing four primary spermatogenous cells, all within the original microspore wall. Forceful ejection of the partially developed microgametophytes may occur at this time by splitting of the upper half of the sporangium along a line of dehiscence. This is followed by differential shrinkage of the lower portion. Whether microgametophytes are shed during this developmental stage or earlier, the final development occurs outside the sporangium wherever the spores may alight. According to Slagg (1932), the primary spermatogenous cells undergo several divisions, forming 128 or 256 spermatocytes which, on disintegration of the jacket cells and rupture of the spore wall along the triradiate ridge, are liberated as free swimming biflagellate sperms (Fig. 8-15).

Just as early stages in formation of the microgametophyte begin while the microspores are still within the microsporangium, megagametophyte development begins while the megaspores are in the megasporangium. After meiosis in a megaspore-mother cell the resulting megaspores soon develop a thick, sculptured outer wall which is designated the exine. Internal to this outer layer and separated from it by some distance is a second wall layer (intine), which is attached to the outer wall at a point along the triradiate ridge. This second wall layer encloses the megaspore protoplast. Very early a conspicuous vacuole develops within the enlarging protoplast which is enclosed by the intine (Campbell, 1902). Associated with this enlargement is the division of the megaspore nucleus. Continued free nuclear divisions and an increase in the amount of cytoplasm results in a thin multinucleate layer of cytoplasm which surrounds a large central vacuole. By this time the intine has become extended and lies next to the exine. According to Pieniążek (1938) the apparent differential growth of the exine and intine is an artifact. He states that the spore coats remain in contact throughout development if the spores are not subjected to unusual physical or chemical changes. He was able to demonstrate that the spore protoplast can be plasmolysed and deplasmolysed.

Concomitant with an increase in the amount of cytoplasm and stored food is the process of cell wall formation. The formation of walls around free nuclei takes place first at the apical end near the triradiate ridge

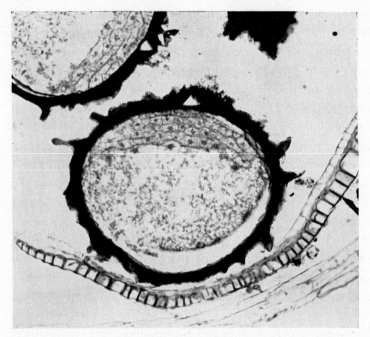

Figure 8-16   Section of developing cellular megagametophyte within megaspore wall of *Selaginella sp.* A large storage vesicle is present beneath the cellular tissue. The triradiate ridge is indicated by a triangular shaped space (white) at the upper end of the spore. The developing endosporic gametophyte is still enclosed within the wall of the megasporangium.

(Fig. 8-16). In some species the cellular portion of the sexually mature megagametophyte may consist of only a few layers of cells separated from the large coenocytic vesicle. Only after the embryo begins development does the vesicle become cellular. In other species cell formation is a continuous process proceeding basipetally from the apical region. Irrespective of the timing of cell wall formation, archegonia soon make their appearance in the apical region (Fig. 8-17, A). Each archegonium develops from a single superficial cell and at maturity consists of eight neck cells (arranged in two tiers of four cells each), a neck canal cell, a ventral canal cell, and an egg cell (Fig. 8-17, B). The megaspore wall breaks along the triradiate ridge, apparently because of the growth of the cellular gametophyte (Figs. 8-16; 8-17, A; 8-19, A). In some species prominent lobes of tissue are produced, with certain cells forming tufts of rhizoids (Bruchmann, 1912).

It has been reported that a certain amount of chlorophyll is present in the upper part of the gametophyte, but this has never been confirmed. The amount of food produced through photosynthesis (if photosynthesis occurs at all) is probably small, and most of the nutritional requirements are met by the storage tissue in the lower part of the megagametophyte.

To achieve continuity in the description of gametophyte development, we have, to this point, made no mention of the time of natural shedding of the megagametophyte from the sporangium. The time of liberation is variable in the genus but may occur (1) at any time before the cellular stage, (2) after the archegonia appear, or (3) after fertilization and development of the embryo (in two cases). In the first two instances the final stages in megagametophyte development and fertilization take place while the megagametophyte rests on decaying portions of the sporophyte or on the soil or humus. In such species the rhizoids undoubtedly play an important role in the absorption of water and in anchorage. The partially developed microgametophytes complete their development while situated on the exposed megagametophyte tissue or in close proximity to it. After the sperms are liberated they swim to the archegonia in a thin film of dew or rain water. In those forms that retain the megaspores (plus megagametophytes) within the sporangium, it is assumed that the partially developed microgametophytes sift down

Figure 8-17   A, section of endosporic, cellular megagametophyte of *Selaginella denticulata;* **B,** details of mature archegonium. [Redrawn from Bruchmann, *Flora* 104:180, 1912.]

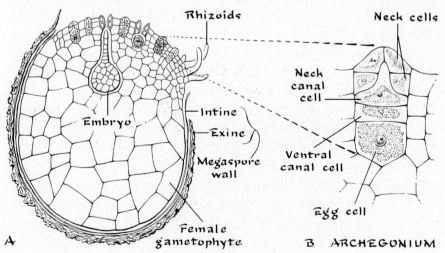

through the strobilus and enter the gaping sporangia, completing their development either on the female gametophytes or in water which may fill the sporangial cavity.

Experimental Study of the Megagametophyte

The successful experiments in culturing the gametophyte of *Lycopodium* have been described earlier in this chapter. The same workers (Wetmore and Morel, 1951b) have cultured the female gametophytes of two species of *Selaginella*. On the culture substrate the gametophytes remain alive for six months, and if vitamins are added large masses of undifferentiated tissue are produced, which are covered with rhizoids and archegonia.

The Embryo

After fertilization has occurred the diploid or sporophyte generation is established. The first division of the zygote is transverse, separating a suspensor cell (that cell toward the archegonial neck), and the embryonic cell (labeled "apex" in Fig. 8-18, A) which will form the remainder of the embryo (see Chapter 6).

The embryo, as can readily be understood, is endoscopic. The suspensor cell may remain undivided or form several cells. In either instance the suspensor serves to thrust the developing embryo proper into the megagametophyte tissue. An apical cell is formed as a result of vertical and oblique divisions of the embryonic cell (Fig. 8-18, D). The apical cell of the future shoot apex is thus established early in embryogeny (Bruchmann, 1909a, 1912). Then, the first two foliar appendages, often referred to as "cotyledons," arise laterally and exogenously from the shoot apical meristem (Fig. 8-18, G). At approximately this stage of development the embryo shoot apex undergoes a 90-degree turn by differential growth (Fig. 8-18, H). Active cell division along the lower side of the developing embryo produces a definable foot (Fig. 8-18, I). Subsequently, periclinal divisions occur in surface cells that are located between the foot and suspensor, and the resulting cells become the root cap. Later, a definable root apical cell makes its appearance some distance from the surface (Bruchmann, 1909a). Considerable variation exists in the origin and position of foot and root (Fig. 6-4).

By continued apical growth, cell enlargement, and differentiation of

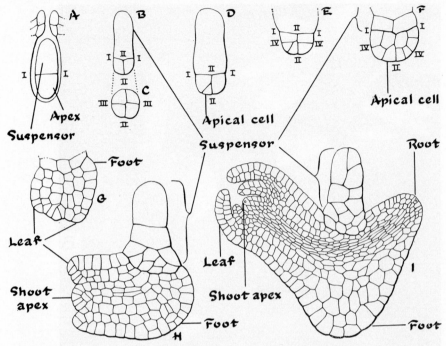

Figure 8-18 Embryogeny in *Selaginella martensii*. In all cases the neck of the archegonium is directed toward the top of the page. The walls resulting from early cleavages are indicated as I-I, II-II, etc. An apical polar view of **B** is shown in **C.** (For details consult text.) [**B-I,** redrawn from Bruchmann, *Flora* 99:12, 1909.]

shoot and root, the young sporophyte emerges from the gametophyte tissue. That portion of the shoot below the first foliar appendages elongates rapidly (Fig. 8-19, B, C). In many species the first dichotomy of the shoot takes place immediately above the cotyledons. The primary root grows downward and enters the soil. The foot remains in close connection with the gametophyte, which, in turn, is surrounded by the megaspore wall. The complete separation of the sporophyte from the gametophyte may not occur until the sporophyte has undergone considerable growth.

Lepidodendrales

A majority of the lycopods of the early Paleozoic were primarily low growing plants, whereas most of those in the late Paleozoic were tree-like

Figure 8-19　Megagametophyte and young sporophyte of *Selaginella kraussiana.*
A, gametophyte tissue protruding through cracked spore wall; **B,** young sporophyte attached to gametophyte showing root (to the right), stem, and first
pair of leaves (oriented in the plane of the page); **C,** older sporophyte (megaspore wall with enclosed gametophyte is still visible at the juncture of stem
and root).

in their growth habit. To the latter belong the genera of the Lepidodendrales. A lepidodendroid plant was arborescent, heterosporous, ligulate,
and had distinctive markings on leaf cushions of the trunk.

Lepidodendron

One genus about which considerable information has been accumulated is *Lepidodendron.* Many species have been described from Europe
and a few from North America. The trunks were well preserved in these
dendroid plants which often attained a height of 100 feet or more. The

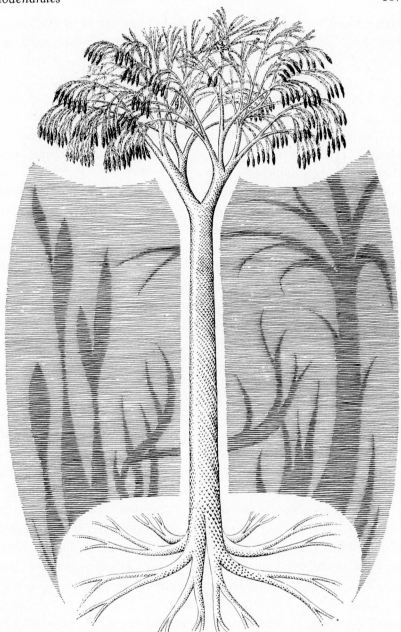

Figure 8-20 Diagrammatic reconstruction of *Lepidodendron*. Note the presence of terminal strobili and the large rhizophores at the base of the trunk. *Form genera* exist for all basic parts of the body of this plant. (Consult text for pertinent information.) [Redrawn from *Handbuch der Paläobotanik* by M. Hirmer, Munich: P. Oldenbourg, 1927.]

unbranched trunk terminated in a dichotomously branched, umbrella-like shoot system in which the branches were clothed with spirally arranged, linear or awl-shaped microphylls (Fig. 8-20). The leaves, on abscission from the trunk and larger branches, left a distinctive persistent scar which is used today as one feature in the separation of different genera. Definite elongate strobili terminated the ultimate branches. The base of the trunk was divided into four large root-like organs (rhizophores), each of which divided again to form two structures. Each of these two organs branched repeatedly.

Anatomically the stem exhibited a rather simple type of organization, although some variation existed among species. Whether the primary vascular cylinder was protostelic or siphonostelic, the exarch primary xylem consisted of tracheids with scalariform pitting. In species which increased in girth, a vascular cambium produced a narrow cylinder of comparatively uniform secondary xylem in which no indication of growth rings is apparent. A relatively small amount of phloem was formed to the outside. The entire vascular cylinder did not exceed several centimeters in diameter. Histologically the broad cortex was much more diverse, consisting of at least three regions.

Form Genera

From the above account the reader would naturally conclude that the discovery of intact remains of this arborescent genus is indeed remarkable. However, the story is not as simple as we have recounted. To uncover a fossil plant with all parts intact is the dream of paleobotanists, but unfortunately, at best only unconnected portions or organs of large plants are generally discovered. This dilemma was appreciated by the early paleobotanists and led to the establishment of *form genera* or *organ genera*. For example, the genus *Lepidodendron* originally referred to portions of the trunk of lycopods with the distinctive leaf-scar pattern. The detached fossil leaves, which have been shown to be related to the branches and trunks of *Lepidodendra*, are placed in the organ genus *Lepidophyllum*. In compressions leaves are frequently found attached to stems and can be compared with those placed in organ genera. The massive root-like organ of lycopods is known as *Stigmaria*, another organ genus. By continued comparative studies and through fortunate discoveries of organs which were connected or in close proximity, paleobotanists were certain of the anticipated conclusion that the above organ genera were merely parts of the same plant type, now designated as *Lepidodendron*.

The strobili of *Lepidodendron*, which are found detached or occasionally in organic connection with a leafy stem, are designated *Lepidostrobus*. These cones were elongate with spirally arranged overlapping ligulate sporophylls. One sporangium was present on the adaxial side of each sporophyll. Microsporangia, enclosing several hundred microspores, occurred in the upper portion of the strobilus, and megasporangia with a limited number of megaspores occupied the lower part of the cone. Megaspores were shed from the sporangia, and development of the megagametophyte was endosporic. Certain species of *Lepidodendron* progressed to an evolutionary level of producing seed-like structures. *Lepidocarpon* applies to the organ genus represented by strobili in which often only one functional megaspore, with its enclosed megagametophyte, was permanently retained within the sporangium. Outgrowths from the sporophyll enclosed the entire structure except for a slit-like opening along the top. At maturity the sporophyll, megasporangium with enclosed megaspore wall, and gametophyte were shed as a unit. Archegonia occurred in the female gametophyte toward the opening at the tip; however, no embryos have ever been discovered. More detailed descriptions of this group of plants can be obtained from paleobotany books; see, for example, Darrah, 1939; Hofmann, 1934; Arnold, 1947; Andrews, 1947).

Herbaceous Lycopods

Not all of the Carboniferous lycopods attained the proportions of the giant species of *Lepidodendron*. From the Carboniferous and even from the Upper Devonian, fossils have been found that resemble very closely those of *Lycopodium* and *Selaginella*. *Lycopodites*, a genus in the Lycopodiales, includes homosporous species in which the sporophylls were not grouped into distinct cones and those in which the cones were distinct. Well-preserved specimens of *Selaginellites* (Selaginellales) have been found and have been identified as being of the Lower Carboniferous Age; in some, megaspores with an enclosed female gametophyte have been described. It has been suggested that these two fossil genera might be the actual forerunners of the living genera *Lycopodium* and *Selaginella*.

Isoetales–Isoetaceae: *Isoetes*

The genus *Isoetes* is a most interesting, provocative, and enigmatic vascular plant. The plant body of all species is relatively small with a greatly shortened axis, and has tufts of leaves and roots which in appearance resemble certain monocotyledonous plants (Fig. 8-21, A). This resemblance to seed plants caused Linneaus, as early as 1751, to characterize the plant as a seed plant; even the "fruit" and "seeds" were described! Even earlier, the herbalist Ray stated that "of this plant, one sees naught but leaves and roots, and knows not from what source it comes directly."

The first popular names recorded for *Isoetes* were "quillwort" and "Merllyn's Grass." The former name is applied to the genus in America; in Europe it is still known as Merlin's Grass. Economically the genus is relatively unimportant today, but there are records of the plants being eaten occasionally in Europe (Pfeiffer, 1922). Great quantities of starch and oil are present in the plant body. Birds, pigs, muskrats, and ducks may eat the fleshy plant body, and cattle often graze on the leaves.

Isoetes includes over sixty species, the majority of which occur in the cooler climates of the world growing immersed in water (at least part of the year) or in swampy areas. There are certain species that have become adapted to existence in a dry environment at least during a part of the year.

Organography

The axial portion of *Isoetes* has been interpreted in various ways, and the descriptive terminology applied to the plant is even more varied in its use and general acceptance by botanists.

As mentioned earlier, the axis is a short, erect structure (commonly referred to as a corm) which, in the mature plant, may be divided into two, three, or, rarely, four lobes. Along the sides of the grooves or clefts are numerous roots. The upper part of the axis is covered with a dense cluster of leaves which have broad overlapping bases (Fig. 8-21, A). The

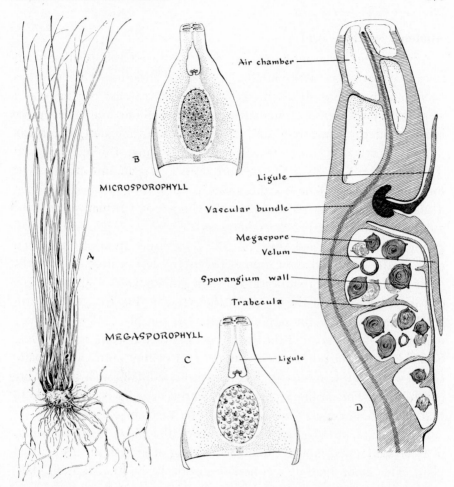

Figure 8-21 **A-C,** *Isoetis howellii.* **A,** habit sketch of sporophyte; **B,** diagram, adaxial view of base of microsporophyll showing microsporangium as seen through the opening in the velum (spores are shown as black dots within the sporangium, the ends of trabeculae as larger black asteroids); **C,** diagram adaxial view of base of megasporophyll with attached megasporangium; **D,** diagram, longisection of megasporophyll and megasporangium of *Isoetes sp.* (markings on spore walls are entirely schematic).

shoot apex is completely hidden in a depression by the tightly imbricated leaves. The sides of mature plants become very rough with layers of sloughing tissues. Each increment includes the leaf bases and severed roots of the previous growing season, and this sloughed tissue decays very rapidly.

Anatomy of the Corm

Any morphological interpretation of the corm of this peculiar plant must necessarily be based partially on internal structure. The corm has been described variously as an erect rhizome; as a stock; as a stem; as a stem combined with a stigmarian type of rhizophore; and as an upper leaf-bearing part, the stem, and a lower root-bearing part, the rhizo-morph (Scott and Hill, 1900; Stokey, 1909; Lang, 1915a; West and Takeda, 1915; Osborn, 1922; Stewart, 1947). If a mature plant is cut longitudinally in a plane at right angles to the basal groove (considering a plant that is two-lobed), a central cylinder of vascular tissue with ascending leaf traces and descending root traces, embedded in a broad ground tissue, is revealed (Fig. 8-22, B). On examination of the central cylinder the line of demarcation between the leaf-bearing part of the plant (stem) and the root-bearing portion (rhizophore) is apparent as a constriction just below the middle of the cylinder (Fig. 8-22, B). A corm cut longitudinally in the opposite plane (in the plane of the groove) makes even more apparent the distinction between the two regions (Fig. 8-22, A). It will be noted that the upper part of the central axis is cylin-drical, whereas the lower part is extended horizontally with slightly up-curved arms. The outline of the entire central cylinder is comparable to that of a garden edging-tool, an anchor, or a vegetable chopper.

Location, identification, and function of the plant body meristems of *Isoetes* are important in the understanding of growth in this unusual plant. The shoot apex, as mentioned previously, is situated at the bot-tom of a depression surrounded by leaves of various ages (Fig. 8-22, A, B). The shoot apical meristem, which includes probably several initial cells, gives rise to new leaves, to cortical tissue, and to tissue that will differentiate into the primary vascular tissues of the leaf traces and central cylinder. Considerable controversy exists as to whether the stem portion of the primary vascular cylinder is composed entirely of the fusion of the lower portions of the leaf traces or whether a portion of it is truly cauline in nature (Scott and Hill, 1900; Lang, 1915b; West and Takeda, 1915). No definite endodermis is present. The apical meristem of the lower portion of the plant occurs as a linear meristem all along the lower edge of the rhizophore. Thus, the meristem is close to the surface in the plane of the groove or grooves (three-lobed corm). To the inside,

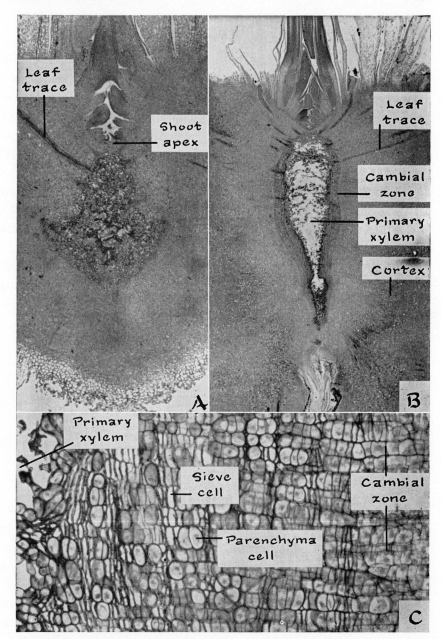

Figure 8-22 Anatomy of the corm in *Isoetes howellii*. **A,** longisection, in the plane of the basal groove; **B,** median longisection, at right angles to the basal groove (several root traces can be seen at lower right); **C,** a portion of the secondary vascular tissues and adjacent tissues.

this meristem gives rise to primary vascular tissues; to the outside, a ground meristem is formed.

It is in this ground meristem that new root primordia take their origin. Following its deep seated initiation (endogenous origin), each root penetrates the ground tissue in reaching the surface and substrate (West and Takeda, 1915). New roots appear on both sides of the groove, and of the linear meristem, in a definite pattern. All roots of a series (those aligned in rows roughly parallel to the groove and meristem) are of the same age. Roots of all series are also aligned in vertical rows (perpendicular to the groove). In a two-lobed corm there are four series, two on each side of the rhizophore. As the plant grows, through extension of the linear meristem, the number of roots constituting a series increases (West and Takeda, 1915).

Roots are produced in such an orderly fashion that the total number of roots produced by a plant can be derived from the following formula (West and Takeda, 1915):

$$x = 2y \, \frac{z(z+1)}{2}$$

Therefore,

$$x = yz(z+1)$$

where

> x = approximate total number of roots produced by a plant
> y = number of lobes
> z = number of series on the flank of a lobe.

So far, only primary growth of the plant body has been described. In *Isoetes* an unusual type of secondary growth takes place which produces a complex and imperfectly known tissue. Also in the process, the plant is divested each year of certain, old non-functional tissues and organs. In contrast with the common situation in seed plants where a cambium arises between the primary xylem and the primary phloem, the cambium in *Isoetes* has its origin in tissue outside the primary phloem. The activity of this cambium is indeed unusual in that parenchyma is produced to the outside, and a specialized type of secondary vascular tissue is formed inwardly (Fig. 8-22, C). The outer parenchymatous layer, which is a storage tissue, is renewed each year. The parenchyma layer of the previous season is pushed outward and is ultimately lost due to the activity of the cambium. Carried upward and off by the sloughed tissue are the decaying leaf bases with their ruptured leaf traces; the non-functional roots and their traces are moved downward and off.

Of the many debatable features of *Isoetes*, interpretation of the secondary vascular tissue has probably caused the most discussion. The cells of this tissue, which are derived from a definite storied cambium, are extremely short, being not much taller than they are wide. The form of these cells, combined with the difficulty of interpretation, led to the general acceptance of the noncommittal term "prismatic layer" for this part of the axis. Nevertheless, this tissue has been interpreted as secondary xylem (Stokey, 1909), as secondary phloem (West and Takeda, 1915), as a secondary tissue containing both tracheids and sieve elements (Scott and Hill, 1900), and as a tissue composed of (1) occasional tracheids, (2) considerable unmodified parenchyma, and (3) specialized parenchyma cells which are concerned with conduction (Weber, 1922).

If the most recent inner derivatives of the cambium from an older plant of *I. howellii* are examined (Fig. 8-22, C), it will be noted that the cells of certain layers have sieve areas and others remain as parenchyma (Esau, *et al,* 1953). The sieve cells have sieve areas on their lateral and end walls. A noticeable clearing of the cell contents occurs, but the nucleus remains, even though seemingly partially degenerated. With age these sieve cells develop irregularly thickened walls (or cell contents that are firmly attached to the walls) which stain similar to lignified or suberized cell walls when certain stains such as safranin are used. Frequently what appears to be a tracheid with helical thickenings may become differentiated within the bands of parenchyma tissue present in the secondary vascular tissue. Certain species are reported as not showing alternate bands of different cells in the secondary vascular tissue (Stokey, 1909).

In summary, the question might be asked: "How is the mature plant form in *Isoetes* related to meristematic activity?" Longitudinal growth, accomplished through the functioning of the apical meristem of the shoot apex and of the linear meristem of the prostrate rhizophore, is very slow, as evidenced by the extremely short axis and the crowding of appendages. The cambium, which surrounds the erect portion of the vascular cylinder and encloses the sides of the rhizophore portion, gives rise yearly to small increments of secondary vascular tissue and a large amount of parenchyma tissue, or secondary cortex. This accounts for the fact that older plants are much broader than tall. Also, the formation of considerable secondary tissue on the sides of the rhizophore would tend to deepen the groove by the presence of overlying dead and dying secondary cortical tissue.

Roots

Roots branch dichotomously after they emerge from the rhizophore ground tissue. The root apical meristem is reported to consist of a group of initials for the root cap, epidermis, and cortex, and a single initial gives rise to tissue of the vascular cylinder (Farmer, 1890; Campbell, 1891).

A transverse section of a mature functioning root reveals a simple type of root of unusual interest. It consists of a cylindrical cortex which surrounds a large air cavity, and it has a vascular cylinder which is attached to the cortex along one side of the cavity. The primary xylem and phloem are collateral in arrangement, the phloem being oriented toward the cavity. An endodermis, with the usual Casparian strips, is present around the primary vascular tissues. The air cavity is formed by a breakdown of cortical cells throughout the length of that portion of the root which has emerged from the rhizophore. Histologically the root of *Isoetes* resembles very closely an appendage on the rhizophore of *Stigmaria*. The similarity is conclusive enough to support the belief, on the part of some botanists, that the phylogenetic relationship between *Isoetes* and some member of the Lepidodendrales is certain.

The Leaf

To this point foliar appendages have been treated simply as leaves, without reference to any special function. Actually each foliar appendage is a potential sporophyll, either a microsporophyll or a megasporophyll. (The terms leaf and sporophyll will be used interchangeably). Each sporophyll has a thickened and expanded base, with a tapering upper portion which is awl-shaped and pointed. Leaves may be a few centimeters long or even up to 50 cm long (*I. japonica*). The lower parts of the leaves may be buried in the soil and lack chlorophyll, and are commonly a glistening white. Some species have black leaf bases. In many species most of the leaves die and decay at the termination of the growing season. In aquatic species leaves may remain on the plant at all times. The upper portion of a leaf is traversed longitudinally by four large air chambers (Fig. 8-21, D) that may be partitioned into compartments by transverse tissue diaphragms—the possession of large air cavities is a feature common to many water plants. Stomata occur on the leaves of all plants except those leaves that are entirely submerged at all times. Running throughout the length of the leaf (a microphyll) is an unbranched vascular bundle composed of primary xylem and phloem.

Located on the adaxial side near the base of each leaf is a sporangium (Fig. 8-21, B, C). A triangular ligule is present just above the sporangium. Covering or partially covering the face of the sporangium is a protective flap of tissue, the velum (Fig. 8-21, D). All sporophylls have normal sporangia except several of the late-formed sporophylls of a growing season. At the end of a growing season a mature plant generally has an outer group of megasporophylls, which encloses a set of microsporophylls, which in turn encloses several poorly developed leaves with abortive sporangia.

Sporophyll and Sporangium Development

Leaves have their origin in surface cells of the apical meristem. At first they are crescent-shaped in outline, and growth in length is initiated by apical initials. When the primordium is only a few cells high, a conspicuous adaxial surface cell of the leaf near the base divides periclinally, giving rise to the ligule (Smith, 1900). By repeated divisions a filamentous structure is formed which soon overtops the leaf apex. The ligule eventually becomes tongue-shaped (Fig. 8-21, B, C) and shows a high degree of histologic specialization (a detailed description is given in Chapter 3). The sporangium and velum have their origin through periclinal divisions in surface cells beneath the ligule. The velum is first to take form, and is followed by growth of the sporangium. As a result of the first periclinal divisions, which localize the sporangial position, a central mass of potentially sporogenous cells is separated from outer layers of peripheral cells. During development the cells of these outer layers may continue to add derivatives to the sporogenous mass (Smith, 1900). Ultimately the outer three or four peripheral layers constitute the sporangial wall. The cells of the sporogenous tissue divide rapidly in all planes.

Microsporangia and megasporangia are indistinguishable during early stages of development, and it is only after the potential microsporocytes or megasporocytes become apparent that the two types of sporangia can be distinguished. In a microsporangium irregular groups of deeply staining cells ultimately become the microsporocytes, and certain bands of lightly staining cells (originally potentially sporogenous) become the trabeculae, which traverse the sporogenous mass but do not divide it into compartments or locules (Fig. 8-23). Covering the trabeculae is a tapetum which may be biseriate or multilayered, the cells of which are derived also from potentially sporogenous cells. The tapetum of the trabeculae is continuous with a tapetal layer lining the sporangial wall. The microspore-mother cells separate from each other prior to the meiotic divisions. Estimates of the number of bifacial microspores produced by a single sporangium range from 300,000 to 1,000,000. The spore number

Figure 8-23 Transection, microsporophyll and developing microsporangium of *Isoetes howellii*. Trabeculae can be seen traversing the mass of potential microsporocytes. The bases of other sporophylls are evident.

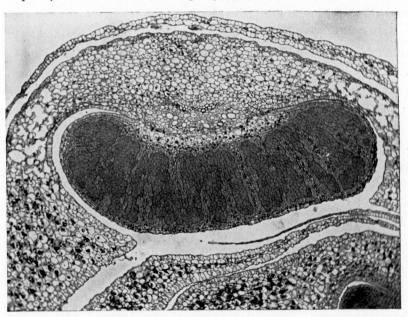

of each sporangium in *Isoetes* is probably greater than it is in any other vascular plant.

In a megasporangium, even before the trabeculae are distinguishable, certain cells are greatly enlarged over their neighbors and will become the megasporocytes (Smith, 1900; Goebel, 1930). Not all of the enlarged cells will become megaspore-mother cells, but some will degenerate and be resorbed. It is only after megaspore-mother cells are in evidence that trabeculae become apparent. As a result of meiosis, each sporangium contains approximately 100-300 tetrahedral megaspores which may range from 200 to 900 microns in diameter (Fig. 8-21, D). Megaspores may be white, gray, or black, and they have distinctive protuberances on their thick cell walls. Microspores are very small, from 20 to 45 microns long, are ridged longitudinally, and have various characteristic wall patterns.

Sporangia are, in general, indehiscent, and liberation of spores is brought about by decay of sporophylls in the fall or winter seasons in cooler latitudes. Certain species of *Isoetes* growing in vernal pools, in which the corm is entirely buried, have a special means of exposing the sporangial contents. In these cases decaying sporophylls of the previous season are forced up by the expansion of mucilage cells at the base of the sporophylls, whereupon the spores are brought to the surface (Osborn, 1922). Distribution of spores is by wind, disturbance of mud in which certain species grow, or wave action in lakes; in some instances earth worms have been reported as carriers (Duthie, 1929).

Chromosome Numbers

There is considerable variation in *Isoetes* as to the reported chromosome number and size. In one instance the chromosome number is $n = 10$, and the chromosomes are very small (1 micron, or less, in length), similar to the genus *Selaginella*. In other species the chromosomes may be 7-8 microns long, and the number may be from 54 to 56 (Dunlop, 1949; Manton, 1950).

Gametophytes

Germination of spores may occur immediately after they are shed from the sporangium, but generally it does not take place until winter, in warm-climate species, or the following spring, in species from colder climates, after decay of the sporophylls. The gametophytes, as in *Selagi-*

nella, are endosporic. The microgametophyte is retained entirely within
the spore wall, though a portion of the megagametophyte may be exposed.

Microgametophyte Development

The first division of the microspore forms a small prothallial cell, and
a large cell that is interpreted as an antheridial initial. By several divisions
the antheridial initial is subdivided into a layer of jacket cells and a total
of four spermatogenous cells (the actual sperm-mother cells, in this
case). After a developmental period of about two weeks, the spore wall
cracks along the flat surface. The jacket cells and prothallial cell degenerate, and four multiflagellate sperms, derived from the metamorphosed
contents of the sperm-mother cells, are liberated (Liebig, 1931). The
general scheme of development is comparable to that in *Selaginella*
(Fig. 8-15). The possession of sperms with many flagella contrasts strikingly with the biflagellate condition of the sperms of other genera
(*Lycopodium* and *Selaginella*) of the Lycopsida.

Megagametophyte Development

A mature megaspore contains a considerable amount of stored food
surrounded by a spore wall of at least three layers. The primary nucleus
is quite large and may be at the base or apex (toward the triradiate ridge)
(Campbell, 1891; LaMotte, 1933). A period of free nuclear division
ensues until about fifty free nuclei are distributed around the periphery
of the protoplast. Wall formation then takes place rapidly around nuclei
at the apex, proceeding basipetally and centripetally at a slower rate.
Stored material is prominent in the basal end of the developing megagametophyte. No large central vacuole, as in *Selaginella,* is ever present.
The megagametophyte may not become entirely cellular until the embryo is quite advanced in development (LaMotte, 1933). With an
increase in volume of the megagametophyte, the megaspore wall breaks
along the triradiate ridge (Fig. 8-24). The first archegonium appears at
the apex (Liebig, 1931), and at maturity consists of four tiers of neck
cells, a neck canal cell, a ventral canal cell, and an egg cell. If fertilization
does not occur, many more archegonia may be formed among rhizoids
that extend above the surface of the gametophyte (LaMotte, 1933).

Figure 8-24 Megagametophytes of *Isoetes howellii* protruding through cracked spore walls. In each case, the megaspore wall was ruptured along the tri-radiate ridge, and three portions of the wall are visible. The dark areas are archegonia, and one tier of four neck cells is apparent in an archegonium of the gametophyte to the left.

The Embryo

After fertilization, the first division of the zygote is transverse or oblique to the long axis of the archegonium (Fig. 8-25, A). The embryo becomes globose, and in some instances quadrants (Fig. 8-25, B) are recognizable (Campbell, 1891, 1940; LaMotte, 1937). The upper half (hypobasal) of the embryo (toward the neck of the archegonium) gives rise to the foot and root, and the lower half (epibasal) produces the first leaf and shoot apex. The embryo is thus endoscopic by definition, but it will be noted that no suspensor is formed as in *Lycopodium* and *Selaginella*. Interpretation of subsequent embryo development is indeed difficult, though the following description may represent a reasonably accurate account of development (LaMotte, 1933, 1937).

That portion of the embryo which will become the foot grows downward obliquely and into the storage tissue of the megagametophyte. At the same time, that portion of the embryo which will produce the first leaf and shoot apex grows laterally or perpendicular to the long axis of the archegonium. The primary root grows in the same plane but in the direction opposite from the leaf. Reorientation of the embryo is thereby

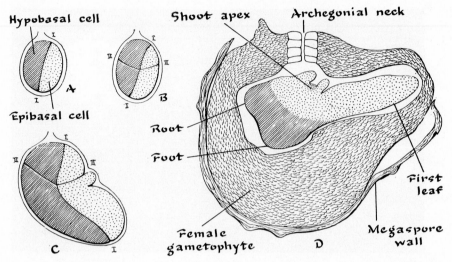

Figure 8-25 Early cleavages and subsequent growth of the embryo in *Isoetes lithophila.* **A**, the first cleavage (*I-I*) in this species is usually as shown, only rarely being at right angles to the neck of the archegonium; **B**, quadrant stage; **C-D**, later stages, each segment being multicellular, but not indicated by cells. More rapid growth occurs in the lower two quadrants, resulting in an apparent rotation of the embryo. [Redrawn from La Motte, *Ann. Bot. N.S.* 1:695, 1937; *Amer. Jour. Bot.* 20:217, 1933.]

achieved (Fig. 8-25, C, D). With further development the first leaf of the sporophyte breaks through the gametophytic sheath; the root emerges and turns downward. The young sporophyte may become firmly established on the substrate, but it remains attached for some time to the gametophyte and surrounding megaspore wall.

Pleuromeiales

The representative member of this order is the Triassic genus *Pleuromeia.* The plant body consisted of an erect, unbranched stem about 1 meter in height and 10 cm in diameter. The stem axis terminated in a strobilus composed of closely overlapping sporophylls with apparently adaxial sporangia (Emberger, 1944). Spirally arranged vegetative leaves occurred beneath the strobilus. A very remarkable structural feature of the genus was the enlargement of the stem base. This basal part was divided commonly into four or eight stigmarian-like lobes (a lobed rhizophore) upon which roots were produced in an orderly fashion.

Understandably comparisons between the root-bearing regions of *Stigmaria*, *Pleuromeia*, and *Isoetes* have been made. It is quite likely that in *Pleuromeia* roots were produced in the same way as they are in *Isoetes*. Anatomically the roots of *Pleuromeia* were of the stigmarian type (large central cavity and eccentrically placed vascular cylinder), a characteristic feature of *Isoetes* today. On the basis of root structure alone, some paleobotanists are convinced of the phylogenetic relationship between the lepidodendrids, *Pleuromeia*, and *Isoetes*. They further visualize the *Isoetes* plant body as a *Pleuromeia* type in miniature, brought about by telescoping of the entire axis. An opposed view is that *Isoetes* has come from a smaller, more herbaceous plant. Plants with all the features of a modern *Isoetes*, and of Lower Cretaceous age, have been found in Portugal and given the generic name *Isoetites*.

Summary and Conclusions

The subdivision Lycopsida includes a wide range of extinct and living forms, the study and comparison of which have shed important light on the morphology and evolutionary trends in primitive vascular plants. The morphological unity of the Lycopsida as a whole is remarkable, and the definitive characters of this subdivision are as follows: (1) the basic pattern of branching is dichotomous; (2) the leaves are typical microphylls, each of which is traversed by a single unbranched vein; (3) the primary xylem is predominantly exarch, the vascular system in the stem is commonly protostelic, and leaf gaps are absent; (4) in all lycopsid plants (extinct or living), a *solitary adaxial sporangium* (eusporangiate in type) is associated with each sporophyll, and is either situated in the axil of the sporophyll or attached adaxially to its basal region.

During the Carboniferous period certain members of the Lycopsida were very large tree-like plants, some of which (e.g., *Lepidodendron*) are believed to have attained a height of 100 feet or more. These giant lycopods exhibited pronounced secondary growth, and their reconstruction has involved the study and synthesis of the fossil remains of trunks, leaves, root-like organs, and strobili. Many of these fossilized structures were at first described as separate "form genera," but subsequently were recognized as portions of one main type of plant now designated as *Lepidodendron*. Other Paleozoic lycopods were apparently relatively small herbaceous plants which resembled rather closely certain living members of the Lycopsida (e.g., *Lycopodium* and *Selaginella*). The comparative morphology of extinct representatives of the Lycopsida has been briefly discussed at appropriate points in this chapter under the orders Lycopodiales, Lepidodendrales, and Pleuromeiales.

The living members of the Lycopsida are worldwide in distribution, and are represented by four genera of comparatively small herbaceous plants: *Phylloglossum* (one species), *Lycopodium* (about 200 species), *Selaginella* (the largest genus with 600-700 described species), and *Isoetes* (over 60 species). Two of these genera, *Phylloglossum* and *Lyco-podium*, are homosporous, with leaves and sporophylls devoid of ligules —they are classified under the family Lycopodiaceae. *Selaginella* and *Isoetes*, in contrast, are heterosporous and ligulate, but differ sufficiently in other characters to justify their segregation into the orders Selagi-nellales and Isoetales, respectively. The salient morphological features of living lycopsids may be conveniently summarized and compared under the following topics:

1. Organography. In marked contrast with the Psilopsida, all living lycopsids form roots which arise and develop in various ways. *Isoetes* is exceptional because a well-defined root system is produced from the basal end of the thick, fleshy corm. In *Selaginella* highly distinctive rhizophores, (stem-like structures which arise at the points of branching of the shoot) produce roots when their tips contact the substratum. The roots of *Lycopodium* arise endogenously within the stems and often traverse the cortex vertically for some distance before emerging into the soil or substrate.

The microphyllous leaves of living lycopsids vary considerably in form and size. In *Phylloglossum* the fleshy tuber-like stem bears a cluster of narrow leaves, whereas the leaves of *Lycopodium* and *Selaginella* are small, scale-like appendages. *Isoetes* develops larger quill-like leaves con-sisting of a basal sheath and a cylindrical or angled lamina; each leaf in *Isoetes* is potentially fertile and bears a large solitary adaxial sporangium near its base.

The pattern of branching of the shoot is fundamentally dichotomous in *Selaginella* and *Lycopodium*, but in each genus asymmetrical develop-ment may result in a pseudomonopodial system. In contrast, *Phylloglos-*

sum and *Isoetes* are typically unbranched; occasional specimens of *Isoetes*, however, may be dichotomously forked.

2. Vascular Anatomy of the Stem. The vascular system in the short axis of *Phylloglossum* is a siphonostele with mesarch xylem; in the other genera, despite considerable variation in stelar type, the primary xylem is *exarch*. The structure of the stele in *Lycopodium* ranges from an actinostele (characteristic of the young stem of most species) to elaborate types of vascular cylinders in which the primary phloem and primary xylem occur as alternating interconnected strips (plectostele), or else the strands of xylem develop as a mesh-like mass with included groups of phloem. Stelar morphology within the species of *Selaginella* is likewise extremely variable; the vascular system may be protostelic or siphonostelic, or in some species a series of concentric meristeles may be formed. Unlike other genera in the Lycopsida, certain species of *Selaginella* develop vessels in the primary xylem. The primary vascular system of the corm of *Isoetes* is interpreted as a protostele, and its detailed form and structure have been discussed in this chapter. One of the many remarkable characters distinguishing *Isoetes* from other living lycopsids is the development of a cambium. This meristem arises just outside the cylinder of primary phloem, and from it are derived externally the parenchyma constituting the so-called secondary cortex and internally the peculiar prismatic layer. The latter may consist of tracheids, and/or sieve cells and parenchyma, and constitutes a tissue of debatable nature, the varied interpretations of which have been briefly considered.

3. Sporangia. As previously noted, the sporangium of the Lycopsida is eusporangiate in type and occurs in an adaxial position with reference to the subtending leaf or sporophyll. In *Isoetes* each leaf of the sporophyte is potentially a sporophyll, and a distinct strobilus is not formed. On the contrary, *Phylloglossum*, *Selaginella*, and most species of *Lycopodium* produce strobili within which the sporangia occur. *Phylloglossum* and *Lycopodium* are homosporous, and each functional sporangium produces a relatively large number of tetrahedral spores. In the two heterosporous genera, *Selaginella* and *Isoetes*, the early stages in development of the microsporangium (which forms numerous microspores) and the megasporangium (which forms fewer megaspores—commonly only four in each megasporangium of *Selaginella*) are entirely similar.

But as development continues in a microsporangium a large portion of the sporocytes undergo meiosis and produce spore-tetrads. In contrast, the further development of a megasporangium in *Selaginella* is characterized by the abortion of all but one sporocyte which divides meiotically to form a single tetrad of large megaspores. The ontogeny of the megasporangium in *Isoetes* is comparable except for the survival of a larger number of functional megasporocytes. The sporangia of *Isoetes* are extremely large, and are structurally distinguished from the sporangia of the other three genera by the development of sterile plates of tissue (trabeculae) which traverse but do not completely separate the mass of spores into compartments.

4. Gametophytes. The exosporic monoecious gametophytes in *Lycopodium* vary, according to the species, as to growth habit. Some may be wholly subterranean and devoid of chlorophyll, others are partially exposed with green aerial branches. In species with subterranean gametophytes an endophytic fungus enters the young gametophyte and becomes localized to certain regions of the mature thallus. Apparently the presence of such a fungus is essential to the normal development of the gametophyte in nature, although recently it has been possible to germinate and to grow gametophytes which, under sterile conditions in culture, formed sex organs. The subterranean types of gametophytes vary widely in form; some are conical, others are discoid with a convoluted or corrugated surface. Normal gametophytes produce abundant archegonia and antheridia and are apparently long-lived. The gametophytes of *Selaginella* and *Isoetes* are highly reduced and essentially endosporic structures. The male gametophyte in these two genera consists of only a few cells, namely, a prothallial cell, a sterile cellular layer, and the spermatogenous tissue. Each male gametophyte in *Selaginella* forms 128-256 sperms, whereas in *Isoetes* only four sperms are formed. The female gametophytes in *Selaginella* and *Isoetes* are more robust and begin development by a process of free nuclear divisions within the megaspores. This is followed by wall formation and the initiation of archegonia from certain of the surface cells of the apical region of the megagametophyte. The megaspore wall ruptures along the triradiate ridge, exposing the female gametophyte and thus facilitating the fertilization of one or more of the archegonia by the sperms. In both *Lycopodium* and *Selaginella*

the mature sperms are biflagellate, and in *Isoetes* the male gametes are multiflagellate.

The polarity of the embryo in *Lycopodium, Selaginella,* and *Isoetes* is endoscopic, although the manner of subsequent growth of the embryo in *Isoetes* results in a re-orientation of parts such that the shoot apex faces upward and the foot lies adjacent to the storage tissue of the megagametophyte. A suspensor is present in the embryos of *Lycopodium* and *Selaginella* but is lacking in the embryo of *Isoetes*.

References

Andrews, H. N. 1947. *Ancient Plants and the World they Lived in.* Comstock Publishing Co., New York.

Arnold, C. A. 1947. *An Introduction to Paleobotany.* McGraw-Hill, New York.

Barclay, B. D. 1931. Origin and development of tissues in stem of *Selaginella Wildenovii. Bot. Gaz.* 91: 452-461.

Blackwood, M. 1953. Chromosomes of *Phylloglossum drummondii. Nature.* 172:591-592.

Bower, F. O. 1935. *Primitive Land Plants.* Macmillan, London.

Bruchmann, H. 1909a. Von den Vegetationsorganen der *Selaginella Lyallii,* Spring. *Flora* 99:436-464.

———. 1909b. Von der Chemotaxis der *Lycopodium*—Spermatozoiden. *Flora* 99: 193-202.

———. 1910. Die Keimung der Sporen und die Entwicklung der Prothallien von *Lycopodium clavatum* L., *L. annotinum* L. und *L. Selago* L. *Flora* 101:220-267.

———. 1912. Zur Embryologie der Selaginellaceen. *Flora* 104:180-224.

Campbell, D. H. 1891. Contributions to the life-history of *Isoetes. Ann. Bot.* 5:231-258.

———. 1902. Studies on the gametophytes of *Selaginella. Ann. Bot.* 16: 419-428.

———. 1940. *The Evolution of the Land Plants (Embryophyta).* Stanford University Press, Stanford, California.

Case, I. M. 1943. Periodicity in the development of fertile and sterile zones in *Lycopodium Selago. New Phytol.* 42:93-97.

Chamberlain, C. J. 1917. Prothallia and sporelings of three New Zealand species of *Lycopodium. Bot. Gaz.* 63: 51-65.

Cusick, F. 1954. Experimental and analytical studies of Pteridophytes XXV. Morphogenesis in *Selaginella Willdenovii.* II. Angle-meristems and angle-shoots. *Ann. Bot. N. S.* 18: 171-181.

Darrah, W. C. 1939. *Textbook of Paleobotany.* Appleton-Century, New York.

Duerden, H. 1929. Variations in megaspore number in *Selaginella. Ann. Bot.* 43:451-457.

———. 1934. On the occurrence of vessels in *Selaginella. Ann. Bot.* 48: 459-465.

Dunlop, D. W. 1949. Notes on the cytology of some Lycopsids. *Bull. Torrey Bot. Club* 76:266-277.

Duthie, A. V. 1929. The method of spore dispersal of three South African species of *Isoetes. Ann. Bot.* 43:411-412.

Eames, A. J. 1942. Illustrations of some *Lycopodium* gametophytes. *Amer. Fern Jour.* 32:1-12.

Emberger, L. 1944. *Les plantes fossiles dans leurs rapports avec les végétaux vivants.* Masson et Cie., Paris.

Esau, K., V. I. Cheadle, and E. M. Gifford, Jr. 1953. Comparative structure and possible trends of specialization of the phloem. *Amer. Jour. Bot.* 40:9-19.

Farmer, J. B. 1890. On *Isoetes lacustris,* L. *Ann. Bot.* 5:37-62.

Goebel, K. 1930. *Organographie der Pflanzen. Dritte Auflage. Zweiter Teil.* G. Fischer, Jena.

Härtel, K. 1938. Studien an Vegetationspunkten einheimischer Lycopodien. *Beiträge zur Biol. der Pflanzen.* 25:125-168.

Harvey-Gibson, R. J. 1897. Contributions towards a knowledge of the anatomy of the genus *Selaginella,* Spr. III. The leaf. *Ann. Bot.* 11:123-155.

Hill, J. B. 1914. The anatomy of six epiphytic species of *Lycopodium. Bot. Gaz.* 58:61-85.

———. 1919. Anatomy of *Lycopodium reflexum. Bot. Gaz.* 68:226-231.

Hofmann, E. 1934. *Paläohistologie der Pflanze.* J. Springer, Wien.

Holloway, J. E. 1909. A comparative study of the anatomy of six New Zealand species of *Lycopodium. Trans. New Zealand Inst.* 42:356-370.

Hsü, J. 1937. Anatomy, development and life history of *Selaginella sinensis.* I. Anatomy and development of the shoot. *Bull. Chinese Bot. Soc.* 3:75-95.

Jones, C. E. 1905. The morphology and anatomy of the stem of the genus *Lycopodium. Trans. Linn. Soc. London* Ser. 2. 7:15-35.

Koster, H. 1941. New *Lycopodium* gametophytes from New Jersey. *Amer. Fern Jour.* 31:53-58.

Kräusel, R. and H. Weyland. 1932. Pflanzenreste aus dem Devon. IV. *Protolepidodendron. Senckenbergiana* 14:391-403.

LaMotte, C. 1933. Morphology of the megagametophyte and the embryo sporophyte of *Isoetes lithophila*. *Amer. Jour. Bot.* 20:217-233.

———. 1937. Morphology and orientation of the embryo of *Isoetes*. *Ann. Bot. N. S.* 1:695-716.

Lang, W. H. 1915a. III. Studies in the morphology of *Isoetes*. I. The general morphology of the stock of *Isoetes lacustris*. *Mem. Proc. Manchester Lit. Phil. Soc.* 59:1-28.

———. 1915b. III. Studies in the morphology of *Isoetes*. II. The analysis of the stele of the shoot of *Isoetes lacustris* in the light of mature structure and apical development. *Mem. Proc. Manchester Lit. Phil. Soc.* 59: 29-67.

Liebig, J. 1931. Ergänzungen zur Entwicklungsgeschichte von *Isoëtes lacustre* L. *Flora* 125:321-358.

Lyon, F. M. 1901. A study of the sporangia and gametophytes of *Selaginella apus* and *Selaginella rupestris*. *Bot. Gaz.* 32:124-141; 170-196.

Ma, R. M. 1930. The chloroplasts of *Selaginella*. *Bull. Torrey Bot. Club* 57:277-284.

Manton, I. 1950. *Problems of Cytology and Evolution in the Pteridophyta*. Cambridge University Press, London.

Mitchell, G. 1910. Contributions toward a knowledge of the anatomy of the genus *Selaginella* Spr. V. The strobilus. *Ann. Bot.* 24:19-33.

Ogura, Y. 1938. Anatomie der Vegetationsorgane der Pteridophyten. *Hand-buch der Pflanzenanatomie*. Gebrüder Borntraeger, Berlin.

Osborn, T. G. B. 1922. Some observations on *Isoetes Drummondii*, A. Br. *Ann. Bot.* 36:41-54.

Pfeiffer, N. E. 1922. Monograph of the Isoetaceae. *Ann. Mo. Bot. Garden.* 9:79-232.

Pieniązek, S. Al. 1938. Über die Entwicklung und das Wachstum der Makrosporenmembranen bei *Selaginella*. *Sprawozdania Towarzystwa Nauk. Warszawskiego Wydziat 4 (Compt. Rend. Soc. Sci. Varsovie Cl. 4)* 31:211-230.

Roberts, E. A. and Herty, S. D. 1934. *Lycopodium complanatum* var. *flabelliforme* Fernald: its anatomy and a method of vegetative propagation. *Amer. Jour. Bot.* 21:688-697.

Scott, D. H. and T. G. Hill. 1900. The structure of *Isoetes Hystrix*. *Ann. Bot.* 14:413-454.

Slagg, R. A. 1932. The gametophytes of *Selaginella Kraussiana*. I. The microgametophyte. *Amer. Jour. Bot.* 19: 106-127.

Smith, R. W. 1900. The structure and development of the sporophylls and sporangia of *Isoetes*. *Bot. Gaz.* 29: 225-258; 323-346.

Sosa, A. and C. Sosa-Bourdouil. 1940. Sur la composition des macrospores et des microspores de *Selaginella*. *Compt. Rend. Acad. Sci., Paris.* 210: 59-61.

Spessard, E. A. 1922. Prothallia of *Lycopodium* in America. II. *L. luci-*

dulum and *L. obscurum* var. *dendroi-deum*. *Bot. Gaz.* 74:392-413.

Stewart, W. N. 1947. A comparative study of stigmarian appendages and *Isoetes* roots. *Amer. Jour. Bot.* 34: 315-324.

Stokey, A. G. 1907. The roots of *Lycopodium pithyoides*. *Bot. Gaz.* 44:57-63.

————. 1909. The anatomy of *Isoetes*. *Bot. Gaz.* 47:311-335.

Sykes, M. G. 1908. Notes on the morphology of the sporangium-bearing organs of the Lycopodiaceae. *New Phytol.* 7:41-60.

———— and W. Stiles. 1910. The cones of the genus *Selaginella*. *Ann. Bot.* 24:523-536.

Treub, M. 1884. Études sur les Lycopodiacées. *Ann. Jard. Bot. Buitenzorg.* 4:107-138.

Tryon, A. F. 1949. Spores of the genus *Selaginella* in North America north of Mexico. *Ann. Mo. Bot. Gard.* 36: 413-431.

Turner, J. J. 1924. Origin and development of vascular system of *Lycopodium lucidulum*. *Bot. Gaz.* 78:215-225.

Wardlaw, C. W. 1924. Size in relation to internal morphology. No. 1. Distri-bution of the xylem in the vascular system of *Psilotum*, *Tmesipteris*, and *Lycopodium*. *Trans. Roy. Soc. Edin.* 53:503-532.

Weber, U. 1922. Zur Anatomie und Systematik der Gattung *Isoëtes*. *Hedwigia.* 63:219-262.

West, C. and H. Takeda. 1915. X. On *Isoëtes japonica*. *Trans. Linnean Soc. London.* 8:333-376.

Wetmore, R. H. 1943. Leaf stem relationships in the vascular plants. *Torreya.* 43:16-28.

———— and G. Morel. 1951a. Sur la culture *in vitro* de prothalles de *Lycopodium cernuum*. *Compt. Rend. Acad. Sci.* 233:323-324.

————. 1951b. Sur la culture du gametophyte de *Selaginelle*. *Compt. Rend. Acad. Sci.* 233:430-431.

Whitebread, C. 1941. Beware of, "*Lycopodium*"! *Amer. Fern Jour.* 31:100-102.

Williams, S. 1931. An analysis of the vegetative organs of *Selaginella grandis* Moore, together with some observations on abnormalities and experimental results. *Trans. Roy. Soc. Edin.* 57:1-24.

————. 1937. Correlation phenomena and hormones in *Selaginella*. *Nature.* 139:966.

Chapter

9 THE SPHENOPSIDA

The Sphenopsida comprises a rather well-defined group of living and extinct plants. Fossil remains are first encountered in strata considered to be of Devonian age. During the Carboniferous the group attained almost worldwide distribution and significant diversity of growth form; a parallel situation, it will be remembered, is encountered in the Lycopsida. During the Carboniferous arborescent and herbaceous sphenopsids were coexistent. By the end of the Triassic only a few representatives remained, and they were relatively small, herbaceous forms. Today only one genus, with about 30 herbaceous species, remains as a remnant of this once conspicuous and diversified group. However, this one genus, *Equisetum*, may itself have been present in the Carboniferous and may not have undergone any significant change in the course of time. If this is so, *Equisetum* may be one of the oldest living genera of vascular plants in the world today.

In characterizing the group, including living and extinct members, the most conspicuous external morphological feature is the subdivision of the sporophyte axis into definite nodes and internodes (Fig. 9-1, B)— that is, the stem is jointed. At the nodes are whorls of relatively small leaves with buds between them. In addition to the stem joints there are definite, easily observed stem ribs. Reproductive structures of the sporophyte are terminal cones or strobili. The strobilus consists of an axis with whorls of stalk-like structures (sporangiophores) to each of which a group of sporangia is attached (Fig. 9-2, A, B).

Classification

The following outline of classification will serve as a possible guide to further descriptions. Only representative orders, families, and genera are included. In conformity with the previous method of presentation, the living member is placed first in the outline and is described in consider-

191

Figure 9-1 **A**, colony of *Equisetum telmateia* growing along roadside embank-
ment, Berkeley, California; **B**, a series of plants arranged to show stages in the
growth and expansion of vegetative shoots. [Courtesy Mr. Louis Arnold.]

able detail later in the text. Descriptions of extinct members are necessarily brief, but their importance in the establishment of morphological unity within the group should not be minimized.

SPHENOPSIDA: Living and extinct plants; sporophyte differentiated into stem, leaf, root and eusporangium; jointed, ribbed stems; buds not on same radii with leaves, but alternate with them; stem protostelic or siphonostelic; xylem exarch or endarch; secondary growth in some forms; sporangia borne on specialized stalks (sporangiophores) which are organized into strobili; largely homosporous with a few reported heterosporous forms (extinct).

EQUISETALES: Living and extinct plants; herbaceous sporophytes, no secondary growth; stem organized into nodes and internodes; siphonostelic and endarch; small microphyllous leaves basally united as a sheath at the node; roots developed from rhizome; sporangia-bearing structures (sporangiophores) organized into strobili. Gametophyte exosporic and green in living members; antheridium produces multiflagellate sperms; the embryo is exoscopic.

EQUISETACEAE: Characteristics as in Equisetales.

Equisetum, Equisetites (extinct).

HYENIALES: Extinct plants of Devonian age; small, shrub-like plants with jointed stems; whorls of short, forked leaves; recurved terminal sporangia grouped into lax strobili.

HYENIACEAE: Characteristics as in Hyeniales.

Hyenia, Calamophyton.

SPHENOPHYLLALES: Extinct plants; small, herbaceous climbing or trailing plants with some secondary growth; exarch protostele in stem; monopodial growth; small, wedge-shaped leaves arranged in whorls at nodes; strobili composed of sterile bracts with axillary sporangiophores; stalked sporangia may be attached to subtending bracts through part of their length.

SPHENOPHYLLACEAE: Characteristics as in Sphenophyllales.

Sphenophyllum (representative of group).

CALAMITALES: Extinct plants; large plants with ribbed stems; endarch siphonostele in stem; considerable secondary growth; relatively small, linear or lanceolate leaves arranged in whorls at nodes; compact strobili consisting of (1) whorls of closely associated sporangiophores and bracts, or (2) alternate whorls of sterile bracts and sporangiophores.

CALAMITACEAE: Characteristics as in Calamitales.

Form genera: *Calamites* (stems), *Annularia* (leaves and small branches), *Calamostachys* (strobili).

Equisetales–Equisetaceae: *Equisetum*

The sporophytes of *Equisetum*, with their characteristic jointed stems and rough texture, have earned several names, of which "horsetails" and "scouring rushes" are most popular. During early American colonial days and undoubtedly in other frontier regions today the scouring rushes were and perhaps are still being used as scouring agents.

The horsetails are worldwide in distribution except for certain parts of Australasia. The majority of species occur in the Northern Hemisphere, with only a few appearing in the tropics and the Southern Hemisphere.

They generally grow in wet or damp habitats, being particularly common along the banks of streams or irrigation ditches (Fig. 9-1, A); some grow in well-drained areas. In some localities they have become a serious weed, and measures must be taken to eliminate or control them. Some have become adapted to dry or mesophytic conditions, for at least a part of the year.

Certain species have been used as indicators of the mineral content of the soil in which they grow (Vogt, 1942). These plants accumulate minerals in their bodies (including gold—up to 4½ oz per ton—Benedict, 1941), and the mineral content can be determined by either chemical or x-ray analysis of the plant tissues. This source of mineral information is therefore of some value in prospecting for new ore deposits, a most important activity in the present world struggle for resources.

Organography

The shoot system of a plant consists of an aerial portion and an underground rhizome portion. The sporophyte is perennial, at least in the sense that the rhizome is perennial, even though the aerial system may die back each fall or winter. In the north temperate regions new aerial shoots are formed each year. Some species are small, particularly those of arctic and alpine regions. One such species occurs within the Arctic Circle in Europe, in Siberia, and in America. Several species are tall in growth form and occur in South America; they are supported partly by surrounding tall grass.

To reiterate, the shoot system of *Equisetum* consists of an underground rhizome and an aerial shoot, each system possessing the same fundamental organization. The stem is divided into definite nodes and internodes, and leaves are attached at nodes, united at least for a part of their length, forming a sheath around the stem (Fig. 9-2, A). The number of leaves per node varies according to species, although the number may fluctuate in a given species. Sporophyte size also seems to have a definite influence on the number of leaves formed at a node. The internodes of the stem are ribbed, and the number of leaves at a node corresponds to the number of ribs on the internode below. Each rib corresponds to a main vascular bundle, the upper part of which is a leaf trace. An internode may continue to grow for some time through the activity of a meristem located at its base. Lateral branches, when evident, are attached at the nodes and are alternate with the leaves. During development each branch breaks through the lower part of the leaf sheath in reaching the exterior. Roots arise at the nodes of the rhizome. Endogenous lateral roots may be formed on main roots. Whether a species is highly branched or not, branch and root primordia are formed at each node. In the rhizome a root primordium develops into a root, whereas a branch primordium may develop into an erect

Figure 9-2 **A,** fertile shoots of *Equisetum telmateia* (the strobili are at different stages of maturity, the youngest is to the left); **B,** median longisection of one sporangiophore showing the vascular bundle in the stalk and its mode of branching (crowded spores with elaters are evident in the sporangia).

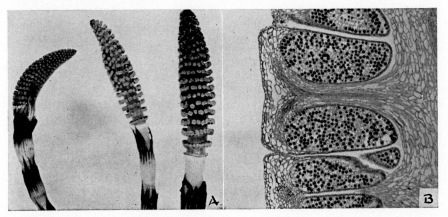

aerial shoot, remain as an arrested bud, develop into a new rhizome, or become abortive. In aerial shoots (if branching is a characteristic of the species) the branch primordia develop while the roots remain in an arrested condition unless the stems become procumbent and come to lie on a moist surface. Use can be made of this information in vegetative propagation. A plant may be propagated vegetatively also from arrested tuberous-like branches which occur at the nodes of rhizomes.

The rhizome, and the aerial stem, can be pulled apart into internodal lengths or "pipes." In one interesting study (Treitel, 1943) it was found that before a rhizome actually breaks under tension its elasticity compares favorably with that of muscle or rubber.

Abnormal growths or monstrosities (teratological forms) are always of interest, and large stands of *Equisetum* generally provide many examples. Certain shoots may have unusually short internodes, the internodal potentiality never having been realized. Other shoots may: have flexuous (snake-like) stems, have continuous spiral leaf sheaths, exhibit dichotomous branching or produce a vegetative shoot beyond the usual terminal cone (Schaffner, 1933). All of these abnormalities undoubtedly are the result of an unbalanced growth-regulating system.

Strobili may occur terminally on many of the main vegetative axes of a highly branched species, but more often a single strobilus terminates the main axis, whether or not the plant is branched (Fig. 9-2, A). Branching in a typically unbranched plant may be induced through injury of the main axis. In a few species there is a segregation of function: some shoots are green and purely vegetative, and others are unbranched and brownish in color and have terminal strobili (e.g., *E. arvense*). Still other species, in addition to having purely vegetative shoots, produce brownish, fertile shoots which may develop chlorophyll after the spores are shed; green branches then grow out from the nodes of the stem.

On the basis of external morphology alone, the evolutionary tendencies in the genus seem to be the following: The more primitive species have perennial, green shoots that are highly branched with green, pointed cones terminating several branches of the same shoot. The most advanced species have annual, branched aerial vegetative shoots that are green and have short-lived, unbranched fertile shoots which lack chlorophyll. Cones are rounded at the tip and are brownish. Naturally there are many species that show intermediate combinations of these characteristics (Schaffner, 1930). The more advanced species occur in the Northern Hemisphere and arctic regions, whereas the more primitive grow in South America, Cuba, and Mexico. In the words of Schaffner (1932), an authority on the genus *Equisetum,* "one immediately sees that the lowest [most primitive] species can be collected as one stands on the equator, while the last and highest species [most advanced] can be gathered for a farewell bouquet as one steps from the farthest northern lands onto the ice of the Arctic Ocean."

Anatomy of the Mature Shoot

The stem of *Equisetum,* as seen in transverse section, is circular in outline with prominent ribs. In the majority of species the cell walls of the epidermis are thick and have a generous deposition of siliceous material. Over the epidermis is a definite cuticle. Stomata often occur in two vertical rows in the regions between the ribs. The stomatal apparatus, which may be in a depression, consists of two guard cells and overarching subsidiary cells. Beneath the epidermis is the cortex, which exhibits a rather complicated structure. The outer cortex is composed of sclerenchymatous tissue, which, in some species, is excessively developed opposite the ribs. Between adjacent ribs there occurs lacunate photosynthetic tissue with a single, large vertical air space (vallecular canal).

Opposite each ridge or rib is a collateral vascular bundle of unusual interest. A transverse section of a mature stem reveals a protoxylem lacuna (carinal canal) associated with each bundle (Fig. 9-3). Frequently one or more stretched protoxylem elements may be attached to one side of the cavity. Differentiated tracheids of the metaxylem occur in two radial files. During development the radial differentiation of primary xylem is endarch (Eames, 1909; Johnson, 1933). Primary phloem is present between the two strands of metaxylem, toward the periphery of the bundle. The remainder of the vascular strand is parenchyma (Fig. 9-3, B).

Depending on the species, one endodermal layer may be present external to the cylinder of vascular bundles, or there may be, in addition, an inner endodermis; in the latter instance the outer endodermis may be

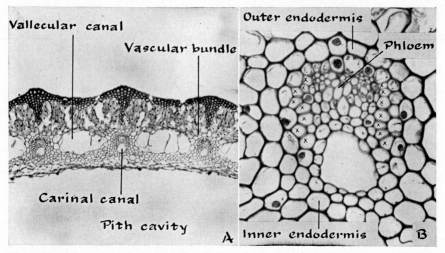

Figure 9-3 Stem anatomy in *Equisetum hyemale*. **A**, transection, portion of stem (note that carinal canals are opposite ridges on stem); **B**, structure of vascular bundle (one protoxylem tracheid is visible along edge of carinal canal at right; metaxylem tracheids are designated X).

irregular in outline. Or, in certain species, an endodermis may completely surround each vascular bundle. A pericycle may or may not be evident. Sometimes the pericycle cells are filled with starch. The vascular cylinder of *Equisetum* has been described as an ectophloic siphonostele of the "*Equisetum* type."

The stem nodes are unusual in that the metaxylem is extensively developed such that there is a conspicuous circular plate of xylem. Carinal and vallecular canals are absent. In addition, a nodal plate of pith tissue separates one internode from another.

The system of vascular bundle connections will be discussed in the following section on shoot development.

The tips of underground rhizomes are covered by scale-like leaf sheaths which may secrete mucilage from their abaxial epidermal cells. Trichomes may also be present on the adaxial side of the sheaths (Francini, 1942). Sclerenchyma occurs in the outer cortex. Vallecular canals and protoxylem lacunae are present. A definite endodermis around each vascular bundle is a common condition. There is often no agreement as to the arrangement and number of endodermal layers (as seen in transverse section) in the aerial stem and rhizome of the same plant.

Development of the Shoot

A large, four-sided inverted pyramidal cell with the rounded base uppermost occupies the apex of the apical meristem (Fig. 9-4). The so-called cutting surfaces are directed downward. The apical cell cuts off daughter cells in a continuous successive manner; each daughter cell

Figure 9-4 Longisection of shoot apex of *Equisetum sp.* showing conspicuous apical cell and its derivative tissues. The pith originates from inner cells derived from periclinally dividing surface cells. Leaf primordia arise from surface initials.

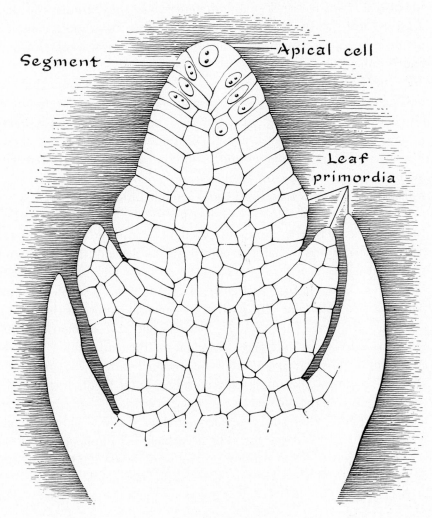

or segment divides anticlinally to form two cells (segment cells). By tangential (periclinal) divisions in segment cells at their innermost ends, a pith meristem is formed. By further divisions (in various planes) of the segment cells, a definable circular bulge is formed below the shoot apex. This bulge consists of five or six layers of cells, the upper two of which produce the future node and leaves; the lower layers will form cortical tissues of the internode.

Very early in development, leaf sheath initials can be distinguished as certain regularly placed cells of the upper two layers of the bulge. A leaf tooth then grows in length and widens at its base, eventually becoming fused to varying degrees with adjacent leaves, thus forming the characteristic leaf sheath (Fig. 9-2, A; also Fig. 9-4). For a more complete discussion of apical growth the student is referred to the work of Golub and Wetmore (1948a).

At the time leaf initials are apparent, procambial cells become differentiated in the nodal and internodal regions near the pith. The results of one study (Golub and Wetmore, 1948b) indicate that the procambium, in one species at least, is acropetally continuous throughout the shoot. External to the procambium, and in internodal regions, an intercalary meristem gives rise, by oriented transverse divisions, to tissues that will differentiate into epidermis, cortex, endodermis, and pericycle.

Equisetum is a favorable plant for descriptive, histogenetic studies. In an investigation on the apical meristem of *E. hyemale* Sinnott (1943) has emphasized that "what a given cell will do depends not upon some general principle of division, common to all cells, but upon the conditions which exist at that particular place and time," (related to the position of the cell in the organized developmental pattern of the plant). On the other hand, Taylor (1939) has described the embryo of *Equisetum* as exhibiting the general principle of the partitioning of cells. According to this concept, the laws of minimal surface and maximum stability are observed in meristematic cells. Sinnott points to the violation of this rule in the division of a segment (cell) in the apical meristem of *Equisetum*. Each segment divides anticlinally, but it should divide periclinally if minimal surface is to be achieved. Morphogenesis is, as yet, little understood, but *Equisetum* and similarly favorable forms provide research tools for both descriptive and experimental studies.

Vascularization

There is considerable controversy regarding the vertical direction of differentiation of primary xylem and phloem (Gwynne-Vaughan, 1901; Queva, 1907; Meyer, 1919; Barratt, 1920; Browne, 1922; Johnson, 1933). From a study of *E. arvense* Golub and Wetmore (1948b) have concluded that differentiation of protoxylem and protophloem within a procambial strand begins at about the fourth node. Differentiation then proceeds acropetally into the developing leaf and basipetally into the internode below. With elongation of the internode the protoxylem and protophloem elements become stretched and torn because the meristem (intercalary meristem) located at the base of each internode does not contribute new cells to the procambial strand. It is during this period of rapid elongation that protoxylem lacunae (carinal canals) are formed. After considerable elongation of an internode, metaxylem and metaphloem differentiation proceeds basipetally from a node through the internode below, and continuity is finally achieved with the same tissues in the node below.

During internodal elongation certain cortical cells do not accommodate themselves to this rapid extension, and they separate from each other, which results in the formation of vallecular canals. The pith cavity is reported to be formed by mechanical tearing of cells (Golub and Wetmore, 1948b).

In following a vascular bundle up through an internode it is found that at the level of leaf attachment a trichotomy of the strand occurs. The median bundle enters the scale leaf, the two laterals diverge right and left, and each is joined laterally with an adjacent strand to form one of the vascular bundles of the next higher internode. As stated before, considerable metaxylem and metaphloem are formed within each bundle at the nodes, resulting in a continuous cylinder of primary vascular tissue.

At this point it is advisable to describe lateral branch development because branches occur at nodes on radii alternating with those of the leaves. At about the sixth node from the shoot tip initiation of a lateral branch is in a single surface mother cell. An apical cell is soon established, and a branch bud with whorled leaves is formed. At about the time the first or second whorl of leaves is formed, a large deep-staining cell becomes apparent near the basal end of each branch. This endogenous cell is a root initial. The vascular tissue at the base of the branch shoot is in the form of a continuous cylinder (siphonostele) and is in continuity with the metaxylem and metaphloem of the nodal region. There is tissue continuity between the pith of the parent axis and the pith of the branch axis. These interruptions in the vascular tissue at the nodes then constitute branch gaps (Jeffrey, 1899). *Equisetum* is cladosiphonic (Chapter 3).

As mentioned earlier, the leaves at each node are united to varying degrees. The thick-walled cells of the abaxial epidermis have various types of ornamentation on their outer tangential walls. Stomata are arranged in longitudinal rows. Internally the mesophyll is lacunate and is traversed by a small collateral bundle. Mesarch xylem has been reported by several workers.

One interesting feature of the *Equisetum* leaf is the presence of specialized "water stomata" (hydathodes) on the adaxial surface of the leaf along the midrib region (Johnson, 1937). *Equisetum* is a convenient plant for demonstrating the secretion of water as it is associated with the conditions of high moisture around the roots and a saturated atmosphere.

The Root

Similar to the type of ontogeny displayed by members of the Lycopsida, the primary root is ephemeral. All other functioning roots in *Equisetum* normally arise at the nodes of underground rhizomes. As seen in transverse section, the mature root has the following organization. The outer cortex is often sclerenchymatous, the inner parenchymatous. The xylem is triarch or tetrarch, or, in the smaller roots, may be diarch. Small roots may have one large metaxylem element in the center of the root (Walton, 1944). The cells of the endodermis and pericycle occur on the same radii, indicating a common origin. Lateral roots have their origin in the pericycle.

The root apical meristem contains an apical cell with four cutting surfaces. To the outside, a root cap is produced. The apical cell produces segments laterally, each of which by two divisions gives rise to three

cells, which in turn produce the vascular tissue, cortex (including endodermis and pericycle), and epidermis (Johnson, 1933).

The Strobilus

Earlier it was noted that a mature strobilus terminates an axis,
whether it be on a vegetative stem or a strictly fertile non-chlorophyllous
axis. The strobilus is composed of an axis with whorls of stalked, peltate
structures termed sporangiophores (Fig. 9-2, A). Each sporangiophore
is umbrella-like in shape, with pendent sporangia (five to ten in number)
attached to the underside of the polygonal, disk-shaped shield (Fig. 9-2,
B; see also Fig. 9-5, A). The flattened tips fit closely together, providing
protection for the sporangia during development. At maturity the cone
axis and sporangiophores shrink, and the sporangia are opened by a
longitudinal cleft that is formed down the inner side of each sporangium. Additional protection during early development is provided by a
rudimentary leaf sheath, the so-called annulus, at the base of the cone.

The vascular cylinder of the cone axis is a network of interconnected

Figure 9-5 Sporangia and spores of *Equisetum*. **A,** a single sporangiophore with
pendant sporangia; **B,** a mature spore (when moist) with coiled elaters; **C,** a
spore (when dry) showing uncoiled elaters.

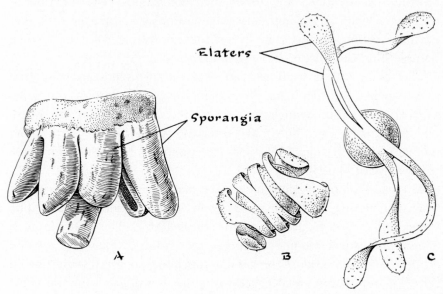

collateral bundles. The vascular cylinder, however, does not reflect a definite organization into nodes and internodes. No large canals are formed as described for the stem. Vascular bundles (sporangiophore traces) diverge from the vascular cylinder at regular intervals and enter the successive whorls of sporangiophores. At the distal end of the sporangiophore the bundle is branched; each strand is recurved and ends near the base of a sporangium (Fig. 9-2, B).

Early in development sporangiophore primordia arise in an acropetal manner on the flanks of the meristematic cone axis. After enlargement of the sporangiophore primordium, sporangia are initiated in single surface cells around the rim of the sporangiophore. The sporangium initial divides periclinally, setting aside an inner and an outer cell. The inner cell, by further divisions in varous planes, produces sporogenous tissue (see Chapter 4, also Fig. 9-6). The outer cell, by anticlinal and periclinal divisions, gives rise to irregular tiers of cells, the inner of which become sporogenous; the outer tiers become the future sporangial wall cells (Bower, 1935). Cells adjacent to the original initials may also contribute to the development of the sporangium (Chapter 4). Before the sporocytes separate and round-off prior to the meiotic divisions, two to three layers of cells adjacent to the sporogenous mass differentiate as the tapetum. In addition, not all of the sporogenous cells function as sporocytes; many degenerate and their protoplasm, together with that of the tapetum, forms a multinucleate nourishing substance which occupies the spaces between the sporocytes.

The results of one study indicate that the first sporangia to mature in a strobilus are sporangia situated in the widest part of the cone. Furthermore, within a single sporangium the sporocytes may be in various stages of meiosis. This may be related to the fact that the spore-mother cells are separated into pockets surrounded by the multinucleate plasma (Manton, 1950).

After the meiotic divisions have taken place the spore tetrads separate from one another, and each spore becomes smooth and spherical. The spore wall is said to be laminated (Beer, 1909). The outer layer is deposited on the spore in the form of four bands, through the activity of the breakdown products of the non-functional sporocytes and tapetal cells. The four bands are attached to the spore wall at a common point and remain tightly coiled around the spore until the sporangium is

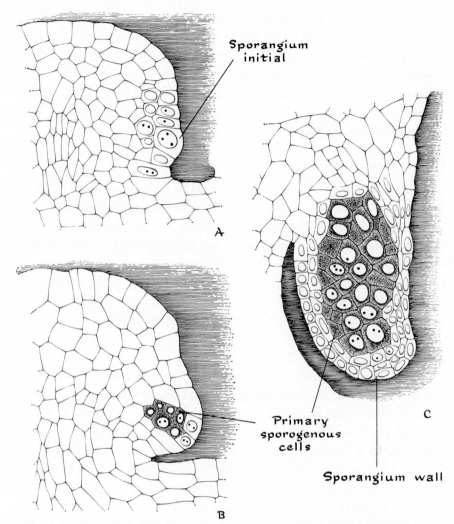

Figure 9-6 A-C, early ontogeny of the sporangium in *Equisetum hyemale.* Initiation occurs in a single surface cell (A), although lateral derivatives of the sporangial initial as well as adjacent surface cells may contribute to the formation of primary sporogenous cells and primary wall cells.

completely mature. The spores are filled with densely packed chloroplasts, a feature quite uncommon to other lower vascular plants.

At maturity a sporangium consists of an outer wall composed of two layers of cells, the inner of which is generally compressed; the cells of the outer layer develop helical thickenings similar to tracheids (Fig.

9-2, B). Internal to the wall is the mass of spores. At the time of dehiscence the free ends of the four bands, or elaters, separate from the spore wall. The elaters are hygroscopic, uncoiling as their water content decreases and recoiling with the addition of moisture (Fig. 9-5, B, C). It has been assumed that through this action the elaters assist in the dehiscence process and also bring about the dispersal of spores in large clumps from the sporangium.

Chromosome Numbers

At this point it is appropriate to discuss the chromosome cycle in *Equisetum*. In certain species that have been studied critically the chromosome number has been determined as approximately $n = 108$. Chromosomes vary in size and shape, but the uniformity of the chromosome number may be indicative of the antiquity and conservativeness of the genus. However, hybridity is suggested in some instances because of peculiarities at meiosis—for instance, lack of chromosome pairing. The spores of such plants are abortive (Manton, 1950).

Gametophyte Generation

Under natural conditions the gametophytic plants may be found growing in damp areas, on mud, along creek banks, and even on the damp floors of abandoned mines and quarries (Matzke, 1941). Mature plants are dull green to brownish, and may range from 1 mm to 1 cm in diameter. In a tropical species (Kashyap, 1914) they may be even as large as 3 cm in diameter and from 2 to 3 mm in height. In some species the plant may be uniform in outline. Viewed from above, it resembles a miniature pin cushion (see Fig. 9-8, D).

The time interval between shedding of spores and germination is quite critical. Spores germinate very readily if they land in a suitable environment; however, the limiting factor seems to be the amount of available water. If the spores do not germinate at once their viability decreases rapidly, and the percentage still capable of germination drops greatly.

The first division of the spore results in two cells unequal in size. The smaller cell, which has fewer chloroplasts, elongates and forms a rhizoid (Fig. 9-7, A, B). The larger cell may divide transversely, or the division may be perpendicular to the original wall. If the developing

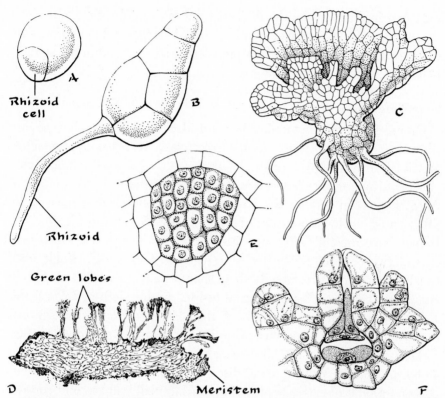

Figure 9-7   A, B, germination of a spore and early development of the gametophyte in *Equisetum hyemale*; **C,** sexually mature gametophyte, *Equisetum
telmateia*; **D,** vertical section of an older gametophyte, *E. telmateia*; **E,**
antheridium as seen in sectional view; **F,** mature archegonium of *E. arvense*
showing two neck canal calls, a ventral canal cell and the egg cell. [C, D, redrawn from Walker, *Bot. Gaz.* 92:1, 1931; F, redrawn from Jeffrey, *Mem.
Boston Soc. Nat. Hist.* 5:155, 1899.]

thallus is growing in water or if the plants are crowded, a filament is
formed with weakly developed branches at the distal end. If the young
plants are widely separated and are terrestrial, divisions in various planes
result in the formation of a dorsiventral, parenchymatous, cushion-like
body attached to the substrate by many rhizoids (Fig. 9-7, C).

Standing upright from the basal portion are irregular branched lobes,
the cells of which contain chloroplasts (Fig. 9-7, D). Chlorophyll is generally lacking in cells of the basal tissue (Walker, 1921). The thallus is

increased in diameter by the derivatives of actively dividing cells along the margins. The derivatives of this marginal meristem differentiate into tissue of the compact base and provide initials for additional upright branches.

Gametangia

On prothallia growing under the most ideal conditions archegonia are formed at about the time the first erect green branches appear. They are situated in the tissue of the basal disc between aerial lobes. Archegonia continue to be produced in derivatives of the marginal meristem. An archegonium follows the common type of ontogeny displayed by other groups of lower vascular plants (Chapter 5; see also Fig. 9-7, F). It may have the following organization: a projecting neck which consists of two or three tiers of cells arranged in four rows, a single neck canal cell or two adjacent cells (boot-shaped cells), a ventral canal cell, and an egg cell at the base of the embedded venter (Jeffrey, 1899; Sethi, 1928). At maturity all the cells of the axial row except the egg cell degenerate, and the upper tier of neck cells separate from one another.

After many archegonia have been formed, antheridia are produced along the periphery of the basal disc (Walker, 1931). They may occur also on upright lobes. Each antheridium is normally sunken and consists of a single layer of from two to four jacket cells which encloses a large number of spermatocytes (Fig. 9-7, E). At maturity the large multi-flagellate sperms escape through a triangular opercular cell of the jacket. The sperms are spirally coiled, with numerous flagella attached to a linear blephroplast (Sharp, 1912). In addition to the nuclear material and flagella, a sac-like vesicle of cytoplasm is attached to the posterior end of the sperm.

To achieve fertilization the thalli must be covered by at least a thin layer of water in which the motile sperms swim to the archegonia. Mature sperms are probably not released until the proper osmotic conditions are achieved. When thalli are flooded, water probably enters the cells of the mature antheridia due to an osmotic gradient. This would bring about swelling of the cells and is possibly the causal factor in the opening of the antheridium.

If fertilization is not achieved, more archegonia and antheridia are formed from derivatives of the marginal meristem.

Gametophyte Nutrition and Culture

As mentioned earlier, gametophyte plants growing under crowded conditions tend to be small and remain filamentous or form branched, flat thalli. Antheridia are formed on these plants, but the development of archegonia is inhibited. Observations of this phenomenon have led to the belief in some quarters that *Equisetum* is truly heterothallic, but reports on naturally occurring gametophytes indicate that the haploid phase is ultimately homothallic. How external influences affect sexuality in *Equisetum* is shown by the study of Schratz (1928), who learned that prothallia of *E. arvense* grown under unfavorable conditions resulted in most of them becoming male plants. He decided that *all* spores have the capability of germinating into male prothallia. Under good growing conditions less than half become heterothallic. Even by enhancing good cultural conditions, some of the originally male plants would not form archegonia. Schratz concluded that sexual determination is phenotypic and that the prothallia are most strongly influenced during early stages of development.

More detailed information is needed on physio-genetic questions of sexuality in all groups of lower vascular plants.

The Embryo

The origin of the diploid phase or sporophyte is the fertilized egg or zygote. Observations on fertilization have indicated that numerous sperms may enter the archegonium (Sethi, 1928), but only one sperm actually penetrates the egg membrane. The first division of the zygote is generally transverse to the long axis of the archegonium, setting aside an upper cell, the epibasal cell, and a lower cell, the hypobasal cell. Obviously the embryo is exoscopic, and in this respect it is similar to the embryos of *Psilotum* and *Tmesipteris* (Fig. 6-1). In one reported instance the first division is longitudinal (Campbell, 1928).

There are conflicting accounts of embryogeny in *Equisetum*, which may indicate that there is considerable variation between species. The early descriptions were presented at a time when embryogeny was considered a precise series of unalterable events. Assignment of the first leaf, stem (future shoot apex), root, and foot to definite segments of the embryo in the quadrant stage was reported by Sadebeck (1878). The first leaf and the shoot apex were reported to develop from the epibasal portion, whereas the first root and a foot originated from quadrants of the hypobasal hemisphere. Later workers reported variations in segmentation and origin of fundamental organs. Until more complete studies are made the following general outline of development may be representative of at least certain members of the genus (such as *E. arvense, maximum, palustre*).

Figure 9-8   **A-C,** development of the embryo in *Equisetum arvense* (the first cleavage of the embryo is indicated as *I-I*); **D,** "leafy" dorsiventral gametophyte of *E. laevigatum* with two attached sporophytes [A-C, redrawn from Sadebeck, *Jahrb. wiss. Bot.* 11:575, 1878; D, redrawn from Walker, *Bot. Gaz.* 71:378, 1921].

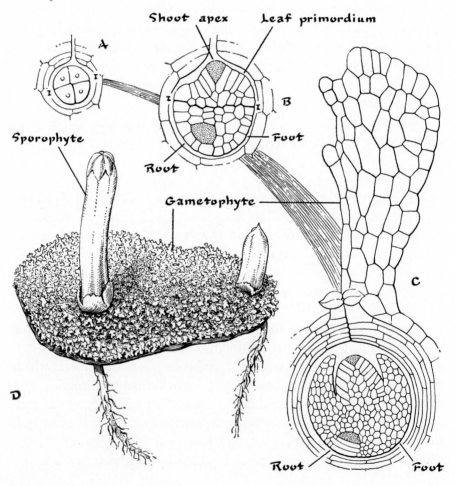

The shoot has its origin from the upper half (epibasal portion) of the embryo, and the root appears rather late in development, in a lateral position, from the hypobasal portion (Fig. 9-8, A-C). A definable haustorial foot may or may not be formed. The shoot grows rapidly, forming whorls of three or four scale-like leaves. Later the root penetrates the gametophytic tissue in reaching the soil. Additional erect shoots are formed from buds on the primary axis during establishment of the sporophyte. Large, sexually mature gametophytic plants may support several sporophytes in varying stages of development (Fig. 9-8, D).

Hyeniales–Hyeniaceae

As stated in the first part of this chapter, the Sphenopsida were widespread in their distribution and flourished particularly during the coal forming age. Representation today is but a vestige of that typical of earlier development. In the following section only brief descriptions will be given for extinct orders of the Sphenopsida.

The earliest known record of plants with sphenopsid features is in the Devonian. The two genera *Hyenia* and *Calamophyton* were small, shrubby plants. The lower branches had forked leaves that were weakly arranged in successive whorls. Certain ultimate branches formed lax strobili (Fig. 9-9). Each strobilus consisted of an axis and whorled fertile branches (sporangiophores). Each of the short fertile side branches (sporangiophores) had recurved terminal sporangia. Little is known of the internal structure of the plants assigned to this group.

Sphenophyllales–Sphenophyllaceae

In the Carboniferous age there were herbaceous, vine-like plants with jointed stems and whorls of wedge-shaped leaves (Fig. 9-10, C). The distal margin was toothed or deeply notched. Unlike the other members of the Sphenopsida, wherein internal structure is unknown, the leaves of this group had a dichotomously branched venation system. The stem was an exarch protostele, which was often triarch. A cylinder of secondary xylem was formed which consisted of tracheids and xylem rays (Fig. 9-10, D). Bordered pits occurred on the radial walls of tracheids. In

Fertile shoot ————

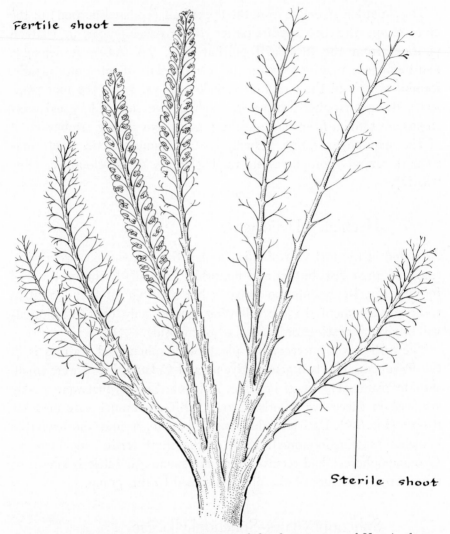

Sterile shoot

Figure 9-9   Diagrammatic reconstruction of the shoot system of *Hyenia elegans*. [Redrawn from Kräusel and Weyland, *Senckenbergische Naturforschende Gesell. Abhandlungen.* 40:115, 1926.]

some species the strobili were elongated branches with whorled bracts that were basally concrescent for some distance. In the axils of bracts were branched sporangiophores (Fig. 9-10, A, B). The terminal, stalked sporangia were recurved, and the stalk was often fused with the bract for some distance. The majority of species were homosporous, but a few forms were heterosporous. The genus *Sphenophyllum* is representative

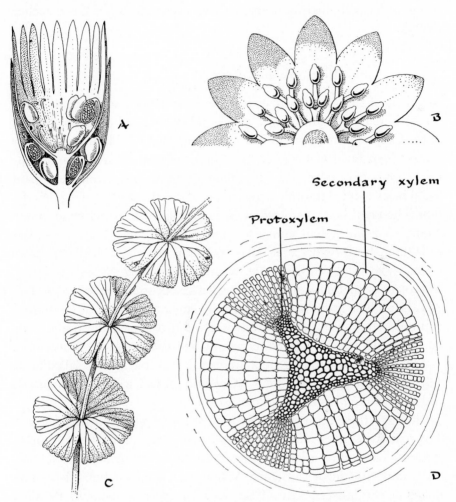

Figure 9-10 Vegetative and reproductive structures of the Sphenophyllales. **A**, longisection, strobilus of *Sphenophyllum dawsoni*; **B**, same as **A**, viewed from above (stalked sporangia were joined with the fused bracts for some distance); **C**, leaves and stem of *Sphenophyllum*; **D**, xylem cylinder, stem of *Sphenophyllum* as seen in transection. [A, redrawn from *An Introduction to the Study of Fossil Plants* by J. Walton, London: Adam and Charles Black, 1953; B, redrawn from *Handbuch der Paläobotanik* by M. Hirmer, Munich: R. Oldenbourg, 1927; D, redrawn from *Les Plantes Fossiles dans leurs Rapports avec les Végétaux Vivants* by L. Emberger, Paris: Masson et Cie, 1944.]

of the order, although form genera have been established for detached strobili.

Calamitales–Calamitaceae

Members of this group were of tree-like proportions (some plants being 1 foot in diameter and 60 feet high) and constituted a significant part of the Carboniferous flora. It is in this group that establishment of *form genera* (explained in Chapter 8) is of great importance because only rarely are connected parts of the plant uncovered. If a complete plant could be assembled it would agree, in general, with the following description. The plant body consisted of an aerial branch system and an underground rhizome system similar to that of *Equisetum*. Roots, as well as aerial branches, originated at nodes along the rhizome. The aerial, articulated shoot exhibited limited or extensive branching. Whorls of linear, lanceolate or spatulate microphyllous leaves occurred at the nodes (Fig. 9-11, D). These leaves were considerably larger than those of *Equisetum* and only rarely were laterally fused. Strobili occupied the tips of side branches and were not placed terminally on major axes as in *Equisetum*.

As noted earlier, form genera are very important in the Calamitales. There are form genera for stems (*Calamites*), leaf whorls (*Annularia*), and strobili (*Calamostachys, Palaeostachya*).

Although these form genera exist, an entire plant is called *Calamites*. The remains of a calamite stem are of two types: pith casts, and petrifactions. The former are formed by infiltration of minerals into the pith cavity and subsequent hardening. When the organic material decays, an image of the inner surface of the vascular cylinder remains. Petrified stems of Calamitales reveal a remarkable similarity to those of *Equisetum*, except for the continuous cylinder of secondary xylem (Fig. 9-11, C). Secondary xylem consisted of tracheids, with bordered pits on radial walls and parenchymatous rays.

Annularia is the genus for whorls of microphyllous leaves attached to small stems (Fig. 9-11, D). Strobili consisted of alternate whorls of bracts and sporangiophores (*Calamostachys*—Fig. 9-11, B) or whorls of peltate sporangiophores that are situated in the axils of sterile bracts (*Palaeostachya*—Fig. 9-11, A). A few forms were heterosporous. The group apparently never attained the seed habit. Some botanists consider

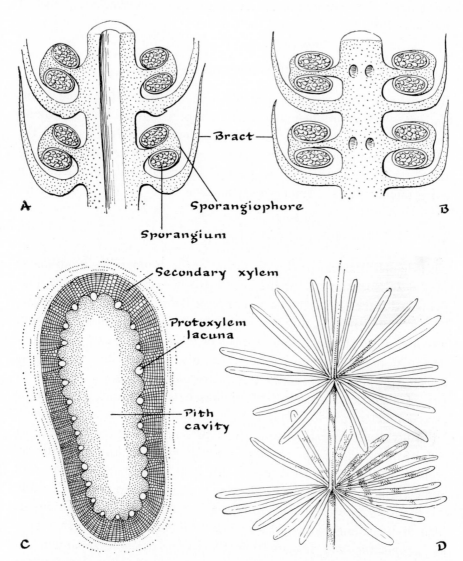

Figure 9-11 Vegetative and reproductive structures of the Calamitales. **A, B,** longisections, strobili of *Palaeostachya* and *Calamostachys*, respectively; **C,** transection, stem of *Calamites*; **D,** leaves and stem of *Annularia*. [A, redrawn from *Studies in Fossil Botany* by D. H. Scott, London: Adam and Charles Black, 1920.]

this group to be a family coordinate with the Equisetaceae and placed in the order Equisetales.

Equisetales–Equisetaceae: *Equisetites*

Before leaving this discussion mention should be made of the genus *Equisetites*. As mentioned above, certain representatives of the Carboniferous resembled the living genus *Equisetum*. From the rocks of the Mesozoic and Coenozoic, plant remains have been discovered and given the name of *Equisetites*. It is extremely difficult to distinguish them from living members of the genus *Equisetum*.

Summary and Conclusions

This chapter has presented a discussion of the comparative morphology of the Sphenopsida, a subdivision of the lower vascular plants that flourished and attained its maximum diversity during the Paleozoic Era. The only surviving member of this ancient group is the genus *Equisetum*, which consists of about 25-30 species of widely distributed herbaceous perennials popularly known as horsetails or scouring rushes. Some of the ancient sphenopsids were large trees with pronounced secondary growth (e.g., *Calamites*), but the modern horsetails are plants which rarely exceed a meter or so in height and which are devoid of secondary vascular tissues. Both the extinct and living representatives of the Sphenopsida differ from other groups of lower vascular plants in the following respects: (1) the shoots are conspicuously jointed with well-defined nodes and elongated internodes; (2) the leaves occur in whorls at each node; (3) branches arise at the nodes in marked contrast with the dichotomous plan of branching characteristic of the *Psilopsida* and of such genera as *Lycopodium* and *Selaginella* in the Lycopsida; (4) the internodal regions of the stem are externally traversed by conspicuous longitudinal ribs; and (5) the sporangia are borne on whorled stem-like appendages termed sporangiophores. These organographic features of the sporophyte have been discussed briefly with reference to the morphology of the extinct orders of the Sphenopsida—that is, the Hyeniales, Sphenophyllales and Calamitales—and in connection with the detailed descrip-

tion of the morphology and reproduction of *Equisetum,* the living representative of the order Equisetales.

The vegetative sporophyte of *Equisetum* consists of an underground
system of rhizomes which form buds and roots at their nodes; certain of
the buds develop into the aerial shoots of the plant. The foliar organs of
Equisetum are small univeined scales which occur in whorls at each node.
The scale leaves are basally united into a cylindrical sheath, and the nodal
branches, which alternate in position with the leaves, must break through
the foliar sheath during their early expansion. In some species of
Equisetum two kinds of shoots arise from the rhizome: unbranched,
brownish, fertile shoots bearing large terminal strobili, and profusely
branched, green, sterile shoots. Other species do not exhibit such dimorphism, and the strobili are borne terminally on the main axis or the
lateral branches of green shoots. The presumable trends in evolutionary
specialization of the varied types of shoots have been briefly discussed.

The anatomy of the stem in *Equisetum* is distinctive, and a detailed
description has been given with particular emphasis on the structure and
ontogeny of the vascular system. In contrast with the predominence of
the protostele (with either exarch or mesarch xylem) in the stems of the
Psilopsida and Lycopsida, the vascular system in the stem internodes of
Equisetum consists of a cylinder of collateral bundles with endarch
xylem; each of these bundles develops a prominent carinal canal (i.e., a
protoxylem lacuna). At the nodes the bundles are joined into a vascular
girdle which is interrupted only by the gaps associated with the nodal
branches. *Equisetum* is thus cladosiphonic and devoid of leaf gaps. The
number of collateral bundles in a given internode agrees with the number
of external longitudinal ribs—each rib lies radially opposite a vascular
bundle.

The mature strobilus of *Equisetum* consists of an axis to which are
attached whorls of peltate sporangiophores. Each sporangiophore bears
on the lower surface of its disk-shaped portion a ring of 5-10 sporangia.
The sporangia are eusporangiate in method of development, and when
ripe contain a large number of spores that are unique in wall structure.
The outermost wall layer—apparently deposited externally through the
activity of a periplasmodium—consists of four strips or bands known as
elaters. These structures are hygroscopic, uncoiling as the spores dry and

recoiling with the addition of water. Possibly the movements of the elaters may aid in the escape of the spores after the sporangium has dehisced.

Spores retain their viability for only a short time, but if moisture is available they germinate readily and give rise to distinctive cushion-shaped gametophytes which produce thin erect photosynthetic lobes. Both antheridia (which produce multiflagellate sperms) and archegonia may develop on vigorous gametophytes which are not crowded during their development. Under less favorable and more crowded conditions, a given gametophyte may produce only antheridia.

Following fertilization in the archegonium, the zygote gives rise to an embryo with exoscopic polarity. No suspensor is formed, and the outer (epibasal) portion of the embryo (i.e., the part directed toward the archegonial neck) develops into the primary shoot; the root arises laterally from the lower (hypobasal) portion. If a definable foot is developed, it arises also from the hypobasal region of the embryo.

References

Barratt, K. 1920. A contribution to our knowledge of the vascular system of the genus *Equisetum. Ann. Bot.* 34:201-235.

Beer, R. 1909. The development of the spores of *Equisetum. New Phytol.* 8:261-266.

Benedict, R. C. 1941. The gold rush: a fern ally. *Amer. Fern Jour.* 31:127-130.

Bower, F. O. 1935. *Primitive Land Plants.* Macmillan, London.

Browne, I. M. P. 1922. Anatomy of *Equisetum giganteum. Bot. Gaz.* 73:447-468.

Campbell, D. H. 1928. The embryo of *Equisetum debile*, Roxb. *Ann. Bot.* 42:717-728.

Eames, A. J. 1909. On the occurrence of centripetal xylem in *Equisetum. Ann. Bot.* 23:587-601.

Francini, E. 1942. La struttura dell'-apice del rizoma in confronto alla struttura dell'apice del fusto aereo in "*Equisetum ramossissimum*" Desf. *Nuovo Gior. Bot. Ital.* 49:337-357.

Golub, S. J. and R. H. Wetmore. 1948a. Studies of development in the vegetative shoot of *Equisetum arvense* L. I. The shoot apex. *Amer. Jour. Bot.* 35:755-767.

———— and ————. 1948b. Studies of development in the vegetative shoot of *Equisetum arvense* L. II. The mature shoot. *Amer. Jour. Bot.* 35:767-781.

Gwynne-Vaughan, D. T. 1901. Remarks upon the nature of the stele of *Equisetum*. *Ann. Bot.* 15:774-776.

Jeffrey, E. C. 1899. The development, structure, and affinities of the genus *Equisetum*. *Mem. Boston Soc. Nat. Hist.* 5:155-190.

Johnson, M. A. 1933. Origin and development of tissues in *Equisetum scirpoides*. *Bot. Gaz.* 94:469-494.

————. 1937. Hydathodes in the genus *Equisetum*. *Bot. Gaz.* 98:598-608.

Kashyap, S. R. 1914. The structure and development of the prothallus of *Equisetum debile*, Roxb. *Ann. Bot.* 28:163-181.

Manton, I. 1950. *Problems of Cytology and Evolution in the Pteridophyta.* Cambridge University Press, London.

Matzke, E. B. 1941. Gametophytes of *Equisetum arvense* L. *Torreya* 41: 181-187.

Meyer, F. J. 1920. Das Leitungssystem von *Equisetum arvense*. *Jahrb. wiss. Bot.* 59:263-286.

Queva, C. 1907. Histogénèse et structure du stipe et de la fronde des *Equisetum*. *Bull. Soc. d'hist. nat. d'Autin.* 20:115-152.

Sadebeck, R. 1878. Die Entwickelung der Keimes der Schachtelhalme. *Jahrb. wiss. Bot.* 11:575-602.

Schaffner, J. H. 1930. Geographic distribution of the species of *Equisetum* in relation to their phylogeny. *Amer. Fern Jour.* 20:89-106.

————. 1932. Diagnostic key to the species of *Equisetum*. *Amer. Fern Jour.* 22:69-75; 122-128.

————. 1933. Six interesting characters of sporadic occurrence in *Equisetum*. *Amer. Fern Jour.* 23:83-90.

Schratz, E. 1928. Untersuchungen über die Geschlechterverteilung bei *Equisetum arvense*. *Biol. Zentralblatt* 48: 617-639.

Sethi, M. L. 1928. Contributions to the life-history of *Equisetum debile* Roxb. *Ann. Bot.* 42:729-738.

Sharp, L. W. 1912. Spermatogenesis in *Equisetum*. *Bot. Gaz.* 54:89-119.

Sinnott, E. W. 1943. Cell division as a problem of pattern in plant development. *Torreya* 43:29-34.

Taylor, T. M. C. 1939. Some features of the organization of the sporophyte of *Equisetum arvense* L. *New Phytol.* 38:159-166.

Treitel, O. 1943. The elasticity, breaking stress, and breaking strain of the horizontal rhizomes of species of *Equisetum*. *Trans. Kansas Acad. Sci.* 46:122-132.

Vogt, T. 1942. Geokjemisk og geobotanisk malmleting III Lift om plante-veksten ved Rörosmalmene. [Geochemical and geobotanical ore prospecting] III. Some notes on the vegetation at the ore deposits at Röros. *K. Nosske Vidensk. Selskab Forhandl.* 15:21-24.

Walker, E. R. 1921. The gametophytes of *Equisetum laevigatum*. *Bot. Gaz.* 71:378-391.

————. 1931. The gametophytes of three species of *Equisetum*. *Bot. Gaz.* 92:1-22.

Walton, J. 1944. The roots of *Equisetum limosum* L. *New Phytol.* 43: 81-86.

Chapter
10 THE PTEROPSIDA

The preceding chapters of this book have been concerned mainly with the comparative morphology and evolutionary relationships of three of the most ancient groups of vascular plants—the Psilopsida, Lycopsida, and Sphenopsida. These groups were conspicuous and highly diversified in the Paleozoic Era, but their surviving descendents today represent a very minor element in modern land floras. Their chief scientific interest, which fully justifies the detailed treatment given them in this book, lies in the information they provide for a clear understanding of the evolution of reproductive mechanisms and for an insight into the organography and vascular anatomy of primitive types of sporophytes. For example, the rootless Psilotales, with their simply vasculated axes, their weakly developed leaves, and their thick-walled terminal sporangia, have been repeatedly considered as the primitive stock from which more complex lines of tracheophytes have arisen. Likewise, the living members of the Lycopsida and Sphenopsida, although less archaic in certain respects than the psilophytes, appear to have retained elemental features in their sporangia, gametangia, and vascular systems which shed considerable light on the phylogeny of these structures in higher groups.

The recognition of the many distinctive morphological characters shared by the psilophytes, lycopods, and sphenopsids resulted many years ago in the proposal by Jeffrey that these plants should be segregated as a single major "group" which he named "Lycopsida." The remaining groups of vascular plants, i.e., the ferns, gymosperms, and angiosperms, were believed to constitute a second contrasting major group which he termed "Pteropsida" (see Jeffrey, 1917, Chapter XVII). This proposed classification of all tracheophytes into two main groups has been somewhat modified as the result of further morphological study of both living and extinct types. As will be discussed in detail later in this chapter, there seems to be both justification and convenience in the recognition of the Pteropsida as a major alliance of vascular plants (Eames, 1936; Arnold, 1947). But the evidence is strongly in favor of discarding the Lycopsida, as conceived by Jeffrey, and of recognizing that the psilopsid, lycopsid, and sphenopsid groups are relatively distinct, ancient alliances between which there are no obvious evolutionary connections linking them together as a single major division of the Tracheophyta.

The remainder of this chapter will be devoted to an analysis of the salient morphological features which have been used to demarcate the Pteropsida from the three other groups of vascular plants. This analysis will not only serve to orient the student regarding the characters common to most members of the Pteropsida, but will also provide a brief review of the contrasted features of the vegetative and reproductive systems of the Psilopsida, Lycopsida, and Sphenopsida.

Vegetative Organography and Anatomy

One of the most distinctive characteristics of the Pteropsida is the presence of a type of leaf known as a megaphyll (a detailed treatment of megaphylls is given in Chapter 3). This organ, which is believed to have originated from the modification of a branch system, reveals its cladode nature most clearly in the ferns. Especially in the Marattiaceae and many of the leptosporangiate types, the leaf has a prolonged period of apical growth, exhibits a characteristic circinate vernation, and is often large and profusely pinnatifid (Figs. 10-1, 10-2). Whether the extremely diversified leaves of living gymnosperms and angiosperms are also to be regarded phylogenetically as derivatives of branch systems is admittedly an open question. But aside from this question, the leaves of seed plants agree with those of ferns in the development of a usually complex venation in the lamina and by the fact that the vascular supply to each leaf is associated with one or more parenchymatous areas in the stele, known as leaf gaps. In these two important anatomical features the leaves of most pteropsid plants differ strikingly from the single-veined microphylls, devoid of leaf gaps, which are characteristic of the majority of the living members of the Psilopsida, Lycopsida, and Sphenopsida (Chapter 3).

Indeed, these differences formed one of the main distinctions originally used by Jeffrey (1910, 1917) in his delimitation of the "Lycopsida" from the "Pteropsida." It is furthermore significant that the presence of

Figure 10-1   Tree fern growing in Golden Gate Park, San Francisco, California. Young leaves, which exhibit circinate vernation, are seen in various stages of growth. The mature fronds are large and profusely pinnatifid. [Courtesy Dr. T. E. Weier, from *Botany, An Introduction to Plant Science*, Ed. 2, by W. W. Robbins, T. E. Weier, and C. R. Stocking, New York: John Wiley and Sons, Inc., 1957.]

Figure 10-2 Greatly enlarged crozier or fiddle head of a fern. Note that the pinnae and further subdivisions exhibit circinate vernation. [Courtesy Dr. T. E. Weier.]

leaf gaps in the Pteropsida and their absence in the other groups is correlated with contrasted types of stelar anatomy in the stem. In the Pteropsida, with the exception of a few protostelic ferns and some aquatic angiosperms (e.g., *Hippuris*), the primary vascular cylinder is a siphonostele with mesarch or endarch xylem, whereas in the majority of the representatives of the other three groups of vascular plants the stem possesses an exarch protostele. (See Chapters 3, 12, and 13 for illustrations of stelar types.) The only exceptions to this general contrast in stelar anatomy in plants below the Pteropsida are provided by the mesarch primary xylem in the stem of *Tmesipteris* and by the endarch bundles typical of the stem of *Equisetum.* Each of these genera, however, differs from the members of the Pteropsida in the absence of leaf gaps.

To summarize, the Pteropsida with but few exceptions are anatomically defined by their usually extensively veined leaves and by the association of their leaf traces with gaps in the vascular cylinder. As explained in some detail in Chapter 3, there is rather general agreement that the siphonostele, which prevails in the stems of the Pteropsida, represents an evolutionary modification of the more archaic protostele typical of the other main groups of vascular plants. It is evident therefore that a close correlation exists between the type of leaf and its vascular supply and the type of vascular system developed in the stem. From a purely onto-genetic viewpoint, this correlation may be expressed as follows. In microphyllous plants, a considerable portion of the primary vascular system of the axis is cauline and unrelated in its development to the initiation and vascularization of the leaves. In this case, each leaf trace appears to represent merely a strand of protoxylem which separates from the periphery of the protostele at the node. On the other hand, in megaphyllous plants the character of the primary vascular system of the axis is apparently affected by the development of the larger leaves and their associated traces.

Indeed, in many of the ferns and in a series of recently investigated seed plants the stele of the stem is interpreted as a composite vascular cylinder made up entirely of the lower portions of leaf traces (cf. Wetmore 1943; see also Esau, 1953, Chapter 15). In the light of these ideas, it seems correct to assume that the progressive evolutionary development of the sporophyte in the Tracheophyta has been accompanied by an increasing interdependence between the vascular systems of the stem and its foliar appendages. This evolutionary trend culminates in the shoots of the Pteropsida in which the primary vascular system of the stem consists of leaf traces. In this connection it should be pointed out that regardless of the stelar pattern of the shoot axis, the primary vascular system of the root is exarch and radial throughout all the groups of vascular plants. This remarkable conservatism of the root seems to be correlated with the absence of foliar appendages and hence lends further support to the idea that the vascularization of stems in higher vascular plants is significantly correlated with the development of leaves and their traces.

Sporangia

In Chapter 4 a distinction between cauline and foliar sporangia was made, and the position of each type in relation to the fertile leaf or sporophyll was briefly discussed with special reference to the lower groups of vascular plants. It will now be appropriate to examine critically those features of sporangial position and number which are more specifically distinctive of the Pteropsida.

Jeffrey (1917, Chapter XVIII) maintained that in addition to possessing megaphylls and leaf gaps, the members of the Pteropsida are further characterized by having sporangia (often in large numbers) on the lower or *abaxial* surface of the sporophyll. In contrast, according to his viewpoint, the microphyllous groups of vascular plants (i.e., the so-called Lycopsida) possess sporangia that are solitary or few and are *adaxial* in position with relation to their sporophylls. In the light of present knowledge, however, it may well be questioned whether a distinction between adaxial and abaxial sporangial positions can serve as a constant criterion in the classification of major groups of vascular plants. For this reason it will be desirable to summarize the essential facts regarding the position of sporangia in the three classes of the Pteropsida.

The ferns, particularly members of the Filicales, provide the best and most striking examples of abaxial sporangia in Pteropsid plants. In contrast with the adaxial, solitary, cauline, or foliar sporangia of the Lycopsida, the sporangia of higher ferns are either marginal (probably the primitive position) or, more commonly, occur on the abaxial surface of the fertile pinnae (Fig. 13-6). Abaxial sporangia, frequently fused into synangia, are also typical of many members of the Marattiaceae. In the Ophioglossaceae, often regarded as the most primitive family in the ferns, the sporangia are either free and terminal on the ultimate divisions of the fertile "leaf segment" (*Botrychium* and *Helminthostachys*) or are embedded and fused with the leaf (*Ophioglossum*). In the light of these facts, it may be concluded that at least in the primitive and non-seed-bearing representatives of the Pteropsida three more or less intergrading sporangial positions occur: terminal, marginal, and abaxial. The first position is likewise found in certain microphyllous plants (e.g., Psilopsida and Sphenopsida) whereas the abaxial position is characteristic of higher ferns and serves to demarcate this group of pteropsid plants.

In seed plants, however, the interpretation of the position of the sporangia represents a complex and controversial series of problems (see Chapters 14-19). At this point, only the general nature of the difficulties will be considered; a more detailed discussion will be reserved for later chapters.

Since all seed plants are characterized by the development of two kinds of sporangia (microsporangia and megasporangia) it will be necessary to consider the position of each type separately. The closest parallel to the abaxial sporangia in ferns is provided by the microsporophylls of certain gymnosperms. In all of the living cycads, for example, the microsporophyll bears on its lower or abaxial surface a relatively large number of microsporangia which are commonly arranged in fern-like soral groups (Fig. 15-7). A somewhat comparable situation is found in certain conifers, but the number of abaxial sporangia on the microsporophyll is much less than in cycads, ranging from two (*Pinus, Cedrus*) to fifteen (*Agathis, Araucaria*). In other groups of the gymnosperms the position of the microsporangia is quite different. *Ginkgo biloba,* for example, has paired and pendent sporangia at the tip of the slender microsporophyll, and in certain of the Gnetales the microsporangia are borne at the tips of short, shoot-like appendages. In the case of the angiosperms, the microsporangia are usually somewhat embedded structures which develop in the anther of the stamen. The stamen, which is apparently equivalent to a microsporophyll, has been variously interpreted as will be shown in a later chapter. But it is important at this point to note that recent investigations on certain primitive members of the Ranales indicate the presence in some genera of foliaceous stamens with clearly defined abaxial microsporangia (Bailey and Smith, 1942, 1943; Canright, 1952). This condition strikingly resembles the position of the microsporangia in certain groups of the gymnosperms, and it may ultimately prove to be the primitive type of stamen in flowering plants.

Although the microsporangia of most gymnosperms and certain angiosperms appear to be foliar, and in many instances are abaxial in their position on the microsporophyll, the position of the ovule or megasporangium in seed plants is much more difficult to determine. In the cycads the ovules are attached to sporophylls which in some species (for instance, *Cycas revoluta*) are pinnatifid megaphyllous-like organs (see Fig. 15-8). But in *Ginkgo*, the conifers, and the Gnetales the position of the ovules has been variously interpreted (Eames, 1952). A classical example of the difficulties involved is furnished by the ovuliferous scale (i.e., cone scale) in the megasporangiate strobilus of certain conifers. This scale bears one, or more commonly two, ovules on its upper or adaxial surface and is usually clearly associated with a subtending bract (Fig. 16-12, G). The evidence from ontogeny and vascular anatomy indicates that this ovuliferous structure is a highly condensed, short shoot and not a simple megasporophyll. Doubts have also been repeatedly expressed by morphologists regarding the foliar nature of the ovule-bearing structure in other gymnospermous plants. Eames (1950, 1952) recently concluded that in the Cordaitales and Ephedrales the ovules are borne on sporophylls and are not cauline, but final conclusions on the gymnosperms as a whole await further investigation. With reference to the angiosperms, similar uncertainties exist, particularly because of the lack of general agreement as to the morphology of the ovule-bearing organ or *carpel*. (See Chapter 18 for a discussion of carpel morphology.)

On the basis of the preceding discussion it is clear that the abaxial position of sporangia, although prevalent in the ferns, is by no means a constant diagnostic feature of the Pteropsida as a whole. Numerous exceptions to the abaxial condition are encountered in pteropsid plants, particularly in the case of the megasporangia of gymnosperms and angiosperms. In these latter classes the organs that bear the megasporangia are difficult to interpret morphologically and in many instances are not strictly comparable to the sporophylls of lower vascular plants. The diversity in the position of sporangia within the Pteropsida is not surprising when we consider the immense variation that has appeared during the evolutionary development of the shoot systems of seed plants. Sporangia are not static structures, and their originally primitive position at the margins or on the abaxial surfaces of fertile leaves has been profoundly modified in the more advanced members of the pteropsid line of development.

From the standpoint of the structure and method of development of their sporangia, the Pteropsida are predominately eusporangiate, in which important respect they closely resemble all members of the Psilopsida, Lycopsida, and Sphenopsida (Chapter 4). The eusporangiate method of sporangial development is characteristic not only of the more primitive orders of the ferns (i.e., Ophioglossales and Marattiales) but occurs also in the seed plants. In the latter the ontogeny of the micro-sporangium conforms more closely to the eusporangiate pattern than does the megasporangium in which there is clear evidence of the reduction or even the elimination of a definable sporangial wall. The higher ferns or Filicales are therefore remarkable among all the Pteropsida by virtue of the presence of leptosporangia, which represent one of the most distinctive morphological features of these plants. As pointed out in Chapter 4, the leptosporangium is evidently an extreme modification of the more archaic eusporangium, and its presence in the Filicales, which are largely homosporous, is a striking example of the result of an independent trend of specialization in spore-producing organs.

With reference to the kinds of spores produced, the Pteropsida are characterized by both homosporous and heterosporous types. The former condition is typical of most ferns; the latter condition prevails through-out the seed plants. Indeed, as we shall see in subsequent chapters, the formation of two kinds of spores in gymnosperms and angiosperms, and the permanent retention of the megaspore within its sporangium, consti-tute definitive features of specialization in these highly evolved seed-bearing plants.

Gametophytes and Embryos

As is true of the other groups of vascular plants, the type and relative prominence of the gametophytes are closely correlated with the conditions of homospory and heterospory in the Pteropsida. Thus, in the homosporous ferns the gametophyte is a freely developed, independent plant which is either photosynthetic or (as in many of the eusporangiate groups) mycorrhizal. In contrast, the male and female gametophytes of the seed plants are typically endosporic and greatly reduced in size.

Antheridia are lacking, and flagellated sperms are restricted to *Ginkgo* and the cycads. As in lower heterosporous plants, archegonia are produced by the female gametophyte in the more primitive seed plants (i.e., most gymnosperms) but have been eliminated from the reproductive cycle of the angiosperms.

Although no single type of polarity characterizes the embryogeny of members of the Pteropsida, the endoscopic condition prevails throughout both classes of the seed plants and occurs also in certain of the eusporangiate ferns (Chapter 6). It is remarkable that the endoscopic type of embryo with a suspensor, which Bower regards as the primitive form in lower vascular plants, has become "standardized" in the most advanced members of the Pteropsida. It is possible that endoscopic polarity carries with it nutritional advantages for the growing embryo and that it has therefore arisen independently in various lines of evolution among the vascular plants.

References

Arnold, C. A. 1947. *An Introduction to Paleobotany.* McGraw-Hill, New York.

Bailey, I. W. and A. C. Smith. 1942. Degeneriaceae, a new family of flowering plants from Fiji. *Jour. Arnold Arboretum* 23:356-365.

—— and ——. 1943. The family Himantandraceae. *Jour. Arnold Arboretum* 24:190-206.

Canright, J. E. 1952. The comparative morphology and relationships of the Magnoliaceae. I. Trends of specialization in the stamens. *Amer. Jour. Bot.* 39:484-497.

Eames, A. J. 1936. *Morphology of Vascular Plants. Lower Groups.* McGraw-Hill, New York.

——. 1950. Again: 'The New Morphology.' *New Phytologist* 50: 17-35.

——. 1952. Relationships of the Ephedrales. *Phytomorphology* 2:79-100.

Esau, K. 1953. *Plant Anatomy.* Wiley, New York.

Jeffrey, E. C. 1910. The Pteropsida. *Bot. Gaz.* 50:401-414.

——. 1917. *The Anatomy of Woody Plants.* The University of Chicago Press, Chicago.

Wetmore, R. H. 1943. Leaf-stem relationships in the vascular plants. *Torreya* 43:16-28.

11 THE FILICINAE

General Characteristics

In the preceding chapter the important features of the Pteropsida were outlined. It is necessary only to review briefly the important morphological characteristics that unify the members of this major group in the Tracheophyta. All of the plants (ferns, cone-bearing plants, and flowering plants) have leaves that are technically designated megaphylls. A megaphyll, whether large or small, usually has a branched venation system, and its leaf trace system is generally associated with one or more leaf gaps in the vascular cylinder of the stem. The results of important studies in comparative morphology and paleobotany indicate that the seed-bearing plants and the ferns, which reproduce solely by spores, have, in the remote past, probably evolved from some common ancestral group.

What general characteristics do we associate with a common garden or house fern? Naturally one thinks of a large fern leaf, commonly called a frond in everyday usage—a term which is used also by many fern specialists. The fern frond may be a simple expanded blade with a petiole or stipe—a term used by students of fern morphology—or, more frequently, the frond is a compound pinnatifid leaf. The stipe is devoid of any expanded blade, and its continuation is the main axis of the frond, called the rachis. Attached to the rachis, and approximately opposite each other, are pairs of leaflets, each division of which is termed a pinna. Each pinna may likewise be subdivided into pairs of pinnules, and further subdivisions may occur (Fig. 13-1). This type of leaf subdivision is known as the pinnate plan of organization. Thus a frond may be once pinnate, bipinnate, tripinnate, and so on.

The manner in which a young fern frond develops or unrolls is a familiar matter to the more careful observer. Unrolling fronds of ferns are often referred to as "fiddle heads," "monkey tails," or "croziers"

(Fig. 10-2). Almost everyone has discovered the brownish to black splotches on the lower surface of a fern frond and perhaps at first has interpreted these structures as being parasitic insects. Actually each spot is a collection of sporangia which are sometimes protected by an outgrowth from the leaf surface. In most ferns the stem is an underground rhizome and is not apparent except in stocky, erect plants. The large trunks of tropical tree ferns, however, compare in size with the trunks of moderately large palms. Roots usually arise from the lower part of an aerial stem or from the lower surface of a rhizome, characteristically related to each leaf.

Today approximately 10,000 species of ferns are widely distributed over the earth's surface. Some species are restricted to narrow environmental niches and are endemic to certain localities. The common bracken fern (*Pteridium aquilinum*), for example, is worldwide in distribution in the tropics and temperate zones. Ferns are quite numerous and are most diverse in the tropical rain forests, many of them becoming trees 20-40 feet high or growing as epiphytes. However, even desert areas and mountains of the temperate regions have a fern population.

The ferns are well known from the fossil record which extends back to about Middle Devonian times. Some of these fossils are not too different from those of certain members of the Psilophytales. In fact, representatives of the familiar "true ferns" are found in strata of the Permian. In addition, certain groups of ferns apparently existed for a period of time without leaving any direct descendants in today's fern flora. Even so, the Filicinae, particularly the Filicales, is a highly successful group in the present epoch, having overcome the rigors of existence in a changing world much better than their frequent plant associates, the lycopods and horsetails.

In the opening of this chapter a general description of a modern fern was presented for orientation purposes. However, the student of fern morphology is interested not only in living ferns but also in ferns of the past. Deviating from the organization of previous chapters, the earliest fossil forms will be introduced first. This departure should not be difficult for the student because he is, by now, familiar with the ancient group, the Psilophytales (Chapter 7), and has gained an insight into the possible evolutionary development of the megaphyll (Chapter 3). In a book of limited scope it is impossible to consider the vast amount of information available on extinct ferns, and we are compelled simply to present certain types which illustrate important morphological steps in the evolution of the group as a whole.

The search for earliest fern records immediately becomes a complicated study, but one not without some degree of hope. The bulk of Paleozoic fern foliage, originally thought to be exclusively that of spore-producing ferns and to which generic names were assigned, was shown to represent actually the leaves of a great many seed-producing ferns—the Cycadofilicales (Fig. 14-3). Thus *form genera* (see the discussion in Chapter 8) exist for the foliage types of both the Filicinae and Cycado-filicales. Identification keys that use shape, method of attachment of pinnules, and type of venation have been established for Paleozoic fern leaves (Fig. 11-1). In certain instances a "natural plant" can be synthesized from the form genus for foliage and from the numerous form genera for other parts of the plant which were originally found as isolated fragments.

The problem, then, in tracing the history of the Filicinae is to separate those fossil forms that may represent morphological steps in the evolution of the fern type of organization but at the same time to recognize that seed ferns probably shared a common ancestry with the Filicinae.

As a result of extensive studies on ferns, Bower (1935) has proposed certain features that would, in his opinion, characterize a primitive fern. The fern archetype would be an upright, dichotomizing plant, if branched at all, in which the distinction between leaf and axis would be either absent or ill-defined. The leaf, where recognizable, would be long-stalked and dichotomously branched with the shanks of the dichotomies free from one another. Sporangia would be relatively large, solitary, and located at the distal ends of leaves. The sporangial wall would be thick, opening by a simple dehiscence mechanism, and the sporangia would contain only one type of spores.

A plant known to exist in the Middle Devonian period in as far-apart places as Belgium and China may well serve as the archetype from which ferns may have had their origin. This plant with psilophytalean form is *Protopteridium* (Fig. 11-2, A). It was a small plant with a sympodial branch system; the ultimate side branches were dichotomized and somewhat flattened. Sporangia occurred at the tips of some of the small lateral branch systems. Another genus, *Iridopteris* (Arnold, 1940), in a better

A. Fronds with differentiated pinnules
  B. Secondary veins forming a network
    C. Pinnules attached by whole breadth of base
                      LONCHOPTERIS

    C'. Pinnules attached by a single point
                      LINOPTERIS

  B'. Secondary veins not forming a network
    D. Pinnules with a distinct midrib
      E. Pinnules small, attached by whole base
                PECOPTERIS

      E'. Pinnules large
        F. Decurrent at base
                ALETHOPTERIS

        F'. Constricted at base
                TAENIOPTERIS

    D'. Pinnules with an indistinct midrib
      G. Pinnules attached by whole base
                ODONTOPTERIS

      G'. Pinnules attached by a point
                NEUROPTERIS

A'. Fronds with pinnules lobed, or dissected;
rarely with rounded pinnules.
        H. Pinnules small, veins radiate
           fan-like from base of pinnule
                SPHENOPTERIS

        H'. Pinnules large, basal pinnule
          decurrent and bifid
                MARIOPTERIS

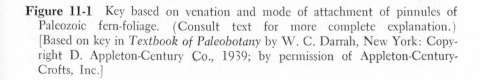

Figure 11-1 Key based on venation and mode of attachment of pinnules of Paleozoic fern-foliage. (Consult text for more complete explanation.) [Based on key in *Textbook of Paleobotany* by W. C. Darrah, New York: Copyright D. Appleton-Century Co., 1939; by permission of Appleton-Century-Crofts, Inc.]

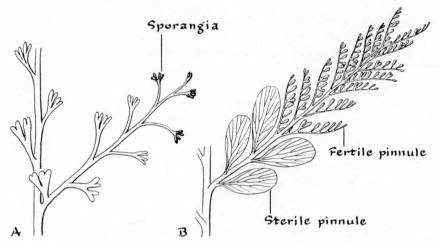

Figure 11-2 Ancestral fern types of Devonian age. **A,** *Protopteridium minutum,*
a presumed early Paleozoic fern of psilophytalean form; **B,** *Archaeopteris* (generalized diagram), of Upper Devonian age. [A, redrawn from Halle, *Palaeon-
tologia Sinica,* Ser. A, vol. i, fasc. 4, 1927.]

state of preservation, had a five-lobed xylem cylinder recalling that of
certain psilophytes (Chapter 7).

Another widely distributed fossil of the Upper Devonian is *Archaeopteris,* which may be cited as representing another evolutionary step in
the organization of the fern frond. The large, bipinnate fern-like frond,
with pinnules apparently arranged in one plane, appears to represent a
system of condensed branches. Sporangia were attached to the axes of
pinnules, often replacing the expanded vegetative pinnules (Fig. 11-2,
B). The plant was apparently heterosporous, nevertheless it vegetatively
represents an intermediate type between the psilophytalean type of
organization and that of later ferns.

In the Lower Carboniferous and Permian there lived a group of plants
that were definitely allied to ferns but which cannot be assigned with
any degree of certainty to modern groups in the Filicinae. These ferns are
classified under the name Coenopteridales, and they present some very
interesting morphological types for comparative purposes.

In general the Coenopteridales can be characterized by the general
lack of distinction between the shoot axis and leaf at the level of frond
attachment. In the simplest example, *Botryopteris,* the stem and stipe
are protostelic, but the vascular cylinder of the stipe is of distinctive

appearance as viewed in transverse section (Fig. 11-3). The xylem is in the form of the letter W in some species (Fig. 11-3, B). The fronds were often pinnately compound and fern-like, with eusporangia borne in tufts on axes of the last order on the pinnate fronds. In some instances the fronds were elaborately branched, often brush-like, and somewhat intermediate between a stem and a more typically foliar structure. Two representative ferns of this type were *Etapteris* and *Stauropteris*. The stalk of the frond (termed a phyllophore) possessed a very complicated vascular

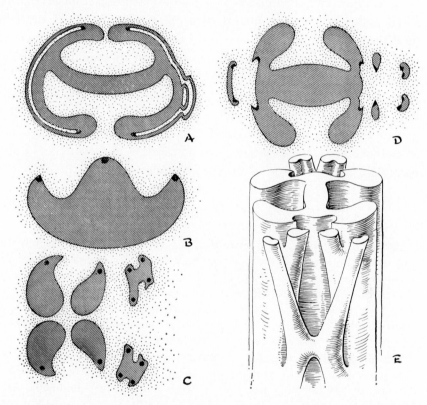

Figure 11-3 Stipes (phyllophores) of the Coenopteridales. **A-D,** xylem cylinders only, as seen in transection (solid black areas represent positions of protoxylem). **A,** *Ankyropteris;* **B,** *Botryopteris;* **C,** *Stauropteris;* **D,** *Etapteris;* **E,** stereogram of xylem cylinder in *Etapteris.* Smaller, peripheral strands in all diagrams are traces departing to subdivisions of the frond. [A, D, E, redrawn from *Handbuch der Paläobotanik* by M. Hirmer, Munich: R. Oldenbourg, 1927; B, C, redrawn from Anatomie der Vegetationsorgane der Pteridophyten by Y. Ogura. In: *Handbuch der Pflanzenanatomie,* Berlin: Gebrüder Borntraeger, 1938.]

cylinder, the xylem in transverse section often having the appearance of the letter H (Fig. 11-3, D). Form genera are common for phyllophores and more distal parts of fronds. Eusporangia were homosporous and grouped in tufts on fertile pinnules, or were solitary and terminal on ultimate small axes of highly branched fronds. In some instances a vascular strand was present in the sporangial stalk, recalling the situation in the Psilophytales. Although the Coenopteridales is a diverse and somewhat enigmatic group, it may well represent a complex from which later ferns were derived. The discovery of additional fossils will serve to test this hypothesis. There are, indeed, fossils that are undoubtedly related to modern day fern families; they will be discussed with the groups listed in the following outline of classification and in subsequent discussions. The Coenopteridales is included in the outline for review purposes. The general characteristics of the Pteropsida have already been discussed in the preceding chapter and reviewed earlier in this chapter. It will be remembered that this large, major division of vascular plants includes the ferns (Filicinae), the seed ferns, cycads, *Ginkgo*, and conifers (Gymnospermae), and the flowering plants (Angiospermae).

Classification

FILICINAE: Living and extinct ferns; plants showing a conspicuous alternation of generations (in modern representatives at least); sporophyte most conspicuous and often elaborately developed; megaphylls present; stems protostelic or siphonostelic, often with complex vascular cylinders; sporangia terminal on ultimate axes, terminal on veins, marginal, or on abaxial surface of fronds; eusporangiate, or more commonly leptosporangiate in living species; homosporous, a few heterosporous; gametophytes: (1) majority exosporic and green, (2) others exosporic, non-chlorophyllous, and subterranean, and (3) endosporic (restricted to heterosporous types); multiflagellate free-swimming sperms; embryo exoscopic, endoscopic, or intermediate.

COENOPTERIDALES: Extinct ferns; only sporophytes known; shoots erect, climbing, or creeping; fronds with pinnate plan or with modified dichotomous type of branching; stem and frond stipe or phyllophore anatomically similar at level of separation; stem protostelic; vascular cylinders of phyllophores often complex; eusporangia grouped in clusters on pinnules or terminal on ultimate branches of a frond and often with a simple dehiscence mechanism; homosporous; form genera common; gametophyte and embryo unknown.

Representative genera: *Botryopteris, Stauropteris, Etapteris* (form genus for fronds), *Zygopteris, Ankyropteris.*

OPHIOGLOSSALES (Chapter 12): Living ferns, fossil record uncertain; sporophyte axis usually short and fleshy; stem siphonostelic; fronds simple or pinnately compound; vernation non-circinate; each fertile frond consists of a fertile segment or spike bearing sporangia and a sterile or vegetative segment; eusporangiate, producing great quantities of spores per sporangium; gametophytes subterranean, non-chlorophyllous, tuberous or wormlike with endophytic fungus; embryo exoscopic with some variation.

OPHIOGLOSSACEAE: Characteristics as in Ophioglossales.

Ophioglossum, Botrychium, Helminthostachys.

MARATTIALES (Chapter 12): Living and extinct ferns; sporophyte stem in most erect and short or may be dorsiventral; stem with complex dictyostelic vascular cylinder; fronds commonly large, simple pinnate to tripinnate, and circinate in vernation; paired, clasping stipules at base of each leaf; eusporangia free and grouped into elongate sori or united into synangia on abaxial surface of fronds; many spores formed per sporangium; gametophyte terrestrial, green, cordate to ribbon shaped with endophytic fungus; endoscopic embryo.

MARATTIACEAE: Characteristics as in Marattiales.

Representative genera: *Angiopteris, Marattia, Psaronius* (form genus for trunks), *Asterotheca* (form genus for synangia).

FILICALES (Chapter 13): Living and extinct plants, of diverse growth habits and habitats; stems vary from protostelic to intricately dictyostelic; fronds simple to compound pinnate; sporangia scattered or grouped into sori; sori marginal or on abaxial side of fronds; sori with or without a protective structure, the indusium; leptosporangiate, most with a definite dehiscence mechanism, the annulus; spores numerous to few per sporangium, tetrahedral or bilateral; prevailingly homosporous, a few heterosporous; gametophytes green, exosporic, primarily thalloid, some filamentous; a few endosporic; embryo "prone." Representative families are Osmundaceae, Schizaeaceae, Gleicheniaceae, Hymenophyllaceae, Dicksoniaceae, Matoniaceae, Cyatheaceae, Polypodiaceae, Marsileaceae, and Salviniaceae. Certain of these families are described in greater detail in Chapter 13.

Before proceeding with a detailed account of the living orders of ferns, that we have just outlined, it is important for the student to have a clear idea of the morphological features that are used for comparative purposes. It was the celebrated British morphologist, F. O. Bower, who realized the importance of exploring and exploiting the totality of morphological features before a reasonable phylogeny of ferns could be achieved. Bower (1923, 1935) concluded that there are at least twelve major morphological and anatomical criteria that should be utilized. These are listed here because discussions of these points are unavoidable in ferns, and because most of them are of great importance in later discussions.

1. External morphology and habit of plant.
2. Apical meristem organization.
3. Architecture and venation of the leaf.
4. Vascular system of the shoot.
5. Morphology of hairs and scales.
6. Position and structure of the sorus.
7. Protection of the sorus by an indusium.
8. Development and mature structure of the sporangium including form of and markings on spores.
9. Number of spores.
10. Morphology of the gametophyte.
11. Position and structure of sex organs.
12. Embryology of the sporophyte.

To this list should now be added the recent important criteria resulting from studies made in the fields of cytology and cytogenetics (Manton, 1950) and experimental physiology and morphology (Wardlaw 1952; Wetmore and Wardlaw, 1951).

References

Arnold, C. A. 1940. Structure and relationships of some Middle Devonian plants from western New York. *Amer. Jour. Bot.* 27:57-63.

Bower, F. O. 1923. *The ferns* (Vol. I). Cambridge University Press, London.

————. 1935. *Primitive Land Plants.* Macmillan, London.

Manton, I. 1950. *Problems of Cytology and Evolution in the Pteridophyta.* Cambridge University Press, London.

Wardlaw, C. W. 1952. *Phylogeny and Morphogenesis.* Macmillan, London.

Wetmore, R. H. and C. W. Wardlaw. 1951. Experimental morphogenesis in vascular plants. *Ann. Rev. Plant Physiol.* 2:269-292.

Chapter

12 THE EUSPORANGIATE FERNS

Ophioglossales–Ophioglossaceae

It is most unfortunate that this particular order has no fossil history; nevertheless most morphologists consider the order to have been derived from the Coenopteridales. Our earliest recorded knowledge of this group dates back to the year 1542 and to one of the herbalists, Leonhard Fuchs (Clausen, 1938).

The family consists of three or four recognized genera, of which two are more commonly seen and known by botanists. One genus, *Botrychium* (grape fern, moonwort), with about 30 or more species, is restricted mainly to the North Temperate Zone. *Ophioglossum* (adder's tongue), with 40 or more species, is widely spread throughout the habitable world but is most abundant in the tropics (Campbell, 1948). Although members of the Ophioglossaceae are typically terrestrial, two species of *Ophioglossum* are epiphytic, occurring in the American tropics. Commonly the stem is short and erect and has a frond that is divided into a flattened, vegetative portion and a sporangium-bearing portion. However, the genera *Ophioglossum* and *Botrychium* can be separated easily (with few exceptions) by examining the fronds. The lamina in *Ophioglossum* is characteristically simple in outline with reticulate venation; it is pinnate in plan in *Botrychium*, with open dichotomous venation. One other genus, *Helminthostachys*, which is native to the Indo-Malayan regions, can be recognized by its creeping rhizome and palmately compound leaves which have an open dichotomous venation system. The genera *Botrychium* and *Ophioglossum* will now be described in detail.

240

Botrychium

The plant axis is a short, stocky, subterranean rhizome from which roots arise adventitiously at the bases of leaves (Fig. 12-1). Generally one frond matures each year in temperate-climate species; the decaying leaves of previous seasons surround the base of the plant. Each frond, all of which are commonly fleshy, has a sheath at its base that encloses the next younger leaf. Although only one leaf matures each year, there are several immature leaves of future seasons in varying stages of development within the terminal bud. During development the leaf does not exhibit circinate vernation—a feature so common to many other ferns. The frond stipe is fleshy and consists of two parts: the vegetative lamina, which usually exhibits a pinnate pattern of branching, and a fertile segment or spike. The fertile spike likewise is constructed on the pinnate plan, bearing eusporangia in two rows on ultimate axes. There is some degree of correlation between the amount of pinnate branching of the fertile and sterile portions of the frond. In certain species the vegetative lamina may be several times pinnate and the fertile segment of the same degree of branching; in others, the blade may be simple and entire with the fertile segment showing the same degree of reduction. This reduction series is considered to be an evolutionary sequence. Morphological interpretation of the frond in *Botrychium* is a lively and controversial subject which will be discussed later in this chapter.

ANATOMY OF THE STEM. Growth of the shoot is reported to be initiated (Campbell, 1911) by an apical cell from which derivative cells are formed; these derivative cells provide initials for leaves, and some of them differentiate into tissues of the axis. The vascular cylinder of well-established plants is an ectophloic siphonostele. The gaps do not overlap, consequently a continuous vascular cylinder or a cylinder with one gap may be present in a stem as seen in a representative transverse section (Fig. 12-2, A). The individual bundles are collateral in arrangement, and the xylem is endarch in development. The tracheids have circular or oval bordered pits in contrast with the scalariform pitting in the vast majority of lower vascular plants. A definite endodermis is present around the vascular cylinder. In contrast with all other living ferns, a vascular cambium is reported to occur in the stem of *Botrychium,* which

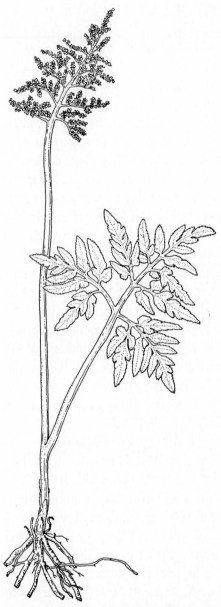

Figure 12-1 Habit sketch of sporophyte of *Botrychium dissectum* var. *obliquum,* showing pinnate fertile and sterile segments of one leaf. [Drawn by Mrs. Emily E. Reid.]

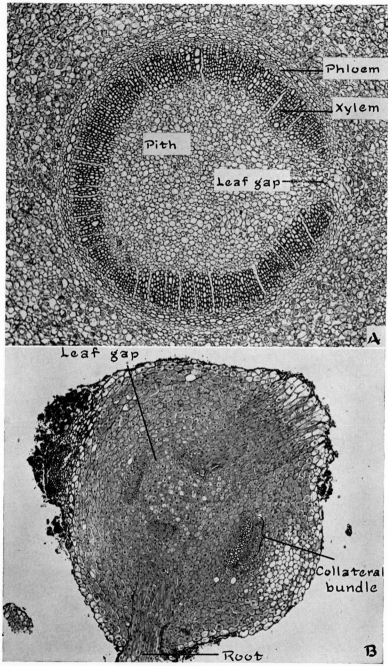

Figure 12-2 Stem anatomy in the Ophioglossales. **A**, transection, stem of *Botrychium* with ectophloic siphonostele; **B**, transection, stem of *Ophioglossum* showing ectophloic siphonostele.

gives rise to some secondary xylem and a limited amount of secondary phloem (Fig. 12-2, A). A critical developmental study of stem anatomy has not been made to date. The sieve cells of the primary phloem are conspicuously thickened except for sieve areas. However, the presence of callose has not been detected in the sieve areas (Esau, Cheadle, and Gifford, 1953). At the periphery of the broad cortex there generally occurs a cork layer.

THE ROOT. Attached near the bases of leaves are hairless, fleshy, storage roots that generally exhibit limited monopodial branching. It is reported that a tetrahedral apical cell is present in the root tips, but cleavages which give rise to the root cap may not be as precise as they are in leptosporangiate ferns (Campbell, 1911; Bower, 1926). Mature roots are tetrarch, often diarch, or even monarch.

THE FROND (LEAF). As stated earlier in this chapter, the vegetative portion of the frond has an open dichotomous venation system with a rather homogeneous mesophyll organization. Transcending the mere knowledge of leaf organization is the important question of the morphological interpretation of the frond. A widely accepted view is that the fertile segment represents two pinnae which have become fused during the course of evolution and which now stand erect (Chrysler, 1925). This hypothesis is based on a study of the vascular system. In general, the leaf trace consists of one vascular bundle which may be dissected into two bundles where it enters the frond. Within the stipes of some species there are two crescent-shaped vascular bundles. This arrangement would appear to be a basic type in the genus *Botrychium*. At the level of the fertile spike the two bundles are branched, one small, branch vascular bundle from each of the original two bundles extends into the fertile spike. The two large vascular strands are continuous up the rachis of the vegetative segment, each one supplying lateral vegetative pinnae with a vascular bundle. Thus the presence of two vascular bundles in the rachis of the fertile segment is the evidence for the assumed evolutionary fusion of two basal fertile pinnae. The occasional occurrence in some species (for example, *B. lanuginosum*) of fertile pinnae occupying the position of otherwise normal vegetative pinnae tends to support this idea (Chrysler, 1925).

More recently the frond has been reinterpreted. This newer theory also is based on the branching of the vascular tissue in the frond. The repeated bifurcations of the vascular tissue are interpreted as being indicative of a once free dichotomous branch system. The first dichotomy is considered to be at a level below the union of the fertile spike and vegetative lamina (or even at the level of the departing leaf trace). Thus this interpretation adds even greater weight to the idea that the "frond" is a modified, reduced dichotomous branch system (Zimmermann, 1942; Chrysler, 1945; Nishida, 1952).

THE SPORANGIUM. The fronds of several future seasons are in varying stages of development within the bud. Therefore the stages of development of the fertile spikes are also variable. Eusporangia are initiated from one or from several surface cells (Bower, 1935) in an acropetal manner on the pinnae. If only one initial surface cell is evident early in development, sooner or later adjacent surface cells may divide periclinally which finally results in the separation of sporogenous cells and wall cells (Chapter 4). The tapetum becomes several layers thick, and its cells break down very early, their contents permeating the spaces between the spore-mother cells.

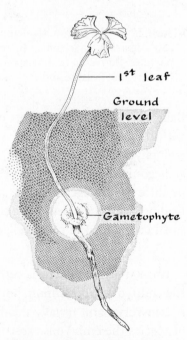

At maturity each sporangium is large and has a vascular strand that extends to the base of the capsule. Each sporangium, which dehisces by means of a terminal slit, produces 2,000, or more, tetrahedral spores. The results of one study have shown that, at least in *Botrychium lunaria*, the haploid number of chromosomes is $n = 45$ (Manton, 1950).

THE GAMETOPHYTE. In *Botrychium* the gametophytic plant is entirely subterranean, tuberous, somewhat longer

Figure 12-3 Subterranean gametophyte of *Botrychium dissectum* with attached sporophyte. [Drawn from specimen, courtesy Dr. A. J. Eames.]

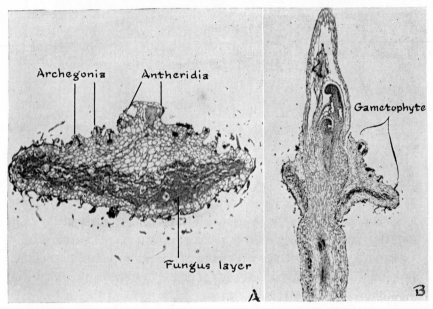

Figure 12-4 **A,** section, gametophyte of *Botrychium* showing antheridial ridge and subjacent archegonia; **B,** section, young sporophyte attached to gametophyte of *Botrychium.* The sporophyte has several immature leaves in the bud; the first root is large and is toward the bottom of the page.

than wide, may be very short or up to ¾ inch in length, and is covered with rhizoids (Fig. 12-3). It is without chlorophyll but it does have an endophytic fungus (Fig. 12-4). Antheridia occur on a dorsal crest with archegonia along each side (Jeffrey, 1897). Antheridia are sunken and produce multiflagellate, free-swimming sperms. Archegonia have protruding necks of a few neck cells, and each one has a binucleate neck-canal cell, a ventral canal cell, and an egg cell.

THE EMBRYO. There is some variation in the early development of the embryo in *Botrychium,* but in all cases the first division of the zygote is transverse, and usually quadrants can be recognized. In the majority of species the embryo is exoscopic. There are no recent studies available, but in general the future shoot apex and first leaf are derived from the apical pole (epibasal cell); the root and foot are formed from the basal pole (hypobasal cell). In one instance the first division of the zygote sets aside a suspensor cell (Lyon, 1905), and the polarity is endoscopic. In this type a foot is absent. Figure 12-4, B shows the relation of a young sporophyte to the gametophyte.

Ophioglossum

Most species are terrestrial except for certain tropical epiphytic forms. The general organization of the plant body is similar to that of *Botrychium*, namely, a short rhizome, adventitious roots, and formation of a single mature frond each year in temperate species (Fig. 12-5). Here also, a leaf sheath encloses the next younger leaf in the bud. The vegetative lamina is generally simple and entire in outline, or it may be palmately lobed or dichotomously branched in epiphytic species. In contrast with *Botrychium*, leaf venation in *Ophioglossum* is of the reticulate type (Fig. 13-4, H). In general the fertile spike consists of an axis with two lateral rows of embedded sporangia. In one tropical epiphytic species (*O. palmatum*) there may be several "fertile spikes" near the base of the lamina. A reductional series (considered to be an evolutionary reductional series) also can be established in the genus beginning with the large epiphytic species and culminating with the minute and inconspicuous types a few centimeters in height (Eames, 1936).

ANATOMY OF THE SHOOT. An apical cell, which may be variable in form

Figure 12-5 Sporophyte of *Ophioglossum lusitanicum* var. *californicum*. Each leaf consists of a simple sterile segment and a compact spike-like fertile segment. One leaf or frond matures each year. The stem is a short upright rhizome bearing roots. [Specimen supplied by Dr. W. H. Wagner, Jr.]

(Bower, 1926), occupies the tip of the shoot axis. The vascular cylinder of the shoot, enclosed by fleshy storage cortical tissue, is described as an ectophloic siphonostele (Fig. 12-2, B). The bundles are collateral and are composed of primary phloem and of endarch primary xylem; the latter consists of scalariformly pitted tracheids. In contrast with the majority of ferns, no definite endodermis is present, at least in older plants. The vascular supply to leaves may be a single vascular bundle or may consist of two bundles. The entire vascular system of the axis, not only in *Ophioglossum* but also in *Botrychium*, has been interpreted as a meshwork of leaf traces and root traces, no part of it being considered as strictly cauline (Baas-Becking, 1921; Campbell, 1921; Maheshwari and Singh, 1934). Carefully devised experiments might prove or disprove this concept.

The base of the frond stipe is traversed by several vascular bundles or by a definite cylinder of bundles which are subdivisions of the leaf trace. Vascular bundles on the adaxial side of the stipe are continuous into the fertile spike; others traverse the vegetative lamina and are branched, forming a reticulate venation system. The morphological interpretation of the fertile spike with its inherent problems is comparable to the situation in *Botrychium* (p. 244). The occurrence in *O. palmatum* of several fertile spikes, arising on the margins of the lamina, is used as evidence for the branched nature of the frond.

THE ROOT. As in *Botrychium* there is generally one fleshy mycorrhizal root attached to the stem near each leaf. Roots arise endogenously, having their origin from cells near the phloem of vascular bundles in the shoot axis. Growth of the root is initiated by a tetrahedral cell; the root becomes monarch or diarch, or even more protoxylem poles of differentiation are formed (Petry, 1914; Joshi, 1940; Chrysler, 1941).

THE SPORANGIUM. Eusporangia, which originate from surface cells along two sides of the young fertile spike, are in varying stages of development before the frond emerges for the season. The sporangia always remain embedded in tissues of the fertile spike; small vascular strands are present between the sporangia and often are turned toward them (Fig. 12-6). At maturity numerous tetrahedral spores are formed which are liberated by a slit in the sporangial wall, perpendicular to the wide surface of the fertile spike. In one study of the meiotic divisions it was reported that the chromosome number in *Ophioglossum lusitanicum* is $n = 125$-130 whereas in the species *O. vulgatum* there is the surprisingly high number of $n = 250$-260 (Manton, 1950).

THE GAMETOPHYTE. Spores germinate slowly, and growth may be extended over a period of years during which time the gametophytes become buried by several inches of humus or soil particles. Growth by an apical cell results in the development of a worm-like, sometimes branched, non-chlorophyllous gametophyte, from ⅛ inch to 1-2 inches in length. An endophytic fungus, essential to the nutrition of the gametophyte, gains entrance early in development and is present in cells of the older parts of the plant body. Sex organs take their origin from meristematic cells distal to the apical cell and are mature within the region of the endophytic fungus. Antheridia and archegonia are scattered and intermingled over the surface of the gametophyte. The gametangia are very similar to those in *Botrychium*.

THE EMBRYO. As is true of most groups of lower vascular plants, the first division of the zygote (in *Ophioglossum*) is transverse, that is, perpendicular to the long axis of the archegonium. The embryo is exoscopic in polarity (Fig. 6-1). A cell division at the apical pole (epibasal cell) and at the basal pole (hypobasal cell) results in the formation of four cells—the quadrant stage of embryogeny. Subsequent cell divisions are irregular, but with little doubt the first leaf and future shoot apex are derived from the epibasal portion of the embryo and the foot is

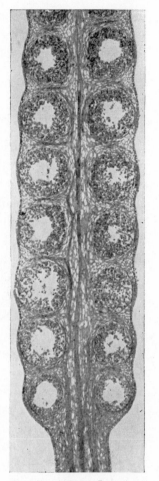

Figure 12-6 Longisection, fertile segment of *Ophioglossum lusitanicum* var. *californicum,* showing two rows of embedded sporangia. Branches of the main vascular system are evident between sporangia at left.

derived from the hypobasal portion. Origin of the root is uncertain, but seemingly it arises near the middle of the embryo and enlarges rapidly in a lateral direction before other parts of the embryo become conspicuous.

Marattiales–Marattiaceae

This is a group of plants the members of which resemble more closely, in general aspect, the so-called true ferns; many of them possess large pinnate fronds with sporangia located on their lower surfaces. It is an ancient group of ferns and has a well-preserved fossil record that extends back to the Carboniferous. It is a tropical group and is generally known only through occasional specimens in conservatories or dried specimens in herbaria. According to one student of ferns, there are six genera and perhaps a hundred or more species (Copeland, 1947). The two better-known genera are *Angiopteris* and *Marattia;* the former is distributed throughout the South Sea Islands and north to Japan, the latter is pantropical in distribution.

In growth habit a marattiaceous fern characteristically has an upright, unbranched tuberous stem or short trunk to which large, pinnately compound leaves (circinate in vernation) and thick, fleshy roots are attached. A pair of clasping fleshy stipules occurs at the base of each leaf, covering a part of the trunk; they persist, along with the leaf base, even after the frond abscisses. On the lower surface (abaxial surface) of the fronds, which may be several feet in length, sporangia commonly occur along veins; the venation is of the open dichotomous type. In *Angiopteris* the sporangia are crowded together in two rows along each side of a vein, and each sporangium dehisces by a longitudinal slit on the side facing the other row of sporangia (Figs. 12-7, A, 12-8). A more specialized condition is observed in *Marattia* where the two rows of sporangia are united into a compact soral group surrounded by a common wall (Fig. 12-7, B). This structure is termed a synagium. At maturity the synangium opens, much like a clam shell, exposing the sporangia which dehisce by longitudinal slits. There are exceptions to the above frond and synangial types. In some genera the fronds may be simple to once pinnate (*Danaea*), or palmately compound with reticulate venation and scattered synangia (*Christensenia*).

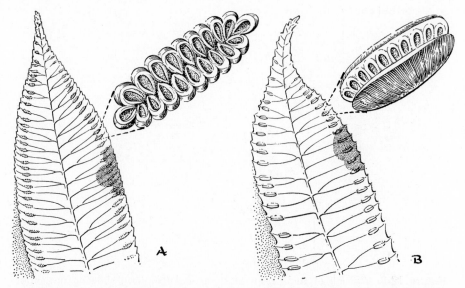

Figure 12-7 Abaxial views of fertile pinnae of *Angiopteris* (**A**) and *Marattia* (**B**). One sorus of each is enlarged. The sporangia in *Marattia* form a definite synangium. [Pinnae redrawn from *The Ferns*, Vol. II, by F. O. Bower, Cambridge: Cambridge University Press, 1926.]

Anatomy of the Shoot

The apical meristem of a mature or adult shoot is reported to have a group of shoot apical initials or an apical cell that is not regular or precise in its divisions (Charles, 1911; Bower, 1923). The apical meristem gives rise to derivative meristematic cells from which leaves take their origin; other derivative cells will differentiate into procambium and pith. A transverse section of a young stem may reveal a cylinder of vascular bundles, but, at a higher level in older plants, the vascular cylinder becomes dis-

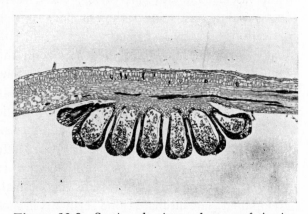

Figure 12-8 Section, lamina and sorus of *Angiopteris*. Note the presence of numerous spores within each thick-walled sporangium.

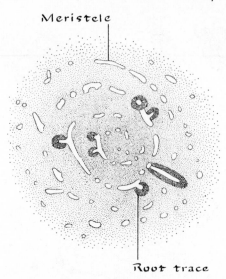

Meristele

Root trace

Figure 12-9 Portion of transection of stem of *Angiopteris*, showing numerous meristeles; root traces are attached to inner meristeles of the stem. [Redrawn from Anatomie der Vegetationsorgane der Pteridophyten by Y. Ogura. In: *Handbuch der Pflanzenanatomie*, Berlin: Gebrüder Borntraeger, 1938.]

sected into a complex polycyclic dictyostele consisting of two or more concentric vascular cylinders (Fig. 12-9). It should be emphasized that the inner vascular cylinders are continuous with the original outer cylinder at a lower level in the stem. It has been shown that the majority of the vascular bundles (meristeles) enter leaves at some level of the shoot axis; however, some of the bundles are reported to be simply interconnections between leaf traces (Farmer and Hill, 1902; Charles, 1911; West, 1917). Additional detailed studies in this group by interested botanists would be desirable. Root primordia have their origin in tissue near the vascular bundles of either the inner vascular cylinders or the outermost cylinder (Fig. 12-9); after their initiation the roots bore their way through the cortex to the surface (Farmer and Hill, 1902). Therefore root traces appear in transverse sections of a stem. In the outer cortex of the stem there are mucilage ducts as well as cells filled with tannin.

The leaves of marattiaceous ferns are circinate in vernation during development. The ultimate frond segments in most species have a single midvein with lateral dichotomous veins. The mesophyll in most forms is differentiated into an adaxial palisade tissue and an abaxial spongy mesophyll. Stomata occur on the abaxial surface. Mucilage cavities, hypodermal sclerenchyma, or collenchyma are often present in the petiole.

The Root

In the primary root and the first-formed adventitious roots there is a definite apical cell; later-formed roots are reported to have a group of about four equivalent initials (West, 1917). Roots become large and fleshy and contain mucilage cavities. Typically the vascular cylinder is polyarch—a feature not generally found in other ferns.

The Sporangium

Sporangia are of the eusporangiate type and commonly originate from mounds of tissue paralleling the veins of developing fronds. At maturity each sporangium has a broad base and a sporangial wall that consists of several layers of cells. When mature the sporangia may be separate from each other (*Angiopteris*), or the sporangial walls may become confluent during development so that each sporangium is actually a pocket or loculus in a compact structure, the synangium (Figs. 12-7; 12-8). Dehiscence of individual sporangia in a synangium is brought about by the drying out of wall cells, which results in longitudinal splitting of each sporangium (after the halves of the synangium separate in *Marattia*), or by the formation of a pore at the tip of each sporangium as in *Danaea*. Spore output is large; spore numbers range from a minimum of 1,000 up to a maximum of 7,000 spores formed by each sporangium (Bower, 1935). In *Marattia sambucina* the spores are yellowish to tan, bilateral and elongate, with a longitudinal ridge (Stokey, 1942). In contrast, tetrahedral spores are formed by other members of the group.

The Gametophyte

The gametophyte is a large, green, dorsiventral ribbon-shaped or heart-shaped structure with a prominent ventral midrib or cushion and thin, lateral wing-like extensions (Fig. 12-10). The thallus, which may be 2 cm, or more, in length is long-lived and has an endophytic fungus which, however, must play only a minor role in the nutrition of the gametophyte because of the presence of chlorophyll. Absorbing rhizoids occur

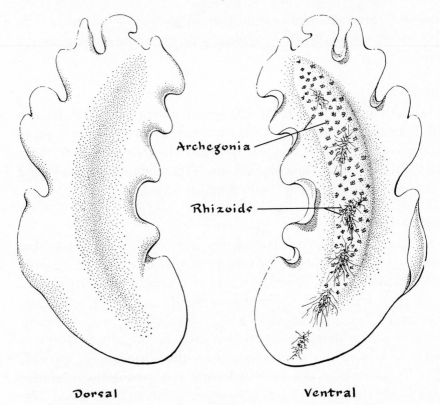

Figure 12-10 Ribbon-shaped gametophyte of *Marattia douglasii*. Antheridia (not shown in drawing) occur mainly on the ventral surface. [Drawn from a specimen supplied by W. H. Wagner, Jr.]

along the ventral midrib. Gametangia show the following pattern of distribution: Antheridia are primarily on the ventral surface but may occur on the dorsal side of the thallus; archegonia are restricted to the projecting ventral midrib (Haupt, 1940). Both antheridia and archegonia are sunken, and the main stages in their development are shown in Fig. 12-11. Mature sperms are coiled and multiflagellate.

The Embryo

Just as in the Ophioglossales the first division of the zygote is transverse, resulting in a two-celled embryo. In contrast with most members of the Ophioglossales, the Marattiaceae exhibit endoscopic polarity (see Fig. 6-1). This means that the future shoot apex and first leaf have their origin from the cell (epibasal cell) directed away from the neck of the archegonium. The cell (hypobasal cell) toward the archegonial neck gives rise to a multicellular foot. The root meristem, appearing late in embryogeny, is endogenous in origin, and in one study it has been reported to be derived from the epibasal portion of the embryo (Campbell, 1911). With subsequent growth of the embryo the young shoot grows up through the gametophyte, emerging from the upper

Figure 12-11 Stages in the development of an antheridium (**A, B**) and of an archegonium (**C-H**) of *Angiopteris evecta*. [Redrawn from Haupt, *Bull. Torrey Bot. Club* 67:125, 1940.]

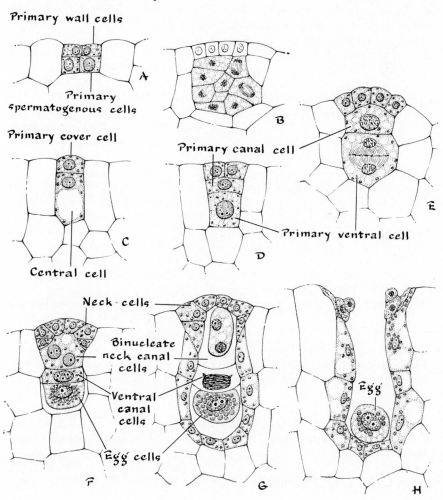

surface. The presence of a suspensor has been reported in some species of *Angiopteris* (Land, 1923) and other genera (Campbell, 1940). The first vascular bundle of the embryo is continuous between the root and first leaf. The vascular bundle of the next leaf is joined to the first vascular strand. The vascular strands of later leaves continue to form essentially an interconnected network of leaf traces and root traces (Campbell, 1911, 1921).

References

Baas-Becking, L. G. M. 1921. The origin of the vascular structure in the genus *Botrychium*; with notes on the general anatomy. *Recueil Trav. Bot. Néerland.* 18:333-372.

Bower, F. O. 1923. *The Ferns (Vol. I).* Cambridge University Press, London.

———. 1926. *The Ferns (Vol. II).* Cambridge University Press, London.

———. 1935. *Primitive Land Plants.* Macmillan, London.

Campbell, D. H. 1911. *The Eusporangiatae.* Carnegie Institute, Washington.

———. 1921. The eusporangiate ferns and the stelar theory. *Amer. Jour. Bot.* 8:303-314.

———. 1940. *The Evolution of the Land Plants (Embryophyta).* Stanford University Press, Stanford, California.

———. 1948. Notes on the geographical distribution of ferns. *Amer. Fern Jour.* 38:122-125.

Charles, G. M. 1911. The anatomy of the sporeling of *Marattia alata. Bot. Gaz.* 51:81-101.

Chrysler, M. A. 1925. *Botrychium lanuginosum* and its relation to the problem of the fertile spike. *Bull. Torrey Bot. Club* 52:127-132.

———. 1941. The structure and development of *Ophioglossum palmatum. Bull. Torrey Bot. Club* 68:1-19.

———. 1945. The shoot of *Botrychium* interpreted as a series of dichotomies. *Bull. Torrey Bot. Club* 72:491-505.

Clausen, R. T. 1938. A monograph of the Ophioglossaceae. *Mem. Torrey Bot. Club* 19:1-177.

Copeland, E. B. 1947. *Genera Filicum (The Genera of Ferns).* Chronica Botanica Co., Waltham, Mass.

Eames, A. J. 1936. *Morphology of Vascular Plants. Lower Groups.* McGraw-Hill, New York.

Esau, K., V. I. Cheadle and E. M. Gifford, Jr. 1953. Comparative structure and possible trends of specialization of the phloem. *Amer. Jour. Bot.* 40:9-19.

References
257

Farmer, J. B. and T. G. Hill. 1902. On the arrangement and structure of the vascular strands in *Angiopteris evecta*, and some other Marattiaceae. *Ann. Bot.* 16:371-402.

Haupt, A. W. 1940. Sex organs of *Angiopteris evecta*. *Bull. Torrey Bot. Club* 67:125-129

Jeffrey, E. C. 1897. The gametophyte of *Botrychium virginianum*. *Trans. Canadian Inst.* 5:265-294.

Joshi, A. C. 1940. A note on the anatomy of the roots of *Ophioglossum*. *Ann. Bot. N.S.* 4:663-664.

Land, W. J. G. 1923. A suspensor in *Angiopteris*. *Bot. Gaz.* 75:421-425.

Lyon, H. L. 1905. A new genus of Ophioglossaceae. *Bot. Gaz.* 40:455-458.

Maheshwari, P. and B. Singh. 1934. The morphology of *Ophioglossum*

fibrosum. Schum. *Jour. Indian Bot. Soc.* 13:103-123.

Manton, I. 1950. *Problems of Cytology and Evolution in the Pteridophyta.* Cambridge University Press, London.

Nishida, M. 1952. Dichotomy of vascular system in the stalk of Ophioglossaceae. *Jour. Jap. Bot.* 27:165-171.

Petry, L. C. 1914. The anatomy of *Ophioglossum pendulum*. *Bot. Gaz.* 57:169-192.

Stokey, A. G. 1942. Gametophytes of *Marattia sambucina* and *Macroglossum smithii*. *Bot. Gaz.* 103:559-569.

West, C. 1917. A contribution to the study of the Marattiaceae. *Ann. Bot.* 31:361-414.

Zimmermann, W. 1942. Die Phylogenie des Ophioglossaceen-Blattes. *Ber. deutsch. bot. Ges.* 60:416-433.

Chapter

13 THE LEPTOSPORAN-GIATE FERNS

Members of this group are popularly termed the "true ferns" and are the types most commonly grown in home gardens.

Almost everyone can recognize a familiar name in the following brief list: cinnamon fern, Boston fern, Christmas fern, male fern, maidenhair fern, sensitive fern, and bracken fern.

Economic Importance

Aside from the purely aesthetic value of ferns they do have moderate economic importance throughout the world; perhaps the most notable use is that of providing food for certain groups of peoples. Young leaf tips of some ferns are eaten throughout the Malayan and adjacent regions. In fact, in the same areas certain ferns are grown commercially in gardens with a value sometimes greater per plot than that of rice (Copeland, 1942). Not only are ferns enjoyed as food in such tropic regions, but "fiddlehead greens" have been imported from Maine to the best hotels in New York (Blake, 1942). One gourmet reputedly remarked, "They taste, simply and beautifully, like the soul of spring." During devastating famines in Europe, precious stores of barley and rye were conserved by mixing small amounts of the grains with dry, ground-up male fern or bracken fern—the mixture being termed *"pain de fougére"* in France (Coquillat, 1950).

Commercially ferns are used extensively by florists in bouquets and floral arrangements, the maidenhair fern being among the most common. A fern with better keeping qualities is the American-shield fern ("fancy fern"). In greenhouses and conservatories orchids often are grown on pieces of the trunk and roots of tree ferns or on *Osmunda* "fiber." In some regions the fibrous material obtained from ferns is used as a stuffing for mattresses.

Medicinally the male fern (*Dryopteris filix-mas*) has been used in the cure of tapeworm since its beneficial effect was discovered by Dioscorides in the days of Nero. Two more uses of the male fern might be cited: tissues of the fern have been substituted for hops in brewing ale, and juices of the fern are said to have been used by witches in concocting love philters!

Distribution and Growth Habit

There are approximately 8,000-10,000 species of "true ferns" and about 300 genera. The number of recognized families varies from 9 to 19, depending on the morphological concepts of fern specialists (Bower, 1935; Copeland, 1947). The Filicales reach their greatest numbers and are most diversified in the tropics. There they are commonly epiphytic, or clamber on other vegetation, or they may form stands of forest trees. Some mountains may have hundreds of species. As an example, a certain mountain in Borneo has at least 437 species (Copeland, 1939). As was pointed out in Chapter 11, ferns are not restricted to the tropics; they may be found within wide ranges of climatic conditions. In temperate regions ferns are largely terrestrial, the shoot being erect or more commonly a prostrate rhizome with no aerial stem, the leaves being the only structures visible above the ground.

It is interesting to note that ferns constitute about one-fiftieth of the total species of vascular plants in California, whereas in Guam (Mariana Islands) one-eighth of the total species are ferns. How can we account for this present unequal distribution of ferns? According to Copeland (1942), who is one of the leading scholars of fern distribution and systematics, the group undoubtedly had its evolutionary beginnings in the Australasian region and spread thence to the north and also across the Pacific Ocean by spores which were left in the wake of tropical storms.

Morphology and Anatomy of the Shoot

It is impossible to describe all of the morphological types and endless variations in the anatomy of the fern sporophyte. We can only look at certain common features, leaving complete surveys to monographic treatments. However, at the end of the chapter the student will find summaries of the important features of selected families and their inter-relationships. In addition there are brief discussions of certain morpho-logical problems in the concluding section of this chapter.

If the aerial stem or rhizome of a fern is short and erect, the plant appears to be a collection of leaves. If, on the other hand, the rhizome is prostrate, the leaves tend to be somewhat farther apart, and nodal and internodal regions can be more easily seen. Branching of the rhizome is usually irregular, but in some ferns it is dichotomous. The majority of true ferns have leaves that are basically organized on the pinnate plan, but many are of the simple type (Fig. 13-1). Members of all families of ferns possess epidermal appendages on the leaf and stem, and fre-quently they are present on the root. These appendages may be only simple hairs, or they may be developed into large chaffy scales called paleae (see Fig. 13-5, C-I). Roots usually arise at definite places along the rhizome; most commonly this position is near the base of the leaves.

The Leaf

Inasmuch as probably everyone has seen a fern frond at some time and noticed the associated reproductive structures, the first detailed organographic account of filicalian organization will deal with the mor-phology of the leaf.

INITIATION AND DEVELOPMENT. A description of the initiation and growth of a foliage leaf should include a description of the shoot apical meristem because of the close ontogenetic relationship of stem and leaf. At the tip of a fern stem is an obvious apical cell which may vary in shape according to the species. In some genera (e.g., *Pteridium, Poly-podium*) the shoot apical cell has three faces, from which cells are cut off on two sides. In others (*Osmunda, Lygodium*) the apical cell is a tetrahedral, pyramidal cell; new cells are initiated from the three oblique basal sides (Fig. 13-2). The apical cell itself divides infrequently, but the derivative cells divide at a rapid rate.

At a rather precise distance from the shoot apex, one cell among a group of dividing cells becomes conspicuous and functions as the initial of a new leaf. This initial soon becomes an apical cell and gives rise to two rows of derivative cells (Fig. 13-2). The leaf then undergoes a period of apical growth which may continue for varying lengths of time

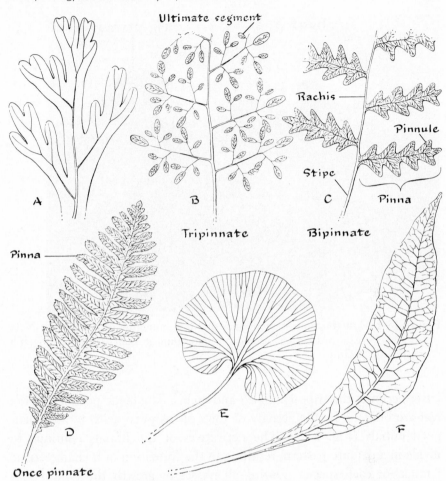

Figure 13-1 Form and organization of fern fronds. **A,** *Hymenophyllum,* portion of a compound pinnate leaf; **B,** *Pellaea;* **C,** schematic only; **D,** *Trichomanes;* **E,** *Trichomanes,* simple leaf with open dichotomous venation; **F,** *Paraleptochilus,* simple leaf with pinnate reticulate venation. [D, redrawn from *The Ferns,* Vol. II by F. O. Bower, Cambridge: Cambridge University Press, 1926; E, *ibid.,* Vol. I; F, redrawn from Edwin Bingham Copeland, *Genera Filicum.* A Chronica Botanica Publication. Copyright 1947, The Ronald Press Company.]

depending on the ultimate size of the foliar structure. A developing vascular bundle may be evident in a leaf that is only a fraction of a millimeter in height. The lamina or pinnae (if the leaf is compound) are formed as lateral outgrowths on the original peg-like structure; the

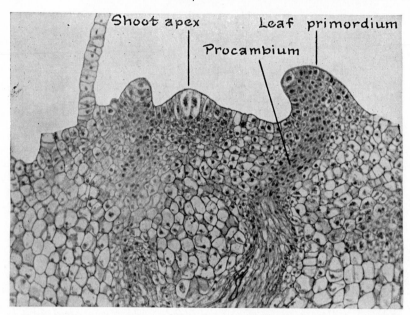

Figure 13-2   Longisection of shoot apex and leaf primordia of *Asplenium*. Note procambial tissue extending into leaf primordium at right. [Photomicrograph courtesy K. Esau.]

latter becomes the stipe (petiole) and rachis. The blade portions of the leaf are built up by the activity of rows of marginal cells, termed marginal initials (Fig. 13-3). The derivatives of the initials continue to divide in a definite pattern, resulting in the formation of a characteristic lamina for each species. During all phases of growth the typical fern leaf displays circinate vernation, not only of the main axis but also of its subdivisions. The occurrence of circinate vernation is undoubtedly related in part to the presence of naturally occurring growth hormones (see Steeves and Wetmore, 1953, for a detailed discussion).

SIZE, FORM, AND TEXTURE.   Some ferns have leaves that are dichotomously branched; the majority, however, have pinnatifid or simple leaves (Fig. 13-1). In size, leaves may vary from the enormous, almost branchlike leaves of tree ferns to the tiny appendages of certain water ferns. In living forms the large, compound, pinnatifid leaves are considered more primitive, whereas the small, simple leaves are considered to have been reduced in size during evolution. The latter type is therefore interpreted as a derived form. There is considerable variation in the texture of fern leaves: they may be thick and leathery, crisp, or very delicate (as in the so-called filmy ferns).

VENATION. The stipe, rachis, and axes of frond subdivisions have prominent veins. The smaller veins of the lamina usually show an open dichotomous type of venation. The dichotomies in some ferns are obscure, the venation pattern being that of the reticulate type (Fig. 13-4). Any degree of vein fusions is considered an advancement. The first steps toward vein fusions are expressed in various ways: sometimes by the appearance of marginal loops which connect the tips of vein dichotomies, or sometimes by the formation of a series of meshes adjacent to the midrib (Fig. 13-4, E) or throughout the pinna (Fig. 13-4, F).

ANATOMY. The typical fern leaf is dorsiventral. Epidermal cells have thickened, outer tangential walls and usually contain chloroplasts, a feature not shared by most other vascular plants. Stomata generally occur on the lower or abaxial surface of leaves. The mesophyll may be uniform in organization, consisting of homogeneous parenchyma with chloroplasts, or the cells may be organized into definite adaxial palisade and abaxial spongy parenchyma layers (Fig. 13-5, A, B). Considerable evolutionary importance is attached to the form and arrangement of the vascular tissue in the stipe and rachis. There may be a simple arc, as seen in transverse section, or the vascular bundle may be convoluted, or the vascular tissue may be broken up into a cylinder of separate bundles

Figure 13-3 Transectional view of a young developing lamina of *Dicksonia.* The epidermal and mesophyll cells have their origins from derivatives of marginal initials. Only one cell of a row of marginal initials is shown.

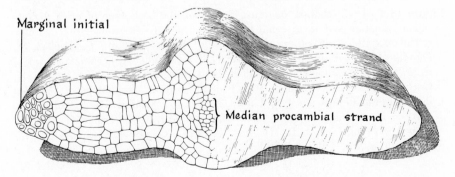

Marginal initial

Median procambial strand

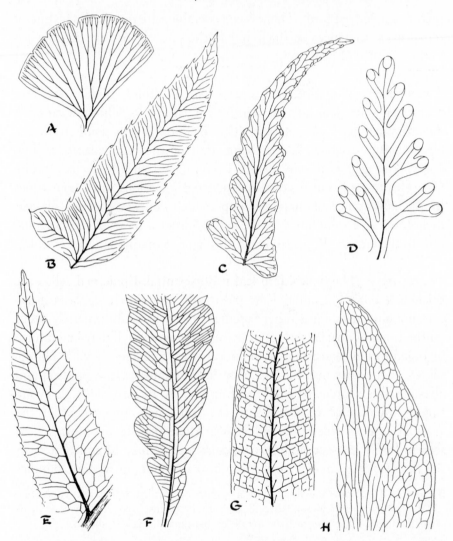

Figure 13-4   Leaf venation in ferns, illustrating the basic type of open dichotomous venation system in some ferns as contrasted with the highly complex
reticulate patterns in others. **A**, *Adiantum*; **B**, *Polystichum*; **C**, *Diellia*; **D**,
Davallia; **E**, *Woodwardia*; **F**, *Onoclea*; **G**, *Polypodium*; **H**, *Ophioglossum*. [A,
redrawn from *Organographie der Pflanzen. Dritte Auflage. Zweiter Teil.* by K.
Goebel, Jena: Gustav Fischer, 1930; B, redrawn from *Morphology of Vascular
Plants. Lower Groups* by A. J. Eames, New York: McGraw-Hill, 1936; C, D,
redrawn from Wagner, Univ. Calif. Publ. in Bot. 26:1, 1952; E-H, redrawn
from *The Ferns*, Vols. I, II, III by F. O. Bower, Cambridge: Cambridge University Press, 1923, 1926, 1928.]

(Fig. 13-5, J-N). The last arrangement is considered a derived condition. As an added complication, the pattern of the vascular tissue may change in passing from the stipe through the rachis to the axes of the pinnae and pinnules.

Figure 13-5 **A, B,** representation of internal leaf structure of ferns; **C-I,** representative types of dermal hairs and scales in ferns [the large peltate scales (E-I) are the more specialized forms]; **J-N,** vascular cylinders of frond stipes as seen in transection (the primitive condition is seen in **J,** and a specialized condition in **N;** xylem black, phloem stippled, protoxylem represented by white dots in **J-L**). **A, B, E, G-I,** *Polypodium;* **C,** *Matonia;* **D,** *Dipteris;* **F,** *Trichomanes;* **J,** *Osmunda;* **K,** *Gleichenia;* **L,** *Asplenium;* **M,** *Histiopteris;* **N,** *Cyathea.* [A, B, E, G-N, redrawn from Anatomie der Vegetationsorgane der Pteridophyten by Y. Ogura. In: *Handbuch der Pflanzenanatomie,* Berlin: Gebrüder Borntraeger, 1938; C, D, F, redrawn from *The Ferns* Vol. I by F. O. Bower, Cambridge: Cambridge University Press, 1923.]

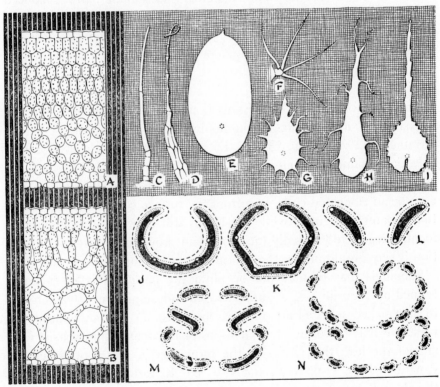

The Sorus

Keeping in mind the main aspects of shoot organography and anatomy, the organization and position of the sorus can more easily be understood. In the vast majority of ferns the foliage leaves serve in both photosynthesis and reproduction. In some species there may be a distinct separation of these functions: certain leaves function in photosynthesis, whereas others are strictly "sporophylls" and nonphotosynthetic. As in all biologic systems, intermediate conditions are present. This is evident in the restriction of sporangia to certain specific portions of a photosynthetic leaf. For the most part, sporangia are crowded in compact groups on leaves, each group being termed a sorus (Fig. 13-6). Sori may be circular or linear in outline. If sporangia are not grouped into definite sori they may form marginal tassels along narrow, reduced leaf segments or be scattered over the lower surface of expanded leaves, along and sometimes between veins. In those species having definite sori the sorus is along the leaf margin or away from the margin on the abaxial side of the frond.

ORGANIZATION. Whether a sorus is marginal or superficial (on the abaxial side) in position, it commonly occurs over a vein or at the terminus of a vein (Fig. 13-6, C, F). That portion of the leaf surface to which sporangia are attached is termed the receptacle (Fig. 13-12). It may be a slight protuberance, it may be a definite bulge, or it may even be an elongated cone. It is from the surface cells of the receptacle that sporangia originate while the leaf is still in a very young developmental stage. Undoubtedly the protection provided by circinate vernation is very important for the delicate sporangia during their ontogeny.

Sporangia may or may not be physically protected by a covering, termed an indusium. If a sorus lacks an indusium it is often referred to as a naked sorus (Figs. 13-6, E, and 13-8, D). If an indusium is present it may be formed by extensions of the adaxial and abaxial margins of the leaf; this results in the formation of a cup or pouch-like structure (Figs. 13-6, A, B, and 13-7, B). In forms that have sori on the abaxial surface the indusium is essentially an outgrowth from the epidermis of the leaf. The form of the indusium is variable: it may be a delicate, linear flap attached along one side only (unilateral indusium);

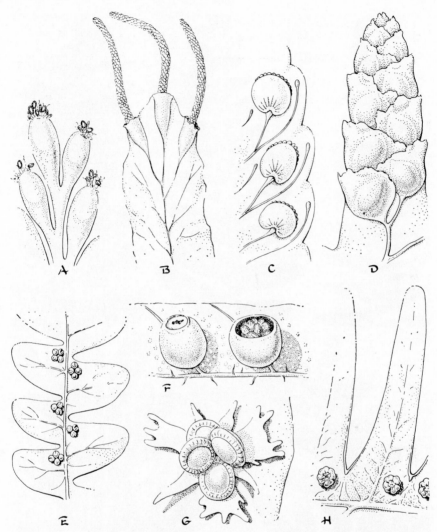

Figure 13-6 Variation in position and form of fern sori. **A,** *Davallia,* marginal position; **B,** *Trichomanes,* marginal, receptacle elongate; **C,** *Nephrolepsis,* indusium attached at one side; **D,** *Lygodium,* each sporangium covered by a laminal flap; **E,** *Gleichenia,* superficial position, no indusium; **F,** *Cyathea,* indusium cup-shaped; **G,** *Woodsia,* basal, membranous indusial segments; **H,** *Matonia,* peltate indusium. [C, redrawn from *The Ferns,* Vol. III by F. O. Bower, Cambridge: Cambridge University Press, 1928; F, adapted from *Morphology of Vascular Plants. Lower Groups* by A. J. Eames, New York: McGraw-Hill, 1936.]

Figure 13-7 Portions of fertile fern leaves showing position of sporangia and types of indusia. **A,** *Pteridium,* young pinna left, older right (the adaxial flap of the indusium of the coenosorus is evident at left); **B,** *Dicksonia,* bivalvate marginal indusia (note that a vein ends at the base of each sorus); **C,** *Lygodium,* individual sporangia covered by a flap of leaf tissue; **D,** *Asplenium,* unilateral indusia.

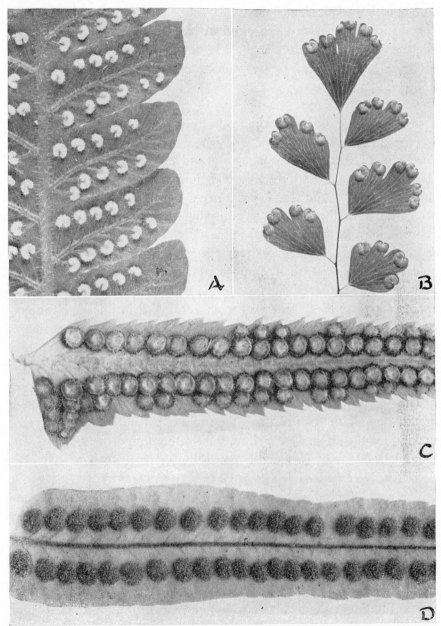

Figure 13-8 Morphology of fern sori. **A,** *Dryopteris,* reniform indusia; **B,** *Adiantum,* each sorus is covered by a reflexed portion of the lamina (note open dichotomous venation); **C,** *Polystichum,* peltate indusia (sporangia can be seen extending beyond the margins of each indusium); **D,** *Polypodium,* naked sori.

it may be horseshoe shaped or circular and elevated (peltate); it may be cup-shaped; it may be a collection of scale-like structures overarching the sporangia; or the leaf margin may be turned back upon itself (false indusium), functioning in the protection of sporangia (see Figs. 13-6, 13-7, 13-8 for types).

DEVELOPMENT AND STRUCTURE OF THE SPORANGIUM. The student is referred to Chapter 4 (pp. 62-69), where a detailed description of the development of both the eusporangium and leptosporangium is presented. It will be recalled that the eusporangium has its origin from several superficial initials and that it has a massive wall and thick base or stalk at maturity. In the Filicales (leptosporangiate ferns) a single surface cell functions as the sporangial initial (Fig. 13-9, A, B). It will also be recalled that the sporangium grows for a time by the activity of an apical cell which eventually forms a jacket cell and a primary sporogenous cell. The latter cell gives rise to the two-layered tapetum and to the sporocytes (Fig. 13-9). The wall remains one cell in thickness throughout development. Space does not permit a more detailed discussion of these features, and the remaining portion of this section will be devoted to an analysis of certain sporangial characteristics of evolutionary and phylogenetic significance.

The two features that are regularly considered in comparing sporangia are final length of the stalk, and the number of cells (or rows of cells) making up the stalk. Short, thick stalks are considered primitive, and long, delicate stalks (frequently consisting of three rows of cells) are derived.

The wall is typically one cell in thickness at maturity. The main point of interest, however, is in the means of dehiscence and in the mechanisms involved. In eusporangiate ferns dehiscence is brought about by a slit which opens down the side of the sporangium, fundamentally longitudinal in all cases. In the Filicales there are various methods of dehiscence, depending on the position of the annulus. It is interesting to note that in the intermediate or transition family, the Osmundaceae, a group of thick walled cells (the annulus), located near the tip but to one side, is responsible for the formation of a cleft that runs over the top of the sporangium and down the opposite side. The sporangium opens like a clam. In other ferns the annulus may form a cap at the distal end of

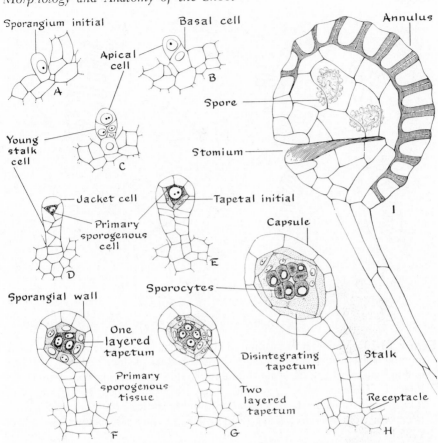

Figure 13-9 Stages in the development of a leptosporangium. Dehiscence has occurred in **I. A-H,** *Polypodium;* **I,** *Polystichum.*

the capsule, be obliquely placed, or run over the top of the capsule in line with the stalk (vertical position). These three positions result in longitudinal, oblique, and transverse dehiscence, respectively (Fig. 13-10). These three types of dehiscence represent a progressive evolutionary series as regards one morphological feature.

MATURATION OF SPORANGIA WITHIN A SORUS. The simplest way in which fern sporangia are borne is singly at the tips or along the margins of leaf segments—each with a vascular bundle leading to its base (as in some extant ferns such as *Botrychium, Osmunda*). This arrangement is the primitive condition. In the majority of Filicales sporangia are aggregrated to form sori which are disposed upon the sporophyll as

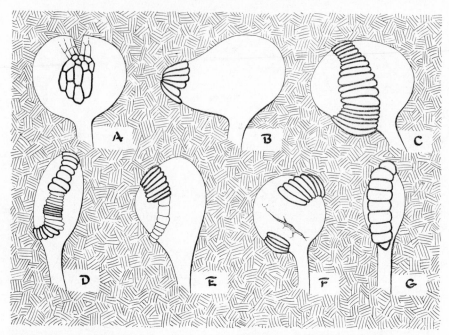

Figure 13-10　Variation in position of the annulus in leptosporangia. **A,** *Todea,* annulus subapical or lateral, results in longitudinal dehiscence; **B,** *Lygodium,* annulus apical; **C,** *Gleichenia,* annulus oblique; **D,** *Plagiogyria,* annulus oblique; **E,** *Loxsoma,* annulus oblique, not all cells thickened; **F,** *Hymenophyllum,* annulus oblique; **G,** *Leptochilus,* annulus vertical, transverse dehiscence. [Redrawn from *Primitive Land Plants* by F. O. Bower, London: Macmillan, 1935.]

described earlier in the chapter. A sorus in which all of the sporangia originate, grow, and mature at the same time is termed a simple sorus (Fig. 13-11). For convenience, ferns having this type of sorus have been placed arbitrarily into a group termed the "Simplices." Members of this group are not necessarily closely related. That the simple sorus is primitive is attested by the fact that members of those extant families, considered to be primitive in the Filicales on other grounds have this type of development.

If sporangia are initiated over a period of time in a definite sequence the so-called gradate sorus is produced ("Gradatae"). The order of sporangial initiation and development is basipetal; the oldest sporangium is near the summit of a receptacle with successively younger sporangia toward the base (Fig. 13-11). When the fossil record is considered and compared with that of living ferns having the simple type of sorus the gradate condition is clearly a derived type. Certain fossils of the Mesozoic had gradate sori. It must be emphasized that all ferns with gradate sori are not necessarily closely related. In summary, the gradate condition represents an evolutionary level of specialization that has been reached by certain species in at least two major lines of fern phylogeny.

The final evolutionary level of development is achieved in the sorus that has intermingled sporangia, all in different stages of growth (Fig. 13-11). This is the mixed sorus and is the means of identifying the group "Mixtae." The more highly specialized and evolved families have this mode of soral development. Bower (1923, p. 271; 1935) has emphasized the physiological importance of extending sporangial development over a longer period of time during the reproductive phase of the sporophyte. Neither should the adaptive value of prolonged spore production be underestimated.

A Survey of Soral Types and Their Positions

Variations in soral morphology are endless. At best only a few of the more common types can be described. Examples most often used for teaching purposes are those that illustrate a generalized type or represent steps in an evolutionary series. Whenever possible, as material is available, the student should not only gain an understanding of soral positions but should also keep in mind the several morphological features of the sorus as described earlier.

MARGINAL POSITION. For a sorus to qualify as *truly marginal* the receptacle and its sporangia must originate strictly from the margins of the developing lamina or leaf segments. This definition of marginal is necessary because during ontogeny the sorus may be shifted toward the abaxial surface. Conversely, sori that have their origin on the abaxial

Figure 13-11 Three types of sporangial maturation in sori of leptosporangiate ferns.

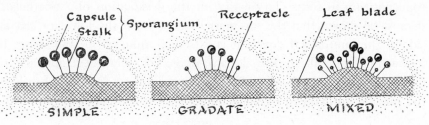

side may appear to be marginal at maturity because of differential growth of the sorus and surrounding tissues. For convenience, however, certain ferns are spoken of as having marginal sori even though the origin of the receptacle may be from tissue on the abaxial side of the leaf near the margin. We are dealing here with an evolutionary trend which will be described in a later section.

A fairly clearcut marginal type of sorus is found in certain members of the genus *Davallia* (a tropical fern). The indusium consists of an adaxial flap and an abaxial flap, together forming a cup-shaped structure. At maturity the sporangia usually extend out beyond the limits of the indusium (Fig. 13-6, A). In *Dicksonia* the indusium is bivalvate; the sporangia are covered by two overlapping flaps, the outer or adaxial flap appearing to be the folded edge of the leaf. The inner or abaxial flap is more delicate. *Pteridium* is an interesting genus because it illustrates how the individuality of sori may be lost in the course of evolution (Fig. 13-7, A). Sporangia are arranged in linear rows along the margins of pinnules and are protected early in development by a larger adaxial flap and a more delicate, inner abaxial flap. At maturity the margins become reflexed, exposing the sporangia. A sorus of this type is termed a continuous marginal coenosorus (common sorus). The sori in *Pteris* are very similar in appearance to those of *Pteridium*, although an inner indusial lip is absent (Fig. 13-12, C). Furthermore, in *Pteris* the adaxial lip appears to be the actual continuation of the leaf margin; the sporangia arise more toward the abaxial side. The genera *Schizaea* and *Lygodium* support the saying—"things are not what they appear to be." Sporangia arise from strictly marginal cells but during development the leaf lamina becomes extended over them, and, as a result, they come to lie on the abaxial side of the leaf. In addition, sporangia occur singly, and not aggregated into sori (Figs. 13-6, D, 13-7, C).

SUPERFICIAL OR ABAXIAL POSITION.　This is the more common type of soral position in ferns. To qualify for the designation of "superficial," it must be shown that the sori actually arise from the lower or abaxial side of the lamina. Of course it is extremely difficult in some cases to follow in detail all of the decisive stages of soral development. In *Gleichenia*, a genus that is undoubtedly related to described fossils of the Jurassic, sori consist of small numbers of sporangia arranged in two

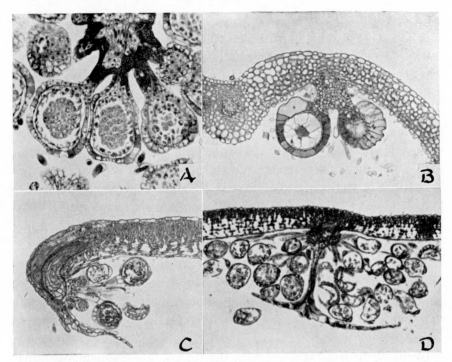

Figure 13-12 Sori and sporangia of ferns as seen in sectional view. **A,** *Osmunda,*
section of leaf segment showing large sporangia, each one with many sporocytes and a massive tapetum (no definite sorus is present); **B,** *Gleichenia,*
showing large sporangia and lack of indusium; **C,** *Pteris,* marginal sorus with
one indusial flap (maturation of sporangia is of the mixed type); **D,** *Polystichum;* peltate indusium.

rows, one on each side of the midvein. There is no indusium (Figs.
13-6, E, 13-12, B). The maidenhair fern, *Adiantum,* familiar to almost
everyone, represents an interesting relationship between sporangia and
protective structures. Sori appear to be marginal, but in reality the sporangia are on the lower surface of leaves near the margin and are
covered by sharply reflexed leaf lobes (Fig. 13-8, B). Some authorities
(e.g., Copeland, 1947) consider the genus to have been derived from
some progenitor that had marginal sori. Others (Bower, 1928) align it
more closely with groups that have never had laminae with truly marginal sori.

In *Asplenium* (spleenwort) sori are elongate, distributed along veins,
and each one is covered by an indusium that is attached only along one
side (unilateral indusium). The indusium is clearly an outgrowth from

the lower leaf surface. In some species the sorus may be very near the leaf margin (Fig. 13-7, D). In the genus *Athyrium*, consisting of about 600 species and distributed throughout the world, the sori are also along veins, but the distal ends of the indusia are usually curved across the vein. Another genus with representatives in nearly all parts of the world, and especially plentiful in the Northern Hemisphere, is *Dryopteris* (male fern, shield fern). Sori occur on the veins and are covered by kidney-shaped (reniform) indusia attached to the receptacle near the sinus (Fig. 13-8, A). The eccentric form of the indusium is particularly well revealed in a sectional view (Fig. 13-22, B, C). Symmetrical, peltate indusia (Figs. 13-8, C, 13-12, D) are characteristic of the genera *Polystichum* (holly fern, sword fern) and *Phanerophlebia* (*Cyrtomium*). Probably one of the most widely used genera for teaching purposes is *Polypodium*. In this genus there is no evidence at all of an indusium (Fig. 13-8, D). The sori are generally round in outline. The absence of an indusium in *Polypodium* has been considered not a primitive condition but the result of a loss of the indusium during evolutionary specialization.

In the chain fern, *Woodwardia*, the sunken sori occur in two interrupted chains very near the midvein of a leaf subdivision and are encircled by larger lateral veins. A unilateral indusium opens toward the midvein (Fig. 13-13, B). These sori are termed coenosori because it has been shown fairly conclusively, on a comparative basis, that this condition has been derived from forms that had long, uninterrupted sori on either side of the midvein (for example, *Blechnum*, Fig. 13-13, A).

Another indusial type is illustrated by *Woodsia* in which the indusium arises as a protective cup around the sorus and at maturity may split into several membranous segments (Fig. 13-6, G). Or, the indusium may be only an investment of hairs. A cup-shaped indusium is also characteristic of certain species in the genus *Cyathea* (Fig. 13-6, F). In water ferns the sporangia are enclosed in highly specialized containers termed sporocarps (Figs. 13-26, A, 13-27, A-D).

While the above descriptions have provided the student with some idea of the variations in soral morphology, reference should be made to the section on special problems in fern morphology, in the later part of this chapter, for a further account of soral evolution.

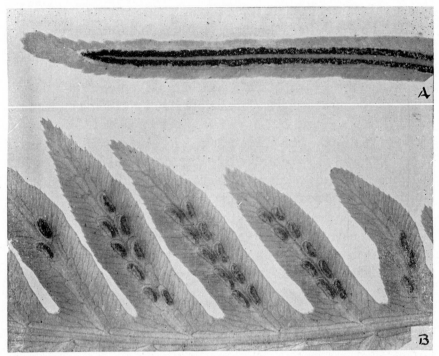

Figure 13-13 **A,** coenosori of *Blechnum,* one at either side of the midvein. **B,** sori of *Woodwardia;* a vein surrounds each sorus and the indusium is attached on the side away from the midvein.

Anatomy of the Stem

A discussion of fern stem anatomy should logically begin, as was done for the leaf, with a description of the apical cell. A variety of structures and tissues take their origin from the meristematic derivative cells of the apical initial; leaves, the protoderm of leaves and of the axis, epidermal hairs and dermal appendages, ground meristem, and procambium. From available studies it appears that procambium in ferns, as is true of the majority of investigated vascular plants, develops in relation to the appearance of leaves. (For a review of this see Esau, 1954.) Very soon after a leaf is initiated a procambial strand becomes differentiated at its base and soon the strand prolongs itself into the leaf. (Fig. 13-2). The development of procambium is acropetal and apparently always in continuity with existing procambium at a lower level in the stem. Within a procambial strand, phloem differentiation also takes place in an acropetal direction (upward into the leaves). In some ferns there is evidence that the differentiation of tracheary elements in the xylem may be discontinuous before a leaf trace, and its continuation into the leaf, has its normal amount of mature xylem. In general, though, the wave of vascular differentiation is in an acropetal direction.

Throughout the Filicales, including the fossil forms, there is no indication of cambial activity resulting in the formation of secondary vascular tissues. There is, however, the development of considerable sclerenchyma in the axes of some ferns, in contrast with its absence in the Ophioglossales and its limited occurrence in the Marattiales. The radial maturation of xylem in a vascular bundle of the stem or leaf is characteristically mesarch. The large tracheids of the metaxylem have tapered ends, and scalariform pitting is present on all sides of the cell. It has been demonstrated that certain ferns (e.g., *Pteridium aquilinum*) possess vessels; actual scalariform perforations instead of pits are present in the oblique end walls between two vessel members (Bliss, 1939).

Types of Vascular Cylinders

What does the fossil record reveal regarding types of vascular patterns in ferns of the past? As in all groups of primitive vascular plants, the protostele is found in ferns from the Paleozoic and even from more recent eras. The extinct eusporangiate fern of the Carboniferous, *Botryopteris*, had a smooth, solid cylinder of xylem in the stem surrounded by phloem. The protostelic condition was also true of *Gleichenites*, a fern of the Triassic, which was undoubtedly related to the living genus *Gleichenia*. Of course the siphonostele is not without representation in the fossil record; it occurred in extinct ferns but at a later date (Late Paleozoic to Coenozoic).

Among living members of the Filicales the protostele has still persisted. For example, it occurs in the genera *Gleichenia* and *Lygodium*, and in the family Hymenophyllaceae. All living ferns having protosteles are considered the more primitive members of the Filicales, not only on the basis of this one feature but on others as well. Most species of *Gleichenia* are protostelic but of a rather special type (Fig. 13-14, A). The bulk of the central column is primary xylem in which tracheids of the metaxylem are interspersed with parenchyma cells. Protoxylem occupies definite loci near the periphery of the xylem. External to the xylem

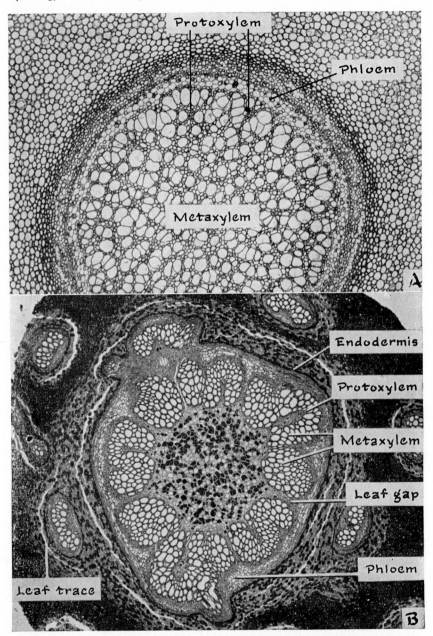

Figure 13-14 Transections of fern stems. **A,** *Gleichenia,* an example of a medullated or "vitalized" protostele; the metaxylem consists of tracheids intermingled with parenchyma; **B,** *Osmunda,* example of an ectophloic siphonostele.

is a cylinder of phloem consisting of relatively large, thin-walled sieve cells and smaller parenchyma cells. The vascular cylinder is enclosed by a rather wide pericycle several cell layers in thickness which, in turn, is surrounded by the endodermis. Frequently the endodermis and particularly the Casparian strips are not well-defined. Topographically the endodermis is located at the boundary between thick-walled cortical cells and thin-walled pericyclic cells. The departure of a leaf trace does not materially affect the outline of the vascular cylinder of the stem. The significance of a "vitalized" protostele in the evolution of the siphonostelic condition has already been considered in Chapter 3.

The most commonly accepted viewpoint is that there are two types of siphonosteles: the *ectophloic siphonostele* (external cylinder of phloem only), and the *amphiphloic siphonostele* (internal and external cylinders of phloem) (see Chapter 3). *Osmunda* is one of the ferns commonly used to demonstrate an ectophloic siphonostele (Fig. 13-14, B). *Osmunda* has a short erect stem upon which is a crown of leaves. The stem axis is completely invested by leaf bases or stipes. A transverse section of an older shoot reveals the crowded condition of the leaves and the presence of a horseshoe-shaped vascular strand in each leaf. Centripetal to the free leaf bases is the outer cortex, consisting of thick-walled sclerenchyma with embedded leaf traces. The inner cortex is parenchymatous, the cells often packed with starch grains. The pith occupies a generous amount of the axis. Along the outer edge of the pith is a cylinder of more or less separate xylem strands, often U shaped in outline with the open side toward the pith. Protoxylem is in the sinus formed by the two arms of metaxylem. For this reason the xylem is mesarch in structure. Surrounding the xylem is a zone of parenchyma, several cells in thickness. External to this layer is the phloem with its relatively large sieve cells, often elongated in an oblique longitudinal direction. This is particularly true of the protophloem. Parenchyma cells also are interspersed among the sieve cells. External to the phloem is the pericycle which, in turn, is surrounded by tannin-filled endodermal cells. The outline of the main vascular cylinder may be somewhat irregular, due to the divergence of leaf traces. Each leaf trace is confronted by a leaf gap which may extend longtitudinally and obliquely for some distance in the xylem. The phloem, however, forms a continuous cylinder. In some species tracheids may be intermingled with parenchymatous pith cells, and in one instance (*O. cinnamomea*) an internal endodermis has been reported.

Ferns with vascular cylinders of the types just described have also been encountered as fossils. The stem anatomy of a Late Paleozoic fern, *Thamnopteris*, resembled closely that of *Osmunda*. In *Thamnopteris* there were tightly packed leaf bases and a continuous cylinder of phloem. The pith consisted of intermingled parenchyma and tracheids surrounded by a compact cylinder of xylem, without leaf gaps. The vascular cylinder was essentially a "medullated" or "vitalized" protostele. Some species of the Mesozoic genus *Osmundites* had stems that were even more similar in anatomy to those of *Osmunda*.

Without doubt many more ferns have the amphiphloic siphonostele rather than the ectophloic type. Fundamentally there are two types of amphiphloic siphonosteles: the solenostele, and the dictyostele. The solenostele, without overlapping leaf gaps, occurs frequently in creeping ferns that have conspicuous internodes. Common examples are *Adiantum* and *Dennstaedtia* (hay-scented fern). A transverse section within an internodal region reveals a complete cylinder of vascular tissue surrounded by the cortex and enclosing a pith that is often sclerified (Fig. 13-15, A). Starting from the outer edge of the vascular cylinder (stele), the outer endodermis can usually be distinguished by tanniferous accumulations in its cells. Internal to the endodermis is the pericycle (one or more layers of cells in width) followed by the phloem (external phloem). As usual the ring of xylem is most conspicuous, being composed of scalariformly pitted tracheids. Internal phloem, pericycle, and inner endodermis follow, in that order, in progressing toward the pith. At a node the seemingly closed cylinder of vascular tissue is broken by the presence of a leaf gap. The leaf gap is not extensive, and the cylinder again appears closed within the next higher internode. This type of stele is not an entirely new innovation because species of *Adiantum* have been found from strata of the Jurassic. The creeping water fern, *Marsilea*, is also solenostelic with a highly lacunate cortex typical of many hydrophytes. Solenosteles may become highly elaborate, as in *Matonia* where there is a variable number of concentric, amphiphloic cylinders. At nodes each cylinder may have a leaf gap, and the entire leaf trace complex also may be a collection of concentric cylinders.

The most specialized type of siphonostele in ferns is the dictyostele.

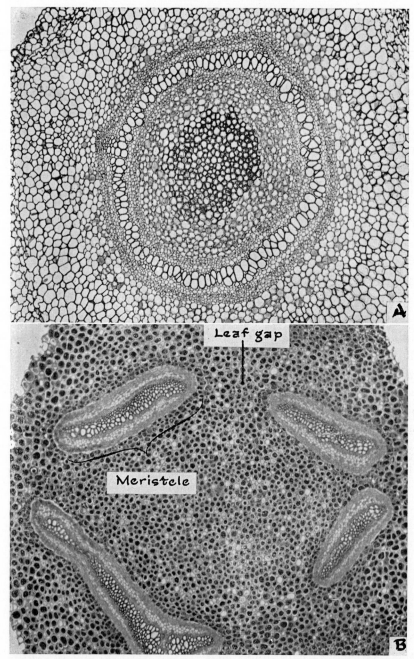

Figure 13-15   Transections of fern steles. **A**, *Dennstaedtia*, solenostele, phloem and endodermis occur on both sides of the xylem (cylinder of large clear cells); section was made at a level between leaf gaps; **B**, *Phyllitis*, dictyostele.

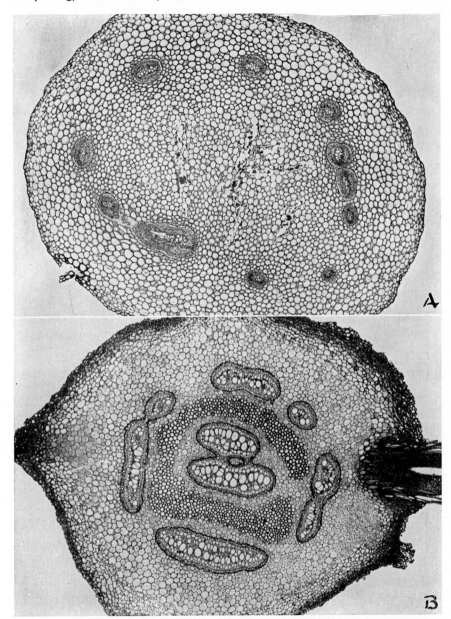

Figure 13-16 Transections of fern rhizomes. **A,** *Polypodium,* example of a dissected dictyostele; **B,** *Pteridium,* a stele with outer and inner vascular cylinders and intervening sclerenchyma.

The dictyostele is an amphiphloic tube of vascular tissue in which parenchymatous leaf gaps overlap. A transverse section made at any level of a well-developed stem shows a ring of separate vascular bundles. These bundles vary considerably in size and shape, but each one consists of primary xylem enclosed by primary phloem. These strands are termed concentric, amphicribral vascular bundles, or meristeles (see Chapter 3, p. 53). The parenchymatous zones between meristeles are leaf gaps (Fig. 13-15, B). Most of the Filicales are fundamentally dictyostelic and of the type just described. This is true of upright as well as creeping species. If the leaf gaps are long and extensive and more than one leaf trace is associated with each gap, or if there are breaks in the cylinder not associated with leaves, the vascular cylinder becomes a tubular network. In one transverse section it is difficult if not impossible in these cases to distinguish the actual limits of the gap. We are describing the so-called dissected dictyostele. *Polypodium* is an example of a common fern with a dissected dictyostele (Fig. 13-16, A). Just as in a solenostele an inner vascular cylinder may be present.

The rhizome of *Pteridium* has medullary strands within an outer vascular cylinder (Fig. 13-16, B). It is difficult to consider the gaps between meristeles as leaf gaps because the main rhizome bears no leaves, these being borne instead on short shoots. The meristeles of the outer ring tend to be smaller than the two strap-shaped medullary strands (Fig. 13-17). Sclerenchyma may entirely or partially enclose the inner strands, or it may appear as two separate bands in transectional view. It should be emphasized that the cylinders of vascular tissue are not entirely independent of each other but are joined at a lower or older level in the rhizome. More highly complicated vascular structures have been described for ferns, namely, species with exceedingly large leaf gaps and numerous leaf traces attached to the sides of the gaps, and species with small innumerable meristeles in the pith and cortex, arranged in intricate patterns and often associated with leaf gaps in various ways. In concluding this section it should be pointed out that critical ontogenetic work, utilizing modern techniques, still remains to be done on fern vasculation before the results of earlier works can be fully accepted without reservation (Esau, 1954). Evolution of the stele in ferns is discussed in more detail in the later section on special problems in fern morphology.

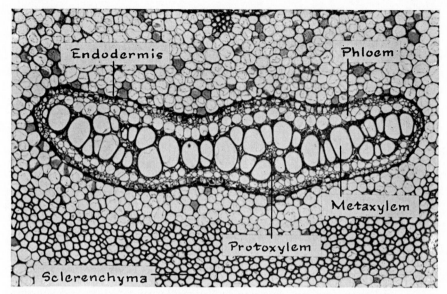

Figure 13-17 Transection of rhizome of *Pteridium* showing structural details of one meristele.

The Root

Except for the first root or primary root of the embryo, all roots of a fern are termed adventitious. (For a critique of the concept of adventitious roots see Esau, 1953.) Roots arise from the rhizome or upright stem, frequently occurring near leaf bases or often below them. They are usually small in diameter, monopodially branched, and dark in color. In some species (e.g., *Dryopteris, Athyrium*) there is but one root associated with the node, whereas in certain species of *Osmunda,* for example, there are two. Three roots per nodal region is typical of *Aspidium.* In the adult stages of some, particularly creeping types (*Adiantum, Pteridium*), there is no relation between nodes and root position. The outer investment of fibrous material on the trunks of tree ferns is a mat of tangled, living, dead, and dying roots. The actual stem axis may be only a relatively small cylinder within the covering of roots.

At the level of mature primary tissues in the root the epidermal cells are usually thin-walled (some cells may form root hairs) followed by parenchymatous cells of the outer cortex. A generous portion of the inner cortex may be sclerenchymatous, or only the cells of a single layer around the endodermis may be thickened. The endodermis is always well-defined, and each cell has the usual Casparian strip; at maturity the cell walls vary in thickness according to the species. Fern roots are usually diarch or triarch with very few tracheids in the xylem. Xylem is exarch in maturation. No secondary growth occurs.

Roots arise endogenously from cells of the stem pericycle. They force their way through the cortex to the outside. Early in their development a conspicuous apical cell makes its appearance and functions throughout the life of the root. In most investigated ferns the apical cell is pyramidal in shape, cutting off cells to the main body of the root on three sides and contributing segments to the root cap on the fourth side. The large apical cell is usually highly vacuolate and apparently divides only infrequently. The three primary meristems—protoderm, ground meristem, and procambium—have their origin from derivative cells of the apical initial, and they, in turn, give rise to the epidermis, cortex, and vascular cylinders, respectively. Lateral roots originate from cells of the endodermis, in contrast with higher plants in which the pericycle is usually the initiating layer (Ogura, 1938; Esau, 1953).

The Gametophyte

The origin of the gametophytic plant or prothallium is normally from a haploid cell, the spore. A majority of the Filicales are homosporous and have exosporic gametophytes. Some water ferns are heterosporous and possess endosporic gametophytes. The latter type of gametophyte is described on p. 311. Not nearly enough is known about the range in variability of the filicalian gametophytic plant, but the type considered to be most common for investigated species will be described. Germination may be signaled by a cell division within the intact wall, or, more commonly, is associated with the cracking of the spore along the line of original contact with other spores. A rhizoid develops from the basal cell; however, the distal cell or prothallial cell may divide transversely several times to form a filament, and later a plate of cells is formed by longitudinal divisions (Fig. 13-18, A, B). Eventually a wedge-shaped apical cell is formed at the growing tip of the plate-like thallus, which cuts off segments in one plane (Fig. 13-18, C). Sooner or later, growth

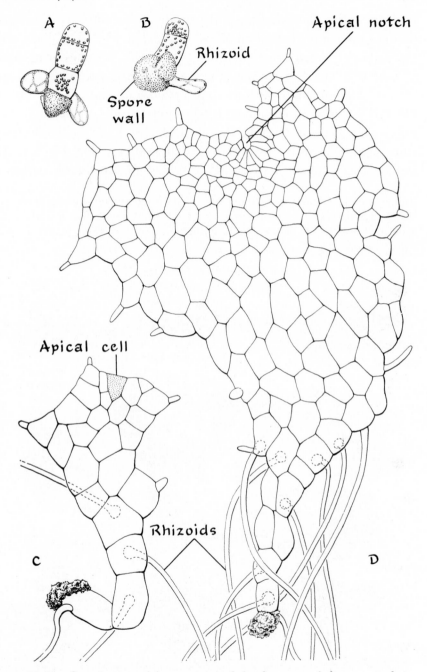

Figure 13-18 Germination of fern spores and development of the gametophyte. **A,** *Athyrium;* **B,** *Pteridium;* **C, D,** *Dryopteris.*

becomes active along the forward margins of the thallus, which commonly results in the formation of two wings (Fig. 13-18, D). The mature prothallium is green, dorsiventral, and commonly becomes heart-shaped or butterfly-shaped in outline (Fig. 13-19, A, also Fig. 13-24). It may vary from a few millimeters to 1 cm or more in width. The wings are one cell in thickness, but the midrib portion, particularly near the apical notch may become several cells in thickness. Early in development, rhizoids arise along the margins of the prothallium (Fig. 13-18, C, D), but eventually most of them are restricted to the midrib region. In

Figure 13-19 Gametophyte and gametangia of a leptosporangiate fern. **A,** form of a typical, sexually mature gametophyte; **B-H,** stages in the development of an archegonium; **I,** nearly mature antheridium. [From slides prepared by Dr. F. V. Ranzoni.]

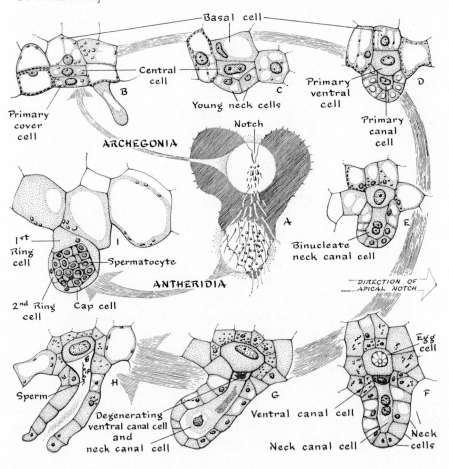

some species characteristic hairs arise from marginal cells. Secondary prothallia may form by dichotomous branching of the original prothallium, or by production of proliferations from the margins, from both surfaces, or from cells near the notch.

Antheridia usually make their appearance before archegonia, and frequently develop as early as two weeks after spores are sown. In healthy mature gametophytes antheridia are usually found in abundance near the basal end of the prothallium among numerous rhizoids (Fig. 13-19, A). They do occur, however, out on the wings and toward the apical notch. Archegonia with recurved necks (directed away from the notch) typically are restricted to the apical pad (Fig. 13-19, A).

The mature antheridium of a specialized or derived leptosporangiate fern consists of three jacket cells—two ring cells and a cap cell—enclosing the spermatocytes or eventual sperms (Fig. 13-19, I). The venter of the archegonium is normally embedded in gametophytic tissue and has a relatively short protruding neck consisting of four rows of from five to seven tiers of cells enclosing a binucleate neck-canal cell, a ventral canal cell, and an egg cell (Fig. 13-19, F). (For a detailed account of antheridial and archegonial development see Chapter 5, pp. 81-84, and Fig. 13-19).

Dynamics of Fertilization and Embryogeny

If sexually mature plants are flooded with water, antheridia may open after 3-15 minutes have elapsed. It has been shown that when flooded the antheridium shows signs of internal pressure followed by the loosening of the cap cell and the escape of the sperms, one by one. In a matter of seconds, or at the most a few minutes, the sperms lose their compact appearance and assume the loose, helical form of the swimming sperm (Ward, 1954). In some ferns a large vesicle of cytoplasm may remain attached to the multiflagellate nuclear band. There have been some interesting studies on sperm morphology in which the electron microscope and ultraviolet microscopy were employed. It has been shown by these studies that each flagellum actually consists of eleven strands, two of which are shorter than the others and centrally located (Manton, 1950; Manton and Clarke, 1951). It is a remarkable fact that the flagella of many animals exhibit this same type of organization.

In one study (Ward, 1954) mature archegonia are reported to open within one or two hours after immersion in water. The impending opening of an archegonium is heralded by enlargement of the distal end and separation of apical neck cells. This allows a tiny stream of mucilaginous material or slime to be released, which is followed by the forceful release of definable protoplasmic bodies—presumably they are entities of the axial row. Following this phase, the upper tiers of neck cells split apart. Swimming sperms are at first not attracted to archegonia, but later, when the slime is diluted, they change direction chemotactically and swim toward an archegonium. In *Phlebodium aureum* from three to five sperms may swim into an open archegonium and occupy the ventral cavity at the same time. However, only one sperm effects syngamy.

The first division of the zygote is reported to take place anywhere from one hour to ten days after fertilization. In *Phlebodium aureum* it is five days (Ward, 1954). Even before the zygote divides, cells of the surrounding gametophyte divide and form a partially ensheathing calyptra. The first division wall of the zygote is generally parallel to the long axis of the archegonium (Fig. 13-20, A). This initial division separates an anterior cell or hemisphere that is directed toward the notch of the prothallium, and a posterior cell or hemisphere that is directed away from the notch. The former cell is in reality the apical pole or epibasal cell, and the latter is the basal pole or hypobasal cell. It can readily be understood why the zygote in the Filicales is said to be "prone" in orientation. Each of the two cells divides and the new cell wall in each is perpendicular to the original or basal wall, resulting in the development of a four-celled embryo or "quadrant stage" of embryogeny (Fig. 13-20, B). Each of the four cells then undergoes (usually by synchronized divisions) more divisions (Fig. 13-20, C). According to the classical descriptions of fern embryogeny, the primary organs may be traced back to specific segments of the quadrant stage. The outer anterior quadrant or cell reportedly gives rise to the first leaf, the inner anterior quadrant to the future shoot apex. The primary root originates from the outer posterior quadrant, the foot from the inner posterior quadrant.

Some workers have questioned the preciseness of fern embryogeny (particularly of later stages) as presented in classical studies. In *Gymnogramme sulphurea* (Vladesco, 1935) the foot is reported to be derived from certain derivatives of the original inner anterior quadrant

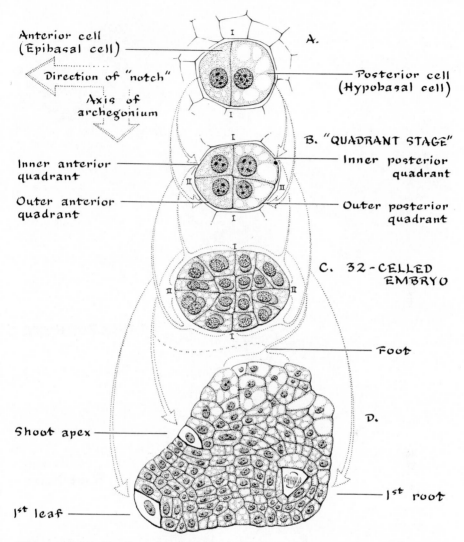

Figure 13-20 Developmental stages in the growth of a leptosporangiate fern embryo (*Gymnogramme sulphurea.*) [Redrawn from Vladesco, *Rev. Gen. Bot.* 47: 513, 1935.]

as well as from the inner posterior quadrant (Fig. 13-20, D). The setting aside of a shoot apical cell is delayed, and frequently it is a cell located very near the equatorial plane of the embryo and not a centrally located derivative of the inner anterior quadrant. In another reported instance (Ward, 1954) the inner two quadrants in *Phlebodium aureum* give rise

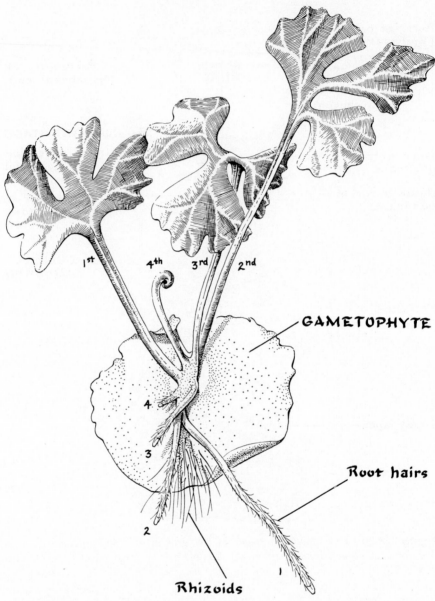

Figure 13-21   Ventral (lower) side of gametophyte of leptosporangiate fern with attached young sporophyte. Note circinate vernation of youngest (fourth) leaf.

to the foot, and the first leaf and root, appearing in that order, have their origin as described earlier. The origin of the future shoot apical meristem cannot be assigned to any definite quadrant but arises from derivative cells of the inner and outer anterior quadrants midway between the organized foot and first leaf.

After whatever manner the organs are delimited, the first root and leaf begin to grow rapidly and pierce the calyptra. The first leaf eventually grows forward and upward through the notch. After the first leaf has unfolded, more leaves are formed by the shoot apical meristem, and adventitious roots are produced from the developing stem axis (Fig. 13-21). Sooner or later, the gametophyte degenerates and dies. Leaves of young sporophytes often do not resemble the leaves of adult plants.

We hope the reader has noted that the morphological features discussed thus far are those that Bower considered to be of utmost importance in fern phylogeny (see Chapter 11, p. 238). Furthermore, the student's attention is directed to Table 13-I, at the end of this chapter, where he will find a comparison of presumed primitive and derived conditions of certain fern characters. Attention should be given to Table 13-I in reading the remainder of this chapter.

Special Problems in Fern Morphology

Changes in Position ("Phyletic Slide") of the Sorus, and Modifications of the Indusium

The primitive position of sporangia is declared by most morphologists to be terminal if the leaf is essentially a branch system. Marginal sporangia of relatively narrow leaf segments or of larger laminae can also be thought of as occupying a primitive position. In the evolution of the fern leaf the processes of overtopping and webbing (see Chapter 3) would ultimately destroy the obvious terminal position of sporangia, but a study of the venation gives us a clue as to their actual morphological position. The genera *Botryopteris*, *Zygopteris*, and *Botrychium* aid us in understanding the essential primitiveness of the marginal position (Chapters 11 and 12).

The location of sporangia on the lower or abaxial side of fronds is not entirely a characteristic of living ferns because certain ferns in the Paleozoic, considered to be members of the Gleicheniaceae, had superficial sori. We can only assume that the transition has taken place several times and in different natural phylogenetic groups of ferns.

The question then is: How has this transition taken place and can we see it still in operation today? In the following discussion certain ferns are used illustratively in tracing the transition from the marginal position to the superficial position. It must be kept in mind that not all of the examples are necessarily closely related. Their sori simply represent graphic examples of possible stages in the evolution of a single fern character—the position of the sorus.

The starting point for our story in one series of ferns is a leaf with sporangia aggregated at the ends of veins. The sorus is clearly marginal, the indusium two-lipped and symmetrical. The receptacle is the continuation of the leaf margin, and the indusial flaps arise as adaxial and abaxial growths distal to the actual margin. A vascular bundle ends at the base of the receptacle or traverses it if elongate in shape. Certain species of *Davallia* described earlier, *Hymenophyllum,* or *Trichomanes* (Fig. 13-6), are illustrative of this condition. In its early development the receptacle of *Dicksonia* (Fig. 13-7, B) is definitely marginal, but subsequently it may be shifted toward the lower surface. The adaxial flap is somewhat larger than the abaxial lip and surrounds the latter. In certain ferns the sorus gradually became shifted phylogenetically to the abaxial side, and during countless years of evolution the original adaxial flap became transformed into a new leaf margin and was provided with vascular tissue (Fig. 13-22). The more delicate lower or abaxial flap or lip became attached only at one point or along one side (as in *Microlepia*).

In this series of ferns it is further postulated that once the receptacle (therefore the sporangia also) assumed the abaxial position, the inner indusium disappeared so that today in certain genera the sporangia appear to be protected by the reflexed leaf margin. Associated with this transition was the fusion and loss of individuality of sori. This transition is well-represented by the genera *Pteridium* (Fig. 13-7, A) and *Pteris.* The genera *Cheilanthes* and *Pellaea,* although having sporangia more or less restricted to the ends of veins, may also be representative of this line of development. Consult Table 13-I for a summary of soral positions and modifications of soral organization.

The occurrence of sporangia on the abaxial side of fronds without protective indusia was true of ferns in the Paleozoic period. The family

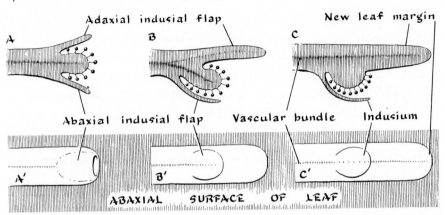

Figure 13-22 Possible evolutionary stages in the movement of the marginal sorus to the abaxial side of the fern leaf (the "phyletic slide"). **A-C**, vertical sections, hypothetical leaf margin; **A'-C'**, surface views. (See text for details.)

Gleicheniaceae represents this condition and contains within it the ancestral stock for another line of development. According to Bower (1928) the primitive indusium in this series has resulted from the progressive evolutionary development of leaf tissue around the receptacle, perhaps from the coalescence of scales. The basal scale-like indusium of *Woodsia* or the cup-shaped indusium of *Cyathea* illustrate the point (Fig. 13-6). With restricted development of the indusium it became reniform (e.g., *Dryopteris, Lastrea*; Fig. 13-8) and eventually assumed radial symmetry by growth of the margins around the sinus (e.g., *Polystichum, Phanerophlebia*; Fig. 13-8). Strictly unilateral indusia, attached along only one side of a vein, can be derived from somewhat zygomorphic indusia by restriction of indusial and receptacular growth to one side of a vein (*Asplenium*; Fig. 13-7). Secondarily, the indusium may be entirely lost at any time during evolution, which results in a naked sorus (*Polypodium*; Fig. 13-8). In other ferns of this series there has been a general spread of originally unprotected sporangia along veins and eventually between them. The end point in this trend is well represented by *Acrostichum* and *Platycerium* (stag-horn fern), in which the sporangia are scattered over the lower surface of the pinnae without any indication of distinct sori. This arrangement is referred to as the acrostichoid condition.

Still another variation in the indusial leaf margin relationships is found in the Blechnoid ferns (Bower, 1935). The starting point for this

series is assumed to be a form possessing superficial coenosori and protected by enrolled leaf margins. A secondary evolutionary trend is the
formation of new leaf wings from the flanks of the enrolled leaf segments. This results in two rows of continuous sori, one on each side of
the midrib. The breaking up of these fertile tracts gave rise to the
Woodwardia type of sorus (Fig. 13-13).

Evolutionary and Ontogenetic Implications of Stem Anatomy

On the basis of comparative morphology of both living and extinct
plants, the protostele, with little doubt, is the truly primitive type of
vascular cylinder. This is true not only in ferns but also in other groups
of vascular plants. Any departure from a simple protostele (haplostele)
is commonly regarded as a derived condition.

The value of studies based on the comparative anatomy of mature
stems should not be underestimated, but the student should be cogni-
zant of the fact that most ferns, during their early ontogeny, have a
vascular pattern quite different from that of the adult plant. For example, it has been shown by many investigators that the base of a fern
stem (older portion) may be protostelic, whereas at a higher level of the
same stem (younger portion) the vascular cylinder may be solenostelic
or dictyostelic. Of course this change is ontogenetic, but it has been
interpreted by some morphologists as representing an evolutionary
recapitulation of stelar types. Rightfully these same morphologists realize
the importance of comparing the steles of plants of comparable age.
Therefore the vascular cylinders of well established adult plants can be
compared, with some degree of assurance. Similarity of vascular cylinders, however, cannot be used in itself as an indication of close relationship between ferns. The attainment of similar levels of structural specialization may be reached in several evolutionary lines. We are dealing here
with parallel evolution or homoplastic development (Bower, 1923, p.
159).

It is a well-known fact that the shoots of many plants, particularly
herbaceous species, become obconical during growth, and, as a result, the
stem at an upper level may be several times larger in diameter than the
base. This phenomenon is particularly well-displayed in ferns. Associated
with this increase in size is generally a change in the form of the vascular
cylinder. Utilizing Galileo's Principle of Similitude, Bower calculated

that a mere increase in size or volume of a smooth cylinder of dead tracheids is not compensated for by a comparable increase in surface of the cylinder. The volume increases as the cube of the linear dimensions, and the surface increases as the square of the linear dimension, if the same shape is maintained. Bower believed that the proper relationship between dead conducting elements and living parenchyma must be maintained. This can be accomplished, then, in any one of several ways or by combinations of these methods: (1) formation of a central pith, (2) formation of flanges or irregular lobes on an otherwise smooth protostele, (3) formation of a highly intricate tubular vascular cylinder, and (4) presence of living cells among dead elements. In living, woody seed plants the necessary parenchyma cells are derived from the vascular cambium, constituting xylem parenchyma and wood rays. Whatever physiological advantages are achieved by these methods they appear to have been favorably acted upon through natural selection.

In recent years there has been a renewed interest in the problem of size and form by morphologists in the United States and Great Britain. In England Wardlaw is the leader of a group that has approached morphological problems from the experimental standpoint. Bower was impressed with the phylogenetic implications of stelar morphology, but he was aware also of the plasticity and variability of the vascular cylinder. Wardlaw (1949) has shown in *Dryopteris* that if the shoot apex is isolated from existing vascular tissue by vertical incisions, the vascular cylinder of the new "plug" of tissue will be solenostelic instead of dictyostelic for a short distance. Eventually the dictyostelic condition is achieved again. If the incisions are made very close to the apical cell, a prostostele is produced. Wardlaw interprets these results as an indication of the importance of non-hereditary factors in determining shoot organization. According to Wardlaw, the availability of nutrients (an extrinsic factor) perhaps has more of an influence on growth than do hereditary factors. Starvation experiments also support this general idea (Bower 1923, p. 179). The pteropsid type of shoot organization has been developed in different phyletic lines under the influence of the same or similar physical and physiological factors. It is hoped that experimentation will be extended to include more diverse plants and will involve a study of those changes induced by treating plants with chemicals without mechanical injury. An account of other experiments on ferns can be found in the following section.

Experimental Morphology

What are the methods or techniques open to the experimental morphologist? Changes in plants can be brought about by altering the culture medium, by applying chemicals directly to the intact surfaces that alter or provoke morphological changes, and through surgical manipulations. The techniques of tissue culture and the culturing of isolated organs should not be overlooked. The experimental morphologist, then, attempts to evoke changes in form and development of the normal plant grown under carefully controlled conditions. When changes are brought about he seeks to relate these changes to the conditions of the experiment, thereby hoping to arrive at a more complete understanding of the basic organization and development of the organism.

The ferns have proven to be particularly good experimental material. A complete discussion of experimental morphology is outside the scope of this book, but the very interesting and stimulating work of Wardlaw in England will be described. His work has been largely directed toward a study of the apical meristem of the fern shoot.

In review, the shoot apical meristem of a leptosporangiate fern is dominated by a definite apical cell situated at the tip of a conical protuberance or cone. In *Dryopteris* there are three different types of structures derived from the apical meristem: leaves, scales, and bud primordia. Leaves arise within the basiscopic margins of the apical cone; scales originate on the margins; buds have their origin outside the base of the cone on the broad sub-apical region. It is a well-known fact that the shoot apex usually exerts physiological dominance over distal buds or bud primordia. That this is controlled by a substance (termed a growth hormone) diffusing basipetally has been demonstrated experimentally. For example, if the tip of a main shoot is removed, dormant buds or bud primordia will begin to grow. If, as in the ferns *Matteuccia* and *Onoclea*, the cut surface is smeared with indole-acetic acid in lanolin, the development of lateral buds does not take place (Wardlaw, 1946a). The applied growth regulating substance performs the same function as the natural growth hormone that is produced at the tip of the intact rhizome.

To determine if the activity of an apical meristem can be modified by experimental treatment, young leaf primordia were constantly removed from a vigorous plant of *Angiopteris*. The apical meristem diminished in size, and eventually the meristematic cells became parenchymatous (Wardlaw, 1946b). Also, when buds of *Onoclea* (sensitive fern) were grown under weak light and high temperature, parenchymatization of the apical meristem and diminution of the vascular cylinder occurred (Wardlaw, 1945).

The question was raised: Does the shoot apex (more specifically the apical cell) determine the position of leaves? In the test experiment great care was taken to puncture only the apical cell; existing primordia and loci of yet-uninitiated leaves were carefully avoided in order to not injure the tissues in any way. After the operation the existing primordia continued to grow, and new ones were formed in a normal pattern until all the space on the apical meristem was used. Apparently the apical cell does not determine leaf position, nor is it responsible for leaf initiation.

As a working hypothesis, Wardlaw assumes that the apical cell and all young leaf primordia constitute growth centers, each with its own physiological "field" (Fig. 13-23, A). This field restricts the initiation of new primordia to within a certain distance from its center. A new or presumptive leaf (I_1) arises in the first available space on the apical meristem—outside the fields of older adjacent leaves. Primordial meristems of lateral buds occupy positions some distance from the apical cell, in interfoliar positions. They, however, remain inhibited during normal growth.

To determine if leaf primordia actually inhibit each other in their development, a series of interesting experiments was performed. If one young primordium was isolated from adjacent primordia by longitudinal radial incisions, it grew very fast and soon became larger than older leaves (Fig. 13-23, B). If an incision was made in the position of a presumptive leaf (I_1), the site of origin of the next leaf in the phyllotactic pattern in that vicinity was shifted toward the incision. These experiments show that leaf primordia have inhibitory effects on each other. In another experiment, I_1 was isolated by both tangential and longitudinal incisions. The primordium, instead of developing as a leaf, became a bud (Fig. 13-23, C). Conversely, experiments were performed that allowed potential bud primordia to develop into leaves. These are only a few of the fascinating experiments performed on ferns.

Studies on growing isolated bits of fern rhizomes on artificial culture media are shedding light on the nutritional aspects of development. Wetmore (1950, 1954) has been able to excise the shoot apices of *Adiantum* and other lower vascular plants and grow normal plants from them on a mineral agar medium supplemented with 2 percent sucrose or

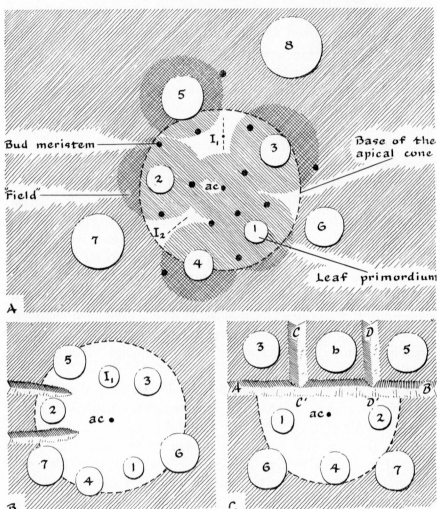

Figure 13-23 **A,** surface view of apical cone of shoot of *Dryopteris* (consult text for explanation); **B,** isolation of young leaf primordium (2) by longitudinal radial incisions; **C,** isolation of I_1, by tangential (*A-B*) and longitudinal incisions (*C-C′, D-D′*) which resulted in formation of a bud (*b*). (*ac*, apical cell; *b*, bud; I_1, position of first presumptive leaf; I_2, position of second presumptive leaf). [Redrawn from *Phylogeny and Morphogenesis* by C. W. Wardlaw, London: Macmillan, 1952.]

dextrose. The addition of auxin, yeast extract, or autoclaved coconut milk speeds up the rate of growth without changing the developmental pattern. The shape of the leaf in *Adiantum* can be modified by varying the concentration of sugar. Allsopp (1951), working with a water fern (*Marsilea*) has been very successful in growing isolated rhizome tips and embryos in culture media. He has shown that the formation of reproductive structures (sporocarps) is favored by strong light. But if the plants are kept at 21°C at a fairly low light intensity, the addition of sucrose in the concentration of 5 percent will favor the formation of sporocarps. Allsopp (1953) has also induced shoots of *Marsilea* to revert to the juvenile type of foliage by depriving the aseptic cultures of either sugar or mineral nutrients. Accompanying this is a reduction from a solenostelic condition to a protostelic one.

So far only the sporophyte generation has been discussed. Recent experiments have been performed on fern prothallia, and they will now be described. Morel and Wetmore (1951) were able to grow gametophytes of *Osmunda cinnamomea* on an agar medium. Green, callus-like outgrowths appeared on the upper surfaces of a few prothallia. These grew very slowly unless given a vitamin-B supplement, whereupon they grew rapidly forming nodules of parenchyma. Certain older parenchyma cells differentiated into tracheids. Because cytological studies revealed that the callus was haploid, Morel and Wetmore concluded that the presence of tracheary tissue is not evidence in itself that apogamy (embryo formed without the fusion of gametes) is an accompanying phenomenon to the formation of tracheary elements.

We have discussed only a few of the recent experimental studies on ferns. The student is referred to a comprehensive review of the entire subject by Wardlaw (1952a, b) and to texts and reviews on tissue culture and its techniques (Gautheret, 1942, 1945; White, 1943, 1946).

Evolution of the Gametophyte

We, the authors, are certain that there can be little doubt in the student's mind that the fern sporophyte has received more attention from botanists than has the gametophyte. Through the continued efforts of Alma G. Stokey and her associates a considerable volume of information is currently being built up relative to the importance of the gametophytic generation in fern classification and phylogeny. The following account is based largely on her published works. (See Stokey, 1951, for a critical review.) Just as in the study of the sporophyte, certain structures and processes in gametophytic development can be used as bases for comparisons. We should consider: (1) type of spore germination, (2) early development and mature form of the prothallium, (3) presence or absence of hairs, and their morphology, (4) color, form, and distribution

of rhizoids, and (5) form and position of sex organs. A primitive gametophyte of present-day members of the Filicales is one that is slow to
develop, perhaps requiring from six to eight weeks, several months, or
even a year or more to mature. Germination results in the formation of
a plate of cells or a cylindrical mass or, rarely, a short filament which
quickly passes to the plate-like dorsiventral thallus. At maturity the
primitive prothallium is large with a prominent, elongate midrib (for
example, prothallia of the Osmundaceae, Gleicheniaceae). The antheridium is large with a layer of several wall cells (from six to eight) enclosing several hundred sperms. Archegonia have relatively long, approximately straight, necks with a wall often present between neck canal
nuclei.

Evolutionary trends involve shortening the time between germination
of the spore and fertilization. There is a tendency to form a filamentous
stage early in development; frequently the filamentous form may be
maintained in older gametophytes, and it is characteristic of certain
epiphytic ferns (e.g., *Hymenophyllum*). In terrestrial ferns the filamentous stage may be greatly shortened. The mature gametophyte may
be cordate without a conspicuous midrib. The antheridium is reduced in
size. The number of wall cells is reduced to three, accompanied by a
great reduction in sperm output. The archegonial neck becomes shorter
and conspicuously curved. In more-specialized ferns the archegonia appear in less than four weeks after spore germination.

The student interested in pursuing this topic in greater detail should
consult the literature, particularly the article by Stokey (1951). Refer
also to Table 13-I at the end of this chapter. In summary, the gametophyte will undoubtedly play an ever increasing rôle in helping to answer
questions involving affinities. The position of a group of genera, for
example, that has not been established to the satisfaction of pteridolo-
gists may well be determined on the basis of gametophyte morphology.

Growing Fern Prothallia

Fern prothallia are easily grown from spores, and provide interesting
material for both the instructor and the student. Ripe, fresh spores of
several common ferns germinate readily and produce good prothallia
when properly cared for. Some of these ferns are the bracken fern
(*Pteridium aquilinum*), the native maidenhair ferns (*Adiantum*), and

Figure 13-24 **A,** culture of fern gametophytes on a clay pot which had been filled with moist peat moss and covered with a glass jar; **B,** enlargment of several gametophytes (note the conspicuous "wings" on the two larger plants).

Dryopteris. There are at least three methods of growing prothallia, but probably the flower-pot culture is the simplest (refer to Fig. 13-24). Fill a clay pot with rich loam or sphagnum moss, and cover with a layer of clear sand. Pour boiling water over the pot and its contents, or place the entire pot in boiling water or an autoclave for a few minutes, to kill harmful organisms. After cooling, dust the fern spores onto the surface, being careful not to sow too many for each culture. Cover the pot with a piece of glass or a bell jar, and set it in a pan for a thorough watering. It is best not to pour water directly on the surface of the sand after the spores have been sown. After the initial watering do not keep the culture too moist. Place the culture in a relatively cool place where it will not be exposed to direct sunlight throughout the day—an eastern or northern exposure is best. The flooding of mature prothallia that have formed gametangia will result in the liberation of sperms and fertilization of the egg. Within a few weeks young sporophytes will be seen emerging from beneath the gametophytic plants. In those ferns that are apogamous, sporophytes may develop without fertilization. (See end of this chapter.)

Prothallia may be grown also on the outer surface of an inverted clay pot filled with sphagnum, sterilized as explained before, and placed in a humid atmosphere. If proper facilities and supplies are available, fern prothallia may be grown on an agar nutrient medium under sterile conditions, or even on the surface of water. For more details consult texts on tissue culture, or read available popularly written notes on plant culture (*Turtox*, 1944; Ward, 1954).

Systematics and Phylogeny

It is entirely beyond the scope of this book to give extensive and intensive descriptions of fern families. We do hope, however, to give the student some idea of the criteria that are used in establishing certain families and arriving at reasonable phylogenies. Although there are several schemes of fern classification, the one by F. O. Bower has undoubtedly been adopted by many botanists. In the discussion of this subject the student is referred to Fig. 13-25 where Bower's ideas are portrayed schematically. Also, Table 13-I should be consulted. The order Coenopteridales is considered to be the ancestral group not only for the Filicales but also for the two orders of eusporangiate ferns—the Ophioglossales and Marattiales. It will be noted in the chart that lines remain unconnected to avoid any connotation of direct and undisputed descent of one group from another.

Osmundaceae

The Osmundaceae, consisting of two living genera, *Osmunda* and *Todea*, has fossil relatives in the rocks of the upper Permian (*Thamnopteris*). They were numerous in the Mesozoic (*Osmundites*) but have declined since. Members of the Osmundaceae combine more eusporangiate and leptosporangiate characteristics in their morphology than do members of any other family in the Filicales. Living plants are terrestrial, erect, and have simple uniseriate hairs. In *Osmunda* large sporangia are attached along the margins of narrow ultimate leaf segments, and are not organized into sori. Certain species exhibit leaf dimorphism in the development of sterile and fertile leaves. In *Todea* there is no marked difference between purely vegetative leaves and fertile leaves. In *Osmunda* the origin of a sporangium is not always easily referrable to a single surface initial, and the mature sporangium has many eusporangiate tendencies (Chapter 4). The sporangium is large with a distal

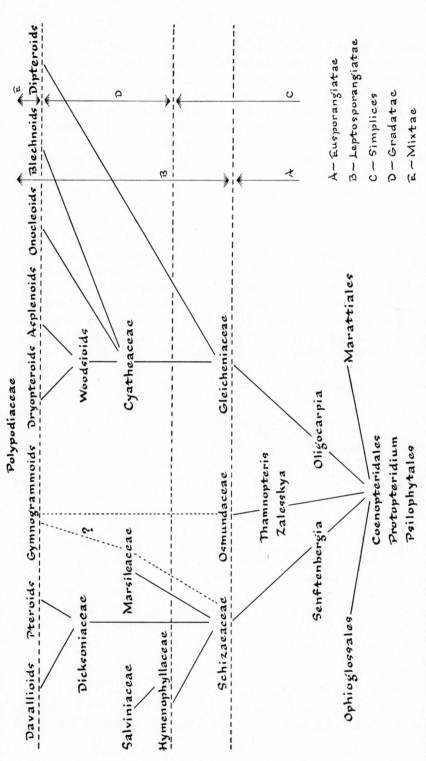

Figure 13-25 Possible interrelationships within the ferns. (Consult text for discussion.) [Based on a table from *Primitive Land Plants* by F. O. Bower, London: Macmillan, 1935.]

305

longitudinal slit and produces a large number of spores (128-512). The gametophyte is a large, green thallus, often cordate in shape, with a conspicuous midrib. Long-lived gametophytes may reach 3-4 cm in length. The antheridium is relatively large and produces a large number of sperms. Many morphologists consider that members of the Osmundaceae have not given rise to any fern group other than perhaps certain members of the so-called gymnogrammoid ferns (ferns with sporangia along veins but with the added development of interveinal or laminar tissue). Copeland (1947), however, considers all gymnogrammoid type ferns more closely allied with members of the "marginal series."

Schizaeaceae

The beginning point for the marginal series is the family Schizaeaceae, which also is an intermediate or transition group. The family is primarily tropical in its distribution. The rhizome is creeping or ascending in growth habit, and the leaves are fundamentally dichotomously branched. Sporangia are regarded as marginal in origin, but are often shifted to the abaxial side during development. They are not grouped into sori. Sporangia are large, they have short stalks and a thick tapetum (*Lygodium*), and they produce a large number of spores (128-256). Each sporangium has a girdling apical annulus which brings about longitudinal dehiscence. Some species are protostelic, others are siphonostelic. The prothallium is the cordate type, except in *Schizaea* where specialization has led to the development of a filamentous form.

Hymenophyllaceae

The Hymenophyllaceae, or filmy ferns, consists of two genera (*Hymenophyllum* and *Trichomanes*), or of many more (Copeland, 1947), depending on the investigator's concept of taxonomic boundaries. Leaves within the group are often finely dissected, and the lamina (except at the vein) is one cell in thickness. The stems are uniformly protostelic. For the most part, the seemingly simple type of vegetative structure exhibited by this family has been secondarily derived and is not primitive. The receptacle of the sorus is always marginal in origin and may become elongated into a bristle and surrounded by an indusium (Fig. 13-6, B). The order of appearance of sporangia on the receptacle is basipetal, and hence of the gradate type. The sporangial stalks are short, and many spores are formed which are liberated by oblique dehiscence of the spore case.

Dicksoniaceae

The Dicksoniaceae, considered by Bower himself somewhat of a synthetic or arbitrary family, occupies an intermediate position between the more primitive families and members of the advanced or derived family, the

Polypodiaceae. In growth habit species vary from creeping types to large dendroid forms (tree ferns). Plant parts in the majority of species have hairs or large dermal appendages. Vascular cylinders in the group are solenostelic or dictyostelic. Sori are marginal in origin and protected by two overlapping indusial flaps (bivalvate) in many species. The annulus of a sporangium may be somewhat oblique, or it may approach a vertical orientation. The family definitely consists of intermediate genera among which there is considerable variation, and the taxonomic limits of the group are variable according to the concepts of individual workers.

Some advanced derivatives of the family Dicksoniaceae have retained the marginal position and individuality of sori (Davalloids), whereas certain other genera have, to some degree, lost the individuality of sori (Pteroids). All these derivative genera show certain common characteristics: a highly specialized sporangium consisting of a long delicate stalk with transverse dehiscence and producing a small number of spores; mixed sorus; and a small specialized antheridium, consisting of three jacket cells and generally producing relatively few sperms. Genera combining these features in their morphology automatically become members of the large family Polypodiaceae.

It is immediately apparent from Fig. 13-25 that additional genera, derived from the other two lines of development, form part of the family Polypodiaceae. The family is large (seven-eighths of the fern genera are included in it) and highly artificial, and it is based arbitrarily on the characteristics just mentioned. Genera of the family have attained the same *evolutionary level*, although they have been derived from different natural phylogenetic lines. In recent reviews and monographic treatments of the Filicales (Copeland, 1947; Holttum, 1949; and others) there is a tendency to establish more natural families out of the polypodiaceous genera. If this procedure is followed, the "natural" family, Polypodiaceae, shrinks in number of genera. The Davalloids become members of the Davalliaceae; the Pteroids become Pteridaceae, and so on. In addition, a lively controversy surrounds the proper designation and limits of the intermediate family shown in Fig. 13-25 as the Dicksoniaceae (Copeland, 1947; Holttum, 1949; Weatherby, 1948).

Marsileaceae–Marsilea, and Regnellidium

GENERAL ORGANOGRAPHY. The two heterosporous fern families, the Marsileaceae and the Salviniaceae, often referred to as the water ferns, clearly represent in their morphology a high degree of specialization. Most morphologists do not consider them closely related to each other but are inclined to believe that they have affinities with homosporous families.

We will not give detailed descriptions of all genera of water ferns. Instead, we will adopt the "type method" and describe the general morphology and life cycle of *Marsilea* (Marsileaceae), leaving detailed

Figure 13-26 Water ferns. **A,** *Regnellidium* (note round sporocarps and bipinnate leaves); **B,** *Azolla,* showing overlapping leaves of the floating shoots and the slender pendulous roots.

analyses of other genera to more specialized works. In growth habit *Marsilea* and *Regnellidium* have creeping rhizomes which may grow in water or be attached by roots to damp soil. Leaves are two-ranked, peltate, and compound. Each leaf blade consists of four pinnae, the entire leaf looking very much like a four-leaf clover; the leaf of *Regnellidium* forms only two pinnae. The venation in each pinna is dichotomous, but there are interconnections between main veins. Leaves exhibit circinate vernation during development. In general, if a plant is not submerged in water, reproductive structures, termed sporocarps and containing sporangia, are formed near the bases of leaves (Fig. 13-26, A). Sporocarps are usually hard, bean-shaped structures and occur singly except in certain species where from two to many may be a characteristic feature.

THE SPOROCARP. It is generally agreed that this specialized structure has been laminar in its origin. The question does arise, however, as to whether it represents a simple, folded basal pinna, or whether in evolution it has arisen from a compound basal pinna or leaflet (for discussions see Puri and Garg, 1953; Eames, 1936; Smith, 1955). There is one main vein in the sporocarp, with lateral side branches that dichotomize (Fig. 13-27, A). Sori occur on the inner side of each half of the sporocarp. An indusium covers each sorus and is a pouch-like structure which extends toward the margin of the sporocarp (Fig. 13-26, B). Developmentally each sorus is of the gradate type, with megasporangia being initiated first, followed by microsporangia. Only one spore in each megasporangium is functional after the meiotic divisions have taken place. The sporangial wall shows no signs of cellular specialization such as the formation of an annulus. Since the overwhelming majority of leptosporangiate ferns are homosporous, the heterosporous condition in *Marsilea* and other water ferns is particularly noteworthy.

ANATOMY OF THE RHIZOME. The prostrate rhizome is typically solenostelic with exarch xylem. The inner portion of the cortex is usually made up of a compact tissue; the outer portion is frequently very lacunate with large air spaces around radiating rows of parenchyma cells.

OPENING OF THE SPOROCARP AND DEVELOPMENT OF GAMETOPHYTES. A mature sporocarp is very long-lived but will open if placed in water. The

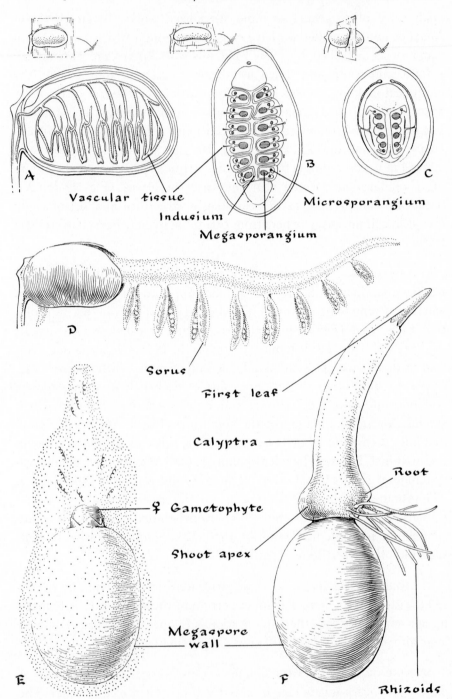

Vascular tissue

Indusium

Megasporangium

Microsporangium

Sorus

First leaf

Calyptra

Root

♀ Gametophyte

Shoot apex

Megaspore wall

Rhizoids

process can be hastened by cracking or scoring the stony covering, whereupon the tissues within immediately begin to imbibe water and swell. As the sporocarp swells the hard sporocarp wall splits open. The events that follow have interested many a student. Within a few minutes a long, worm-like gelatinous structure emerges, attached to which are the sori (Fig. 13-27, D). The indusia and sporangial walls are intact at first, but with continued imbibition there is a general breakdown of the cells and the spores are released.

The numerous microspores immediately begin to germinate (cell division within the spore wall). After several divisions the endosporic microgametophyte consists of a jacket of cells enclosing 16 spermatocytes. Each spermatocyte will become metamorphosed into a multiflagellate sperm on the bursting of the spore wall. The sperms are unusually good for demonstrating swimming male gametes. The main body of the sperm (mostly nuclear material) is a tightly coiled structure attached initially to a large vesicular body of cytoplasm. As the sperm continues to swim the tightly coiled "spring" becomes looser and looser until it is corkscrew in form.

Development of the female gametophyte or megagametophyte, also begins early within the megaspore wall. Each megaspore is roughly egg-shaped with an apical nodule at one end (Fig. 13-27, E). The first division within the megaspore wall takes place at the apical end. This separates a small, densely cytoplasmic apical cell from a large, highly vacuolate starch-containing basal cell. The small apical cell functions as the archegonial initial. The one archegonium consists of a few neck cells, one neck canal cell, a ventral canal cell, and an egg cell. By the time the

---

Figure 13-27 **A-C,** structure of sporocarps of *Marsilea.* **A,** *Marsilea minuta,* longitudinal section in the dorsiventral plane, showing the vasculature of one half of the sporocarp as viewed from the inside; **B,** *Marsilea sp.,* longitudinal section at right angles to **A,** showing soral organization; **C,** *Marsilea sp.,* transverse section at right angles to **A. D-F,** germination of sporocarp and subsequent development of the megagametophyte. **D,** *M. quadrifolia,* extrusion of gelatinous cylinder to which sori are attached; **E,** *M. vestita,* megaspore wall with megagametophyte surrounded by gelatinous sheath in which sperms (shown as spirals) are embedded; **F,** *M. vestita,* external appearance of young sporophyte attached to gametophyte. [A, redrawn from Puri and Garg, *Phytomorphology* 3:190, 1953; B-D, adapted from *Morphology of Vascular Plants. Lower Groups* by A. J. Eames, New York: McGraw-Hill, 1936.]

archegonium is mature the megaspore wall has become gelatinous, and forms a wide, watery colloidal jacket. Sperms, swimming in the vicinity, are attracted to the megagametophyte. Some of them penetrate the gelatinous sheath to the vicinity of the archegonium and swarm around the mouth of the gametangium. Other sperms never reach the archegonium but may be found embedded in the matrix of the sheath. From liberation of the spores to fertilization requires from 12 to 18 hours.

THE EMBRYO.   Early embryogeny is much like that already described for leptosporangiate ferns (p. 290). After a few days a young sporophyte can be seen, attached to the large megaspore. Externally the first leaf, root, and enclosing gametophytic sheath (calyptra), from which numerous rhizoids emerge, are easily identified (Fig. 13-27, F).

Other Water Ferns

Two other genera, *Regnellidium* and *Pilularia*, are similar to *Marsilea* in many respects. *Regnellidium* (Fig. 13-26, A), however, has only two leaflets, whereas *Pilularia* lacks any definable blade. *Salvinia* and *Azolla*, usually placed in the family Salviniaceae, are highly reduced and specialized genera (Fig. 13-26, B). Leaves exhibit erect vernation, and each has a single vascular bundle. The vascular cylinders of the stems are reduced. The sporocarps are modified indusial structures rather than modified pinnae. The development of sori, sporangia, and gametophytes is more complex in *Salvinia* and *Azolla* than in *Marsilea*; the student is referred to the pertinent literature on the subject for additional reading and further study.

Gleicheniaceae

The family Gleicheniaceae, considered to be the most primitive one in the superficial series, is a most natural group, according to Copeland (1947). It is primarily a tropical family of both hemispheres, often forming dense thickets at the edges of forests. The family occupies the same evolutionary level as does the Schizaeaceae in the other line of development. There were undisputed relatives in the Triassic, with soral impressions from the Upper Carboniferous resembling the sori of modern-day species.

Members of the Gleicheniaceae are terrestrial ferns with long creeping rhizomes, and the leaves may clamber on other vegetation. Fronds are once or more pinnately compound, but often they are pseudodichotomously branched by the abortion of terminal pinnae and the repetitive development of lateral pinnae. The ultimate veins end freely. Stems are usually protostelic and of the "vitalized" type (Fig. 13-14, A). The sori of extinct and living plants occur in two rows, one on each side of the leaf segment (Fig. 13-6, E). There are a relatively few large sporangia in each sorus. Each sporangium produces a large number of spores (128-800), and dehiscence is brought about by the functioning of a transverse, to a transverse-oblique, girdling annulus. The gametophyte or prothallium is of the primitive type, namely, a large, green, dorsiventral plant with a conspicuous midrib or cushion. Considering all morphological features of this family, it obviously occupies a primitive position in the Filicales. With little doubt, the family Matoniaceae is related to the Gleicheniaceae, and the basis for this conclusion rests primarily on the position of sori (Fig. 13-6, H) and the type of sporangium. Divergence of the two families probably occurred not later than the Mesozoic.

Cyatheaceae

The family Cyatheaceae occupies the same intermediate position in the superficial series as does the Dicksoniaceae in the marginal series. It is truly the family of tree ferns, and there are species in all tropical lands south to Chile, New Zealand, and South Africa (Copeland, 1947). Individual trees may reach heights of from 60 to 80 feet.

The typical tree fern has a trunk 4-12 inches, or more, in diameter, on which the leaf scars or leaf bases may be seen (Fig. 13-28). A crown of unusually large, pinnately compound leaves is present at the top of the trunk. The sight of large unrolling fiddle-heads has evoked comment from many an observer. Older trunks are covered with masses of inter-tangled roots; the base of a trunk is often enlarged, due to the presence of innumerable roots which have grown downward through the trunk from positions near leaf bases located high on the stem (Fig. 13-28). The vascular cylinders of all tree ferns are intricate dictyosteles of the dissected type (see p. 284).

Sori are located abaxially and are round without an indusium, or with a cup-shaped indusium that enclosed the sorus during early development (Fig. 13-6, F). Each sorus is of the gradate type, and each sporangium has an oblique annulus.

The prothallium is the usual cordate type, although older specimens may have a conspicuous midrib.

Emerging from the superficial line are certain derivatives that have the polypodiaceous characteristics outlined earlier (p. 307). Members of the Woodsioids have reached the mixed condition of the sorus, and in some of them the indusium has become zygomorphic. On the one hand, individuality of the sorus and zygomorphy of the indusium have been

Figure 13-28 Trunk of tree fern showing conspicuous leaf scars and dense mat of roots forming a buttress at base of stem. Many roots have grown downward from points high on the trunk. [Courtesy Dr. T. E. Weier.]

carried through to the Dryopteroids; in some, radial symmetry has been achieved secondarily (*Polystichum*). The Blechnoids, on the other hand, have formed long coenosori (*Blechnum*), only to be broken up secondarily into smaller coenosori (*Woodwardia*). In the Asplenoids the sori have become extended along veins and are covered by unilateral indusia.

Chromosome Numbers

This chapter should not be closed without some discussion of the very important contributions made to fern systematics, based on chromosome studies. The most intensive work on this subject has been carried out by I. Manton (1950), of the University of Leeds, England. Studies of this type get to the very basis of evolution and permit clarification of some of the uncertainties in fern phylogeny. Counting chromosomes in ferns is often difficult because of the large chromosome numbers, and it is somewhat perplexing because of obligate apogamy in many ferns. In these instances the chromosome complements may be reduplicated in premeiotic divisions of the sporogenous cells with the result that the spores have the unreduced number of chromosomes. Sporophytes develop apogamously from the gametophytes in these cases, and therefore chromosome numbers are the same for the two generations.

Chromosome numbers vary considerably (for example, $n = 250\text{-}260$ in *Ophioglossum*; $n = 40$ in *Athyrium*; $n = 22$ in *Osmunda*), but the cytological approach to phylogeny becomes extremely important, particularly in studies of restricted groups. For example, in Britain the male fern, *Dryopteris filix-mas*, long considered to be the most common and best-known British fern, turned out to be an assemblage of different forms (Manton, 1950). *D. filix-mas* (*sens. strict.*) itself is a hybrid between *D. abbreviata* and some unknown species. Proof of this comes from a cross between *D. filix-mas* and *D. abbreviata*. Half of the chromosome complement of the former are homologous with those of the latter, as revealed by pairing at the metaphase plate. *D. borreri*, the other species of the complex, is exclusively apogamous because the chromosome number of sporophyte and gametophyte are the same, sex organs are imperfect, and some sporangia are abortive. This is only one example of how knowledge of chromosome number and behavior can be utilized in fern taxonomy.

Chromosome numbers can be important evidence for the placement of a genus. The genus *Diellia* has generally been aligned with the marginal ferns, but Wagner (1952) has shown that on the basis of chromosome number the genus is more closely aligned with the asplenoids of the superficial line. In addition, the totality of morphological characteristics substantiates this conclusion.

Information on chromosome numbers in ferns will accumulate gradually and will play an important role in establishing the proper phylogenetic positions of species, genera, and higher taxa.

Although this section on fern systematics has necessarily been brief, it is hoped that the student will be encouraged to carry out additional reading in the references cited. If he does he will encounter new and stimulating ideas on fern classification and phylogeny.

TABLE 13-I *Primitive and Derived Conditions of Certain Characters in the Filicales*

I Sporophyte	Primitive	Derived
Leaf	Large, compound	Small, simple; filmy
	Open dichotomous venation	Modified dichotomous to reticulate
	Single simple arc of vascular tissue in stipe	Dissected cylinder of tissue
	Simple uniseriate hairs	Scales; capitate hairs
Stem	Terrestrial	Epiphytic; hydrophytic; lianas
	Prostrate, rhizomatous	Erect to columnar; stoloniferous
	Protostelic	Solenostelic to dictyostelic
	Simple uniseriate hairs	Scales; capitate hairs
Sorus	Sporangia single	Sporangia few in a sorus to many
	Marginal position	Superficial position
	Indusium absent	Present to secondarily absent
	Simple (simultaneous) maturation	Gradate to mixed
Sporangium	Large, short stalks	Delicate, long stalks
	Massive, irregular tapetum	Two-layered tapetum
	Apical or lateral annulus	Oblique annulus to vertical annulus
	Longitudinal dehiscence	Oblique dehiscence to transverse dehiscence
	Numerous spores (e.g., 128, 256)	Few spores (e.g., 32, 64)
Spores	Spores tetrahedral	Spores bilateral
	Without perispore	With perispore
	Homospory	Heterospory

II
Gametophyte

	Exosporic, green	Endosporic (water ferns)
Form and Growth	Large, winged, with elongate midrib	Cordate; filamentous
	Maturing slowly	Maturing rapidly
Antheridium	Large, several wall cells	Small, wall of 3 cells
	Several hundred sperms	Commonly 14, 16, 32
Archegonium	Relatively long, straight neck	Shorter, strongly curved neck
	Often a wall between neck canal nuclei	No wall between neck canal nuclei
Embryo	Early divisions irregular	More precise cleavages

References

Allsopp, A. 1951. *Marsilea* spp.: materials for the experimental study of morphogenesis. *Nature* 168:301-302.

———. 1953. Experimental and analytical studies of pteridophytes. XIX. Investigations on *Marsilea. Ann. Bot. N.S.* 17:37-55.

Blake, S. F. 1942. The ostrich fern as an edible plant. *Amer. Fern Jour.* 32: 61-68.

Bliss, M. C. 1939. The tracheal elements in the ferns. *Amer. Jour. Bot.* 26:620-624.

Bower, F. O. 1923. *The Ferns (Vol. I).* Cambridge University Press, London.

———. 1928. *The Ferns (Vol. III).* Cambridge University Press, London.

———. 1935. *Primitive Land Plants.* Macmillan, London.

Copeland, E. B. 1939. Antarctica as the source of existing ferns. *6th Proc., Pacific Sci. Congress* 4:625-627.

———. 1942. Edible ferns. *Amer. Fern Jour.* 32:121-126.

———. 1947. *Genera Filicum (The Genera of Ferns).* Chronica Botanica Co., Waltham, Mass.

Coquillat, M. 1950. Au sujet du "pain de fougère" en Mâconnais. *Bull. Mens. Soc. Linn. Lyon.* 19:173-175.

Eames, A. J. 1936. *Morphology of Vascular Plants. Lower Groups.* McGraw-Hill, New York.

Esau, K. 1953. *Plant Anatomy.* Wiley, New York.

————. 1954. Primary vascular differentiation in plants. *Biol. Rev.* 29: 46-86.

Gautheret, R. 1942. *Manuel Technique de Culture des Tissus Végétaux.* Masson et Cie., Paris.

————. 1954. *La Culture des Tissus.* Gallimard, Paris.

Jeffrey, E. C. 1902. The structure and development of the stem in the Pteridophyta and Gymnosperms. *Phil. Trans. Roy. Soc. London Ser. B.* 195:119-146.

Holttum, R. E. 1949. The classification of ferns. *Biol. Rev.* 24:267-296.

Manton, I. 1950. Demonstration of compound cilia in a fern spermatozoid by means of the ultra-violet microscope. *Jour. Exptl. Bot.* 1:68-70.

————. 1950. *Problems of Cytology and Evolution in the Pteridophyta.* Cambridge University Press, London.

————. and B. Clarke. 1951. Demonstration of compound cilia in a fern spermatozoid with the electron microscope. *Jour. Exptl. Bot.* 2:125-128.

Morel, G. and R. H. Wetmore. 1951. Fern callus tissue culture. *Amer. Jour. Bot.* 38:141-143.

Ogura, Y. 1938. Anatomie der Vegetationsorgane der Pteridophyten. *Handbuch der Pflanzenanatomie.* Gebrüder Borntraeger, Berlin.

Puri, V. and M. L. Garg. 1953. A contribution to the anatomy of the sporocarp of *Marsilea minuta* L. with a discussion of the nature of sporocarp in the Marsileaceae. *Phytomorphology* 3:190-209.

Smith, G. M. 1955. *Cryptogamic Botany Vol. II.* Ed. 2. McGraw-Hill, New York.

Steeves, T. A. and R. H. Wetmore. 1953. Morphogenetic studies on *Osmunda cinnamomea* L.: some aspects of the general morphology. *Phytomorphology* 3:339-354.

Stokey, A. G. 1951. The contribution by the gametophyte to classification of the homosporous ferns. *Phytomorphology* 1:39-58.

Turtox, 1944. *Turtox* service leaflets Nos. 30 and 44. *Turtox* General Biological Supply House, Chicago, Illinois.

Vladesco, M. A. 1935. Recherches morphologiques et expérimentales sur l'embryogénie et l'organogénie des fougères leptosporangiées. *Rev. Gen. Bot.* 47:513-528; 564-588.

Wagner, W. H., Jr. 1952. The fern genus *Diellia*, its structure, affinities and taxonomy. *Univ. Calif. Publ. in Bot.* 26:1-212.

Ward, M. 1954. Fertilization in *Phlebodium aureum* J. Sm. *Phytomorphology* 4:1-17.

Wardlaw, C. W. 1945. An experimental treatment of the apical meristem in ferns. *Nature* 156:39-41.

————. 1946a. Experimental and analytical studies of pteridophytes. VIII. Further observations on bud development in *Matteuccia struthiopteris, Onoclea sensibilis,* and species of *Dryopteris. Ann. Bot.,* N.S. 10:117-132.

―――. 1946b. Experimental and analytical studies of pteridophytes. IX. The effect of removing leaf primordia on the development of *Angiopteris evecta. Hoffm. Ann. Bot.,* N.S. 10: 223-235.

―――. 1949. Further experimental observations on the shoot apex of *Dryopteris aristata* Druce. *Phil. Trans. Roy. Soc. London. Ser. B.* 223:415-451.

―――. 1952a. *Phylogeny and Morphogenesis.* Macmillan, London.

―――. 1952b. *Morphogenesis in Plants.* Methuen, London.

Weatherby, C. A. 1948. Reclassifications of the Polypodiaceae. *Amer. Fern Jour.* 38:7-12.

Wetmore, R. H. 1950. Tissue and organ culture as a tool for studies in development. *Rept. Proc. 7th Internat. Bot. Congr.,* Stockholm. p. 369.

―――. The use of *"in vitro"* cultures in the investigation of growth and differentiation in vascular plants. *Brookhaven Symposium in Biology* 6:22-40.

White, P. R. 1943. A *Handbook of Plant Tissue Culture.* The Jaques Cattell Press, Lancaster, Pa.

―――. 1946. Plant tissue cultures. II. *Bot. Rev.* 12:521-529.

Chapter

14 THE GYMNOSPERMS

General Characteristics

Gymnosperm means literally naked seed, and serves to designate an important character of all those members of the Pteropsida in which the ovules (i.e., megasporangia) are borne in an exposed position on the sporophylls or equivalent structures. In contrast, the angiosperms or flowering plants develop their ovules and seeds within a closed ovary. As we shall see in subsequent chapters, this distinction between "naked" and "enclosed" seeds, although of considerable importance, is by no means the only salient morphological distinction between gymnosperms and angiosperms, and indeed is not even a completely valid difference in all cases.

As a class the gymnosperms include extremely ancient lines of seed-bearing plants, and their long evolutionary history contains many examples of organisms which flourished and finally became extinct. One of the most important and interesting of these extinct gymnospermous lines was an assemblage of plants decidedly fern-like in foliage and general appearance but which possessed a primitive type of seed. Indeed, the leaves of some of these plants were for a long time classified as parts of fossil ferns, and it was not until seeds were found attached to the pinnatifid fronds that their unique nature could be fully appreciated. This group has been well-named seed ferns, or Cycadofilicales, and their former existence is evidence of the origin of the gymnosperms from an ancient stock of fern-like pteropsid plants (Fig. 14-1). In addition to the Cycadofilicales, several other ancient extinct lines of seed plants are recognized as gymnosperms—for example, the Cordaitales and the Bennettitales (Fig. 14-2). The former were conspicuous in the Paleozoic and have often been regarded as the ancestral stock from which the modern conifers and Gnetales may have originated (Eames, 1952). The Bennettitales, which strikingly resembled modern cycads in their vegeta-

320

Figure 14-1 Reconstruction of a specimen (12-15 feet high) of *Medullosa noei*. [Redrawn from W. N. Stewart and T. Delevoryas, *Bot. Rev.* 22:45, 1956.]

tive appearance and structure, were highly diversified and widely distributed during the Mesozoic Era; together with the extinct representatives of the cycads, they flourished during the age of the giant dinosaurs.

The remaining members of the gymnosperms are represented in the modern flora and are commonly grouped in four orders: the Ginkgoales, Cycadales, Coniferales, and Gnetales. A detailed account of the anatomy and reproduction of selected representatives of these orders will occupy the next three chapters. At this point, however, it is important to empha-

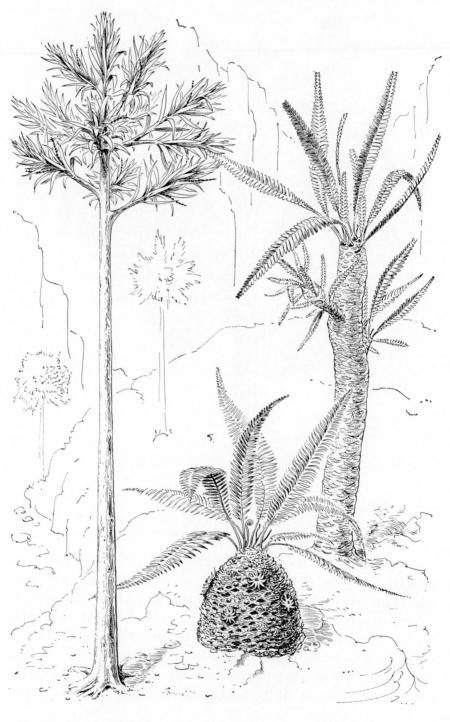

size briefly the general nature and geographical distribution of these surviving gymnosperms. The largest group, and the one containing the most familiar and most economically important plants, is the Coniferales. Examples of this order are pines, spruces, firs, and cedars. Some conifers are not only among the largest plants on the earth but also represent, as in *Sequoia gigantea*, organisms with a life span which may reach 4,000 years. The Coniferales are worldwide in distribution and commonly form extensive forests in both the northern and southern hemispheres. In contrast, the Ginkgoales and Cycadales represent the surviving members of extremely ancient groups and in the modern world are veritable living fossils. *Ginkgo biloba*, for example, is the sole living representative of a formerly widely distributed and diversified group of gymnosperms, and there has been considerable doubt as to whether it actually exists in the wild state today. The living cycads likewise appear as relicts of a once large and considerably diversified group of Mesozoic plants. At the present time the cycads are confined to limited areas of the subtropics or tropics, but very rarely do they form extensive or conspicuous features of the vegetation. The final order of living gymnosperms, the Gnetales, contains but three living genera, which differ in general aspect not only from one another but from all other known gymnospermous plants. One of them, *Welwitschia mirabilis*, is monotypic and restricted to certain deserts in southwest Africa. *Ephedra* and *Gnetum* each contain a number of species; *Ephedra* occurs in tropical and temperate Asia and in North and South America, and *Gnetum* is restricted to tropical areas in Africa, Asia, and South America. As will be described in a later chapter, the Gnetales have many puzzling features in their method of reproduction, and because their evolutionary history is obscure they constitute a somewhat isolated and poorly understood group of seed-bearing plants.

A very convenient, broad classification of living and extinct gymno-

Figure 14-2 Reconstructions showing the habit and general organography of extinct types of gymnosperms. Left, *Dorycordaites*, a member of the Cordaitales; center, *Cycadella*, right, *Williamsonia Sewardiana*, both members of the Bennettitales. Although *Dorycordaites* was not coexistant with other genera shown, it has been included in the figure to emphasize contrasts in growth habits. [*Dorycordaites* redrawn from *Studies in Fossil Botany* by D. H. Scott, London: Adam and Charles Black, 1920; *Williamsonia* adapted from *An Introduction to Paleobotany* by C. A. Arnold, N. Y.: McGraw-Hill Book Co. Inc., 1947.]

sperms (exclusive of the Gnetales) was proposed by Chamberlain (1935). He recognized two major evolutionary groups, each of which may be traced back to the Paleozoic Era. One group, the "Cycado-phytes," includes those gymnosperms with fern-like pinnatifid leaves, relatively short and usually unbranched trunks, and large and conspicu-ously developed pith and cortical zones in the stems (Figs. 14-1, 14-2; Fig. 15-2). The cycadophytes are essentially a group of extinct gymno-sperms which includes the Cycadofilicales and Bennettitales—the only surviving representatives today are the modern cycads. The other major group, the "Coniferophytes," comprises gymnosperms with simple and often needle-like or scale-like leaves, tall and often profusely branched trunks, and relatively small pith and cortical zones in the stem. Typical coniferophytes also develop a conspicuous amount of secondary xylem, whereas, in contrast, there is noticeably less cambial activity in the stems of cycadophytes. The coniferophytes include the Coniferales, *Ginkgo biloba*, the extinct order Cordaitales, the Paleozoic conifers (e.g., the Voltziales), and the extinct members of the Ginkgoales (Fig. 14-2; Fig. 15-11; Fig. 16-1). In Chamberlain's view, the cycadophytes and conif-erophytes represent distinct and parallel lines of evolution in the gymno-sperms, but their ultimate origins in the Paleozoic remain to be dis-covered. Further light on this problem depends on the evidence which paleobotany can produce regarding the origin of the seed habit itself. It seems reasonably clear that the seed, as a definitive morphological struc-ture, evolved independently in various groups of ancient vascular plants. But whether seeds developed from the modification of terminal sporan-gia of some remote psilopsid group or whether they initially arose from the sporaniga or the sori of the megaphylls of an ancient fern stock are questions that must await further paleobotanical discoveries for an answer (Arnold 1938, pp. 227-232).

Ontogeny and Structure of the Seed

At present there are too many serious gaps in the fossil record to permit a satisfactory reconstruction of the evolutionary history of the gymno-spermous seed. As Coulter and Chamberlain (1917, p. 416) have clearly pointed out "the ovules of Cycadofilicales and of Cordaitales are so well organized, even in the modern sense, that their connection with the

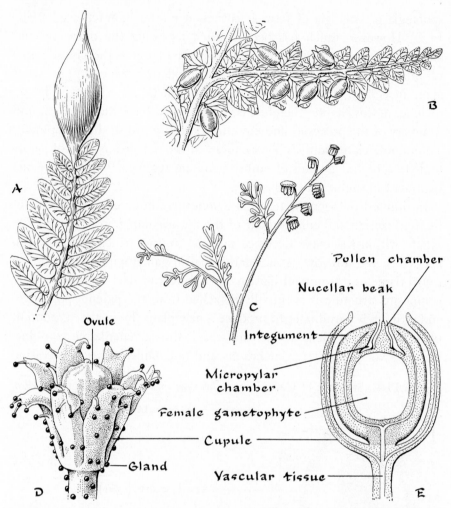

Figure 14-3 Reproductive structures in seed ferns. **A,** pinna with terminal seed of *Neuropteris heterophylla;* **B,** *Emplectopteris triangularis,* seeds attached to subdivisions of leaf; **C,** portion of fertile leaf of *Crossotheca* bearing clusters of pendant microsporangia; **D,** reconstruction of the ovule and cupule of *Lagenostoma Lomaxi;* **E,** longisection of ovule of *Lagenostoma* showing details of internal structure. [A, redrawn from *Textbook of Paleobotany* by W. C. Darrah. N. Y.: Copyright, D. Appleton-Century Co., 1939, by permission Appleton-Century-Crofts, Inc.; B, redrawn from *Ancient Plants and the World They Lived In* by H. N. Andrews. N. Y.: Comstock Publ. Co., 1947; C and D from *Les Plantes Fossiles dans leurs Rapports avec les Végétaux Vivants* by L. Emberger. Paris: Masson et Cie, 1944; E, adapted from *An Introduction to Paleobotany* by C. A. Arnold. N. Y.: McGraw-Hill Book Co. Inc., 1947.]

sporangia or synangia of ferns is entirely a matter of inference." (Fig. 14-3.) However, much has been learned regarding the ontogeny and anatomy of the seeds of living gymnosperms. Despite the considerable variation in the *details* of their structure, modern gymnospermous seeds agree in certain basic morphological and functional respects. The remainder of this chapter therefore is concerned with a critical analysis and summary of the processes and structures common to seed development. To promote clarity and emphasis, many of the detailed aspects of gametophyte morphology and of embryogeny are reserved for more specific treatment in the next two chapters.

In simplest ontogenetic terms, a gymnospermous seed is the result of the fertilization and enlargement of the megasporangium or ovule. The zygote within the ovule develops into an embryo which becomes embedded in the nutritive tissue of the female gametophyte, and the external tissue or integument hardens as a protective seed coat. The entire composite structure is eventually detached from the parent sporophyte and ultimately germinates to produce a new plant. From the standpoint of Alternation of Generations, the seed is thus a remarkable combination of two sporophytic generations and one gametophytic generation

Figure 14-4   Structure of a gymnospermous type of seed in longisectional view.

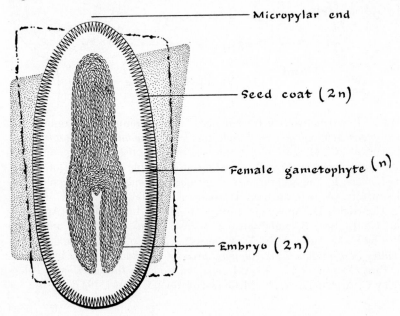

Micropylar end

Seed coat (2n)

Female gametophyte (n)

Embryo (2n)

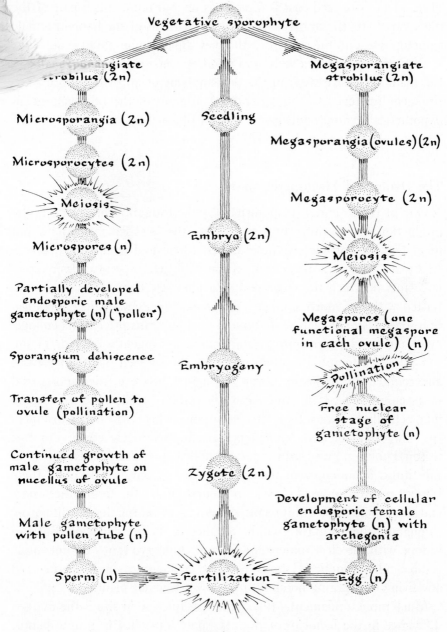

Figure 14-5 Generalized representation of the reproductive cycle in gymnosperms.

(Fig. 14-4). The seed coat is diploid tissue and represents a part of the old sporophyte, the nutritive tissue is the remains of the haploid female gametophyte, and the embryo is the new diploid sporophyte generation.

With this general orientation in mind, it is now appropriate to discuss the main successive steps in the development of an ovule into a seed. Frequent reference to the generalized diagram of the life cycle of an hypothetical gymnosperm given in Fig. 14-5 will greatly aid in understanding the following discussion.

The Ovule and Megasporogenesis

One of the essential prerequisites for the formation of a seed is the production of two different spore types—the so-called microspore and megaspore. Unfortunately these names, when used with reference to a seed plant, suggest a direct comparison with heterosporous lower vascular plants in which the megaspore is a relatively enormous cell as contrasted with the much smaller microspore. Precise statistical investigations on the size of each spore type in gymnosperms *prior* to its enlargement and development into a gametophyte are urgently needed. Thomson (1927) attempted such an investigation for seed plants in general and found little to justify a size distinction between microspores and megaspores. Indeed, in some cases (in certain cycads) the microspore may actually be larger than the megaspore, whereas in other instances the dimensions of both spore types are approximately equal. For this reason Thomson proposed the terms "pollen spore" and "seed spore" as substitutes for microspore and megaspore, respectively. Although there is merit in this proposed change in nomenclature, the terms microspore and megaspore are so universally employed in morphological literature throughout the world they will be retained in the present book. But this is done with the clear understanding that these two terms do not imply a direct phylogenetic relationship between modern gymnosperms and any living free-sporing heterosporous lower vascular plant.

Much more fundamental than a mere distinction in size is the marked difference in the *behavior* of the two spore types in the gymnosperms. The numerous microspores develop in distinct microsporangia of the eusporangiate type, and the endosporic male gametophytes have already begun their development at the time of dehiscence of the sporangium

(Fig. 16-15). In contrast, the usually solitary functional megaspore arises deeply within the tissue of the ovule and is never released by dehiscence from this type of sporangium. On the contrary, the megaspore enlarges and gives rise to an endosporic female gametophyte which is nourished and sheltered by the enveloping tissues of the ovule. This characteristic *retention of the megaspore* and its growth and development into a female gametophyte within its own sporangium represent additional fundamental prerequisites for seed development. For this reason it will now be necessary to examine briefly the structure of the gymnospermous ovule, which differs in a number of respects from a typical megasporangium.

Figure 14-6, A, depicts somewhat diagrammatically an ovule in median longisectional view. The main body of the ovule is known as the nucellus and consists of parenchymatous tissue. Deeply embedded within the nucellus there is evident a linear tetrad of four well-defined haploid megaspores which have originated by meiosis from a single megasporocyte. The lowermost of these megaspores (i.e., the one farthest away from the micropyle) is destined to enlarge and to give rise to the female gametophyte, whereas the remaining spores above it will ultimately degenerate (Fig. 14-6, B). Surrounding the upper free end of the nucellus is a collar or rim-like integument which is pierced by a small central opening or micropyle. As will be described more fully later, the micropyle in gymnospermous ovules provides the means of entrance to the interior of the ovule for the endosporic male gametophytes. Except for the Gnetales, which develop ovules with two integuments, all other living gymnosperms consistently form a single integument which is free from the nucellus only near the upper or micropylar end of the ovule. The lower portion of the ovule, where integument and nucellus are firmly joined, is termed the chalaza.

Although the nucellus of the ovule clearly appears to be functionally equivalent to a megasporangium, the integument represents an accessory structure which is not duplicated in the megasporangia of lower heterosporous vascular plants. It has been conjectured that the integument represents phylogenetically an indusium-like structure and that the nucellus may represent the only surviving sporangium of a hypothetical fern sorus. But as Schnarf (1937) has emphasized, this theory and other hypotheses regarding the origin of the integument have little evidence

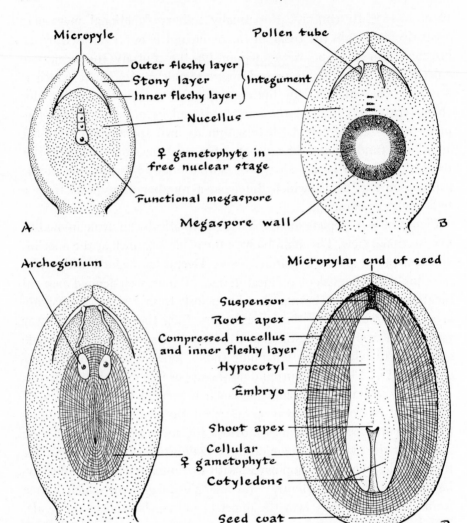

Figure 14-6 The processes and structures concerned in the development of a seed in gymnosperms. **A,** longisection of ovule, showing linear tetrad of megaspores, the lowermost of which will develop into the female gametophyte; **B,** female gametophyte in free nuclear stage of development (note early phases in growth of pollen tubes in nucellus); **C,** cellular female gametophyte with two archegonia (note that a pollen tube has reached the archegonium at the right); **D,** mature seed, consisting of seed coat, remains of the nucellus, female gametophyte tissue, and endoscopically oriented embryo.

in their favor, and at present the evolutionary history of the integument is an unsolved problem.

From an anatomical standpoint, however, the integument has been rather thoroughly studied, and certain facts deserve brief mention at this point. Throughout the gymnosperms the integument is histologically differentiated into three zones or layers: an outer fleshy layer, a middle "stony" or sclerenchymatous layer, and an inner fleshy layer (Fig. 14-6, A). The degree of development of each of these layers during seed ontogeny varies within the different groups of the gymnosperms; in some (e.g., many conifers) the outer fleshy layer is rudimentary, whereas in others (e.g., the cycads and *Ginkgo*) this layer is thick, and conspicuously pigmented in the mature seed. In all cases, however, the inner fleshy layer tends to collapse and in the mature seed appears as a papery layer lining the inner surface of the stony layer. Further indication of the histological complexity of the integument is shown in many gymnosperms by the development of a vascular system (Fig. 15-9, D). In the cycads vascular strands traverse *both* the outer and inner fleshy layers, but in *Ginkgo* only the inner bundle system is developed. In members of the pine family both sets of vascular bundles have been eliminated. These varying conditions are of interest when compared with the structure of certain types of Paleozoic seeds in which the nucellus itself, as well as the outer fleshy layer of the integument, contained vascular tissue (Coulter and Chamberlain, 1917; Oliver, 1903; Arnold, 1938). Therefore it seems reasonable to conclude that there has been a general tendency in seed evolution to eliminate vascular strands first from the nucellus and then from one or both fleshy layers of the integument (Fig. 14-3, E).

Very commonly reference is made to the process of megasporogenesis in *Selaginella* as an approach to one of the processes underlying the seed habit. In two reported instances the development of the female gametophyte and the embryo may occur within the sporangial cavity (see Chapter 8). However, the megasporangium of *Selaginella* lacks an integument; in this respect and in the absence of any vascular system it differs markedly from a gymnospermous ovule. Furthermore, the growth of the female gametophyte and the embryo in *Selaginella* is at the expense of food previously stored in the megaspore itself, whereas the gametophyte and embryo of a seed depend for nutrition on the food material supplied to them by the closely adjacent tissue of the ovule.

The Female Gametophyte

A detailed description of the structure and development of the female gametophyte of various gymnosperms will be found in the next three chapters. At this point, discussion will be restricted to the more general morphological aspects of the female gametophyte with special reference to seed development.

As in lower heterosporous vascular plants, the first phase of development of the gymnospermous female gametophyte is characterized by an extensive series of free-nuclear divisions (Fig. 14-6, B). Ultimately wall formation begins at the periphery and proceeds centripetally until the entire gametophyte consists of cells which later become richly stored with reserve food materials (Fig. 14-6, C). Throughout the ontogeny of the gametophyte this structure is encased by the well-defined megaspore wall, which appears in some cases to increase in thickness during the development of the ovule. It may attain a thickness of 9 or 10 microns in the adult seeds of some of the cycads. As Schnarf (1937, p. 18) has emphasized, the presence of a conspicuous megaspore wall surrounding the female gametophyte is one of the most important and definitive features common to gymnospermous seeds; it may serve to indicate the phylogenetic connection between the megagametophytes of free-sporing plants and those of primitive gymnosperms.

During or following the process of wall formation, certain individual superficial cells of the gametophyte—usually those near its micropylar end—give rise to archegonia (Fig. 14-6, C). The number of archegonia varies considerably, ranging from usually two in *Ginkgo,* to many as in some of the conifers. All living gymnosperms, with the exception of *Gnetum* and *Welwitschia,* are thus archegoniate plants, despite the fact that the female gametophyte is no longer a freely exposed sexual plant. (See Chapter 5 for a general discussion of the Archegoniatae.)

Pollination, the Formation of Pollen Tubes, and Fertilization

Since the ovules of gymnosperms are exposed, the process of pollination consists in the transferral (usually by wind) of the partly developed endosporic male gametophyte (pollen) to the micropylar end of the ovule. In many gymnosperms the microspore wall adheres to a drop of sticky fluid (the so-called pollination drop) which exudes from the micropyle of the ovule. When this liquid begins to dry it retracts, drawing the male gametophyte down into the ovule. This is commonly followed by the closure of the micropyle. In some of the gymnosperms a somewhat well-defined recess termed the pollen chamber is developed in the free apical end of the nucellus (Fig. 15-9, D; Fig. 17-7, B). Pollen chambers were highly developed in the ovules of Paleozoic gymnosperms and are believed to have served as liquid-containing cavities within which the flagellated sperms were liberated by the dehiscence of the microspore wall (Fig. 14-3, E). Among living gymnosperms, pollen chambers occur only in *Ginkgo*, the cycads, and *Ephedra*. In the conifers, on the other hand, the endosporic male gametophyte is brought into direct contact with the surface of the nucellar beak.

One of the distinctive morphological characters of *living* gymnosperms is the production of a more or less tubular outgrowth of the male gametophyte known as the pollen tube (Fig. 14-6, B, C). In *Ginkgo* and the cycads the pollen tube is largely haustorial in function, and grows, often for several months, like a fungal hypha *laterally* into the tissue of the nucellus; its function seems to be the absorption of food materials which are used by the gametophytic cells at the lower end of the tube. At the time of fertilization the basal end of the pollen tube bursts, liberating the two large flagellated sperms together with some liquid into the cavity directly above the female gametophyte (Fig. 15-9, C). One or both sperms may then enter an archegonium, and one of them fertilizes the nucleus of the large egg cell. In contrast, the pollen tubes of the conifers are sperm carriers, and after growing downward through the intervening nucellar tissue they convey the non-flagellated male gametes directly to the archegonium (Fig. 14-6, C).

The term "siphonogamous" has been used collectively to designate plants in which the sperms are directly conveyed to the egg by means of a pollen tube. Lower vascular plants, by contrast, have been designated as "zooidogamous" because the motile flagellated sperms are freely liberated from the antheridium into water through which they must move (often for some considerable distance) to reach and fertilize the eggs. The evolutionary steps in the transition from zooidogamy to siphonogamy are by no means entirely clear, but the development of sperm-carrying pollen tubes, typical of higher gymnosperms and of all angiosperms, was surely a significant achievement. By means of the pollen tube the considerable chances and hazards of the aquatic zooidogamous method were eliminated, and much greater assurance of fertilization was made possible. In the three extinct orders of gymnosperms—Cycadofilicales, Cordaitales, and Bennettitales—there is no evidence of the existence of pollen tubes. It is possible that in these groups the motile sperms were liberated directly into the pollen chambers by the rupture of the spore wall. Among living types the cycads and *Ginkgo* appear to have a rather primitive type of pollen tube which serves primarily as a haustorium. It seems significant in this connection that these are the only known living seed plants that have retained the flagellated type of sperm characteristic of zooidogamous tracheophytes.

Embryogeny and the Maturation of the Seed

One of the remarkable features of the ontogeny of most gymnosperms is the occurrence of a free-nuclear period in embryogeny. The only known exceptions to this condition are *Welwitschia, Gnetum,* and *Sequoia sempervirens* (Buchholz, 1939). The phase of free-nuclear divisions in embryogeny is unknown in the angiosperms and lower vascular plants. In these the first division of the zygote is followed directly by the development of a new wall separating the two cells, and this process is repeated throughout the further cellular development of the embryo. In the gymnosperms, beginning with the first division of the nucleus of the fertilized egg, there is a somewhat protracted phase of nuclear multiplication unaccompanied by the formation of walls. Thus this initial phase of embryogeny bears a striking resemblance to the earliest stage in development of the female gametophyte (Fig. 15-10). The number of free nuclei formed varies widely. In certain of the cycads as many as 1,000 free nuclei are developed before wall formation begins, whereas in *Pinus* the number is four. In seeking an explanation of the distinctive free-nuclear phase of embryogeny in gymnosperms Chamberlain suggested that it may be the result of the very large size of the gymnospermous egg and the consequent inability of the first-formed cell plate to subdivide it. This idea seems highly speculative and certainly sheds no light on the phylogenetic origin or morphological meaning of the free-nuclear period.

Following the free-nuclear phase, the embryo in gymnosperms becomes cellular and gradually becomes differentiated into a suspensor, shoot apex, cotyledons, hypocotyl, and radicle. From the standpoint of polarity, the embryo of gymnosperms is strictly endoscopic with the shoot end directed away from the micropyle (Fig. 14-6, D).

In most of the gymnosperms there is a marked tendency toward the condition of polyembryony; i.e., the formation of several embryos in a single gametophyte. This is possible because more than one archegonium is commonly fertilized, and hence several zygotes may be produced. But more remarkable is the process of cleavage polyembryony, which is characteristic of a majority of the conifers. In this process, which will be described in more detail in Chapter 16, certain cells of the young embryo become separated from one another and give rise to a system of four or more distinct embryos. In some of the conifers both types of polyembryony may occur in the same developing seed. Physiological competition between the various embryos usually results in the elimination of all but one, which continues its differentiation and becomes the dominant embryo in the fully developed seed.

During the last phases of embryogeny the nucellar tissue of the ovule becomes disorganized and frequently persists only as a paper-like cap of dry tissue at the micropylar end of the seed. Further histological maturation of the various layers of the integument continues, and the stony layer becomes an extremely hard, resistent shell which effectively encloses and mechanically protects the female gametophyte and the embryo. Except for the cycads and *Ginkgo*, the detached seed of gymnosperms remains dormant for some time. Under favorable conditions the embryo resumes growth and, rupturing the seed coat, develops into a new sporophyte plant (Fig. 16-19).

References

Arnold, C. A. 1938. Paleozoic seeds. *Bot. Rev.* 4:205-234.

Buchholz, J. T. 1939. The embryogeny of *Sequoia sempervirens* with a com parison of the Sequoias. *Amer. Jour. Bot.* 26:248-257.

Chamberlain, C. J. 1935. *Gymnosperms: Structure and Evolution.* University of Chicago Press, Chicago.

Coulter, J. M. and C. J. Chamberlain. 1917. *Morphology of the Gymnosperms.* University of Chicago Press, Chicago.

Eames, A. J. 1952. Relationships of the Ephedrales. *Phytomorphology* 2:79-100.

Oliver, F. W. 1903. The ovules of the older gymnosperms. *Ann. Bot.* 17: 451-476.

Schnarf, K. 1937. Anatomie der Gymnospermen-Samen. *Hand. der. Pflanzenanatomie.* Band. X. Gebrüder Borntraeger, Berlin.

Thomson, R. B. 1927. Evolution of the seed habit in plants. *Proc. and Trans. Roy. Soc. Canada* 21:229-272.

Chapter

15 THE LIVING CYCADS AND GINKGO BILOBA

It is indeed a matter of rare good fortune to the student of evolution that there exist on the earth today a few surviving types of ancient primitive seed plants. These organisms are the cycads and the remarkable *Ginkgo biloba* or maidenhair tree. These living fossils, as they are sometimes called, clearly represent the last vestiges of formerly diversified and widely distributed lines of gymnospermous plants. The living cycads are the only extant members of the archaic cycadophyte branch in evolution, and *Ginkgo*, which is represented by a single species, is the sole living remnant of an ancient branch of the coniferophyte stock.

A comparison of Figs. 15-1 and 15-11 will immediately show the striking organographic and habit differences between an arborescent cycad and *Ginkgo*. The cycad, with its columnar unbranched trunk and crown of large pinnate leaves, is quite unlike the profusely branched sporophyte of *Ginkgo*, with its fan-shaped, bilobed leaves. But the significant fact, worthy of emphasis, is that despite these dissimilar vegetative features the cycads and *Ginkgo* resemble one another rather closely in many details of their reproductive structures and processes. These similarities include the method of pollination and pollen-tube development, the morphology of the gametophytes, the possession of motile, multiflagellated sperms, the long-extended free nucleate period in embryogeny, and the general structure of the ovule and ripe seed. Such points of morphological similarity are impressive but cannot by themselves be used to prove a close phylogenetic relationship between these two groups of gymnosperms. On the contrary, such similarities appear as the result of the retention, by both cycads and *Ginkgo*, of certain very ancient patterns of reproduction which probably were shared by many of the

Paleozoic and Mesozoic gymnosperms. The nature of these patterns, however, provides the student with an indispensable basis for understanding gymnosperms as a whole and hence will receive considerable emphasis in the chapter.

The Cycads

Distribution

According to recent paleobotanical studies, present-day cycads were derived from a rather extensive cycad flora that extended widely over the earth during much of the Mesozoic Era. The age of the cycads as a group has been estimated at 200 million years, and remains of these plants have been found in Triassic and Cretaceous deposits in such widely separated regions as Siberia, Oregon, Greenland, Sweden, central Europe, and Australia. Thus the period of maximum development of the extinct cycads coincided with the age of the giant dinosaurs. Indeed, according to Schuster (1932) there is good reason to believe that the young leaves and seeds of the ancient cycads provided a source of food for certain of the herbivorous dinosaurs. At the present time the cycads are a comparatively small remnant of a previously widespread group and are confined to isolated areas in the subtropics and tropics of the New and Old World.

Figure 15-1 A microsporangiate plant of *Microcycas calocoma* growing in the colony at Cayo Ramones, Province of Pinar del Río, Cuba. The trunk of this large specimen measured 28 feet in height and was 44 inches in circumference near the base. [From Foster and San Pedro, *Memorias Soc. Cubana Hist. Nat.* 16:105, 1942.]

The living cycads are classified into nine well-defined genera and about a hundred species. The systematics of certain of the genera is currently under investigation, but the great difficulties involved in field and laboratory studies make progress in our understanding of species relationships extremely slow. The pattern of present-day distribution of the genera of cycads is peculiar and difficult to interpret. In the Western Hemisphere four genera occur: *Microcycas* (a Cuban endemic), *Ceratozamia*, *Dioon* (endemic to Mexico), and *Zamia*, which occurs in southern Florida (the only cycad native to the United States), the West Indies, Mexico, Central America and northern and western South America. In the Eastern Hemisphere, the important cycad areas are: *Australia*, where two endemic genera, *Bowenia* and *Macrozamia* as well as the more widely distributed *Cycas* occur and *Africa*, where the endemic genera *Stangeria* and *Encephalartos* are found. The genus *Cycas* exists, in addition to Australia, in India, China, parts of southern Japan, Madagascar and certain of the Pacific Islands. As Arnold (1953) points out, it seems unlikely that Mexico and Australia represent the main centers from which the diffuse patterns of migration of present-day cycads have radiated. In his view it is more probable that such isolated genera as *Microcycas*, *Encephalartos*, and *Stangeria* "evolved at or near the places where they now occur and they are leftovers of a former larger more extensive cycadophytic population." In our opinion, a similar hypothesis seems reasonable for the other genera of cycads as well.

Because of their large, attractive palm-like leaves, many of the cycads are widely grown as ornamentals. The commonest species in cultivation throughout most of the Northern Hemisphere is the so-called Sago Palm (*Cycas revoluta*). This form requires greenhouse protection in regions of cold winters but is quite hardy outdoors in Southern California, parts of Louisiana, and Florida (Fig. 15-2, A). The most extensive outdoor collections of cycads in the United States are found in the Coconut Grove Palmetum, Coral Gables, Florida, and the Huntington Botanical Gardens, San Marino, California. The growth and general aspects of the species found at the latter institution are interestingly described and photographically illustrated in a recent book by Hertrich (1951).

Figure 15-2 Habit and general organography of cycads. **A,** specimen of *Cycas revoluta* growing in cultivation in Pasadena, California (note the crowded zones of persistant leaf bases which comprise the armor of the trunk); **B,** specimen of *Dioon spinulosum* growing in the Conservatory at Golden Gate Park, San Francisco, California (note the enormous size of the pendulous megasporangiate cone and the conspicuous armor of leaf bases). [B, courtesy Dr. T. E. Weier.]

Vegetative Organography and Anatomy

The general habit of cycads ranges from types in which the stem is tuberous and partly or wholly subterranean (species of *Zamia, Macrozamia,* and *Encephalartos;* and the genera *Stangeria* and *Bowenia*) to relatively tall plants with the general aspect of tree ferns or palms. The latter category is illustrated by the Cuban cycad *Microcycas calocoma* (Fig. 15-1). The columnar trunk of this inappropriately named genus was found by Foster and San Pedro (1942) to attain a height of about 30 feet as measured from the ground to the base of the terminal crown of leaves. According to Chamberlain (1919), the tallest of the cycads is *Macrozamia hopei,* a native of Queensland, Australia, which may reach a height of 60 feet. The same author records specimens of the Mexican cycad *Dioon spinulosum,* which measured 50 feet in height. Since cycads in general are conspicuously sluggish in their rate of growth, large arborescent types probably are extremely old. Estimates of the age of large specimens have been based on a study of the persistent leaf bases which constitute the characteristic armor of the trunk (Fig. 15-2). If one can determine the average number of leaves produced each year, this figure divided into the total number of leaf bases on the entire trunk yields some approximation of the age of the plant. By this method Chamberlain concluded that a plant of *Dioon edule* with a trunk only six feet in height was at least 1,000 years old. Age determinations based on the study of the leaf armor, however, are probably conservative because the sluggish period of development of the seedling and the prolonged periods of dormancy of older plants are not taken into consideration.

Cycads as a whole, particularly the arborescent types, are unbranched, but exceptions occur in both the tuberous as well as the columnar habits of growth (Swamy, 1948). In *Cycas revoluta*, for example, lateral buds commonly develop from various areas of the trunk, and their irregular expansion into shoots results in the production of irregularly or grotesquely branched individuals. These lateral buds, which apparently originate from the living tissue of the persistent leaf bases, are capable of rooting and producing new plants if detached from the trunk. But in other instances branching is clearly the result of the injury or destruction of the main terminal bud. Striking examples of this were discovered by Foster and San Pedro (1942) in *Microcycas*. In this genus adventitious buds arise following injury (often as a result of wind) to the upper part of the trunk, and may give rise to large candelabra-like branches.

As viewed in transverse section, the stem of cycads is distinguished by several anatomical characteristics. First, the cortex and pith are exceptionally large, as compared with the relatively narrow diameter of the vascular cylinder (Fig. 15-3). For example, the diameter of the pith in large trunks of *Cycas revoluta* may measure as much as 6 inches. Secondly, the course of the vascular strands or traces which supply each of the leaves is complex. Since the various strands entering a given leaf extend horizontally through the cortex before entering the leaf base, a girdling arrangement is seen in thick or cleared sections of the stem. Although secondary growth by means of a vascular cambium occurs in the stems of many genera, the amount of secondary vascular tissues produced is relatively small, and the xylem is traversed by numerous broad

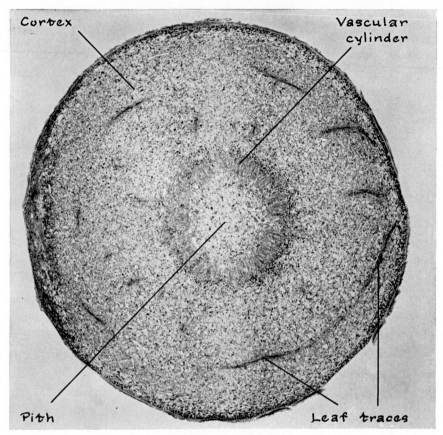

Figure 15-3 Transection of stem of *Zamia sp.* demonstrating the large pith and cortex and the characteristic girdling leaf traces. (X4.)

parenchymatous rays. Seward (1917, p. 7) designated the loose-textured wood of cycads as "manoxylic," in contrast with the more compact and dense xylem of conifers which he termed "pycnoxylic." Moreover, although concentric and definable growth rings may be seen in certain genera, they do not appear to represent true annual increments or annual rings. According to Chamberlain's study of *Dioon spinulosum*, the rings correspond to those periods in development when new crowns of leaves were produced by the terminal bud.

Cycads are distinguished from all other living gymnosperms by their pinnate leaves which, in certain genera, may reach a length of from four to five feet. The genus *Bowenia* is exceptional in having large bipinnate leaves; in all other living cycads the leaf develops a single series of leaflets (Fig. 15-4, A). Except during the juvenile phases of development, the leaves in most of the genera are produced in crowded clusters, or crowns, which thus impart a palm-like aspect to many of the arborescent types (Figs. 15-1, 15-2, A). Prior to the expansion of a crown of new foliage leaves the latter are overlaid and protected by an extensive imbricated series of tough bud scales. These structures, like the bases of the foliage leaves, persist for many years on the trunk and thus further contribute to the characteristic leaf armor. In many cycads the new leaves are erect, and the leaflets are flat during the period of expansion of the crown. But in the genus *Cycas*, the vernation of the young leaflets is distinctively *circinate* as in many ferns. Figure 15-4 shows that the unrolling of the successive coiled pinnae of each leaf occurs from the base upwardly and is thus properly designated as occurring acropetally. In addition to the fern-like vernation of the leaflets in *Cycas*, the *venation* of the leaflets in all genera of the cycads (except *Cycas*) is dichotomous and hence comparable to the vasculature of a great many ferns (Fig. 15-5). Perhaps the most fern-like foliage among all the cycads is that produced by *Stangeria*. The broad leaflets of this genus have a conspicuous midrib and dichotomously branched lateral veins (Fig. 15-5, B). Indeed, until cones with seeds were discovered *Stangeria* had been incorrectly classified as a member of the Polypodiaceae!

Certain important aspects of leaf anatomy may be briefly noted at this point. In *Cycas* the vascular tissue of each leaflet is confined to the midrib, and the laminar halves are devoid of veins. Of particular interest in this genus is the occurrence of both endarch and exarch primary xylem in the midrib bundle as well as in the vascular strands in the rachis. This

Figure 15-4 Circinate vernation in *Cycas revoluta*. **A,** adaxial view of foliage leaf showing the acropetal unrolling of the rows of circinate pinnae; **B,** transection of rachis of leaf showing two circinate pinnae. [Drawn by Mrs. Emily E. Reid.]

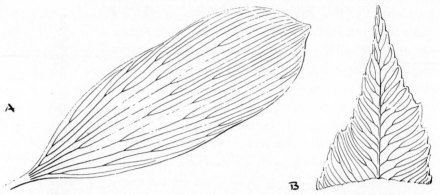

Figure 15-5 Dichotomous venation in leaflets of cycads. **A,** *Zamia Wallisii;* **B,**
Stangeria schizodon, tip of leaflet (note midvein, dichotomously branched lateral veins, and union of certain vein endings). [From *Vergleich. Morphologie
der höheren Pflanzen* by W. Troll. Berlin: Gebrüder Borntraeger, 1938.]

development of exarch or so-called cryptogamic wood is regarded by
some investigators as the retention of the primitive type of primary
xylem typical of many of the lower vascular plants (see Jeffrey, 1917,
pp. 199-202). Another feature, of particular importance in the study
and interpretation of extinct cycadophytes, is the structure and development of the stomatal apparatus in the cycads. Intensive comparative
studies have shown that the method of development of the paired
guard cells and their accompanying subsidiary cells is fundamentally
different in the Cycadales (living and extinct) from the condition
found in the Bennettitales (Arnold, 1953). Thus an important criterion
has been made available for the accurate interpretation and classification
of the epidermal structures of fossil cycads and their presumed allies
(see Fig. 16-7).

According to the celebrated student of cycad morphology, Dr. C. J.
Chamberlain (1935), the sporophytes of all cycads develop peculiar
apogeotropic roots which extend above the surface of the soil as cor-
alloid, dichotomously branched structures. Apogeotropic roots occur
almost universally in seedlings and are also very evident in cultivated
cycads (e.g., *Cycas revoluta*), particularly if the plants are confined in
pots or tubs. The function (if any) of apogeotropic roots is still problematical, but it is interesting that, according to Chamberlain's descriptions and figures, a zone of blue-green algae (*Anabaena*) is present in
the central portion of the cortex of these remarkable roots.

The Reproductive Cycle

STROBILI. All carefully investigated species of cycads are strictly dioecious in the sense that microsporangiate and megasporangiate strobili are borne on separate plants. Chamberlain stated emphatically that "in thirty years of study in the field and in greenhouses I have never seen anything to indicate that the cycads are not absolutely dioecious." In all genera, with the exception of *Cycas*, both types of strobili are compact cone-like structures with determinate growth; in position they are apparently terminal in such genera as *Dioon*, although in certain species of *Macrozamia*, *Bowenia*, and *Encephalartos* they are axillary and lateral. According to Chamberlain (1935), the *first* cone produced by *Dioon* is terminal, and a new vegetative meristem, developing *laterally* at the base of this cone, gives rise to the next crown of leaves and a new cone. The possible occurrence of this type of "sympodial growth" in other cycad genera deserves study.

The unique feature of *Cycas* consists in the fact that the megasporophylls are produced, like the foliage leaves, in a relatively loose crown which surrounds the shoot apex of the terminal bud (Fig. 15-6, B). After seed maturation, a new crown of foliage leaves expands above the cluster of megasporophylls; the latter persist as dead or dying structures below this new foliage. The microsporangiate strobilus of *Cycas*, however, is a terminal, compact, determinate cone as in the other genera (Fig. 15-6, A).

According to Chamberlain, "the largest cones that have ever existed are found in the living cycads." Apparently the largest dimensions and greatest weight are characteristic of the megasporangiate strobili of certain species of *Encephalartos*, *Dioon*, and *Macrozamia* (Fig. 15-2, B). Weights up to 90 pounds have been recorded for *Encephalartos*, and Chamberlain describes the seed cones of *Macrozamia denisoni* as measuring two feet in length, nearly a foot in diameter at the base, and with a weight of 50-70 pounds. In comparison with such gigantic cones, the cones of the more familiar gymnosperms, such as pine, indeed seem insignificant in size.

SPOROPHYLLS AND SPORANGIA. The microsporophylls in the cycads, although varying in size and form, all are rather thick, scale-like struc-

Figure 15-6   Strobili of *Cycas revoluta*. **A,** microsporangiate strobilus (cultivated specimen, Pasadena, California); **B,** megasporangiate strobilus (note pinnatifid form of megasporophylls). [B, courtesy Dr. T. E. Weier.]

tures that bear the microsporangia on their lower or abaxial surfaces (Fig. 15-7, B). This resemblance to the abaxial position of sporangia typical of many ferns is strengthened by the fact that the microsporangia are arranged in somewhat definite soral clusters. The number of microsporangia borne by a single sporophyll varies from over a thousand in *Cycas media* to several dozen in *Zamia floridana*. Although much remains to be done in the study of the origin and early ontogeny of the microsporangium, it is known that its structure at maturity is typically eusporangiate with a wall several cell layers in thickness, a tapetum, and numerous small microspores (Fig. 15-7, A). The surface cells of the microsporangium are large and very thick-walled (except at the point where dehiscence will occur) and have collectively been regarded by Jeffrey (1917, fig. 160) as an annulus.

The megasporophylls vary considerably in size and form; in many cases their shape is of great systematic value in the characterization of genera or even species. Two extreme types occur. In *Zamia, Microcycas,* and *Ceratozamia,* for example, the megasporophylls are peltate, scale-like organs, each bearing two ovules (Fig. 15-8). In marked contrast, the megasporophylls of *Cycas revoluta* are conspicuously pinnatifid, leaf-like structures that bear 6-8 ovules laterally arranged on the sporophyll axis below the terminal group of rudimentary pinnae (Fig. 15-6, B; Fig. 15-8). In other genera, such as *Dioon* and *Encephalartos*, the sporophylls although essentially scale-like in form may show extended tips or marginal serrations suggestive of reduced leaf blades. The common interpretation of this range in sporophyll form and ovule number is to regard the condition in *Cycas revoluta* as primitive and the other conditions the result of varying degrees of suppression and ultimate elimination of a definable lamina in the megasporophyll (Fig. 15-8). Although such a series is morphologically plausible, the paleobotanical evidence is still inconclusive as to the true nature of the ovuliferous structure in the ancestors of modern cycads.

The ovules of cycads are erect in orientation, the micropyle lying oppo-

Figure 15-7 *Zamia sp.* **A,** transection of microsporophyll; **B,** abaxial view of microsporophyll, showing soral clusters of microsporangia. Note thick walls of the stalked microsporangia and the abundant microspores produced in each of them.

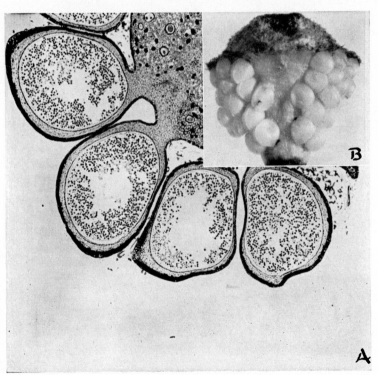

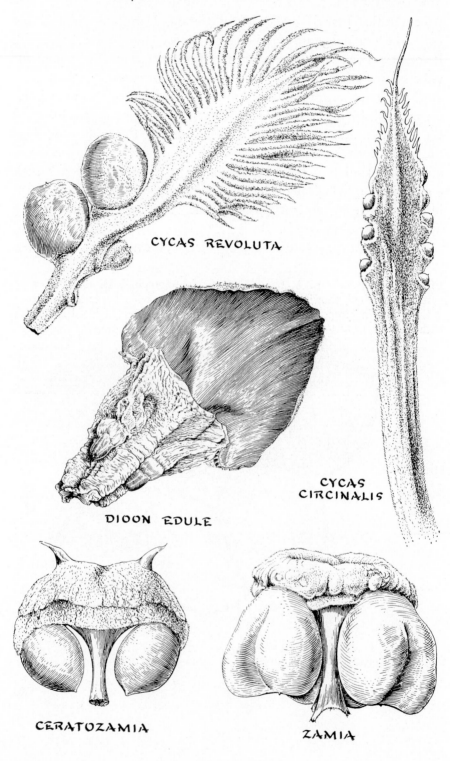

CYCAS REVOLUTA

CYCAS CIRCINALIS

DIOON EDULE

CERATOZAMIA

ZAMIA

site the point of attachment of the ovule to the megasporophyll. In the genus *Cycas* the micropyles of the ovules are turned obliquely outward and because of the loose arrangement of the pinnatifid megasporophylls are a striking example of veritable naked ovules (Fig. 15-8). In the other genera the micropyles of the paired ovules of each sporophyll are directed inward toward the axis of the strobilus and, except during the brief period when pollination occurs, are not directly exposed to the air (Fig. 15-8).

On the whole, cycad ovules are large as compared with the ovules of other gymnosperms. According to Chamberlain, the ovules of *Cycas circinalis* and *Macrozamia denisoni* may reach 6 cm in length; in other genera the ovules are smaller, the most diminutive being those in *Zamia pygmae* which measure only 5-7 mm in length. Structurally the cycad ovule consists of a massive nucellus and a single integument which is free from only the upper portion of the nucellus (Fig. 15-9, D). As was briefly mentioned in the preceding chapter, the integument is histologically differentiated into an outer and an inner fleshy layer, and a middle layer which becomes sclerified and stony during seed development (Fig. 15-9, E). Both the outer and inner fleshy layers of the ovule possess a vascular system; according to Reynolds (1924), in *Microcycas* branches of the inner vascular system extend into the free portion of the nucellus. The inner layer of the integument usually breaks down during seed development, but the outer portion is conspicuous in the ripe seed and is often brilliantly colored.

GAMETOPHYTES. Our knowledge of the gametophytes, fertilization, and embryogeny in cycads is still somewhat fragmentary, and the brief discussion of these topics here necessarily represents a composite picture derived from the available data. In many respects the investiga-

Figure 15-8 Megasporophylls in Cycads. *Cycas revoluta*, pinnatifid type of megasporophyll with developing seeds; *Cycas circinalis*, note very rudimentary pinnae [redrawn from *Die natür. Pflanzenfamilien* by Engler and Prantl. Leipzig: Wilhelm Englemann, 1926]; *Dioon edule*, megasporophyll with expanded lamina tip and two ovules; *Ceratozamia*, peltate type of megasporophyll bearing two ovules (the two spines at the top of the sporophyll are characteristic for this genus) [redrawn from *Syllabus der Pflanzenfamilien* by A. Engler and E. Gilg. Berlin: Gebrüder Borntraeger, 1924]; *Zamia*, peltate type of megasporophyll with two ovules.

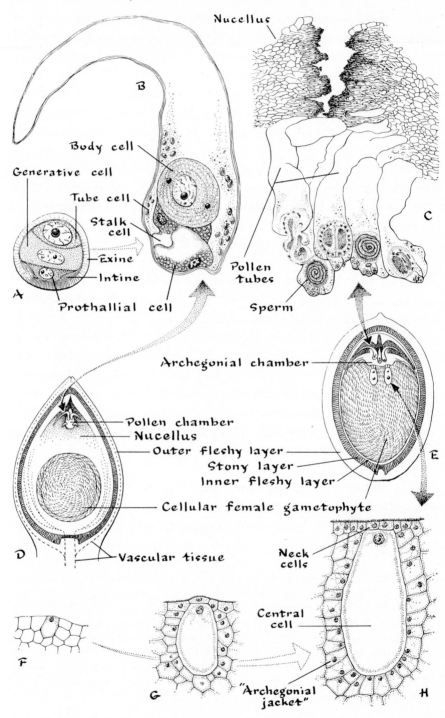

Nucellus

B

Body cell

Generative cell

Tube cell

Stalk cell

Exine

Intine

A

Prothallial cell

Pollen tubes

Sperm

C

Archegonial chamber

Pollen chamber

Nucellus

Outer fleshy layer

Stony layer

Inner fleshy layer

Cellular female gametophyte

E

Vascular tissue

D

Neck cells

Central cell

"Archegonial jacket"

F

G

H

tions of Chamberlain, especially on *Dioon*, are classical and have pro-vided the firm basis for most of the subsequent investigations on other species.

The male gametophyte is strictly endosporic and begins its devel-opment within the confines of the microsporangium. Two successive mitotic divisions result in a gametophyte consisting of a basal prothallial cell, a generative cell, and a tube cell; at this stage the partially developed gametophyte, surrounded by the microspore wall, is released into the air by the dehiscence of the microsporangial wall. This three-celled stage of the male gametophyte is apparently the characteristic "shedding stage" of most cycads (Fig. 15-9, A).

The exact manner in which the endosporic gametophytes are con-veyed to the ovules in such dioecious plants as cycads needs wide field study. Although insect pollination has been suggested, Chamberlain con-cluded from very extensive field observations that all cycads are wind pollinated. The excessive amount of light, dry "microspores" produced by cycads makes this conclusion quite plausible. On reaching the micro-pylar end of the ovule the young endosporic gametophyte adheres to the pollination droplet which exudes from the micropyle and is subsequently drawn into the pollen chamber. This chamber is an irregular cavity formed by the breakdown of the cells in the upper part of the nucellus (Fig. 15-9, D).

The interval between pollination and fertilization in some of the cycads is 4-6 months. During this period a pollen tube, produced by the

---

Figure 15-9 The reproductive cycle in cycads. **A-C,** development of male game-tophyte in *Cycas*. **A,** the three-celled stage at time of shedding; **B,** the genera-tive cell has divided forming the body cell and the stalk cell. This stage occurs after pollination and during the invasion of the nucellus by the pollen tube; **C,** reconstruction of adjacent serial sections showing five pollen tubes with sperms in various stages of development, hanging from the nucellus in the archegonial chamber (note the spirally-arranged band of flagella on two of the mature sperms); **D,** diagram of longisection of ovule of *Dioon edule* showing early stage in development of pollen tubes and the cellular stage of the female game-tophyte; **E,** diagram of longisection of ovule of *Dioon edule* showing pollen tubes hanging downward in the archegonial chamber and the position of the archegonia in the female gametophyte; **F-H,** ontogeny of archegonium in *Dioon edule*. [A-C redrawn from Swamy, *Amer. Jour. Bot.* 35:77, 1948; D-H, redrawn from *Gymnosperms. Structure and Evolution* by C. J. Chamberlain. Chicago: The University of Chicago Press, 1935.]

tubular extension of the upper end of the microspore wall (i.e., the end *opposite* the basal prothallial cell), invades the tissues of the nucellus (Fig. 15-9, D, E). In some cycads this haustorial portion of the pollen tube may become irregularly branched. Commonly the tube nucleus migrates into the intrusively growing region of the tube. Concomitantly with the haustorial growth of the upper portion of the tube, the lower swollen prothallial end of the tube becomes extended downward into the expanding pollen chamber (Fig. 15-9, E). The generative cell finally divides into a stalk cell, located next to the prothallial cell, and a terminal body cell (Fig. 15-9, B). From the latter, by a single division, two flagellated sperms are ultimately produced. * Figure 15-9, C, based on the reconstruction of several serial sections, depicts the structure of pollen tubes and their contained male gametophytes just prior to the release of the sperms in *Cycas.* A more detailed description of the structure of the remarkable motile sperms found in cycads will be given in the discussion of fertilization.

As stated in the previous chapter, the female gametophyte in gymnosperms arises by the enlargement and division of a single functional megaspore which is deeply situated within the nucellar tissue of the ovule. However, because of the many technical difficulties involved in securing young ovules at the critical stage, our present knowledge of the details of megasporogenesis in the cycads is extremely meagre. The most complete study is that made by Smith (1910), who found that in *Zamia floridana* a linear series of four megaspores is produced from the single megasporocyte; the upper three megaspores degenerate, and the lowermost spore enlarges and gives rise to the female gametophyte. Since this is the general pattern of megasporogenesis in a good many gymnosperms and angiosperms, comparative studies may ultimately show it to be the prevailing condition throughout the other genera of the cycads.

Studies of a number of cycads show that the first step in the differentiation of the female gametophyte is an extended period of free nuclear divisions which, for some time, are simultaneous. Chamberlain estimated that about 1,000 free nuclei are produced during the early ontogeny of the female gametophyte in *Dioon edule.* During its free nuclear phase

* *Microcycas* is exceptional among all investigated cycads because 16-22 sperms may be produced by a single male gametophyte. This is the result of the formation of a series of 8-11 body cells (Downie, 1928).

the gametophyte becomes jacketed by one or more layers of nucellar cells which constitute the "endosperm jacket"; this jacket apparently functions somewhat as a tapetum, and conveys soluble food materials from the nucellus to the enlarging gametophyte.

The period of free nuclear divisions is followed by the progressive development of cell walls which enclose single nuclei and associated masses of cytoplasm. Wall formation begins at the periphery of the gametophyte and continues centripetally until the entire gametophyte is cellular (Fig. 15-9, D). A well-defined megaspore wall, several microns in thickness, clearly demarcates the gametophyte from the adjacent tissue of the nucellus.

The development of the archegonium has been studied in a number of genera and seems to follow a rather uniform pattern (Fig. 15-9, E-H). Certain of the surface cells near the micropylar end of the gametophyte function as archegonial initials, the number fluctuating among different genera or even within the same species. The first division of the initial is periclinal, yielding a small outer primary neck cell and a large inner central cell. The primary neck cell then divides to form two neck cells, the prevailing condition in most cycad archegonia (Fig. 15-9, H). The central cell continues to enlarge and the cytoplasm becomes vacuolated. At this time the gametophytic cells that surround the archegonium become definable as a jacket, which presumably functions in the translocation of food materials to the archegonium. A short while before fertilization—only a few days in *Dioon*, according to Chamberlain— the nucleus of the central cell divides, forming a ventral canal cell nucleus and a large egg nucleus (Fig. 15-9, E). In most cycads studied no wall is produced between these two nuclei, and the ventral canal cell nucleus soon degenerates. As a result, the ripe archegonium at the time of fertilization consists of two neck cells and an extremely large uninucleate egg cell, the membrane of which is tough. This type of archegonium is predominant in the majority of gymnosperms, and on comparative grounds it represents a highly reduced structure as contrasted with the archegonia of lower vascular plants. (See Chapter 5 for a general description of the structure and development of archegonia in the tracheophytes.)

The number of functional archegonia in cycads is usually small, in *Dioon* ranging from 3 to 10. *Microcycas* is unique because as many as from 4 to 6 distinct groups of developing archegonia are scattered over the surface of the gametophyte. However, it is only the micropylar group of initials that produces fully developed archegonia; the other groups become disorganized (Reynolds, 1924).

FERTILIZATION.   A short time before the archegonia complete their development, the upper micropylar region of the female gametophyte becomes depressed and separated from the overlying nucellus, resulting in the formation of the so-called archegonial chamber (Fig. 15-9, E). As the prothallial ends of the pollen tubes lengthen they finally lie suspended within this chamber, and the flagellated sperms together with some liquid are discharged into it. Many detailed studies have been made of the structure of the remarkable sperms in cycads and their behavior prior to their entrance into the archegonium. In size, the sperms are the largest known in vascular plants, those of *Dioon*, according to Chamberlain, attaining a diameter of 200 microns and a length of 300 microns; consequently they are visible to the unaided eye. In form and structure, the sperms are top-shaped with a spirally coiled band bearing tufts of flagella (Fig. 15-9, C). Using sections of living ovules, Chamberlain observed that the two sperms in each pollen tube swim up and down the tube by means of their flagella, and also exhibit various types of pulsating and amoeboid movements. Such movements are believed by Swamy (1948) to facilitate the entrance of the sperm into the egg. Once inside the cytoplasm of the egg, the flagellated band becomes detached and remains plainly visible near the neck of the archegonium. The nucleus of the sperm then sinks down into the egg cytoplasm and comes into direct contact with the egg nucleus. This is fertilization. Although several sperms may pass through the neck, only one sperm nucleus fuses with the egg nucleus; the others remain near the top of the egg and finally disintegrate.

EMBRYOGENY AND SEED DEVELOPMENT.   In the previous chapter it was emphasized that the embryogeny of most gymnosperms begins with a period of free nuclear divisions. The cycads as a whole are distinguished by the relatively large number of free nuclei produced before wall formation starts.

Following the division of the zygotic nucleus, successive divisions for some time are definitely synchronized. But after about eight successive divisions, which result in 256 nuclei, irregularities appear, some of the nuclei either failing to divide or at least not keeping pace with the rate of division of the remainder. Hence the ultimate number of free nuclei is likely to be less than the theoretical expectation. In *Dioon edule* Chamberlain found about 1,000 free nuclei before the initiation of cell walls. Other cycads have smaller numbers; the lowest recorded is 64 in the genus *Bowenia*.

Wall formation in the embryo begins at the lower end of the archegonium and progresses toward the neck end. In some genera this segmentation process extends completely throughout the entire mass of multinucleate protoplasm. But in others only the inward-facing portion of the embryo develops cell walls—the remainder retains the free nuclear condition and ultimately disintegrates. This is the situation in *Zamia*, and the salient features of its early embryogeny will now be outlined on the basis of the recent study by Bryan (1952).

At the final phase of the free nuclear period a large number of nuclei are aggregated at the inward-directed end of the embryo (Fig. 15-10, A). Two successive, simultaneous divisions of these nuclei occur, and during these divisions cell walls form progressively in an upward direction (Fig. 15-10, B, C). As a result, the embryo now consists of two well-defined regions: a tissue of walled cells, and a region of vacuolated cytoplasm with scattered nuclei. This latter portion of the embryo apparently serves a nutritive function for a time but finally disintegrates. Active cell division in the cellular part of the embryo results in the gradual differentiation of (1) a conspicuously meristematic zone, from which the main organs of the embryo ultimately arise, and (2) a posterior region of elongating cells arranged in vertical series which mark the origin of the massive suspensor typical of cycad embryos (Fig. 15-10, D). The cells lying above the suspensor region are smaller and constitute a zone that possibly serves as a buffer, which may, to some degree, direct the downward extension of the suspensor. A distinctive feature of the young embryo of *Zamia* is the layer of discrete surface cells that constitutes a cap over the meristematic zone (Fig. 15-10, D). Bryan found that the outer walls of the cap cells are extremely thick. Gradually the cap cells distintegrate, and the outermost cells of the meristematic zone become organized as a new surface layer. The functional significance,

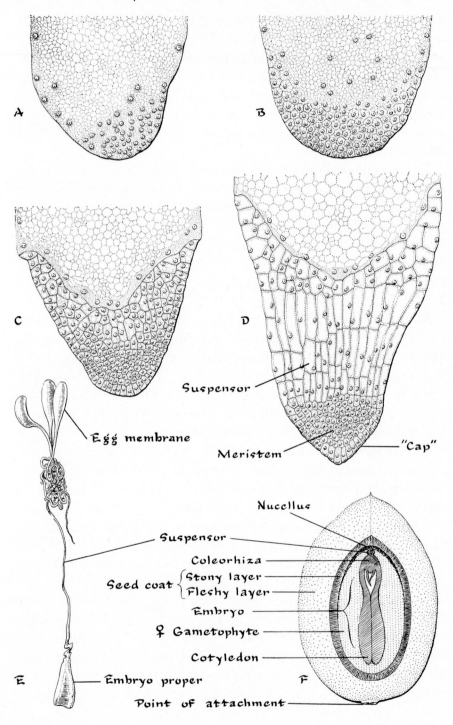

Suspensor

Egg membrane

Meristem   "Cap"

Nucellus

Suspensor

Coleorhiza

Seed coat { Stony layer
          { Fleshy layer

Embryo

♀ Gametophyte

Cotyledon

Embryo proper

Point of attachment

if any, of this "deciduous" cap in the embryo of *Zamia* is problematical. It may constitute a protective layer during the early period when the meristematic zone is pushed deeply into the gametophytic tissue by the elongating suspensor. Comparative embryological studies are highly desirable in order to determine whether caps occur in the young embryos of other cycad genera.

In *Zamia*, as well as in other genera, the elongation of the suspensor forces the apex of the embryo through the tough membrane of the original egg into contact with the nutritive tissue of the large gametophyte. During this invasion the suspensor usually becomes coiled or twisted and often reaches a considerable length. Simple polyembryony (i.e., the development of the zygotes of several archegonia in the same ovule) is extremely common in cycads. According to Chamberlain's investigations, the coiled suspensors of several young embryos may intertwine to form a compound structure (Fig. 15-10, E). Typically, only one embryo normally survives and is functional.

As stated above, the main organs of the embryo develop from the meristematic, inward-facing end of the embryo which is thus of the endoscopic type. (See Chapter 6 for a general discussion of endoscopic polarity in embryos.) Usually two cotyledons, which flank the shoot apex, are soon differentiated, although *Ceratozamia* is characterized by having a single cotyledon. The posterior end of the embryo in direct contact with the suspensor develops into the radicle. In some cycads the shoot apex forms several bud-scale primordia and possibly the primordium of the first foliage leaf before seed development is completed. The structure of a ripe cycad seed is shown in longisectional view in Fig. 15-10, F.

Figure 15-10   A-D, early embryogeny in *Zamia umbrosa*. **A,** free nuclear period; **B,** formation of walls between nuclei in lower end of embryo; **C,** beginning of cellular differentiation (note lower region of small actively dividing cells above which occur the first elongating cells of the future suspensor); **D,** later stage showing clear differentiation of surface layer or "cap," meristem, suspensor, and "buffer" region (note that upper portion of embryo has remained in the free nuclear condition); **E,** young embryo of *Cycas* dissected from seed (note long, slender suspensor and, above, the persistent membranes of several egg cells); **F,** diagram of a longitudinal section of a cycad seed. [A-D, redrawn from Bryan, *Amer. Jour. Bot.* 39:433, 1952; E, redrawn from Swamy, *Amer. Jour. Bot.* 35:77, 1948.]

THE SEEDLING. According to Chamberlain (1935), there is no fixed period of dormancy in cycad seeds. The micropylar end of the seed coat is ruptured by the emerging radicle, and this is followed by the shoot apex and its foliar appendages. A distinctive feature of the germination process is the fact that most of the blade region of the two cotyledons remains within the seed coat, apparently absorbing food materials from the gametophyte and conveying them to the developing shoot and root systems. In seedlings one or two years old the seed may still remain attached by the withered cotyledons to the young sporophyte. For several years after germination the young sporophyte bud produces at intervals, single foliage leaves. Continued growth of the shoot ultimately results in the formation of well-defined crowns of foliage leaves. The shoot apex of large sporophytes in the cycads is distinguished by a complex zonal structure; in *Cycas revoluta* the shoot apex may measure about 3.5 mm in diameter, a dimension greatly exceeding that typical of the apices of other vascular plants. (See Foster, 1939, 1940, 1941, 1943; and Johnson, 1944, for detailed descriptions of the shoot apices in the cycads.)

Ginkgo biloba

The first European botanist to study the maidenhair tree was Kaempfer, who observed it in Japan in 1690. He proposed for it the name "Ginkgo," and Linnaeus adopted this generic appelation in 1771, adding the descriptive species name "biloba" in reference to the frequent notched character of the fan-shaped leaves. There has been considerable argument regarding the etymology of the word Ginkgo, but according to the recent study of Li (1956) there is no reason for rejecting this word on the basis that Ginkgo is a misspelling of "Ginkyo," as several writers have contended. Li believes that the maidenhair tree has been correctly designated as Ginkgo for nearly 250 years "and certainly will be known as such forever."

Like the cycads, *Ginkgo* is a surviving relic of a once widely distributed group of ancient gymnosperms, which are conveniently grouped under the order Ginkgoales. Arnold (1947, p. 277) concludes that "*Ginkgo biloba* is one of the oldest of living plants, and may indeed be the oldest living genus of seed plants." Leaf remains of *Ginkgo* and its close allies occur abundantly in rocks of the Triassic and Jurassic Periods, during which time these plants were apparently worldwide in distribution. The extinct species *Ginkgo digitata* for example, occurred in Oregon, Alaska, Australia, Japan, England, and other parts of the world. Following the period of its vigorous development in the Mesozoic Era *Ginkgo* declined progressively in its distribution, and, according to Seward (1938), China was the last home of this ancient seed plant.

Whether *Ginkgo* still exists in the wild state in the more remote and poorly explored forests of China has been regarded an unsettled question by many writers. Some evidence has been produced in favor of the existence of native stands of *Ginkgo* trees, though many botanists contend that such trees may represent the offspring of cultivated specimens. In a recent and thorough discussion, however, Li (1956) presents evidence that *Ginkgo* still exists in the wild state in southeastern China, and that the last refuge of this living fossil is a mountainous area "along the northwestern border of Chekiang and southeastern Anhwei." From a broad evolutionary viewpoint, *Ginkgo* is to be regarded "as one of the wonders of the world; it has persisted with little change until the present through a long succession of ages when the earth was inhabited by animals and plants for the most part far removed, in kind as in time, from their living descendants. *Ginkgo* is one of a small company of living plants which illustrates continuity and exceptional power of endurance in a changing world" (Seward, 1938, p. 424).

Ginkgo biloba is widely cultivated as a park specimen, or street tree in many temperate areas of the world (Fig. 15-11). In accordance with the vitality which has enabled it to survive as a distinct organism for millions of years, the modern *Ginkgo* appears exceptionally resistant to the attacks of insects and fungi, and grows successfully amidst the smoke and gasoline fumes of modern cities. The outer fleshy coat of the seed emits an odor like rancid butter, and for this reason the male or microsporangiate trees are preferable to female trees for park or street planting.

Although there is no known way of separating male from female trees on the basis of external morphological characters, prior to the formation of reproductive structures, the recent work of Lee (1954) and Pollock (1957) suggests that it is possible to differentiate between chromosomal complements in the two sexes. If a study of chromosome morphology by means of stem-tip and leaf primordia smears proves

Figure 15-11 A large, microsporangiate specimen of *Ginkgo biloba* in leafless condition, University of California Campus, Berkeley. Note very irregular pattern of branching.

practical in distinguishing the sex of young *Ginkgo* plants, it would then be possible to eliminate potential female trees from street plantings.

The kernel of the seed (i.e., the female gametophyte tissue and the embryo) of *Ginkgo* is highly nutritious and is used as food in China and Japan. *Ginkgo* seeds are imported into this country, and we, the authors, secure seeds for class study from the various markets in San Francisco's Chinatown.

Vegetative Organography and Anatomy

Young *Ginkgo* trees have a pronounced excurrent habit of growth, resembling in this respect many conifers. With increasing age the crown becomes broad and irregular and the pattern of branching variable (Fig. 15-11). Large specimens may attain a height of 100 feet; exceptionally robust individuals are found near certain temples and shrines in Japan and China.

Among the truly unique and distinctive organographic features of *Ginkgo* is the shape and venation of the deciduous foliage leaves. The leaf consists of a slender petiole, traversed by two collateral vascular bundles, and a fan-shaped lamina with very regular open dichotomous venation (Fig. 15-12). The resemblance in form and venation of the *Ginkgo* leaf to the pinna of the leaf of *Adiantum*, the maidenhair fern, formed one of the reasons for the binomial "*Salisburia adiantifolia*," the scientific

Figure 15-12 *Ginkgo biloba*. Mature foliage leaf with very regular dichotomous venation. [From *Vergleich. Morphologie der höheren Pflanzen* by W. Troll. Berlin: Gebrüder Borntraeger, 1938.]

name for *Ginkgo* proposed by Smith, the English botanist in 1797. The leaves of the same individual differ considerably in their degree of lobing—many are nearly entire, others are notched or very conspicuously two-lobed. On vigorous sucker shoots, arising from wounds or near the base of the tree, the lamina may be divided into a series of wedge-shaped lobes. Such leaves closely resemble the multilobed foliar organs characteristic of some of the ancient members of the Ginkgoales. The presence of a regular open type of dichotomous venation in *Ginkgo* recalls the existence of a similar type of venation pattern in the leaflets of certain cycads (Fig. 15-5). In both cases dichotomous venation seems to represent a retention of an ancient fern-like type of vasculature, and hence is of considerable morphological and evolutionary interest.

Unlike the cycads the pith and cortical regions of young stems of *Ginkgo* are relatively small in volume, and cambial activity is vigorous and sustained, producing a massive development of secondary xylem of the compact pycnoxylic type as in typical conifers and woody angiosperms.

During the development of a *Ginkgo* tree a marked distinction becomes apparent between *long shoots*, which develop widely spaced

Figure 15-13   *Ginkgo biloba.* **A,** spur shoot with expanding leaves and microsporangiate strobili; **B,** spur shoot with young leaves and pairs of ovules borne on slender stalks.

internodes and many leaves, and *spur shoots*, which are characterized by short, crowded internodes and the annual expansion of only a few leaves (Fig. 15-13, A); the terminal buds of both types of shoots and the axillary buds of the long shoots are covered, during the dormant period in winter, by an overlapping series of bud scales. An anatomical study has shown that the cellular structure of the apical meristem is identical in the terminal buds of both long and spur shoots; the difference between them depends on the duration of cell division and cell elongation in the stem tissues derived from the shoot apex (Foster, 1938). Furthermore, the pattern of growth in the two types of shoots is reversible: a spur shoot, several years in age, may give rise at its tip to a long shoot, whereas the terminal growth of a long shoot may be greatly retarded for several seasons and thus resemble the growth of a lateral spur shoot (Gunckel and Wetmore, 1946). The physiological basis for shoot dimorphism in *Ginkgo* is difficult to determine, but there is experimental evidence that spur shoots are the result of the inhibitory effects of auxins produced by the tissues of the long shoots (Gunckel, Thimann, and Wetmore, 1949).

The Reproductive Cycle

Ginkgo resembles the cycads in being strictly dioecious, but the spore-producing structures are relatively small and bear no resemblance to the strobili of the cycads. Both the microsporangiate and the megasporangiate structures in *Ginkgo* arise in the axils of scales, or foliage leaves and are restricted in occurrence to the ends of the spur shoots (Fig. 15-13).

THE MICROSPORANGIATE STROBILUS. The microsporangiate strobilus is a loose, pendulous, catkin-like structure, consisting of a main axis to which are attached numerous slender microsporophylls (Fig. 15-13, A). The stalk-like portion of each microsporophyll bears usually two pendant microsporangia at its tip. Such terms as "sporangiophore" and even "stamen" have been applied to the microsporophylls of *Ginkgo*, thus indicating the uncertainty which prevails as to their phylogenetic origin and homology. Although the method of initiation of the microsporangium still remains to be accurately studied, the general plan of development is eusporangiate as in the cycads. At maturity the microsporangium consists of a wall several layers in thickness, the remains of the tapetum (apparently sporogenous in origin), and a large number of small microspores.

THE OVULIFEROUS STRUCTURE. In striking contrast with the cycads, the ovuliferous structure in *Ginkgo* is not a foliaceous or scale-like sporophyll. It consists rather of a stalk or peduncle bearing at its tip two (occasionally three, or more) erect ovules (Fig. 15-13, B). Each ovule is subtended basally by a rim-like outgrowth termed by Chamberlain (1935) the "collar." This structure has been interpreted as a reduced and vestigial sporophyll, and the entire ovuliferous structure as a strobilus. However, the strictly terminal naked ovules and seeds of *Ginkgo* more closely resemble the stalked ovules of some of the extinct Bennettitales rather than a single modified strobilus (Fig. 15-14). The general anatomy of the ovule is much like that in the cycads, except the weakly developed vascular system is restricted to the inner fleshy layer of the seed coat. Megasporogenesis proceeds as in the cycads, and the basal member of the row of four megaspores enlarges to form the female gametophyte.

GAMETOPHYTES. Both the male and female gametophytes of *Ginkgo* closely resemble, in their development and morphology, the corresponding structures in the cycads. The male gametophyte is strictly endosporic, begins its development within the microsporangium, and when shed consists of two prothallial cells (one of which is abortive), a generative cell, and a tube cell. Pollination is apparently achieved by the wind, and after the grain reaches the pollen chamber of the nucellus of the ovule an haustorial pollen tube is produced as in the cycads. During the growth of the pollen tube the generative cell divides, forming the stalk cell and the body cell. The latter, by a single division, produces two large multiflagellated sperms, the structure and behavior of which in the tube and at fertilization have been investigated most recently by Shimamura (1937), Lee (1955), and Favre-Duchartre (1956). In *Ginkgo*, unlike the situation in cycads, no wall separates the sperms within the body cell. The mature sperm is top-shaped, possesses a flagellated spiral band at one end, and in Shimamura's material measured 90 microns in length and 72 microns in width.

Figure 15-14 *Ginkgo biloba.* Tip of spur shoot with mature foliage leaves and ripening seeds.

According to Chamberlain (1935), the development of the female gametophyte begins at the time of pollination of the ovule. The functional megaspore enlarges, and this is accompanied by an extended period of free nuclear divisions, followed by the centripetal development of cell walls (Lee, 1955; Favre-Duchartre, 1956). The central cells of the gametophyte, however, are not joined, and a definite suture is produced along which the gametophyte can be split apart. There are two or three archegonia situated at the micropylar end of the gametophyte. Their ontogeny closely resembles cycad archegonia, except a wall is produced between the nucleus of the egg and the ventral canal cell. The latter ultimately degenerates, and the mature archegonium consists of four neck cells and a large egg.

FERTILIZATION.   Fertilization has been observed by several investigators, and is interestingly described by Shimamura (1937) and Lee (1955). The flagellated sperms escape into the archegonial chamber through an opening near the prothallial end of the pollen tube. During their passage between the neck cells of the archegonium the sperms apparently become considerably stretched but are evidently not injured. Although two sperms may enter the archegonium, only one functions. As in cycads, the male nucleus slips out of its cytoplasmic sheath and contacts the egg nucleus, and the flagellated band is left near the top of the egg cytoplasm.

EMBRYOGENY.   Eames (1955) has confirmed earlier reports that fertilization and embryogeny in *Ginkgo* may occur either on the tree or after the ovule has fallen to the ground. He regards the latter condition as phylogenetically important to our understanding of primitive seed plants, in some of which the embryo may, like *Ginkgo*, have begun development only after the shedding of the ovule.

The early phase of embryogeny in *Ginkgo* is characterized by numerous free nuclear divisions, as in the cycads. After a series of about eight successive divisions (256 nuclei), centripetal wall formation begins and the young embryo becomes cellular throughout. In contrast with cycad embryogeny, no well-defined suspensor is formed. The lower end of the embryo, by means of active cell divisions, becomes a meristem from which the shoot apex and cotyledons are developed; the cells immediately behind this portion ultimately differentiate into the primary root or radicle (Ball, 1956a, b). Usually there are two cotyledons, but occasionally three are developed. In addition to the cotyledons, the embryo of ripe seeds commonly contains the primordia of several additional foliar structures which, together with the shoot apex, constitute the first terminal bud of the plant.

The germination of the seed closely resembles that typical of cycads. The primary shoot and root emerge by the rupture of the micropylar end of the seed, but the tips of the cotyledons remain within the nutritive tissue of the female gametophyte. The original seed may still cling to the base of a seedling a year or more in age.

The apical meristem of both the long and spur shoots of *Ginkgo* has a characteristic zonal structure. As shown in Fig. 15-15, the subsurface zone

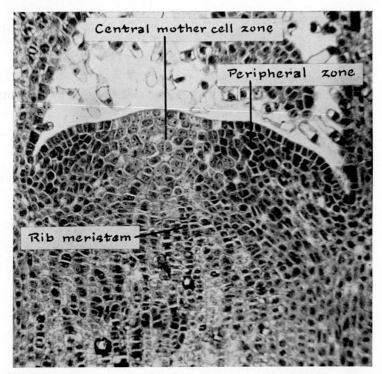

Figure 15-15 *Ginkgo biloba.* Median longisection of shoot apex showing typical zonal structure.

of the shoot apex consists of a conspicuous group of enlarged, highly vacuolated, central mother cells from which the more actively dividing and smaller cells of the peripheral and rib-meristem zones take their origin. The type of zonation in the apical meristem of *Ginkgo* has been very helpful in the interpretation of the structure and growth of the shoot apex in the cycads and in certain genera of the coniferales. (For details see Foster, 1938; Johnson, 1951; Esau, 1953; Gifford, 1954.)

Summary and Conclusions

In this chapter we have presented a discussion of the salient aspects of sporophyte structure and reproductive cycles in the living cycads and *Ginkgo biloba*. The most obvious differences between these two groups of primitive gymnosperms are shown in the habit and in the organography and general anatomy of certain portions of the sporophyte generation. Cycads are distinctive because of their large pinnate leaves, the un-branched or weakly branched nature of their stems, the large pith and cortex, the sluggish character of secondary growth in the stems, and the frequently enormous size of the strobili. The microsporangia are fern-like in structure and in their abaxial position on the microsporophylls; the megasporangia are borne in pairs on the scale-like megasporophylls, except in *Cycas* where from six to eight ovules develop on a more or less pinnate type of sporophyll. In contrast, *Ginkgo biloba* is a large, pro-fusely branched tree with spur and long shoots. The deciduous leaf is petiolate, with a fan-shaped, dichotomously veined lamina. Secondary growth is vigorous and sustained, and the pith and cortical regions of the twigs are relatively small. The microsporophylls develop in loose catkin-like strobili, each sporophyll consisting of a stalk terminated usually by two pendent microsporangia; the ovules are also terminal, and are borne in pairs at the tip of a stalk-like peduncle. Both the micro-sporangiate strobili and the ovuliferous structures are axillary in position, and are restricted to the tips of the spur shoots.

With reference to the reproductive cycle, there are many points of close similarity between cycads and *Ginkgo*. Among the most important of these resemblances are the development of haustorial pollen tubes and large multiflagellated sperms, the formation of large nutritive female gametophytes bearing archegonia with exceptionally large eggs, and the extended period of free nuclear divisions during early embryogeny. The ripe seed in both *Ginkgo* and the cycads consists of an endoscopic em-bryo, usually with two cotyledons, imbedded in the tissue of the female gametophyte which, in turn, is surrounded by a thick seed coat. When the seed germinates, the laminal portions of the cotyledons remain as haustorial structures within the gametophyte tissue.

On the basis of these differences and similarities, what may be con-cluded regarding the evolutionary origin of the living cycads and *Ginkgo*? As pointed out at the beginning of this chapter, the similarities in repro-ductive structures probably represent the persistence of certain of the generalized characters shared by many of the ancient gymnosperms, par-ticularly the pteridosperms. If this view is correct the living cycads and *Ginkgo* would represent two terminal and independent lines of evolu-tion. From the standpoint of vegetative morphology the cycads may have evolved, together with the Bennettitales, from a common pteridosperm stock—both are cycadophytes. On the other hand, the anatomy and organography of *Ginkgo* include typical coniferophyte characteristics, and this relic plant may have developed, along with the Paleozoic Cordaitales and the extinct conifers, from a separate, but at present unknown, group in the seed ferns.

References

Arnold, C. A. 1947. *An Introduction to Paleobotany*. McGraw-Hill, New York.

————. 1953. Origin and relationships of the cycads. *Phytomorphology* 3: 51-65.

Ball, E. 1956a. Growth of the embryo of *Ginkgo biloba* under experimental conditions. I. Origin of the first root of the seedling in vitro. *Amer. Jour. Bot.* 43:488-495.

————. 1956b. Growth of the embryo of *Ginkgo biloba* under experimental conditions. II. Effects of a longitudinal split in the tip of the hypocotyl. *Amer. Jour. Bot.* 43:802-810.

Bryan, G. S. 1952. The cellular proembryo of *Zamia* and its cap cells. *Amer. Jour. Bot.* 39:433-443.

Chamberlain, C. J. 1919. *The Living Cycads*. University of Chicago Press, Chicago.

————. 1935. *Gymnosperms. Structure and Evolution*. University of Chicago Press, Chicago.

Downie, D. G. 1928. Male gametophyte of *Microcycas calocoma*. *Bot. Gaz.* 85:437-450.

Eames, A. J. 1955. The seed and *Ginkgo*. *Jour. Arnold Arboretum* 36: 165-170.

Esau, K. 1953. *Plant Anatomy*. Wiley, New York.

Favre-Duchartre, M. 1956. Contribution a l'etude de la reproduction chez le *Ginkgo biloba*. *Rev. Cyto. et Biol. Veg.* 17:1-216.

Foster, A. S. 1938. Structure and growth of the shoot apex in *Ginkgo biloba*. *Bull. Torrey Bot. Club* 65: 531-556.

————. 1939. Structure and growth of the shoot apex of *Cycas revoluta*. *Amer. Jour. Bot.* 26:372-385.

————. 1940. Further studies on zonal structure and growth of the shoot apex of *Cycas revoluta*. *Amer. Jour. Bot.* 27:487-501.

————. 1941. Zonal structure of the shoot apex of *Dioon edule Lindl.* *Amer. Jour. Bot.* 28:557-564.

————. 1943. Zonal structure and growth of the shoot apex in *Microcycas calocoma* (Miq.) A.D.C. *Amer. Jour. Bot.* 30:56-73.

————. and M. R. San Pedro. 1942. Field studies on *Microcycas calocoma. Memorias Soc. Cubana Hist. Nat.* 16: 105-121.

Gifford, E. M., Jr. 1954. The shoot apex in angiosperms. *Bot. Rev.* 20: 477-529.

Gunckel, J. E. and R. H. Wetmore. 1946. Studies of development in long shoots and short shoots of *Ginkgo biloba* L. I. The origin and pattern of development of the cortex, pith and procambium. *Amer. Jour. Bot.* 33:285-295.

————. K. V. Thimann and R. H. Wetmore. 1949. Studies of development in long shoots and short shoots in *Ginkgo biloba* L. IV. Growth habit, shoot expression and the mechanism of its control. *Amer. Jour. Bot.* 36: 309-316.

Hertrich, W. 1951. *Palms and Cycads.* Privately printed, San Marino, California.

Jeffrey, E. C. 1917. *The Anatomy of Woody Plants.* University of Chicago Press, Chicago.

Johnson, M. A. 1944. On the shoot apex of the cycads. *Torreya* 44:52-58.

————. 1951. The shoot apex in gymnosperms. *Phytomorphology* 1:188-204.

Lee, C. L. 1954. Sex chromosomes in *Ginkgo biloba. Amer. Jour. Bot.* 41: 545-549.

————. 1955. Fertilization in *Ginkgo biloba. Bot. Gaz.* 117:79-100.

Li, Hui-Lin. 1956. A horticultural and botanical history of *Ginkgo. Bull. Morris Arboretum* 7:3-12.

Pollock, E. G. 1957. The Sex Chromosomes of the Maidenhair Tree. *Jour. Hered.* 48:290-294.

Reynolds, L. G. 1924. Female gametophyte of *Microcycas. Bot. Gaz.* 77: 391-403.

Schuster, J. 1932. Cycadaceae. *Das Pflanzenreich* Vol. IV.

Seward, A. C. 1917. Fossil Plants. Vol. 3. Cambridge University Press, London.

————. 1938. The story of the Maidenhair tree. *Science Progress* 32:420-440.

Shimamura, T. 1937. On the spermatozoid of *Ginkgo biloba. Cytologia.* Fujii Jublilee volume: 416-423.

Smith, F. G. 1910. Development of the ovulate strobilus and young ovule of *Zamia floridana. Bot. Gaz.* 50:128-141.

Swamy, B. G. L. 1948. Contributions to the life history of a *Cycas* from Mysore (India). *Amer. Jour. Bot.* 35: 77-88.

16 THE CONIFERALES

The most dominant and conspicuous gymnosperms in the floras of the modern world belong to the order Coniferales.

Included under this order are such familiar and widely cultivated trees as pine, spruce, fir, cedar, yew, and redwood (Fig. 16-1). Many genera are of great economic importance to man as sources of lumber, wood pulp, and turpentine. Their evolutionary history is as long as or probably longer than that of the cycads, and extends from the Carboniferous and Permian periods up to the present. But unlike the living cycads, which consist of a few relict genera, modern conifers are represented by 50 genera and about 500 species, and occur widely in both the Northern and Southern Hemispheres. Western North America and Eastern and Central China are regions characterized by an exceptional diversity of conifers, some of the genera forming extensive forests in these regions. Portions of Australia and New Zealand are likewise notable for the abundance and diversity of certain coniferous genera. As a group, the conifers are plants of the more temperate regions of the world; in contrast with the cycads, only a few are strictly tropical in distribution.

Because of their diversity, prominence, and economic value, conifers have attracted much varied study, and the literature devoted to investigations of their comparative anatomy, methods of reproduction, systematics, and phylogeny is extremely voluminous. Although the reproductive cycles of many conifers are now rather well-known, both intensive and extensive research still remains to be accomplished on a great many genera and species before a complete understanding is possible. This chapter therefore does not pretend to give a full résumé of present knowledge of the comparative morphology of the conifers. Its main objectives are twofold: (1) to outline those general aspects of systematics, organography, and anatomy which form the basis of our present concept of the Coniferales as a whole, and (2) to present in detail the salient features of the reproductive cycle of *Pinus*, including brief com-

Figure 16-1 *Cedrus deodara,* growing on campus of University of California, Berkeley. Note large erect seed cones on specimen at right.

parisons with other well-investigated genera. Despite the weakness of a "type" method of approach to reproduction, it seems preferable to a more diffuse and involved résumé of the fluctuations in the details of the life history of a large number of forms. For more exhaustive treatments of conifer morphology the student should consult the works of Coulter and Chamberlain (1917), Chamberlain (1935), and Florin (1938-1945, 1951) in which extensive bibliographies are also given.

Systematics

The evidence from comparative studies of both living and fossil material indicates that modern conifers are the surviving members of lines of evolution which began in the Paleozoic Era. Many efforts have been made to establish the boundaries of genera and to group these genera into tribes or families. Probably all the proposed schemes of classification are artificial to some degree, because of the large amount of parallel evolution of the structures used as the basis for separating genera and families. As is true for other groups of related organisms, the ideal classification of conifers should rest on the evaluation of the *totality* of morphological characteristics, including features of the gametophytes and embryos. This goal may ultimately be attained, but at present the systematic treatment of conifers is largely based on characters derived from the strobili, leaves, and, to a lesser degree, the pollen grains.

Figure 16-2 *Pinus*. **A,** terminal portion of branch showing clusters of microsporangiate strobili below the expanding leaf fascicles (spur shoots); **B,** tip of branch showing large terminal bud, and below it, three young megasporangiate strobili. [Courtesy of Dr. T. E. Weier.]

As a group, the conifers are monoecious, that is, each individual produces both megasporangiate and microsporangiate strobili (Fig. 16-2). The latter are uniformly cone-like and simple throughout the order, but the ovuliferous structures are of two rather distinct types. In the majority of conifers the ovules are borne in pairs on the surface of scale-like structures which collectively form a conspicuous cone—the familiar pine cone. Buchholz (1933) proposed the subordinal name Phanerostrobilares to include all conifers with this type of megasporangiate cone; other morphologists (e.g., Coulter and Chamberlain, 1917) utilized this character as the basis of the family Pinaceae. By contrast, a few conifer genera, which are segregated into the families Taxaceae and Podocarpaceae, develop ovules that are exposed (they do not occur in well-defined cones); furthermore, the seed proper in the Taxaceae is enclosed completely or partially by a fleshy covering known as the aril (Fig. 16-14, B). Buchholz segregated these plants under the subordinal group Aphanostrobilares. This subdivision of living conifers into two main groups may truly correspond to distinct lines of phylogenetic development. Rudolph Florin (1951), the great student of the conifers, says that the Taxaceae "differ from the true conifers by their lack of inflorescences or cones, and there is no indication at all that this is the result of reduction. On the contrary, the morphological conditions in the fossil and living forms favors the view that the taxads have always had isolated female flowers in the axils of foliage or scale leaves."

Within each of the major suborders of the Coniferales the various genera may be conveniently segregated into families. Pilger's (1926) scheme has found rather wide acceptance and will be adopted here. In this classification, which is reproduced below, seven families are recognized. The first four are members of the Phanerostrobilares, the last three are the representatives of the Aphanostrobilares. For the sake of brevity, only a limited number of the genera belonging to each family are included in the following conspectus; for a full listing of genera the student should consult Pilger (1926) or Chamberlain (1935).

1. Pinaceae (*Pinus, Picea, Abies, Pseudolarix,* etc.)
2. Taxodiaceae (*Taxodium, Sequoia, Metasequoia,* etc.)
3. Cupressaceae (*Cupressus, Juniperus, Libocedrus, Thuja,* etc.)
4. Araucariaceae (*Araucaria, Agathis*)
5. Podocarpaceae (*Podocarpus, Dacrydium,* etc.)

6. Cephalotaxaceae (*Cephalotaxus, Amentotaxus*, etc.)

7. Taxaceae (*Taxus, Torreya*, etc.)

Certain aspects of the geographical distribution of these families deserve brief mention. The majority of the Pinaceae occur in the Northern Hemisphere, with *Pinus*, consisting of about 90 species, being the largest genus. In contrast, the Araucariaceae and most of the Podocarpaceae are restricted to the Southern Hemisphere, the largest genera being *Podocarpus* and *Dacrydium*. *Podocarpus* is cultivated in the warmer parts of the United States, and the genus *Araucaria* includes the so-called Monkey Puzzle tree, popular as an ornamental in certain areas in California. The families Cupressaceae and Taxodiaceae have representatives in both hemispheres. The latter family is of particular botanical and general interest for several reasons. First, it includes the coast redwood (*Sequoia sempervirens*), limited to a narrow coastal belt in northern California and southern Oregon, and the giant redwood or "Big Tree" (*Sequoia* or *Sequoiadendron gigantea*) found only in a few groves in the Sierra Nevada mountains in California. The sequoias are remarkable for their enormous size and longevity; *S. gigantea* attains an age of 4,000-5,000 years (Molisch 1938). The Taxodiaceae is also notable because it now includes as one of its members the very recently discovered Dawn Redwood (*Metasequoia glyptostroboides*). The genus *Metasequoia* had been known only from the fossil record, and the discovery of a living representative in Szechuan Province, China, in 1944, by Chinese botanists, was of exceptional scientific importance. The systematic affinities of the living species with other genera of the Taxodiaceae have been discussed in detail by Sterling (1949). According to Chaney (1950), who has investigated in great detail the paleobotanical aspects of fossil *Sequoia* and *Taxodium*, *Metasequoia* "was the most abundant and widely distributed genus of the Taxodiaceae in North America from Upper Cretaceous to Miocene time. There is no known record of its occurrence on this continent in rocks younger than Miocene; it survived into the Pliocene epoch in Japan, and a few hundred trees are still living in the remote interior of China." Thus *Metasequoia*, somewhat like *Ginkgo* and the living cycads, is truly a living fossil, and further studies of its structure and reproduction should result in discoveries of considerable evolutionary interest.

General Organography and Anatomy

The conifers, as a group, are trees that often attain an enormous size, as in the case of *Sequoia, Pseudotsuga,* certain species of *Pinus* and *Abies,* and the Southern Hemisphere genus *Agathis.* Very commonly the habit is prominently excurrent with a persistent central trunk and a tiered or whorled arrangement of branches. Some species, however, may exhibit a more diffuse or deliquescent pattern of growth, as is true of the Monterey Cypress (*Cupressus macrocarpa*) and several species of *Pinus* and *Juniperus.* Except for a very few deciduous genera (*Larix, Pseudolarix, Taxodium,* and *Metasequoia*), the members of the Coniferales are "evergreens"; i.e., the foliage leaves function for more than one season. In some species of *Araucaria* the dead foliage leaves remain attached for many years to the branches. Usually the leaves of conifers are individually deciduous, but in *Pinus, Taxodium,* and *Sequoia sempervirens* entire shoots are abscissed from the older portions of the branch system.

Foliage Leaves

EXTERNAL MORPHOLOGY AND VENATION. In marked contrast with the pinnate leaves typical of the cycads, the foliage leaves of all members of the Coniferales are simple, and most commonly are scale-like or needle-like in form (Figs. 16-3, 16-4). Particularly in such genera as *Thuja* (arbor vitae), *Cupressus* (cypress), *Libocedrus* (incense cedar), and *Juniperus* (red cedar), the vegetative shoots with their small appressed scale-like leaves superficially resemble the shoots of *Lycopodium* or *Selaginella* (Fig. 16-4). From an anatomical standpoint, however, it is clear that conifer leaves are like those of other gymnosperms in that the vascular supply to each leaf is associated with a well-defined leaf gap. (See p. 53 for a general discussion of leaf gaps in the Pteropsida.) Furthermore, while the leaves of perhaps the majority of the conifers are univeined, the broad leaves of *Agathis* and certain species of *Araucaria* and *Podocarpus* exhibit a complex open dichotomous venation. It should therefore be evident that in the strict anatomical sense the foliage leaves of the conifers are not microphylls; microphylls, as pointed out in Chapter 3, are always univeined and leaf gaps are absent. The ultimate phylogenetic origin of the type of leaf characteristic of the living conifers is a problem that will be discussed briefly later in this section.

Figure 16-3   Seed cones of conifers. **A,** *Cryptomeria japonica;* **B,** *Cedrus deodara.* [A, courtesy Dr. T. E. Weier.]

Variations in the phyllotaxy, form, venation, and general histology of conifer leaves provide useful criteria in the systematic treatment of genera and families. However, because a full discussion of these matters lies outside the scope of this book, the discussion is limited to the most important and general aspects of leaf morphology and anatomy.

In most conifers the leaves develop on long shoots, and the phyllotaxy is spiral and alternate. A conspicuous exception is the Cupressaceae, all members of which have decussate or whorled phyllotaxy. The pattern of branching with reference to phyllotaxy is complex and variable. In such genera as *Pinus, Picea, Abies,* and *Pseudotsuga* a large proportion of the needle-like leaves produced during a growing season are devoid of axillary buds; in these plants branching proceeds from a few axillary buds located in a pseudowhorl just below the terminal bud. The ramification of members of the Cupressaceae, by contrast, is often very profuse, and commonly results in the development of flattened spray-like branch systems (Fig. 16-4).

A few genera (*Larix, Cedrus, Pseudolarix*) produce their foliage leaves on spur as well as long shoots, thus recalling the marked dimorphism of shoots characteristic of *Ginkgo biloba* (see Chapter 15).

Figure 16-4 *Thuja,* portion of shoot with seed cones. Note appressed scale-
like leaves.

With reference to spur shoots, the situation in *Pinus* is unique among all
living conifers (Fig. 16-2). In this genus the photosynthetic needle
leaves of well-developed sporophytes are restricted to lateral spur shoots
which are ultimately shed as units from the tree; following the seedling
stage, the foliar appendages produced on the primary axes are exclusively
nonphotosynthetic scale leaves. The spur shoots are often referred to as
"leaf fascicles," a misleading term which tends to obscure the real
morphological nature of these structures. A spur shoot in pine arises
from a bud developed in the axil of a scale-leaf produced on the main
axis. The young spur consists of a very short stem, a series of imbricated
membranous bud scales and, depending on the species, from one to five
foliage leaves. (See Sacher, 1955a, for a detailed study of bud scale

ontogeny in *Pinus*.) The diminutive shoot apex is usually recognizable in a longisection of a mature spur, but the cells composing it are vacuolate and inactive in appearance, and the surface and subsurface cells may ultimately die, become desiccated, and collapse (Sacher, 1955b). Under conditions of unusual stimulation, fully mature spur shoots may proliferate into long shoots through the reactivation of their shoot apices. The peculiar segregation of the foliage leaves to spur shoots can be followed in the progressive development of the pine seedling. When a pine seed germinates, the leaves following the whorled cotyledons are green and needle-like, but are borne in a spiral series on the *main axis* of the seedling (Fig. 16-19). The first spurs arise as buds in the axils of certain of these juvenile leaves; all subsequently formed spurs, however, arise from buds subtended by nonphotosynthetic scale leaves. The deciduous spur shoots of *Pinus* not only are an interesting example of the vegetative specialization in the Coniferales but have figured prominently as an aid in the interpretation of the ovuliferous scales of the megasporangiate strobili in the conifers (Doak, 1935).

In a number of living conifers there is a marked difference in form between the seedling or juvenile foliage leaves and the leaves produced during the subsequent growth of the sporophyte. This heterophylly is particularly striking in certain genera of the Cupressaceae where the juvenile leaves are needle-like and are ultimately followed by the appressed scale-like leaves characteristic of the adult plant. By means of cuttings it is possible to propagate the juvenile phase and to produce well-developed trees or shrubs bearing only (or largely) juvenile foliage. The various horticultural forms produced in this way are popular ornamentals and are often collectively designated Retinospora.

It should be evident from the preceding paragraphs that the external form of the foliage leaf not only varies between genera or families but may even change during the ontogeny of the individual. For this reason it is difficult to trace the ultimate phylogenetic origin of the leaf of modern members of the Coniferales. Laubenfels (1953), on the basis of a recent comprehensive survey, has grouped the leaves of living conifers into the following major categories: type 1 includes needle-like leaves which are univeined and tetragonal in transection. This type is regarded by Laubenfels as the commonest form in fossil conifers, and it is widely distributed among the Pinaceae, Araucariaceae, Podocarpaceae, and

Taxodiaceae; type 2 comprises leaves which also are univeined, but which are linear or lanceolate in contour and bifacially flattened. This type is regarded as the most common among living conifers, and members of all families "have type II in some genus at some period in ontogeny"; type 3 comprises all scale-like forms of leaves, e.g., the adult foliage leaves of the Cupressaceae; type 4 includes the broad, multiveined leaves of *Agathis*, and of species of *Araucaria* and *Podocarpus*. From a phylogenetic standpoint it would be tempting to regard the leaves of type 4 as the primitive condition from which the smaller and more simply veined types of leaves have been derived. However, the evidence from paleobotanical research does not support this conjecture (see Laubenfels' discussion).

Florin (1950, 1951) has shown that in Paleozoic conifers two distinct types of leaves (sometimes connected by intermediate forms on the same individual) were present (Fig. 16-5, B). In the probably more primitive of the two types, the leaf, although vascularized by a single trace, was dichotomously lobed or bifurcated, and was dichotomously veined. Bifurcated leaves occurred on the main axis and principal branches of *Lebachia* and *Ernestiodendron*, and were followed in branches of the ultimate order by a second type which were needle-like or scale-like and very probably univeined. The occurrence of heterophylly in these very ancient conifers is of considerable interest, and led Florin to conclude that the simple leaf arose by reduction. In certain genera, such as *Carpentieria*, even the leaves of small lateral shoots were forked (Fig. 16-5, A). This condition is interpreted by Florin as a slightly modified persistence of the juvenile type of foliage. From this brief discussion it may be concluded that (1) the needle-like type of leaf probably arose early in the phylogeny of the Coniferales from a dichotomously branched appendage, and (2) this simple leaf type, modified to varying degrees, has persisted to the present time as the characteristic foliar appendage of most living conifers.

HISTOLOGY. Numerous comparative studies have shown that the histology of relatively small simple leaves of conifers is extremely complex. The epidermal, fundamental, and fascicular tissue systems (see Chapter 3), are characteristically well-defined, but the cellular structure of these systems, particularly the last two, varies widely even among genera or species. Despite our present incomplete knowledge of the comparative leaf anatomy of the conifers as a whole, two aspects of leaf

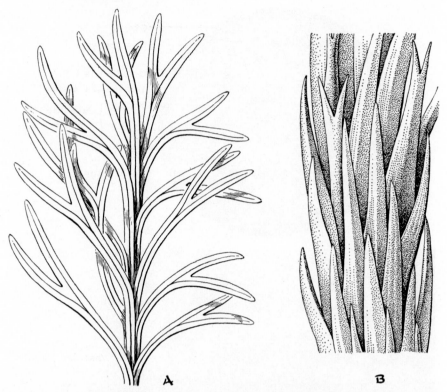

Figure 16-5 Foliage leaves of extinct conifers. **A,** dichotomously forked leaves of *Carpentieria frondosa*; **B,** simple and forked leaves at base of an ovuliferous cone of *Lebachia piniformis*. [Redrawn from Florin, Palaeontographica Abt. B, Bd. 85, 1944.]

histology—the stomata and the transfusion tissue—have been widely studied and discussed in the literature, and these deserve brief consideration at this point.

In many of the conifers the stomata occur on both surfaces of the leaf, but in certain families the stomata are sharply restricted to either the abaxial or adaxial epidermis. The leaf of *Pinus*, for example, is termed amphistomatic, since stomata occur on all surfaces of the needle (Fig. 16-6, A). A typical example of a hypostomatic leaf (stomata confined to the lower surface) is provided by *Pseudotsuga*.

In most genera the stomata are arranged in rather well-defined longitudinal rows. Without question, the most comprehensive study of the structure, ontogeny, and systematic value of stomata in gymnosperms

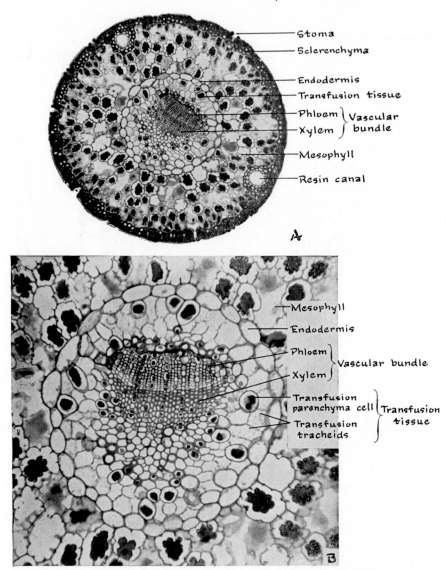

Figure 16-6 Histology of the leaf of *Pinus monophylla.* **A,** transection of leaf; **B,** details of endodermis, transfusion tissue, and vascular bundle.

has been made by Florin (1931, 1951). The impetus for Florin's very detailed investigations was the extraordinarily well-preserved cuticular pattern of the epidermis of fossil gymnospermous leaves. To secure a reliable basis for the interpretation and classification of fossil material, Florin has studied the ontogeny and structure of the stomata in all

groups of living gymnosperms (i.e., cycads, *Ginkgo*, Coniferales, Gnetales). From his work there has emerged a classification of gymnospermous stomata into two main types: the *haplocheilic type,* in which the
two guard cells originate from a common mother cell and certain of the
neighboring epidermal cells become modified as subsidiary cells (Fig.
16-7); and the *syndetocheilic type,* in which a common mother cell gives
rise by two divisions to three cells, the median one dividing to form two
guard cells, the lateral cells becoming specialized as subsidiary cells (Fig.
16-7).

It is particularly significant, from an evolutionary viewpoint, that these

Figure 16-7   The two main types of stomata in gymnosperms. (See text for
discussion.) [Redrawn from Florin, *Acta Horti Bergiana* 15:285, 1951.]

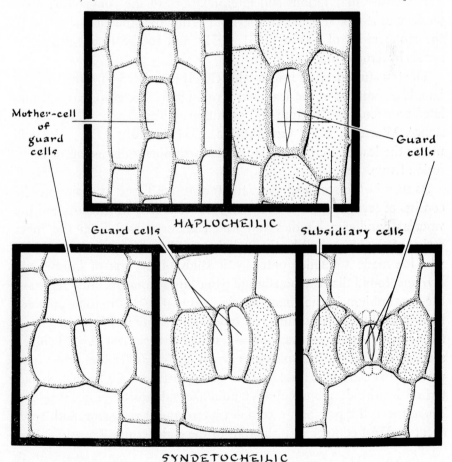

two types of stomatal apparatus can be traced through the fossil record
to the Paleozoic Era, and that they serve so consistently in the separation
of main groups in the gymnosperms. The haplocheilic type is regarded
by Florin as the more primitive of the two, and is a feature peculiar to the
leaves of (1) extinct and living conifers (including *Lebachia* and *Ernestiodendron*), (2) the Cycadofilicales, (3) Cordaitales, (4) Cycadales,
(5) Ginkgoales, and (6) the genus *Ephedra* in the Gnetales. The more
advanced or syndetocheilic type occurs, among gymnosperms, only in the
extinct Bennettitales and in the living genera *Welwitchia* and *Gnetum*
in the Gnetales. Florin has also demonstrated the great utility of stomatal
morphology in the taxonomic study of living conifers, since considerable
variation occurs in the details of construction of the haplocheilic type.
For extensive descriptions and interpretations of the comparative morphology of stomatal apparati in gymnosperms the student is referred to
the monographs of Florin (1931, 1951) and to the recent article on
cycads by Arnold (1953).

The transfusion tissue is invariably closely associated with the vascular
bundle or bundles in the leaf, and a voluminous literature has accumulated regarding its structure and evolutionary significance. (See, for instance, Worsdell, 1897; van Abbema, 1934; Griffith, 1957.) We will
utilize the leaf of *Pinus* as a basis for a preliminary discussion of transfusion tissue.

As seen in transectional view, the transfusion tissue in a pine needle
consists of several layers of compactly arranged cells which surround the
vascular bundle or bundles and which are separated from the inner
region of the mesophyll by the endodermis (Fig. 16-6). Sacher (1953),
who has made a detailed ontogenetic study of the leaf of *Pinus Lambertiana*, found that the transfusion tissue arises from the outer region of
the procambium in the young needle, and that its maturation proceeds
basipetally and centripetally. The transfusion tissue in *Pinus* consists of
two principal cell types: transfusion tracheids, which have thick, lignified
secondary walls with conspicuous circular bordered pits; and transfusion
parenchyma cells, which retain their protoplasts and are further characterized by the development of tannin-like substances (Fig. 16-6, B).
These two cell types form a complex interconnected system; both types
occur in direct contact with the cells of the endodermis. The physiologi-

cal role of the transfusion tissue in *Pinus* and other gymnosperms is generally considered to be that of conduction of materials between the vascular bundle and the mesophyll.

In other genera of the Coniferales the transfusion tissue consists entirely of tracheids and occurs in a variety of patterns, with reference to the vascular system (Griffith, 1957). In *Araucaria*, for example, the transfusion tissue forms a sheath completely surrounding the xylem in the lower portion of the leaf, and nearer the leaf tip it encloses also the lateral portions of the phloem; this appears to be a very common pattern of distribution in a wide variety of gymnosperms (Griffith, 1951). Members of the Cupressaceae develop the transfusion tissue as two lateral wings which extend from the sides of the vascular bundle. Furthermore, the secondary wall pattern of the transfusion tracheids is quite variable, ranging from reticulate or trabeculate to pitted, and includes transitional conditions between these types of sculpturing (Al-Sherifi, 1952).

The occurrence of a separate zone of transfusion tracheids external to the tracheids of the xylem poses an interesting but exceedingly difficult morphological problem. According to one widely expressed view, transfusion tissue originated from the primitive, centripetal primary xylem, which is characteristic of the leaves of certain Paleozoic gymnosperms (Worsdell, 1897; Jeffrey, 1917). A contrary view holds that transfusion tissue represents the modified development of the original parenchyma surrounding or flanking the vascular bundle (van Abbema, 1934). Both of these ideas appear somewhat conjectural and a better understanding of the nature and history of transfusion tissue will depend on the study of fossil leaves as well as on the intensive ontogenetic investigation of this tissue in a wide range of living gymnosperms (see Griffith, 1957).

Stem Anatomy

It will be possible only to review here certain of the main anatomical features of the stem in the Coniferales. The transection of the young stem of *Pinus* will be used to illustrate the general topography and cellular structure of the various tissues (Fig. 16-8, A). Unlike stems in the cycads, this stem is characterized by a prominent vascular system. At the developmental stage illustrated in Fig. 16-8, A, this system is almost entirely composed of secondary phloem and secondary xylem, both

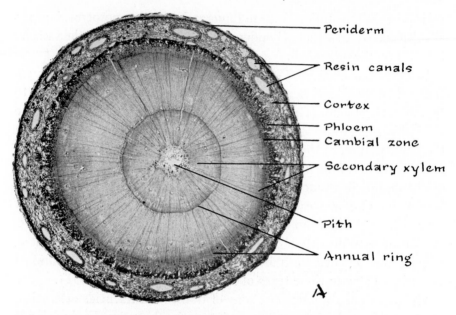

Periderm

Resin canals

Cortex

Phloem

Cambial zone

Secondary xylem

Pith

Annual ring

A

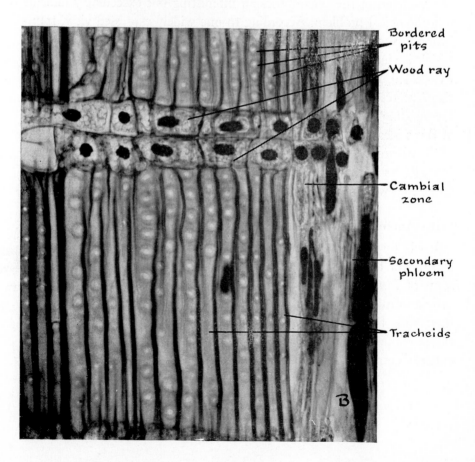

Bordered pits

Wood ray

Cambial zone

Secondary phloem

Tracheids

B

developed from the persistent type of cambial activity characteristic of all conifers. Aside from the frequent resin ducts, the secondary xylem consists of tracheids, which are elongate cells arranged in regular radial rows, and xylem rays, which consist of living parenchyma cells arranged in radially directed sheets. Figure 16-8, B, shows the form and relationship of the tracheids and rays in longitudinal section and the conspicuous circular bordered pits and pit-pairs of the tracheids. The wood of *Pinus*, like that of all gymnosperms except the Gnetales, is characterized by the absence of vessels, and in this respect is more homogeneous and primitive than the xylem of the majority of angiosperms. As shown in Fig. 16-8, the secondary phloem resembles the xylem in its relatively simple structure, and consists of elongated sieve cells, phloem parenchyma and rays; in many conifers, fibers and sclereids may also develop in the secondary phloem. The pith and cortex of the pine stem are composed largely of parenchyma tissue, but the cortex is particularly distinguished by the presence of numerous, large resin ducts. The epidermis has thickened outer walls overlaid by a massive cuticle, and during later stages in the increase in circumference of the stem it is sloughed away by the development of a cylinder of periderm.

Because of the continued activity of the vascular cambium for hundreds or even thousands of years (e.g., *Sequoia*), the stems of many conifers attain enormous diameters. Usually, as shown in Fig. 16-8, A, the so-called annual rings are clearly defined, each ring representing the increment of secondary xylem produced annually by the cambium. Not infrequently false annual rings are produced as the result of abnormal cambial activity; they, of course, must be considered when attempting to estimate the age of a given stem.

The scientific interest in conifers and their importance as sources of lumber have been responsible for the numerous studies on cambial activity and wood histology in these plants. For more detailed treatments of these topics and other aspects of stem anatomy the student should consult Esau (1953), and Brown, Panshin, and Forsaith (1949).

Figure 16-8 Stem anatomy in *Pinus*. **A,** transection of two-year-old stem; **B,** radial longisection of secondary vascular tissues and cambial zone. Note especially the conspicuous circular bordered pits of the tracheids and the living cells of the wood ray.

Strobili and Sporangia

One of the most uniform characteristics of the Coniferales is the mono-sporangiate nature of their cones or strobili. This means that in all normal cases two distinct types of strobili are formed: the microsporan-giate or pollen-bearing cone, and the megasporangiate or seed cone (Fig. 16-2). The latter is the larger, and is exemplified by the familiar cones of pines, firs, and spruces (Figs. 16-3, B; 16-14, A). Bisporangiate cones (structures that develop both microsporangia and ovules) have been observed in many genera of living conifers, but they clearly represent abnormalities and do not provide evidence as to the phylogenetic history of the two cone types in living forms. According to Florin, no bisporan-giate cones have been encountered in the fossil remains of either Paleo-zoic or Mesozoic conifers—he concludes that monosporangiate cones represent a primary and fundamental condition in the evolutionary his-tory of conifers.

As stated earlier in the chapter, the living conifers are predominantly monoecious, both kinds of cones occurring on the same individual. This was very probably the prevailing situation in the extinct conifers also. The dioecious condition, in which the two kinds of cones are produced by separate individuals of a species, is found in the Taxaceae, in a ma-jority of the Araucariaceae, in *Podocarpus*, and in a number of genera in the Cupressaceae.

The Microsporangiate Strobilus

As compared with the cycads, the microsporangiate strobili of most conifers are relatively small, commonly measuring only a few centi-meters or less in length. The longest that have been recorded occur in *Araucaria bidwilli* where they may reach a length of 10-12 cm. The position of the microsporangiate strobili varies considerably within the Coniferales. In *Pinus* these strobili arise in the axils of scale leaves and are produced in subterminal clusters (Fig. 16-2, A), whereas in *Cedrus* solitary microsporangiate cones develop at the tips of certain of the spur shoots. In other families, e.g., the Cupressaceae, the strobili are de-veloped terminally on certain specialized lateral shoots.

The microsporophylls vary in form from flattened leaf-like appendages

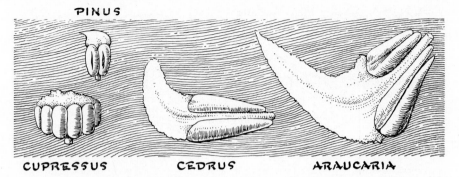

Figure 16-9 Microsporophylls in the conifers showing variations in their form and in the number of microsporangia. [Redrawn from *Gymnosperms. Structure and Evolution* by C. J. Chamberlain, Chicago: The University of Chicago Press, 1935.]

with expanded tips to peltate organs. In all cases the microsporangia develop on the lower surface of the sporophylls, but the number of sporangia is not constant throughout the order (Fig. 16-9). In the Pinaceae the number is consistently two, whereas in the other families from two to seven sporangia may occur on each sporophyll. Certain species of *Araucaria* and *Agathis* are notable because from thirteen to fifteen sporangia may be produced by a single sporophyll.

Throughout much of the current literature it is stated that the microsporangium of conifers, although eusporangiate in its general pattern of development, *originates* from the division of a series of hypodermal cells (Chamberlain, 1935; Campbell, 1940; Haupt, 1953). In other words, in marked contrast with the *superficial* position of sporangial initials in lower vascular plants, the parent cells of the microsporangia of conifers are asserted to occur *below* a surface or epidermal layer. According to this interpretation, the outermost cell layer of the adult microsporangium would be morphologically a part of the epidermis of the sporophyll. Several recent investigations have shown that, on the contrary, the method of origin of the microsporangium is not standardized but that two different patterns of initiation occur. In two members of the Pinaceae—*Pseudotsuga taxifolia* (Allen, 1946b) and *Cedrus deodara* (Erspamer, 1952)—the sporangial initials are two groups of surface cells near the base of the abaxial surface of the young sporophyll. As in the lower vascular plants, these initials divide periclinally, forming an outer

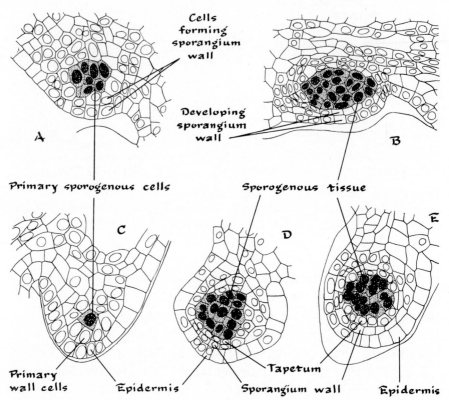

Figure 16-10 Initiation and early development of the microsporangium in
conifers. **A-B,** *Cedrus deodara,* showing origin of microsporangium from
superficial initials; **C-E,** *Chamaecyparis Lawsoniana,* showing origin of microsporangium from hypodermal initials (note that epidermis is a distinct cell
layer throughout development). [Redrawn from J. L. Erspamer, Ph.D. dissertation, University of California, Berkeley, 1952.]

series of cell layers which compose the sporangium wall and an inner
group of sporogenous cells (Fig. 16-10, A, B). In these plants therefore
the surface cells of the mature microsporangium are morphologically a
part of the sporangial wall and not epidermal cells. The contrasted pattern of sporangial initiation was found by Erspamer (1952) in representatives of three other families: *Cryptomeria japonica* (Taxodiaceae),
Chamaecyparis lawsoniana (Cupressaceae), and *Taxus baccata* (Taxaceae). In these species the sporangial initials are strictly hypodermal in
origin, and after the usual eusporangiate development has been com-

pleted the microsporangium is externally bounded by a true epidermis (Fig. 16-10, C-E).

These recent studies emphasize the great need for a comprehensive survey of the method of initiation and early ontogeny of the microsporangium throughout the Coniferales as well as in the other groups of living gymnosperms. Furthermore, as was pointed out in Chapter 4, studies on sporangial development should, in all cases, be made in the light of detailed knowledge of (1) the structure and growth of the vegetative and reproductive apices, and (2) the method of initiation of foliage leaves and sporophylls. Allen and Erspamer showed that in the Pinaceae the superficial position of the initials of the microsporangium is matched by the active contribution of surface cells to the formation of leaf and sporophyll primordia. In contrast, the hypodermal position of sporangial initials in *Cryptomeria, Chamaecyparis,* and *Taxus* is closely correlated with the presence in the apical meristem of a well-defined surface layer, which does not contribute to the inner tissue of either the foliage leaf or the microsporophyll. When studied in this broad way the method of sporangium initiation becomes part of the problem of general morphogenesis rather than simply an isolated aspect of morphological study.

At maturity the wall of the microsporangium consists of one, or, as in *Cedrus,* several layers of cells. Commonly many or all of the internal layers of the wall become crushed or obliterated. The outermost layer consists very often of cells with reticulate, helical, or annular thickenings which closely resemble the patterns of the secondary wall of tracheary elements. This surface layer is concerned with the mechanical rupturing of the sporangium at the period of release of the pollen grains. Although a tapetum is characteristically developed, its origin is quite variable (Fig. 16-10, D, E), since it may represent the innermost layer of the sporangial wall (*Chamaecyparis*), or else is a derivative of the sporogenous tissue (*Taxus*). In most genera, particularly in the Pinaceae and Araucariaceae, a large number of microspores is produced in each sporangium (Fig. 16-11). A very characteristic feature of the microspores of most of genera in the Pinaceae is the development of two air-filled lateral bladders or wings (Fig. 16-15). Winged microspores are present also in members of the Podocarpaceae.

The Megasporangiate Strobilus

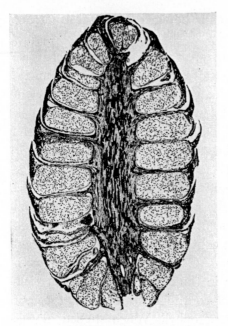

Figure 16-11 Longitudinal section of mature microsporangiate strobilus in *Pinus.*

In this section we are concerned with the morphological nature of the megasporangiate strobilus or seed cone which is characteristically developed in the majority of the families of living conifers. It would not be an exaggeration to state that the interpretation of the structure and evolution of the seed cone represents one of the most difficult and controversial problems in plant morphology. In recent years Rudolf Florin (1938-1945, 1950, 1951) has made highly significant contributions to a better understanding of the structure and evolutionary history of the megasporangiate cone in the Coniferales. The necessarily brief discussion given here is based largely on his discoveries and conclusions, and we hope that from it the student will gain a fairly clear understanding of the nature of the problems and the kinds of evidence that have been used to solve them.

The essence of the morphological problem is clearly exemplified by such a familiar plant as *Pinus.* If one dissects a young seed cone, or examines it in longisectional view, it will be evident that its general structure is quite different from that of a typical microsporangiate cone. As shown in Fig. 16-12, C, the seed cone consists of an axis which bears a spirally arranged series of small appendages termed bracts. In the axil of each bract is a thick, woody scale upon which are borne two ovules; the latter are attached to the upper or adaxial surface of the cone scale near its base. Since the ovuliferous scales are lateral structures, each subtended by a bract, the entire cone is thus a "compound" strobilus and has often been likened in this respect to an inflorescence. By contrast, the microsporangiate strobilus is "simple" in organization because the sporangia are borne directly upon the primary appendages or microsporophylls (compare Fig. 16-11 with Fig. 16-12, C).

Reduced to simplest terms, the problem of the seed cone in *Pinus* and other members of the Phanerostrobilares centers on the debatable nature of the ovuliferous scale. Although this structure is sporophyll-like in that it bears the ovules, its axillary position with reference to the bract creates a very puzzling situation. Of all the conflicting and involved theories that have been proposed during the last century* the most plausible and best supported view holds that the ovuliferous scale is a highly modified lateral fertile shoot and hence not a sporophyll. In other words, the scale has developed, phylogenetically, from an originally leafy, ovule-bearing dwarf shoot, and its present simple appearance is the result of the fusion and specialization of both the sterile and fertile components of such a composite ancestral structure.

One of the earliest precursors of the modern ovuliferous scale occurs in *Lebachia* and *Ernestiodendron*, two genera of Paleozoic conifers which have been studied in great detail by Florin. In *Lebachia* the megasporangiate cone consisted of a series of spirally arranged, bifid bracts, in the axils of which developed short, uniovulate, radial, leafy shoots. Usually all but one of the scale-like leaves were sterile; the fertile appendage or megasporophyll, situated near the base or middle region of the dwarf shoot, faced the main axis of the cone and bore a single erect ovule (Fig. 16-13, A). The structure of the axillary fertile shoots in the cone of *Ernestiodendron* was somewhat similar to that in *Lebachia* except for the larger number of ovuliferous appendages (Fig. 16-13, B). Florin has termed the fertile shoots in these and other conifers "seed-scale complexes," and believes they demonstrate that the compound type of megasporangiate strobilus is a primary condition in the Coniferales, with the exception of the Taxaceae. The latter he regards as having a separate evolutionary history because they lack definable seed cones. Very little is known as to the internal structure of the ovule in such ancient conifers as *Lebachia* or *Ernestiodendron*. A single integument was present, and it is thought that the female gametophyte produced two archegonia at its micropylar end.

In certain conifers of the Upper Permian the fertile ovuliferous dwarf shoots were characterized by a significant series of structural modifications. The cone of *Pseudovoltzia*, for example, consisted of spirally

---

* For a critical discussion of many of the older interpretations of the ovuliferous scale, the student is referred to Worsdell (1900), Coulter and Chamberlain (1917), and Chamberlain (1935).

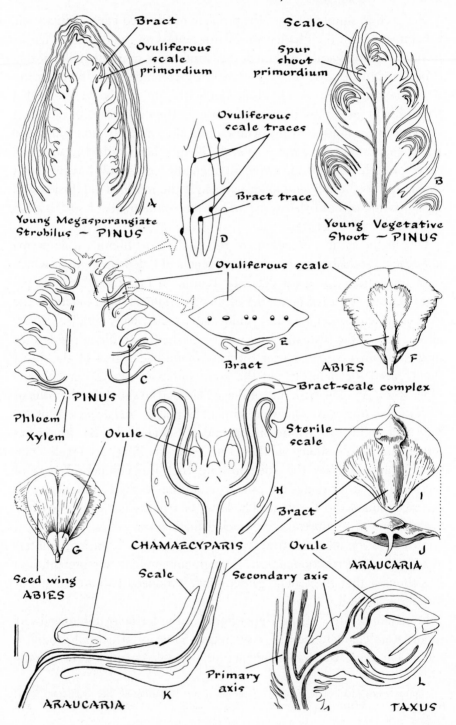

Bract

Ovuliferous
scale
primordium

Young Megasporangiate
Strobilus ~ PINUS

Scale

Spur
shoot
primordium

Young Vegetative
Shoot ~ PINUS

Ovuliferous
scale traces

Bract trace

Ovuliferous scale

Bract

ABIES

Bract-scale complex

Sterile
scale

Bract

Ovule

ARAUCARIA

PINUS

Phloem
Xylem

Ovule

Seed wing
ABIES

CHAMAECYPARIS

Scale   Secondary axis

Primary
axis

ARAUCARIA   TAXUS

arranged entire bracts. Each axillary seed-scale complex was more or less flattened and was composed of a short axis bearing five sterile scales and two or three stalked megasporophylls. Each sporophyll bore a single inverted ovule (Fig. 16-13, C, D). Florin concludes that this type of fertile shoot "corresponds to the ovuliferous scale of a recent pine cone with its two inverted ovules." Additional reduction and modification of the seed-scale complex occurred in the Triassic genus *Voltzia*. The significant features here are that the five sterile scales are basally fused to form a flat sterile component, and that the three megasporophylls were adnate for most of their length to the inner surface of these united scales (Fig. 16-13, E, F).

The further evolutionary development of the seed-scale complex in the Coniferales is still imperfectly understood, and reference to Florin's various papers will show the many gaps in the fossil record. Essentially, however, the general trend seems to have been toward (1) the elimination of all but a few sterile scales which became fused into the so-called ovuliferous scale, and (2) the ultimate suppression of the sporophylls which finally became incorporated with the lower part of the ovuliferous scale.

Figure 16-12 Morphology of ovuliferous structures in various conifers. **A,** *Pinus banksiana,* longisection of young seed cone showing relation of developing ovuliferous scales and their associated bracts; **B,** *Pinus banksiana,* longisection of vegetative bud showing the general structure and axillary position of spur-shoot primordia; **C,** *Pinus maritima,* longisection of immature seed cone showing several examples of the orientation of phloem (white) and xylem (black) in the vascular traces of the ovuliferous scale and its associated bract; **D,** *Pinus maritima,* longisection showing separate origin of bract trace and ovuliferous scale traces; **E,** *Pinus maritima,* transection showing vascular system of bract and ovuliferous scale (note inverted orientation of scale bundles); **F-G,** *Abies balsamea,* abaxial and adaxial views, respectively, of ovuliferous scale; **H,** *Chamaecyparis Lawsoniana,* longitudinal section of seed cone showing union between ovuliferous scale and bract; **I-J,** *Araucaria Bidwillii.* Adaxial and end views, respectively, of ovuliferous scale joined with its bract; **K,** *Araucaria Balansi,* longisection showing vascular supply of bract and scale (note single basal ovule); **L,** *Taxus canadensis,* median longitudinal section of vegetative shoot and of secondary lateral fertile shoot which terminates in a single ovule. [Redrawn from following sources: A-B, from *Gymnosperms. Structure and Evolution* by C. J. Chamberlain, Chicago: University of Chicago Press, 1935; C, D, E, H, K, from Aase, *Bot. Gaz.* 60:277, 1915; F, G, I, J, L, from Florin, *Acta Horti Bergiana* 15:285, 1951.]

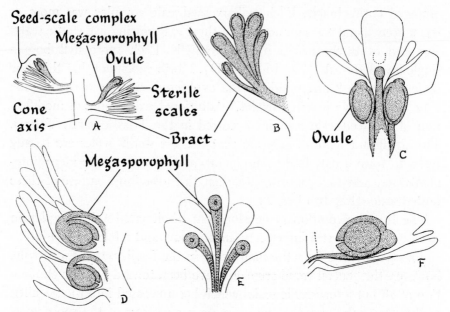

Figure 16-13 Various types of ovuliferous structures in extinct conifers. **A,** *Lebachia Goeppertiana*; **B,** *Ernestiodendron filiciforme*; **C-D,** adaxial and side views, respectively, in *Pseudovoltzia Liebeana*; **E-F,** adaxial and side views, respectively, in *Voltzia sp.* [Redrawn from Florin, Palaeontographica Abt. B, Bd. 85, 1944.]

In modern conifers evolutionary specialization is also shown by the various degrees of fusion between the seed-scale complex and its subtending bract (Fig. 16-12, C, F-K). Throughout the Pinaceae the bract is conspicuous and almost entirely free of its associated scale. Indeed, in *Pseudotsuga* and certain species of *Abies* the bracts are prominently exserted in the mature seed cones and may be tridentate in form (Fig. 16-14, A). In the Taxodiaceae, Cupressaceae, and Araucariaceae, however, the bract is partially or entirely fused with the scale as can be seen in Fig. 16-12, H-K. In these groups, as well as in the Pinaceae, anatomical study has shown that the vascular system of the bract is separate from the bundles which extend through the seed-scale complex. In *Pinus*, for example, a single vascular strand, with the xylem oriented toward the *upper* surface, as in a normal leaf, supplies the bract (Fig. 16-12, C, D). The vascular supply of the scale consists of four bundles, the upper two of which may fuse to form a median strand. Within the ovuliferous scale the bundles dichotomize (Fig. 16-12, E), and a small vein diverges from each lateral and enters the base of an ovule. Since the xylem portions of these scale bundles face toward the *lower* surface of the scale, the vascular strands appear inverted in orientation when compared with the bract bundle. This so-called inversion is evidently the result of the close union, for a longer or shorter distance, between the bract and the seed-scale complex (Fig. 16-12, C, H). Both systems of bundles may appear as a closed vascular cylinder below the point of fusion of the bract and the seed-scale complex.

Florin (1951) has applied his evolutionary views in a reinterpretation of the composition of the seed-scale complex in various living conifers. Several examples of his interpretation may be mentioned. In the Pinaceae the flattened seed-scale complex normally consists of a rudimentary axis, two basal megasporophylls, and two or three distal sterile scales; the last are fused and constitute the so-called ovuliferous scale. In *Araucaria* an extreme example of reduction occurs, according to Florin. Here the seed-scale

Figure 16-14 **A**, seed cones of *Pseudotsuga* (note exserted tridentate bracts); **B**, portion of branch of *Taxus* showing a seed surrounded by cup-shaped aril. [A-B, from *Botany. An Introduction to Plant Science*, Ed. 2, by W. W. Robbins, T. E. Weier, and C. R. Stocking. N. Y.: John Wiley and Sons, Inc., 1957.]

complex, which bears only a single ovule, consists of a rudimentary axis, a single, basal, extremely reduced megasporophyll, and a single, distal, sterile scale located in front of the ovule (Fig. 16-12, I-K). Certain genera in the Taxodiaceae appear to have retained a more primitive type of seed-scale complex; in this family, the ovuliferous scale appears to arise from two or more scales which develop as separate primordia usually located in front of the ovules. Although collaterally joined on a common elongating base, they retain their free tips in the mature scale.

This section may be terminated by a brief reference to the ovuliferous structures in the Taxaceae. As shown in Figs. 16-14, B, and 16-12, L, the ovule of *Taxus* is terminal on a short lateral shoot and, furthermore is partly enclosed by a fleshy aril. Such ovuliferous branches seem far removed, in their structural organization, from the seed cones of most conifers. Both *Taxus* and *Torreya* existed during the Mesozoic Era, and in Florin's opinion there is no evidence that they developed from types with distinct ovuliferous strobili. Further comparative studies of the Taxaceae as well as the Podocarpaceae, in which the ovuliferous structures are sometimes strobiloid, are very much needed. For details of their reproductive structures, which cannot be treated in this book, the student should consult Coulter and Chamberlain (1917), Chamberlain (1935), and the extensive bibliographies included in these books.

The Reproductive Cycle in *Pinus*

Numerous comparative studies have demonstrated the wide variation in the details of sporogenesis, gametophyte development, and embryogeny within the living conifers. To choose one genus from the large number of investigated plants as being typical of the Coniferales as a whole is doubtless impossible. Most conifers, on the contrary, prove to have a blend of gametophytic and embryological characters, some advanced, some primitive, and still others shared by even the cycads and *Ginkgo*. For these reasons there is probably no living genus which can serve alone as the measure of phylogenetic trends within the order.

The selection of *Pinus* as the basis for the following discussion of reproduction in the conifers is therefore admittedly arbitrary but yet not without some justification. The life history of pine has been studied more intensively than that of probably any other conifer (Ferguson, 1904; Buchholz, 1918; Haupt, 1941; Johansen, 1950). As a result it will be possible to present a complete, connected account of the successive stages of its life cycle. For the student, the advantages of a coherent description of the steps in reproduction of a familiar type of conifer are obvious. But in order to illustrate some of the apparently significant variations between *Pinus* and other genera, brief comments will be included at the end of the description of the life cycle. This procedure, we hope, will broaden the student's view of reproductive structures in the conifers without seriously interrupting the general continuity of the discussion. Figure 14-5 presents a diagrammatic life cycle of a conifer, and should provide additional orientation for the following detailed descriptions.

Sporogenesis

MICROSPOROGENESIS.   The entire developmental history of the micro-sporangiate strobilus in certain species of pine extends over a period of approximately a year (Ferguson, 1904). The strobili are initiated in the spring or early summer, and by winter the microsporangia contain well-defined sporogenous tissue. Meiosis and the formation of the character-istic winged microspores, however, are processes that do not occur until the following spring. Each functional microsporocyte gives rise to four haploid microspores, which are enclosed by the wall of the microsporo-cyte for some time (Fig. 16-15, A). According to Ferguson, the air sacs or wings of each spore are formed by the separation of the outer (exine) and inner (intine) layers of the microspore wall; this occurs while the members of a spore tetrad are still surrounded by the common mother cell wall. The outer wall of the mature microspore, especially in the two wings, exhibits a reticulate sculpture. At the lower end of the spore the wall is relatively thin and smooth; this region is the point at which the emergence of the pollen tube later takes place (Fig. 16-15, E, F).

MEGASPOROGENESIS.   Before describing the process of megasporogen-esis, it will be essential to discuss the general ontogeny of the ovuliferous scale in *Pinus*. Figure 16-12, A, represents somewhat diagrammatically a longisection of a young megasporangiate strobilus enclosed within a series of overlapping bud scales. This stage of development is apparently attained during the late summer or autumn of a given year. The still-embryonic strobilus consists of an axis bearing a series of lateral bracts, in the axil of each of which is a structure that resembles a young, undif-ferentiated, vegetative axillary bud (Fig. 16-12, A, B). These bud-like structures, shown in Fig. 16-12, A, are the primordia of the ovuliferous scales, and their axillary position with reference to the bracts gives addi-

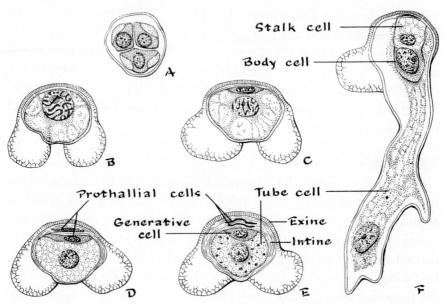

Figure 16-15   Development of the male gametophyte in *Pinus laricio*. **A,** tetrad
of young microspores enclosed within wall of microsporocyte (note developing
wings of microspores); **B,** prophase of first division of microspore nucleus; **C,**
the first prothallial cell has been formed and the microspore nucleus is preparing to divide again; **D,** a second prothallial cell has been formed; **E,** the
microspore nucleus ("antheridial nucleus") has divided, producing the tube
and generative cells; at this four-celled stage the male gametophyte is liberated
from the microsporangium; **F,** young pollen tube as it would appear in the
nucellus of ovule after pollination (note that generative cell has divided to
form the stalk and body cells). [Redrawn from *Gymnosperms. Structure and
Evolution* by C. J. Chamberlain. Chicago: University of Chicago Press, 1935.]

tional support to the interpretation of the scale as a modified, condensed
shoot. (See page 393 for the morphological interpretation of the ovuliferous scale.) As the development of the megasporangiate strobilus
continues, the embryonic protuberances subtended by the bracts differentiate into thick scales bearing two ovules on their upper surface (Fig.
16-12, C, G). As in the microsporangiate strobilus, however, the differentiation of the young seed cone is interrupted by the onset of winter.
According to Ferguson (1904), the first indications of ovule development do not occur in certain species until April or late May of the
year following the initiation of the cone. Just prior to megasporogenesis,
the pine ovule consists of a nucellus and a single integument; the

conspicuous micropyle is directed inward toward the axis of the cone (Fig. 16-16, A).

In the species of *Pinus* that have been intensively studied the single megasporocyte of each ovule is deeply situated within the tissue of the nucellus, and there is no evidence of its origin from a hypodermal cell (Fig. 16-16, A). The megasporocyte is demarcated from other adjoining cells by its large size and prominent nucleus. Soon after its differentiation, the megasporocyte is surrounded by a zone of modified nucellar cells which have been collectively termed spongy tissue. This tissue continues to grow throughout the periods of megaspore formation and gametophyte development, and its physiological rôle seems to be related especially to the nutrition of the female gametophyte.

Theoretically the meiotic division of the megasporocyte should yield a tetrad of four haploid megaspores (Fig. 14-6, A). Ferguson's (1904) detailed investigations, however, showed variation in the number of cells produced by the megasporocyte, not only among different species

Figure 16-16 *Pinus sp.* **A,** median longisection of ovule showing a single deeply embedded megasporocyte (note large radially elongated cells of the middle layer of the integument and the pollen grains); **B,** longisection of ovule showing young pollen tube penetrating the nucellus.

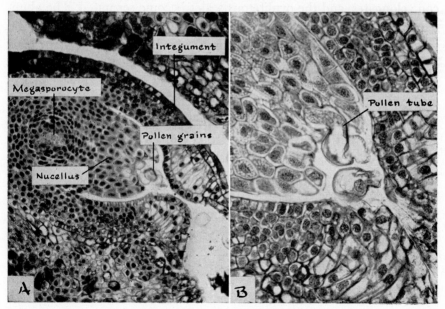

of pine but even within the same species. In *P. austriaca* a linear tetrad of four megaspores results from the division of *each* of the first two cells produced by the division of the sporocyte. In *P. strobus* and *P. rigida,* however, only three cells are formed. This condition is the result of the degeneration of the upper cell of the two formed by the division of the sporocyte; in this case, only the lower cell (i.e., the cell farthest from the micropyle) of the two divides. Regardless of these variations, the lowest cell of the series produced by the sporocyte becomes the functional haploid megaspore, the two or three cells above it soon disintegrating.

Gametophytes

As in the cycads and *Ginkgo,* the early development of the endosporic male gametophyte occurs before the dehiscence of the microsporangium. As a result of three successive nuclear divisions, the young male gametophyte consists of two prothallial cells (which soon become flattened and dead), a generative cell, and a tube nucleus (Fig. 16-15, E). This is the usual stage in *Pinus* at which the pollen grains are set free into the air by the dehiscence of the microsporangium.

As in most conifers, the ovules of *Pinus* are wind pollinated. At the time of pollination, in late spring, the axis of the young megasporangiate cone elongates, and the ovuliferous scales become separated. The abundant pollen grains, borne by wind and gravity, sift down between the scales, and one or several grains become lodged in the micropylar canals of the ovules. According to Chamberlain (1935) the pollen grains adhere to the pollination drops that exude from the micropyles of the ovules. Ferguson (1904) found that the free end of the nucellus is slightly depressed in *Pinus* and that the pollen grains lie in this cavity. According to her observations the radial elongation of the cells of the middle layer of the integument, a short distance above the tip of the nucellus, forms a rim-like protuberance that seals off the outer part of the micropylar canal (Fig. 16-16, A). After pollination the ovuliferous scales become drawn together and remain compact until the seeds are released from the mature cones.

A salient feature of the reproductive cycle in *Pinus* is the relatively long interval between pollination and fertilization. In many pines this interval is about twelve months. At the time of pollination the male

gametophyte has not completed its development, and megasporogenesis has just begun in the ovules. Following pollination there is a
slow period of development of the male gametophyte; this comprises
the emergence of the pollen tube from the concave side of the spore
and usually the division of the generative cell to form a stalk cell and
a body cell (Figs. 16-15, F, 16-16, B). Concomitantly the single functional megaspore within the nucellus of the ovule enlarges, and a series
of free nuclear divisions occur. According to Ferguson (1904), about
five successive nuclear divisions, yielding 32 nuclei, occur before the period of dormancy is reached. Thus both the male and female gametophytes are in a comparatively rudimentary stage in *Pinus* throughout the
winter, and the development of sperm nuclei and archegonia takes place
during the renewal of growth the following spring.

The details of development of the female gametophyte in pine are
very similar to those already described for the cycads and *Ginkgo* (Fig.
14-6, B). At the end of the first period of development the female
gametophyte is a more or less spherical sac, containing about 32 nuclei,
embedded in a parietal layer of cytoplasm, and a large central vacuole.
When development resumes in the spring there is a very rapid formation of free nuclei within the female gametophyte. Ferguson observed
about 2,000 free nuclei in the gametophyte of *Pinus strobus*. During
the latter part of the spring centripetal wall formation begins and ultimately the female gametophyte becomes a massive cellular body. At
this period, the megaspore wall enclosing the gametophyte is very evident
and in some species of pine may be 3-4 microns in thickness.

The development of archegonia may be deferred until the female
gametophyte is completely cellular, but not infrequently archegonia are
initiated before wall formation has terminated. According to Ferguson
archegonia are detectable about two weeks before fertilization. The
ontogeny of the archegonium is markedly like that of a cycad (Fig.
15-9, F-H). The initial which is a surface cell differentiated at the micropylar end of the gametophyte divides periclinally into a small outer
primary neck cell and a larger inner central cell. By means of two successive anticlinal divisions, the primary neck cell forms four neck cells, a
condition apparently rather common in *Pinus strobus*. In other species,
however (e.g., *P. austriaca, P. rigida,* and *P. resinosa*), these four neck
cells may divide periclinally, forming an eight-celled neck with the cells

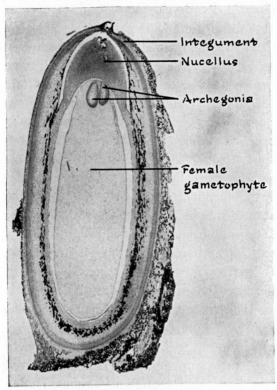

Figure 16-17 *Pinus sp.* Median longisection of ovule showing female gametophyte with two archegonia.

arranged in two tiers. Apparently the number of neck cells varies somewhat even in the same species. The central cell enlarges, but its nucleus
remains close to the neck of the archegonium. Ultimately the nucleus
of the central cell divides, forming a small ventral canal cell which is
separated by a definite wall from the large egg cell. The ventral canal
cell eventually degenerates, and the nucleus of the egg cell becomes
enlarged and descends to a central position in the egg (Fig. 16-17).
When mature, the egg of the archegonium is jacketed by a distinct layer
of cells, and numerous proteinaceous bodies (so-called protein vacuoles)
become evident in the cytoplasm; these bodies superficially resemble
nuclei (Fig. 16-18, A).

The number of archegonia produced by a single gametophyte varies
considerably, depending somewhat on the species. According to Johansen
(1950) there is usually a single archegonium in the Monterey Pine

(*P. radiata*), whereas in the majority of the other species investigated the number of archegonia ranges from two to six (Fig. 16-17).

Fertilization

During the resumption of growth by the female gametophyte in the spring, the stalk and body cells of the male gametophyte move down toward the lower end of the pollen tube. Approximately a week before fertilization the nucleus of the body cell divides to form two sperm nuclei which are unequal in size. In marked contrast with the large motile sperms found in *Ginkgo* and the cycads, these sperm nuclei are not individualized "cells," and they are entirely devoid of flagella. Following the formation of the two sperm nuclei in *Pinus*, the pollen tube grows actively down through the nucellus. Since several pollen grains may lodge within the micropylar canal of the ovule, a corresponding number of tubes may begin development; usually only two or three persist in development and reach the female gametophyte. The tip of the pollen tube forces itself between the neck cells of the archegonium and then ruptures, discharging the two male gametes, the tube nucleus, and the stalk cell into the cytoplasm of the egg. However, the pollen tube itself does not extend into the archegonium. Syngamy consists in the union of the larger of the two male gametes with the nucleus of the egg (Fig. 16-18, A); usually the other gamete, the tube nucleus, and the stalk cell can be seen at the top of the egg after sexual fusion has been accomplished. Eventually these three nuclei disintegrate

Embryogeny and Seed Development

The early embryogeny of *Pinus*, like that of the majority of the members of the Coniferales, is characterized by an extremely short period of free nuclear divisions. Following syngamy the nucleus of the fertilized egg contains two distinct haploid groups of chromosomes, one paternal, the other maternal (Fig. 16-18, B). These two sets of chromosomes soon become arranged at the equatorial region of a common spindle, and at this time Ferguson (1904) and Haupt (1941) were able to count 24 chromosomes, apparently the typical diploid number for various species of *Pinus* (Fig. 16-18, C).

The division of the zygote nucleus yields two nuclei, each of which promptly divides forming a total of four free nuclei located near the

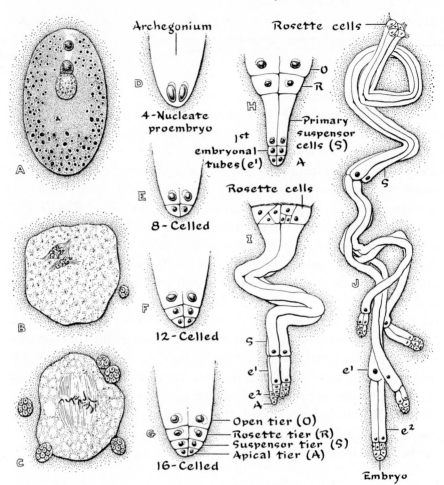

Figure 16-18 Fertilization and early embryogeny in *Pinus*. **A,** longisection showing the larger of the two sperm nuclei in contact with egg nucleus (note abundant proteinaceous bodies in cytoplasm of egg cell); **B,** fertilized egg cell showing distinct groups of paternal and maternal chromosomes; **C,** chromosomes derived from sperm and egg nuclei arranged at equatorial region of a common spindle; **D,** free nuclear phase in embryogeny with four nuclei; **E-G,** development of the four superposed cell tiers of the proembryo; **H,** elongation of primary suspensor cells and formation of first embryonal tubes (e^1); **I,** the lower end of the proembryo has begun to separate (cleavage polyembryony) into four vertical series of cells [note the formation of a second series of embryonal tubes (e^2) and the divisions which have occurred in the rosette cells]; **J,** series of four competing embryos formed by cleavage (note conspicuous apical cell in each embryo). [A-C, redrawn from Haupt, *Bot. Gaz.* 102:482, 1941; D-J, redrawn from Buchholz, *Trans. Illinois Acad. Sci.* 23:117, 1931.]

middle of the cytoplasm of the egg. These four nuclei represent the extent of the free nuclear period in *Pinus*. Soon after their formation, they move to the lower end of the archegonium where a third division accompanied by wall formation occurs (Fig. 16-18, D, E). The first wall formed is transverse to the long axis of the archegonium and separates the eight nuclei into two tiers, then vertical walls appear separating the nuclei in each tier; the embryo now consists of a lower tier of four cells, completely bounded by walls and an upper tier devoid of walls adjacent to the cytoplasm of the egg (Fig. 16-18, E). The next division usually occurs in the cells of the upper tier and is followed by a similar transverse division in the lower tier. The proembryo, as it is termed, now consists of sixteen cells arranged in four superposed tiers (Fig. 16-18, F, G). This tiered arrangement of the cells of the proembryo occurs in many genera of the Coniferales, and the precision with which it originates offers a marked contrast with the comparatively unstratified cell arrangement characteristic of the early embryogeny of the cycads and *Ginkgo* (see Chapter 15).

One of the outstanding features of the later phases of embryogeny in *Pinus* (and in many other conifers) is the development, from the walled cells of the proembryo, of from four to eight separate competing embryos. This early formation of multiple embryos becomes particularly remarkable when one recalls that embryogeny in pine—as in all tracheophytes—begins with a single fertilized egg cell.

To understand clearly the process of polyembryony it is essential to begin with the structure and further development of the cell tiers of the sixteen-celled proembryo shown in Fig. 16-18, G. The uppermost cell tier, sometimes termed the open tier, is in open communication with the egg cytoplasm and possibly serves for a short time to transmit reserve food materials to the lower portion of the proembryo; soon, however, the cells of this tier disintegrate. The next tier comprises the so-called rosette cells which earlier investigators of pine embryogeny considered functionless. Buchholz (1918, 1931), however, has clearly demonstrated that several, or all four, rosette cells may give rise during early embryogeny to small embryos which often become twisted or curved in orientation (Fig. 16-18, I). The development of the rosette embyros however is not extensive—they soon abort and do not include more than a dozen or so cells.

The dominant aspect of polyembryony in *Pinus* is the result of the ultimate separation of the lower cell tiers of the proembryo into four filamentous embryos (Fig. 16-18, I). This process has been termed cleavage polyembryony, and its salient features may now be discussed. Shortly before the proliferation of the rosette cells into embryos, the cells in the tier below them elongate markedly (Fig. 16-18, H, I). These are the primary suspensor cells, and their vigorous extension forces them and the apical tier of cells through the membrane of the original egg into the female gametophyte. Buchholz (1918) has described in detail the breakdown of the starch-containing cells in the upper part of the female gametophyte and the formation of a "corrosion cavity" into which the growing system of embryos intrudes. Because of the limited confines of the corrosion cavity, the primary suspensors soon become coiled and buckled (Fig. 16-18, I, J). During the early elongation of the primary suspensors the apical tier of embryonal cells gives rise, by a series of transverse divisions, to several additional cell tiers (e^1, e^2, etc. in Fig. 16-18, H, I). These cells quickly elongate, like the primary suspensor cells behind them, and are termed embryonal tubes; their extension serves to push the embryo system farther into the corrosion cavity of the gametophyte. Following the formation of the first series of embryonal tubes the lower end of the embryo system separates or cleaves into four distinct vertical series of cells. Each series consists of an apical cell, two or more embryonal tubes, and a primary suspensor cell, and represents an independently developing embryo (Fig. 16-18, I, J). Prior to elongation any of the successively formed embryonal tubes may divide by vertical walls; as a consequence, each unit embryo may be attached to a complex and collaterally arranged series of embryonal tubes. In contrast, the primary suspensor cells never divide but eventually collapse and die later on in embryogeny.

Within the system of embryos derived by the cleavage of one proembryo, there is apparently intense competition. One of the four embryos, usually the lowest and most aggressive member of the group, continues to develop and becomes the differentiated embryo of the pine seed; the other embryos abort and cannot be detected in the mature seed.

From the foregoing discussion it should be clear that each proembryo in *Pinus* is theoretically capable of forming eight embryos, four derived from the rosette tier and four from the cleavage process just outlined.

If all the archegonia of a single gametophyte are fertilized, an extraordinary number—as many as 48—separate embryos might begin development. Buchholz (1918) actually found as many as four separate embryo systems, each the product of a fertilized archegonium, in some species of pine. These embryo systems grow in competition for variable periods of time, but only a single embryo among them normally reaches a fully developed condition in the ripe seed.

The later stages of development of the successful embryo are complex and can be only considered very briefly in this chapter. According to Buchholz the terminal cell of the embryo soon takes on the character of a pyramidal apical cell which forms derivative cells or segments very much like the apical cell of *Equisetum* or a leptosporangiate fern (Fig. 16-18, J). Buchholz (1931) and Chamberlain (1935) regard the presence of an apical cell in conifer embryogeny as a "primitive character." After the main body of the pine embryo consists of several hundred cells a definitive apical cell is no longer apparent, and the extreme apex of the embryo is occupied by a group of equivalent apical initials. The further histogenesis of the embryo includes the differentiation, at the suspensor end, of the initial cells of the root apex, and the ultimate formation of a series of cotyledon primordia from the lower or shoot apex region. For a detailed description of tissue and organ formation during the later stages of embryogeny the student is referred to the work of Spurr (1949) on *Pinus strobus*.

The fully developed embryo of *Pinus* consists of a whorl of cotyledons [the average number in the genus, according to Butts and Buchholz (1940), is 8.1] which surrounds the shoot apex, a short hypocotyl, and a primary root or radicle. The embryo is embedded in the tissue of the massive female gametophyte which, in turn, is surrounded by the seed coat. The seed coat consists primarily of a hard outer coat, which is derived from the stony layer of the integument. The inner fleshy layer of the integument degenerates during seed development, and in the ripe seed is reduced to a thin papery membrane. Usually the remains of the nucellus can be seen at the micropylar end of the female gametophyte.

When the pine seed germinates, the entire embryo emerges from the ruptured seed coat which may adhere for a short time to the tips of the cotyledons (Fig. 16-19, A). The primary shoot formed by the terminal

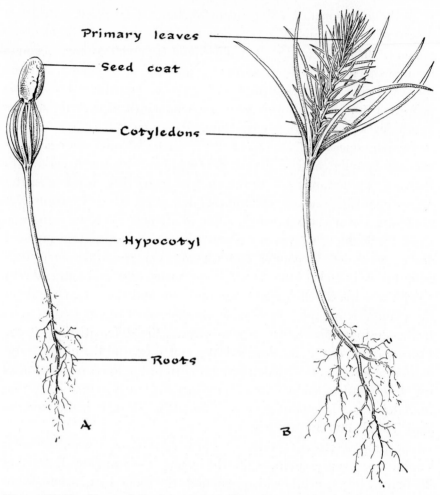

Primary leaves

Seed coat

Cotyledons

Hypocotyl

Roots

A   B

Figure 16-19 *Pinus edulis.* **A,** young seedling showing whorl of cotyledons and remains of seed coat; **B,** older seedling showing cotyledons and spirally arranged primary leaves. [Redrawn from *Gymnosperms. Structure and Evolution* by C. J. Chamberlain. Chicago: University of Chicago Press, 1935.]

bud of the seedling at first bears only a spiral series of needle-like leaves (Fig. 16-19, B). Later, as we have described on page 379, the first spur shoots arise in the axils of some of the primary leaves. The zonal structure and growth of the shoot apex of well-developed trees of *Pinus Lambertiana* and *Pinus ponderosa* have recently been described in detail by Sacher (1954).

Comparisons of Pinus and Other Conifers

In this book it is not possible to present a detailed contrast between the gametophytic and embryological features of *Pinus* and the voluminous data on these topics which have accumulated for other coniferous genera. Chamberlain (1935) has briefly reviewed much of the pertinent literature on reproduction in conifers, and a résumé of comparative embryogeny has been given by Johansen (1950). Our discussion at this point will be restricted to a brief comparison of certain selected aspects of the reproductive cycle in which *Pinus* differs significantly from other genera in the order.

THE MALE GAMETOPHYTE.   Although prothallial cells are a consistent feature of *Pinus* and other genera in the Pinaceae, they are absent in most members of the Taxodiaceae, in many genera of the Cupressaceae, and throughout the Taxaceae, according to Chamberlain's (1935) summary. On the other hand, the Araucariaceae are notable for the very large number (as many as 18-20) of prothallial cells. If, as Chamberlain assumes, prothallial cells represent the remains of the purely vegetative body of the male gametophyte, *Pinus* with two prothallial cells would be relatively advanced in this character.

In a great many conifers the male gametes are represented by two nuclei, as has been described for *Pinus*. But in a number of genera of the Taxodiaceae and Cupressaceae the male gametes are well-defined cells which except for the absence of flagella resemble the sperms of cycads and *Ginkgo*. Since the pollen tubes of conifers function primarily to convey the male gametes directly to the archegonia, the organized male gametes of *Taxodium* and similar plants may conceivably represent structures which have only recently (geologically speaking) lost their flagella. From this hypothetical viewpoint, the male gamete of *Pinus* would appear to represent a very highly evolved condition.

EMBRYOGENY.   As compared with *Ginkgo* and the cycads, the period of free nuclear divisions in most conifers is brief, and very commonly, as in *Pinus*, terminates after four nuclei have been formed. In some genera, such as *Taxus*, walls do not form until 16-32 free nuclei have developed (Sterling, 1948). The early embryogeny of the Araucariaceae, however, is unique. The free nuclear period in this group is relatively protracted, and 32-64 nuclei are present before walls are formed. Unlike most conifers, the free nuclei do not migrate to the base of the egg but remain in the center. A massive suspensor develops from the upper cells of the proembryo, whereas the outer cells of its lower portion form a protective cap, recalling the analogous structure formed during the early embryogeny of *Zamia* (see Chapter 15, p. 355). The free end of the araucarian embryo, after the cap cells have degenerated, gives rise to the main body of the embryo (Johansen, 1950).

As far as is known, *Sequoia sempervirens* is the only conifer devoid of a free nuclear period in embryogeny. The first division of the zygote is followed by a transverse wall yielding a bicellular embryo. This is a puzzling problem, especially because in the rather closely allied species *Sequoia gigantea* embryogeny begins with the formation of eight free nuclei (Buchholz, 1939).

Polyembryony is widespread among members of the Coniferales, and, according to the extensive investigations of Buchholz, cleavage poly-embryony occurs in 30 of the 37 genera which have been intensively studied. The occurrence of cleavage polyembryony, however, is variable even among genera of the same family. In the Pinaceae, for example, *Pinus, Cedrus, Tsuga,* and *Pseudolarix* exhibit cleavage polyembryony, whereas *simple polyembryony* seems to prevail in *Abies, Picea,* and *Pseudotsuga.*

Simple polyembryony designates the condition where each of the several fertilized eggs of one gametophyte produce separate but undivided embryos. In other words, each proembryo directly produces a single embryo, and the four terminal embryonal cells function as a unit without cleaving. Allen's (1946a) investigations on *Pseudotsuga* showed, however, that very frequently two of the terminal cells of the proembryo may overtop the others in growth and ultimately function as the origin of the embryo proper. The suppressed units apparently contribute only to the development of the suspensor system. Although cleavage poly-embryony in conifers has been regarded as being more primitive than simple polyembryony, the phylogenetic aspects of this problem are still in an unresolved condition (Buchholz, 1926; Schofp, 1943; Allen, 1946a).

Summary and Conclusions

In this chapter we have attempted to present certain of the important morphological features of the leaf, stem, and strobili of the Coniferales as a whole. In addition, we have given a rather full and connected description of the reproductive cycle in *Pinus*, a genus that seems to illustrate some of the widespread characteristics of the gametophytes and embryo that are common to many conifers.

Although the leaves of conifers are simple and commonly univeined, these organs are not microphylls in a morphological sense because their traces are associated with definable leaf gaps. In certain of the Paleozoic conifers the foliage leaf was bifid or dichotomously lobed; from this primitive foliar type the simple leaf of modern conifers may have evolved.

With reference to leaf histology, emphasis has been placed on the structure and method of development of stomata because of their systematic and phylogenetic importance in the study of ancient as well as living conifers. Attention has been directed also to the characteristic transfusion tissue which accompanies the vascular system in conifer leaves. The need for comprehensive ontogenetic and comparative studies on transfusion tissue was emphasized.

The histology of the stem of *Pinus* was briefly described and the absence of vessels in the secondary xylem was shown to be a general feature of all conifers.

Throughout the Coniferales the microsporangiate strobilus is "simple," consisting of an axis bearing a series of microsporophylls. The microsporangia are borne on the lower surface of the sporophylls and vary from two to seven, depending upon the genus. In the light of recent study we have shown that there is no standardized method of initiation of the microsporangium. In *Pseudotsuga* and *Cedrus* the sporangial initials are surface cells, whereas in a series of other genera these parent cells are hypodermal in position. In each type, however, the pattern of development of the microsporangium is of the eusporangiate type.

With the exception of the Taxaceae and related forms, the megasporangiate strobilus of the Coniferales is "compound" and consists of an axis bearing a series of bracts, each of which subtends or is more or less

fused with an ovuliferous scale which develops one or more ovules. According to Florin's extensive studies on the megasporangiate strobili of Paleozoic and Mesozoic conifers, the so-called ovuliferous scale of modern conifers is the evolutionary modification of a primitive, radially organized, leafy, ovule-bearing lateral shoot.

The reproductive cycle of *Pinus* exhibits many features shared by the majority of gymnosperms including the cycads and *Ginkgo,* namely: endosporic and reduced male gametophytes; a protracted period of free nuclear division followed by centripetal wall formation in the female gametophyte; highly specialized archegonia with neck cells, an evanescent ventral canal cell, and a large egg cell; and a period of free nuclear divisions in embryogeny. The absence of flagellated sperms and the development of pollen tubes which convey the male gametes to the archegonia are important features distinguishing *Pinus* and other conifers from both *Ginkgo* and the cycads. Additional characters which *Pinus* shares with many other conifers include highly evolved non-flagellated male gametes; a very restricted period of free nuclear divisions in embryogeny; and the tiered arrangement of the cells of the proembryo. This structure in *Pinus* and in many other genera typically produces, by cleavage of the two lowermost cell tiers, four separate competitive embryos; the rosette cells in *Pinus* also proliferate to small and abortive embryos.

References

Abbema, T. van. 1934. Das Transfusiongewebe in den Blättern der Cycadinae, Ginkgoinae und Coniferen. *Travaux. Bot. Neerlandais* 31: 310-390.

Allen, G. S. 1946a. Embryogeny and development of the apical meristems of *Pseudotsuga.* I. Fertilization and early embryogeny. *Amer. Jour. Bot.* 33:666-677.

———. 1946b. The origin of the microsporangium of *Pseudotsuga. Bull. Torrey Bot. Club* 73:547-556.

Al-Sherifi, K. A. 1952. Histological studies on the shoot apices and leaves of certain Cupressaceae. Ph.D. Diss., Univ. Calif., Berkeley.

Arnold, C. A. 1947. *An Introduction to Paleobotany.* McGraw-Hill, New York.

———. 1953. Origin and relationships of the cycads. *Phytomorphology* 3: 51-65.

Brown, H. P., A. J. Panshin and C. C. Forsaith. 1949. *Textbook of Wood*

Technology, vol. I. Structure, Identification, Defects, and Uses of the Commercial Woods of the United States. McGraw-Hill, New York.

Buchholz, J. T. 1918. Suspensor and early embryo of *Pinus*. *Bot. Gaz.* 66: 185-228.

———. 1926. Origin of cleavage polyembryony in conifers. *Bot. Gaz.* 81: 55-71.

———. 1931. The pine embryo and the embryos of related genera. *Trans Illinois Acad. Sci.* 23:117-125.

———. 1933. The classification of Coniferales. *Trans. Illinois Acad. Sci.* 25:112-113.

———. 1939. The embryogeny of *Sequoia sempervirens*, with a comparison of the Sequoias. *Amer. Jour. Bot.* 26:248-257.

Butts, D. and J. T. Buchholz. 1940. Cotyledon number in conifers. *Trans. Illinois Acad. Sci.* 33:58-62.

Campbell, D. H. 1940. *The Evolution of the Land Plants.* Stanford University Press, Stanford, California.

Chamberlain, C. J. 1935. *Gymnosperms. Structure and Evolution.* University of Chicago Press, Chicago.

Chaney, R. W. 1950. A revision of fossil *Sequoia* and *Taxodium* in western North America based on the recent discovery of *Metasequoia.* *Trans. Amer. Phil. Soc.* 40:172-262.

Coulter, J. M. and C. J. Chamberlain. 1917. *Morphology of Gymnosperms.* University of Chicago Press, Chicago.

Doak, C. C. 1935. Evolution of foliar types, dwarf shoots, and cone scales in *Pinus*. *Illinois Biol. Monographs* 13:1-106.

Erspamer, J. L. 1952. Ontogeny and morphology of the microsporangia in certain genera of the Coniferales. Ph.D. Diss., Univ. Calif., Berkeley.

Esau, K. 1953. *Plant Anatomy.* Wiley, New York.

Ferguson, M. C. 1904. Contributions to the knowledge of the life history of *Pinus* with special reference to sporogenesis, the development of the gametophytes and fertilization. *Proc. Wash. Acad. of Sci.* 6:1-202.

Florin, R. 1931. Untersuchungen zur Stammesgeschichte der Coniferales und Cordaitales. *Svenska Vetensk. Akad. Handl.* Ser. 5. 10:1-588.

———. 1938-1945. Die Koniferen des Oberkarbons und des unteren Perms. *Paleontographica* 85B:366-654.

———. 1950. Upper Carboniferous and Lower Permian Conifers. *Bot. Rev.* 16:258-282.

———. 1951. Evolution in Cordaites and Conifers. *Acta Horti Bergiana* 15:285-388.

Griffith, M. M. 1951. A study of the shoot apex and leaf histogenesis in certain species of *Araucaria*. Ph.D. Diss., Univ. Calif., Berkeley.

———. 1957. Foliar ontogeny in *Podocarpus macrophyllus*, with special reference to transfusion tissue. *Amer. Jour. Bot.* 44:705-715.

Haupt, A. W. 1941. Oögenesis and fertilization in *Pinus Lambertiana* and *P. monophylla*. *Bot. Gaz.* 102: 482-498.

———. 1953. *Plant Morphology*. McGraw-Hill, New York.

Jeffrey, E. C. 1917. *The Anatomy of Woody Plants*. University of Chicago Press, Chicago.

Johansen, D. A. 1950. *Plant Embryology*. Chronica Botanica Co., Waltham, Mass.

Laubenfels, D. J. de. 1953. The external morphology of coniferous leaves. *Phytomorphology* 3:1-20.

Molisch, H. 1938. *The Longevity of Plants*. Eng. Trans. by E. H. Fulling, New York.

Pilger, R. 1926. Coniferae. In: Engler and Prantl's "Die natürlichen Pflanzenfamilien. Ed. 2. 13:164-166.

Sacher, J. A. 1953. Structure and histogenesis of the buds of *Pinus lambertiana*. Ph.D. Diss., Univ. Calif., Berkeley.

———. 1954. Structure and seasonal activity of the shoot apices of *Pinus*

lambertiana and *Pinus ponderosa*. *Amer. Jour. Bot.* 41:749-759.

———. 1955a. Cataphyll ontogeny in *Pinus lambertiana*. *Amer. Jour. Bot.* 42:82-91.

———. 1955b. Dwarf shoot ontogeny in *Pinus lambertiana*. *Amer. Jour. Bot.* 42:748-792.

Schopf, J. M. 1943. The embryology of *Larix*. *Illinois Biol. Monographs* 19: 1-97.

Spurr, A. R. 1949. Histogenesis and organization of the embryo in *Pinus strobus*. *Amer. Jour. Bot.* 36:629-641.

Sterling, C. 1948. Proembryo and early embryogeny in *Taxus cuspidata*. *Bull. Torrey Bot. Club* 75:469-485.

———. 1949. Some features in the morphology of *Metasequoia*. *Amer. Jour. Bot.* 36:461-471.

Worsdell, W. C. 1897. On "transfusion tissue": its origin and function in the leaves of gymnospermous plants. *Trans. Linn. Soc. London. Bot.* Ser. II. 5:301-319.

———. 1900. The structure of the female "flower" in Coniferae. *Ann. Bot.* 14:39-82.

Chapter

17 THE GNETALES

This chapter presents a brief discussion of a small group of
gymnosperm-like plants that seems extremely isolated, in most
respects, from the cycads, *Ginkgo*, and the Coniferales. This
group comprises three genera: *Ephedra*, *Welwitschia*, and *Gnetum*. In
the past these genera were considered to be the only living members of
the family Gnetaceae and the order Gnetales. But as knowledge of the
many remarkable differences in structure and reproduction between the
genera increased, the tendency was to assign each genus to a separate
family. At present, as Eames (1952) has indicated, there seems excellent reason to split the Gnetales into three orders, namely, Ephedrales,
Welwitschiales, and Gnetales. In this classification each order would
comprise a single family and a single genus. In this book the three
genera are included in the single order Gnetales purely for convenience
in discussion and with the recognition of the probable artificiality of
such a classification. Eames (1952), in particular, has shown the numerous morphological differences between *Ephedra* on the one hand, and
Gnetum and *Welwitschia* on the other.

Throughout much of the voluminous literature on the Gnetales a
repeated effort has been made to demonstrate that these plants represent
a connecting link between the gymnosperms and angiosperms. Among
the assumed angiospermic features which are usually cited are (1) the
"compound" nature of *both* the microsporangiate and megasporangiate
strobili which have been likened to the inflorescences of angiosperms,
and (2) the presence of vessels in the xylem. It will not be possible in
this book to review the various complex theories proposed to explain the
relation of the angiosperms to gnetalean plants. Students interested in
these theories should consult Arber and Parkin (1908), in addition to
Pearson's (1929) monograph on the Gnetales and the extensive literature cited therein and in Chamberlain (1935). At this point it is sufficient to emphasize that despite their stimulating effect on morphological

417

research, such theories are very largely conjectural. On the contrary, the totality of evidence from comparative morphology and geographical distribution seems to indicate that the living members of the Gnetales are specialized and are, at most, remotely interrelated end points of gymnosperm evolution. The relation of the three genera to any known angiosperms is highly improbable, and their affinities with modern gymnospermous types seem almost equally obscure.

Because of the considerable botanical interest of the Gnetales, a brief description of their habit, geographical distribution, and general organography and anatomy will be given first. This will be followed by a concise description of the main steps in the life cycle of *Ephedra*. This genus was selected because it is quite conifer-like in many aspects of its morphology and because its gametophytes and embryogeny are now fairly well understood. Furthermore, *Ephedra* is represented by several species in the United States and thus is available for laboratory study. The reproductive cycles of *Gnetum* and *Welwitschia*, however, are extremely complex, and many details of their gametophytes and embryos are either unknown or subject to varied interpretations. At the close of the chapter an effort will be made to point out certain of the more important differences in reproduction between these genera and *Ephedra*.

Habit and Distribution

The three genera of the Gnetales are strikingly unlike in their general habit and geographical distribution. *Ephedra*, a genus of about 35 species, is usually a profusely branched shrub, although the South American *E. triandra* becomes tree-like and a few species are climbers. The young stems and twigs are green, and the leaves are small, scale-like, and inconspicuous (Fig. 17-1, B). *Ephedra* occurs in both the Western and Eastern Hemispheres, and most of the species inhabit arid or desert areas. In North America the six known species are found in the deserts or steppes of California, Nevada, Arizona, Utah, New Mexico, and northern and central Mexico.

Gnetum, in marked contrast, inhabits moist tropical forests in parts of Asia, Africa, northern South America, and certain islands between Asia and Australia. Most of the 30 or so described species of *Gnetum*

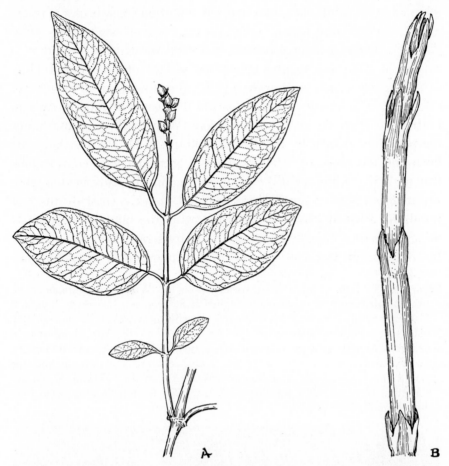

Figure 17-1 **A,** *Gnetum indicum.* Terminal portion of shoot showing seeds
and three pairs of simple leaves with pinnate-reticulate venation (X1); **B,**
Ephedra sp. Tip of a vegetative shoot to illustrate the whorled arrangement of
the reduced scale-like leaves (X4). [Drawn by Mrs. Emily E. Reid.]

are lianas which climb to the tops of tall trees; a few species, such as
G. *gnemon,* are arborescent. One of the many remarkable and distinctive
features of *Gnetum* is the leaf, which closely simulates the simple reticu-
lately veined type of leaf common in the dicotyledons (Fig. 17-1, A).

The most bizarre and geographically restricted of all gnetalean plants
is the African genus *Welwitschia,* which consists of a single species, W.
mirabilis. The specific name is very appropriate because the adult sporophyte is unlike that of any known plant on the earth! Most of the stem

is buried in the sandy soil, and the exposed portion consists of a massive, woody, concave disc which bears two huge strap-shaped leaves (Fig. 17-2, B). These structures become split and frayed, and extend in a twisted or contorted manner along the surface of the ground (Fig. 17-2, B). According to Pearson (1929) the leaves of old plants are often six feet in length. *Welwitschia* was discovered in 1860 in Angola, Portuguese West Africa, by Dr. Frederic Welwitsch, in whose honor the plant was named by the British botanist, J. D. Hooker. Since its discovery, the range of *Welwitschia* has been extended considerably. Rodin (1953a), discovered the plant growing in the Kaokoveld, a semi-desert region about a hundred miles inland from the coast. In most of the desert areas in which *Welwitschia* exists the rainfall is extremely meagre; the exceptionally long tap root characteristic of old plants may be an important factor in survival in such inhospitable areas. Possibly,

Figure 17-2 Habit and general organography of *Welwitschia mirabilis*. **A,** plant about twenty years old photographed at Stellenbosch University Botanical Gardens, South Africa. The specimen is growing in a section of pipe to provide space for development of the tap root. Note the two, long twisted foliage leaves; **B,** a large microsporangiate plant photographed at Brandberg, S. W. Africa, showing the abundant branched clusters of strobili and the frayed and longitudinally split foliage leaves. [A from R. J. Rodin, Ph.D. dissertation, University of California, Berkeley, 1951; B, from Rodin, *Amer. Jour. Bot.* 40:280, 1953.]

as suggested by Rodin, prior to the development of a tap root young plants may utilize the condensed moisture of fog and dew.

Vegetative Organography and Anatomy

In this section our discussion will be limited to only a few of the unique and well-investigated aspects of structure and development of the sporophyte in the Gnetales. Despite the voluminous literature, which is reviewed in detail by Pearson (1929) and Chamberlain (1935), it is evident that much remains to be done before an adequate comparative treatment of the sporophytes of gnetalean plants as a whole can be accomplished. *Gnetum* and particularly *Welwitschia* are extremely complex anatomically and require further intensive ontogenetic study.

The Leaf

Despite the marked differences in size and form of the leaves in the Gnetales, the phyllotaxis is prevailingly decussate except that in certain species of *Ephedra* the leaves develop in whorls of three at each node. The reduced leaves of *Ephedra* are commonly united to form a basal sheath, and the shoot superficially resembles a branch of *Equisetum* (Fig. 17-1, B). The organography of the shoot of *Welwitschia* presents a situation which apparently is without parallel among vascular plants. Except for a pair of cotyledons, which are short-lived, the permanent photosynthetic system is represented by a *single pair* of evergreen leaves which persist throughout the entire life of the plant (Fig. 17-2, A). Although the terminal portions of these leaves become cracked and dead, their bases remain continuously meristematic, and new tissue (including additional vascular bundles) is formed throughout the life of each leaf (Rodin, 1958a, 1958b). Ontogenetic study of the seedling of *Welwitschia* has revealed that shortly after the initiation of the pair of foliage-leaf primordia, further growth of the shoot apex is completely suppressed (Rodin, 1953b). Thus, in contrast with all other vascular plants, the shoot of *Welwitschia* exhibits a closed rather than an open system of growth, and most of its post-seedling development centers on (1) an increase in size of the underground stem, and further growth of the tap and lateral roots; (2) the slow basal elongation of the two foliage leaves, and (3) the production of strobili (Fig. 17-2, B). The latter originate from the inner ridge of tissue lying above the groove within which the leaf bases are inserted.

Several aspects of leaf histology are worthy of mention at this point. As in many gymnosperms the leaf trace in the Gnetales (at least in *Ephedra* and *Welwitschia*) is double, but in each of the three genera the venation of the lamina is different. In *Ephedra*, according to Marsden and Steeves (1955) the two traces are related to a single gap in the eustele and remain distinct and unconnected within the leaf. *Gnetum*, in contrast, develops a broadly elliptical lamina with pinnate-reticulate venation (Fig. 17-1, A). The large linear leaves of *Welwitschia* are traversed by a series of prominent longitudinal veins interconnected by pairs of oblique-lateral veins; the latter may be joined in various ways to form irregular areoles or meshes, or their fused, upwardly directed tips may end blindly in the mesophyll. This peculiar venation pattern also occurs in the blades of the cotyledons and, as compared with the venation of other gymnospermous leaves, seems unique in type (Rodin, 1951, 1953b).

In contrast with the uniformly haplocheilic stomata characteristic of the cycads, *Ginkgo*, and the conifers, both of the main types of stomatal apparati recognized by Florin (1931), as discussed in Chapter 16, are represented in the Gnetales. *Ephedra* has the primitive haplochelic type, whereas *Welwitschia* and *Gnetum* are alike in developing the syndetocheilic type (see Fig. 16-7). This situation is regarded by Eames (1952) as additional evidence of the phylogenetic isolation of *Ephedra* from other gnetalean forms.

The Shoot Apex

During the past fifteen years numerous studies have been made on the structure and growth of the shoot apex in gymnosperms. [See the review by Johnson (1951).] These investigations have been stimulated by the need for a full knowledge of the apical meristem and of the ways in which foliar organs and tissues are derived from it, and by the idea that the comparative study of shoot apices in gymnosperms might provide data of phylogenetic importance. Although there are still many gaps in our knowledge, one significant phylogenetic trend seems evident in the shoot apex of gymnosperms: the elimination of periclinal divisions in *all* the surface cells of the apex and the consequent development of a discrete superficial cell layer or tunica. From this standpoint the apices of the cycads, *Ginkgo*, and many members of the Pinaceae are relatively primitive because of the great frequency of surface periclinal divisions. In the Taxodiaceae and Cupressaceae periclinal divisions are largely restricted to the uppermost initial cells of the apex, and below them a well-defined protoderm is maintained. Finally, a very marked approach to the angiosperm type of shoot apex is exhibited by *Araucaria*. In a comparative study of this genus, Griffith (1952) found that, depending on the species, one or several discrete tunica layers are sharply defined in the shoot apex.

In the light of these facts it is interesting—and possibly phylogenetically significant—that the shoot apices of several species of *Ephedra* and of a species of *Gnetum* likewise possess a well-demarcated tunica layer (Fig. 17-3). This has been observed in *E. altissima* by Gifford (1943), in *E. fragilis var. campylopoda* by Seeliger (1954), and in *G. gnemon* by Johnson (1950). In *Welwitschia*, however, the continuity of the surface

Figure 17-3 Median longisection of the shoot apex of *Ephedra altissima*. Note the single, clearly defined tunica layer.

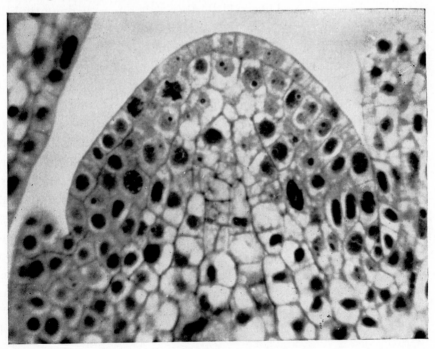

layer of the shoot apex is interrupted by the periclinal division of the apical initials, recalling the situation in some of the conifers (Rodin, 1953b). From these observations it may be concluded that the shoot apices of *Ephedra* and *Gnetum* are relatively advanced in structure and, *in an anatomical sense*, have attained an "angiosperm-like" condition. This may, however, represent the result of parallel evolution of similar structures, and it is by no means a proof of a direct phylogenetic relationship between the Gnetales and the angiosperms.

Vessels

As stated in the beginning of this chapter, the occurrence of vessels in the Gnetales distinguishes them from other living gymnosperms and has often been used as an argument for their presumed evolutionary relationship to the angiosperms. But it has now been clearly established that the *method* of origin of the perforations in the vessel members of the Gnetales differs from that of all other vascular plants including the angiosperms. In the angiosperms, as well as in certain species of *Pteridium* and *Selaginella*, the initial step in vessel evolution was the loss of the membranes from the *transversely elongated* bordered pits situated at each sloping end of a tracheid-like cell. Further elaboration of these slit-like perforations led to the development of vessel members with well-defined scalariform perforation plates. The most advanced vessel members in angiosperms possess large circular or oval simple perforations which originated by the elimination (phylogenetically and ontogenetically) of the bars between the slit-like openings. In contrast, as Thompson (1918) has shown, the initial step in vessel evolution in the Gnetales began with the loss of membranes from a series of *circular* bordered pits located near the ends of long tracheid-like cells. In *Ephedra*, transitional conditions between intact bordered pits and bordered foraminate perforations occur, i.e., there are clear transition forms between typical tracheids and vessel members (Fig. 17-4). The vessel members of *Gnetum* commonly possess large circular or elliptical simple perforations and thus markedly resemble the specialized vessel members of many angiosperms. Thompson (1918) found, however, that the *Gnetum* type of vessel perforation is the result of the further enlargement of a series of circular perforations and the elimination of the portions of the end wall between them.

Thus in the initial steps of their origin as well as in their subsequent

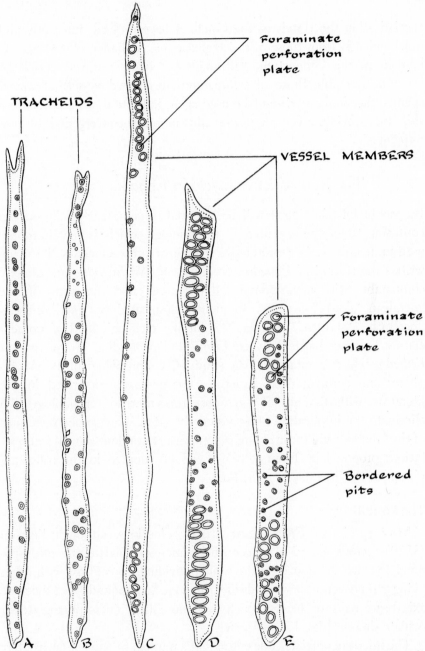

TRACHEIDS

Foraminate
perforation
plate

VESSEL MEMBERS

Foraminate
perforation
plate

Bordered
pits

A   B   C   D   E

Figure 17-4 Tracheary elements from the secondary xylem of *Ephedra cali-fornica.* **A-B,** tracheids with numerous circular bordered pits; **C-E,** vessel members with foraminate perforation plates on end walls. [From *Plant Anatomy* by K. Esau. N. Y.: John Wiley and Sons, Inc., 1953.]

specialization the vessels of the Gnetales have evolved differently and independently from those in the angiosperms. As Bailey (1953) has remarked in this connection, "although the highly evolved vessels of *Gnetum* resemble those of comparably specialized vessels of angiosperms, the similarity cannot be used as an indication of close relationship, but provides a very significant illustration of convergent evolution in plants."

The Reproductive Cycle in Ephedra

By way of introduction it will be essential to comment briefly on the confusing "angiosperm-centered" terminology which is so commonly used in describing the reproductive structures in the Gnetales. To many writers the strobili of *Ephedra, Gnetum,* and *Welwitschia* are directly comparable with angiospermic inflorescences, and the parts of the gnetalean "flower" are very frequently designated by such terms as "perianth," "stamen," "anther," "column," etc. This kind of nomenclature becomes particularly confusing and misleading in the case of *Ephedra,* which is notable for the conifer-like morphology of its gametophytes and embryo; these structures are invariably described in the literature with the aid of "gymnosperm-centered" terminology! To eliminate the implication of homology between sporogenous structures of the Gnetales and those of angiosperms, the terms and general interpretations proposed by Eames (1952) will be adopted in the following résumé of the life cycle of *Ephedra.*

The Strobili

Most species of *Ephedra* are strictly dioecious, although Pearson (1929) records several instances where microsporangiate and megasporangiate cones developed on the same individual. In contrast with other living gymnosperms, both kinds of strobili are "compound," i.e., the cone axis bears pairs of bracts which subtend either microsporangiate or ovulate shoots (Figs. 17-5; 17-6, A).

The microsporangiate cone consists of a number of pairs of decussately arranged bracts, the lowest pairs of which are sterile while usually each of the remainder develops a microsporangiate shoot in its axil. This shoot consists of a pair of fused bracteoles (the so-called perianth) and

Figure 17-5 *Ephedra chilensis.* Microsporangiate (left) and megasporangiate (right) strobili. Note protrusion of tubular inner integument of the ovules from the axils of the bracts of the megasporangiate strobili.

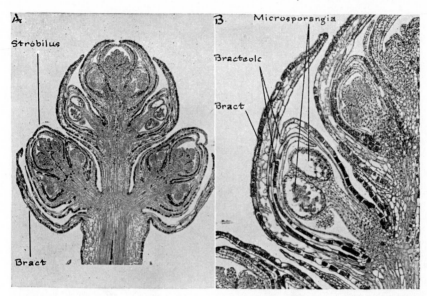

Figure 17-6 Structure of microsporangiate strobili in *Ephedra chilensis.* **A,** longisection of tip of reproductive shoot (each of the microsporangiate strobili is situated in the axil of a bract); **B,** enlargement of portion of **A** showing a microsporangiate shoot which consists of an axis ("column") with apical microsporangia enclosed by a pair of fused bracteoles.

a short axis terminating in from one to eight microsporangia, the number varying with the species (Fig. 17-6, B). According to Eames (1952) the axis or column of the microsporangiate shoot is the result of the phylogenetic fusion of a pair of microsporophylls; in certain species which he regards as primitive the two microsporophylls are free, and each bears four terminal microsporangia.

The megasporangiate cone of *Ephedra* also consists of an axis with decussately arranged bracts. However, most of these appendages are sterile, and the cones of many species contain only two ovules, one in the axil of each of the upper bracts (Fig. 17-7, A). In some species the cones are uniovulate; this is commonly the result of the abortion of one ovule and the crowding of the other into a false terminal position.

The ovules of *Ephedra, Gnetum,* and *Welwitschia* are usually regarded as being unique among gymnosperms because of the presence of two integuments. Particularly notable is the marked elongation of the inner integument as a tube which extends freely out of the cone at the time of pollination (Figs. 17-5; 17-7, B). The evidence from ontogeny

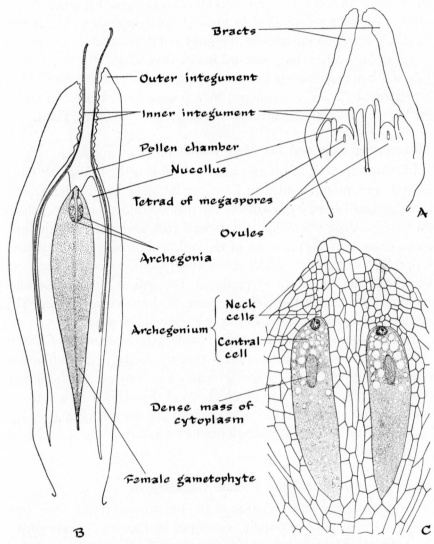

Figure 17-7 The ovule and mature female gametophyte of *Ephedra foliata*. **A,** longisection of megasporangiate strobilus showing two young ovules, each with a linear tetrad of megaspores; **B,** median longisection of an ovule showing the female gametophyte, the conspicuous pollen chamber, and elongated inner integument; **C,** details of micropylar region of female gametophyte showing structure of archegonia. [From Maheshwari, *Proc. Ind. Acad. Sci.* 1:586, 1935.]

and vascular anatomy, however, indicates that the so-called outer integument in *Ephedra* is equivalent to a pair of fused appendages and is not, strictly speaking, an integument. This fact and the nature of the vascular supply of the ovulate shoot have led Eames to conclude that the ovule of *Ephedra* is not cauline—in his view it terminates a greatly reduced basal megasporophyll, and is enveloped by a pair of fused bracteoles which are homologous with the bracteoles of the microsporangiate shoot.

Microsporogenesis and the Male Gametophyte

Microsporogenesis has been carefully studied in *E. trifurca* by Land (1904), and, more recently, in *E. foliata* by Maheshwari (1935). The sporangial initials are hypodermal, as in many conifers, and by periclinal divisions produce externally primary wall cells, and internally the first sporogenous cells. As the result of the periclinal division of the primary wall cells, a single layer of wall cells—which soon become flattened and stretched—and a tapetum are produced. The cells of the latter become multinucleate during the differentiation of the microsporocytes. The mature microspore has a thick exine and is devoid of wings.

The ontogeny of the endosporic male gametophyte of *Ephedra* closely resembles that typical of many conifers. As the result of four successive nuclear divisions, a young male gametophyte consists of two prothallial cells (the second of which is not demarcated by a wall), a tube nucleus, a stalk cell nucleus and a body cell nucleus (Fig. 17-8, F). In this five-nucleate stage of development the gametophyte is shed from the microsporangium.

Megasporogenesis and the Female Gametophyte

Just prior to the differentiation of the megasporocyte the ovule consists of a well-developed nucellus enveloped by the two "integuments." According to Maheshwari's (1935) detailed investigation the so-called archesporial cell is hypodermal in position in the nucellus. Several parietal (i.e., wall) cells are produced by the repeated periclinal division of the archesporial cell, and similar divisions occur in the overlying epidermal cells of the nucellus (see also Seeliger, 1954). As a result, the megasporocyte is ultimately situated deep within the tissue of the nucellus (Fig. 17-9, A). The usual meiotic divisions yield a linear tetrad of megaspores, although in several instances Maheshwari observed a row

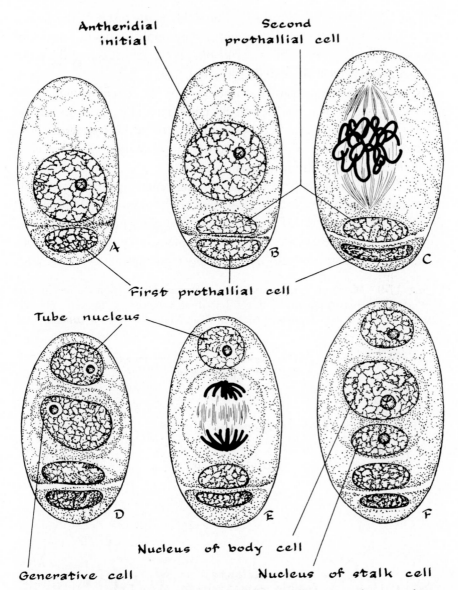

Figure 17-8 Development of male gametophyte of *Ephedra trifurca*. **A,** formation of first prothallial cell; **B,** gametophyte with two prothallial cells; **C-D,**
formation of tube and generative cells; **E-F,** division of nucleus of generative
cell and formation of nuclei of stalk and body cells. [Redrawn from Land, *Bot.
Gaz.* 38:1, 1904.]

of three cells (Fig. 17-9, B, C). This probably is the result of the failure of the upper dyad cell to divide, as not uncommonly occurs in *Pinus* (see Chapter 16, p. 402). In both cases in *Ephedra* the lowest cell in the series enlarges and produces the female gametophyte.

As in other gymnosperms, the initiation of the female gametophyte involves a process of active free nuclear divisions (Fig. 17-9, D). Land (1904) found about 256 free nuclei in *E. trifurca* before walls were formed, and Maheshwari (1935) counted approximately 500 nuclei at the comparable stage in ontogeny in *E. foliata.*

The formation of walls in the developing female gametophyte prob-ably occurs as in other gymnosperms, but neither Land nor Maheshwari describes the details of this process. Soon after the gametophyte has be-come cellular it differentiates into two well-defined regions: a lower zone of compact food-storing cells, and an upper micropylar region of more

Figure 17-9   Megasporogenesis and the young female gametophyte of *Ephedra foliata*. **A-C,** development of linear tetrad of megaspores; **D,** four nucleate stages of female gametophyte. [Redrawn from Maheshwari, *Proc. Indian Acad. Sci.* 1:586, 1935.]

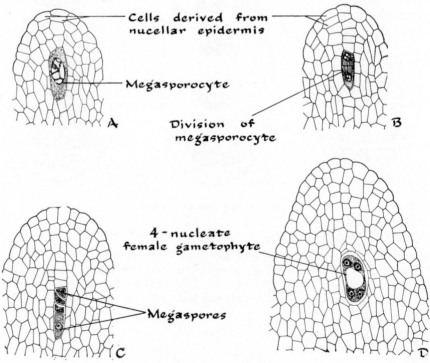

delicate tissue, certain surface cells of which give rise to the archegonia. These vary somewhat in number, according to the species—three are most commonly produced in *E. foliata,* whereas two or occasionally only one are characteristic of *E. trifurca.*

As in *Pinus,* the archegonium of *Ephedra* arises from a superficial cell at the micropylar end of the gametophyte. This initial divides periclinally into an outer primary neck cell and an inner central cell. The most distinctive feature of archegonial development in *Ephedra* is the many-celled neck which arises from the repeated periclinal and anticlinal division of the primary neck cell. At first the divisions are so regular that the neck cells are arranged in tiers; subsequent anticlinal divisions finally result in a less orderly arrangement, the cells merging with the adjacent elements of the gametophyte (Fig. 17-7, C). The mature neck consists of about 30-40 cells, and Land (1904) remarks: "of all gymnosperms *Ephedra* has the longest-necked archegonium." The enlargement of the central cell is soon followed by a nuclear division which forms the ventral canal cell nucleus and the egg nucleus. Sometimes the ventral canal cell nucleus appears to degenerate soon after its formation, but it may remain intact near the upper part of the archegonium. As the central cell enlarges, the adjacent cells of the gametophyte form an archegonial jacket consisting of one or two layers of cells.

Pollination and Fertilization

During the early phases of archegonial development the nucellar tissue lying directly above the female gametophyte becomes disorganized and then obliterated, producing a very conspicuous pollen chamber (Fig. 17-7, B). A unique feature of *Ephedra* is the fact that the upper portion of the gametophyte is freely exposed at the bottom of this pollen chamber. As a consequence, the young endosporic male gametophyte, conveyed by the wind to the tip of the exserted integument, is drawn—or falls—into the pollen chamber and thus lies directly in contact with the exposed female gametophyte.

According to Land (1907) the interval between pollination and fertilization in *Ephedra trifurca* may be as short as ten hours, a remarkable contrast with the extended interval typical of *Pinus* and many other conifers. Shortly before the emergence of the pollen tube the exine of the microspore is shed, and the body cell divides forming two sperm nuclei. At this time, or earlier, both of the prothallial cells degenerate.

The pollen tube pushes its way between the neck cells of the archegonium, and when the tip ruptures, the tube nucleus, stalk-cell nucleus, and two sperm nuclei are discharged into the cytoplasm of the egg.

Although one of the sperm nuclei unites in the expected manner with the egg nucleus, the behavior of the other sperm nucleus is extraordinary. According to Khan's (1943) observations on *E. foliata* the second male nucleus may fuse with the ventral canal cell nucleus near the upper part of the archegonium. Although an embryo does not result from this fusion, Khan observed in one case two nuclei which he considered the results of the division of the fertilized ventral canal cell nucleus. The union of *both* sperms in *Ephedra* with nuclei in the archegonium recalls the process of double fertilization so characteristic of most angiosperms (see Chapter 19). But Khan concludes that "the type of 'double fertilization' seen in *Ephedra* may have no phylogenetic significance at all and may simply be the natural outcome of a tendency towards fusion between any two nuclei of opposite sexual potencies that happen to lie free in a common chamber."

Embryogeny

In both *E. trifurca* and *E. foliata* a process of free nuclear division occurs, beginning with the division of the fertilized egg nucleus. Each of the eight diploid nuclei that are produced first becomes surrounded by a densely staining sheath of cytoplasm; later each cell differentiates an external wall (Fig. 17-10, A). Since each of these cells may independently develop into an embryo, *Ephedra* exhibits a distinctive and precocious type of cleavage polyembryony. In a functional sense these free proembryonal cells in *Ephedra* are the equivalents of the eight walled-cells of the tiered proembryo of *Pinus* (see Fig. 16-18, E). From an ontogenetic standpoint, polembryony in *Ephedra* has thus been pushed back to the free nuclear stage in embryogeny. According to Land it is usually the lower proembryonal cells that successfully develop into embryos. Khan observed in one of his preparations six embryos in different stages of development (Fig. 17-10, B).

In *E. foliata* the proembryonal cell first produces a tubular projection, termed the suspensor tube, into the tip of which the nucleus descends and then divides; the two nuclei become separated by a transverse wall,

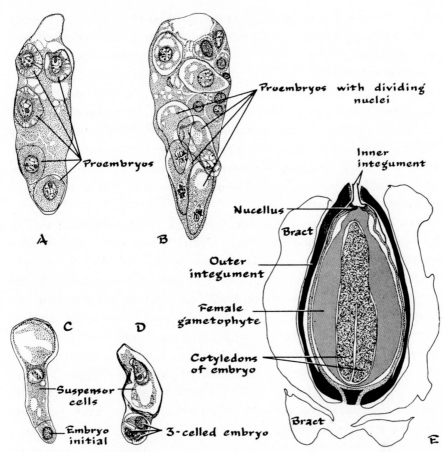

Figure 17-10 Embryogeny and seed structure in *Ephedra foliata*. **A,** longisection of egg cell showing five proembryos; **B,** reconstruction from several sections showing six proembryos in various stages of development (note mitoses and origin of suspensor tubes in the four lower proembryos); **C,** embryo consisting of an enlarged suspensor cell and an embryo initial; **D,** three-celled embryo resulting from divisions of embryo initial; **E,** longisection of mature seed. [A-E redrawn from Khan, *Proc. Nat. Acad. Sci. India* 13:357, 1943.]

and the embryo then consists of a terminal embryo initial and the elongating suspensor cell (Fig. 17-10, C). A similar condition is characteristic of *E. trifurca* except that the nucleus of the proembryonal cell divides before the suspensor tube is initiated, and there is a long interval between this nuclear division and the production of a transverse wall. A periclinal division of the embryo initial, followed by the longitudinal division of the lower of the two cells, yields three cells from which, on further division, the embryo proper originates (Fig. 17-10, D). A multi-cellular secondary suspensor differentiates next to the suspensor cell, and the lower end of the embryo produces two cotyledons and the shoot apex. In connection with the discussion on the shoot apex of the Gnetales given earlier in the chapter (p. 423), it is interesting to note that a well-defined tunica layer originates in the embryo even before the cotyledons develop. Of the several embryos which competitively develop within a single ovule, only one reaches a fully developed stage in the seed. Khan observed in one ovule 18-19 separate developing embryos. He interpreted this large number as the result of a combination of simple and cleavage polyembryony.

The general structure of a ripe seed of *E. foliata* is shown in Fig. 17-10, E. The conspicuous embryo, with its two large cotyledons, is embedded within the tissue of the female gametophyte, and the remains of the nucellus are evident as a disorganized sheath of cells. At the micropylar end of the seed the "true" integument, consisting of two layers of cells, has persisted, and the entire seed is externally enclosed within the so-called outer integument, the cells of which have thick walls. As the seed matures in *E. foliata* the subtending adjacent bracts of the strobilus become thick and fleshy, forming an additional investment. According to Land's (1907) observations on *E. trifurca* there appears to be no resting period for the seed, which may even germinate within the parent strobilus.

Morphological Contrasts between Ephedra, Gnetum, and Welwitschia

As many writers have pointed out, the sporophytes of the three genera of the Gnetales have certain morphological features in common: compound microsporangiate and megasporangiate strobili, vessels in the secondary xylem, extended micropylar tubes of the integuments of the ovules, opposite or whorled leaf arrangement, and embryos with two cotyledons. Whether these characteristics indicate close phyletic relationship between the genera is difficult to prove, since some of them (e.g., decussate phyllotaxis and dicotyledonous embryos) are shared by other gymnosperms and others (e.g., secondary xylem vessels) may be the result of parallel evolution. Pearson (1929) concluded that "the relationships of the three genera of the Gnetales are perhaps as obscure now as they have been at any time within the last decade," and Eames (1952) has emphasized in detail the wide morphological divergence between *Ephedra* and the other two genera.

When one attempts to compare the gametophytes and embryogeny, the differences between the genera are striking and very difficult to interpret. The closest agreement is probably shown by the male gametophyte. As we have already indicated, this structure is conifer-like in *Ephedra*, consisting of two ephemeral prothallial cells, a stalk cell, a tube nucleus, and two male gametes (Fig. 17-8, F). The male gametophytes of *Welwitschia* and *Gnetum* are comparable although more reduced in structure. In both a prothallial nucleus has been observed, but the formation of the stalk cell is suppressed and the generative nucleus directly produces the two male gametes.

The differences between the development and structure of the female gametophyte in the three genera are, however, very remarkable. *Ephedra* has a typical gymnospermous type of gametophyte with clearly demarcated archegonia (Fig. 17-7, B, C). Definable archegonia are absent in the other two genera, and the female gametophyte, particularly that of *Gnetum*, has been interpreted as angiospermic in organization. In *Welwitschia* numerous superficial cells at the micropylar end of the gametophyte become bi- or multinucleate, and have been regarded as multinucleate eggs or the equivalents of archegonial initials (Battaglia, 1951). Each of these multinucleate cells develops a tube into which the "female nuclei" migrate, and this tube grows *upward* into the nucellar tissue above the female gametophyte. These curious, tubular, gamete-containing structures in *Welwitschia* are apparently without parallel in living seed plants—Pearson (1929) has termed them "embryo-sac tubes." The growth of an embryo-sac tube continues, and ultimately its tip may meet the tip of a *downward* developing pollen tube. The walls of the two tubes break at the point of contact, and one of the nuclei of the embryo-sac tube unites, *within the pollen tube itself*, either with a sperm nucleus or with the still undivided generative nucleus. Thus, unlike any other known seed plant, the process of fertilization occurs in the pollen tube rather than in an archegonium or an embryo sac! Following fertilization, the other nuclei in the embryo-sac tube seem to degenerate in most cases.

In *Gnetum* the details regarding the formation of female gametes and the process of fertilization are poorly understood, and the meagre data have been variously interpreted. Apparently one or more of the free nuclei at the micropylar end of the female gametophyte become differentiated as egg cells. Each of these gametes may be fertilized by the sperm nucleus of a pollen tube. Because of the origin of the egg cells from free nuclei, *Gnetum* has been considered by some morphologists to approximate the condition typical of the sexual reproduction in the angiosperms. There a single micropylar cell of the embryo sac functions directly as an egg cell.

According to some writers a further resemblance to angiosperms is illustrated by the remarkable free nuclear divisions and fusions that occur in the lower part of the female gametophytes of *Gnetum* and *Welwitschia*. The tissue that results from such nuclear activity has been regarded as being equivalent to the endosperm tissue in angiosperm seeds although its origin is not dependent on a male gamete participating in the fusion.

With reference to embryogeny, all three genera present remarkable differences. In *Ephedra* separate diploid proembryonal cells give rise to a series of independently growing embryos (Fig. 17-10, A, B). The embryogeny of *Gnetum* still awaits intensive study, but in certain species the zygote gives rise to filamentous, suspensor-like tubes, and the cells produced at their tips develop into embryos (Johansen, 1950). *Welwitschia* also exhibits polyembryony, and each of the numerous zygotes may develop into a filamentous proembryo at the tip of which a multicellular embryo is formed.

Summary and Conclusions

This chapter has been devoted to a brief résumé of the important features of organography, anatomy, and reproduction in three very remarkable genera of gymnosperm-like plants—*Ephedra*, *Welwitschia*, and *Gnetum*. The morphological differences between these genera are so extensive and peculiar that each may be appropriately regarded as a member of a distinct family and order. Purely for convenience, they are grouped in this chapter under the order Gnetales.

Following a brief description of the habit and geographical distribution of the Gnetales, certain important features of the sporophyte generation have been briefly discussed. Although the phyllotaxis is prevailingly decussate, the leaves of the three genera differ widely in size, form, and venation. In *Ephedra* the leaves are scale-like, basally fused to form a sheath, and are traversed by two unbranched veins. The leaves of *Welwitschia* are long and strap-shaped, and the numerous longitudinal veins are interconnected by anastomosing veinlets which form irregular areoles or meshes. *Gnetum* is particularly unusual among gymnosperms because of the pinnate-reticulate venation of its broad, angiosperm-like leaf blades. With reference to stomata, those of *Ephedra* are *haplochelic*, as in most gymnosperms, whereas the *syndetochelic* condition occurs in both *Gnetum* and *Welwitschia*.

Particular attention has been given to the structure of the shoot apices in *Ephedra* and *Gnetum* which agree in the presence of a well-defined tunica layer. In the light of recent investigations on the shoot apices of other gymnosperms, the situation in *Ephedra* and *Gnetum* is considered advanced, in an anatomical sense. *Welwitschia* is unique among vascular plants because its shoot apex, after initiating a single pair of foliage-leaf primordia, ceases all further activity. The long-lived foliage leaves of *Welwitschia* grow by means of a perennial basal meristem.

Although the xylem of the Gnetales is different from that of other gymnosperms, due to the presence of vessels, the perforations of the vessel members originated by the loss of the membranes of circular bordered pits. Since vessel perforations in the angiosperms initially developed from the disappearance of the membranes of transversely elongate pits (scalariform pitting), the evolution of vessels in angiosperms and the Gnetales illustrates parallel evolution and is no evidence of phyletic relationship between the two groups of plants.

In all members of the Gnetales both the microsporangiate and megasporangiate strobili are "compound." In *Ephedra*, which we have described in detail, the microsporangiate shoots arise singly in the axils of bracts; each fertile shoot consists of a pair of connate bracteoles enclosing an axis which terminates in one to eight microsporangia. The fertile ovulate shoot consists of a greatly reduced axis or sporophyll, a husk-like envelope (the so-called outer integument), and usually a single ovule. In all gnetalean plants, the single true integument of the ovule becomes elongated as a tube.

Ephedra was selected as the basis for a discussion of the reproductive cycle in the Gnetales because sporogenesis and the development of the gametophytes follow rather closely the pattern typical of many gymnosperms, particularly the conifers. Just prior to pollination and fertilization a conspicuous, deep pollen chamber develops in the upper end of the nucellus; the top of the female gametophyte is exposed at the base of the chamber, and the endosporic male gametophytes ultimately rest in the vicinity of or on the necks of the archegonia. Following the union of one of the sperm nuclei with the egg nucleus, the zygote gives rise, by free nuclear divisions, to eight diploid proembryonal cells, each of which is capable of producing a separate embryo. In a functional sense, the proembryonal nuclei are equivalent to the eight walled-cells of the proembryo of *Pinus* and other conifers which exhibit cleavage polembryony. Sometimes, in *Ephedra*, the second sperm nucleus fertilizes the ventral canal cell of the archegonium, but this does not give rise to an additional embryo.

Finally a brief comparison has been made between *Ephedra, Gnetum,* and *Welwitschia*. Although the sporophytes of these remarkable plants seem to agree in a number of respects, the complex female gametophytes of both *Gnetum* and *Welwitschia* are devoid of archegonia, and the female gametes are represented by peculiar uninucleate or multinucleate cells at the micropylar end of the female gametophytes.

Many attempts have been made to interpret the female gametophyte of *Gnetum* as a structure which typifies a stage in the evolution of the embryo sac of angiosperms. In view of our complete ignorance of the evolutionary history of the angiosperms, however, their origin from gnetalean ancestors comparable to any of the modern genera seems highly improbable. The living members of the Gnetales should, on the contrary, be regarded as extremely specialized end-points in evolution which are not closely related to any present-day gymnosperms or angiosperms.

References

Arber, E. A. and J. Parkin. 1908. Studies on the evolution of the angiosperms. The relationship of the angiosperms to the Gnetales. *Ann. Bot.* 22:489-515.

Bailey, I. W. 1953. Evolution of the tracheary tissue of land plants. *Amer. Jour. Bot.* 40:4-8.

Battaglia, E. 1951. The male and female gametophytes of angiosperms—an interpretation. *Phytomorphology* 1: 87-116.

Chamberlain, C. J. 1935. *Gymnosperms. Structure and Evolution.* University of Chicago Press, Chicago.

Eames, A. J. 1952. Relationships of the Ephedrales. *Phytomorphology* 2:79-100.

Florin, R. 1931. Untersuchungen zur Stammesgeschichte der Coniferales und Cordaitales. *Svenska Vetensk. Akad. Handl.* Ser. 5. 10:1-588.

Gifford, E. M. 1943. The structure and development of the shoot apex of *Ephedra altissima.* Desf. *Bull. Torrey Bot. Club* 70:15-25.

Griffith, M. M. 1952. The structure and growth of the shoot apex in *Araucaria. Amer. Jour. Bot.* 39:253-263.

Johansen, D. A. 1950. *Plant Embryology.* Chronica Botanica Co., Waltham, Mass.

Johnson, M. A. 1950. Growth and development of the shoot of *Gnetum gnemon* L. I. The shoot apex and pith. *Bull. Torrey Bot. Club* 77:354-367.

————. 1951. The shoot apex in gymnosperms. *Phytomorphology* 1:188-204.

Khan, R. 1943. Contributions to the morphology of *Ephedra foliata.* Boiss. II. Fertilization and embryogeny. *Proc. Nat. Acad. Sci. India* 13:357-375.

Land, W. J. G. 1904. Spermatogenesis and oögenesis in *Ephedra trifurca. Bot. Gaz.* 38:1-18.

————. 1907. Fertilization and embryogeny in *Ephedra trifurca. Bot. Gaz.* 44:273-292.

Maheshwari, P. 1935. Contributions to the morphology of *Ephedra foliata.* Boiss. I. The development of the male and female gametophytes. *Proc. Indian Acad. Sci.* 1:586-606.

Marsden, M. P. F. and T. A. Steeves. 1955. On the primary vascular system and the nodal anatomy of *Ephedra. Jour. Arnold Arboretum* 36:241-258.

Pearson, H. H. W. 1929. *Gnetales.* Cambridge University Press, London.

Rodin, R. J. 1951. Anatomical studies of the foliar organs of *Welwitschia mirabilis.* Ph.D. Diss., Univ. Calif., Berkeley.

————. 1953a. Distribution of *Welwitschia mirabilis. Amer. Jour. Bot.* 40:280-285.

————. 1953b. Seedling morphology of *Welwitschia. Amer. Jour. Bot.* 40: 371-378.

————. 1958a. Leaf anatomy of *Wel-witschia*. I. Early development of the leaf. *Amer. Jour. Bot.* 45:90-95.

————. 1958b. Leaf anatomy of *Wel-witschia*. II. A study of mature leaves. *Amer. Jour. Bot.* 45:96-103.

Seeliger, I. 1954. Studien am Spross-vegetationskegel von *Ephedra fragilis* var. *campylopoda* (C. A. Mey.) Stapf. *Flora* 141:114-162.

Thompson, W. P. 1918. Independent evolution of vessels in Gnetales and angiosperms. *Bot. Gaz.* 65:83-90.

Chapter

18 GENERAL MOR-PHOLOGY AND EVOLUTON OF THE ANGIOSPERMS

As contrasted with all the preceding groups of the Tracheo-phyta, the angiosperms or flowering plants constitute the dom-inant and most ubiquitous vascular plants of modern floras on the earth. The term angiosperm (literally, a vessel seed) was devised to designate one of the most definitive characteristics of flowering plants, namely the enclosure of the ovules or potential seeds within a hollow ovary. In this respect angiosperms are considered to be advanced, as compared with the naked seeded gymnosperms.

Angiosperms far exceed in number and diversity of form and structure all other major groups of living plants, and more than 200,000 different species have been named and classified. Flowering plants occupy a very wide range of ecological habitats (including representatives in both salt and fresh water), and extend far toward the polar extremities of the earth. Although scientific study of the classification, morphology, and geographical distribution of angiosperms has been pursued for over 200 years, we still do not possess even a reasonably complete census of living flowering plants. Modern scientific botany had its origin in the studies of the north temperate angiosperms of England and Europe, and our knowledge of the richly diversified floras of tropical areas is still extremely incomplete. Such regions of the earth as New Guinea, New Caledonia, tropical Asia and Africa, and the vast Amazon rain forest still await comprehensive botanical exploration. A fuller knowledge of the angio-sperms in these regions may ultimately modify many of our present con-

443

cepts which, it must be emphasized, still are based largely on the intensive study of north temperate plants.

Aside from bacteria and pathogenic fungi, angiosperms are the plants which most obviously affect the existence of man on earth. The basic food supply of the world is derived from the seeds and fruits of angiosperms (rice, wheat, corn, are outstanding examples), and fibers, wood, drugs, and other products are further illustrations of the great economic value of flowering plants in our daily lives.

Thus far the known fossil record of the angiosperms has failed to provide any reliable clues as to their origin and evolutionary development. The fragmentary evidence provided by fossilized wood, and especially by impressions of leaf form and venation, shows that by the Middle Cretaceous period angiosperms had reached a high stage of morphological specialization. Even if due allowance is made for errors in identifying genera by means of leaf impressions, it seems clear that by the latter part of the Mesozoic Era many modern families were clearly defined. How should this apparently sudden appearance of highly specialized angiosperms in the Cretaceous period be interpreted? Does it indicate—as has been commonly argued—that angiosperms evolved at a much faster rate than was true of the gymnosperms and lower vascular plants? Or is this abrupt appearance of angiosperms in the fossil record a clear demonstration of a long pre-Cretaceous period in their evolutionary development?

Because of the very meagre fossil record, it is not possible to answer these questions in any satisfactory manner. Fragmentary evidence, however, is accumulating in support of the inference that, like other groups of vascular plants, the angiosperms have probably developed over an extremely long period of time. Their so-called abrupt rise to dominance during the Mesozoic may thus be an illusion. Axelrod (1952) has discussed the paleobotanical evidence suggesting the existence of angiosperms during the Triassic and Jurassic periods—they may even, as he postulates, have been in existence at the end of the Paleozoic Era. A most discouraging aspect of the paleobotanical study of angiosperms is the probability that they initially developed in upland areas, i.e., in regions most unlikely to provide conditions for the preservation of fruits, flowers, leaves, wood, and pollen. If this commonly held view is correct, we may search in vain for tangible fossil records of the nature of truly ancient and primitive angiosperms.

Because of the unconvincing nature of the fossil record, the theories regarding the ancestral stock from which angiosperms originated are extremely speculative and contradictory. Engler (1926) proposed that the angiosperms arose from a hypothetical Mesozoic group of seed plants which he termed the Protangiospermae. Other botanists have sought to derive angiosperms from various gymnospermous stocks such as the Hemiangiosperms (Arber and Parkin, 1907) or Bennettitales (Lemesle, 1946). Fagerlind (1946) postulated that several primitive lines of angiosperm evolution (which he collectively termed the Urangiospermen) originated from the same ancestral stock which gave rise to the modern genera of the Gnetales.

It has also been suggested that the angiosperms may have been derived from the seed ferns or pteridosperms (Andrews, 1947; Arnold, 1947; Thomas, 1955), and there is much to be said in favor of this hypothesis. But in criticism of all these varied suggestions, it must be realized that they are made (1) in the absence of a comprehensive knowledge of the comparative morphology of existing angiosperms, and (2) without a full recognition of the results of parallel evolution, i.e., the independent origin, in unrelated groups, of similar end products. As will be pointed out later in this chapter, a reliable body of data derived from the study of *surviving* types of primitive angiosperms is now developing. This holds considerable promise in orienting and guiding the continued search of paleobotanists for fossil records of ancient angiosperms.

Organography and Anatomy

In Chapter 3 an effort was made to characterize the fundamental aspects of organography and anatomy illustrated by vascular plants. That chapter should be carefully studied as an essential background to the necessarily brief and condensed treatment of the vegetative sporophyte of angiosperms now to be presented.

The extensive descriptions and interpretations of organography given by Goebel (1905) and Troll (1935, 1937, 1938, 1939), and the comprehensive accounts of comparative anatomy found in the treatises by Solereder (1908), Metcalfe and Chalk (1950), Bailey (1954), and Esau (1953), ably demonstrate the structural complexity and diversity of living angiosperms. Moreover, it should be emphasized that many of our present concepts and generalizations, especially in anatomy, are based on a knowledge of the dicotyledons rather than on a comprehensive balanced knowledge of the angiosperms as a whole. Indeed, some of the classical textbook distinctions between monocotyledons and dicotyledons* have many exceptions in the light of present knowledge. In fact, there is no reliable set of morphological criteria which serve to separate rigidly the monocotyledons from the dicotyledons. This is strikingly demonstrated if contrasts are attempted with reference to the reproductive cycle (see Chapter 19). Maheshwari (1950) states that "there are no essential differences between the monocotyledons and dicotyledons as regard the development and organization of the male and female gametophytes and the endosperm, and the process of fertilization is the same in both subgroups." Cotyledon number, which formed the basis for the original distinction between the two groups, may also fluctuate. Certain "monocotyledons" develop embryos with two cotyledons, whereas, conversely, the embryos of some "dicotyledons" produce only a single cotyledon. In view of these facts, generalizations regarding the evolutionary trends of organographic or anatomical characters must be made with great caution and are subject to continual revision as our knowledge of the angiosperms increases.

Leaves

MORPHOLOGY AND VENATION.   In marked contrast with the relatively few major types of foliage leaves in gymnosperms, the foliar organs of angiosperms are extraordinarily diverse in size, morphological organization, and histology. The foliage leaf in some angiospermous genera is sessile and appears to consist only of a blade region. More commonly, however, the foliage leaf consists of several well-demarcated parts: the leaf base, the petiole, and the lamina (Fig. 18-1, H). The form, structure, and proportions of each of these parts vary widely and provide the basis for the typological classification of foliage leaves. (See Troll, 1935, for a very detailed treatment of the major types of angiospermous leaves.)

The leaf base in a large number of dicotyledonous genera develops a pair of appendages which are termed stipules. These structures may be

---

* For example, the numerical plan of the flower (three in monocotyledons, four or five in dicotyledons), the type of foliar venation (parallel in monocotyledons, pinnate or palmate reticulate in dicotyledons), and the vascular anatomy of the stem (scattered vascular bundles in monocotyledons, bundles in a cylinder in dicotyledons).

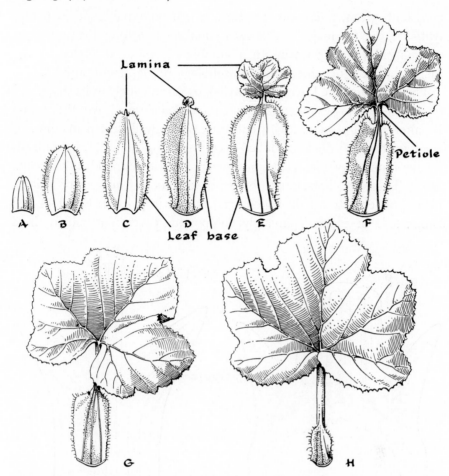

Figure 18-1 *Ribes sanguineum.* **A-D,** outer scales of a bud showing enlarged leaf-base and rudimentary lamina; **E-F,** transitional forms between bud scales and foliage leaves (note enlarged lamina and short petiole of the appendages); **G-H,** foliage leaves each with a well-developed palmately lobed lamina, an elongated petiole, and a sheathing leaf base. [Redrawn from *Vergleich. Morphologie der höheren Pflanzen* by W. Troll. Berlin: Gebrüder Borntraeger, 1939.]

adnate to the leaf base or they may appear as two free appendages (Fig. 18-2). Ontogenetic study has shown, however, that free lateral stipules originate as paired outgrowths of the leaf primordium. Although the morphological nature of stipules is at present a debatable question, these structures provide characters of considerable diagnostic value to the taxonomist. The stipules of some plants (e.g., pansy and sweet pea) are

persistent, green, foliaceous structures which presumably aid in photosynthesis, but the major rôle of most stipules seems to be the protection
of young developing leaves. In a number of woody dicotyledons the
tough scales of the winter buds morphologically represent stipules.

The lamina of the leaves of dicotyledons varies widely in its shape and
type of morphological organization. In so-called simple leaves the lamina
is either a unit structure with entire or variously dissected margins, or
else is more or less obviously lobed in contour (Fig. 18-1, H). In contrast,
a large number of dicotyledonous genera form compound or branched
leaves. These are characterized by the development—in place of a single
blade—of separate leaflets which are arranged in pairs on the elongated
lamina-axis or rachis (pinnately compound leaves), or radiate in a

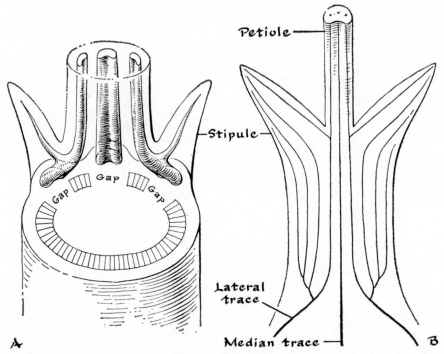

Figure 18-2 Vasculation of stipules. **A,** diagram of a trilacunar node showing
that the vascular supply of each stipule arises as a branch from the adjacent
lateral leaf trace; **B,** *Trifolium medium,* diagram showing that the veins entering the paired adnate stipules represent branches of the corresponding lateral
leaf traces. [A, redrawn from Sinnott and Bailey, *Amer. Jour. Bot.* 1:441, 1914;
B, redrawn from *Vergleich. Morphologie der höheren Pflanzen* by W. Troll.
Berlin: Gebrüder Borntraeger, 1939.]

digatate manner from the very short rachis (palmately compound leaves). A peculiar and distinctive type of lamina—illustrated by the common garden nasturtium—is termed peltate. In this type the petiole is attached near the center of the lower surface of the lamina. Peltate leaves, according to Troll's (1935) detailed survey, occur more commonly in the angiosperms than had previously been recognized.

The foliage leaf in the majority of the monocotyledons has a simple blade, and the leaf base region is often developed as a conspicuous sheath which may completely encircle the node (Fig. 19-28). In a relatively few monocotyledons (for example, the family Araceae) the lamina is palmately or pinnately dissected. The large, apparently pinnately compound leaves of the palms, however, are unique because the subdivisions of the lamina are said to arise by a process of splitting of the tissue of the young blade rather than as distinct lateral outgrowths of the leaf primordium as in the dicotyledons.

In addition to the photosynthetic foliage leaves, the sporophyte of angiosperms produces other types of foliar appendages, among which are included cotyledons, cataphylls (i.e., the scale leaves of rhizomes and the scales of winter buds), floral bracts, and, according to the classical interpretation, the sepals, petals, stamens, and carpels of the flower (Fig. 18-1, A-E). A discussion of the ontogeny and morphology of bracts and floral organs will be presented later in the chapter.

One of the outstanding structural features of the angiospermous leaf is the intricate and diversified nature of its venation, which consists of an extremely complex interconnected system of veins and veinlets (Figs. 18-3; 18-4). This reticulate type of venation is developed in a wide variety of patterns which have long been used in the determination of leaf fossils and in the taxonomic definition of genera, families, and even classes in the living angiosperms (Foster 1950a, 1950b, 1951, 1953). Nearly a century ago von Ettinghausen (1861) published an extensive monograph on the venation patterns of a wide range of living species, as an aid to the paleobotanist in the identification and classification of fossilized leaves. Some of his terminologies for describing the course of the main veins in the lamina have proved useful, and several examples are given in Fig. 18-3. Unfortunately, however, we still have a very meager idea of the range and degree of consistency of venation patterns within genera and families, and relatively little attention has been given

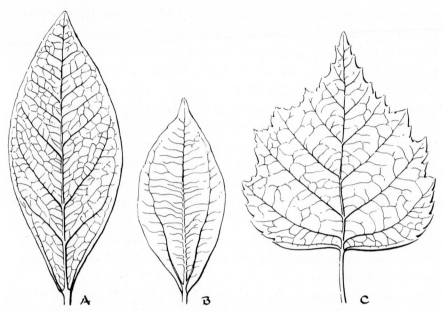

Figure 18-3   Venation patterns in the foliage leaves of dicotyledons. **A,** *Oreo-daphne sp.,* camptodromous type of venation, the pinnately arranged secondary veins interconnected and not terminating at the lamina margin; **B,** *Cinamomum glabrum,* acrodromous type of venation, with two strong basal secondary veins extending nearly to lamina tip; **C,** *Betula alba,* craspedodromous type of vena-tion, the pinnately arranged secondary veins extending to the lamina margin. [Redrawn from *Die Blatt-Skelete der Dikotyledonen* by C. R. von Ettinghausen. Wien: Kais. Kon. Hof-und Staatsdruckerei, 1861.]

to the ontogenetic aspects of the problem (see Foster, 1952; Pray, 1955a, 1955c). As a consequence, we have no reliable clues regarding the trends of specialization in angiospermous venation. A good example of our present difficulties is found in the widespread but incorrect use of the term "parallel" to describe the type of venation characteristic of the monocotyledons. Although it is true that the *major veins* in some mono-cotyledonous leaves extend vertically through the lamina (e.g., in the laminae of grasses), in many cases these primary veins are by no means parallel (in a geometric sense) but extend as a series of arches towards the leaf apex (Fig. 18-4, A). Moreover, in all carefully investigated species the primary veins not only converge and join near the apex, but are interconnected by smaller veinlets throughout their course. These minor veinlets may appear as a series of transverse or oblique commissural veinlets, but in many genera develop as a complex reticulum (Fig. 18-4, B). In some families in the monocotyledons (the Liliaceae, Araceae, and Orchidaceae) the network of anastomosed veins and veinlets is extremely complex and dicotyledonous in aspect. From the above critique it should be evident that there is no single definitive type of

Figure 18-4 Venation patterns in angiosperms. **A,** the campylodromous venation of *Hosta caerulea* (note the arcuate course and the progressive union, from base of lamina upwards, of the primary veins); **B,** details of network of veinlets from area indicated in the circle of **A** (note the freely terminating vein endings); **C,** major venation in the leaf of *Liriodendron tulipifera*; **D,** details of area indicated in the circle of C, showing complex reticulum of veinlets and numerous branched vein endings. [A-B redrawn from Pray, *Amer. Jour. Bot.* 42:611, 1955; C-D, redrawn from Pray, *Amer. Jour. Bot.* 41:663, 1954.]

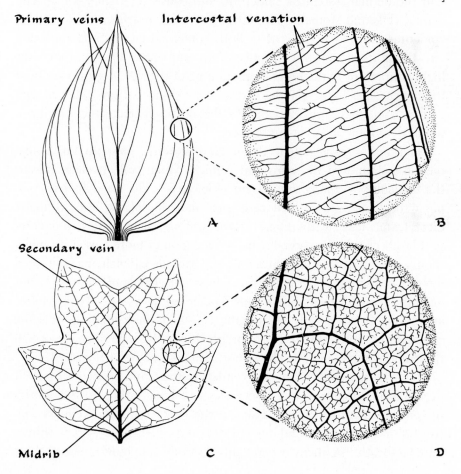

foliar venation which serves to distinguish the leaves of monocotyledons from those of dicotyledons. It therefore must be emphasized that further progress in our understanding of the vasculation of angiospermous leaves depends on fresh information to be secured from ontogenetic study and comparative surveys.

HISTOLOGY.   In Chapter 3 (p. 39), the general application of Sach's scheme of tissue systems to the description of leaf anatomy was briefly discussed. Figure 18-5 represents transections of portions of the leaf blades of *Pyrus* (a dicotyledon) and *Lilium* (a monocotyledon), and will serve to illustrate the necessarily brief account of foliar anatomy presented here. The abaxial and adaxial surface layers collectively represent the dermal system or epidermis, and consist of tightly joined epidermal cells and stomata. The latter are often restricted to the lower epidermis but may be present in both epidermal layers. Stomata represent the ports of exit and entrance of air and water vapor and are thus highly important to the normal functioning of the leaf. A great variety of trichomes (i.e., hairs, glands, scales) may develop from the leaf epidermis, and often provide valuable diagnostic characters in the taxonomic definition of species and genera.

The internal tissue systems of the lamina are the mesophyll or fundamental system, and the veins and veinlets which collectively represent the fascicular or *conducting system* (Fig. 18-5). The mesophyll is composed of living, thin-walled cells rich in chloroplasts, and in many dicotyledons it is clearly differentiated into one or more relatively compact layers of palisade parenchyma and a region of more loosely arranged spongy parenchyma. Very commonly the palisade parenchyma is situated directly below the upper epidermis (dorsiventral type of anatomy), but not infrequently occurs below both epidermal layers (isolateral type of anatomy). Palisade cells are usually columnar in form, but in some angiosperms these cells are armed or lobed (Fig. 18-5, B). The mesophyll functionally represents the chief photosynthetic tissue of the plant.

The histology of the veins and veinlets in the lamina depends on their degree of development, and also varies widely according to the species or genus of plant concerned. Each of the larger veins and veinlets consists of a collateral strand of phloem and xylem enclosed within a bundle sheath. In many woody dicotyledons the bundle sheaths are

Palisade parenchyma   Upper epidermis   Bundle-sheath extention

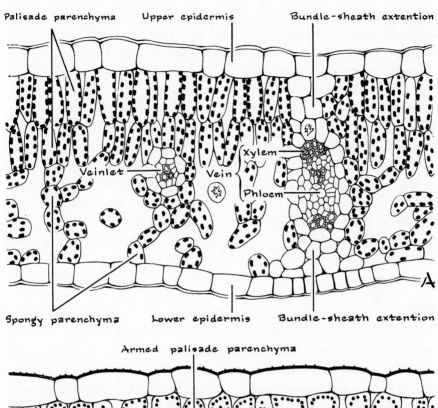

Veinlet   Vein   Xylem

Phloem

Spongy parenchyma   Lower epidermis   Bundle-sheath extention

Armed palisade parenchyma

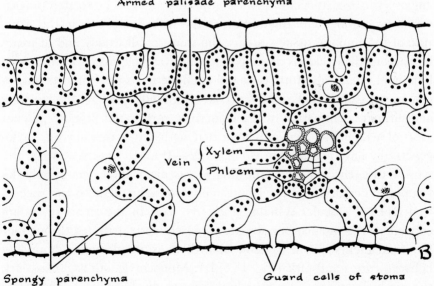

Vein { Xylem
       Phloem

Spongy parenchyma   Guard cells of stoma

Figure 18-5 Transections illustrating the histology of the lamina of leaves in angiosperms. **A,** *Pyrus;* **B,** *Lilium* (see text for discussion of this figure). [Redrawn from *Plant Anatomy* by K. Esau. N. Y.: John Wiley and Sons, Inc., 1953.]

connected with one or both epidermal layers by plates of cells known as bundle-sheath extensions (Fig. 18-5, A). These structures are believed to participate in the conduction of liquids between the veins and the epidermis. The vascular tissues of the smaller veinlets and veinlet-ends in the leaf are derived from the procambium, and are thus exclusively primary in nature. Cambial activity, if it occurs in a given leaf, is therefore restricted to the coarser veins in the lamina and to the vascular system of the petiole. Generally speaking, relatively little secondary xylem and phloem occur in the fascicular system of the leaf.

This account of leaf histology reflects very little of the wide range in the details of structure of the dermal, fundamental, and fascicular tissue systems of the leaf. Students interested in more extensive discussions of the structure and histogenesis of angiospermous leaves should consult Solereder (1908), Metcalfe and Chalk (1950), and Esau (1953).

Stems

GENERAL STRUCTURE. The comparative anatomy of the stem in angiosperms is a subject of great complexity and can be treated only in very brief outline here. In addition to the wide fluctuation in the structure of the primary tissue systems, the stems of all woody and of many herbaceous dicotyledons develop secondary vascular tissues from a cambium and usually also form cork and phelloderm tissues from the phellogen or cork cambium. Extensive secondary growth results in the crushing and ultimate elimination of the epidermis, cortex, and primary phloem areas of a stem. It is generally held that herbaceous angiosperms phylogenetically have arisen from woody types—from this point of view, the narrow vascular cylinder or the ring of vascular bundles commonly developed in herbaceous dicotyledons represent highly reduced and specialized types of vascular systems (Fig. 18-6, A). In the stems of monocotyledons the vascular bundles are very frequently scattered throughout the fundamental tissue system, and there is no definable boundary between cortex and pith (Fig. 18-6, B). Monocotyledons as a class lack the cambial activity so commonly present in dicotyledons, but in a few aborescent genera in the Liliaceae (e.g., *Yucca, Dracaena, Cordyline*) a peculiar type of secondary growth occurs which adds new vascular bundles and additional parenchyma to the primary body.

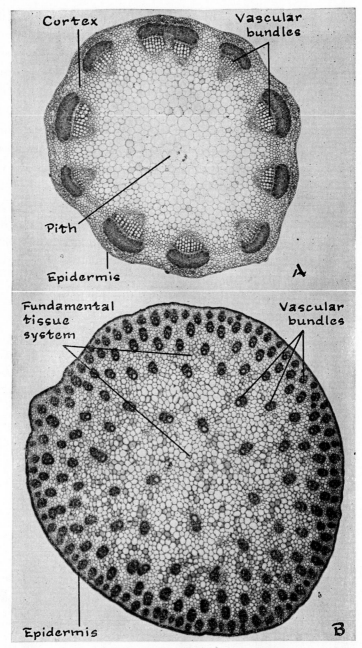

Figure 18-6 Types of stem anatomy in angiosperms. **A**, transection of stem of *Trifolium* (a dicotyledon); **B**, transection of stem of *Zea Mays* (a monocotyledon) (note scattered arrangement of vascular bundles and the absence of definable cortex and pith).

NODAL ANATOMY.   The angiosperms, particularly the dicotyledons, are typical pteropsid plants, with reference to stem anatomy. The primary vascular cylinder is interrupted at each node by the divergence of one or more leaf traces, and, depending on the number of leaf gaps, the nodal anatomy is described as unilacunar (a single gap), trilacunar (three gaps), or multilacunar (five or more gaps). See Fig. 18-7, A, B, E. Following the original discovery and designation of these patterns by Sinnott (1914), extensive use has been made of nodal anatomy in the comparative and systematic study of the angiosperm leaf and in the interpretation of the morphology of floral organs. Sinnott postulated that the trilacunar type of nodal structure is primitive in the angiosperms and that the unilacunar node arose phylogenetically either by the elimination of the two lateral gaps and their traces or by the approximation of the two lateral traces which together with the median formed a tripartite trace related to a single gap (Fig. 18-7, C, D). In contrast, the multilacunar node was considered to have evolved by the addition of extra independently developed gaps and traces (Fig. 18-7, E).

Figure 18-7   Transections illustrating some of the main types of nodal anatomy in dicotyledons. **A,** unilacunar node of *Eucalyptus sp.,* **B,** trilacunar node of *Ilex opaca;* **C,** trilacunar node of *Sisymbrium leiocarpum* (Cruciferae); **D,** unilacunar node of *Barbarea* (Cruciferae); **E,** multilacunar node of *Acanthopanax.* [Redrawn from Sinnott, *Amer. Jour. Bot.* 1:303, 1914.]

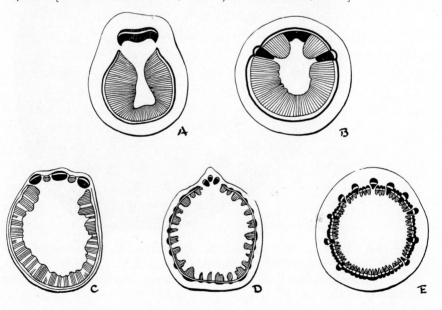

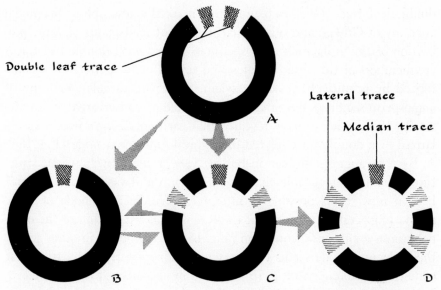

Double leaf trace

Lateral trace

Median trace

A

B

C

D

Figure 18-8 Phylogenetic origin of the uni-, tri-, and multilacunar types of nodal anatomy in dicotyledons. **A,** primitive type of unilacunar node with double leaf trace; **B,** unilacunar node derived from A by fusion of two traces; **C,** trilacunar node derived from either A or B by addition of a pair of lateral traces and gaps (arrow pointing left indicates possible origin of **B** from **C** by secondary elimination of lateral gaps and traces); **D,** multilacunar node derived from C by addition of a pair of lateral traces and gaps. [Redrawn from Marsden and Bailey, *Jour. Arnold Arboretum* 36:1, 1955.]

The assumption that the trilacunar node is the ancient or primitive condition in angiosperms has very recently been criticized in the light of new evidence derived from a broad survey of nodal anatomy in the Pteropsida. (See Marsden and Bailey, 1955; Marsden and Steeves, 1955; Bailey, 1956a.) In many ferns, as well as in *Ginkgo*, the seed ferns, the Cordaitales, the Bennettitales, the Coniferales, and *Ephedra* the strand or strands diverging into a foliar appendage are associated with a single gap. As Bailey emphasizes, it is thus reasonable to assume that the unilacunar node is the primitive condition in ancient types of pteropsid plants, and that therefore "the trilacunar and multilacunar structures of angiosperms must have been derived at some evolutionary stage from a unilacunar condition." The comparative investigations made by Bailey and his associates on families and genera in the dicotyledons have further revealed that the unilacunar condition is very often associated with a double leaf trace (Fig. 18-8, A), thus markedly resembling the nodal anatomy of *Ginkgo* and other ancient types of seed plants. A large proportion of the unilacunar angiospermous genera with double leaf traces are members of the order Ranales, and several of the genera are characterized by primitively vesselless xylem. Since the vascular anatomy of angiosperm seedlings has often been regarded as conservative, it is noteworthy that Bailey's survey revealed that each cotyledon often is vascularized by a double trace related to a typical unilacunar node (Fig. 18-9, A, B). The angiosperm leaf, in Bailey's view, is a relatively plastic structure, capable of reversible changes in its form and vasculature. On this basis it now seems possible to interpret the unilacunar node of some genera (e.g., certain members of the Ranales) as a retention of the original primitive pteropsid condition (Fig. 18-9, C), whereas in other genera the unilacunar node seems to represent a reduction from the trilacunar condition. Reference to Fig. 18-8 will aid in visualizing the possible evolutionary development and relationships of the main types of nodal anatomy in the dicotyledons. Further comparative surveys of nodal anatomy obviously constitute an important aspect of future morphological research.

WOOD ANATOMY. One of the most productive aspects of modern investigations on angiosperm anatomy is the comparative study of the xylem (Cheadle, 1956). The virtually endless variations in the structure and arrangement of tracheids, vessels, fibers, wood rays, and vertical wood parenchyma (particularly in the secondary xylem) have been widely used in the characterization of families and genera and in support of phylogenetic conclusions. (See Metcalfe and Chalk, 1950, for a detailed treatment of the extensive literature.) Of great interest is the discovery by Bailey and his associates that in certain woody members of the Ranales [the Winteraceae (six genera), *Trochodendron, Tetracentron, Amborella,* and *Sarcandra*] the xylem of *all organs* is devoid of vessels (Bailey, 1953). On the basis of detailed evidence, it is clear that these ranalian plants are *primitively* vesselless and therefore of exceptional evolutionary interest. In this connection it is significant that relatively primitive stages in the presumed evolutionary development of vessels from tracheids are extensively preserved in a wide range of dicotyledonous families. With reference to the monocotyledons, Cheadle's

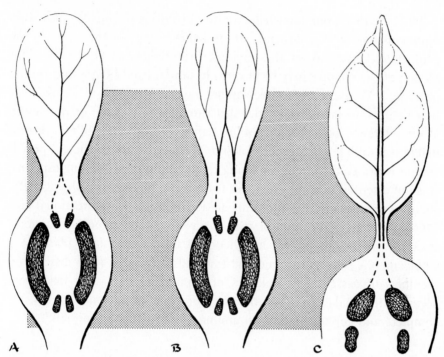

Figure 18-9 **A-B**, unilacunar nodal anatomy of cotyledons in dicotyledonous
seedlings (note that in **A** the cotyledonary traces unite directly to form a
midvein, whereas in **B** each trace dichotomizes, the two central strands joining
to form a midvein); **C**, unilacunar nodal anatomy and vascularization of the
foliage leaf in *Austrobaileya* (note that the two bundles remain separate in
their course through the petiole and lamina). [A-B redrawn from Bailey, *Jour.
Arnold Arboretum* 37:269, 1956; C, redrawn from Bailey and Swamy, *Jour.
Arnold Arboretum* 30:211, 1949.]

comprehensive survey reveals that vessels in this group, as in the dicotyledons, very probably originated by the disappearance of the pit membranes in the scalariformly pitted ends of tracheids (Cheadle, 1953).
However, in monocotyledons vessels appeared first in the metaxylem
tissue of the root, whereas in dicotyledons vessels initially developed in
the secondary xylem of the stem. Cheadle concluded, on this basis, that
vessels evolved independently in monocotyledons and dicotyledons. If
this view is correct—and there is much evidence to support it—it seems
entirely possible, as suggested by Constance (1955) that monocotyledons
and dicotyledons originated from a common, woody, vesselless ancestral
type.

The growth of our knowledge of the evolutionary history of vessels represents one of the most important achievements in the study of the comparative anatomy of the angiosperms (Bailey, 1944, 1957). This section of the chapter may be effectively summarized by quoting from a paper by I. W. Bailey, whose researches have contributed so significantly to a better understanding of the structure and phylogeny of the vessel. With reference to vessel evolution Bailey (1953) concludes: "Fortunately, a complete phylogenetic picture of this trend of tracheary specialization is preserved among surviving representatives of the angiosperms. It is not essential to comb the rocks for missing links in the phylogenetic chains. Furthermore, the morphogenetic trend is an unidirectional and irreversible one, and cannot be read in reverse, as so frequently happens, since in view of our present knowledge of the vascular land plants as a whole, no one is likely to argue that tracheids originated from dissociated members of vessels. The volumes of supporting data that have now accumulated make this evolutionary story one of the most extensive, complete and convincing known among either plants or animals."

The Flower

General Concept

Since angiosperms are commonly designated the flowering plants one might assume that rather general agreement exists as to the scientific concept of a flower. Unfortunately this is not the case, and the literature on floral organography, ontogeny, and structure displays widely divergent viewpoints with respect to the fundamental nature of the flower as well as to the interpretation of its varied component organs (sepals, petals, stamens, and carpels) (Fig. 18-10).

One of the basic difficulties lies in our complete ignorance of the evolutionary history of the flower. Floral organs are generally fragile, ephemeral structures and are rarely preserved in the known fossil record. Thus it becomes largely a matter of conjecture whether one is justified in drawing comparisons between modern angiospermous flowers and the spore-producing structures of other tracheophytes. If such comparisons are attempted, it is quite possible to reach either a very broad or a very restricted concept or definition of a flower.

As an example of the excessively broad concept, favored particularly by

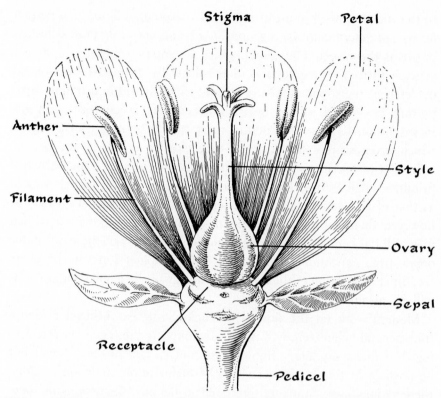

Stigma

Petal

Anther

Style

Filament

Ovary

Sepal

Receptacle

Pedicel

Figure 18-10 Organography of a flower. [Redrawn from *Lehrbuch der allgemeinen Botanik* by H. Von Guttenberg, Ed. 2. Berlin: Akademie-Verlag, 1952.]

certain German morphologists, we cite the definition of Goebel (1905, p. 469): "I understand here by the term 'flower' a shoot beset with sporophylls, that is to say, leaves bearing sporangia." From this standpoint, and with the additional qualification that the flower is a shoot of limited growth, "flowers," according to Goebel, occur in all the strobilus-bearing lower vascular plants as well as in the gymnosperms. From a similar viewpoint, Engler (1926) refers to the microsporangiate and megasporangiate strobili of the conifers as "male" and "female" flowers, respectively. We have also pointed out in Chapter 17 that the strobili of the Gnetales have been likened to inflorescences which bear flowers with a vestigial perianth (see also Fagerlind, 1946).

On the other hand, there has been a strong tendency on the part of many morphologists and taxonomists to limit the concept of the flower to the angiosperms. From this *restricted* viewpoint, a flower is a *particular type of determinate sporogenous shoot,* and one of its most definitive organs is the carpel. The carpel, which resembles a megasporophyll in general *function,* is regarded as morphologically distinctive because the ovules (i.e., megasporangia) are usually enclosed within a hollow basal portion designated as the ovary. Furthermore, in contrast with the megasporophylls of gymnosperms, most carpels terminate in a stigma, which serves as a receptive structure for the pollen.

In view of the absence of paleobotanical evidence as to the nature of primitive angiosperms, the evolutionary history of the carpel as well as that of the stamen, petal, and sepal remain unknown. Fortunately, however, there still exist angiosperms with carpels and stamens which may well typify early steps in the evolutionary history of these debatable organs from some more elemental type of sporophyll. Later in this chapter a brief description of the floral morphology of these relict angiosperms will be given.

Modern work on the flowers of angiosperms has utilized evidence from general organography, vascular anatomy, and ontogeny in attempting to define morphologically a flower and its appendages. It will not be possible in this book to review the major results of enquiry along these various lines. Students interested in detailed discussions of these important areas of morphological research should consult review articles and special treatises written in recent years by Eames (1931, 1951), Eames and McDaniels (1947), Puri (1951), and Wilson and Just (1939), where the pertinent literature is to be found.

In the present volume it is necessary to emphasize, however, that, despite the still controversial status of many aspects of floral morphology, the so-called classical theory of the angiosperm flower has much evidence in its favor (Mason, 1957). This theory, which stems from the early writings of Goethe (1790) on metamorphosis in plants and which was developed in detail by De Candolle (1844), holds that the flower is a shoot, the appendages (i.e., floral organs) of which are the morphological equivalents or homologues of leaves (Arber, 1937, 1946). In the light of modern ideas concerning the origin of the megaphyllous leaf of pteropsid plants from a branch system, the question of the presumed homology between *foliage leaves* and floral appendages is indeed a controversial matter, at least from the standpoint of phylogeny (Wilson,

1953). But marked *resemblances* can be demonstrated between vegetative leaves and floral appendages, with respect to their initiation, early ontogeny, and basic plan of vasculation. It will therefore be desirable to present concisely some of the evidence from vascular anatomy and ontogeny on which the present widespread adherence to the classical theory of the flower depends.

Vascular Anatomy

Since the classical investigations of Van Tieghem (1875) on the anatomy of the pistil and fruit, much labor and considerable enthusiasm have been devoted to the study of the vasculation of the flower.

In addition to providing data of importance in the morphological interpretation of fusion, adnation, and the inferior ovary, the anatomical method has, in general, furnished strong support for the classical theory of the flower. A. J. Eames (1931), an outstanding leader in the modern study of floral anatomy, maintains that "flowers, in their vascular skeletons, differ in no essential way from leafy stems." He emphasizes, however, that because of the determinate pattern of growth of a flower and the crowding and fusion of the frequently numerous appendages on the short floral axis, anatomical interpretation is often difficult, and, to be successful, requires broad comparative knowledge of the vasculature of both flowers and vegetative shoots. Puri (1951), who has reviewed in detail the very extensive literature on floral anatomy, concludes that evidence derived from the anatomical method has made a significant contribution to a better understanding of the angiosperm flower. But he emphasizes the necessity of regarding vasculation as only *one* of the important sources of morphological ideas—the evidence from organography and floral ontogeny also needs full consideration.

Numerous comparative studies on the vasculation of angiosperm flowers make it possible to select relatively simple types of flowers for brief consideration. In many respects, the flower of *Aquilegia,* a genus in the Ranunculaceae, is ideal because the successive floral appendages are free from one another and are borne on a well-defined stem-like axis or receptacle. According to the recent detailed investigations of Tepfer (1953) the flower of *Aquilegia formosa* var. *truncata* commonly consists of an axis bearing 70 appendages as follows: a calyx of five sepals, a corolla of five petals, an androecium of 45 stamens and ten staminodia (petaloid organs devoid of anthers) and a gynoecium of five carpels, free at first but becoming basally concrescent later. Serial transactions of the flower of *Aquilegia* reveal that the vascular system of the pedicel and receptacle is stem-like, consisting of a dissected cylinder of phloem and xylem from which are derived the traces to the successive floral appendages (Fig. 18-11, A-J). These floral traces, like leaf-traces, are associated with definable gaps in the stele of the receptacle, as is clearly revealed in completely mature flowers (Fig. 18-11, K).

As is true of a great many flower types which have been studied anatomically, there are remarkable differences in *Aquilegia* with reference to the number of traces and the venation characteristic of the

Figure 18-11 **A-J**, transections illustrating vascular anatomy of the flower of *Aquilegia*. **A**, transection of pedicel; **B-C**, departure of sepal and petal traces; **D-E**, departure of stamen traces; **F**, departure of dorsal traces of each carpel; **G**, departure of ventral carpel traces; **H**, transection of basal region of united carpels; **I**, the five carpels nearly free; **J**, the carpels at higher level, each with a dorsal and two ventral bundles; **K**, pattern of the vascular cylinder of a mature flower of *Aquilegia* split longitudinally and spread out in one plane (this diagram shows only a portion of the floral traces and gaps depicted in A-G). [A-J, redrawn from Eames, *Amer. Jour. Bot.* 18:147, 1931; K, redrawn from Tepfer, *Univ. Calif. Pub. in Bot.* 25:513, 1953.]

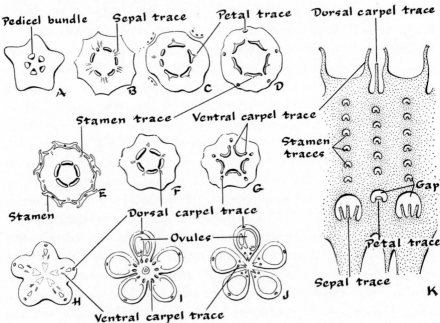

successive sets of floral appendages. Figure 18-11, K, illustrates the basic plan of vasculation in the flower, and Fig. 18-12 depicts the venation patterns typical of the sepal, petal, stamen, staminode, and carpel. At the nodal level of the calyx each of the five sepals receives three traces which typically are associated with a single gap (Fig. 18-11, K). The three traces become more or less joined as a single bundle in the base of the sepal, and then separate into a palmate series at the base of the lamina, the venation of which consists of a series of irregularly dichotomizing and interconnected bundles (Fig. 18-12, A). The five petals, and each of the numerous stamens and staminodia, in contrast, are vasculated by single traces, each trace related to a distinct and separate gap (Fig. 18-11, C-E, K). Like the sepals, petals of the flower exhibit a complex pattern of venation that differs markedly from the simple unbranched vascular strand which traverses each of the stamens and the staminodia (Fig. 18-12, B-D). Each of the five carpels receives three traces (associated with a single gap)—a dorsal trace which extends up the abaxial side of the carpel into the terminal region of the style, and two ventral traces which traverse the fused adaxial margins of the ovary and end in the style a short distance below the dorsal bundle (Fig. 18-11, F-K). As shown in Fig. 18-12, E, F, these ventral carpellary bundles give rise to lateral dichotomizing veins, one series of which enters the stalks of the ovules, the other series constituting the venation of the two walls of the ovary. From the above description it is evident that the basic vasculation of the flower of *Aquilegia* closely resembles that typical of a vegetative shoot. In both the shoot and the flower the successive appendages are vascularized by traces associated with gaps in the vascular cylinder of the axis (i.e., stem or receptacle). Indeed, the vascular plan of the flower in *Aquilegia* appears to lend strong support to the classical interpretation of the flower, and serves as an example of a simple and possibly primitive type of floral vasculature in the angiosperms.

Many flowers, however, are more complex because of the reduction in size or phylogenetic loss of certain organs, or because of the very frequent tendency toward the fusion between floral organs. Fusion may consist in partial or complete lateral union or cohesion between the adjacent members of the calyx, corolla, androecium, or gynoecium of a flower (Fig. 18-13, A, K-M); or it may consist in adnation between

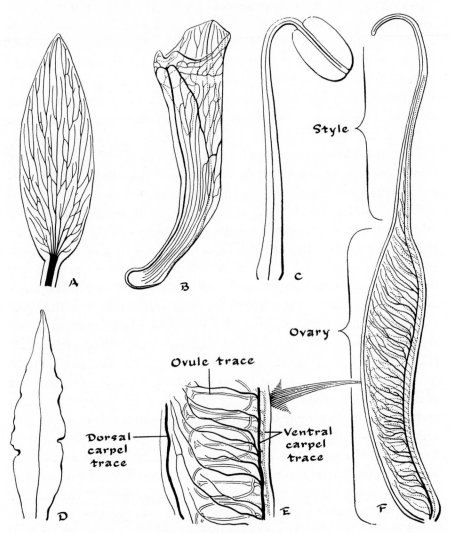

Figure 18-12 Venation patterns in the floral organs of *Aquilegia formosa* var. *truncata.* **A,** sepal; **B,** petal; **C,** stamen; **D,** staminodium; **E,** details of vasculature of portion of ovary (note the lateral, dichotomizing branches of the ventral traces and the derivation of the ovule traces); **F,** total venation of a carpel (the ovules, ovule traces, and wall venation of lower side shown by dotted lines). [Redrawn from Tepfer, *Univ. Calif. Pub. in Botany* 25:513, 1953.]

members of successive floral whorls, for example, the frequent union of stamens to petals or to the tube of a sympetalous corolla (Fig. 18-13, B-F). These organographic specializations are, in turn, reflected in corresponding modifications of the vasculature of complex types of flowers.

It will not be possible in this volume to discuss fully the application of the anatomical method to the interpretation of the diversified levels of specialization in angiosperm flowers, but a few examples, selected from anatomical studies on the gynoecium, will serve at least to illustrate the effects of cohesion. In a free carpel the margins may become closely appressed without fusion, or, as in *Aquilegia,* may fuse during early phases in carpel ontogeny (Tepfer, 1953). In either case, the two ventral bundles are separate and distinct throughout the carpel (Figs. 18-12, F; 18-13, G). In instances where the fusion of the carpellary margins occurs earlier in ontogeny, the two ventral bundles may be joined as a double or an apparently single bundle at various levels in the carpel (Fig. 18-13, I-J). Syncarpous gynoecia reflect in their vasculature the varied degrees of lateral cohesion between adjacent carpels. In the simplest cases, the paired ventral bundles remain distinct and constitute the vascular system of the axile placenta (Fig. 18-13, K). When the carpels are closely united to form a tri- or multiloculate ovary, the placental region is often vascularized by one-half the expected number of bundles. This is interpreted as the result of fusion either between the ventrals belonging to each carpel or between the ventral bundles of laterally adjacent carpels (Fig. 18-13, L, M). Students interested in the further complications in the vasculature of gynoecia, stamens, sympetalous corollas and synsepalous calyces of specialized flowers should consult Eames (1931), Puri (1951) and Eames and MacDaniels (1947).

Ontogeny

The recent revival of interest, throughout the world, in problems of growth and differentiation in plants has resulted in a rich literature, particularly on the subject of apical ontogeny in vegetative shoots, inflorescences, and flowers (Gifford, 1954). In addition to numerous studies on the structure of the shoot apex and the development of leaves and stem tissues, much attention has been devoted to the ontogeny of the flower. A few ontogenetic investigations have yielded conclusions

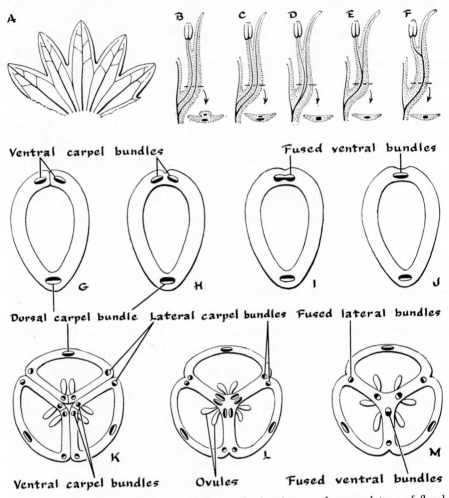

Ventral carpel bundles   Fused ventral bundles

Dorsal carpel bundle Lateral carpel bundles Fused lateral bundles

Ventral carpel bundles   Ovules   Fused ventral bundles

Figure 18-13 The effects of cohesion and adnation on the vasculature of floral organs. **A,** the calyx of *Ajuga reptans* showing the five basally fused sepals (the adjacent lateral veins of each sepal are united below the sinus); **B-F,** corresponding longitudinal and transectional diagrams showing the results of successive degrees of adnation between stamen and petal upon the pattern of vasculature; **B-C,** weak adnation, with traces of stamen and petal separate; **D-F,** progressive steps in the radial fusion between stamen and petal bundles; **G-J,** transectional diagrams showing effect of union of carpel margins on ventral bundles; **G-H,** the ventral bundles are distinct; **I,** a double ventral bundle; **J,** fusion of ventrals to a single bundle; **K-M,** transections showing effects of cohesion between three carpels; **K,** carpels in close contact but with distinct margins and paired ventral bundles; **L,** carpels fused, the ventral and lateral bundles of adjacent carpels arranged in pairs; **M,** the pairs of ventral and lateral bundles united. [Adapted from *An Introduction to Plant Anatomy,* Ed. 2, by Eames and MacDaniels. N. Y.: McGraw-Hill Book Company, Inc., 1947.]

radically opposed to the classical view that a flower is a special or modified type of shoot (see Thompson, 1934; Grègoire, 1938; Buvat, 1952). But, in general, developmental studies appear to strengthen the classical interpretation and to complement the conclusions reached through the study of the vasculature of adult flowers. As an example, a brief discussion will now be presented of Tepfer's (1953) detailed study of floral ontogeny in *Aquilegia* and *Ranunculus*.

In both of these genera the sepals, petals, stamens, and carpels are produced in an acropetal sequence from the meristematic floral apex (Fig. 18-14). During the period of initiation of the appendages, however, rather striking changes occur in the dimensions and cellular structure of the floral apex. These changes involve a transition from a relatively small apex of uniformly and densely staining cells to a broad dome-like apical meristem with a conspicuously vacuolated parenchymatous core overlaid by several layers of meristematic cells. The latter condition is particularly characteristic of the apex of *Ranunculus* during the formation of the carpel primordia. The massive parenchymatous core of the floral apices of *Aquilegia* and *Ranunculus*, however, is correlated with the elongated floral receptacle in these genera, and therefore does not demonstrate a fundamental difference between vegetative and floral meristems as was postulated by Grègoire (1938). In other

Figure 18-14 Organogeny of the flower of *Aquilegia formosa* var. *truncata*. **A-B,** outlines of longisections of the floral apex illustrating acropetal development of sepals (*Se*), petals (*Pe*), stamens (*St*), staminodes (*St*), and carpels (*Ca*); **C,** outline of a transection of a developing flower showing the five sepals and the primordia of petals and stamens. [Redrawn from Tepfer, *Univ. of Calif. Pub. in Botany*, 25:513, 1953.]

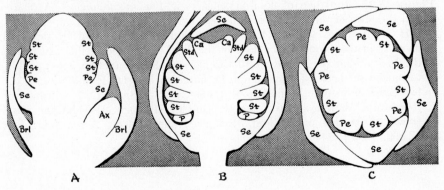

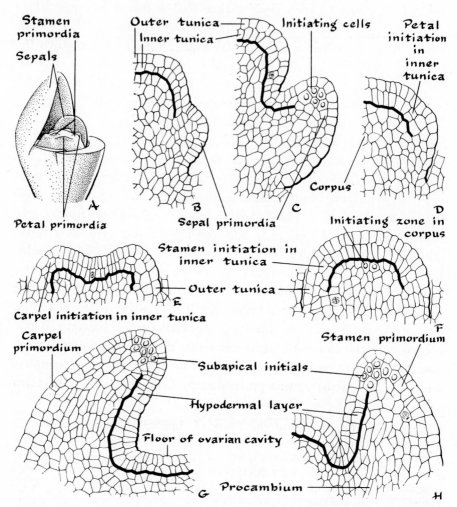

Figure 18-15   Initiation of floral appendages in *Frasera carolinensis.* **A,** flower bud with two of the sepals removed showing primordia of petals and stamens. **B-H,** longisections showing that all floral organs are initiated by periclinal divisions in the second tunica layer of the floral apex (a heavy line demarcates the tunica from the corpus in all the figures); **B-C,** initiation and early development of the sepal primordium; **D,** initiation of petal; **E,** initiation of the two carpel primordia; **F,** initiation of stamen primordium; **G,** longisection of young carpel showing group of subapical initials; **H,** longisection showing apical growth of stamen primordium. [Redrawn from McCoy, *Amer. Jour. Bot.* 27:600, 1940.]

angiosperms, for example, *Vinca, Umbellularia, Laurus,* and *Frasera* (Fig. 18-15) the structure and growth of the floral apex during the formation of appendages resemble closely the organization of a vegetative shoot apex (McCoy, 1940; Boke, 1947; Kasipligil, 1951; Philipson, 1947, 1949).

Tepfer's investigations further demonstrate that the method of initiation and the early phases of cellular differentiation of sepal, petal, stamen, and carpel primordia are fundamentally similar and closely agree with the early ontogeny of bracts and foliage leaves (Fig. 18-16). These striking resemblances include the method of development of the procambium which is produced acropetally in *both* vegetative and floral apices. The early ontogeny of the carpels in *Aquilegia* is of particular morphological interest. Soon after their initiation from the floral meristem, the carpel primordia appear horseshoe-shaped in transectional view

Figure 18-16 Similarity in initiation and early histogenesis of the leaf, bract, and floral organs in *Aquilegia formosa* var. *truncata*. Nuclei (shown as circles) in the drawings of stages in initiation indicate cells derived from the second tunica layer and the outer corpus of the floral apex. In the trans- and longisections of primordia, the procambium is represented by the cells with nuclei. [Redrawn from Tepfer, *Univ. of Calif. Pub. in Botany* 25:513, 1953.]

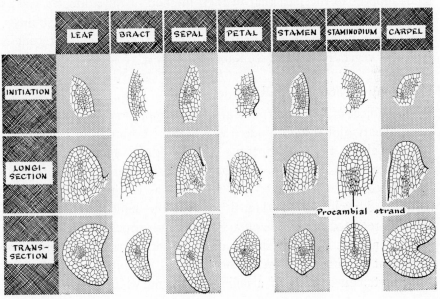

(Figs. 18-16; 18-17, D). Well-defined marginal growth—resembling the marginal growth of a vegetative leaf—results ultimately in the *actual* ontogenetic fusion of the margins of each carpel and the formation of the ovarian region. Ovules are initiated from hypodermal cells situated about midway between the fused edges of the carpel and the inner surface of the ovarian cavity (Fig. 18-17, A). Because of this, Tepfer regards the placentation of the ovules as laminal rather than marginal. During the early phases of development of the gynoecium, the five carpel primordia are free from one another (Fig. 18-17, B, D). Later the bases of adjacent carpels become fused by the cohesion of their meristematic epidermal layers (Fig. 18-17, C). At maturity the original, separate epidermal layers of the joined carpels can no longer be distinguished (Fig. 18-17, E). Thus in *Aquilegia* the union of the carpel margins and the fusion between the bases of adjacent carpels are truly ontogenetic processes. Many examples of such post-genital carpel fusions occur in the angiosperms (Baum, 1948a, 1948b).

In concluding this discussion of floral ontogeny it must be admitted that our present knowledge rests on a relatively small number of histogenetic studies. Comprehensive surveys of floral histogenesis throughout the angiosperms are badly needed. But the evidence secured thus far lends support to the idea that in their method of initiation, as well as in the early critical stages of their differentiation, sepals, petals, stamens, and carpels parallel to a remarkable degree the general histogenesis typical of vegetative leaves (see Kaussmann, 1941).

Phylogeny of Stamens and Carpels

The subject of floral morphology may be appropriately concluded by a consideration of certain modern views on the evolution of the stamen and carpel in the angiosperms. Usually these sporangium-bearing organs are quite different from foliage leaves in their general form and appearance, and conflicting views still exist as to their morphological nature and evolution (Parkin, 1951). In the light of the evidence already presented in this chapter, stamens and carpels seem to be leaf-like appendages. But how should one attempt to visualize a primitive stamen or a primitive carpel? The common or conventional type of modern stamen consists of a delicate filament, which bears at its tip

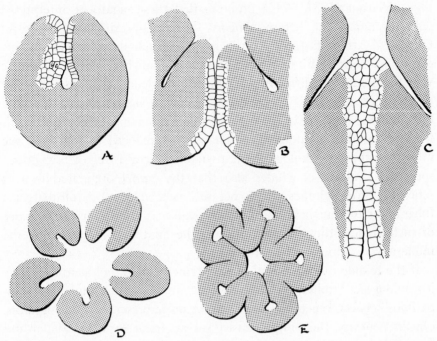

Figure 18-17 Carpel primordia and fusion of adjacent carpels in *Aquilegia truncata* var. *formosa*. **A,** transection of carpel showing initiation (two hypodermal cells with nuclei) of ovule distal to margin; **B-C,** stages in the ontogenetic fusion of the edges of two adjacent carpels; **B,** carpel edges in contact with distinct epidermal layers; **C,** edges of carpels fusing, boundary of epidermal layers becoming indistinct; **D,** transection showing typical horseshoe shape of the free carpel primordia; **E,** transection showing postgenital fusion of carpel primordia. [Redrawn from Tepfer, *Univ. Calif. Pub. in Botany*, 25:513, 1953.]

the anther containing usually four embedded microsporangia (see Fig. 18-10, also Fig. 19-1). Is this widespread type of stamen highly specialized or relatively conservative in character? As for the carpel, the classical view regards this organ fundamentally as a foliar organ in which the fused involute margins serve as the point of attachment of the enclosed ovules. Does this concept of an involutely folded, leaf-like structure provide a reliable idea of the nature and method of origin of the carpel in ancient flowering plants? Provisional answers to these questions have been recently attempted, and they merit careful consideration.

On the basis of a series of investigations on the vasculation of stamens, Wilson (1937, 1942) proposes that these organs be interpreted with the aid of the Telome Theory. This theory, discussed earlier in Chapter 3, attempts to derive vegetative megaphylls as well as sporogenous organs from primitive, dichotomously branched axes. In Wilson's view the modern angiosperm stamen, with its slender filament and compact anther, represents the end product of reduction and fusion of a dichotomous branch system with terminal sporangia. According to his idea the number of sporangia ultimately was reduced to four, and the modern anther morphologically is a synangium consisting of four microsporangia. Wilson concludes also that the carpel originated from a series of fertile telomes which became webbed to form ultimately a foliar-like structure bearing marginal ovules. Infolding of the margins of such an hypothetical structure was the final step in producing the modern ovary which encloses the ovules.

If the telome interpretation of the stamen and carpel were accepted, it would appear somewhat futile to draw any *direct* morphological comparisons between vegetative and floral organs in present-day angiosperms. On the contrary, the comprehensive surveys made by I. W. Bailey and his associates on the comparative morphology of many families in the order Ranales have produced a new and hopeful line of attack on the problem of stamen and carpel evolution (Bailey, 1954). These surveys indicate that within *living* woody members of the Ranales there have persisted not only primitive trends of wood specialization—including primitively vesselless xylem—but also types of stamens and carpels which appear relatively primitive and unspecialized in character (Figs. 18-18; 18-19; 18-20).

Degeneria, a recently investigated ranalean genus native to Fiji, provides a striking illustration of primitive stamens and carpels. The stamen of *Degeneria* is *not* differentiated into filament, anther, and connective but is a broad, foliaceous, three-veined sporophyll which develops four, slender, elongated microsporangia deeply embedded in its abaxial surface (Fig. 18-18, C, E). It should be noted that the paired sporangia are laminal rather than marginal in position, and that they lie between the lateral veins and the midvein of the stamen. Closely similar types of broad microsporophylls occur in other ranalean genera (Figs. 18-18; 18-19) such as *Austrobaileya, Himantandra* and certain members of the Magnoliaceae (Canright, 1952; Ozenda, 1952), and in the genus *Sphe-*

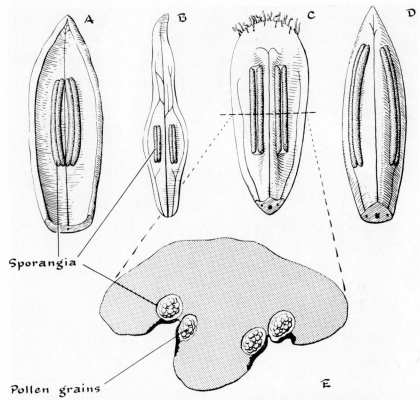

Figure 18-18 Primitive types of stamens in the Ranales. **A,** *Austrobaileya maculata,* adaxial surface showing paired sporangia at each side of midvein; **B,** *Himantandra baccata,* abaxial surface showing sporangia and relatively complex venation; **C,** *Degeneria vitiensis,* abaxial view showing pairs of sporangia between lateral veins and midvein; **D,** *Magnolia maingayi,* adaxial view showing venation and paired sporangia; **E,** diagrammatic view of transection of stamen of *Degeneria* showing the four sporangia embedded in abaxial surface. [Redrawn from Canright, *Amer. Jour. Bot.* 39:484, 1952.]

nostemon (Bailey, 1956b). In the Magnoliaceae Canright was able to arrange the various stamen types in an evolutionary series, beginning with broad, three-veined microsporophylls and culminating in types with marginal sporangia and with a definable differentiation into anther and filament. He regards the stamen of *Degeneria,* however, as "the closest of all *known* types to a primitive angiosperm stamen."

The megasporophyll of *Degeneria* differs in many fundamental respects from the typical angiosperm carpel with its differentiation into a closed ovary, style, and stigma. When studied in transectional

Figure 18-19   Flower of *Liriodendron tulipifera* showing external perianth, numerous stamens with abaxially embedded sporangia, and central group of closely crowded carpels. [From *Botany. An Introduction to Plant Science*, Ed. 2, by Robbins, Weier and Stocking. N. Y.: John Wiley and Sons, Inc., 1957.]

view during early ontogeny, the carpel of *Degeneria* is a conduplicately folded structure, the closely adjacent margins of which flare outwardly but remain unfused for a considerable time (Fig. 18-20). Thus, during this stage in development, the open carpellary margins form a narrow cleft extending from the exterior to the inner cavity or locule.

Swamy's (1949) investigation shows that, beginning with the flared carpellary margins an extensive development of epidermal hairs proceeds inwardly toward the locule, ultimately extending beyond the points of attachment of the ovules (Fig. 18-20). The space between the closely adjacent carpellary margins becomes filled with interlocking hairs, whereas the trichomes on the inner surface of the carpel are short and papillate. Collectively, all these hairs represent a stigmatic surface. Pollination involves the deposition of pollen grains on the adaxial hairy divergent margins of the open carpel. Swamy observed that the developing pollen tubes grow into the cavity of the carpel between the hairs and along the papillate surface—in no instance do the tubes penetrate the tissue of the carpel. The position and source of vascular supply of the ovules in *Degeneria* are remarkable also. The two rows of ovules are remote during initiation and development from the true margins of the carpel, and some are vascularized from branches of the ventral bundles, some from branches of the dorsal bundles, and still others by strands derived from both the main ventral and dorsal bundles. Following pollination and the fertilization of the ovules, the adjacent adaxial surfaces of the carpel become concrescent, and the recurved portions of the margins persist as parallel corky ridges on the mature fruit.

Additional examples of conduplicate carpels with extensive marginal stigmatic surfaces occur in the Winteraceae, another highly interesting ranalean family exhibiting many primitive morphological characters including the total absence of vessels in the xylem. According to Bailey and Swamy (1951) "the least modified form of surviving carpel" occurs in *Drimys piperita* and allied species of this genus. The young carpel is stalked, but, like the carpel of *Degeneria*, consists of a conduplicately folded lamina enclosing a series of ovules attached to the adaxial inner surface, distal to the carpellary margins (Fig. 18-21, B, D). This carpel, during the period of anthesis, can readily be unfolded and cleared, revealing that the ovules are attached to areas between the dorsal and two lateral veins (Fig. 18-21, C). As in *Degeneria*, the ovules of *Drimys piperita* are vascularized by extensions from either the dorsal or ventral carpellary bundles or by bundles that arise from strands derived from both the median and lateral systems. Pollen grains adhere to the external stigmatic marginal hairs, and, as in *Degeneria*, the pollen tubes reach the ovules by growing through the mat of hairs which extend inwardly

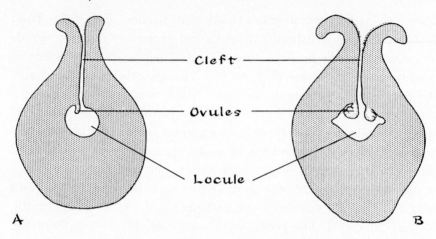

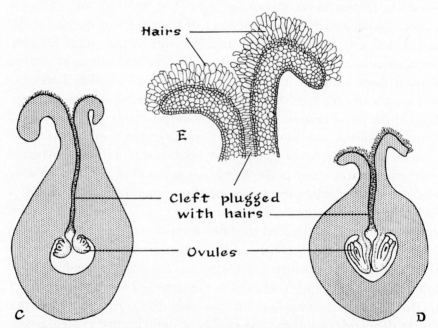

Figure 18-20 Transections of conduplicate carpel of *Degeneria* showing position of ovules and gradual occlusion of cleft between margins by development of hairs. **A,** young stage with open glabrous cleft; **B,** showing initiation of hairs on adaxial surface of flared ventral halves of the carpel; **C-D,** progressive inward development of hairs and occlusion of the cleft; **E,** detailed structure of dense mat of hairs within the cleft and on the adaxial flared ventral edges of the carpel. [Redrawn by Mrs. Emily E. Reid from Swamy, *Jour. Arnold Arboretum* 30:10, 1949.]

Figure 18-21 The primitive conduplicate carpel of *Drimys piperita*. **A,** side view showing the paired stigmatic crests; **B,** transection showing attachment of ovules and growth of a pollen tube through the mass of hairs which lies between the ventral surfaces of the carpel; **C,** cleared unfolded carpel show vasculature and variations in derivation of ovule traces; **D,** unfolded carpel showing the course of the pollen tubes and the laminal placentation of the ovules. [Redrawn from Bailey and Swamy, *Amer. Jour. Bot.* 38:373, 1951.]

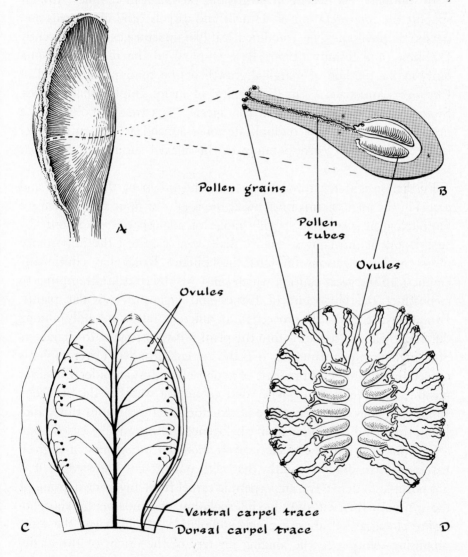

to the surface of the locule (Fig. 18-21, B, D). The varied and complex trends of carpel specialization that have presumably arisen from the primitive condition exemplified in *Degeneria* and *Drimys piperita* are described in detail by Bailey and Swamy (1951) but will not be discussed in this book.

In summary, the recent investigations on ranalean families strongly support the interpretation of stamens and carpels (and also sepals and petals) as phyllomes, i.e., modified leaf-like appendages. Very recently Periasamy and Swamy (1956) have emphasized the remarkable similarity in the method of marginal growth of the conduplicate carpel of *Cananga* (Annonaceae) to that typical of many simple foliage leaves. Swamy states that the carpel of this species "is a true homologue of a nearly mature, adaxially conduplicate foliar appendage, the entire inner surface of the cleft corresponding to the adaxial surface of the foliar lamina."

Further insight regarding the nature and origin of the stamen and carpel in the angiosperms must await the results of more comprehensive morphological surveys of a wide range of angiosperms. It is only by such laborious procedures that we shall be able to test the importance of recent investigations on ranalean families. Bailey has continually emphasized the great caution which must be observed in attempting to reconstruct the phylogeny of tissues and organs in vascular plants. Evolution has evidently proceeded at different rates, not only among different organs or tissues within the plant but with respect to characters of a single organ or structure. It is thus essential to avoid overemphasis on certain selected end products of evolution and to consider whenever possible the *totality* of evidence derived from a study of the ontogeny and morphology of a wide range of structural features. From this standpoint, the sound development of phylogenetic ideas must be based upon a full consideration of the *successively modified ontogenies* of a given tissue or organ. Bailey remarks that with our present knowledge "it is not possible to derive the angiospermic carpel from any known group of the gymnosperms without the interpolation of fundamental morphological changes that are excessively speculative." In his view, the most promising solution to the abiding mystery of the origin of the angiosperms would appear to be in the paleobotanical study of plant remains in the Austro-Malayan and Indo-Malayan regions.

Pollination, Gametophytes, and Fertilization

One of the salient and definitive characteristics of the angiosperms is the greatly reduced nature of the gametophyte generation. Following the classical investigations on the nature of sexual reproduction which were made during the nineteenth century, numerous studies have been devoted in the past fifty years to gametophyte development, fertilization, and the ontogeny of the embryo and endosperm in the flowering plants. As a result we now possess extensive information on the details of angiosperm reproduction, and admirable discussions of the facts and interpretations are presented by several recent authors (Maheshwari, 1950; Johansen, 1950; Battaglia, 1951; Wardlaw, 1955). The final chapter in this book attempts to present a connected account of sporogenesis, the gametophytes, and seed development in angiosperms. In concluding this chapter, however, it will be desirable to comment briefly on certain broad aspects of the sexual reproduction of angiosperms, which serve, like the stamen and carpel, to distinguish the flowering plants from all other tracheophyta.

In contrast with the direct pollination of the ovule typical of gymnosperms, the pollen grains of angiosperms are deposited, by various means (e.g., wind, or insects), on a special receptive surface. In the majority of angiosperms this receptive surface is the stigma of the carpel, but in a few primitive types (*Degeneria, Drimys*) the hairy, more or less open margins of the conduplicate carpel serve as a stigmatic area (Figs. 18-20; 18-21, B, D).

From a comparative viewpoint, the male gametophyte in angiosperms is a highly reduced structure because all traces of prothallial cells have been eliminated, and the generative cell gives rise to two non-flagellated male gametes (Fig. 19-6). These cells are conveyed directly to the female gametophyte by the pollen tube. From a phylogenetic standpoint, Maheshwari (1950) concludes that "the male gametophyte of angiosperms may be assumed to have been derived from that of some gymnospermous ancestor by further simplification and elimination of the single prothallial or the stalk cell."

Much attention has been devoted in recent years to the details of development and structure of the female gametophyte or embryo sac

in various families of the angiosperms. As a result, a typology of embryo
sacs has gradually arisen, and it will be considered in some detail in the
next chapter. One of the most interesting results of comparative studies,
however, is the suprisingly uniform organization of the embryo sac in
widely separated families and genera. According to Maheshwari, in
approximately 70 percent of all investigated angiosperms the mature
embryo sac consists of eight nuclei or cells as follows: an "egg apparatus"
(situated at the micropylar end) composed of a *single egg* flanked by
two synergids, a group of three or sometimes many *antipodal cells*
(located at the lower end), and two *polar nuclei* (which may fuse prior
to fertilization) found in the central region of the embryo sac (Fig.
19-11). This common type of eight-nucleate embryo sac has often been
adduced as an argument in favor of the idea that the angiosperms are
monophyletic in origin. However, in this connection it must be emphasized that efforts to derive the angiosperm embryo sac by reduction from
any of the types of female gametophytes found in living gymnosperms
rest upon highly speculative assumptions. In particular, the repeated
attempts that have been made to homologize the egg apparatus—and
even the group of antipodal cells—with reduced archegonia seem entirely
conjectural and devoid of substantial evidence. (See Maheshwari, 1950,
and Battaglia, 1951, for discussions of the archegonial theories of embryo
sac organization.) According to Battaglia (1951), "an archegonial
homology between angiosperms and gymnosperms does not exist." This
conclusion serves to emphasize our present ignorance of the phyletic
origin and evolutionary history of the flowering plants.

In marked contrast with the gymnosperms, *both* of the male cells
introduced into the embryo sac of angiosperms normally are concerned
in a fusion process. One male gamete unites with the egg cell (syngamy),
resulting in a zygote, while the other male gamete fuses with the two
polar nuclei, producing a primary endosperm nucleus. The cells or
tissue resulting from the latter constitute the endosperm of the developing seed. The participation of both male gametes in fusion processes has
long been designated double fertilization, and, regardless of how it may
be interpreted, this process represents one of the most definitive aspects
of reproduction in the angiosperms. Obviously the interpretations of the
meaning of double fertilization directly affect the morphological inter-

pretation of the endosperm in the angiosperm seed, as will be discussed at some length in the final chapter of the book.

Fruits and Seeds

Pollination and fertilization normally result in the development of a fruit which contains one or more seeds. The word "fruit" is often used in botany in a very general sense to designate structures that serve, in some way, to propagate new individual plants. In a strict sense, however, the term fruit is most appropriately restricted to that structure in angiosperms that results from the enlargement and specialization of the gynoecium, often accompanied by the modified development of adjacent floral organs, e.g., the receptacle. Many classifications of angiosperm fruits have been proposed, and are presented in one form or another in elementary or advanced textbooks. The suggested classifications and terminologies are somewhat contradictory and confused, and a discussion of this problem cannot be included in the present book. (See Winkler, 1939, for a proposed revised classification of angiosperm fruits.) It should be emphasized, however, that a more natural classification of fruit types fundamentally still awaits a more comprehensive knowledge of the comparative ontogeny and vasculation of the flower in the angiosperms.

Because of the similarity in origin and development, there is considerable agreement between the general structure of angiosperm and gymnosperm seeds. But a striking contrast is provided by the origin of the nutritive or reserve-food tissue in the two living groups of seed plants. In gymnosperms the reserve food utilized by the embryo and early seedling is the haploid female gametophyte itself. The endosperm tissue in angiosperm seeds arises from a fusion nucleus and, as will be discussed in the last chapter, varies widely in chromosome number although very commonly it is triploid. On the basis of chromosome number therefore, the endosperm tissue of angiosperms is usually neither sporophytic nor gametophytic in its morphological nature.

Summary and Conclusions

The angiosperms or flowering plants are the dominant tracheophytes of the modern floras of the earth. In structure and reproduction they are extremely diversified and complex, and they do not appear to have evolved from any of the existing groups of pteropsid plants. In this chapter we have attempted to discuss critically certain aspects of the vegetative organography, anatomy, floral morphology, and sexual reproduction of angiosperms from the standpoint of evolution.

The foliage leaves of angiosperms are highly diversified in form and morphological organization and, early in the chapter a brief discussion was given of simple, compound, and peltate types of leaf blades. An outstanding structural feature of angiosperms, urgently in need of ontogenetic and comparative study, is the complex venation of the leaf. The use of venation patterns in the identification and classification of fossilized and modern angiospermous leaves has been emphasized, and a critical treatment was given of the use of the term "parallel" as applied to the course of the veins in the leaves of monocotyledons. Finally, we presented a brief description of the histology of the epidermis, mesophyll, and veins in the leaf blades of angiosperms.

Certain of the general anatomical features of stems have been briefly outlined, and the effects of secondary growth on the primary body noted. Angiosperms are typical pteropsid plants because the vascular cylinder at each node is interrupted by the divergence of one or more leaf traces. A short discussion was given of phylogenetic interpretations of nodal anatomy, with particular reference to the possibility that the unilacunar type of node may represent the original condition from which the trilacunar and multilacunar patterns have evolved.

The important rôle of wood anatomy in the systematic and phylogenetic study of angiosperms was emphasized. In particular, the origin of vessels from tracheids and the independent and unidirectional paths of evolution of vessels have been clearly determined. Recent studies indicate that vessels originated independently in the monocotyledons and dicotyledons. This interpretation suggests that the two classes of angiosperms may have evolved from a common vesselless ancestral type.

Considerable attention also was given to the vexed problem of the morphological nature of the flower in the angiosperm. From the restricted concept, a flower is a determinate sporogenous shoot, and one of its most definitive organs is the carpel. According to the classical theory, the sepals, petals, stamens, and carpels of the flower are the morphological equivalents of leaves. Although there is no decisive paleo-botanical evidence to support this idea, the evidence from vascular anatomy and ontogeny emphasizes the marked resemblances between vegetative and floral appendages. The shoot-like vasculation of the flower of *Aquilegia* has been described in detail as an example of the application of anatomy in the interpretation of floral structure. A few selected instances of the effects of fusion on the vasculature of single carpels as well as of syncarpous gynoecia have also been briefly discussed, and the shoot-like nature of the flower was examined from the stand-point of ontogeny. In *Aquilegia*, for example, there is close similarity in the initiation and early cellular development of foliage leaves, bracts, and floral organs. The resemblances are emphasized by the acropetal pattern of development of the procambium, which is common to the primordia of all these types of appendages.

Because there is no fossil record of primitive angiosperm flowers, the phylogeny of floral organs has been the subject of much conjecture and speculation. Recent studies on certain woody genera of the Ranales were reviewed with particular reference to the structure of presumably primitive types of stamens and carpels. According to current views, primitive stamens are broad, foliaceous, three-veined structures with deeply embedded microsporangia. These organs do not show the familiar distinction between filament, anther, and connective illustrated in typical angiospermous stamens. Primitive carpels likewise differ in many ways from the conventional type of carpel which is demarcated into ovary, style, and stigma. Perhaps the least modified type of existing carpel occurs in *Drimys* (Winteraceae) and *Degeneria* (Degeneriaceae). In these the carpel is a conduplicately folded sporophyll which bears two rows of ovules on its inner adaxial surface. During pollination the pollen tubes grow into the cavity of the carpel through the dense mat of hairs which occupy the space between the closely adjacent but unfused carpel-lary margins.

The chapter terminates with a brief résumé of the reproductive cycle in angiosperms. Particular emphasis was placed on the conspicuously reduced structure of the gametophytes. The female gametophyte, commonly known as the embryo sac, most frequently consists of an egg apparatus composed of a single egg flanked by two synergids, a group of three (sometimes more) antipodal cells, and two polar nuclei (which may fuse before fertilization). Attempts to homologize the angiosperm embryo sac with the female gametophyte of gymnosperms appear, in the light of present knowledge, highly speculative in character.

A salient and definitive characteristic of angiosperms is the participation of *both* male gametes in a fusion process with cells in the embryo sac. One male gamete unites with the egg, resulting in a zygote from which the embryo develops, and the other fuses with the polar nuclei, resulting in a primary endosperm nucleus. The cells or tissue arising from the primary endosperm nucleus constitute the endosperm distinctive of angiosperm seeds. The functioning of both male gametes in the embryo sac is commonly designated double fertilization, but the evolutionary origin of this process is still a mystery.

References

Andrews, H. N. Jr. 1947. *Ancient Plants and the World they Lived in.* Comstock Publishing Co., Ithaca, N. Y.

Arber, A. 1937. The interpretation of the flower: a study of some aspects of morphological thought. *Biol. Rev.* 12:157-184.

————. 1946. Goethe's Botany. *Chronica Botanica* 10:67-124.

Arber, E. A. N. and Parkin, J. 1907. On the origin of angiosperms. *Jour. Linn. Soc. Bot.* 38:29-80.

Arnold, C. A. 1947. *An Introduction to Paleobotany.* McGraw-Hill, New York.

Axelrod, D. I. 1952. A theory of angiosperm evolution. *Evolution* 6:29-60.

Bailey, I. W. 1944. The development of vessels in angiosperms and its significance in morphological research. *Amer. Jour. Bot.* 31:421-428.

————. 1953. Evolution of the tracheary tissue of land plants. *Amer. Jour. Bot.* 40:4-8.

————. 1954. *Contributions to Plant Anatomy.* Chronica Botanica Co., Waltham, Mass.

————. 1956a. Nodal anatomy in retrospect. *Jour. Arnold Arboretum* 37: 269-287.

————. 1956b. The relationship between *Sphenostemon* of New Caledonia and *Nouhuysia* of New Guinea. *Jour. Arnold Arboretum* 37:360-365.

————. 1957. The potentialities and limitations of wood anatomy in the study of the phylogeny and classification of angiosperms. *Jour. Arnold Arboretum* 38:243-254.

————. and B. G. L. Swamy. 1951. The conduplicate carpel of dicotyledons and its initial trends of specialization. *Amer. Jour. Bot.* 38:373-379.

Battaglia, E. 1951. The male and female gametophytes of angiosperms —an interpretation. *Phytomorphology* 1:87-116.

Baum, H. 1948a. Über die postgenital Verwachsung in Karpellen. *Österreich Bot. Zeit.* 95:86-94.

————. 1948b. Postgenitale Verwachsung in und zwischen Karpell—und Staubblattkreisen. Sitzungsber. *Österr. Akad. Wiss. Math-naturw Kl. Abt. I.* 157:17-38.

Boke, N. H. 1947. Development of the adult shoot apex and floral initiation in *Vinca rosea.* L. *Amer. Jour. Bot.* 34:433-439.

Buvat, R. 1952. Structure évolution et fonctionnement du méristème apical de quelques Dicotylédones. *Ann Sci. Bot. Nat. XI* 13:199-300.

Canright, J. E. 1952. The comparative morphology and relationships of the Magnoliaceae. I. Trends of specialization in the stamens. *Amer. Jour. Bot.* 39:484-497.

Cheadle, V. I. 1953. Independent origin of vessels in the monocotyledons and dicotyledons. *Phytomorphology* 3:23-44.

————. 1956. Research on xylem and phloem—Progress in fifty years. *Amer. Jour. Bot.* 43:719-731.

Constance, L. 1955. The systematics of the angiosperms. From: A Century of Progress in the Natural Sciences, 1853-1953. California Academy of Sciences. 405-483.

De Candolle, A. P. 1844. *Organographie végétale. Vol. 1.* Germer Bailliere, Paris.

Eames, A. J. 1931. The vascular anatomy of the flower with refutation of the theory of carpel polymorphism. *Amer. Jour. Bot.* 18:147-188.

————. 1951. Again: 'The New Morphology.' *New Phytologist* 50:17-35.

————. and L. H. MacDaniels. 1947. *An Introduction to Plant Anatomy.* Ed. 2. McGraw-Hill, New York.

Engler, A. 1926. Angiospermae In Engler and Prantl's "Die natürlichen Pflanzenfamilien." Bd. 14a.

Esau, K. 1953. *Plant Anatomy.* Wiley, New York.

Fagerlind, F. 1946. Strobilus und Blüte von *Gnetum* und die Moglichkeit, aus ihrer Struktur den Blütenbau der angiospermen zu deuten. *Arkiv för Botanik* 33A (No. 8):1-57.

Foster, A. S. 1950a. Morphology and venation of the leaf in *Quiina acu-*

tangula Ducke. *Amer. Jour. Bot.* 37: 159-171.

―――. 1950b. Venation and histology of the leaflets in *Touroulia guianensis* Aubl. and *Froesia tricarpa* Pires. *Amer. Jour. Bot.* 37:848-862.

―――. 1951. Heterophylly and foliar venation in *Lacunaria*. *Bull. Torrey Bot. Club* 78:382-400.

―――. 1952. Foliar venation in angiosperms from an ontogenetic standpoint. *Amer. Jour. Bot.* 39:752-766.

―――. 1953. Venation patterns in the leaves of angiosperms, with special reference to the Quiinaceae. *Proc. Seventh Int. Bot. Congress* (Stockholm, 1950), p. 380.

Gifford, E. M. Jr. 1954. The shoot apex of angiosperms. *Bot. Rev.* 20:477-529.

Goebel, K. 1905. *Organography of Plants.* Eng. Ed. by I. B. Balfour. Part II. Clarendon Press, Oxford.

Goethe, J. W. von. 1790. Versuch die Metamorphose der Pflanzen zu erklären. Gotha.

Grégoire, V. 1938. La morphogénèse et l'autonomie morphologique de l'appareil floral. I. Le carpelle. *La Cellule* 47:287-452.

Johansen, D. A. 1950. *Plant Embryology.* Chronica Botanica Co., Waltham, Mass.

Kasapligil, B. 1951. Morphological and ontogenetic studies of *Umbellularia california* Nutt. and *Laurus nobilis* L. *Univ. Calif. Publ. Bot.* 25:115-240.

Kaussmann, B. 1941. Vergleichende Untersuchungen über die Blattnatur der Kelch, Blumen und Staubblätter. *Bot. Archiv.* 42:503-572.

Lemesle, R. 1946. Les divers types de fibres à ponctuations aréolées chez les dicotylédones apocarpiques le plus archaïques et leur rôle dans la phylogénie. *Ann. Sci. Nat. Bot. et Biol. Végétale.* XI. 7:19-40.

Maheshwari, P. 1950. *An Introduction to the Embryology of Angiosperms.* McGraw-Hill, New York.

Marsden, M. P. F. and I. W. Bailey. 1955. A fourth type of nodal anatomy in dicotyledons, illustrated by *Clerodendron trichotomum* Thunb. *Jour. Arnold Arboretum* 36:1-50.

―――. and T. A. Steeves. 1955. On the primary vascular system and the nodal anatomy of *Ephedra*. *Jour. Arnold Arboretum* 36:241-258.

Mason, H. L. 1957. The concept of the flower and the theory of homology. *Madroño* 14:81-95.

McCoy, R. W. 1940. Floral organogenesis in *Frasera carolinensis*. *Amer. Jour. Bot.* 27:600-609.

Metcalfe, C. R. and L. Chalk. 1950. *Anatomy of the Dicotyledons.* 2 v. Clarendon Press, Oxford.

Ozenda, P. 1952. Remarques sur quelques interprétations de l'étamine. *Phytomorphology* 2:225-231.

Parkin, J. 1951. The protrusion of the connective beyond the anther and its bearing on the evolution of the stamen. *Phytomorphology* 1:1-8.

Periasamy K. and B. G. L. Swamy. 1956. The conduplicate carpel of *Cananga odorata*. *Jour. Arnold Arboretum* 37:366-372.

Philipson, W. R. 1947. Some observations on the apical meristem of leafy and flowering shoots. *Jour. Linn. Soc. Bot.* 53:187-193.

————. 1949. The ontogeny of the shoot apex in dicotyledons. *Biol. Rev.* 24:21-50.

Pray, T. R. 1954. Foliar venation in angiosperms. I. Mature venation of *Liriodendron*. *Amer. Jour. Bot.* 41: 663-670.

————. 1955a. Foliar venation of angiosperms. II. Histogenesis of the venation of *Liriodendron*. *Amer. Jour. Bot.* 42:18-27.

————. 1955b. Foliar venation of angiosperms. III. Pattern and histology of the venation of *Hosta*. *Amer. Jour. Bot.* 42:611-618.

————. 1955c. Foliar venation of angiosperms. IV. Histogenesis of the venation of *Hosta*. *Amer. Jour. Bot.* 42:698-706.

Puri, V. 1951. The rôle of floral anatomy in the solution of morphological problems. *Bot. Rev.* 17:471-553.

Sinnott, E. W. 1914. Investigations on the angiosperms. I. The anatomy of the node as an aid in the classification of angiosperms. *Amer. Jour. Bot.* 1: 303-322.

Solereder, H. 1908. *Systematic Anatomy of the Dicotyledons*. 2 v. Clarendon Press, Oxford.

Swamy, B. G. L. 1949. Further contributions to the morphology of the Degeneriaceae. *Jour. Arnold Arboretum* 30:10-38.

Tepfer, S. S. 1953. Floral anatomy and ontogeny in *Aquilegia formosa* var. *truncata* and *Ranunculus repens*. *Univ. Calif. Pub. in Bot.* 25:513-648.

Thomas, H. H. 1955. Mesozoic Pteridosperms. *Phytomorphology* 5:177-185.

Thompson, J. McLean. 1934. Studies in advancing sterility. VII. The state of flowering known as angiospermy (with special reference to placentation and the origin and nature of follicles and achenes). *Univ. Liverpool, Hartley Bot. Lab. Pub.* 12:5-47.

Troll, W. 1935, 1937, 1938, 1939. *Vergleichende Morphologie der höheren Pflanzen*. Gebrüder Borntraeger, Berlin.

Van Tieghem, P. 1875. Recherches sur la structure du pistil et sur l'anatomie comparée de la fleur. *Mem. Acad. Sci. Inst. Imp. France* 21:1-262.

Von Ettinghausen, C. R. 1861. Die Blatt-Skelette der Dicotyledonen mit besonderer Rücksicht auf die Untersuchung und Bestimmung der fossilen Pflanzenreste. Kais. Kön. Hof und Staatsdruckerei, Wien.

Wardlaw, C. W. 1955. *Embryogenesis in Plants*. Wiley, New York.

Wilson, C. L. 1937. The phylogeny of the stamen. *Amer. Jour. Bot.* 24:686-699.

————. 1942. The telome theory and the origin of the stamen. *Amer. Jour. Bot.* 29:759-764.

————. 1953. The telome theory. *Bot. Rev.* 19:417-437.

————. and T. Just. 1939. The morphology of the flower. *Bot. Rev.* 5:97-131.

Winkler, H. 1939. Versuch eines "natürlichen" Systems der Früchte. *Beitr. Biol. Pflanz.* 26:201-220.

Chapter

19 THE REPRODUCTIVE CYCLE IN ANGIOSPERMS

In the great majority of lower vascular plants the gametophyte generation, although comparatively small in size, is completely independent of the sporophyte and is a free-living plant. In marked contrast, the gametophyte generation of gymnosperms is not only reduced in size but, in the case of the female gametophyte, is permanently enclosed within the ovule and thus entirely dependent for its nutrition on the sporophyte. This general evolutionary trend toward simplification and dependence reaches its culmination in the small, few-celled gametophytes of the angiosperms, the study of which, even today, with the best of technical methods, offers considerable difficulty to investigators.

Our present ontogenetic concepts of angiospermous gametophytes and our interpretation of the striking, novel aspects of sexual reproduction and seed formation in this group go back to the inspired and careful investigations that were made in Europe during the latter part of the nineteenth century. (See Maheshwari, 1950, for an excellent historical sketch of these early pioneering studies.) Modern studies on the details of the reproductive cycle in angiosperms are both voluminous and diversified, and they include systematic-phylogenetic surveys as well as the initiation of experimental work on the gametophytes and the developing seed. Some of these studies have resulted in clarification of the proper systematic disposition of certain genera or families. Others have greatly enriched our knowledge of the wide range in patterns of development of the endosperm tissue and the embryo. Hopefully, the continuous accumulation of knowledge in this area will eventually throw new and important light on the abiding mystery of the evolutionary relationships of flowering plants.

490

The publication of Maheshwari's invaluable book, "An Introduction to the Embryology of Angiosperms," has provided morphologists with an able, coherent résumé of the salient aspects of sporogenesis, gametophyte development, double fertilization, endosperm formation, and embryogeny in flowering plants. In addition to this work, extensive discussions of the reproductive cycle have been prepared by Schnarf (1927-1928, 1931, 1941), Johansen (1950), Maheshwari (1948, 1949), and Wardlaw (1955). These references will supplement the necessarily brief outline of the structures and processes in the reproductive cycle of angiosperms given in this chapter.

One of the characteristic features of sexual reproduction in angiosperms is the marked telescoping of the processes of sporogenesis and gametophyte development. Microsporogenesis, for example, is directly followed by only two mitoses, which yield the pollen grain with its typical, endosporic, three-celled male gametophyte. Megasporogenesis may involve, as in gymnosperms, the formation of a linear tetrad of morphologically discrete megaspores. But in many angiosperms, wall formation does not occur between the haploid megaspore nuclei, all four of which, by further divisions, contribute to the development of the female gametophyte. In short, the demarcation between the spore and the early phase in ontogeny of the gametophyte is frequently not sharp, and correct interpretation depends on a full appraisal of cytological details, especially the point at which meiosis occurs and the subsequent behavior and fate of the haploid nuclei.

In Chapter 18 the angiosperm flower was discussed from a broad morphological point of view, with particular emphasis on the interpretation of floral organs on the basis of their ontogeny and vasculation. In this chapter we are concerned with the rôle of the flower in reproduction, and we will attempt to present a coherent account of sporogenesis, the development of the gametophytes, pollination, fertilization, and the formation of endosperm and embryo in the seed. Because of the rapid accumulation in recent years of information on the life cycles of a wide range of angiosperms, it is now possible to present a synthetic description of the *basic features* common to all reproductive cycles in the angiosperms. This is done with full realization of the numerous— and possibly significant—departures in detail from the general situation as illustrated, for example, by the various types of embryo-sac development that are now recognized. To promote clarity in exposition, important deviations from what appears to be the typical condition will be reserved for brief discussion at the end of each topic.

Structure and Development of Microsporangia

The microsporangia of angiosperms are located in the anther of the stamen, and in certain respects appear very similar to the microsporangia of many living gymnosperms (see Fig. 18-10). In both groups of seed plants the fully developed microsporangium is provided with a thick wall, usually develops a tapetum, and contains tetrads of microspores. Further resemblances are shown by the eusporangiate pattern of development of the microsporangium in both gymnosperms and angiosperms. However, it is generally recognized that the parent cells or initials of the microsporangia in angiosperms are *consistently hypodermal* in position. As a result, the microsporangia of angiosperms are embedded in the anther, and the surface cell layer represents the epidermis rather than a component of the sporangial wall (Fig. 19-1). But it should be recalled that a rigid distinction cannot be made with reference to the position of microsporangial initials in gymnosperms and angiosperms. In the conifers, for example, the initials may be superficial, as in *Cedrus* and *Pseudotsuga*, or hypodermal, as in *Cryptomeria*, *Chamaecyparis*, and *Taxus* (see Fig. 16-10).

Despite the wide range in the external form and size of angiosperm stamens, the anther, just prior to its dehiscence, usually contains four microsporangia arranged in pairs in the two anther lobes. Members of each pair of microsporangia are separated from one another by sterile tissue, and the central tissue or connective of the anther is traversed by a strand of vascular tissue (Fig. 19-1). Since the ontogeny of all four microsporangia is similar, the following account will mainly describe the origin and development of a single microsporangium.

Shortly after its differentiation in a stamen primordium, an embryonic anther, as seen in transection, consists of a mass of ground meristem enveloped by a discrete protoderm (Fig. 19-2, A). According to Boke (1949), in *Vinca rosea* the single median procambial strand becomes well-differentiated and apparently is in continuity with the vascular system of the receptacle in stamen primordia about 150 microns in height.

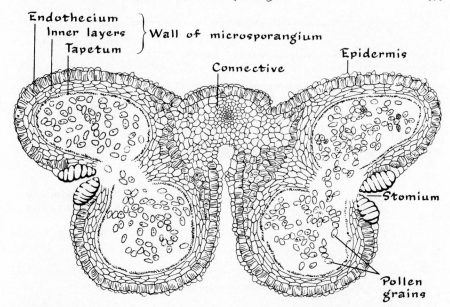

Figure 19-1 Transection of a nearly mature anther of *Lilium philadelphicum*. The sterile tissue, which originally separated the pairs of microsporangia in each half of the anther, has broken down forming a cavity within which the pollen grains occur. [Redrawn from *Morphology of Angiosperms* by J. M. Coulter and C. J. Chamberlain. N. Y.: Copyright, D. Appleton and Co., 1903, by permission Appleton-Century-Crofts, Inc.]

The entire subepidermal layer of the young anther may well be sporogenous in potentiality, as is indicated by the variable number of cells which function to produce the microsporangia. Usually, however, sporangium initiation is restricted to four separated areas which correspond to the corners of the developing anther (Fig. 19-2, B). At each of these discrete regions a more or less extensive series of hypodermal cells divide by periclinal walls. This characteristic eusporangiate pattern of initiation establishes two well-defined cell lineages, the fate of which may now be described.

The *inner* cells produced by the first periclinal division of the initials are the *primary sporogenous* cells, which may divide further or function directly as microsporocytes. The *outer* cells derived from the sporangial initials are the *primary parietal* cells; by periclinal and anticlinal divisions these cells form the several cell layers of the sporangial wall and a large part of the tapetum (Fig. 19-2, B, C). Although there is evidently no

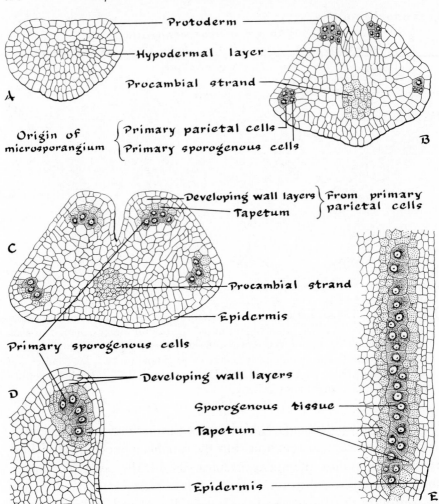

Figure 19-2   Origin and development of microsporangia in the stamen of *Vinca rosea*. **A-D,** transections of successively older stages in development of the anther. **A,** young anther with clearly defined hypodermal layer; **B,** later stage showing origin of microsporangia by periclinal divisions in four separate groups of hypodermal cells; **C,** stage illustrating the origin of a portion of the tapetum from the primary parietal cells; **D,** details of a later stage in development of a single microsporangium showing the developing wall layers and the group of sporogenous cells surrounded by the tapetum; **E,** longisection of portion of anther showing origin of inner portion of tapetum from cells adjacent to the sporogenous tissue (note the continued development of the wall layers below the epidermis). [Redrawn from Boke, *Amer. Journ. Bot.* 36:535, 1949.]

fixed sequence in the appearance of anticlinal and periclinal divisions in the differentiating parietal cells, the young wall of the microsporangium frequently consists of a series of concentric layers of cells (Fig. 19-2, D). The outermost of these layers is situated directly beneath the epidermis of the anther, and prior to the release of the pollen it develops very distinctive fibrous bands of thickenings on certain of its walls (Fig. 19-1). This well-marked outer layer of the microsporangium wall is usually designated as endothecium, and appears to function as a dehiscence mechanism in a manner somewhat similar to that of the external annulus in fern sporangia. The middle layer or layers of the wall tend to become stretched and compressed as development continues, and are often collapsed or difficult to define at the period of dehiscence of the anther (Fig. 19-1).

The innermost layer of the wall progressively differentiates into a well-defined tapetum. As noted above, a considerable portion of the tapetum morphologically represents the innermost layer of the sporangial wall; the remainder of the tapetum originates from cells, derived by fairly regular divisions, which lie adjacent to the inner boundary of the primary sporogenous tissue (Fig. 19-2, C-E). According to Boke's (1949) investigation the inner portion of the tapetum in *Vinca* is frequently several layers of cells in thickness; a comparable condition probably occurs in other angiospermous genera.

Tapetal cells in the microsporangia of angiosperms are often conspicuously enlarged and may be multinucleate or polyploid. Maheshwari's (1950) survey of the literature indicates that, despite mitotic irregularities and peculiar nuclear fusions, tapetal nuclei generally divide by normal mitosis and that amitosis (direct cleavage of the nucleus) does not occur. As in other groups of vascular plants, the tapetum (of the microsporangium of angiosperms) appears to serve as a source of nutrition for the developing spores. Two major types of tapeta, based on the behavior of the cells during sporogenesis, are recognized: the glandular or secretory tapetum, the cells of which remain in their original position but which eventually become disorganized and possibly absorbed by the adjacent sporocytes (Fig. 19-1), and the amoeboid tapetum, which is characterized by the intrusion of the tapetal protoplasts among the developing sporocytes or spores and the fusion of these protoplasts to form a tapetal periplasmodium (Fig. 19-3). It is of physiological interest

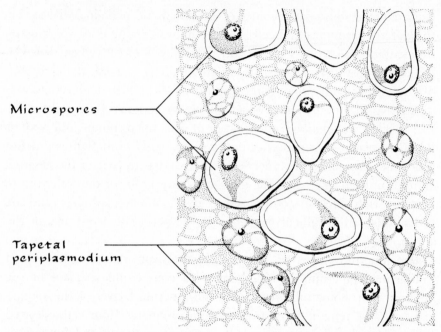

Microspores

Tapetal
periplasmodium

Figure 19-3 Section of developing microsporangium of *Symphoricarpos racemosus* illustrating the structure of the tapetal periplasmodium. [Adapted from *An Introduction to the Embryology of Angiosperms* by P. Maheshwari. N. Y.: McGraw-Hill Book Company, Inc., 1950.]

to recall at this point the two entirely comparable types of tapetal behavior in the sporangia of lower vascular plants (see Chapter 4, p. 62).

Microsporogenesis

During the formation of the sporangial wall the primary sporogenous cells may divide in various planes, the cells finally separating and functioning as microsporocytes. The microsporocytes or pollen mother cells (PMC) of angiosperms provide important and readily accessible material for the study of meiosis in the angiosperms. Indeed, it is possible, under favorable or controlled conditions, to predict the stage in stamen development at which the various phases of meiosis will be most abundantly displayed. The laborious method of sectioning fixed anthers and subsequently staining the serial sections has been replaced by the simple procedure of "squashing" the anthers in iron aceto-carmine solution directly on the slide. (See Johansen, 1940, for a detailed account of this technique.) As a result, much has been learned regarding the meiotic process and the development of pollen grains in a wide range of angiospermous species.

Each functional microsporocyte, by means of meiosis and wall formation, gives rise to a tetrad of haploid microspores or pollen grains. As shown in Fig. 19-4, wide variation occurs among species or even within the same species with reference to the arrangement of the spores in the tetrad. Apparently the two most common patterns of arrangement are the tetrahedral and the isobilateral. Much study has been devoted to the process of cytokinesis or wall formation in the developing microsporocyte, and two well-contrasted types are recognized. In the so-called *successive type* each of the two meiotic divisions of the nucleus is followed by the formation of a wall (Fig. 19-5, A-E). In the *simultaneous type* walls are formed by "furrowing" *after* the four nuclei have been produced (Fig. 19-5, F-I). Although the simultaneous type seems prevalent in dicotyledons and the successive type is characteristic of many monocotyledons, there are frequent exceptions to this systematic correlation. Moreover, there is apparently no exact correlation between the method of spore arrangement in the tetrad and the mode of wall formation.

Most commonly the spore members of each tetrad separate from one another and lie freely within the microsporangium (Fig. 19-1). In a number of genera, however, clusters of spore tetrads adhere in groups,

Figure 19-4 Various types of arrangement of microspores in a tetrad. [Adapted from *An Introduction to the Embryology of Angiosperms* by P. Maheshwari. N. Y.: McGraw-Hill Book Company, Inc., 1950.]

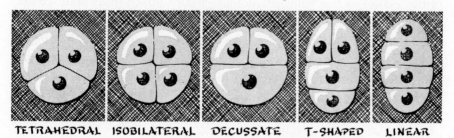

TETRAHEDRAL   ISOBILATERAL   DECUSSATE   T-SHAPED   LINEAR

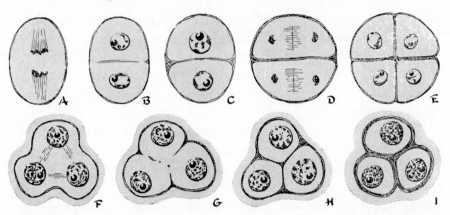

Figure 19-5 Types of cytokinesis in microsporocytes. **A-E,** the successive type in *Zea Mays*; **F-I,** the simultaneous type in *Melilotus alba* (note centripetal direction of furrows separating the microspore protoplasts as shown in **G-H**). [Adapted from *An Introduction to the Embryology of Angiosperms* by P. Maheshwari. N. Y.: McGraw-Hill Book Company, Inc., 1950.]

and, in the Asclepiadaceae, for example, all of the microspores of a sporangium cohere in a single mass termed the pollinium.

When mature, the microspores or pollen grains of angiosperms exhibit a thick exine, which is apparently deposited on the surface of the cell as it develops. The range in form, size, and types of wall sculpture in pollen grains is very extensive and of considerable value in the identification of fossil spores, the systematic definition of species, genera, or even larger taxa, and in the validation of theories as to the evolutionary relationship between angiosperms and other groups of vascular plants. The rapidly growing interest in the comparative morphology of pollen grains has recently emerged in the form of a separate division of plant morphology designated as palynology. As conceived by Erdtman (1952), who is one of the leaders in this field, palynology "means pollen and spore science. It deals chiefly with the walls of pollen grains and spores, not with their live interior." During the rapid development of modern palynology a complex series of new concepts and new terminologies has been proposed. A discussion, even brief, of these matters lies beyond the scope of this book, and the interested student should turn to the works of Wodehouse (1935) and Erdtman (1952) for comprehensive treatments of the varied aspects of pollen morphology.

The Male Gametophyte

As was pointed out in earlier chapters, the male gametophyte of gymnosperms varies as to the number and types of sterile cells present. Commonly, however, one or more strictly vegetative prothallial cells occur, and the generative cell produces a stalk and body cell, the latter representing the parent cell of the two male gametes. In contrast, the male gametophyte of angiosperms is characterized, with few exceptions, by a consistent and simple type of morphological structure and by the remarkably uniform pattern of its development. A total of two successive mitoses yield a three-celled gametophyte consisting of two male gametes and a vegetative cell (Fig. 19-6, H). The conspicuous absence of prothallial cells and the direct origin of the two gametes from the generative cell lead to the conclusion that the male gametophyte generation in angiosperms is the end product of a profound phylogenetic reduction, possibly from some hypothetical gymnospermous-like condition (see Maheshwari, 1950, pp. 411-412; Battaglia, 1951).

Figure 19-6 presents schematically the main steps in the ontogeny of the male gametophyte in angiosperms. Prior to the first mitosis the nucleus of the microspore becomes displaced toward the wall. It then divides into the generative cell and the vegetative cell (Fig. 19-6, B-D). According to Maheshwari's review of the literature, in plants in which the pollen grains remain attached in tetrads, variation occurs as to the relative position of the generative nucleus. Sometimes it lies next to the inner wall (i.e., the wall facing the center of the spore tetrad), whereas in other cases it may lie near the outer wall of each pollen grain or even adjacent to one of the sides or corners. Apparently there is marked uniformity as to the early position of the generative cell in certain species or genera, and hence this feature may be of taxonomic importance.

Soon after its formation, the generative cell loses contact with the spore wall and appears as a lenticular or ellipsoidal cell lying in the cytoplasm of the vegetative cell (Fig. 19-6, E, F).

In many instances the male gametophyte is in the two-celled stage shown in Fig. 19-6, F, at the time the pollen grains are liberated by the dehiscence of the anther. According to Maheshwari, however, an increasing number of cases have been observed where the generative

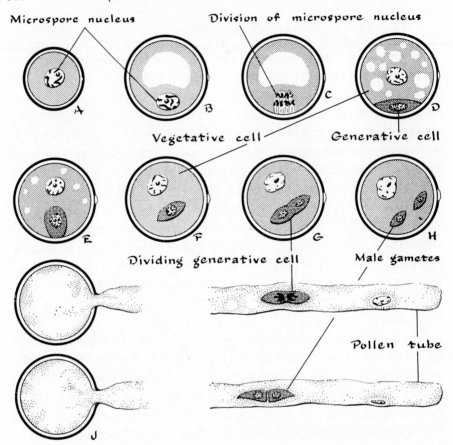

Figure 19-6 Development of the male gametophyte in angiosperms (see text for full discussion of this diagram). [Redrawn from Maheshwari, *Bot. Rev.* 15:1, 1949.]

nucleus divides prior to the release of the pollen grains. Probably a sharp distinction between two-celled and three-celled pollen grains should not be drawn since some observers report that the generative cell may be in prophase or even metaphase at the time the pollen is shed. Whether the generative cell divides within the pollen grain (Fig. 19-6, G, H), or after it has descended into the pollen tube (Fig. 19-6, I, J), considerable technical difficulties arise in attempting to study the details of spindle and cell-plate formation. In many cases, when proper fixation and staining are employed, the two male gametes are at first separated by a delicate and ephemeral cell plate.

Considerable attention has been devoted to the cytological aspects of the development, structure, and behavior of the two gametes in the male gametophyte of angiosperms (for details see Maheshwari, 1950). In contrast with the flagellated sperms of all lower vascular plants and lower types of gymnosperms, the male gamete of an angiosperm is devoid of flagella and consists of a nucleus surrounded by a sheath of cytoplasm; the latter can be recognized, in a number of cases, up to the time the sperms are discharged into the embryo sac. The mechanism involved in the movement of the gametes in the developing pollen tube is still a debatable problem. Originally it was suggested that the two gametes move passively in the streaming cytoplasm of the tube. Observations on living pollen tubes, however, suggest the possibility that the gametes are capable of autonomous movement, since their descent toward the tip of the tube does not entirely coincide with the direction of cytoplasmic streaming.

In concluding this section a few comments are needed regarding the behavior and possible significance of the vegetative nucleus during the growth of the pollen tube. The assumption has commonly been made that the vegetative nucleus—also termed the tube nucleus—functions in some manner to control the intrusive advance of the pollen tube. Maheshwari (1950, pp. 169-170), however, has presented evidence from the literature which casts doubt on the physiological rôle if any, of the vegetative nucleus. In some plants the vegetative nucleus begins to degenerate soon after its formation (Fig. 19-6, G, H). Even when it can be recognized in the developing pollen tube, the vegetative nucleus does not always precede the male gametes (as commonly stated) but may lie behind them. In the light of these facts, the function and phylogenetic nature of the vegetative nucleus appear very problematical and clearly deserve further investigation.

The Ovule

Before discussing megasporogenesis and the various patterns of origin and development of the female gametophyte, it will be essential to describe the salient features of the ovule or megasporangium.

Since the ovule is the structure within which meiosis and megaspore formation occur, it *functionally* represents a megasporangium. But, as in the gymnosperms, the ovule of angiosperms is relatively complex *structurally,* since it normally consists of a stalk or funiculus, which bears the nucellus, surrounded by one or two integuments (Fig. 19-7, J). Commonly a single hypodermal cell at the micropylar end of the nucellus is the parent cell of the megaspores (or megaspore nuclei), which thus are strictly embedded within the sterile tissue of the nucellus (Fig. 19-7, D). This condition is strikingly parallel with the embedded character of the microsporangium in the sterile tissue of the anther (Fig. 19-2, B).

On the whole, angiosperm ovules are relatively small as compared with the ovules of gymnosperms, and often develop in large numbers from the plancentae of the ovary. The primordium of an ovule arises by the localized periclinal divisions of the hypodermal cell layer and rapidly differentiates into the young nucellus (Fig. 19-7, A). As the nucellus enlarges, growth may be unequal, resulting in various degrees of curvature of the main body of the ovule. The type of development illustrated in Fig. 19-7 leads to the common anatropous type of ovule in which the micropyle becomes directed inwardly toward the point of attachment of the funiculus. If the ovule develops in an erect position, it is designated as orthotropous. During the enlargement of the nucellus the integument or integuments arise as rim-like outgrowths from the surface cells of the nucellus. When two integuments occur the inner integument arises first and is followed by the initiation of the outer integument (Fig. 19-7, A, B). The micropyle in the mature ovule very commonly is a narrow tubular opening in the inner integument, although in some plants both integuments contribute to the formation of the micropyle. In the higher groups of the dicotyledons (i.e., the Sympetalae) the ovule is usually provided with a single integument, whereas in lower dicotyledons and many monocotyledons the ovule forms two integuments. Because of the still problematical phylogenetic nature of the integuments of ovules, the evolutionary significance of unitegmic (one integument) and bitegmic (two integuments) ovules is by no means clear.

The ovule in angiosperms is vascularized by a single bundle which often is restricted to the funiculus and terminates blindly in the chalazal region of the nucellus. According to Maheshwari's survey of the literature, the integuments of the ovules in a wide range of dicotyledonous families are also vasculated by strands derived from the main bundle of

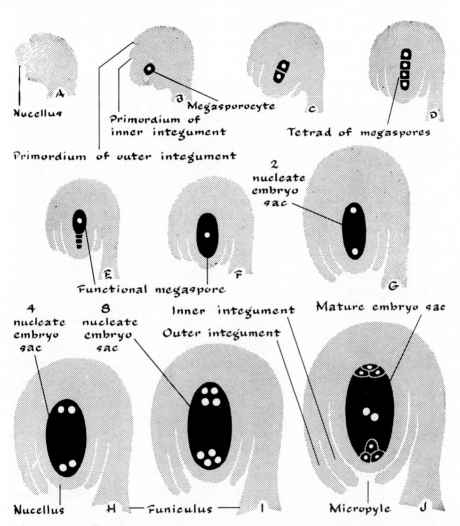

Figure 19-7 Development of an angiosperm ovule, beginning with the formation of the integuments and the single megasporocyte (A-B), continuing through the formation of megaspores (C-E), and concluding with the successive stages in development of the embryo sac (F-J) (see text for detailed discussion of this figure). [Redrawn from A *Textbook of General Botany*, Ed. 4, by R. M. Holman and W. W. Robins. N. Y.: John Wiley and Sons, Inc., 1951.]

the ovule. This condition recalls the highly vasculated nature of the integuments in the ovules of cycads and many of the extinct lines of gymnosperms.

Origin of the Megasporocyte

Although examples have been discovered of the formation of several megasporocytes in a single ovule, megasporogenesis in most angiosperms results from the meiotic divisions of a single hypodermal cell. In a great many cases the megasporocyte originates *directly* from a hypodermal cell

Figure 19-8   Megasporogenesis in the ovule of *Hydrilla verticillata*. **A,** hypodermal sporangial initial; **B,** periclinal division of sporangial initial into parietal cell and primary sporogenous cell; **C,** results of anticlinal division of parietal cell; **D,** megasporocyte situated below the layer of wall cells; **E-F,** formation of dyad cells; **G,** linear tetrad of megaspores. [Adapted from *An Introduction to the Embryology of Angiosperms* by P. Maheshwari. N. Y.: McGraw-Hill Book Company, Inc., 1950.]

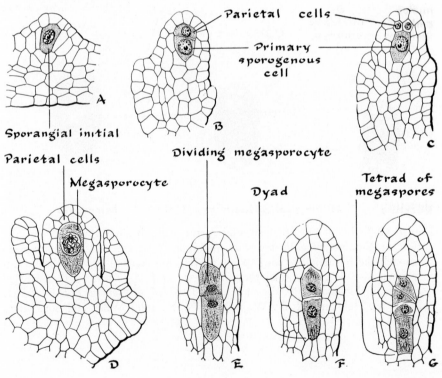

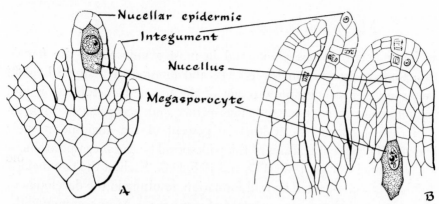

Figure 19-9 **A,** tenuinucellate type of ovule in *Orchis maculatus,* in which the megasporocyte occurs directly below the nucellar epidermis; **B,** crassinucellate type of ovule in *Quisqualis indica* (note deeply embedded position of mega-sporocyte and the active periclinal divisions in the nucellar epidermis). [Adapted from *An Introduction to the Embryology of Angiosperms* by P. Maheshwari. N. Y.: McGraw-Hill Book Company, Inc., 1950.]

which becomes differentiated from its neighbors by its larger size, more conspicuous nucleus, and denser cytoplasm (Fig. 19-9, A). An *indirect* method of origin of the megasporocyte, however, has been recorded in a number of species. In these cases, a hypodermal cell first divides (often unequally) into an outer parietal cell and an inner primary sporogenous cell (Fig. 19-8, A, B). The latter usually functions directly as the mega-sporocyte, while the parietal cell may give rise by anticlinal or periclinal divisions to a variable number of wall cells (Fig. 19-8, C). Not infrequently the formation and division of parietal cells is accompanied by active periclinal divisions in the nucellar epidermis. As a result, in some angiosperms the functional megasporocyte becomes deeply embedded in the tissue of the nucellus, and ovules of this structural type are designated in the modern literature crassinucellate (Fig. 19-9, B). On the other hand, the term tenuinucellate is applied to ovules in which parietal cells are absent and in which the functional megasporocyte lies directly below the nucellar epidermis (Fig. 19-9, A). The phylogenetic significance of parietal cells is problematical, although it has been argued that there is a strong tendency toward the elimination of such cells in angiosperm evolution.

Megasporogenesis

In lower heterosporous plants and in most gymnosperms the female gametophyte arises from the growth and division of a *single* haploid megaspore. This monosporic origin of the female gametophyte is also commonplace throughout the angiosperms, and, according to Maheshwari (1950) "occurs in at least 70 percent of the angiosperms now known." The salient features of this widespread type of megasporogenesis are illustrated in Figs. 19-7, B-D, and 19-8, D-G. Each of the two meiotic divisions is accompanied by wall formation, resulting in the development of a well-defined linear row or tetrad of megaspores. Most commonly, the three upper megaspores nearest the micropyle degenerate, and the lower surviving megaspore enlarges and by three successive nuclear divisions gives rise to an eight-nucleate female gametophyte or embryo sac (Fig. 19-7, E-J). Thus, if we begin with the megasporocyte, a total of five nuclear divisions, two of which represent meiosis, occur to produce the embryo sac.

However, striking deviations from this typical pattern of megasporogenesis and embryo-sac development have been discovered as the result of comparative studies on a wide range of angiosperm genera. One of the most remarkable deviations—which apparently is without parallel in other vascular plants (except *Gnetum?*)—is the participation of *more than one spore* in the development of the female gametophyte. This highly peculiar—and probably highly specialized condition—fundamentally is the result of the partial or complete failure of wall development during meiosis. As a result, megasporogenesis results in the production of haploid nuclei, some or *all* of which take part, by further divisions, in the production of the mature embryo sac (Fig. 19-10).

Types of Embryo Sac Development

Maheshwari (1950, p. 86) has developed a classification of the various types and subtypes of embryo sac development in the angiosperms. His classification is fundamentally based on: (1) the number of spores or spore-nuclei which enter into the formation of the embryo sac, (2) the total number of nuclear divisions which occur during megasporogenesis

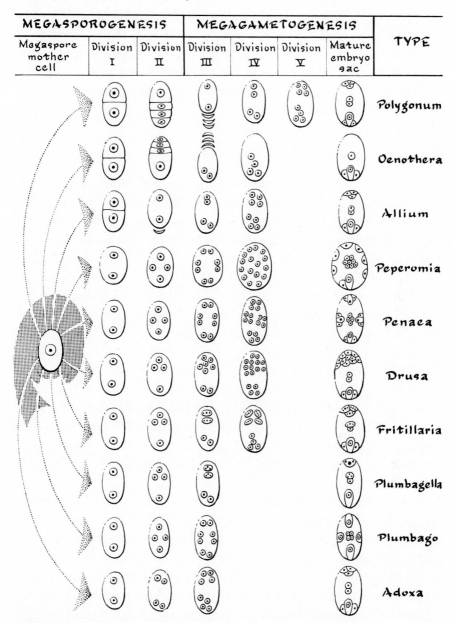

MEGASPOROGENESIS			MEGAGAMETOGENESIS				TYPE
Megaspore mother cell	Division I	Division II	Division III	Division IV	Division V	Mature embryo sac	
							Polygonum
							Oenothera
							Allium
							Peperomia
							Penaea
							Drusa
							Fritillaria
							Plumbagella
							Plumbago
							Adoxa

Figure 19-10 Origin and development of the main types of embryo sacs in angiosperms (see text for detailed discussion of the *Polygonum*, *Oenothera*, *Allium*, *Adoxa*, and *Fritillaria* types of embryo-sac development). [Redrawn and modified from Maheshwari, *Bot. Rev.* 14:1, 1948.]

and megagametogenesis, and (3) the number, arrangement, and chromosome number of the nuclei in the mature embryo sac. A consideration of each of the ten types of embryo sac development recognized in Maheshwari's classification is not attempted in this book. But it will be necessary to consider, briefly, selected examples from each of his three major types of embryo sac development.

Monosporic Type

In this type megasporogenesis results in four well-defined megaspores, one of which gives rise to the embryo sac. Most commonly the megaspore farthest from the micropyle is functional. As this spore enlarges the nucleus divides, and the daughter nuclei move apart to the two poles of the sac (Fig. 19-10, *Polygonum*). Each of these nuclei then divides, and a final division of the four nuclei yields a total of eight nuclei, arranged in quartets at the micropylar and chalazal ends of the embryo sac. Three of the nuclei at the micropylar pole become organized as naked cells and constitute the egg apparatus; at the time of fertilization this consists of the female gamete or egg cell flanked by the two synergids (Fig. 19-11). At the opposite end of the embryo sac three nuclei differentiate as antipodal cells, which, in certain plants, may give rise to additional cells by further division. The two polar nuclei, migrating from opposite ends of the embryo sac, may fuse to form a diploid fusion or secondary nucleus (Fig. 19-11). This pattern of embryo sac development is so widespread that it is often designated the Normal type. Inasmuch as the monosporic, eight-nucleate, seven-celled embryo sac was first clearly described for *Polygonum* in 1879 by Strasburger, Maheshwari suggests that it be designated the Polygonum type.

An interesting variant of the monosporic type of embryo sac development is apparently characteristic of the family Onagraceae, and has been termed the Oenothera type by Maheshwari. In this type the micropylar megaspore is functional, and a total of two (rather than three) mitotic divisions result in a well-defined four nucleate four-celled type of embryo sac consisting of an egg apparatus and a *single* polar nucleus (Fig. 19-10, *Oenothera*). Because of the elimination of the third division in megagametogenesis, the other polar nucleus and the antipodal cells are not formed. The Oenothera type is of particular morphological interest be-

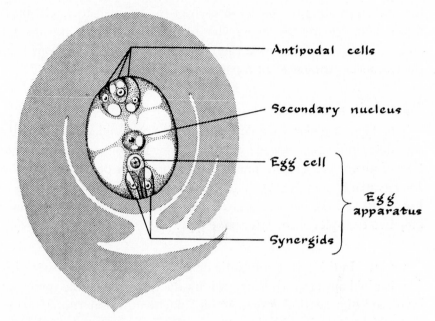

Antipodal cells

Secondary nucleus

Egg cell ⎤
⎥
⎥ Egg
⎥ apparatus
Synergids ⎦

Figure 19-11 Longisection of ovule of *Anemone patens* showing structure of mature embryo sac. [Adapted from *Plant Morphology* by A. W. Haupt. N. Y.: McGraw-Hill Book Co., Inc., 1953.]

cause, following double fertilization, the primary endosperm nucleus is *diploid* rather than triploid or polyploid as in other angiosperms.

Bisporic Type

This type is based on the condition in *Allium*, but, with minor variants, it occurs also in a number of other monocotyledons and in several dicotyledonous families. The definitive feature of the bisporic type arises from the *abortion* of one of the two dyad cells produced after the first meiotic division of the megasporocyte (Fig. 19-10, *Allium*). The nucleus of the surviving dyad cell (commonly the lower chalazal dyad cell) divides to form two haploid nuclei which are interpreted as megaspore nuclei. This is the definitive feature of the bisporic type. Two further nuclear divisions yield a total of eight nuclei which eventually become organized as in the Polygonum type of embryo sac (Fig. 19-10). The ontogeny of the embryo sac in *Convallaria majalis* appears to represent a condition transitional between the mono- and bisporic types. Megasporogenesis in *Convallaria* results in a tetrad of megaspores, but soon the walls separating the nuclei of each of the original dyad cells break down. Subsequently the micropylar binucleate dyad cell degenerates, and, as in *Allium*, the mature eight-nucleate embryo sac develops from the two megaspore nuclei of the lower or chalazal dyad cell.

Tetrasporic Type

This type of embryo sac development is remarkable because of the complete elimination of wall formation during meiosis, and the participation of all four megaspore nuclei in the formation of the embryo sac. Many variants are recognized, and for details the student is referred to Fig. 19-10 and the discussion given by Maheshwari. We shall consider only two examples of the tetrasporic type.

ADOXA.   In this type the meiotic divisions of the megasporocyte yield four haploid nuclei which lie free within the cytoplasm of the young embryo sac (Fig. 19-10, *Adoxa*). A third nuclear division (mitotic) produces eight nuclei which become organized to form a typical eight-nucleate seven-celled embryo sac (Fig. 19-10). The Adoxa type is apparently limited in occurrence to *Adoxa*, *Sambucus*, and *Ulmus* in the dicotyledons, and to certain species of *Erythronium* and *Tulipa* in the monocotyledons.

FRITILLARIA.   This peculiar type of embryo sac development is of particular interest because it occurs in a wide range of angiospermous genera including *Lilium*, which has long been employed in botany courses to demonstrate embryo sac development in the angiosperms (Fig. 19-10, *Fritillaria*). It was only after the careful investigations of Bambacioni (1928a, 1928b) and Cooper (1935) that the true sequence of events in the embryo-sac development of *Lilium* and *Fritillaria* was fully understood.

In *Lilium* and *Fritillaria* the four megaspore nuclei behave in a peculiar and distinctive manner (Fig. 19-12). Three of these nuclei migrate to the chalazal end of the sac, and the remaining nucleus is situated at the micropylar pole (Fig. 19-13, A). This 3 + 1 arrangement —as it is designated by Maheshwari—represents the *first, four-nucleate stage* in the development of the embryo sac. This phase is followed by

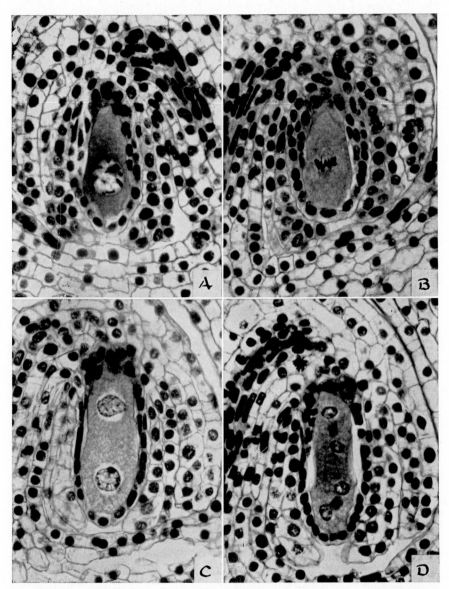

Figure 19-12 Megasporogenesis in *Fritillaria*. **A,** megasporocyte with nucleus in prophase; **B,** nucleus of megasporocyte in metaphase; **C,** two megaspore nuclei; **D,** four megaspore nuclei. [From slides prepared by Dr. F. V. Ranzoni.]

the division of the micropylar nucleus to form two haploid nuclei, and the fusion of the three chalazal nuclei and the subsequent division of the fusion nucleus to form two triploid nuclei (Fig. 19-13, B, C). As a result, a *second, four-nucleate stage* is observable, consisting of two haploid micropylar nuclei and two triploid chalazal nuclei. A final (fourth) nuclear division occurs, producing a micropylar quartet of haploid nuclei and a chalazal quartet of triploid nuclei (Fig. 19-13, D). As a result of these events in development, the mature embryo sac of *Fritillaria* or *Lilium* has the following construction: a normal haploid egg apparatus, three triploid antipodal cells, and, most remarkable of all, a tetraploid secondary nucleus formed by the union of a haploid and a triploid polar nucleus. When double fertilization occurs the polar nuclei join with one of the male gametes, and the primary endosperm nucleus is thus $5n$ (Fig. 19-14).

From an ontogenetic-cytological point of view it seems natural to assume that the bisporic and tetrasporic types of embryo sac represent modifications of the monosporic type. Indeed, there is remarkable structural similarity among the mature Polygonum, Adoxa, Allium, and Fritillaria types of embryo sacs, despite the remarkable differences in their ontogeny. From a phylogenetic viewpoint, the interpretation of the embryo sac in the angiosperms raises many difficult questions. The monosporic Polygonum type most closely resembles, in *method of origin*, the condition typical for gymnosperms, and several ingenious theories have been developed in an effort to demonstrate the equivalence between gymnosperm archegonia and certain cell groups in the angiosperm embryo sac.

Detailed discussions of the various archegonial theories applied to the interpretation of the embryo sac are given by Swamy (1946), Maheshwari (1950), and Battaglia (1951) but cannot be considered in this book. Maheshwari is highly critical, and states that "it seems far more likely instead that the angiosperms have long passed the stage of archegonia or that they never had them at any time in their fossil history." A comparable viewpoint is shared by Battaglia, who maintains that "the reduction of the female gametophyte from gymnosperms to angiosperms is characterized by the disappearance of the archegonium." These skeptical ideas serve to emphasize again our present ignorance as to the nature

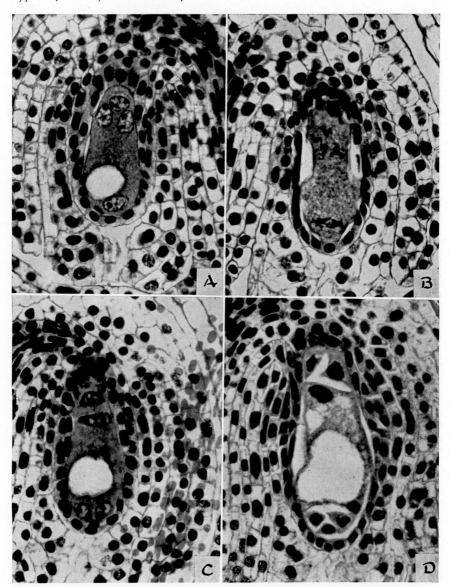

Figure 19-13 Development of embryo sac in *Fritillaria*. **A,** first four-nucleate stage consisting of a single micropylar and three chalazal megaspore nuclei; **B-C,** origin of second four-nucleate stage (note differences in size and shape of the micropylar and chalazal nuclei); **D,** eight-nucleate embryo sac consisting of a group of four haploid micropylar nuclei (lower end of sac) and a quartet of triploid chalazal nuclei. [From slides prepared by Dr. F. V. Ranzoni.]

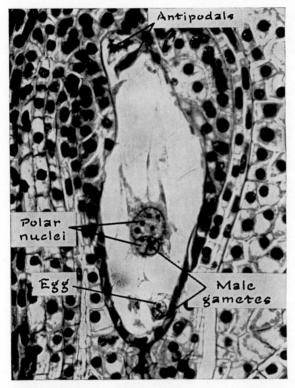

Figure 19-14 Double fertilization in the embryo sac of *Fritillaria*. Note difference between large triploid chalazal polar nucleus and the much smaller haploid micropylar polar nucleus.

of sexual reproductive structures in the ancestors of present-day angiosperms.

Fertilization

As described earlier in this chapter, the pollen grain when released from the anther encloses the reduced male gametophyte consisting of two or three cells (Fig. 19-6). Various agencies, particularly insects or wind currents, convey the pollen to the stigmatic surface of the carpel or the gynoecium. Germination of the pollen grain often occurs rapidly, and the emerging pollen tube grows intrusively between the stigmatic cells downward into the style. The latter in many angiosperms is hollow, and the pollen tubes grow along the epidermal surface (or transmitting tissue) which lines the surface of the stylar canal. But in many cases the style is a "solid" column of tissue, and the pollen tube must push its way through the intercellular spaces and between the cells which lie in its path.

In the majority of cases the tip of the pollen tube enters the ovule through the micropyle. This condition is termed porogamy. Less commonly the pollen tube penetrates the chalazal region of the ovule. This condition is designated chalazogamy and occurs in *Casuarina* (Swamy, 1948) and certain genera of the Amentiferae. The phenomenon of chalazogamy was for a long time considered a mark of primitiveness which could be used to establish the systematic position of a genus. At the present time, chalazogamy seems to present a problem of physiological rather than evolutionary importance.

After its entrance into the ovule, the tip of the pollen tube pushes into the micropylar end of the embryo sac, passing either between the egg and one synergid or between a synergid and the wall of the sac. Usually one of the synergids in the egg apparatus is destroyed by the entrance of the pollen tube.

Following penetration of the sac, the tip of the pollen tube ruptures, discharging the two male gametes (and often the vegetative cell or its remains) into the cytoplasm of the female gametophyte.

Accurate observations on the actual behavior of the two gametes in fertilization are beset with innumerable technical difficulties, and many of the critical steps have been observed in only a few plants. One of the present gaps in our knowledge concerns the possibility that the two gametes may differ from one another in size and behavior, the larger uniting with the polar nuclei (or the secondary nucleus) and the smaller fertilizing the egg cell. According to Maheshwari, however, there is insufficient reliable evidence at present to support such a generalization.

As mentioned in Chapter 18, the participation of each of the two male gametes in a fusion process is uniquely characteristic of angiosperms, and is usually designated by the expression "double fertilization." The union of one male gamete with the egg represents syngamy, and the diploid zygote which results normally develops into the embryo. The other male gamete unites with the two polar nuclei, or, if they have fused prior to fertilization, with the secondary nucleus (Fig. 19-14); the primary endosperm nucleus which results initiates the development of the endosperm tissue. Since in a great many angiosperms this latter type of fusion actually involves three nuclei, it has been separately designated triple fusion. However, the appropriateness of this phrase has progressively declined as a broader knowledge of the wide variation of structural types of embryo sacs has been secured. In the Onagraceae, for example, there is only a single polar nucleus, and hence the expression "triple fusion" is meaningless (Fig. 19-15, *Oenothera*). At the opposite extreme, cases are now known in certain angiosperm genera where four, eight, or as many as fourteen polar nuclei join with one of the male gametes in the formation of the endosperm (Fig. 19-15). Further discussion of such exceptional conditions will be given in the following section.

Endosperm Development

The term "endosperm" designates the tissue, formed during the development of an angiospermous seed, which provides the essential food ma-

Figure 19-15   Embryo sacs. Note the wide variation in the number of polar nuclei which join with the sperm nucleus (shown in black) in the initiation of endosperm. [Adapted from *An Introduction to the Embryology of Angiosperms* by P. Maheshwari. N. Y.: McGraw-Hill Book Company, Inc., 1950.]

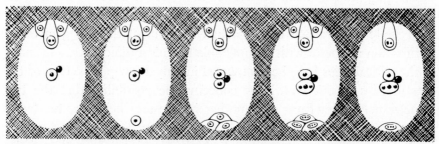

OENOTHERA BUTOMOPSIS POLYGONUM FRITILLARIA PLUMBAGELLA

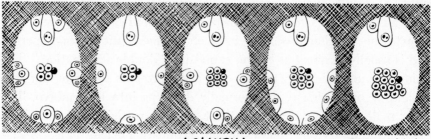

PENAEA   PLUMBAGO   ACALYPHA INDICA   PEPEROMIA   PEPEROMIA HISPIDULA

terials utilized in the growth of the embryo, and, in many cases, the young seedling. Although in a functional sense endosperm performs the same role as the haploid female gametophyte tissue of a gymnospermous seed, the two structures are analogous rather than homologous, from a morphological point of view. In some angiosperms (e.g., beans and peas) the endosperm tissue is completely digested by the developing embryo— such exalbuminous seeds frequently develop thick food-storing cotyle- dons which provide nutrition to the seedling during germination (Fig. ·19-25, E, F). Other angiosperms (corn, wheat, castor bean) have al- buminous seeds in which copious amounts of endosperm tissue are pres- ent at the time of seed germination (Figs. 19-25, A, B; 19-26, A-C). The histological structure of endosperm is highly variable—often the cells are densely packed with starch grains, granules of protein, or oils. In certain palms (for example, the so-called ivory-nut palm) the endosperm cells develop very thick, hard walls composed of hemicellulose. Endo- sperm is characteristic of the developing or mature seeds of the majority of angiosperms, and in only a few families, notably the Orchidaceae, is its development suppressed or ephemeral.

Endosperm formation is initiated by the mitotic division of the primary endosperm nucleus. This usually occurs prior to the division of the zygote. Extensive comparative studies have revealed considerable variation in the mode of development of endosperm, and the following main ontogenetic types are now recognized.

Nuclear Type

In this type a variable number of free nuclear divisions occur and at first are unaccompanied by the formation of walls (Fig. 19-20, B, C). During this period of free nuclear divisions the center of the embryo sac is often occupied by a large vacuole, and the nuclei lie peripherally in the cytoplasm which lines the wall of the embryo sac (Fig. 19-21, A). In some plants endosperm formation ceases after the production of a few or a large number of free nuclei. Not uncommonly, however, as in *Capsella* (Figs. 19-20, D; 19-21, B), walls may eventually develop be- tween the nuclei, resulting in a definable cellular tissue, at least in certain parts of the sac. Sometimes more than one of the original free nuclei becomes enclosed within a single endosperm cell; in such cases nuclear fusions may subsequently take place.

Cellular Type

This type is well-contrasted with the nuclear type because the division of the primary endosperm nucleus is followed by either a transverse or longitudinal wall dividing the embryo sac into two cells or chambers

Figure 19-16   Early stages in development of the cellular type of endosperm in various angiosperms. In A and D, the plane of the first wall is vertical; in E, the first division wall is transverse. **A-C,** successive stages in *Adoxa moschatellina;* **D,** first longitudinal wall in *Centranthus macrosiphon;* **E-J,** successive stages in *Villarsia reniformis.* [Adapted from *An Introduction to the Embryology of Angiosperms* by P. Maheshwari. N. Y.: McGraw-Hill Book Company, Inc., 1950.]

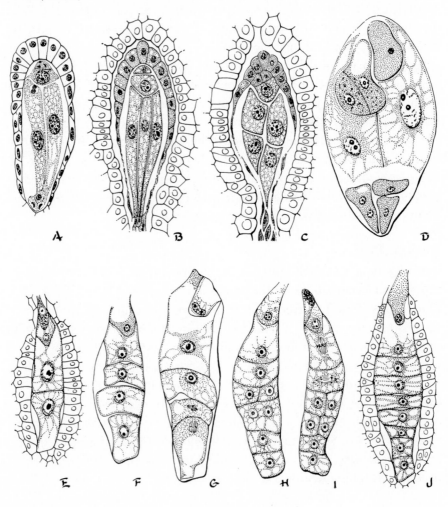

(Fig. 19-16). The subsequent planes of division in these first two cells may at first coincide with the plane of the first division, but soon the new walls are inserted in variable planes, and the mature endosperm then consists of a tissue of irregularly arranged cells. In some plants, characterized by the formation of the cellular type of endosperm, remarkably bizarre haustoria develop from one or both ends of the endosperm. These haustoria may penetrate for a considerable distance into the adjacent tissue of the ovule, and are believed to contribute significantly to the movement of food materials into the growing endosperm. (See Maheshwari, 1950, for descriptions and illustrations of endosperm haustoria.)

Helobial Type

This type, so named because of its occurrence in the order Helobiales (monocotyledons), is characteristic of a widely scattered series of angiosperm genera. In mode of development the Helobial type seems to combine in a remarkable way the main features of the two preceding types. The first division of the primary endosperm nucleus is followed by a transverse wall which divides the embryo sac unequally into a small chalazal chamber and a large micropylar chamber (Fig. 19-17). Free nuclear divisions then occur in each chamber, but those in the chalazal member are relatively few in number, and this region of the endosperm often degenerates and may eventually become obliterated. Commonly the formation of free nuclei in the micropylar chamber is followed by wall formation and the development of cellular endosperm tissue.

Beginning with the classical studies of the past century and extending to the present, the endosperm of angiosperm seeds has been the subject of varied interpretation and controversy by morphologists. Strasburger (1900) regarded the process of triple fusion as "vegetative fertilization" —in his view the union of one of the male gametes with two polar nuclei constitutes a needed stimulus for the development of the nutritive endosperm. He interpreted the endosperm phylogenetically as a gametophytic structure, a view later adopted by Coulter and Chamberlain (1912). On the other hand, if triple fusion is regarded as an act of true fertilization or syngamy, the endosperm might be regarded as a malformed or unorganized second embryo, the normal development of

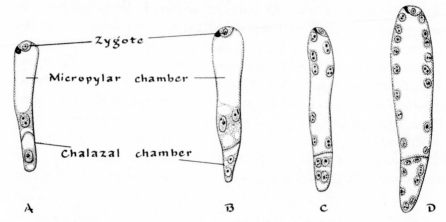

Figure 19-17   Development of the Helobial type of endosperm in *Eremurus himalaicus.* [Adapted from *An Introduction to the Embryology of Angiosperms* by P. Maheshwari. N. Y.: McGraw-Hill Book Company, Inc., 1950.]

which is inhibited by the participation of the chalazal polar nucleus in the formation of the primary endosperm nucleus. This theory, developed by Sargant (1900) obviously cannot account for the development of endosperm in the Onagraceae, where the primary endosperm nucleus, like the zygote, is a diploid cell (Fig. 19-15). In more recent years the fertilization of polar nuclei by a male gamete has been interpreted from a genetical-physiological point of view. This hypothesis maintains that (1) triple fusion is necessary as a stimulation for the early rapid development of endosperm, and (2) since endosperm nuclei contain paternal and maternal chromosomes, endosperm tissue possesses hybrid vigor and hence physiological aggressiveness (Brink and Cooper, 1947).

The young endosperm of coconut, known as coconut milk, contains certain important growth promoting factors and has proved beneficial as a component of the media used in *in vitro* cultures of embryos and excised plant structures. Experimental studies that utilize coconut milk seek to discover the biochemical organization of endosperm and its possible significance in morphogenesis.

In the authors' opinion, none of the theories proposed for the interpretation of endosperm provides an explanation of either the phylogenetic origin of this tissue or the remarkable range in chromosome number of endosperm cells that fluctuates from $2n$ (*Oenothera*), $3n$

(*Polygonum*), or 5*n* (*Fritillaria*), to high degrees of polyploidy. The wide range in the number of nuclei that fuse to form the primary endosperm nucleus is presented diagrammatically in Fig. 19-15. As Coulter and Chamberlain (1912) stated so clearly many years ago, "the phylogeny of the endosperm must be traced, and the place of the triple fusion in its history determined before opinions cease to differ as to its morphological character." (See Swamy and Ganapathy, 1957.)

Embryogeny

The embryogeny of the majority of gymnosperms begins with a period of free nuclear divisions which is then followed by the formation of cell walls (see Chapters 15, 16, and 17). Angiosperm embryogeny, in contrast, is fundamentally like that in lower vascular plants because the first nuclear division of the zygote is accompanied by the formation of a distinct wall—the cell lineages derived from these first two cells contribute in various degrees to the formation of the suspensor and the embryo proper.*

With very rare exceptions, the plane of the first division of the zygote is transverse, and the two-celled embryo, as in the majority of other vascular plants, is strictly endoscopic in polarity (Figs. 19-18, B; 19-22, B; 19-24, A). The lower or terminal cell, by subsequent divisions, forms the bulk of the embryo, and the upper or basal cell (lying nearer the micropyle) forms the suspensor and, in some plants, also contributes to the hypocotyl-root end of the embryo.

During the present century much attention has been devoted to intensive as well as comparative studies of the details of cell formation in developing embryos. In an effort to systematize and coordinate the mass of detailed information which now exists, certain embryologists have devised elaborate and complex typological classifications and have even proposed a series of laws which are said to regulate the sequence, position, and fate of cells in the embryo. Leaders in this typological approach to embryogeny are Schnarf (1929), Souèges (1938, etc.), and

---

* A striking exception to the usual situation in angiosperms has recently been described by Yakovlev and Yoffe (1957). According to these investigators a free nuclear period is characteristic of the early phases of embryogeny in several species of *Paeonia*.

Johansen (1950), and students interested in detailed descriptions and analyses of angiosperm embryogeny should consult these references as well as the briefer treatments given by Maheshwari (1950) and Wardlaw (1955).

A critical review of the various typological classifications of embryo development cannot be attempted in this book. Although the successive steps in the embryogeny of a given species often seem remarkably precise and are doubtless under genic control, there appears to be considerable overlapping among the various types. As Wardlaw (1955) remarks, conceptions of the kind advanced by Souèges and others should be received with caution "until much more is known about organismal reaction systems and the effect on them of genic mutations and other genetical changes on the resulting segmentation pattern." In order to illustrate the *principles* of angiosperm embryogeny it will, however, be essential to consider a few well-recognized types of dicotyledonous and monocotyledonous embryos.

Capsella bursa-pastoris

The embryogeny of *Capsella* was first carefully investigated by Hanstein in 1870 and subsequently has served as an instructional model for the discussion of the dicotyledonous embryo. Souèges has reinvestigated the successive steps in the developing embryo of this plant, and the essential events based on his study are shown in Fig. 19-18.

The first division of the zygote yields a terminal and basal cell (*t* and *b*, Fig. 19-18, B). Then the basal cell divides transversely and a *longitudinal division* follows in the terminal cell (Fig. 19-18, C-E). As a result, a four-celled proembryo is developed.* It will be necessary at first to trace separately the further division of the upper and lower pairs of cells. Each of the two terminal cells divides longitudinally, resulting in a quadrant of cells (Fig. 19-18, F-J). Transverse divisions then occur in each of these four cells, yielding the octant stage of the embryo (Figs. 19-18, K; 19-20, A). A critical histogenetic event now occurs: each of the eight cells divides periclinally into an outer der-

---

* At this point it should be noted that the longitudinal plane of division of the terminal cell is considered a highly significant event in the typological classification of the embryo of *Capsella*, which, on this basis, is assigned to the "Onagrad Type" by Johansen (1950).

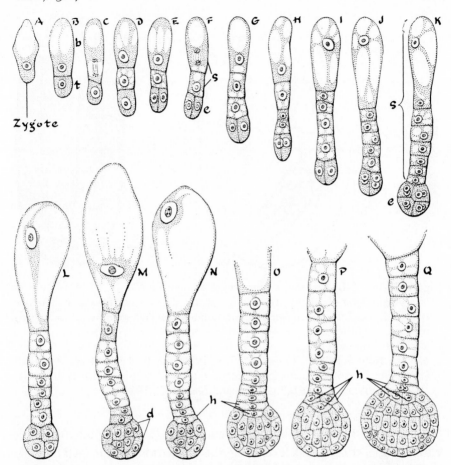

Figure 19-18 Early embryogeny in *Capsella bursa-pastoris.* **A-B,** division of zygote into terminal (*t*) and basal cells (*b*); **C-D,** development of three-celled proembryo; **F-H,** formation of suspensor cells (*s*) and division of terminal cells resulting in the quadrant (**J**) and octant (**K-L**) stages of embryo proper (*e*) (note progressive enlargement of uppermost suspensor cell); **M,** origin of "dermatogen" (*d*) representing the surface cells or epidermis of the embryo; **N-Q,** origin and division of hypophysis cell (*h*) and continued increase in number of surface and internal cells in the globular embryo. [Redrawn from Souèges, *Ann. Sci. Nat. Bot.* X. 1:1, 1919).

matogen cell and an inner cell; as a consequence the young embryo proper now consists of eight external dermatogen cells, destined to produce by further anticlinal division the embryonic surface layer or epidermis, and eight internal cells, from which the ground meristem and

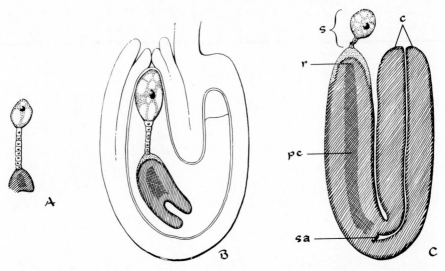

Figure 19-19   A-B, late stages in embryogeny of *Capsella*. **A,** the cordate form
of a longisection of an embryo at stage of initiation of cotyledons; **B,** longisection of developing seed showing orientation and general structure of an embryo
with two cotyledons; **C,** longisection of an embryo from a mature seed (*c,* cotyledons, *pc,* procambium, *r,* tip of root, *s,* suspensor, *sa,* shoot apex). (A and C
redrawn from Schaffner, *Ohio Nat.* 7:1, 1906; B, after Bergen and Caldwell,
and redrawn from A *Textbook of General Botany,* Ed. 4, by R. M. Holman and
W. W. Robbins. N. Y.: John Wiley and Sons. Inc., 1951.]

procambial system of the hypocotyl and cotyledons will gradually differentiate (Fig. 19-18, L-N). During the formation of the octant stage
of the embryo proper the suspensor is developed from the two upper
cells of the proembryo (Fig. 19-18, F-M). As is shown in this figure and
in Fig. 19-21, A, the suspensor cell next to the micropylar end of the
embryo sac usually fails to divide, but, instead, progressively enlarges
to form a very conspicuous vesicular cell. A variable number of transverse divisions of the upper cell and its descendents produce 5-7 additional suspensor cells. The uppermost cell of the suspensor was originally
termed the hypophysis by Hanstein (Fig. 19-20, B). This cell, by
transverse and longitudinal divisions, produces two four-celled tiers of
cells (Fig. 19-18, N-Q). Derivatives of the lower tier contribute to the
cortex of the embryonic root, and derivatives of the tier nearest the
suspensor form the earliest cells of the root cap and the adjacent root
epidermis.

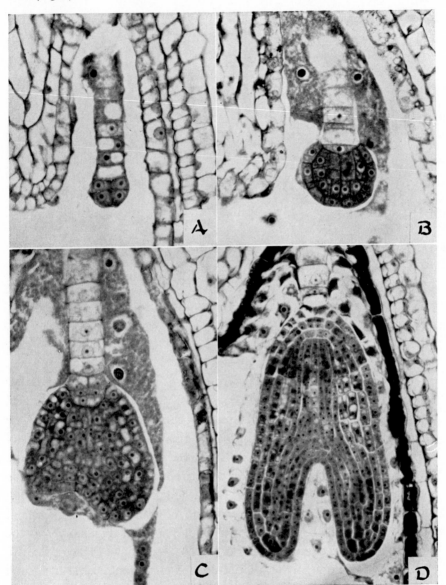

Figure 19-20 Embryogeny in *Capsella*. **A,** octant stage of proembryo, comparable with Fig. 19-18 L; **B,** later stage with "dermatogen" comparable with Fig. 19-18 O; **C,** later stage showing initiation of cotyledons, comparable with Fig. 19-19 A; **D,** embryo with well-developed cotyledon primordia and procambium, comparable with Fig. 19-19 B. Free nuclear stage in endosperm shown in **B-C;** cellular endosperm in **D.**

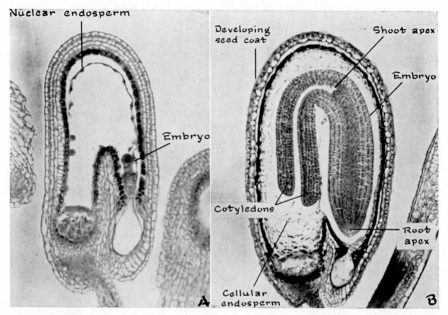

Figure 19-21 Longisections of developing seeds in *Capsella*, showing early embryogeny and free nuclear endosperm in **A** and nearly mature embryo and cellular endosperm in **B**.

To recapitulate, the young embryo of *Capsella*, as a result of a rather well-coordinated sequence of cell divisions, now consists of a spherical group of cells attached to a filamentous suspensor (Fig. 19-18, Q). The paired cotyledons arise as two ridges of tissue derived from the distal tier of the embryo, and a few cells situated between the bases of the cotyledon primordia remain undifferentiated and constitute the future shoot apex of the embryo (Figs. 19-19; 19-20, C, D). During cotyledon initiation the division and differentiation of cells in the lower tier of the embryo gradually produce the young axis or hypocotyl of the embryo. At this general stage the embryo is somewhat heart-shaped, as seen in longisectional view. Continued enlargement of the hypocotyl and cotyledons results in a pronounced curvature of the cotyledons which lie parallel to the axis of the embryo in the mature seed (Figs. 19-19; 19-21, B).

Nicotiana

In the construction of current schemes for classifying types of embryogeny, considerable importance is attached to the plane of division of the terminal cell of the two-celled proembryo. As we have seen, in *Capsella* the terminal cell divides by a *longitudinal* wall, and on this basis *Capsella* is assigned to the Onagrad type of embryogeny. In contrast, in a wide series of dicotyledons the plane of division of the terminal cell is *transverse*. Embryos developing according to this pattern are further classified into groups or types on the relative contribution of the basal cell of the proembryo to the development of the suspensor and the main body of the embryo. As an example we may select the embryogeny of *Nicotiana*, which is classified under the Solanad type (Fig. 19-22). Both the terminal and basal cells of the two-celled proembryo divide transversely, and the result is a filamentous embryo of four superposed cells (Fig. 19-22, F). The two lower cells (*t′* and *t″*) divide by longitudinal walls to form two, four-celled tiers (Fig. 19-22, G). The lowermost of these tiers of cells divides further and produces the cotyledons and shoot apex, and from the upper tier originate the hypocotyl and a portion of the root. Meanwhile the two upper cells of the four-celled proembryo divide transversely (Fig. 19-22, F-H). Cells derived from *n* form the root tip, and cell *s* produces a short suspensor.

Figure 19-22 Early embryogeny in *Nicotiana*. **A-F**, development of four-celled proembryo (note, in contrast with *Capsella*, Fig. 19-18, E, that the plane of division of the terminal cell, *t*, is transverse; **G, H**, vertical division of cells *t′* and *t″*, and formation of octant stage (*r*, cell from which portion of root tip is derived; *s*, suspensor cells). [Redrawn from Souèges, *Bull. Soc. Bot. France* 69:163, 1922.]

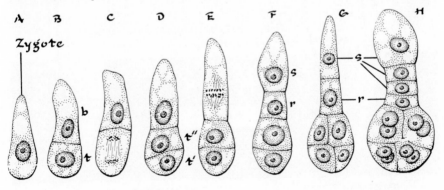

Monocotyledons

The differences between the organography of the *mature embryo* in monocotyledons and dicotyledons are striking and have long been used to demarcate these two major classes in the angiosperms. With a few notable exceptions (e.g., the development of a single cotyledon in *Ranunculus ficaria,* and certain genera in the Umbelliferae) the embryo of most dicotyledons has a pair of lateral cotyledons between the bases of which is situated the rudimentary terminal shoot apex (Fig. 19-23). In contrast, the typical embryo in monocotyledons develops a single, terminal cotyledon, and the shoot apex appears lateral in position (Fig. 19-23).

Despite these organographic differences, the early stages in embryogeny, *prior* to the differentiation of the solitary or paired cotyledons, are very similar in both monocotyledons and dicotyledons. Indeed, with reference to the sequence of cell divisions leading to the proembryo, certain of the proposed types of embryogeny include examples from

Figure 19-23 Differences between the organography of the embryo in dicotyledons and monocotyledons.

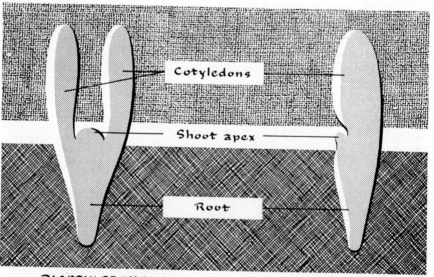

DICOTYLEDONOUS
TYPE OF EMBRYO

MONOCOTYLEDONOUS
TYPE OF EMBRYO

both classes of angiosperms (see Wardlaw, 1955, pp. 240-244). Apart from variation of detail, the salient aspect of the *late embryogeny* of many monocotyledons consists in the differentiation of all or a large part of the lower cell tiers of the embryo into a relatively massive and apparently terminal cotyledon. As an illustration, the main steps in the embryogeny of *Sagittaria sagittifolia* may now be described briefly.

The zygote of *Sagittaria* divides by a transverse wall into a terminal and a basal cell (Fig. 19-24, A). The latter divides no further, but progressively enlarges during embryogeny to form a conspicuous vesicular cell (Fig. 19-24, A-H). Meanwhile the terminal cell divides transversely, and the proembryo at this stage consists therefore of three superposed cells (Fig. 19-24, C). The lowermost cell t' then divides by a longitudinal wall, and further longitudinal and transverse divisions yield eight cells arranged in two tiers (Fig. 19-24, C-G). The middle cell t'' of the three-celled proembryo gives rise, by transverse division, to two cells; from the lower of these two cells (a) the lateral shoot apex originates, and the decendents of the upper cell h form the hypocotyl, the tip of the root, and a short suspensor (Fig. 19-24, D-H). Soon periclinal divisions that produce the dermatogen, occur in the eight cells at the distal end of the embryo, and this entire region, by further growth and differentiation, develops into the single terminal cotyledon (Fig. 19-24, H-J). During the final phases of embryogeny the future shoot apex lies in a shallow lateral depression situated about midway between the base of the cotyledon and the axis of the embryo (Fig. 19-24, I, J).

Seeds and Seedlings

The development of an ovule into a seed includes not only the origin and formation of the embryo and endosperm but also a series of complex modifications of the nucellus and integuments. Although in some cases a definable remnant of nucellar tissue—the so-called perisperm—is present at maturity, most or all of the nucellus usually becomes crushed and obliterated as the seed reaches maturity. On the other hand, the cells of the integument or integuments often develop into a great variety of cell types characterized by their peculiar orientation and often greatly thickened walls. These outer cell layers—derived mainly from the integu-

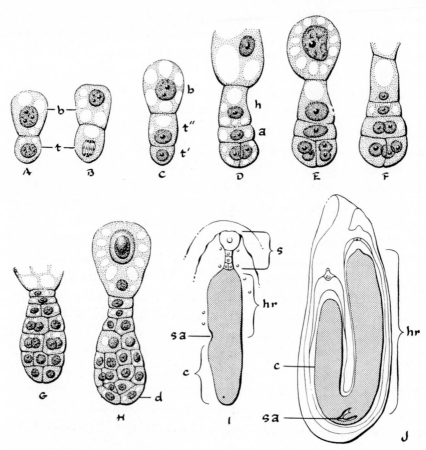

Figure 19-24   **A-H,** early embryogeny in *Sagittaria sagitifolia*. **A,** transverse division of zygote into terminal (*t*) and basal (*b*) cells (note progressive enlargement of the basal cell in later stages, C-H); **B-C,** transverse division of terminal
cell into cells *t'* and *t''*; **D,** transverse division of *t''* forming cells *a* and *h*, and
vertical division of *t'*; **E,** cells derived from *t'* again divide longitudinally (quadrant stage); **F,** vertical division of cell *a* and transverse division of cell *h*; **G,**
the four terminal cells divide transversely (octant stage); **H,** origin of "dermatogen" (*d*); **I-J,** late stages in embryogeny of *Sagittaria variabilis*; **I,** longisection of embryo with terminal cotyledon (*c*), shoot apex (*sa*), hypocotyl-root
(*hr*), and suspensor (*s*); **J,** longisection of curved embryo in mature seed (la-
bels as in I). [A-H redrawn from Souèges, *Ann. Sci. Nat. Bot.* X. 13:353, 1931;
I-J, redrawn from Schaffner, *Bot. Gaz.* 23:252, 1897.]

ment—collectively form the tough or stony coat of the seed. (See Neto-litzky, 1926, for a detailed monograph on the extremely variable structure of seed coats.)

The behavior of angiospermous seeds, after their separation from the parent plant, varies widely. In some cases (e.g., in certain maples and oaks) the seeds promptly germinate if environmental conditions, such as temperature and moisture, are favorable. But in a large number of species the detached seeds enter into a somewhat protracted period of dormancy. Because of its scientific as well as practical interest, much attention has been given to the physiological aspects of dormancy in seeds. The mechanical rupture of the seed coat alone may be sufficient to induce germination. In other instances, however, it appears that the embryo itself is in a physiological state of dormancy which can artificially be broken only by relatively drastic measures such as exposure of the seeds to low temperature or treatment with special chemical reagents. In nature the seeds of certain species retain their viability for many years. A classical example is provided by the seeds of an Indian species of lotus (*Nelumbo*) which germinated after lying dormant in a peat bog for several centuries!

The first stage in the germination of an angiosperm seed consists in the emergence of the radicle or embryonic root, which, after rupturing the seed coat at the micropylar end of the seed, normally grows downward into the soil or substrate and forms root hairs and, very often, lateral roots. Following this first step, the cotyledons and shoot apex of the embryo may emerge (further rupturing the seed coat) and, because of the elongation of the hypocotyl, become elevated above the level of the soil. This extremely common type of germination is termed *epigeous* and is illustrated by many plants such as radish, sunflower, pumpkin, and castor bean (Fig. 19-25, A-C). The cotyledons of seedlings with epigeous development are extremely varied in form and function. In the common bean the cotyledons are thick, fleshy, food-storing organs which soon shrivel and drop off. But in a wide range of dicotyledons the epigeous cotyledons are green, foliaceous appendages which evidently carry on photosynthesis. Students interested in the wide range in form and structure of epigeous cotyledons should consult the extensive monograph written by Lubbock (1892).

A contrasted type of germination, termed *hypogeous*, occurs in a

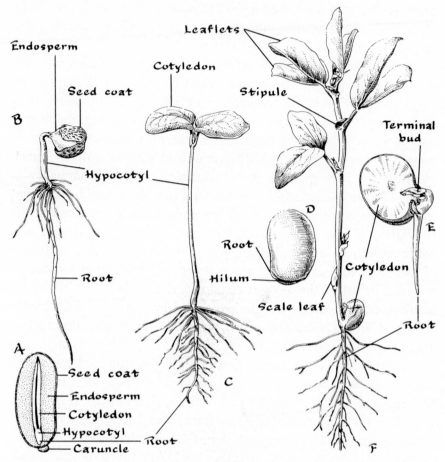

Figure 19-25   **A-C,** epigeous type of seed germination in castor bean (*Ricinus communis*). **A,** diagram of longisection of ripe seed showing the embryo surrounded by the copious endosperm tissue; **B,** young seedling showing the cotyledons still embedded in the endosperm; **C,** later stage (the elongation of the hypocotyl has elevated the two cotyledons and terminal bud above the surface of the ground). **D-F,** hypogeous type of seed germination in vetch (*Vicia Faba*). **D,** lateral view of seed showing position of embryonic root with reference to hilum; **E,** early stage in germination (seed coat removed) showing terminal bud of epicotyl, the two fleshy cotyledons, and the primary root; **F,** well-developed seedling, showing the elongated primary shoot (epicotyl) with scale leaves and stipulate foliage leaves (the cotyledons remain below ground because of the failure of growth in length of the hypocotyl). [Redrawn from *Vergleich. Morphologie der höheren Pflanzen* by W. Troll. Berlin, Gebrüder Borntraeger, 1935.]

variety of angiospermous genera. For example, in Vetch (*Vicia faba*) the fleshy, food-storing cotyledons remain within the seed coat, and there is little or no elongation of the hypocotyl. As a result, the primary shoot or epicotyl of *Vicia* originates by the internodal elongation of the embryonic terminal bud of the embryo (Fig. 19-25, E, F). The seedlings of *Nasturtium* and *Quercus* provide further examples of hypogeous cotyledons.

In addition to functioning as food-storing or photosynthetic organs, cotyledons may serve, to varying degrees, as haustorial organs, that is, organs that digest the food materials in the endosperm and transmit

Figure 19-26 Seed germination and seedling morphology in *Allium Cepa*. **A,** longisection of ripe seed showing coiled embryo surrounded by endosperm tissue; **B,** longisectional view of early stage in germination (the intercalary elongation of the single cotyledon has ruptured the seed coat and pushed out the root and shoot apex of the embryo; note that coiled haustorial tip of cotyledon remains in the seed); **C,** longisection of later stage in germination showing characteristic loop-like form of cotyledon, the sheathing base of which encloses the shoot apex and first leaf primordium; **D,** seedling in which the withered tip of cotyledon has separated from the seed (note emergence of first foliage leaf from cotyledonary sheath). [Redrawn from *Vergleichende Morphologie der höheren Pflanzen* by W. Troll. Berlin: Gebrüder Borntraeger, 1935.]

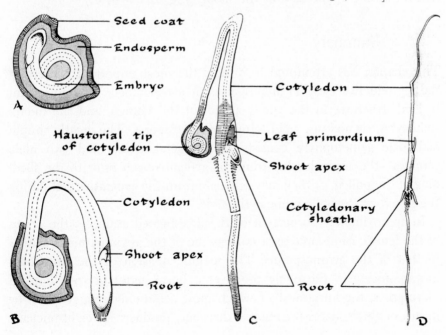

them to the growing root and shoot systems of the seedling. Numerous examples of this relationship occur in the monocotyledons. When the seed of onion (*Allium*) germinates, the cotyledon elongates and pushes the root end of the embryo out of the seed; the tip of the cotyledon, however, remains for some time within the endosperm of the seed, functioning as an absorbing structure (Fig. 19-26, A-C). Ultimately the withered tip of the cotyledon separates from the seed, and the green, photosynthetic portion of the cotyledon assumes an erect position (Fig. 19-26, D). An additional striking illustration of the haustorial function of the cotyledon is found in the young seedlings of the date-palm (*Phoenix dactylifera*) as shown in Fig. 19-27. Perhaps the most extreme examples of a haustorial cotyledon in monocotyledons occur in the seedlings of grasses, e.g., *Zea*, *Avena*, and *Triticum*. In these plants the single cotyledon is a thick, shield-shaped organ, termed the scutellum, which remains permanently in the grain in direct contact with the copious endosperm tissue (Fig. 19-28, A, B). The young primary shoot of the seedling is at first enclosed within a tubular sheathing leaf, which is termed the coleoptile. As the foliage leaves enlarge and the internodes elongate the coleoptile is ruptured at its open end but per-sists for a time at the base of the shoot (Fig. 19-28, B, C)

Summary

This chapter has attempted to outline the most important aspects of the reproductive cycle in angiosperms. Microsporangia develop as em-bedded structures in the young anther of the stamen, and the micro-sporocytes, by meiosis, yield tetrads of microspores. The greatly simpli-fied male gametophyte consists of a vegetative cell and two male gametes—the latter develop from the generative cell prior to the shed-ding of the pollen, or they may originate from the generative cell during the growth of the pollen tube in the style.

In approximately 70 percent of the investigated examples the *origin* of the female gametophyte or embryo sac of the angiosperms is similar to that of the gymnosperms. The meiotic division of the functional megasporocyte in the ovule produces a linear series of four haploid megaspores, the lowermost of which most commonly enlarges and, by means of three successive nuclear divisions, produces an eight-nucleate

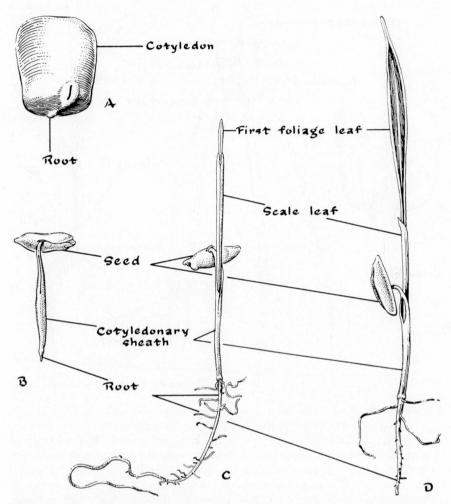

Figure 19-27 Seed germination and seedling morphology in the date palm (*Phoenix dactylifera*). **A,** embryo showing position of root and opening at base of cotyledon through which the first scale leaf will later emerge (see B-C); **B,** early stage in germination showing haustorial end of cotyledon still within the seed; **C, D,** later stages in seedling development showing seed attached to cotyledon and the elongation of the scale and foliage leaf. [Redrawn from *Vergleichende Morphologie der höheren Pflanzen* by W. Troll. Berlin: Gebrüder Borntraeger, 1935.]

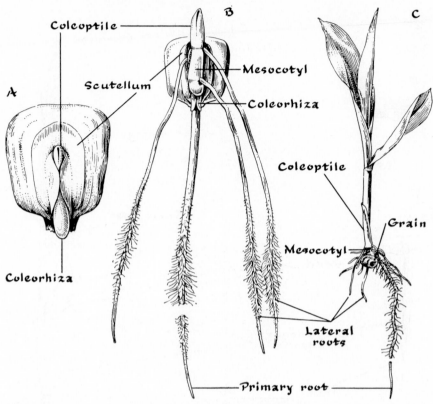

Figure 19-28 Seed germination and seedling morphology in corn (*Zea Mays*). **A,** corn grain with pericarp removed showing the embryo with its coleorhiza, coleoptile, and scutellum attached to the endosperm tissue; **B,** early stage of germination showing elongation of primary root, the lateral roots developed from mesocotyl, and the sheath-like coleoptile; **C,** seedling showing that scutellum remains within grain below ground (note conspicuous sheath of the young foliage leaves and the persistent coleoptile). [Redrawn from *Vergleichende Morphologie der höheren Pflanzen* by W. Troll. Berlin: Gebrüder Borntraeger, 1935.]

embryo sac. This embryo sac at maturity consists of (1) an *egg apparatus*, composed of two synergids and the egg cell, situated at the micropylar end of the sac; (2) a group of three *antipodal cells*, formed at the lower or chalazal end of the gametophyte; and (3) two *polar nuclei*, which often fuse prior to fertilization to form a centrally placed secondary nucleus.

A critical discussion is given of those types of megasporogenesis characterized by the partial or complete suppression of walls between the haploid megaspore nuclei. Depending on the number of megaspore nuclei which enter into the development of the embryo sac, *two* principal types may be recognized: the bisporic, or Allium, type, and the tetrasporic type illustrated by *Adoxa* and *Fritillaria*.

Normally, both male gametes participate in an act of fusion within the embryo sac, and this process, apparently definitive for the angiosperms, is designated as double fertilization. One male gamete fertilizes the egg, and the resulting diploid zygote develops into the embryo. The other male gamete unites with the polar nuclei (or their fused product), yielding the primary endosperm nucleus from which the endosperm takes origin.

The ontogeny of the endosperm, which usually begins in advance of embryogeny, occurs in a variety of ways. In the *nuclear type* a series of free nuclear divisions first occur; later these nuclei may become separated by wall formation as the component cells of the endosperm tissue. The *cellular type of* endosperm formation is distinctive because cell walls are produced each time the nucleus divides, and hence the endosperm from the beginning is a cellular tissue. The *Helobial type* of endosperm appears to combine certain features of each of the two preceding types. The first division of the primary endosperm nucleus is accompanied by a transverse wall dividing the sac into a small chalazal chamber and a larger micropylar chamber. In the latter, free nuclear divisions followed by wall formation produce the bulk of the endosperm, and the chalazal chamber, after a few nuclear divisions, usually degenerates.

A critical discussion is given of the difficulties of interpreting the endosperm from a morphological standpoint. Depending on the number of polar nuclei that are fertilized, the chromosome number in endosperm cells varies from $2n$ (*Oenothera*), to $3n$ (common condition), to higher polyploid conditions.

With very few exceptions the polarity of the embryo in angiosperms is endoscopic, and the first division of the zygote is transverse, yielding a lower or terminal cell and a basal cell. By further divisions the terminal cell forms the bulk of the embryo, while the basal cell forms the suspensor and in some species contributes to the differentiation of the hypocotyl-root end of the embryo. One of the widespread types of embryogeny found in dicotyledons is discussed in detail with reference to *Capsella*. It is emphasized that there is close agreement between the very early phases of embryogeny in dicotyledons and monocotyledons. The salient aspect of late embryogeny in monocotyledons, as illustrated by *Sagittaria*, is the development of the distal cell tiers of the embryo into the single terminal cotyledon and the lateral origin of the shoot apex. In contrast, the comparable region of a dicotyledonous embryo develops into a pair of lateral cotyledons and the terminal shoot apex which lies between them.

References

Bambacioni, V. 1928a. Ricerche sulla ecologia e sulla embriologia di *Fritillaria persica* L. *Ann. di Bot.* 18:7-37.

———. 1928b. Contributo alla embriologia di *Lilium candidum* L. R. C. *Accad. Naz. Lincei* 8:612-618.

Battaglia, E. 1951. The male and female gametophytes of angiosperms— an interpretation. *Phytomorphology* 1:87-116.

Boke, N. H. 1949. Development of the stamens and carpels in *Vinca rosea* L. *Amer. Jour. Bot.* 36:535-547.

Brink, R. A. and D. C. Cooper. 1947. The endosperm in seed development. *Bot. Rev.* 13:423-541.

Cooper, D. C. 1935. Macrosporogenesis and development of the embryo sac of *Lilium henryi. Bot. Gaz.* 97:346-355.

Coulter, J. M. and C. J. Chamberlain. 1912. *Morphology of Angiosperms.* Appleton, New York.

Erdtman, G. 1952. *Pollen Morphology and Plant Taxonomy.* Almqvist and Wiksell, Stockholm.

Johansen, D. A. 1940. *Plant Microtechnique.* McGraw-Hill, New York.

———. 1950. *Plant Embryology.* Chronica Botanica Co., Waltham, Massachusetts.

Lubbock, Sir John. 1892. A *Contribution to our Knowledge of Seedlings.* 2 v. Kegan Paul, Trench, Trübner and Co. Ltd., London.

Maheshwari, P. 1948. The angiosperm embryo sac. *Bot. Rev.* 14:1-56.

———. 1949. The male gametophyte of angiosperms. *Bot. Rev.* 15:1-75.

———. 1950. *An Introduction to the Embryology of Angiosperms.* McGraw-Hill, New York.

Netolitzky, F. 1926. Anatomie der Angiospermen—Samen. In: K. Linsbauer. *Handbuch der Pflanzenan-*

atomie. Band 10. Lief. 14. Gebrüder Borntraeger, Berlin.

Sargant, E. 1900. Recent work on the results of fertilization in angiosperms. *Ann. Bot.* 14:689-712.

Schnarf, K. 1927-1928. *Embryologie der Angiospermen.* In: K. Linsbauer. Handbuch der Pflanzenanatomie. Band 10. Gebrüder Borntraeger, Berlin.

————. 1931. *Vergleichende Embryologie der Angiospermen.* Gebrüder Borntraeger, Berlin.

————. 1941. Contemporary understanding of embryo sac development among angiosperms. *Bot. Rev.* 2:565-585.

Souèges, E. C. 1914. Nouvelle recherches sur le développement de l'embryon chez les Crucifères. *Ann. Sci. Nat. IX. Bot.* 19:311-339.

————. 1919. Les premièrs divisions de l'oeuf et les différenciations du suspenseur chez le *Capsella bursa-pastoris. Ann. Sci. Nat. X. Bot.* 1:1-28.

————. 1938, 1939, 1948, 1951. Embryogénie et classification. Hermann, Paris.

Strasburger, E. 1900. Einige Bemerkungen zur Frage nach der "doppelten Befruchtung" bei den Angiospermen. *Bot. Zeit.* 58:293-316.

Swamy, B. G. L. 1946. Inverted polarity of the embryo sac of angiosperms and its relation to the archegonium theory. *Ann. Bot. N.S.* 10:171-183.

————. 1948. A contribution to the life history of *Casuarina. Proc. Amer. Acad. Arts and Sci.* 77:1-32.

————, and P. M. Ganapathy. 1957. On endosperm in dicotyledons. *Bot. Gaz.* 119:47-50.

Wardlaw, C. W. 1955. *Embryogenesis in Plants.* Wiley, New York.

Wodehouse, R. P. 1935. *Pollen grains. Their Structure, Identification and Significance in Science and Medicine.* McGraw-Hill, New York.

Yakovlev, M. S. and M. D. Yoffe. 1957. On some peculiar features in the embryogeny of *Paeonia. Phytomorphology* 7:74-82.

Index